MACWORLD
COMPLETE MAC® HANDBOOK

By Jim Heid
Macworld *Getting Started* Columnist

ULTIMATE MAC REFERENCE ■ SOFTWARE & HARDWARE FROM SOUP TO NUTS ■ INCLUDES CLASSIC, IIsi, LC, PERSONAL LASERWRITER LS, & STYLEWRITER ■ 100s TIPS & SHORTCUTS ■ INSIDER NOTES & BACKGROUNDERS ■ EXPERT ADVICE ON SYSTEM 7 ■ THE ONE BOOK YOU NEED TO BECOME A MAC AFICIONADO

"A GREAT GUIDE...FULL OF GREAT TIPS ON HOW TO BUY AND USE MACS...I ACTUALLY LEARNED A FEW THINGS!"–FRANK CASANOVA, PRODUCT LINE MANAGER, HIGH PERFORMANCE MACINTOSH, APPLE COMPUTER

IDG
BOOKS

MACWORLD COMPLETE MAC HANDBOOK
SYSTEM 6.x QUICK REFERENCE

FINDER SHORTCUTS

To accomplish this...	Do this...
Bypass the warning dialog box	Press Option while dragging when you discard an application or the System file to the Trash.
Close all open disk/folder windows	Press Option while clicking any window's close box or choosing the Close command (if not using MultiFinder, press Option immediately after quitting a program).
Move an inactive window without activating the window	Press Command while dragging the inactive window's title bar (works in applications, too).
Copy a file from one folder to another instead of moving it.	Press Option while dragging the file to the destination folder.
Quickly determine whether a file is locked or unlocked.	Select the file, then move the pointer over the file's name. If the I-beam pointer appears, the file is not locked.
Align all icons in a window	Press Option while choosing Clean Up from the Special menu.
"Program" a directory window to close automatically when you return to the Finder	Press Option while opening the directory window (doesn't apply to MultiFinder).

FINDER KEYBOARD COMMAND SHORTCUTS

File menu

New Folder	Command-N
Open	Command-O
Close	Command-W
Get Privileges	Command-P
Get Info	Command-I
Duplicate	Command-D
Eject	Command-E

Edit menu

Undo	Command-Z
Cut	Command-X
Copy	Command-C
Paste	Command-V
Select All	Command-A

MAKING YOUR TEXT LOOK TYPESET (ALL SYSTEM VERSIONS)

The special characters and tips below can make your text look professionally typeset.

Character	Key Combination	Example of Usage
"	Option-[	He said, "I think so."
"	Shift-Option-[	That's the way to do it.
'	Option-]	She said, "That's 'odd.'"
'	Shift-Option-]	I'll be back—you'll see.
—	Shift-Option-hyphen	5–10 feet long.
–	Option-hyphen	

MORE TYPE TIPS
- Type one space after punctuation, not two.
- Don't type "1" for 1 or "0" for zero.
- Commas and periods go inside quotes.
- Colons and semicolons go outside quotes.
- Use italics, not underlines, for emphasis.
- Use tabs, not the spacebar, to align text.
- For better legibility, avoid all CAPITALS.

MACWORLD COMPLETE MAC HANDBOOK
SYSTEM 6.x QUICK REFERENCE

OPEN AND SAVE DIALOG BOXES

All Mac programs use the same basic Open dialog box, whose standard components and keyboard shortcuts are shown here. The Save dialog box is not shown, but works similarly.

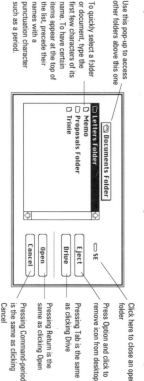

Use this pop-up to access other folders above this one

To quickly select a folder or document, type the first few characters of its name. To have certain items appear at the top of the list, precede their names with a punctuation character such as a period.

Click here to close an open folder

Press Option and click to remove icon from desktop

Pressing Tab is the same as clicking Drive

Pressing Return is the same as clicking Open

Pressing Command-period is the same as clicking Cancel

DIALOG BOXES WITH TEXT-ENTRY BOXES

In dialog boxes containing multiple text-entry boxes, you can jump from one text box to the next by pressing the Tab key. Other shortcuts for the Print dialog box are shown here.

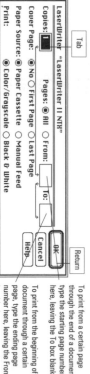

To print from a certain page through the end of a document, type the starting page number here, leaving the To box blank.

To print from the beginning of a document through a certain page, type the ending page number here, leaving the From box blank.

CONTROLLING THE MOUSE POINTER WITH EASY ACCESS

The Mouse Keys feature of the Easy Access system extension lets you control the mouse pointer using the numeric keypad. To activate and deactivate Mouse Keys, press Command-Shift-Clear. When the Mouse Keys feature is active, the keypad's keys control the pointer as shown below, at left.

MULTIFINDER NAVIGATION

You have three ways to switch between programs when running MultiFinder: you can click the visible part of a different program's window; you can click the small icon at the right end of the menu bar (above, right); or you can choose the desired program's name from the Apple menu (left).

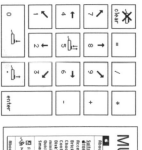

MACWORLD COMPLETE MAC HANDBOOK
SYSTEM 7 QUICK REFERENCE

by Jim Heid

Open and Save Dialog Boxes

System 7.0 uses new Open and Save dialog boxes, whose components and keyboard shortcuts appear here. Programs developed prior to System 7.0 may not use the new components of the Save dialog box.

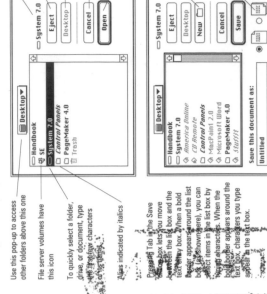

Click here to close an open folder

Command-E is the same as clicking Eject

Command-D is the same as clicking Desktop

Command-period is the same as clicking Cancel

Return is the same as clicking Open

Use this pop-up to access other folders above this one

File server volumes have this icon

To quickly select a folder, drive, or document, type the first few characters of its name.

Alias indicated by italics

Pressing Tab in the Save dialog box lets you move between the list box and the text-entry box. When a bold border appears around the list box (as shown here), you can select items in the list box by typing characters. When the bold border appears around the text box, characters you type appear in the text box.

Lets you create a new folder (keyboard shortcut: Command-N). If you've already opened a folder, the new folder is created within it.

Lets you create a stationery pad. Stationery pads let you reuse a document's contents without accidentally saving over them.

Switching Between Programs

Hides current application (here, the Finder)

Hides windows of inactive applications

Displays all hidden windows

Check mark denotes active application

Press Option and choose to hide active application

Dimmed icons indicate inactive applications whose windows are hidden

To switch to a different program, click within one of its windows, if any are visible. You can also use the application menu (at the right edge of the menu bar) to switch between programs and hide the windows of programs you aren't using.

File Sharing Icons and Access Priviliges

ICONS IN DIRECTORY WINDOW HEADINGS

You can't make changes to this folder.

You can't see files within this folder.

You can't see folders within this folder.

Icon	What it means
	You can put items in this folder but you can't open the folder or access its contents
	You can't access or modify this folder
	You can use this folder normally
	You own this folder and can use it normally

MACWORLD COMPLETE MAC HANDBOOK
SYSTEM 7 QUICK REFERENCE

Finder Shortcuts

To accomplish this...	do this...
Eject a disk and remove its icon	Drag the icon to the Trash or select the disk and choose Put Away (Command-Y).
Bypass the warning dialog box	Press Option when choosing Empty Trash.
Select an icon from the keyboard	Type the first few characters of its name.
Hide the current application when switching to another application	Press Option while choosing the desired application from the application menu.
Rename an icon	Select it, press Return, and then start typing.
Quickly determine whether a file is locked or unlocked	Select the file and press Return. If no border appears around the name, the file is locked.
Organize icons by name	Choose By Name from View menu, then choose By Icon or By Small Icon. Next, press Option and choose Clean Up by Name.
Clean up everything	Press Option and choose Clean Up All.
Clean up selected items only	Press Shift and choose Clean Up Selection.
Close all disk/folder windows	Press Option while clicking a close box or choosing Close.
Copy a file from one folder to another instead of moving it	Press Option while dragging the file to the destination folder.
Open an item and close its window	Press Option and double-click on the item.
Open the folder or disk window that holds the current directory window	Press Command while clicking on the window title, then choose the desired folder or disk name.
Abort a program that seems to have crashed	Press Command-Option-Esc and click Force Quit.
Open a document using an application that may not have created it	Drag the document's icon to the application's icon.

FINDER WINDOW SHORTCUTS

• Command-down arrow opens icon
• Tab selects next icon alphabetically; Shift Tab selects previous or previous icon
• Left and right arrow selects next or previous icon
• Command-right arrow expands folder outline; Command-Option-right arrow expands entire outline (Left arrow to collapse)
• Command-up arrow opens the window that holds active window

Finder Keyboard Command Shortcuts

File menu		Edit menu	
New Folder	Command-N	Undo	Command-Z
Open	Command-O	Cut	Command-X
Print	Command-P	Copy	Command-C
Close	Command-W	Paste	Command-V
Duplicate	Command-D	Select All	Command-A
Put Away	Command-Y		
Find	Command-F	**Special menu**	
Find Again	Command-G	Eject Disk	Command-E

MACWORLD

Complete Mac Handbook

By Jim Heid

Macworld *Getting Started* Columnist

Foreword by Jerry Borrell

Editor-in-Chief, *Macworld* magazine

IDG Books Worldwide, Inc.
An International Data Group Company
San Mateo, California 94402

Macworld Complete Mac Handbook

Published by
IDG Books Worldwide, Inc.
An International Data Group Company
155 Bovet Road, Suite 730
San Mateo, CA 94402
(415) 358-1250

Library of Congress Catalog Card No.: 91-70289

ISBN 1-878058-17-7

Printed in the United States of America

10 9 8 7 6 5 4 3 2

Project Manager: Jeremy Judson, Associate Editor
Editor-in-Chief: Michael E. McCarthy
Production Manager: Lana Olson
Edited by Dennis Cohen
Information graphics by Arne Hurty
Interior design by Peppy White; section opening illustrations by Mimi Fujii
Production by University Graphics

Distributed in the United States by IDG Books Worldwide.
Distributed in Canada by Macmillan of Canada, a Division of Canada Publishing Corporation.
For information on translations and availability in other countries, contact IDG Books Worldwide.

For sales inquiries and special prices for bulk quantities, write to the address above or call IDG Books Worldwide at (415) 358-1250.

Dedication

To Maryellen and to my mother;

and in loving memory of Suzanne Raynak, who started it all.

(The publisher would like to thank especially Bill Murphy, without whom this book would not be possible.)

Acknowledgements

The Getting Started columns you read in *Macworld* and the chapters you'll read in this book aren't the product of one person; they're the result of a collaborative effort of many, and they all have my sincere thanks and gratitude.

Topping the list is *Macworld* magazine's talented staff, the best group of computer journalists and consumer advocates I've ever had the honor of working with. In the departments section, thanks go to Nancy Dunn, who originally proposed the Getting Started column to me and who was instrumental in shaping the column's style and scope; to Cathy Abes, who picked up the torch when Nancy left and has since whipped dozens of columns into shape; and to Deborah Branscum, who has expertly supervised the magazine's departments section and whose Conspicuous Consumer column always educates and enlightens.

On the features side, my thanks and respect go to Brita Meng, Charlie Piller, Cheryl Spencer, Suzanne Stefanac, and Liza Weiman. Their work has been an inspiration over the years, and their tolerance of the occasional missed deadline — especially as this book came together — is truly appreciated. Thanks also to *Macworld's* expert copy editors, whose love of language makes *Macworld's* writers look good and whose attention to detail never fails to amaze.

On the design and production side, warm gratitude goes to Arne Hurty, who created the gorgeous technical illustrations in this book and generously provided several illustrations that appeared in the magazine's features section. Arne can make Aldus FreeHand sing, and his cheerful personality and dedication to his art make him a pleasure to work with. And I'm indebted to Assistant Managing Editor Luis Camus, Production Editor Joanne Villalobos, and Senior Designer Leslie Barton who dusted off megabytes of old archives to supply me with disk files of the published columns, illustrations, and icons. (See Appendix B for a look at how this book was produced.)

Special thanks go to Jerry Borrell for his support of my work and of this project; and to Adrian Mello, who has been a steadfast supporter and friend since 1984, and who always has the reader's best interests in mind. I also appreciate the efforts of everyone in Macworld Lab and on the administrative side, especially Jane Lagas and Lyn Taylor.

I also want to thank all the experts of the Macintosh world who have shared their knowledge with me over the years, and the press and marketing representatives who helped supply me with company and product information. They include (but aren't limited to) Peggy J. Day, Joel West, Mike Marks, Dan Shramek, Steve Carlson, Julie Larson, Mark Craemer, Ben Bauermeister, Robin O'Leary, Gary Amstutz, Marvin Carlberg, Josh Rosen, Suz Howells, Peter Gotcher, Joan Haber, Sue Nail, Larry Miller, Joe Ryan, Erik Smith, Richard Fontana, Wendy Keough, Gary and Jim McIntosh, Bruce Bradshaw, Robert Capon, Margaret Lee, David Weinberger, Paul Kerr, Allan Joseph, Paul Debenidictus, Sarah Charf, Karen Merideth, Jeff Harbers, John Marvaides, John Mitchell, Tim Tully, Stuart Henigson, Steve Lipson, Lisa Shaw, Cathy Sang, Royal Farros, Dave Varney, Terry Harbin, Riz Reed, Kevin Frost, Jeff Nichols, and Bill Darney.

My warm thanks also go to Dennis Cohen, the technical editor of this book and a good friend. Dennis has forgotten more about the Mac than I'll ever know, and he's been a superb source of technical information and insights over the years. The Macintosh world is lucky to have him in its ranks. If he had stayed at the Jet Propulsion Laboratory, we'd have colonized the solar system by now.

Then there's Apple. I may not agree with everything that comes out of Cupertino, but I've always been impressed with the skill and dedication of Apple's engineers and product managers. There is a corporate culture at Apple, but it has nothing to do with sunny Silicon Valley or Friday beer busts. It has to do with a commitment to the philosophy behind the Macintosh — that a powerful computer can be easy to use and fun. I'd like to thank all the engineers and product managers who have taken time from their incredibly hectic schedules to answer questions from some bozo up in Mendocino county. They include Frank Casanova, Steve Goldberg, Steve Rea, Duane Schulz, Charlie Oppenheimer, Paul Hudspeth, Jim Stoneham, Karen Ebert, Mark Orr, Paul Prebin, Mario Diaz, Fred Parker, Jack Palevich, Jim Gable, Dave Garr, Michael Mace, Jim Stair, Neil Selvin, Bryan Stearns, Donn Denman, Kevin Jones, and Randy Carr. Thanks also to Martha Steffen, for her support of this book and for supplying me with prerelease copies of System 7.0; and to Kate Paisley and Patty Tulloch, for their assistance in arranging interviews and briefings and for their support of my coverage of the Personal LaserWriter LS, the StyleWriter, and System 7.0.

My heartfelt thanks also go to the folks at IDG Books Worldwide, the most innovative book publisher I've ever worked with. Specifically, I want to thank John Kilcullen, for his inspiring enthusiasm and for having the vision to realize what a nifty book this could be; Milissa Koloski, for her creative sales and marketing efforts and her highly contagious good humor; Mike McCarthy, for support that never waivered, even when schedules did; and Jeremy Judson, for expertly shepherding the book through the production process and for patiently listening to my answering machine more often than he should have had to. Thanks also go to Ty Koontz for his indexing expertise, and to Peppy White and the rest of the gang at University Graphics who handled this book's tricky production demands with aplomb.

And finally, the home front. My buddy Kevin Fraser helped get me through the worst of it and introduced me to the wonders of the Northern California coast. Trixie was a sweet and constant companion who always seemed to know when it was time for a squeak-squeak break. And the love of my life, Maryellen Kelly, was there, as always, reading every word, running everything, and providing love and support that continues to make it all worthwhile.

About the Author

Jim Heid has been writing for *Macworld* since 1984, and has appeared in every issue since March 1985. He writes the monthly *Getting Started* column as well as feature articles and reviews. Heid specializes in page printers, desktop publishing, typography, MIDI, and digital audio — a mix that exploits his background as a typographer, musician, and audio buff. (He grew up in his father's recording studio, which was Pittsburgh's first.)

Prior to writing for *Macworld,* Heid was Senior Technical Editor for *Kilobaud Microcomputing* magazine, where he began working with the Mac prior to its introduction. He has been working with and writing about personal computers since the late seventies, when he computerized his home-built ham radio station with one of the first Radio Shack TRS-80s. He is the author of six books on Macintosh and IBM PC personal computing and frequently speaks at user group meetings, developer's conferences, and Macworld Expos. He and his wife live on California's scenic Mendocino coast.

About IDG Books Worldwide

Welcome to the world of IDG Books Worldwide.

International Data Group (IDG) is the world's leading publisher of computer periodicals, with more than 150 weekly and monthly newpapers and magazines reaching 25 million readers in more than 40 countries. If you use personal computers, IDG Books is committed to publishing quality books that meet your needs. We rely on our extensive network of publications — including such leading periodicals as *ComputerWorld, InfoWorld, MacWorld, PC World, Portable Computing, Publish, Network World, SunWorld, AmigaWorld,* and *GamePro* — to help us make informed and timely decisions in creating useful computer books that meet your needs.

Every IDG book strives to bring extra value and skill-building instruction to the reader. Our books are written by experts, with the backing of IDG periodicals, and with careful thought devoted to issues such as audience, interior design, use of icons, and illustrations. Our editorial staff is a careful mix of high-tech journalists and experienced book people. Our close contact with the makers of computer products helps ensure accuracy and thorough coverage. Our heavy use of personal computers at every step in production means we can deliver books in the most timely manner.

We are delivering books of high quality at competitive prices, on topics customers want. At IDG, we believe in quality, and we have been delivering quality for 25 years. You'll find no better book on a subject than an IDG book.

Jonathan Sacks
President
IDG Books Worldwide, Inc.

International Data Group's publications include: ARGENTINA'S Computerworld Argentina; ASIA'S Computerworld Hong Kong, Computerworld Southeast Asia, Computerworld Malaysia. Computerworld Singapore, Infoworld Hong Kong, Infoworld SE Asia; AUSTRALIA'S Computerworld Australia, PC World, Macworld, Lotus, Publish!; AUSTRIA'S Computerwelt Oesterreich; BRAZIL'S DataNews, PC Mundo, Automacao & Industria; BULGARIA'S Computer Magazine Bulgaria, Computerworld Bulgaria; CANADA'S ComputerData, Direct Access, Graduate CW, Macworld; CHILE'S Informatica, Computacion Personal; COLUMBIA'S Computerworld Columbia; CZECHOSLOVAKIA'S Computerworld Czechoslovakia, PC World; DENMARK'S CAD/CAM WORLD, Computerworld Danmark, PC World, Macworld, Unix World, PC LAN World, Communications World; FINLAND'S Mikro PC, Tietoviikko; FRANCE'S Le Mond Informatique, Distributique, InfoPC, Telecoms International; GERMANY'S AmigaWelt, Computerwoche, Information Management, PC Woche, PC Welt, Unix Welt, Macwelt RD; GREECE'S Computerworld, PC World, Macworld; HUNGARY'S Computerworld SZT, Mikrovilag; INDIA'S Computers & Communications; ISRAEL'S People & Computers; ITALY'S Computerworld Italia, PC World Italia; JAPAN'S Computerworld Japan, Macworld, SunWorld Journal; KOREA'S Computerworld, PC World; MEXICO'S Computerworld Mexico, PC Journal; THE NETHERLAND'S Computerworld Netherlands, PC World, AmigaWorld; NEW ZEALAND'S Computerworld New Zealand, PC World New Zealand; NIGERIA'S PC World Africa; NORWAY'S Conputerworld Norge, PC World Norge CAD/CAM, Macworld Norge; PEOPLE'S REPUBLIC OF CHINA'S China Computerworld, China Computerworld Monthly; PHILLIPPINE'S Computerworld Phillippines, PC Digest/PC World; POLAND'S Komputers Magazine, Computerworld; ROMANIA'S Infoclub; SPAIN'S CIM World, Communicaciones World, Computerworld Espana, PC World, AmigaWorld; SWEDEN'S ComputerSweden, PC/Nyhetherna, Mikrodatorn, PC World, Macworld; SWITZERLAND'S Computerworld Schweiz, Macworld; TAIWAN'S Computerworld Taiwan, PC World, Publish; THAILAND'S Computerworld; TURKEY'S Computerworld Monitor, PC World/ Turkiye; UNITED KINGDOM'S Graduate Computerworld, PC Business World, ICL Today, Lotus UK, Macworld UK; UNITED STATES' AmigaWorld, A+, CIO, Computerworld, Digital News, Federal Computer Week, GamePro, InfoWorld, Lotus, Macworld, Network World, NextWorld, PC Games, PC World, Portable Office, PC Letter, Publish!, Run, SunWorld Journal; USSR'S MIR PC, Computerworld, Computer Express, Network, Manager Magazine; VENEZUELA'S Computerworld Venezuela, Micro Computerworld; YUGOSLAVIA'S Moj Mikro

Contents at a Glance

Table of Contents

Section One: Using the Mac

1 Buying a Mac 3

2 Macintosh Basics 17

Section Two: Mastering the Mac

Section Three: Expanding the Mac

Foreword

By Jerry Borrell
Editor-in-Chief
Macworld magazine

Jim Heid has been writing for *Macworld* for six years. He has also written several books on Macintosh software. As the author of *Macworld's* monthly column "Getting Started," Heid is already familiar to hundreds of thousands of Macintosh users.

To those who do not know Jim, let me recommend this book. Like his column in *Macworld*, *The Complete Mac Handbook* seeks to provide Macintosh users with clear, insightful, and reliable advice on how to get the most out of whatever you need to do on your Mac. *The Complete Mac Handbook* is one of those reference volumes you'll want to have next to your computer.

You should also consult the relevant chapter of the book the next time you're wondering "why my Mac does (or doesn't) do that" or before you wander off to the computer store in search of the next great Mac product.

Jim will save you endless time and trouble.

Introduction

In 1986 — back when the Mac Plus was Apple's flagship and a year before the first Mac II was christened — the editors of *Macworld* magazine approached me about writing a column that would focus on a different aspect of Macintosh fundamentals each month. The Mac world was becoming more complex, they explained, and even seasoned veterans were increasingly likely to encounter unfamiliar terms or concepts.

The first installment of "Getting Started" appeared in the November 1986 issue. I've written several dozen columns since then, and the book you're reading now contains the best of them, up to and including the May 1991 installment.

But these aren't just reprints. I've updated every column to reflect new or discontinued products, evolving Mac technology, and Apple's growing product line. I've also expanded every column, adding new illustrations, tables, product listings, and sidebars containing additional background, tips, and insights. And you'll find an all-new chapter containing expanded coverage of Apple's new System 7.0 software, and a pull-out quick reference card that's packed with shortcuts and tips for using the Mac. New and improved, I think they call it.

At the same time, I've retained the magazine-style format of the original columns. You'll find sidebars, comprehensive figure captions (not just "Figure 2-1: A dialog box"), and top-notch technical illustrations — items you'd expect from a magazine, not a book. I've aimed for the best of both worlds — magazine-style layout and graphics along with the depth and scope only a book can provide.

Whom This Book is For

From its inception, my Getting Started column has been aimed at the beginner. But by "beginner," I don't always mean someone who's just unpacked his or her Mac and isn't sure what to do next. I refer instead to anyone unfamiliar with the subject at hand. The Mac world has so many facets, everyone's a beginner at something.

To be a bit more specific, this book is intended for:

❖ people who are thinking about buying a Macintosh and need introductions to Mac terminology and operating concepts and on what you can do with a Macintosh

❖ experienced Mac users who want overviews of Macintosh application categories and hardware concepts to help them choose products and brush up on areas they're unfamiliar with

❖ regular Getting Started readers who want an updated and expanded collection of columns for convenient reference.

How This Book is Organized

Most computer books begin with chapter after chapter of technical background on bits and bytes and how computers work. Not this book. In my experience, the first questions people ask about the Mac aren't, How does it work and what do all those weird words mean? Instead, they ask, Which machine should I buy and what can I do with it? That only makes sense: whether you're shopping for a car, a house, or a computer, your first priorities are making an informed purchase and then applying that purchase to your daily life. Learning the technical details behind your plumbing, engine, or central processing unit usually comes later.

For this reason, this book is organized a bit differently than the rest:

❖ In Section I, "Using the Mac," we get right down to business, examining issues you'll want to investigate when shopping for a Mac system, and looking at the many ways you can put a Mac to work. We'll explore the worlds of word processing, desktop publishing, spreadsheets, database management, animation, music, computer-aided design, and more. Each chapter in this section describes the concepts behind an application category and spotlights the leading products in the field. You'll also find tips for using your programs more effectively and shopper's guidelines that will help you choose programs that meet your needs.

❖ In Section II, "Mastering the Mac," we'll take a closer look at what makes the Mac tick. We'll unscramble the acronyms and demystify the jargon you'll encounter as you use the Mac, and we'll look at more advanced topics such as protecting your Mac from computer viruses, backing up, exchanging data between programs and computers, troubleshooting, and working with digital sound.

❖ In Section III, "Expanding the Mac," we'll look at the kinds of add-ons you might buy to round out your Mac system. Scanners, monitors, laser printers, high-capacity disks, and expansion cards are among the hardware vying for your checkbook's attention. You'll learn what each type of add-on has to offer and what to look for when shopping.

The back of the book contains two appendices. Appendix A, "Where to Buy," lists the phone numbers of the companies whose products are mentioned in this book. Appendix B, "Production Notes," spotlights the remarkable roles the Mac played in the production of this book. And last but not least, there's a comprehensive index that will help you locate the terms, concepts, and products discussed here.

Because the chapters in this book began life as magazine columns, you may find that some information and definitions appear in more than one place. As I revised each column, I removed most of this duplicated information, but there are some common terms or concepts that are so important that I've left them in each place they appear. This will allow you to skip around from chapter to chapter without worrying about encountering too many unfamiliar terms.

Conventions Used in This Book

This book also contains BACKGROUND, TIPS, and INSIGHTS to keep in mind as you learn Macintosh concepts and are indicated by icons in the margins. Here is what to look for:

Background gives you the nuts-and-bolts technical explanations of how certain components work or the ideas behind them.

Quick Tips are shortcuts that have been learned over the years to save you time and trouble.

Shopping Tips give you tips on what to look for when shopping for hardware and software and how much money you can expect to pay for them.

Insights are comments given to better inform the reader on the core of an issue or category of products.

Also, in the left-hand margins of this book you'll find vertical rules which serve to separate your thoughts from the author's. Feel free to take notes or jot down ideas in this area we have provided. Whether you're a student with that fast-approaching mid-term coming, or a casual Mac user learning at your own pace, we think you'll find this feature helpful in your learning experience.

A Word About System 7

While I was wrapping up this book, Apple programmers were putting the finishing touches on a major enhancement of the software that enables the Mac to run. This enhancement, called *System 7.0,* is scheduled to be available by the middle of 1991. I've included detailed information on System 7.0 gleaned from interviews with Apple engineers and other Mac experts, from preliminary versions of the System 7.0 manuals, and from working with prerelease versions of the System 7.0 software itself. If you read this before System 7.0 is available, you'll be prepared, ready to make the transition and able to assemble the hardware necessary to run the new software effectively.

Other Titles to Enhance Your Mac Knowledge

When you're through reading this book and you've got to know all the ins and outs of System 7.0, you'll want to look at *Macworld Guide To System 7.0* — the authoritative guide to Apple's new system software which reveals undocumented tips not found in the manual.

For those interested in making Music with the Macintosh, there's *Macworld Music & Sound Bible* — the only comprehensive and authoritative guide to using music, sound, digital audio, and multimedia on the Mac.

Both these books contain the same kind of quality information found in this book and throughout the IDG Books book lines. They can be found in better bookstores everywhere. To order by phone call: (800) 28BOOKS or (800) 282-6657.

Feedback, Please!

The letters and comments I've received from Getting Started readers have helped set the column's direction. Similarly, your feedback to this book will help make future editions better. Please write to me, in care of IDG Books Worldwide, with questions or comments. You can also contact me directly using electronic mail (if you don't know what that is, don't worry — it's covered here). On CompuServe, send messages to 76174,556. On America Online, I'm JimHeid. On MCI Mail, they call me JHEID.

Let's get started!

Section One
USING THE MAC

MACWORLD

Chapter 1
Buying a Mac

In This Chapter:

✔ Details on how to determine which Macintosh will meet your present and future needs.

✔ An introduction to the hardware features you'll want to examine when shopping for a Mac.

✔ A look at the used Mac market: which models are worth considering?

✔ An introduction to Macintosh printers and other add-ons.

✔ Tips for buying a Mac and saving money when assembling a system.

✔ A summary of how the Macintosh family compares to the IBM PC.

Today's Macintosh shopper faces more decisions than the president on a bad day. Apple offers seven Macs, ranging in price from under $1000 for a bare-bones Macintosh Classic to over $10,000 for a Mac IIfx with all the trimmings. Hundreds of independent, or *third-party*, manufacturers supply thousands of programs and hardware add-ons. You can outfit a system using only Apple hardware, or combine components from different firms. You can shop at a local dealer, or through the mail. Buy the right system, and you'll wonder how you got along without it. Buy the wrong one, and you'll feel betrayed by technology as you watch it depreciate and collect dust.

In this chapter, we'll make our way through the maze of issues you need to consider when assembling a Mac system, with the goal of helping you decide what combination of hardware is best for you.

Money Is Everything

Many consultants and experienced users will suggest that you answer the following questions to determine what to buy:

1. What tasks do I want to use the Mac for?

2. Which programs can perform them?

3. What kinds of hardware do those programs require?

This is a valid approach, but I like to preface it with a more pragmatic question: How much can you spend? The fact is, what you *want* a Mac to do and what the system you can afford *can* do are often two different things. Thus, you can't accurately answer the first question until you determine your budget.

Addressing your finances is especially important in the Mac world, where "bargain" often means "less than a new car." I'm exaggerating, but it is true that most Macs generally cost more than the other major microcomputing standard, the IBM PC and its work-alikes, or *clones.* (Actually, Macs often cost less than similarly equipped IBM machines; it's those low-cost clones that offer the real

Mac Versus PC

If you've browsed some mail-order advertisements in IBM-oriented magazines, you've probably noticed a big price difference between Macs and PC-class hardware. Apple's prices are competitive with those of firms such as IBM and Compaq, but mail-order retailers such as Dell Computer Corporation and PC Brands, both of which sell IBM-compatible machines, offer some real bargains.

So why buy a Macintosh? Several reasons:

❖ Ease of use. The Mac's *graphical user interface* — the on-screen menus and other devices you use to control your programs — makes the machine easier to learn and use. PCs can run a Mac-like graphical user interface called *Microsoft Windows,* but it isn't as polished or mature as the Mac's interface. The Mac was designed from the ground up to be a graphical computer; PCs weren't, and it shows. Macintosh hardware is generally easier to set up, too.

❖ Larger software base. More programs are available that take advantage of the Mac's graphical personality than are available for Windows. This will be the case for some time to come.

❖ Superior video display options. It isn't surprising that a highly graphical computer would have superior video talents. Mac owners can choose from a large array of sophisticated video cards, including ones that display images with photographic realism and ones that can connect to video cassette recorders. Some such boards are available for PCs, but the selection is relatively small. What's more, there's no guarantee that a board will work with all PC programs. The Mac's standardized system software eliminates such compatibility concerns.

❖ More built-in hardware. Macs include hardware that usually costs extra on PCs. This hardware makes it easier and less expensive to connect multiple add-ons and to interconnect Macs to form a network that lets you share expensive add-ons and information.

❖ Sophisticated sound output. PCs can beep; Macs can play digitally recorded sounds. The Mac Classic, LC, and IIsi can also record sounds (other Macs can, too, with inexpensive third-party hardware). This not only means you can hear amusing beep sounds when you make a mistake, you can also integrate sound into presentations and other documents you create. Products are available that even let you send recorded voice messages to other Macs on an office network. **M**

bargains.) But the Mac is easier to set up and learn. If your time is worth money, the system's higher cost may easily be offset by the time you save learning it, especially if you or someone else will be training employees. (For more comparisons between the Mac and PC worlds, see the sidebar "Mac versus PC.")

Hardware Decisions

You've thought about what you want to do with the Mac and you've determined which programs you want to use. You're now ready to start shopping for hardware. That means addressing the seven basic areas that differentiate each Mac model. The table "Comparing Macs" shows how the members of the Mac family fare in each category. We'll take a detailed look at most of these categories in later chapters; for now, here's an overview of what to think about before opening your checkbook.

❖ *Size* If portability is important, you'll want to consider the Mac Portable or one of the members of Apple's *compact Mac* line: the Classic or SE/30. (The members of the Mac II family form the *modular Mac* line.) Of these, the Portable is the only one that runs on batteries. It fits on airline tray tables, but at

Comparing Macs

	Classic	SE/30	LC	IIsi	IIci	IIfx	Portable
Portability	good (weighs about 20 lbs., has built-in screen, but requires power source	good (weighs about 20 lbs., has built-in screen, but requires power source	fair (weighs about 8 lbs., but requires monitor and power source	fair (small system unit, but requires external monitor and power source	fair (small system unit, but requires external monitor and power source	poor (large system unit, requires external monitor and power source	very good (weighs under 16 lbs., has built-in screen, runs on batteries
Speed (1=slowest, 6=fastest)	1	4	3	4	5	6	2
Internal Expandability	poor (no slots)	good (1 slot)	good (1 slot)	good (1 slot)	very good (3 slots)	very good (6 slots)	good (3 specialized slots)
Video Flexibility	poor (supports single built-in screen only)	very good (supports 1 external monochrome or color/grey-scale monitor)	very good (contains built-in color/grey-scale circuitry)	very good-excellent (contains built-in color/grey-scale circuitry; also accepts one video board)	excellent (contains built-in color/grey-scale circuitry; also accepts up to 3 video boards)	excellent (supports up to 5 color/grey-scale)	very good (highly legible built-in screen; supports external color/grey-scale monitors with Apple adapter)
Memory Capacity*	very good (up to 4MB)	excellent (up to 8MB)	excellent (up to 10MB)	excellent (up to 17 MB)	excellent (up to 8MB)	excellent (up to 8MB)	fair (up to 2MB)
Virtual Memory Support	no	yes	no	yes	yes	yes	no

*Macs with NuBus expansion slots can also accept memory boards to extend their memory beyond the values listed here.

16 pounds, it's no lightweight. Straddling the fence between the compact and modular Macs is the Macintosh LC. The LC isn't battery powered like the Portable, but at only eight pounds (not including the display *monitor*), it's easy to move around.

❖ *Speed* The Mac SE/30, LC, and the II family are faster than the Classic and Portable, and therefore are better able to handle applications that demand fast processing speed. Even the lowly Mac Classic can handle such tasks as simple word processing and filing, black-and-white drawing, telecommunications, light-duty desktop publishing and spreadsheet work, and creating and using HyperCard stacks. (HyperCard is covered in Chapter 9.) You'll probably want a faster Mac, however, for working with large databases or spreadsheets, large word processor documents with indexes and tables of contents, color illustrations or animations, or large desktop publications containing color.

❖ *Expandability* The SE and II families and the LC contain internal *expansion slots* into which you can plug *cards* or *boards* that add to the machine's capabilities. *Accelerator boards* boost performance, *video boards* control monitors, and *communications boards* let you connect to other computers over the phone or to high-speed office networks. Expansion slots are also an excellent defense against obsolescence. For example, an accelerator board can make a Mac SE roughly as fast as a Mac IIci.

❖ *Video features* The Macintosh Portable and Classic can display only black screen dots and white screen dots, or *pixels*. If you want to work with color or true shades of grey (like those displayed by televisions), you'll want a Mac equipped with color or *grey-scale* video hardware. That means an LC, or an SE/30 or member of the II family equipped with color video circuitry.

Just as some cameras include built-in lenses while others require separately purchased ones, some Macs contain built-in video circuitry, while others require you to buy a separate video card. Black and white, or *monochrome,* video circuitry and screens are built into the Mac Classic, Portable, and SE/30 (and into the now-discontinued Plus). The LC, IIsi, and IIci contain video circuitry that can create up to 256 colors or grey shades (see the figure "True Grey"). For business graphics, presentations, black-and-white scanned images, and many desktop publishing applications, 256 colors are more than enough, but they may not be adequate for working with scanned color photographs or illustrations. For those tasks, you may want a *24-bit* color video card such as Apple's Macintosh Display Card 8•24, SuperMac's Spectrum/24, or RasterOps's ColorBoard 264. These cards are also often called *true-color* cards, since they can display color images with photographic realism. You can add a true-color

True Grey

The Mac LC and members of the II family can display true grey shades (top), while the Classic, SE/30, Portable, and other compact Macs simulate grey shades (bottom). For applications that involve working with illustrations or scanned images, you'll want a Mac with color or grey-scale video hardware.

card to any member of the Mac II family, to the SE/30, and eventually, to the LC (at this writing, no true-color cards were available for the LC — that will change in time).

For desktop publishing, electronic drawing and drafting, and word processing applications, consider a large-screen monitor such as Apple's Portrait Display or Two-Page Monochrome Monitor, which show one or two letter-size pages, respectively. Or you might consider one of the large-screen color monitors offered by firms such as SuperMac, Radius, and RasterOps.

❖ *Memory capacity* If your applications demand speed, chances are they'll devour memory and disk space, too. In its least-expensive configuration, the Mac Classic comes standard with 1 megabyte (MB) of memory, also called *RAM*. That's barely enough. (These days, it's rarely enough.) 2MB of memory — the minimum amount you'll find in all other Macs except the Portable — will provide better performance and let you run at least two programs at the same time and switch between them in a flash. You'll also need at least 2MB of memory to run Apple's System 7.0 software — that major enhancement to the Mac's fundamental operating software that I mentioned in the Introduction.

If you plan to work extensively with sounds and color images — or if you want to be able to run several programs simultaneously — you'll probably want (if not need) 4MB. You can add that extra memory by purchasing memory boards called *SIMMs*, short for *Single Inline Memory Module*. If you want to be able to run several memory-devouring applications at once, consider an SE/30, LC, or a modular Mac. They can accommodate more than 4MB of RAM.

❖ *Disk-storage capacity* Every Mac model except the entry-level versions of the Classic and Portable includes one built-in, or *internal, hard disk.* That's good, because hard disks hold far more information and transfer it far more quickly than do floppy disks. Today's complex programs require that speed and capacity. Without a hard disk, you'll endure slow performance and you'll swap floppy disks until your hands hurt. With one, the Mac starts programs and opens documents swiftly, and you'll be able to switch between programs and documents without shuffling floppies.

You can supplement your internal hard disk with an external hard disk (or add an internal or external hard disk to an entry-level Portable or Classic). Prices for external hard drives have dropped sharply in recent years. By shopping from mail-order firms such as MacConnection, you can buy a 20MB or 40MB drive for just a little more than what Apple charges for a second floppy drive. (By the way, you don't need a second floppy drive if you're buying a Mac with a hard disk, although one will make copying floppy disks far more convenient — and you should always make backups of any software you purchase. Without a hard disk, a second floppy drive is all but essential.)

❖ *Virtual memory support* System 7.0 provides a *virtual memory* feature that lets the Mac treat a hard disk as an extension of RAM, thus allowing you to run more programs than would otherwise fit into memory. Although all Macs from the Plus on can run System 7.0, the Classic, LC, and Portable don't support the virtual memory features. (The original Mac II doesn't either, unless you add a $200 chip.) So, to take best advantage of System 7.0, consider an SE/30, IIsi, IIci, or IIfx. But don't base a purchase on this factor alone. Add a few megabytes of memory, and any Mac can run several large programs at once.

The Used Mac Lot

In October 1990, Apple revamped the Macintosh line, adding three new machines and discontinuing the Plus, SE, IIcx, and IIx. But you may still find these discontinued machines on dealer shelves for a while, and they'll be showing up in classified ads and on college dorm bulletin boards for years. Should you consider one? That depends on the model:

❖ Avoid the Mac Plus if your budget allows it. It's true that the Plus runs virtually all of today's software, and given 2MB of memory, it can run System 7.0 (although it won't support virtual memory). But its weakling power supply and lack of an expansion slot make obsolescence-shattering upgrades such as accelerator boards impractical and risky. What's more, as the Mac family as a whole gets faster, software developers are creating increasingly complex programs that often run sluggishly on the Plus. The Plus is still a workhorse for tasks that don't demand blazing speed, but elsewhere it's showing its age.

❖ As for the SE, its single expansion slot gives it a brighter future. Indeed, its expansion slot makes the SE less prone to obsolescence than the Mac Classic that replaced both it and the Plus. Unlike the Plus, the SE can reliably accommodate an accelerator board and an internal hard disk. It's also about 25 percent faster than the Plus, and about as fast as a Classic.

❖ The IIcx was a fine machine, and many Mac buffs were sad to see it go. Its three expansion slots (two, after you add a required video card) provide plenty of room to grow. The IIcx is slower than the Mac IIsi that replaced it, but it's faster than the Mac LC. The IIcx remains a good choice for someone who wants the performance of the Mac II line, can't afford a IIci, but needs more expandability than the single-slot Mac IIsi provides.

❖ The IIx was a slow seller before Apple phased it out, and for some good reasons. It cost more than the other members of the Mac II line, yet it's slower. Its large case also requires a significant chunk of desktop real estate. The IIx's primary (and enduring) strength is that it provides six expansion slots — enough for the most avid card collector. Another IIx advantage is that you can upgrade it to the top-of-the-line Mac IIfx for $2999 plus another $300–$500 for memory. A used, reasonably priced IIx (or II, for that matter) could be an ideal stepping stone to a IIfx.

Finally, what about the Macs prior to the Plus — the 512K Enhanced, 512K, and 128K? All three can be upgraded to a Mac Plus, but their future ends there. Unless the price is right and your budget won't budge, avoid these Macs.

Dot Matrix and Laser Printers

Chances are you'll want to commit your work to paper. If your budget is very tight, consider a *dot matrix* printer such as Apple's ImageWriter II or ImageWriter LQ — both print by striking a cloth ribbon with a series of fine wires. ImageWriter output looks good, but it has that computer-printer look. However, because ImageWriters are *impact* printers and can accept *continuous-feed* paper stock, they're the scribes of choice for printing on multipart business forms and mailing labels. Both the ImageWriter II and the LQ accept optional expansion cards that let you share the printer with numerous Macs that are interconnected by *LocalTalk* network cables.

If you plan to do desktop publishing, you'll probably want a *laser printer.* These use photocopier-like mechanisms to produce sharp output that looks similar to the output of a typesetting machine, with print resolution of 300 dots per inch (dpi) versus an ImageWriter II's 140 dpi and an LQ's 216 dpi. A laser printer's resolution is still short of a typesetter's (1270 dpi and up), but it's sharp enough to render the subtle line strokes and serifs of most typefaces, or *fonts.*

One of the least expensive laser printers is Apple's Personal LaserWriter LS, which retails for approximately $1200. The LS produces first-rate output, thanks to its use of Apple's *TrueType* fonts, which I'll examine in later chapters. When you use Adobe Systems' Adobe Type Manager utility, you can choose from thousands of additional fonts. You can't share a Personal LaserWriter LS with other Macs on a network, however.

If you're serious about publishing — or if you want to share your printer with other Macs in your office — you'll want a printer that uses Adobe Systems' *PostScript* page-description language. PostScript printers such as Apple's Personal

LaserWriter NT and LaserWriter IINTX contain powerful computers that can produce remarkable graphic and type effects. They also contain software and built-in network connectors that let you share a printer with other Macs and even with IBM PCs.

PostScript printers cost more than non-PostScript ones, but costs are coming down. Numerous PostScript printers are available for between $2000 and $3000, including Texas Instruments' microLaser PS17 and PS35, QMS' PS-410, GCC's Business LaserPrinter II (BLP II), and Apple's Personal LaserWriter NT.

PostScript clones — printers that act like PostScript printers but don't use Adobe's version of the language, such as Qume's CrystalPrint Publisher II and Abaton's LaserScript — sometimes sell for less or are a bit faster at printing documents containing a variety of fonts and sizes, but I've had mixed results with them. If you're shopping for a PostScript printer, I recommend buying one that contains an Adobe PostScript interpreter.

It's worth mentioning that you can get PostScript output without buying a printer: simply carry a floppy disk containing completed documents to a desktop publishing *service bureau* for printing. Many printing companies and college libraries also rent time on Macs and PostScript printers. These alternatives aren't as convenient as having a printer in your home or office, but saving a few thousand dollars can make a little inconvenience palatable. (In Chapter 36, I'll spotlight another alternative: PostScript *emulation* software that lets you print PostScript documents on non-PostScript printers.)

Ink Jet Printers

If you're on a tight budget but crave that laser printer look, an excellent alternative is an *ink jet* printer such as Apple's remarkably compact StyleWriter or Hewlett-Packard's DeskWriter. Ink jet printers straddle the fence between lasers and inexpensive dot matrix printers. Like a dot matrix printer, an ink jet printer contains a relatively simple print mechanism containing a print head that glides from left to right, applying ink as the paper advances. But where a dot matrix printer uses fine wires that strike an inked ribbon (whining all the while), an ink jet printer uses microscopic jets that silently spray fine streams of ink at the paper — it's spray painting on a microscopic level. Like a laser, an ink jet printer is a *non-impact* printer, and thus, it can't print on carbon or carbonless multipart forms. But more to the point, ink jets are capable of laser-like resolution — the HP DeskWriter yields 300-dpi resolution, while the somewhat slower StyleWriter prints 360 dpi.

Good, Better, Best
The output of a dot-matrix printer such as an ImageWriter II isn't bad (top), but it can't compare to the near-typeset look of ink-jet (middle) or laser (bottom) output. The higher resolution of ink jet and laser printers allows them to more accurately render the subtleties of true typographic fonts. But note the fuzzy-edged quality of ink jet output caused by the ink spreading into the paper's fibers as it dries.

NEWS FLASH!

The quick brown fox jumped over the lazy dog's back!

Film at eleven.

NEWS FLASH!

The quick brown fox jumped over the lazy dog's back!

Film at eleven.

NEWS FLASH!

The quick brown fox jumped over the lazy dog's back!

Film at eleven.

But an ink jet's output still isn't in the laser league. Up close, even the naked eye can discern sloppy character edges created by ink seeping into the paper's fibers as it dries (see the figure "Good, Better, Best"). Scanned images and large black areas have a mottled look. You can minimize these flaws by photocopying printed pages, but handle them gently — ink jet output can smear in its first few seconds of life. Indeed, until improved ink formulations arrived only recently, a drop of water caused even dry ink jet output to run like Tammy Faye's mascara.

Today's ink jet printers no longer require special paper as did some pioneering models of the mid-80s, but they're still more finicky than lasers. They generally can't handle heavy card stocks, and can't automatically feed multiple envelopes.

Output quality varies dramatically depending on the quality of paper you use, and you'll also wait longer to see it — most personal laser printers can churn out several pages in the time it takes an ink jet to produce one.

But it's hard to argue with an ink jet printer's price. Apple's StyleWriter retails for just over $599, while HP's DeskWriter is often discounted by dealers and mail-order retailers to below $700. GCC Technologies' WriteMove, which offers 192-dpi resolution instead of the DeskWriter's 300 dpi, retails for $549.

Other Add-Ons

Another peripheral you might consider is a *modem,* which lets you connect to other computers using phone lines. Team a modem with *communications software,* and you can send electronic mail on services such as MCI Mail, America Online, and CompuServe. As we'll see in Chapter 13, you can also tap into a vast network of fellow computer users to exchange ideas and obtain free or nearly free software.

If you'll be doing desktop publishing or computer illustration, you might want a *scanner,* which lets you turn artwork and photographs into digital images that you can alter, or trace over and include in publications. Combine a scanner with *optical character recognition* (OCR) software such as Caere's OmniPage, Olduvai's Read-It, and DEST's Recognize!, and you can scan pages of text and edit the results using your word processor. We'll look at scanners and OCR in detail in later chapters.

Which Route for You?

Before you buy a Mac, you need to weigh the differences between each model and determine which features are most important to you. This will help you get the machine best suited to your present and future computer needs.

Aside from actually writing out the check, deciding which machine is right for you is one of the hardest steps in the purchasing process. It's at this juncture that you'll realize just how many ways exist for you to reach your hardware goals. For example, say you've determined that you need a fast Mac with a hard disk and 4MB of memory. Should you buy an SE/30 or a member of the II family? Or should you get a used SE and install an accelerator board? Should you buy a stripped-down Mac and a mail-order memory upgrade and hard disk? Or should you spring

SAMPLE SYSTEMS

Low-Cost System

Macintosh Classic
External floppy drive
ImageWriter II or
StyleWriter
Future additions:
External SCSI hard disk,
2400-baud modem,
memory upgrades (to
maximum of 4MB).

Portable System

Macintosh Portable
Memory upgrade
StyleWriter printer with
battery pack
Future additions:
Internal modem, video
adapter and monitor

Economical Business/Professional System

Monochrome: Macintosh Classic with 40MB hard disk
Color: Macintosh LC with 40MB or 80MB hard disk
Apple Personal LaserWriter LS or NT
Memory upgrade to 4MB
Future additions:
Accelerator board, upgrade from Personal LaserWriter LS to NT,
24-bit color board (LC only), 2400-baud modem.

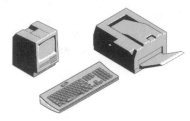

Performance-Oriented Business/Professional System

Mid-range: Macintosh IIci with 80MB hard disk
High-end: Macintosh IIfx with 80MB or 160MB hard disk
Apple Keyboard or Apple Extended Keyboard II
PostScript laser printer
Memory upgrade to 5–8MB
Video card (for IIfx only; IIci contains video circuitry)
Color or monochrome monitor
Future additions:
More memory, additional monitors, 9600-baud modem,
additional disk storage, cache memory card (IIci only), 24-bit video board

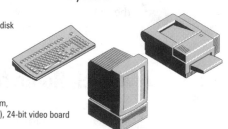

Listed here are several ways to assemble a Mac system, each geared to different needs and price ranges. Suggested retail prices aren't listed here because they change frequently; also, you may find dealers offering discounts of 20 percent or more, especially if you shop in urban areas. Remember, for hard disks, memory, monitors, and other peripherals, you're likely to find less-expensive alternatives from third-party manufacturers.

When you buy any Mac except the Classic, LC, or Portable, you purchase the keyboard separately. The Apple Extended Keyboard II costs more than the Apple Keyboard but provides additional keys, including cursor control keys, which make it easier to navigate large word processing documents, and function keys, which many programs let you use as an alternative to choosing commands with the mouse.

for a system in which those components are factory installed? The figure "Sample Systems" shows several routes you might consider. Here are a few more buying tips to steer you in the right direction.

❖ Buy the fastest Mac you can afford, even if your present needs are simple. You'll enjoy top-notch performance, and your hardware will be better suited to running System 7.0 and the programs that exploit its talents. At the very least, your system will retain its value better should you decide to sell it.

❖ Don't be afraid to mix and match components. There may be a certain comfort that comes with buying all your components from one company, but that comfort will cost you. You can often save money by buying non-Apple hard disks, printers, modems, network connectors, and memory upgrades. And many third-party hard disks and laser printers are faster than Apple's. On the other hand, many third-party products lack the "plug and play" setup convenience of Apple's add-ons, which are designed to mesh tightly with the rest of your Mac system. Also, some companies strip away features to arrive at a lower list price — some low-cost laser printers, for example, require you to purchase extra memory if you want to print on legal-sized (8½ by 14-inch) paper. The bottom line: You can save money and often get superior hardware by buying third-party products, but assess your needs and compare features carefully.

❖ To save even more, buy your third-party gear through the mail. Items available through most mail-order firms include printers, hard disks, external floppy drives, modems, scanners, video monitors, network cables, software, and memory upgrades. (The latter require careful hands but no special tools to install in a Mac LC or II-class machine; for compact Macs, you're better off having a dealer install extra memory.) The drawbacks: you're likely to suffer delays if a defective component needs to be returned, and you won't be able to turn to one source for technical assistance. Some consumers have also been burned when the manufacturer of their mail-order hard disks filed for bankruptcy after charging their credit cards for goods never delivered. *Caveat emptor.* And ask fellow Mac users to recommend prompt, reliable mail-order houses that they've dealt with.

❖ Join a user group. Asking other people about products and places to buy them is a good idea no matter how much experience you have. Call 800/538-9696, extension 500, to find the group closest to you. As your experience grows, you may evolve from a question asker to a question answerer, helping newcomers tread the same path you did.

Good Buy for Now

One more piece of advice: don't put off a purchase in the hopes that some future Mac will offer dramatic new features at half the price. If you really need a machine now, buy a machine now. It will be supplanted by faster machines with new features, but if you buy a Mac with expansion slots, chances are you'll be able to buy boards that boost performance or add those new features to your existing machine.

More to the point, if you wait to buy a Mac, you'll miss out on the productivity-boosting benefits one can provide. It's like waiting to buy a car in the hopes that next year's model will be cheaper or get better gas mileage. Maybe it will, maybe it won't, but one thing is certain: you'll do a lot of walking in the meantime.

Summary:

✔ Finding the right Macintosh requires assessing your needs in the areas of portability, speed, expandability, video features, and memory and disk-storage capacity.

✔ Of the used or discontinued Macs, ones with expansion slots are the least prone to obsolescence.

✔ For the hard copy, you can buy a dot matrix, ink jet, or laser printer. Each is progressively more expensive, but provides sharper, faster output. PostScript printers are preferable for publishing and can be shared on a network.

✔ Other peripherals to consider include a modem for connecting to other computers via the phone lines, and a scanner for digitizing images and scanning text.

✔ You can often save money by buying non-Apple products, but be aware that some third-party products may not offer the same features or plug-and-play convenience as Apple's.

Chapter 2
Macintosh Basics

In This Chapter:

✔ An introduction to the Mac's easy operating style.

✔ Explanations of the fundamental software you'll encounter.

✔ Details on how to navigate through the Mac and its programs.

✔ Navigational shortcuts not found in manuals.

✔ Suggestions on how to master your Mac.

The Mac is an easy-to-use machine, but it's also powerful and complex. And because it's so easy to learn basic Mac tasks, many people never venture into the nooks and crannies that help make the machine so powerful.

Before we look at ways to put the Mac to work, we're going to venture into some of those nooks and crannies. This chapter isn't a step-by-step tutorial on Mac basics — the Mac's manuals contain detailed tutorials, and I'd be wasting space by repeating them here. Instead, this chapter is a sound overview of the Mac's interface and of basic Mac operating techniques. If you're a Mac veteran, you probably talk about these things in your sleep. If you're new to the Mac or you use it only occasionally, the information in this chapter will form the foundation that we'll build on in the rest of this book.

The Mac's Way of Doing Things

The cornerstones of the Mac's easy operating style are its graphical user interface and its mouse. Many computers require you to memorize and type cryptic commands or choose them from option lists whose workings vary from program to program — not the Mac. You control the Mac by using the mouse to control the position of an on-screen arrow, called the *pointer*. By rolling the mouse and pointing to the elements you see on the screen and then *clicking* the button on top of the mouse, you can issue commands, work with disks, and much more.

The figure "Face to Interface" shows the key elements of the Mac's user interface. Your Mac manual describes them in detail, so I'll just summarize them here.

❖ The *desktop* is your electronic work surface, upon which rest *icons,* pictorial representations of objects such as disks, or of functions such as the Trash can.

❖ The *menu bar* contains *menu titles.* When you point to a menu title and then press and hold the mouse button, a list of *commands* called a *menu* appears. To choose a command, move the mouse pointer while pressing the mouse button until the command is *highlighted,* then release the button. The leftmost menu is the *Apple menu;* it's always available regardless of the program you're using. The remaining menus change depending on the program you're using. When you start a program, it takes over the menu bar, replacing the menus that were there with its own. Nearly all programs provide File and Edit menus, but the menus' commands usually differ between programs.

The Apple menu lists your available *desk accessories,* which are handy programs you can select while running another program such as a word

▼ **Face to Interface**

The Mac's user interface relies on these standard elements. The icon labelled "Startup" is that of an Iomega Bernoulli Box II, which stores 44MB on a removable cartridge. Icons for hard disks and other non-floppy mass storage drives will vary depending on the brand of drive.

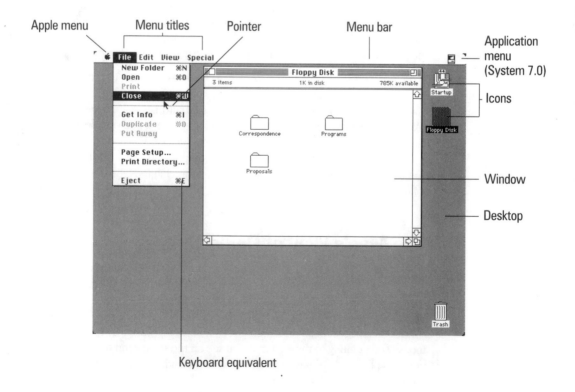

processor. The Mac comes with numerous desk accessories. Some, such as the Calculator and Alarm Clock, mimic real-world desk accessories. Others, such as the Control Panel and Chooser, let you manage certain aspects of the Mac's operation. We'll look at both types of desk accessories in later chapters, and I'll spotlight some third-party desk accessories you might want to add to your collection.

❖ *Windows* are viewing portals that let you see the contents of a disk or document. Windows themselves have standard elements that let you move them on the desktop, change their size, *close* them (make them disappear), and *scroll* through them (view information that isn't currently visible within a window's boundaries). The figure "Looking at Windows", on the next page, shows each of these elements. You can have many windows open on the screen at once, but only one is *active.* The active window has thin horizontal stripes in its title bar; an inactive window doesn't.

❖ *Dialog boxes* contain *buttons, check boxes, text boxes,* and other elements that let you provide more information and select various options after you've chosen a command. For example, when you choose the Print command, you get a dialog box that, among other things, lets you specify which pages you want to print and how many copies you want.

Finder and MultiFinder Basics

The first piece of software you encounter when you start up your Mac is the *Finder.* The Finder is the link between you and the rest of the Mac's *system software,* the fundamental software that enables the Mac to run. You use the Finder to start or *launch* programs, to delete files, and to copy, eject, and erase disks. The Finder also provides disk-management conveniences — the Get Info command for attaching descriptive text to files, for example — and it lets you organize a disk's contents by creating folders and moving documents, programs, or other folders into them. And the Finder's Print Directory command (in the File menu) lets you print *directory* print-outs that show what's on a disk or in a certain folder.

Then there's *MultiFinder,* which enhances the Finder by allowing the Mac to run more than one program at once, eliminating the need to quit one program to start another. MultiFinder also makes working with files and disks more convenient, since the Trash and the rest of the Finder's features are always available. And if you have an Apple Personal LaserWriter SC, LS, or a PostScript-based laser printer, MultiFinder provides a *background printing* option that lets you save time when printing.

Close box   Window title   Title bar

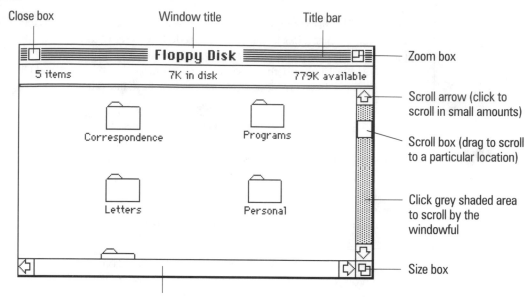

Zoom box

Scroll arrow (click to scroll in small amounts)

Scroll box (drag to scroll to a particular location)

Click grey shaded area to scroll by the windowful

Size box

Scroll bar is unshaded and lacks a scroll box when there's nothing beyond the window's boundaries

▲ **Looking at Windows**

Windows provide standard components, shown here, that let you move, close, scroll through, and resize them. These components operate similarly in all Mac programs, so once you've learned how to work with a window such as this Finder directory window, you can work with windows in any program.

Of course, these extra capabilities will cost you — in memory. You can run MultiFinder on a 1MB Mac, but you probably won't have enough memory left over to run any of today's powerful programs. To get the most from MultiFinder, you'll want at least 2MB, and preferably more. The more memory your Mac has, the more programs you'll be able to run simultaneously.

Choosing Between the Finder and MultiFinder

In system versions preceding 7.0, you can choose whether to use MultiFinder or the "single" Finder. To specify whether or not the Mac uses MultiFinder, select your disk's icon, choose the Set Startup command from the Finder's Special menu, select the MultiFinder or Finder option as desired, and then click the OK button. Finally, choose Restart from the Special menu.

When you choose to run under the single Finder, the Finder's disk- and file-management features aren't available when you're using an application program. To throw away a file or create a folder, you'll need to quit the program you're using. Despite this limitation, using the single Finder is a good idea if your Mac has only 1MB of RAM; otherwise, you'll probably want to use MultiFinder to gain its benefits.

If your Mac is running System 7.0, you're running MultiFinder all the time. (Indeed, in System 7.0, the Finder and MultiFinder are one and the same.) The fact that MultiFinder is always active under System 7.0 is one reason why System 7.0 requires a minimum of 2MB of memory.

We'll look at memory and MultiFinder issues again in Section II. In the meantime, check your Mac manual; it explains MultiFinder's benefits in detail. Pay particularly close attention to the section that describes how to fine-tune your program's memory requirements. As we'll see in Section II, by fine-tuning program memory requirements, you can get better performance or squeeze more programs into memory at once.

Clipboard 101

The Mac's *Clipboard* enables you to move information between programs, and has always been one of the Mac's greatest strengths. Thanks to the Cut, Copy, and Paste commands that virtually all Mac programs provide, you can include graphics in a word processor document — or paragraphs of text in a drawing.

Apple's ads often showcase this ability by depicting a fancy business report with a chart shoehorned into it. Combining text and graphics to create what are often called *compound documents* is certainly one way to put the Clipboard to work. But don't ignore its more mundane uses. Recycle text or part of a graphic by copying it from an older version of a document. If you're always typing a finger-twisting scientific term, copy it to the Clipboard and paste it in each time it's needed. To remind yourself of what's in a word processor document, copy the first few lines of it and paste them into the Finder's Get Info window for that document — more about Get Info shortly.

If you use the Calculator desk accessory (DA, for short), you can copy the result of a calculation and then paste it into a document; simply choose Copy after performing the calculation. You can also paste numbers or math symbols from the Clipboard to the Calculator. You'll even see the Calculator's keys flash to reflect what you've pasted. (You'll also hear a lot of error beeps if you paste characters that don't correspond to keys on the Calculator.) And here's a handy way to "stamp" a document with the time you started working on it: select the Alarm Clock DA from the Apple menu, choose Copy to put the current time and date on the Clipboard, and then paste it at the beginning of your document.

The Clipboard's contents vanish when the Mac is switched off, but you can save them using the Scrapbook DA: just open the Scrapbook and choose Paste. Doing so adds a new "page" containing the Clipboard's contents to the Scrapbook (see

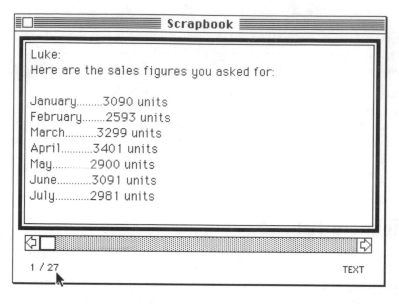

```
┌──────────────────────────────────────────────────┐
│ ▤□▤▤▤▤▤▤▤▤▤▤▤▤ Scrapbook ▤▤▤▤▤▤▤▤▤▤▤▤▤ │
│ ┌──────────────────────────────────────────────┐ │
│ │ Luke:                                        │ │
│ │ Here are the sales figures you asked for:    │ │
│ │                                              │ │
│ │ January.........3090 units                   │ │
│ │ February........2593 units                   │ │
│ │ March...........3299 units                   │ │
│ │ April...........3401 units                   │ │
│ │ May.............2900 units                    │ │
│ │ June............3091 units                    │ │
│ │ July............2981 units                    │ │
│ │                                              │ │
│ └──────────────────────────────────────────────┘ │
│ ◁ ▢▒▒▒▒▒▒▒▒▒▒▒▒▒▒▒▒▒▒▒▒▒▒▒▒▒▒▒ ▷ │
│   1 / 27                              TEXT        │
└──────────────────────────────────────────────────┘
```

the figure "Compiling a Scrapbook"). To retrieve an item from the Scrapbook, use the scroll bar to get to the desired page, then choose Copy from the Edit menu (or Cut to remove the item from the Scrapbook).

The Scrapbook's contents are stored in a file called Scrapbook File, located in the System Folder. If you want to move your Scrapbook to a different Mac, copy the Scrapbook File to a floppy

▲ **Compiling a Scrapbook**
The Clipboard's contents vanish when the Mac is switched off, but you can save them by opening the Scrapbook (choose its name from the Apple menu) and choosing Paste. To retrieve an item from the Scrapbook, use the scroll bar to get to the desired page, then choose Copy from the Edit menu.

disk and then copy it to the System Folder on the second Mac. Note that you'll replace the existing Scrapbook; you might want to stash the existing one in a different folder first.

If you use the Scrapbook extensively, consider one of the more powerful Scrapbook alternatives such as Solutions International's SmartScrap or Olduvai Software's MultiClip. Both support multiple Scrapbook files, allowing you to create separate ones for, say, text and graphics. Each also provides a table of contents feature that shows lots of pages reduced to fit within a window and allows you to jump to a specific page in a flash (see the figure "A Smarter Scrapbook").

What's Your Version Number?

That isn't a line from a Silicon Valley singles bar. Software evolves over time — bugs are fixed, features are added, performance is improved — and *version numbers* indicate just how far along the evolutionary timeline a particular program is.

There are a few good reasons to know how to determine version numbers. When you call a dealer or software firm for technical help, you'll probably be asked which version of the Mac's system software you're using. When you buy a program, you'll want to be sure you're buying the latest version. And you'll want to verify its compatibility with the version of the Mac's system software you use.

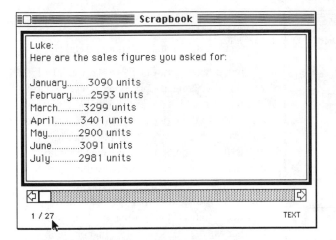

A Smarter Scrapbook

Alternatives to Apple's bare-bones Scrapbook desk accessory (top) include Olduvai's MultiClip and Solutions' SmartScrap (bottom), which provides a table of contents feature that shows numerous Scrapbook pages in reduced form. You can jump to a specific page by double-clicking it, and you can name pages for fast searching. You can also switch between different Scrapbook files. Apple's Scrapbook limits you to just one Scrapbook file and shows only one page at a time.

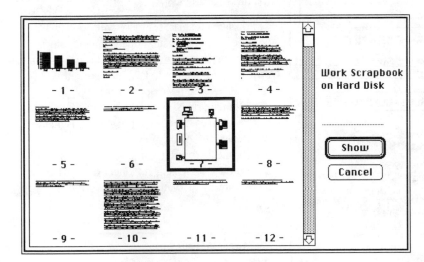

One way to determine a version number is to use the *About command*, which always appears first in the Apple menu. To learn the version number of your Mac's system software, for example, choose the About the Finder command. (In System 7.0, the command reads About This Macintosh.) To learn the version number of an application program, start that program and choose its About command.

Another way to determine a program's version number is to use the Finder's Get Info command: Select the program's icon and choose Get Info from the File menu. The file's version number appears in the Get Info window (see the figure "What's Your Version?" on the next page).

The Get Info command also works for documents you create. A document file doesn't have a version number to appear in the Get Info window, but you can use

```
▤□▥▥▥▥▥▥▥▥ Info ▥▥▥▥▥▥▥▥
```

Aldus FreeHand   Locked ☐

Kind: application
Size: 716,421 bytes used, 700K on disk

Where: Hard Disk (SCSI #1)

Created: Mon, Nov 21, 1988, 6:13 PM
Modified: Mon, Nov 21, 1988, 6:15 PM
Version: 2.0, © Altsys Corporation, 1988

Suggested Memory Size (K): 750
Application Memory Size (K): [1200]

```
▤□▥▥▥▥ QuarkXPress® Info ▥▥▥▥▥
```

QuarkXPress®
QuarkXPress® 3.0

Kind: application program
Size: 1.6 MB on disk (1,724,901 bytes used)
Where: System 7.0 Startup: QuarkXPress Folder: QuarkXPress®

Created: Fri, Aug 3, 1990, 10:38 AM
Modified: Mon, Dec 24, 1990, 3:48 PM
Version: 3.0 © 1986–1990 Quark, Inc.

Comments:

☐ **Locked**

┌─ **Memory** ──────────
Suggested size: 1,500 K
Current size: [1,500] K

the text box at the bottom of the window to type descriptive information about the file (or to hold a few sentences from it, as mentioned earlier).

Among manufacturers, there is no standard for version numbering, though there is a general rule. When a product is significantly improved, the number before the decimal point increases. When the revision fixes bugs or has only minor improvements, the number after the decimal goes up. A product label may say "requires System version 6.x." In this case, you need any version that begins with 6. A manufacturer may also state that its product requires "System version 6.0 or later" — in other words, a version with a higher number will probably also work.

I qualified that last sentence with "probably" because system software enhancements sometimes cause a program that worked fine under an earlier system version to fail. Sometimes this happens because developers bend Apple's programming rules. Other times, it happens because Apple changes the rules or spells them out ambiguously to begin with. Whatever the reason, the end result is the same: A program that used to run reliably no longer does. When these software growing pains surface, the

---

What's Your Version?

Choosing the Finder's Get Info command displays a window containing statistics about the selected application or document, a check box for locking the file to prevent accidental modification or deletion, and a text box that can contain several paragraphs of descriptive text. The Get Info window for an application also lists the program's memory requirements. By boosting the Application Memory Size value, you can often improve a program's performance. Lowering the value will probably make the program more sluggish, but can allow you to squeeze more programs into memory. At bottom, a Get Info window from System 7.0. Note the slightly different (and clearer) wording of the memory size text boxes, and the new location of the Locked check box.

program's developer will release a revised version that is compatible with the new system software.

But the new version may not be available immediately, and you don't want to be out of operation in the meantime. For that reason, before upgrading your Mac's system software to a new version, it's a good idea to verify its compatibility with the programs you use. Go straight to the source: call the technical support hotlines operated by the companies that published your programs.

Basic Navigation Techniques

An old bicyclists' maxim says that the easiest way to make your bike 5 pounds lighter is to lose 5 pounds. There's a variation of that truism for the Macintosh: the easiest way to boost your productivity with the Mac is to learn how to control it efficiently. Today's fast Macs and high-performance add-ons are great, but you won't get the most out of them until you master all the navigation options the Mac and its programs provide.

You might think that Mac navigation concepts could be summed up in one word: mouse. The mouse doesn't have exclusive domain over Mac manipulation, but there's no denying the rodent's role as the primary link between you and your Mac. That's why navigational expertise is built on three basics: the click, the double-click, and the drag.

Clicking — pressing the mouse's button once — is your way of telling the Mac, "Here's where I want to work." *Here* is where the mouse's on-screen pointer is. In the Finder, pointing to an icon and clicking tells the Mac to *select* the icon — to highlight it for a subsequent action. In a word processor, clicking produces a blinking *insertion point* where you've situated the pointer. In a dialog box, clicking a button performs an action, such as OKing or canceling your choices; clicking on a radio button or a check box selects an option. Most Macintosh programs follow these basic rules. "Buttons and Bars," on the following page, shows the differences between check boxes and radio buttons and spotlights some other components of the Mac interface.

Double-clicking — pressing the mouse button twice in rapid succession — creates a kind of super click, a cut above a single click in the mouse-maneuvering hierarchy. Double-clicking an icon in the Finder is the same as clicking it once, then choosing Open from the File menu. When you're editing text, whether in a word processor, a spreadsheet, or the text-entry portions of a dialog box, double-clicking while the pointer is on a word selects that word — it's faster than manually dragging the pointer across the entire word.

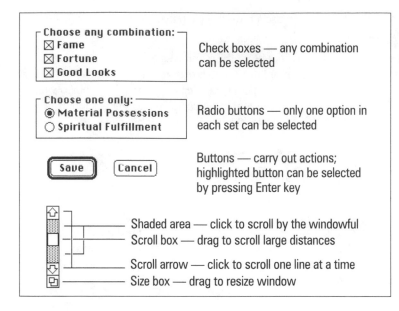

Check boxes — any combination can be selected

Radio buttons — only one option in each set can be selected

Buttons — carry out actions; highlighted button can be selected by pressing Enter key

Shaded area — click to scroll by the windowful
Scroll box — drag to scroll large distances

Scroll arrow — click to scroll one line at a time
Size box — drag to resize window

▲ **Buttons and Bars**
A guided tour of the interface elements you're likely to encounter in dialog boxes.

In programs that provide *palettes* — rows of icons that control program functions — double-clicking an icon often performs an action that's an extended version of the icon's normal purpose. In Claris' MacPaint and most other painting programs, for example, double-clicking the eraser icon clears the entire drawing window. In Claris' MacDraw II and MacDraw Pro, double-click on a tool and you can draw one shape after another without having to reselect the tool each time. In Claris's FileMaker II and FileMaker Pro database managers, double-click on a field name to modify it. In QuarkXpress, double-click on a text block or graphic to display the Modify dialog box. The list goes on — and you'll find it in your manuals.

(Incidentally, if you find that the Mac isn't treating two clicks as a double-click, you may not be clicking quickly enough. Either speed up your clicking or use the Mouse Control Panel option to tell the Mac to give you more time to double-click. Your Mac manual describes the latter option in detail.)

Dragging is the process of moving the mouse while holding down its button. You move windows by dragging their title bars. In the Finder, you move icons by dragging them. In a graphics program, dragging lets you draw with the tool that's selected in the program's palette. You can also reposition items by selecting them, then dragging. And in programs and dialog boxes that let you edit text, you can select text by dragging the pointer across it.

Natural Selection

Next to the big three, the most important Mac technique to perfect is selecting. A primary precept of the Macintosh says that selection is always the first step in an action: you select something, then tell the Mac what to do with it.

To select an object such as an icon in the Finder or a graphic element in a drawing or publishing program, point at the object and click — once. Don't be what my colleague Lon Poole calls a "hapless double-clicker": someone who habitually clicks twice when once will suffice. You can also select multiple objects by enclosing them in a selection rectangle, often called a *marquee* because its dotted lines flow like a movie marquee (see the figure "In the Marquee"). To draw a marquee, position the pointer at one corner of the area you want to enclose, hold down the mouse button and drag to the opposite corner; releasing the button highlights all selected objects. The technique works differently in certain applications — in some, like the Finder, you need only touch an object with the marquee, while in others, the whole object must be enclosed.

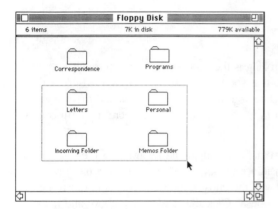

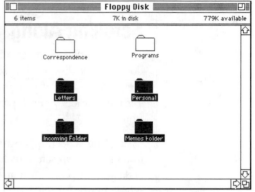

In the Marquee

In the Finder and in most desktop publishing and drawing programs, you can select multiple objects by enclosing them within a marquee (left). When you release the mouse button, the objects are selected (right).

You can combine the two main text-selection moves — selecting a word by double-clicking on it and selecting a range of text by dragging the pointer across it. Just double-click to select a single word, then without releasing the button after the second click, drag to select additional text, one word at a time. And if you selected the text as a prelude to replacing it, don't press Backspace or Delete before typing the new text. Just start typing; the first key you press clears the selected text.

When you need to alter a lengthy passage of text, dragging through it all can be a drag in itself. A better solution is to use the *Shift-click* technique. Locate the beginning of the passage you're changing and click to the left of its first character to create a blinking insertion point. Next, locate the end of the section, then hold down the Shift key and click to the right of the last character or, to include a Return character, at the beginning of the next line.

Shift-clicking also lets you extend a selection — that is, add additional items to an existing selection. Should you realize you didn't select enough text, just hold down the Shift key again and click at the appropriate place. To select a slew of icons, you might combine the marquee and Shift-clicking techniques: select icons adjacent to each other by enclosing them in a marquee, then add ones that are scattered throughout the window by Shift-clicking on them. These same techniques also apply in most graphics and desktop publishing programs, as well as in database managers that let you create customized forms.

The Shift key takes on an additional function in drawing and publishing programs: it lets you *constrain* a drawing action. For example, pressing Shift while drawing with an oval tool produces a perfect circle; with the rectangle tool, you get a perfect square; with a line tool, you get horizontal, vertical, or diagonal lines.

Scrolling Along

As I mentioned earlier, scrolling is the process of moving through a document or disk window so that you can see things that aren't visible within the window's size. If you imagine your document as a scroll and the window as a frame that lets you see part of it, you can understand where the term comes from.

Scrolling is such a pervasive activity, you should be aware of the three ways to do it. You can scroll in small increments (usually one line at a time) by clicking the Up or Down arrow at the ends of the scroll bar; hold down the mouse button to scroll continuously. Click the shaded area above and below the scroll box to scroll by the windowful, again holding down the mouse button to do so continuously. To scroll large distances in a single bound, drag the scroll box itself (for instance, to reach the end of a document, drag the box to the bottom of the scroll bar). With the third approach, an outline of the scroll box follows the pointer as you drag; when the outline is where you want it, release the mouse button and the window scrolls.

But for searching through a lengthy word processor document, scrolling can be cumbersome and time consuming. If your word processor provides one, use the Go To command to jump to a specific page. If you don't know the general vicinity of the text you're looking for, the Find command is a better option — if possible, select an unusual word or phrase that appears only in the section you're looking for and the Mac will take you there swiftly with no stops in between.

The Keys to Navigation

In the navigational realm, the Macintosh keyboard used to be considered a second-class citizen. Apple's philosophy held that keys should be used only for text entry, because keyboard commands were considered intimidating and far less intuitive than mouse movements.

That was true to an extent, but wordsmiths and data-entry artisans soon began moaning about how constant jumping between keyboard and mouse slowed them down. Fortunately, Apple listened. The Mac Plus keyboard debuted with *direction keys,* which let you move the insertion point, and from then on the Mac's keyboard maneuvering aids have steadily improved.

One keyboard control the Mac has always provided is the *Command-key shortcut,* which involves pressing the Command key along with a letter or number key. (The Command key is the key with the freeway cloverleaf and Apple symbols on it.) Command-key sequences let you execute commands from the keyboard so you can bypass the mouse. These shortcuts are especially useful in text-oriented programs like word processors, since they let you issue commands without moving a hand from the keyboard. A program's designers decide which commands will have Command-key shortcuts and list them alongside the corresponding menu commands. The most common are Command-Q to quit the application, Command-O to open a document that you've previously saved, Command-S to save your work on disk, and Command-P to print. Most programs with Font or Style menus offer Command-key shortcuts that let you access other type styles, such as italic or bold. Most word processors also use Command-F to summon the Find command. But you shouldn't assume that all applications use the same shortcuts — it's best to explore each application's menus to find out for sure.

> **The best navigation habit you can develop is to periodically press Command-S to save your document as you work.**

The best navigation habit you can develop is to periodically press Command-S to save your document as you work. Do it every few minutes — every time you pause for inspiration or get a phone call — and you won't lose much if a power failure or system error occurs. (Incidentally, don't be alarmed if a program doesn't have a Save command — many programs, including HyperCard and most database managers, save automatically as you work.)

Commands like Open and Find always lead to dialog boxes, which have keyboard-control options of their own. In an Open dialog box you can locate a specific document or folder by typing the first character of its name. If more than one document or folder starts with the same character, type a few characters. (Unless you type them in fairly rapid succession, though, the Mac

▼ **Dialog Box**
Shortcuts

In dialog boxes with multiple text-entry boxes, pressing Tab moves the insertion point from one text box to the next. Pressing Return or Enter selects the bold-outlined button. To print a partial range of pages rather than an entire document, you often don't need to type values in both the From and To boxes. For example, to print pages 1 through 5, type 5 in the To box and leave the From box blank. Similarly, to print starting at page 3 and continuing to the end of the document, type 3 in the From box and leave the To box blank.

assumes each keystroke is the first character in a different name.) Many people exploit this trick by preceding the names of often-used folders or documents with a number or punctuation character such as a period (.). That way, they can jump to a particular item by typing a single number or character. Any character will work except for the colon (:), which is the one character the Mac doesn't let you use in a document or folder name.

If your keyboard has direction keys, you can use them to scroll through the list of document and folder names. To open a document or a folder, select its name and press Return. To close a folder and move up one level in the folder hierarchy, press the Command-key along with the Up arrow key. To access a different disk, press Tab instead of clicking Drive (this doesn't work in System 7.0, where Tab lets you move between the list box and text-entry portions of the Open dialog box). To cancel the dialog box, press Command-period (.). Some people find these key sequences more cumbersome than using the mouse, but keyboard afficionados swear by them. It's another example of how the Mac lets you choose the navigation style that suits you.

Speaking of dialog boxes, you can use the Tab key to move between their text-entry boxes (see the figure "Dialog Box Shortcuts"). For example, to perform a search-and-replace in Microsoft Word, press Command-H to summon the Change dialog box, type the text you want located, press Tab to jump to the Replace With box, and type the new text. When you're ready to begin the search, there's still no need to reach for the mouse. Because the Start Search button is highlighted with a heavily outlined border, pressing the Enter key automatically chooses it. In any dialog box with a heavy-bordered button, pressing Enter is the same as clicking that button. Pressing the Return key usually (although not always) performs the same result.

When you use Tab to jump between text boxes, the Mac selects any text previously entered. That means you can type new text without having to backspace over an existing entry. Most database managers also let you move from one field to the next using Tab, and to the previous field using Shift-Tab. Spreadsheets use Tab and Shift-Tab to move one cell to the right or left, and Return and Shift-Return to move up or down one cell.

Assessing Your Options

In many programs, holding down the Option key while choosing a command or using the mouse produces a different result than that of the original action. Many times, these modified effects aren't discussed in the program's manual; you're left to discover them on your own or hear about them from other sources.

In the Finder, you can close all open windows by holding down Option while clicking a window's close box (see the sidebar "Finder 6.x Shortcuts"). Pressing Option while choosing the Finder's Eject command (or while clicking the Eject button in an Open or Save dialog box) tells the Mac to eject the disk and remove its icon from the desktop — as if you dragged the disk's icon to the Trash. For this

Finder 6.x Shortcuts

To accomplish this...	Do this...	To accomplish this...	Do this...
Bypass the warning dialog box	Press Option while dragging when you discard an application or the System file to the trash.	Copy a file from one folder to another instead of moving it.	Press Option while dragging the file to the destination folder.
Close all open disk/folder windows	Press Option while clicking any window's close box or choosing the Close command — or — Press Option immediately after quitting an application (not in MultiFinder).	Quickly determine whether a file is locked or unlocked.	Select the file, then move the pointer over the file's name. If the I-beam pointer appears, the file is not locked.
		Align all icons in a window.	Press Option while choosing Clean Up from the Special menu.
Move an inactive window without activating it.	Press Command while dragging the inactive window's title bar (works in applications, too).	"Program" a directory window to close automatically when you return to Finder.	Press Option while opening the directory window (doesn't apply to MultiFinder).

trick to work, you need to hold down the Option key until the disk has been ejected from the drive.

In most painting programs, pressing Option while dragging a selection duplicates that selection. Adobe Illustrator uses the Option key to modify the effects of numerous commands. In all of Claris' products except MacPaint, pressing Option while choosing the About command from the Apple menu displays a window containing technical information about your Mac. Sometimes the Option key even unlocks secret messages created by mischievous programmers.

While Option seems to be the favored modifier key, some programs use Shift, Command, or both. In Word, for example, pressing Shift while choosing Open tells the program to display a list of all files, instead of just word processing documents.

Navigation Nooks and Keyboard Crannies

For Mac users who like navigation shortcuts, Microsoft's programs, especially Word and Excel, are what musty second-hand stores are to antique hounds. In dialog boxes, you can double-click on a radio button to select it and confirm the dialog box. Double-click on a window's title bar, and the window shrinks to half size; double-click again, and it returns to normal. (Many other Mac developers have adopted this one.) Press Command-period (.) to cancel a dialog box. You can also press the Esc key on keyboards that have one. Faced with a Save Changes? dialog box, press Y, N or C to answer yes, no or cancel. (This works with QuarkXpress and many other programs, too.)

Word even lets you choose menu commands and dialog-box options with the keyboard. Press the period key on the Mac's numeric keypad (or Command-Tab on those lacking keypads), then the first letter of the menu. When the menu appears, press the first letter of the desired command (or use the direction keys to highlight the command) then choose it by pressing Return. In dialog boxes, you can "press" a button by holding down the Command key while typing the button's first letter. You can even select radio buttons from the keyboard, but doing so requires such a finger-tangling combination of keystrokes that it's only worth doing if your mouse goes feet up. (System 7.0, as we'll see in Chapter 25, also provides many of these options.)

Word, Excel, and File also provide a unique dialog-box feature called the local undo. By clicking the title above a list of radio buttons, you can undo any selections made in that list (see the figure "Local Undo").

```
┌─────────────────────────────────────────────┐
│ ≡≡≡≡≡≡≡≡≡≡ Character ≡≡≡≡≡≡≡≡≡≡             │
│ Font:                Size:       ┌────────┐  │
│ ┌──────────────┐⊞   ┌──┐⊞       │   OK   │  │
│ │ Courier      │     │12│         └────────┘  │
│                                  ┌────────┐  │
│ Underline:           Color:      │ Cancel │  │
│ ┌──────────────┐⊞   ┌────────┐⊞ └────────┘  │
│ │ None         │     │ Black  │   ┌────────┐  │
│                                   │ Apply  │  │
│ ┌─Style────────┐ ┌─Position──────────────┐  │
│ │ ☒ Bold       │ │ ◉ Normal    By:       │  │
│ │ ☐ Italic     │ │ ○ Superscript ┌─────┐ │  │
│ │ ☐ Outline    │ │ ○ Subscript   └─────┘ │  │
│ │ ☐ Shadow     │ └───────────────────────┘  │
│ │ ☐ Strikethru │ ┌─Spacing───────────────┐  │
│ │ ☐ Small Caps │ │ ◉ Normal    By:       │  │
│ │ ☐ All Caps   │ │ ○ Condensed  ┌─────┐  │  │
│ │ ☐ Hidden     │ │ ○ Expanded   └─────┘  │  │
│ └──────────────┘ └───────────────────────┘  │
└─────────────────────────────────────────────┘
```

Of course, Microsoft doesn't have a monopoly on clever shortcuts. Symantec's More and some other programs let you select dialog-box buttons by pressing the Command key along with the button's first letter. Claris's HyperCard provides *power keys* that let you issue commands with a single keystroke when a drawing or other non-text-entry tool is active; that is, when there's no blinking insertion point on screen. In HyperCard, for example, pressing A chooses Select All, H chooses Flip Horizontal, and V chooses Flip Vertical.

▲ **Local Undo**
In several Microsoft programs, you can undo changes in a dialog box by clicking the title above the list of options you've changed. Shown here: the Character dialog box from Microsoft Word 4.0.

Consider a Copilot

Any pilot will tell you that navigation is easier if you have a copilot. You can create your own keyboard shortcuts using a *macro* utility such as Apple's MacroMaker (included with System 6.x), or the more powerful QuicKeys from CE Software and Tempo II from Affinity Microsystems, both of which we'll look at in Chapter 19.

Other Stops on the Road to Mastery

Familiarizing yourself with the concepts, shortcuts, and commands I've presented in this chapter will take you a long way toward mastering your Mac. Here are a few more suggestions:

❖ Read. Many advanced Mac users brag that they never crack a manual — even when learning a new program. It's a testament to the Mac's graphical interface and to software designers that this is possible. Nonetheless, every program has its subtle points, and you're unlikely to find them unless you read or at least browse the manual. If you haven't already, work through the tutorials in the Mac's manual and in your program's manuals. More good places to uncover the hidden treasures of your favorite applications are in *Macworld*'s Quick Tips columns and in user-group newsletters. Or, you might browse through a tip anthology, such as Lon Poole's *Amazing Mac Facts* (Microsoft Press) and *The Macintosh Bible* (Goldstein and Blair).

❖ Register your software. By sending in the registration cards that accompany new programs, you'll be eligible for technical support and be notified when new versions are developed. Many companies offer newsletters containing tips and insights on their wares, and some also operate customer support forums on communications services such as CompuServe and America Online.

❖ Join a user group. As I mentioned in the last chapter, they're among the best sources of information, assistance, and free or nearly free software.

❖ Take time to play. Set aside time to experiment with your programs and desk accessories and with the Finder's many commands and options. Try selecting text by double clicking, dragging, and Shift-clicking. Conquer the scroll bars. Use a marquee to select groups of icons in the Finder. Press Option or Command while choosing menu commands or clicking palette icons. Keep exploring. You'll become more adept at using the Mac's interface, you'll develop a better understanding of how the Mac works, and you'll be able to tailor your Mac to your tastes.

Many people use the phrase "power user" to describe someone who's mastered the Mac. To me, a power user is something that plugs in. It isn't power that makes a Mac expert; it's knowledge, experience, and perseverance. You're on your way to attaining that expertise. More power to you.

Summary:

✔ The Mac is an easy-to-use machine primarily because of its graphical user interface and mouse.

✔ The Finder and MultiFinder are the links between you and the Mac's system software.

✔ To get the most out of your Mac, master all the navigation options the Mac and its programs provide.

✔ You can choose certain commands from the keyboard by pressing the Command key along with a letter key.

✔ The best way to master the Mac is to read the manuals, experiment and register your software to get technical support.

Chapter 3
Word Processing

If you're like most Macintosh users, you'll use a word processor more than any other program. Whether you peck out occasional memos or write reams of technical manuals, a word processor's benefits — convenient text entry, easy revision, and formatting flexibility — are among the best reasons to use a computer.

Regardless of which word whacker you use, chances are your word processing life will take you through similar formatting terrain. In this chapter, we'll look at the basics behind word processing, and then I'll show how to conquer common formatting chores with today's most popular word processors. Perhaps you'll find an insight that your manual shrouded in fog. If you're still shopping, you can assess how each program handles each task. The sidebar "Shopping for a Word Processor" spotlights some advanced features you may want to consider, too.

The Basics

At its simplest level, word processing means using a computer to supplant a typewriter by typing and editing your words on screen, and sending them to paper only when you're satisfied with the results. The cornerstone of a word processor's text-slinging skills is a function called *word wrap,* which brings words that don't fit on a line down to the next line as you type. Word wrap means not having to visit the Return key at the end of every line, and it allows a word processor to quickly adjust line breaks when you add or remove text.

(Continued on page 39)

Shopping for a Word Processor

Here's a look at some helpful word processing features and at some points to consider when shopping.

❖ *Editing shortcuts* When the creative juices are flowing, you don't want to have to move a hand from the keyboard to choose common commands. Better word processors provide a selection of keyboard shortcuts for choosing commands and moving text. Microsoft Word, WordPerfect, Paragon's Nisus, and FullWrite provide keyboard shortcuts for every command and even let you access dialog box options. Word also has slick shortcuts for copying and moving text without replacing the Clipboard's contents. WordPerfect and Nisus let you create *macros* to automate command sequences. For example, if your last step in creating a document involves selecting all of its text, changing its font, and then choosing the Print command, you can create a macro that performs these tasks for you when you press a single keystroke. Nisus offers the most sophisticated macro features. It can be a tricky program to learn, but it's fast and powerful, and has attracted a loyal, if relatively small, following.

❖ *Outliners* Many writers develop outlines to flesh out the structure of a piece. Word, WordPerfect, and FullWrite contain built-in outliners that let you use the mouse to rearrange your thoughts (see "Outlining Your Ideas"). Or you might consider an outliner desk accessory such as the one in Symmetry Corporation's Acta Advantage. One advantage to using a desk accessory outliner is that it's available regardless of the program you're using.

❖ *Glossaries* A glossary feature lets you store and name lengthy words or paragraphs that can then be inserted into a document with a couple of keystrokes. You'll find glossary features in Word, FullWrite, and Nisus. You can also use WordPerfect macros to insert repetitive text.

❖ *Style sheets* A style sheet is a collection of typographic, line spacing, and margin formats to which you assign a name. Style sheets allow you to switch between formats with a few keystrokes instead of manually choosing formatting commands. Word, FullWrite, and MacWrite II provide style sheet features (MacWrite II's and FullWrite's are somewhat limited), and you can get the same results with WordPerfect or Nisus macros.

❖ *Spelling checkers* Many word processors provide built-in spelling checkers and thesauri. They're useful, but do have limitations. Spelling checkers don't guarantee accurate spelling or word usage. For example, if you substitute the word *there* for *their,* a spelling checker won't catch the error. But it can still be valuable, especially if your writing contains brand names or industry-specific words. By adding such words to a *user dictionary, you* can tailor your silicon lexicon to your work. Because a thesaurus typically offers numerous (and often quite different) synonyms for a given word, it's up to you to choose the one whose meaning fits the context in which the word will be used. When you find a synonym you like, consult a dictionary to make sure it's appropriate.

❖ *Table editing* Word 4.0 is currently the only Mac word processor to offer table-editing features. If you prefer a different program, however, you might combine a standalone table-editing program such as Macreations' Tycho with your word processor. FullWrite and Aldus' PageMaker desktop publishing program include serviceable table-editing programs, too. After creating a table with one of these programs, you can use the Clipboard to paste it into your word processor. ☞

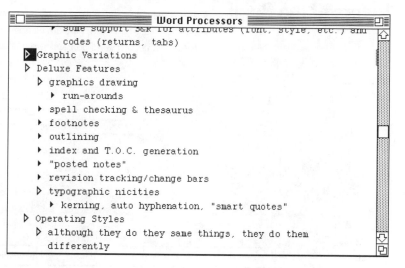

Outlining Your Ideas

Outliners let you sketch out the overall structure of what you're writing and reorganize topics and subtopics by dragging them with the mouse. Some people also use outliners to create to-do lists and small databases. Symmetry Corporation's Acta Advantage outliner desk accessory is shown here. The item "Graphic Variations" has been *collapsed*— its subtopics aren't visible.

❖ *Mail merge* This feature lets you combine your word processor and a database management program to produce "personalized" form letters — it's how those publishing clearinghouses churn out those giveaway notices. You'll find mail merge features in Word, Microsoft Works, MacWrite II, WordPerfect, and Nisus.

❖ *Revision tracking* In many organizations, documents must journey through an approval loop. Revision tracking features such as those found in FullWrite help you manage this process by placing vertical *change bars* in the margin alongside changed text. A *document comparison* feature, provided by Nisus and by Word (using a separate program included with the package) allow you to scan two documents and highlight the differences between them. FullWrite's *document annotation* feature lets you attach comments to a document. Called posted notes, they're electronic versions of Post-It notes. In FullWrite versions 1.5s and later,

these notes can take the form of recordings that you create using the microphone included with the Mac IIsi and LC, or with third-party recording hardware such as Farallon's MacRecorder.

❖ *Index and table of contents generation* Word, WordPerfect, Nisus, and FullWrite can automatically generate tables of contents and indexes. Nisus' tables of contents and indexes go into a separate file and are fully editable but need to be regenerated each time you change the document; the other programs update automatically but the indexes they generate are usually not fully editable.

❖ *Equation processing* Word lets you create and edit complex mathematical equations, albeit by typing formatting codes that are almost as complex. If you work with equations extensively, consider an equation editor such as Expressionist from Prescience Corporation, Formulator from Icom Simulations, or MathWriter from Cooke Publications. **M**

Rulers of the Road

A ruler is the gateway to a word processor's tab, margin, line spacing, and justification features. Shown here are components you'll find in the rulers of today's most popular word processing programs.

Word 3.0

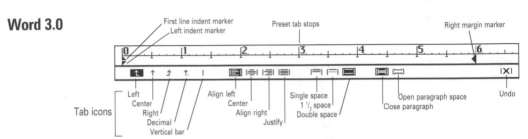

First line indent marker
Left indent marker
Preset tab stops
Right margin marker

Tab icons
Left
Center
Right
Decimal
Vertical bar
Align left
Center
Align right
Justify
Single space
1 ½ space
Double space
Close paragraph
Open paragraph space
Undo

Word 4.0

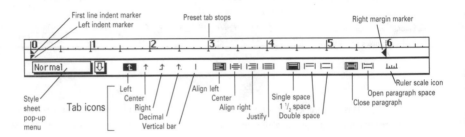

First line indent marker
Left indent marker
Preset tab stops
Right margin marker

Style sheet pop-up menu
Tab icons
Left
Center
Right
Decimal
Vertical bar
Align left
Center
Align right
Justify
Single space
1 ½ space
Double space
Close paragraph
Open paragraph space
Ruler scale icon

Write Now 2.1

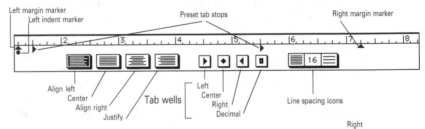

Left margin marker
Left indent marker
Preset tab stops
Right margin marker

Align left
Center
Align right
Justify
Tab wells
Left
Center
Right
Decimal
Line spacing icons

WordPerfect 1.x

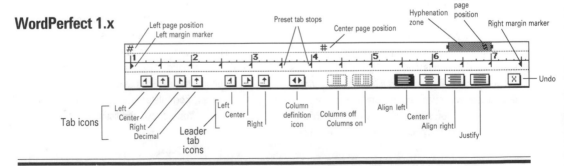

Left page position
Left margin marker
Preset tab stops
Center page position
Hyphenation zone
Right page position
Right margin marker

Tab icons
Left
Center
Right
Decimal
Leader tab icons
Left
Center
Right
Column definition icon
Columns off
Columns on
Align left
Center
Align right
Justify
Undo

All word processors also provide *formatting* features — the ability to specify margin widths, line spacing, and *justification*. The latter is a leap forward from typewriting; if you've struggled with typewriters, you'll be delighted with the ease with which word processors let you center lines of text or align them against the left or right margins (or both). And with most Mac word processors, you can usually perform all these formatting tasks by clicking icons on an on-screen ruler. You can display most programs' rulers by choosing a Show Ruler command. The figure "Rulers of the Road" shows the components of the rulers used by today's most popular word processors.

Word processors also let you adorn the top and bottom of every page with page numbers and *headers* and *footers*, text that repeats at the top or bottom of each page. Most Mac word processors let you create different headers and footers for

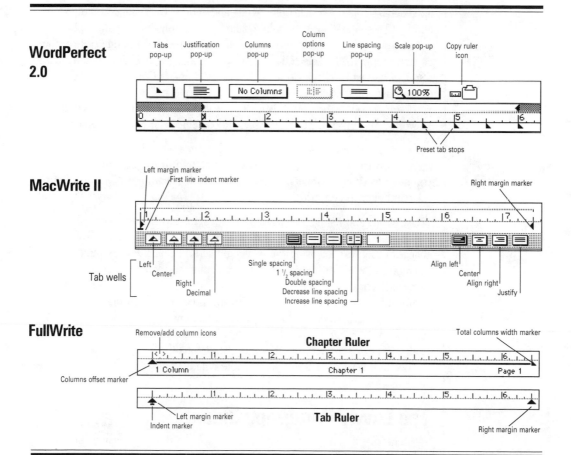

WordPerfect 2.0

Tabs pop-up · Justification pop-up · Columns pop-up · Column options pop-up · Line spacing pop-up · Scale pop-up · Copy ruler icon

No Columns · 100%

Preset tab stops

MacWrite II

Left margin marker · First line indent marker · Right margin marker

Tab wells · Left · Center · Right · Decimal · Single spacing · 1 ½ spacing · Double spacing · Decrease line spacing · Increase line spacing · Align left · Center · Align right · Justify

FullWrite

Remove/add column icons · **Chapter Ruler** · Total columns width marker

1 Column · Chapter 1 · Page 1

Columns offset marker

Indent marker · Left margin marker · **Tab Ruler** · Right margin marker

odd- and even-numbered pages, a useful feature if your final product will be bound in book form.

Macintosh word processors also exploit the Mac's text talents, letting you format a document using a variety of fonts, styles, and sizes. And they support the Mac's Clipboard, allowing you to use the Copy and Paste commands to include text and graphics created in other programs in your documents.

Know Thy Rulers

Before you tackle any word processing job, it's vital to understand your program's approach to storing such formatting *attributes* as line spacing, paragraph indents, margins, justification, and tabs. All Mac word processors have on-screen rulers for adjusting those settings, but they don't all use them in the same way. Two schemes predominate. With the *attached-to-paragraph* approach — taken by Microsoft's Word and Works, by T/Maker's WriteNow, and by Claris' MacWrite II — ruler changes apply only to the paragraph containing the blinking insertion point. If you've selected a range of text, the changes apply to the selected paragraphs. To change an entire document, select all its text. You can do this in Word by pressing Command and clicking in the selection bar along the window's left edge. (The bar is invisible, but you'll know you're there when the pointer changes to a right-pointing arrow.) In Works, MacWrite II, and WriteNow, choose Select All from the Edit menu.

Ashton-Tate's FullWrite uses the *ruler-to-ruler* method, in which the current format is governed by the last ruler setting in the document. When you need to change formats — margin widths, for example — you insert a new ruler and alter it as needed.

Like Word and its ilk, WordPerfect versions 1.x and 2.x have only one ruler. But instead of attaching formats to paragraphs, WordPerfect applies ruler changes to all text following the blinking insertion point. For example, if the insertion point is in the third line of a paragraph and you click on the justified-text icon, WordPerfect inserts a carriage return at the cursor's position and then justifies everything below that, leaving preceding lines unchanged. Variations of this scheme apply to many formatting options not on the ruler, such as line spacing. It's confusing at first, but with practice you will master it. (Unless otherwise noted, the tips and instructions in this chapter apply to WordPerfect versions 1.x and 2.x. I'll note where things differ between the two versions.)

The Lowly Paragraph Indent

Indents are indents, right? Wrong. There's more than one way to bump a paragraph's first line to the right. My favorite method is to press Tab. All programs offer *preset* tab settings, usually spaced at ½-inch intervals. So by pressing Tab at the beginning of a paragraph, you indent its first line ½-inch.

Another method is to use the ruler to create *a first-line indent,* in which the first line of every paragraph — that is, each line following a carriage return — is indented. To create a first-line indent in Microsoft Word, WriteNow, or MacWrite II, place the insertion point in the paragraph to be changed (or before the point where you'll begin typing), and then drag the ruler's indent marker to the right. In Word, you can also use the Command-Shift-F keyboard shortcut. In FullWrite, insert a tab ruler (if none exists already) and then drag its indent marker to the right. You can also edit the default ruler by choosing Base Styles from the Style menu. In WordPerfect 2.0, drag the ruler's first-line indent marker (the right-pointing, hollow triangle), or choose Paragraph from the Layout menu and type the desired indent value.

There's a drawback to the first-line indenting approach: because any line ending in a carriage return is considered a paragraph, single-line "paragraphs" such as subheads will appear indented, too, unless you reformat each one to appear flush against the left margin. That's one reason I prefer using the Tab key to create first-line indents.

Using Tab to indent is essential if you need to save your document in *text-only format* for transmission over the phone lines or to transfer to a program that can't read your word processor's document files. Text-only files discard formatting information such as fonts and indents, but they *do* retain rudimentary formatting codes such as tabs and carriage returns. We'll look at data exchange issues in detail in Chapter 29.

More Ins and Outs of Indents

A variation on the indenting theme is the *hanging indent,* in which the first line of a paragraph begins to the left of subsequent lines. These often appear in numbered or bulleted lists of items (see the figure "Hanging Indents" on the next page). Creating a hanging indent is easier if you've typed at least one of the numbered or bulleted items, so do that first. (If you use bullets, put a space between the bullet and the first character of the item. If you want more space, press Tab.)

Next, if you are using Word, place the insertion point within the item, or select all the items if you've already typed them. Now press Shift and drag the lower indent marker to the right about ¼-inch, and all the lines except the first jump to the right. While still pressing Shift, fine-tune the marker's position until the margins align with the first character after the bullet or decimal point.

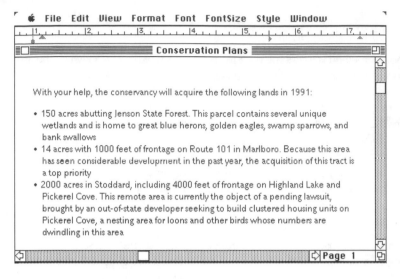

In FullWrite, position the insertion point before the first item and insert a tab ruler. Next, press Shift and drag the triangular left-margin indent marker to the right, and then fine-tune the marker's position. To restore the normal left margin, move the insertion point to the end of the item list, insert a new ruler, and drag its left-margin marker to the left.

▲ **Hanging Indents**

Hanging indents are often used to align the left margins in a list of bulleted or numbered items. WriteNow, shown here, lets you create a hanging indent by positioning the indentation marker to the left of the left margin marker. Most word processors use a similar technique.

In MacWrite II, drag the left indent marker to set the width of the paragraph and then drag the first line indent marker (the upside-down T) to the left. To specify a more precise hanging indent, use the Format menu's Paragraph command.

In WordPerfect 1.x, first position the cursor before the list of items. Next, create a tab stop roughly ½-inch to the right of the left margin, and then choose Indent from the Paragraph submenu to create a hanging indent for the first item. To indent each remaining item, move the cursor to the beginning of each and choose Indent (or press Command-Shift-T). To adjust the indent's size, position the cursor after the tab-set code and drag the tab stop to the left or the right. Working with formatting codes is easier if you choose Show Codes from the Edit menu. In WordPerfect 2.x, use the ruler's indent marker.

Paragraphs in a legal document or lengthy quotes from another author's work are often indented from both margins. To indent both margins in Word, Works, MacWrite II, or WriteNow, first place the insertion point within the paragraph you're indenting (or select the paragraphs to be indented), and then drag the left and right indent markers toward each other by ½-inch or so. With FullWrite, insert a new ruler before and after the text to be indented, and then adjust the margins of the ruler that precedes the text. In WordPerfect 1.x, open the Format menu's Paragraph submenu and choose Left-Right Indent. In WordPerfect 2.x, choose Left-Right Indent from the Layout menu.

Hands On the Table

Another common word processing job involves creating *columnar tables,* typically used for such items as tables of contents and financial statements. Tables often contain *leader characters,* usually lines of periods, which run across the column and guide the eye along the line to the next column.

Creating tables means mastering tab features. Most programs let you center text within tabs or align it against a tab's left or right edge. And all provide *decimal tabs,* which align the decimal points in columns of numbers.

Rulers are the gateways to tabs. With Word, Works, or WriteNow, first be sure the cursor is located where the table will begin before you create the tab stops. To create a tab in Word, click on the ruler at the tab's position. Word and most other programs are preset to create left-aligned tabs. To create a different kind, first select the ruler icon for that kind. In WriteNow and MacWrite, drag the desired tab out of its *tab well* and position it on the ruler.

In FullWrite, insert a tab ruler if necessary. Then, to create left-aligned tabs, click the ruler at each tab position. For a right aligned tab, press Command and click the ruler. For a centered tab, press Shift; for a decimal tab, Command-Shift. To change a tab's alignment setting or leader character, double-click the tab and make adjustments in the subsequent dialog box.

In WordPerfect, begin by clearing the preset tabs, which appear at ½-inch intervals: choose Tabs from the Line submenu, click the Delete button, then click OK. Next, if you're using WordPerfect 1.x, select the tab icon for the type of tab you want, and then click the *tab pointer* on the ruler at each tab's location. To switch to a different type of tab, click that tab's ruler icon. To change an existing tab's alignment, click on the new alignment's icon, and then on the existing tab. If you're using WordPerfect 2.x, you can create and clear tabs by using the ruler's Tabs pop-up menu and clicking on the ruler. You can also use the Tabs dialog box, which you can display by choosing Tabs from the Line submenu or double-clicking on any tab in the ruler. With all these programs, you adjust a tab's position by dragging it left or right on the ruler.

Word, FullWrite, MacWrite II, and WordPerfect also accept measurements in a dialog box for precise positioning. All programs except WordPerfect 1.x let you remove a tab by pointing to it and dragging away from the ruler. To expunge a WordPerfect 1.x tab, first click the tab icon that matches the style of the doomed tab, then click on the tab to remove it, then click the same tab-style icon to reset the pointer. Remember, with attached-to-paragraph programs, the cursor must be in the line whose tabs you're refining. If you're refining the entire table, select all of it first. With WordPerfect you can mutilate

 File Edit Format Font Document Utilities Window Work

Ch28—Virus Fighters.Word4

Product	Developer	Distribution	Description
AntiPan	Michael Hamel	free	Removes nVIR infections and prevents future nVIR infections. Detects nVIR clones.
Antitoxin	Mainstay	commercial	Includes watchdog INIT and scan/repair application. Awkward design; not recommended.
Disinfectant	John Norstad	free	Scan/repair application with superb on-line help. Highly recommended.
Eradicat´Em	Dave Platt	free	INIT that repairs and protects against WDEF infections.
GateKeeper	Chris Johnson	free	INIT/cdev that protects system files and applications

Page 1   Normal

Editing on the Table
Microsoft Word 4.0's table-editing features in action.

a table by carelessly dragging tabs left and right. You'll get the best results by selecting the entire table and then fine-tuning.

Microsoft Word 4.0 boasts a labor-saving Insert Table command that creates a grid of rows and columns. You can type tables within this grid without fussing with tabs and rulers (see the figure "Editing on the Table").

Take Me to Your Leader

Word, FullWrite, WriteNow, MacWrite II, and WordPerfect let you include leader characters in tables (see the figure "Fearless Leaders"). In most programs, you assign the leader character to the tab whose column the leaders will point to. For example, to create a leader between columns two and three, assign the leader to column three's tab. To create leaders in Word, first create tabs for each column. Next, double-click on an existing tab to display the Tabs box, click on the tab you want the leaders to point to, and then choose the kind of leader character you want. Click OK to apply the changes and close the dialog box.

In FullWrite, double-click on an existing tab to summon the Tabs dialog box, and then choose the desired leader. (The second button gives the best dot leaders.) In WordPerfect, use the ruler's leader tab icons. If you prefer the Tabs dialog box, you can assign a leader to a given tab by clicking the Dot Leader check box (in version 1.x) or choosing the desired leader from the dialog box's Type pop-up menu (in version 2.x).

WriteNow lets you create leaders, albeit in an odd way. To create a leader between columns one and two, type column one's information, then while holding down the Tab key type a period. Release Tab and type column two's information. In MacWrite II, choose the Tab command from the Format menu and type the desired leader character (usually a period) in the Fill Character text box.

File Edit Search Format Font Document Window

Financial Report

Elements of Increase in Working Capitol

	Proprietary Fund Type	Fiduciary Fund Type	Totals
Cash	$125,295	$ (60,631)	$223,187
Account receivable	(7,529)	—	768
Investments	—	116,1364	1,000
Inventory	241	—	(1,647)
Accounts payable	2,229	(19,340)	8,955
Accrued interest payable	1,623	—	1,308
Current portion of long-term debt	267	—	32,974
Increase in working capital	$122,126	$ 3,165	$316,545

Page 1   Normal+...

▲ Fearless Leaders

Leader characters guide your eye across a line to the next column in a table. In this Microsoft Word 4.0 table (top), the leader character has been assigned to the tab near the ruler's 2 ½-inch mark.

Changing Your Style

All programs offer *search-and-replace* features for finding and changing text — changing, for example, all occurrences of "East Germany" to simply "Germany." But not all programs let you search for one type of formatting attribute (such as tabs and font information) and replace it with another. Want to change all 10-point Helvetica text to 12-point Times Bold? Without the ability to search and replace attributes, it's a laborious chore. The ability to search for and replace formatting attributes is a useful feature that lets you quickly change a document's appearance.

Word lets you locate tab characters and carriage returns by typing ^t or ^p in the Find What text box. You can search for a specific format by selecting a character or entire paragraph (including the carriage return) with the desired format, and then press Command-Option-R. You can't use the Change command to replace one font or style with another, but you can use the command to reformat paragraphs. First, copy the carriage return of the paragraph whose format you want to apply elsewhere (choose Show ¶ from the Edit menu to see carriage return codes). Then select the carriage return of the paragraph to be

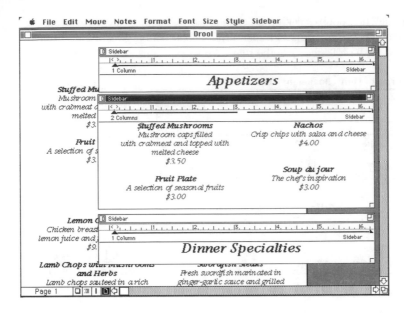

changed and choose Paste. To automate the process, type ^p in the Find What box, and ^c in the Replace With box. The latter tells Word to replace the text to be changed with the Clipboard's contents.

FullWrite, WordPerfect 2.0, and MacWrite II can search for and replace nearly any formatting attribute. In FullWrite, specify the attributes by using the Font, Size, or Style menus while the

▲ Columns on the Mac

To mix various column widths on the same page with FullWrite, you must create multiple sidebars. Here, each section of the page is a separate sidebar. Editing and positioning multiple sidebars can be cumbersome, but it allows formatting feats that would be difficult or impossible with other word processors.

blinking cursor is in the Find What or Change To box. For example, to change all 12-point Times text to 10-point Helvetica, first choose 12-point and Times from the Size and Font menus. Next, press Shift-Option-? to get the wildcard character ¿ (which means *any character*). Next, tab to the Change To box and choose 10-point and Helvetica from the Size and Font menus, respectively. Finally, type another ¿ and click Change All. (FullWrite can't undo a Change All operation, so consider saving the document first. That way, if you change your mind after using Change All, you can revert to the previously saved version.)

To search and replace attributes in MacWrite II, choose Find/Change from the Edit menu and check the Use Attributes check box in the Find/Change dialog box that appears. The dialog box changes to include lists of fonts and attributes that you can select. If you're just searching for text attributes (not attributes as well as specific characters), you'll need to uncheck the Use Text check box.

In WordPerfect 2.0, use the Match and Affect menus in the Find window to specify which attributes you're searching for and replacing. To display the Find window, choose Find/Change from the Search menu.

Citizen Mac

One way in which most Mac word processors infiltrate the desktop publishing camp is by letting you create multiple *columns* of text on a page.

Multicolumn pages are common in newsletters, brochures, and menus (see the figure "Columns on the Mac"). In Word, WriteNow, and MacWrite II creating multiple columns involves choosing a command and specifying the number of columns you want. In Word, use the Section command. In WriteNow, use Page Setup. In MacWrite II, choose the Page command from the Format menu or double-click the column border at the top of MacWrite II's ruler or the page number indicator in the lower left corner of the document window. In FullWrite, choose the Columns On and Columns Off commands after you've specified column characteristics. In FullWrite, you can also click the little arrows at the top left of the chapter ruler to change the number of columns. In WordPerfect 2.0, you can choose the number of columns desired using the ruler's Columns pop-up menu. You can also adjust the columns' widths by dragging the shaded borders in the ruler.

The Last Word

If you're still shopping a word processor, test drive some programs to find one whose operating style you like. This is especially important if you'll be spending a great deal of time writing. Every word processor has its own feel, and you'll want to find one that feels good to you.

And don't be wowed by endless lists of features. Gimmicky formatting and drawing features won't help you put your thoughts into words — indeed, they might tempt you to play with fancy formats instead of making another round of revisions. Word processors exist to make writing easier. That's a miraculous feat in itself.

Summary:

✔ Automatic word wrap, easy editing, and effortless formatting features are what set a word processor apart from a typewriter.

✔ The gateway to most common formatting tasks is a word processor's on-screen ruler.

✔ Some word processors provide time-saving features such as glossaries, which store often-used text; and style sheets, which store formatting information.

✔ Some word processors encroach on desktop publishing territory by providing features that let you create multicolumn pages.

✔ More powerful word processors can automatically generate indexes and tables of contents.

✔ When shopping for a word processor, features to consider include editing shortcuts, outlining, glossaries and style sheets, spelling checkers, table-editing, mail merge, revision tracking, and equation processing.

Chapter 4
Spreadsheets

In This Chapter:

✔ The basic components and benefits of a spreadsheet.

✔ An introduction to using mathematical functions.

✔ Tips on how to best format and design spreadsheets.

✔ How to manage spreadsheets.

✔ How to use spreadsheets to store data and create tables.

The spreadsheet has been around in one form or another for centuries. In the 1800s, spreadsheets were big, leather-bound books — the kind Cratchet scratched his quill in. In this century, leather gave way to leatherette, and Cratchet evolved into a paunchy guy in baggy pants who played a mechanical adding machine like a Stradivarius.

For years the spreadsheet remained essentially the same: a large ledger with pages divided into rows and columns for convenient organization of text and numbers. Then in the late 70s, a Harvard MBA candidate named Dan Bricklin got the idea that a computer program could mimic a ledger and also calculate numbers. His finance professor dismissed the idea as having no commercial value, but Bricklin was undaunted, and teamed up with programmer Bob Frankston to create a wildly successful program called VisiCalc. The electronic spreadsheet was born, and the skeptical professor joined the ranks of history's great antivisionaries.

Since then, the spreadsheet program has become as much a mainstay of business as the expense account. And deservedly so. A spreadsheet lets you record numbers more neatly and efficiently than a ledger does, and it lets you calculate and analyze them. You can plug in new values and watch the spreadsheet recalculate accordingly. You can ask "what if?" questions: What if interest rates rose to 15 percent? What if we got a 20-year mortgage instead of a 30-year?

A spreadsheet does for you what a flight simulator does for a pilot: it lets you explore different approaches to a problem — without the risk. And because life is full of problems and risks, spreadsheets have 1001 uses. You can use them to create business plans and profit-and-loss statements, to forecast sales figures and track stock market data, and to print loan-amortization tables — in short, any endeavor that involves playing with numbers. And their orderly approach to storing information makes them ideal for other tasks, from managing address files to creating columnar tables (see the sidebar "A Spreadsheet's Other Lives").

Everything in Its Cell

The secret to a spreadsheet's organizational virtues is its gridlike approach to storing information. A blank spreadsheet is divided into horizontal and vertical lines that create a grid of boxes called *cells* (see the figure "Spreadsheet Basics"). The horizontal lines form rows, and the vertical lines form *columns.* Rows are labeled by number, columns by letter, to give every cell its own address: A1 is the cell in the upper-left corner of the spreadsheet. B4 is the cell in the second column, four rows down. (Some spreadsheets number both rows and columns: A1 becomes R1C1, and B4 is R4C2. Many programs let you choose the numbering scheme you prefer.)

Each cell can hold a number, some text, or a *formula.* A simple spreadsheet contains text *labels* that describe the numbers in adjacent cells and a formula —

A Spreadsheet's Other Lives

Spreadsheets' abilities to neatly pigeonhole text and numbers make them good database managers. When using a spreadsheet for data management, label columns with your field names (such as Name, Address, Phone) and build down from there, making each row a record. There's no need to fuss with field definitions and maximum character lengths: every cell will accept any combination of text or numbers, and most spreadsheets can hold 255 characters per cell. And you can use the spreadsheet's library of functions and math features to analyze data and create reports.

Many spreadsheets provide additional commands for managing data. Excel lets you sort and search through your data. Microsoft Works provides data-entry forms that show one record at a time. Excel, Wingz, and Full Impact also have data management features. But remember, spreadsheets generally don't offer the sophisticated form-layout features or the extensive entry-checking features of true databases.

Finally, spreadsheets' columnar bent make them wonderful "table processors." (Indeed, most of the large product-features tables you see in *Macworld* articles began life as spreadsheets.) You can add new columns or rows with a mouse click and resize columns in a flash — instead of struggling with rulers and tab settings. If you need fancy formatting, move the completed table into a word processor by copying its cells to the Clipboard or by saving it as a text-only file. **M**

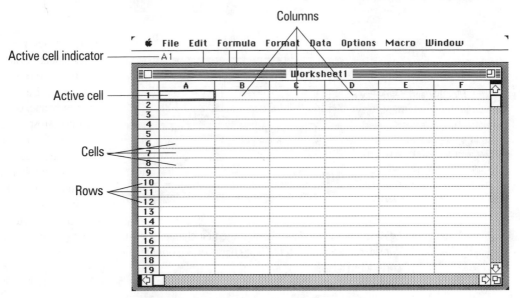

Columns

Active cell indicator — A1

 File   Edit   Formula   Format   Data   Options   Macro   Window

Worksheet1

Active cell —

Cells —

Rows —

▲ **Spreadsheet
Basics**

Horizontal and vertical
lines divide a
spreadsheet's window
into a grid of boxes
called cells, each with
its own address (A1 is
the cell in the upper-left
corner). A bold
rectangle indicates the
active cell.

a combination of cell addresses and math symbols that tell the program what to do with those numbers (see the figure "Weekly Pay").

But the real power of a spreadsheet surfaces when you create formulas that manipulate the results of other formulas. In the figure "Monthly and Yearly Pay" on the next page, I've tied two new formulas to the result of "Weekly Pay." This causes any changes in the Hours Worked or Hourly Wage cells to show up in the Weekly Pay, Monthly Pay, and Yearly Pay cells. To answer the question, "What if I earned $15 an hour instead of $10?" simply type 15 in cell B2 and press Return.

That brings us to spreadsheet navigating. In all Mac spreadsheet programs, you select a cell by pointing to it with the mouse and then clicking, or by using your keyboard's direction keys to move the *cell pointer,* a dark rectangle that encloses the current cell. Once you've homed in on a cell, simply begin typing. The characters you type appear within the cell and also within the formula *bar;* a text-entry box just below the spreadsheet's menu bar. You can edit text in the formula bar just as you would in other Mac applications. Pressing the Return key stores the text in the cell.

 File   Edit   Formula   Format   Data

B4   =B1*B2

Worksheet-1

	A	B
1	Hours Worked	40
2	Hourly Wage	10
3		
4	Weekly Pay	400
5		

Weekly Pay

This spreadsheet uses a formula to calculate weekly income based on number of hours worked and hourly wage. The formula itself appears in cell B4, and tells the spreadsheet program, "Multiply the contents of cell by the contents of cell B2, and display the result here."

```
     File   Edit   Formula   Format   Data
        B5              =B4*4
```

	A	B
1	Hours Worked	40
2	Hourly Wage	$10
3		
4	Weekly Pay	$400
5	Monthly Pay	$1,600
6	Yearly Pay	$19,200
7		
8		

Monthly and Yearly Pay ▶

Building on the formula in "Weekly Pay," the monthly Pay formula multiplies weekly pay by 4, while the Yearly Pay formula multiplies monthly pay by 12. As you enter different wage and hour values, the spreadsheet instantly recalculates the weekly, monthly, and yearly pay.

How does the spreadsheet know whether you've typed a label, a numeric value, or a formula? Most programs follow this approach: if you type only numbers, the entry is treated as a value. If it contains any letters or spaces, it's treated as a label. If the first character is an equal sign (=), it's considered a formula. If the first character is a double quote ("), the text is considered a label.

Manipulate Data with Functions

Spreadsheet programs also contain a number of preprogrammed formulas *called functions,* which provide advanced math skills. You needn't remember any complex math symbols to use a function; simply type its name (or choose it from a dialog box or menu), and enclose the required values, called *arguments,* within parentheses. The function performs its preprogrammed calculation on the arguments and returns a result.

One *statistical function* that all spreadsheets provide is SUM, which adds its arguments. In a spreadsheet function, a colon (:) between two cell addresses indicates a *range* of cells, while a comma between them denotes individual cells. For example, the Excel formula = SUM(B1:B3) adds the contents of cells B1 *through* B3 (the short form of = B1+B2+B3), while the formula = SUM(B1,B5,B7) adds the contents of cells B1, B5, and B7. (Unless otherwise noted, I use Excel in all the examples in this chapter, since it's the Mac world's most popular spreadsheet program. All of the concepts here apply to other spreadsheets, too, but the exact spelling — the *syntax* — of formulas or functions may differ.)

Other statistical functions include AVERAGE, which calculates the average value of given arguments; and MAX and MIN, which return the largest and smallest values, respectively, within the list of arguments. Spreadsheets also provide *mathematical functions* such as ABS, which returns the absolute value of an argument; and ROUND, which rounds it off to a specified number of digits. Then there are *trigonometric functions* like COS, which gives the cosine; and TAN, which calculates the tangent. *Text functions* search and manipulate text. *Financial functions* calculate present and future values, rates of return, and more. *Date functions* return the current date and time. A spreadsheet's seemingly endless library of functions is its ultimate weapon for manipulating text and numbers.

Functions become even more powerful when you nest them within other functions so that one function uses the value returned by another function as an argument. For example, the Excel formula =MID(A1,1,SEARCH(", ",A1,1)-1) uses two text functions, MID and SEARCH, to extract the last name from a cell (A1) containing names in "last name, first name" format. Excel first executes the SEARCH function to locate the comma. SEARCH reports its findings to MID, which takes over to extract all the characters up to the comma.

Then Spruce It Up with Formats

Spreadsheets calculate numbers with a high degree of precision, using droves of decimal places (14, in Excel's case) to represent fractional values as accurately as possible. But that kind of precision is overkill for some data. A dollars-and-cents value doesn't look like one when 14 digits follow the decimal point.

Cell *formats* enable you to specify how you want numbers and text to be displayed. You can have dollars-and-cents figures appear with a dollar sign and only two digits after the decimal point. You can have percent signs appear after values that represent a percentage of other values. For date values, you can specify display formats such as 8/17/91 or 17-Aug-91. Appropriate display formats can make spreadsheet values more meaningful.

Another aspect of spreadsheet formatting involves specifying the *alignment* of data within cells. Numbers, for example, are usually aligned against the right edge of their cells, with their decimal points aligned. Text is usually aligned against the left edge. You can also choose to center text within a cell — handy for a title that appears above a column of numbers.

Mac spreadsheets provide other formatting options as well, including the ability to format cells in different fonts and styles. Excel, Ashton-Tate's Full Impact, Informix's Wingz, and RagTime Inc.'s RagTime 3 all support color graphs and cell formats. So when you're in the red, your spreadsheet figures can be, too. These programs also let you create boxes and lines to highlight key figures or underscore totals.

Making Things Manageable

A single spreadsheet document provides many thousands of blank cells, ready for facts and formulas. But you'll probably run out of memory long before filling all of them. And if you don't, you'll run out of patience as you struggle to scroll from one area of the spreadsheet to another.

One solution to both problems is a program that enables you to *link* separate documents, causing changes made in one to appear in the other. Linking separate spreadsheets lets you work around memory limitations and simplifies creating and using a complex spreadsheet application.

While the specific steps vary between products, you usually link spreadsheets by creating a formula in one spreadsheet that refers to one or more cells in the second spreadsheet. For example, assume you're working with two spreadsheets, named Income and Expenses, and you want to link them so that the contents of the Income spreadsheet's Net Income cell are copied into the Net Income cell of the Expenses worksheet. To do so in Excel, you'd create formula in the Net Income cell of the Expenses worksheet reading =Income!$E2.

Other Labor Savers

Another way to tame a spreadsheet is through *macros,* series of formulas and commands that carry out actions at your command. A macro facility is an electronic autopilot that you can program to perform repetitive tasks — anything from choosing commands to entering formulas to performing complex calculations. You'll find basic macro features in Microsoft Works, and far more advanced ones in Excel, Full Impact, and Wingz. You can create macros from scratch by typing their statements one at time, but an easier way is to use the program's *macro recorder.* Activate the macro recorder, and the program watches you work, translating your actions into macro statements. You can replay the resulting macro as-is to repeat the steps you performed, or edit it to add additional functions.

The macro languages in Excel, Full Impact, and Wingz go even further to allow you to create customized dialog boxes, menus, on-screen buttons, and other user interface elements. You (or a consultant) can use these features to create customized spreadsheets that work like standard Mac applications. For example, a business might create an accounting system with menu commands such as Display Outstanding Invoices or Display Cash Flow Graph. Behind these commands would be macro statements that perform the appropriate tasks. Such a spreadsheet could be used by an administrative assistant or temporary employee who might not otherwise know how to generate graphs or display outstanding invoices. These kinds of customized applications are often called *turnkey* applications, since, metaphorically speaking, all a user has to do is turn the key to be off and running. You might also hear a turnkey spreadsheet application described as a *template.* A large library of Excel templates is available from Heizer Software.

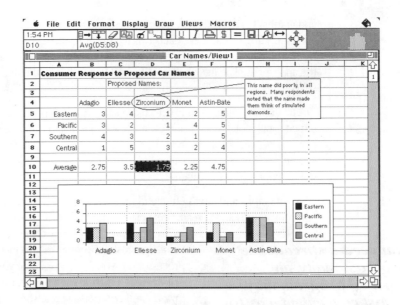

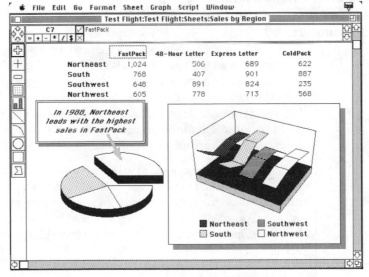

Tables and Charts

Full Impact (top) and Wingz (bottom) let you mix graphs and spreadsheet cells in the same document. Both programs also support 3-D graphs and color. Excel 3.0, due for shipment before the middle of 1991, will provide all of these features, too.

Choosing a Spreadsheet

Besides number-analyzing prowess, most Mac spreadsheet programs also have built-in graphing features that transform numbers into spiffy bar, line, or pie charts. Full Impact, Wingz, and RagTime 3 even let you mix spreadsheets and graphs on the same page (see the figure "Tables and Charts"). Excel version 3.0, which is scheduled to be released by the middle of 1991, will also let you mix spreadsheets and graphs. In Excel 3.0, you can even resize a bar or line in a graph and change its corresponding spreadsheet data. This feature is useful for *goal-seeking* tasks — for example, if you want sales to increase by ten percent next year, you can drag the appropriate line in a chart, and Excel 3.0 will change the underlying spreadsheet to show what will need to take place in order for you to meet your goal.

Full Impact, Wingz, and Excel 3.0 can also create graphs that have a three-dimensional look to them, and even allow you to rotate the graph and change its perspective. Graphs and spreadsheets team up well for analyzing numbers and spotting trends; a rising or falling line tells a more compelling story than a nondescript table of numbers.

Since graphs and tables often end up in reports, all spreadsheet programs let you copy graphs and spreadsheet cells to the Clipboard for subsequent pasting into a word processor or desktop publishing program. Some spreadsheet programs also include built-in word processors so you can consolidate your efforts. Excel 3.0 provides a built-in outlining feature that lets you *expand* and *collapse* a spreadsheet to show various levels of detail.

> 66 *If you need a spreadsheet only occasionally, an integrated program may be the most convenient way to include spreadsheet data in your documents.* 99

For spreadsheet tasks that can benefit from the power of a high-end database manager, consider Acius' 4th Dimension and 4D Calc. 4D Calc is a sophisticated spreadsheet program that runs within 4th Dimension. With 4D Calc, you can assign a spreadsheet to a particular record in a database. A real estate office could use this feature to store information on available properties and simultaneously generate amortization schedules for prospective buyers based on the house and decorating options they choose. We'll look at database management again in Chapter 7.

For more basic needs, it's hard to beat Microsoft Works, which takes a Swiss-army-knife approach by consolidating spreadsheet, word processing, graphing, database management, and telecommunications features in one program. Another integrated program, RagTime 3 wraps its spreadsheet within a desktop publishing framework, making it well suited for creating financial reports that need to be updated on a regular basis.

Integrated programs such as Works and RagTime are convenient, but remember that the Mac's Clipboard and Scrapbook let you create your own integrated workplace by cutting and pasting information between programs. And with MultiFinder and System 7.0, you can do so without quitting and restarting each application (provided your Mac has enough memory, of course). If you need a spreadsheet only occasionally, an integrated program may be the most convenient way to include spreadsheet data in your documents. But if you plan to spend a great deal of time asking "what if?" you'll be better served by a powerhouse spreadsheet like Excel, Full Impact, or Wingz, using the Clipboard and MultiFinder to exchange and combine data within other applications as needed.

If you create complex formulas containing flocks of functions and parentheses, look for a program that lets you "attach" notes to cells. Cell notes, electronic versions of Post-It notes, are an effective way to describe how large formulas work or how the spreadsheet is structured — details that are easy to forget and difficult to decipher. Full Impact and Wingz let you attach roughly a page of text to each cell.

As you shop for heavy-duty spreadsheets, look for these two techie-sounding features: *sparse matrix memory management* and *minimal recalculation.* Sparse matrix memory management is an efficient method of spreadsheet storage that doesn't waste memory on empty cells, and thus lets you squeeze more into the machine's memory. Programs that use minimal recalculation recalculate spreadsheets by keeping track of which cells depend on the contents of other cells. Thus, they recalculate only those cells that are dependent on the cells you've changed, which takes far less time than checking and recalculating every cell in the spreadsheet. (In Ashton-Tate's Full Impact 2.0, this feature is called *intelligent recalculation.*)

If you work in an office that uses IBM PCs as well as Macs, look closely at Excel and Wingz. Both are also available for PCs; the PC versions use the Microsoft Windows graphical environment I mentioned in Chapter 1, and operate nearly identically to their Mac cousins. By standardizing on the Mac and PC versions of either of these programs, you can easily move spreadsheets between Macs and PCs and minimize training time, since both versions are so similar.

Finally, if your Mac has only 1MB of memory, consider Bravo Technologies' MacCalc. It's fast, easy to use, and compares favorably against its more corpulent competitors. There's also Zedcor's Desk, a collection of desk accessories, one of which, DeskCalc, is a mini spreadsheet. In the shareware arena, there's BiPlane, which comes in both application and desk accessory versions. (See Chapter 13 for details about shareware.)

The Power of Numbers

As you master the workings of your spreadsheet program, don't forget the importance of good spreadsheet design. Creating a spreadsheet that's easy to understand and maintain requires forethought and an understanding of the problem you're analyzing. You'll find some tips for creating effective spreadsheets in "Spreadsheet Design Basics."

Finally, don't underestimate the potential for spreadsheet abuse. These days, business plans and sales forecasts come with an entourage of facts and figures depicting profits and prosperity. Often, those statistics are supplied by the project's proponents, and therein lies the potential problem. Anyone can doctor a spreadsheet to give the desired results by simply beginning with preselected figures, and then designing a spreadsheet to produce them. In such cases, the spreadsheet changes from a tool for evaluating options to a tool that supports decisions that have already been made.

The moral? Don't take a spreadsheet's numbers at face value. Question the spreadsheet's underlying assumptions: did its creator assume that profits will increase 20 percent each year, that interest rates will fall, that no competition exists, that costs will remain the same?

George Canning, a prime minister of Britain in the nineteenth century, said it best: "I can prove anything by statistics — except the truth."

Spreadsheet Design Basics

Creating an effective, easily understood spreadsheet requires an organized approach and plenty of advance planning. According to John M. Nevison's excellent *The Elements of Spreadsheet Style* (1987, Brady), a spreadsheet "should be straightforward to build, easy to read, receptive to change, and, above all, free of error." Here are a few of Nevison's 22 spreadsheet rules:

❖ *Make a formal introduction.* Explain the spreadsheet's purpose and design, as well as how to use it: describe cells holding key information, and provide a "table of contents" listing key data sections.

❖ *Label every assumption.* So that your readers can better understand your spreadsheet's structure, state — up front — all its assumptions (say, a 5 percent annual growth rate with a 7 percent annual depreciation rate).

❖ *Explain tricky formulas.* If your spreadsheet offers cell-notation features, use them. Later, when you have to modify your formulas, you'll be glad you did.

❖ *Use cell naming.* If your spreadsheet program lets you, assign names to a cell or range of cells to explain key formulas. The formula =HoursWorked*HourlyWage says a great deal more than =B7*B6.

❖ *Graph to illuminate.* Be sure that graphs summarize their data well. Proofread them for style and content. And put each graph's conclusion in its title. For example, the title "Sales Up 20 Percent This Year" says more than "Year-to-Date Sales Results." **M**

Summary:

✔ A spreadsheet is divided into horizontal and vertical lines that create a grid of boxes called cells which hold numbers, text, or a formula.

✔ Spreadsheet programs contain pre-programmed formulas called functions which perform calculations on given values and return results.

✔ You can format your spreadsheet by specifying how you want numbers and text to appear and how you want the data aligned within the cells.

✔ Ways to manage spreadsheets include linking separate spreadsheets together and using macros, series of formulas and commands often used to perform repetitive tasks.

✔ If you only use a spreadsheet for basic needs, consider a package that combines spreadsheet, word processing, graphing, database management and telecommunications in the program. For frequent spreadsheet users, a stand alone program that suits your particular needs is the best bet.

Chapter 5

Desktop Publishing

In This Chapter:

✔ Why desktop publishing is replacing traditional layout techniques.

✔ Desktop Publishing Systems: the more you spend, the more you get.

✔ An introduction to desktop publishing software.

✔ Finding a program that meets your needs.

✔ The design and typographic responsibilities involved in desktop publishing.

I n the last thirty years, the graphic arts industry has seen more revolutions than any third-world country. In the sixties, the turn-of-the-century Linotype and Monotype hot-metal typesetters based on medieval printing technologies rapidly began to be displaced by phototypesetting machines whose speed and output improved in quantum leaps — each machine becoming obsolete within a few years of its introduction. The seventies saw large publishing houses, printers, and newspapers begin to use on-screen page-makeup systems that allowed graphic artists to lay out pages electronically — without T squares, X-acto knives, and the other tools of mechanical pasteup.

Although electronics played a prominent role in the evolution of phototypesetting and electronic page-makeup equipment, microcomputers didn't. They lacked the processing power to calculate precise character widths and line endings, and the graphics to display various fonts and sizes. Then the Macintosh appeared. Armed with *desktop publishing programs,* the Mac has picked off the expensive page-layout systems, sniped at typesetters, and forced established type houses either to join the revolution or to retreat.

As a computer user, I'm excited to see that technology has advanced enough to enable non-professionals to set type and paste up pages with a $1000 Macintosh. But as a former typographer, I cringe when that technology is misused. Properly producing a printed piece takes time, patience, and at least a rudimentary knowledge of design and typographic concepts. In this chapter, we'll examine desktop publishing — and the responsibilities you assume when you start producing your own publications.

The Desktop Difference

In the world of electronic page makeup, a video screen and a mouse (or some other pointing device) replace the traditional layout table and its tools (see the sidebar "Layout and Pasteup the Old-Fashioned Way"). Rules, halftone windows,

Layout and Pasteup The Old-Fashioned Way

Before you can fully grasp what desktop publishing is, you should learn how printed materials are produced without it. Initially a graphic designer develops a concept by drawing rough, or *thumbnail,* sketches. Later, comprehensive drawings, called *comps,* are produced, which show how the final piece will look.

Next the designer chooses the typefaces and type sizes for the text, using a tedious process called *copyfitting* to make sure it will fit the available space. From there, the text is *marked up* with specifications for line lengths, fonts (a typeface in a particular size), and spacing. The typesetter may key in the text from the marked-up copy or convert the author's disk files, adding the necessary typesetting codes.

The layout artist then creates a *dummy,* a preliminary layout that shows how and where the text and graphics will go on each page. The artist refers to the dummy when pasting up the finished type on cardboard sheets, using T squares, triangles, and sharp eyes to make sure everything's straight. If the design calls for them, the artist will draw lines (called *rules)* with a drafting pen, or add stick-on *rule tape* (clear adhesive tape on which rules have been machine drawn).

If the page includes photographs, a screened negative for a *halftone* must be made from each photo to convert its various shades into dots that can be printed. The artist cuts a matching *window* from opaque film (such as Parapaque or Zipatone) and pastes it down on the board to show the printer where to position the halftone. *Line* art — graphs or line drawings — does not require halftones.

The artist then draws *crop marks* to denote the page's boundaries and may attach a protective sheet of tissue paper on which to mark ink colors or paper stock. Finally, when the cardboard sheet (called a *mechanical)* is *camera ready,* the printer shoots an actual-size negative from which the printing plate is made. **M**

Opposite page ▶
Elements of a Page
The pasted-up page, called a mechanical, as it should look when it's camera ready — with headlines and body text aligned, line art and halftone windows in place, and crop marks, registration marks, and fold lines to guide the printer.

and crop marks are added with electronic drawing tools; then the whole shebang is sent to a phototypesetting machine that delivers a camera-ready page. With desktop publishing, these basic steps are the same, except that they're accomplished within the friendly confines of a Macintosh.

If you're willing to invest some time and effort in learning a sophisticated word processor or a desktop publishing program and some fundamentals of publishing design, you can do what used to require several specialists and quite expensive typesetting equipment. Using the Mac, you can write and proofread *copy,* design a layout, and create camera-ready pages on a laser printer or a phototypesetter, or

ELEMENTS OF A PAGE

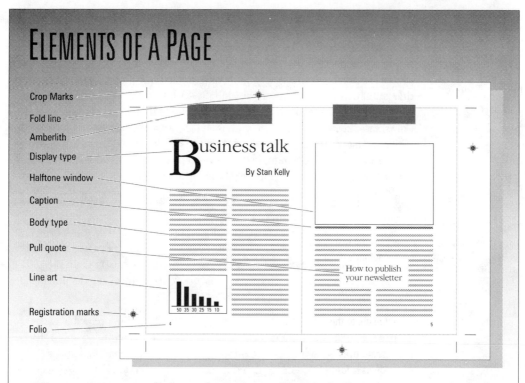

The pasted-up page, called a mechanical, as it should look when it's camera ready—with headlines and body text aligned, line art and halftone keyline in place, and crop marks, registration marks, and fold lines to guide the printer.

imagesetter. If you don't own a laser printer, you can use one at any of the growing number of copy shops and computer stores that rent time on desktop publishing systems.

With commercial typesetting and graphic arts firms charging $20 an hour and up *(way* up), it doesn't take long for a desktop publishing system to pay for itself. And there's the convenience factor. You can experiment with different designs or make last-minute type corrections in the time it would take to call a typesetting service and place an order. Best of all, the Mac can serve you in other areas when you aren't wearing your printer's apron.

Toll Road Ahead

But you have to spend before you can save. The road to desktop publishing has a number of alternate routes, and each takes a progressively higher toll on your bank account. The least expensive involves combining the Mac's typographic prowess with conventional pasteup methods. By preparing text with a word processor, printing it on a laser printer, and then pasting it up by hand, you can dramatically reduce your typesetting and production costs, which are often the most expensive part of a job. If you're willing to rent time on a laser printer, the only vehicle needed to travel this path is a Mac with a word processor; a used 128K Mac and the original version of MacWrite will do, but I'd suggest at least a two-drive Mac Plus and a more powerful word processor, such as Microsoft Word (I'll have more to say about software shopping shortly).

A more direct route, the one most desktop publishers take, involves using a desktop publishing program to paste up pages electronically. Most desktop publishing programs mimic conventional pasteup methods. After you specify basic information about your publication — its page size, number of pages, and whether the final product will be printed on both sides — the program presents you with a blank page into which you can *import* word processing documents and graphics created with drawing or business graphics programs.

The toll: a Mac with at least one megabyte of memory, but preferably two. Aldus PageMaker and Letraset's DesignStudio are billed as requiring only 1MB, but they perform sluggishly with that amount. Xerox's Ventura Publisher and QuarkXpress, on the other hand, require 2MB as a minimum. You'll also need a hard disk; earlier versions of these programs could run on a system with only two floppy drives, but those days are gone. (The truth is, they were never really here: two floppy drives delivered slow performance and forced you to perform some creative disk-swapping to transfer files from your word processing and graphics disks to those used for page layout.)

The third route to desktop publishing traverses the same terrain as the second but includes some high-priced stopovers to pick up a large-screen display and a *scanner*. Large-screen displays are just that: big screens that let you view an entire 8½ by 11 inch page (or even two, side by side) without having to scroll.

Scanners are add-ons that use optical sensors to convert photographs or other artwork into graphic documents where the original image is represented by a series of dots (see Chapter 39). Scanners range in price from a few hundred dollars for *hand held* scanners such as Thunderware's LightningScan to over $1500 for scanners such as Apple's Apple Scanner and Hewlett-Packard's ScanJet Plus, which can produce images that look at least as good as a high-quality newspaper photo.

Scanners can earn their keep in another way: when driven by the appropriate software, they become *optical character recognition* (OCR) devices, able to "read" typed or typeset pages of text from which they create disk files you can edit and reformat with a word processor (see Chapter 14).

The Software Side

Most Mac desktop publishing programs create on-screen versions of an artist's layout table. You can zoom in on the page to position something precisely, or zoom out to get the big picture of a single page or a two-page *spread*. You can position text and graphic elements by dragging them with the mouse. In keeping with the Mac's what-you-see-is-what-you-get (WYSIWYG, pronounced *wizzy-wig*) philosophy, the screen accurately reflects the appearance of the final page.

Most publishing programs offer similar features: on-screen rulers for measuring and aligning elements; the ability to import word processing documents with formatting attributes and style sheets intact; rudimentary text editing for making corrections or typing short passages; *master pages* for holding page numbers and other elements that repeat on each page; and formatting commands that let you change the appearance of text and create tables. The two most popular publishing programs — Aldus PageMaker and QuarkXpress — are shown in the figure "Electronic Layout Tables."

Publishing programs can also import images from graphics programs, and they provide tools for drawing rules, boxes, and circles. They also let you create *spot color* — a single color dropped into certain page elements (such as a headline or a horizontal bar) used to grab readers' attention. When you print a publication containing spot color, the program prints a separate sheet of paper for each

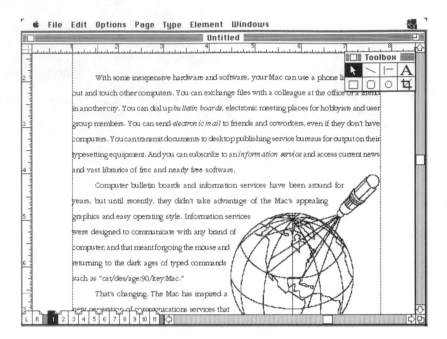

Electronic Layout Tables

Desktop publishing programs such as Aldus PageMaker (top) and QuarkXpress (bottom) provide on-screen layout tables upon which you electronically attach text and graphics. Here, both programs have wrapped text around an irregularly shaped graphic—a difficult job for many conventional typesetting machines. Note the drawing tools for creating boxes, lines (also called rules), and other shapes. Clicking on the page-number icons takes you to different pages in the publication.

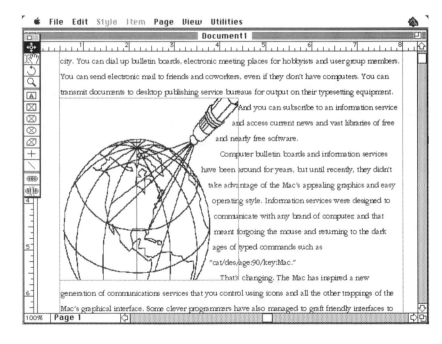

color. Each sheet contains *registration marks* that a printer will use to align colors.

Aldus PageMaker, QuarkXpress, and DesignStudio can also import color images, and can (with additional software) print *process color separations* that a professional printer uses to create the four printing plates (cyan, yellow, magenta, black) used to print color images on offset printing presses. This is the leading edge of desktop publishing, and you'll need a sense of adventure and some pioneer spirit to attain it. Many publishing pros have learned the hard way that it's often easier and more economical to stick with traditional color-separation techniques, which usually involve sending color images to separation houses that use ultra-expensive computer systems from firms such as Crossfield and Scitex. The resulting separations are then *stripped* into place by hand.

Some publishers strike a middle ground, using a desktop publishing program's color features for proofing, and then using conventional separation techniques for the final product. Technology is improving rapidly, however, and companies like Crossfield and Scitex are building their next-generation separation systems around the Macintosh. The next few years will bring more affordable and less experimental desktop color separation products.

Workstation Publishing

A notch or two above PageMaker, QuarkXpress, Ventura Publisher, and DesignStudio, you'll find so-called *workstation publishing* programs such as Frame Technology's FrameMaker and Interleaf Corporation's Interleaf (see the figure "High-End Publishing" on the next page). These programs provide interactive layout features, too, but they supplement them with features aimed at the production of lengthy documents such as books and technical manuals. Both programs let you create and manage footnotes, tables of contents, and indexes. Both can automatically revise page numbers in cross references (such as "see 'mouse' on page 150") as you add text to or remove it from a publication. And both provide *template* features that automate the production of documents where each page has a similar layout. (Ventura Publisher has many of these features, too; indeed, the program's prowess at handling lengthy, structured documents has helped make it one of the IBM PC world's most popular publishing programs. The Macintosh version appeared in late 1990.)

Besides handling lengthy documents, workstation publishing programs allow you to produce complex publications without having to use separate word processing and graphics programs. Both FrameMaker and Interleaf provide powerful drawing features you can use to create technical illustrations and schematics. And both provide built-in word processors with advanced features such as revision tracking and equation editing.

High-End Publishing

Frame Technology's FrameMaker (top) is a workstation publishing program designed for the production of lengthy documents. FrameMaker (and Interleaf Corp.'s Interleaf) provide built-in word processing and drawing features that go far beyond those of general-purpose publishing programs like PageMaker. Note the extensive object-manipulation features in FrameMaker's tool palette (which can be collapsed to show only the most often-used tools). FrameMaker's equation editor is visible at the bottom of the screen. Xerox's Ventura Publisher (bottom) straddles the fence between general-purpose and workstation publishing programs. Ventura Publisher lacks the sophisticated drawing features found in FrameMaker and Interleaf, but it does provide automatic cross-referencing, equation editing, and other features designed for the production of lengthy, complex documents.

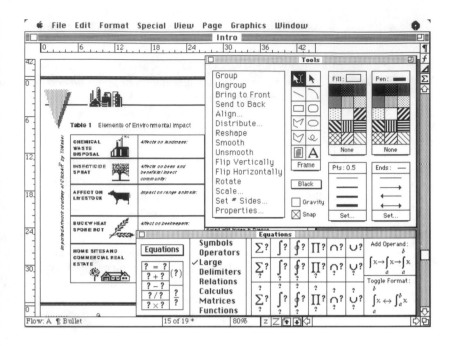

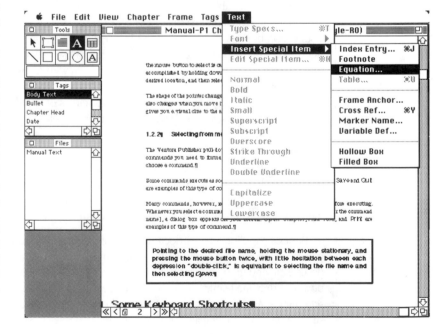

Workstation publishing programs get their name because they were originally developed for minicomputer-based workstations such as those made by Sun Microsystems and Digital Equipment Corporation. Indeed, both FrameMaker and Interleaf are still available for such workstations, and you can transfer publications between the Mac and workstation versions of each product. On the negative side, both FrameMaker and Interleaf have steep hardware requirements (4–5MB of memory and a Mac II-class machine with a big hard disk) and they can be difficult to learn. Also, their all-in-one approach makes sense for high-end workstations, where there isn't a huge selection of third-party software, but it's less of an advantage in the Mac world, where you can choose from — and combine — dozens of powerful word processors and graphics programs.

On the fringes of the desktop publishing world are *code-oriented* (also known as *command-driven* or *batch-processing*) programs that require typed formatting codes in the text. With code-oriented programs, typed codes such as \hsize = 155mm replace the mouse and menus for positioning and formatting text. This makes them more difficult to use; indeed, you'll need mountain climbing gear to scale the learning curve of programs like FTL Systems' MacTeX. But there are rewards at the summit. Not only can code-oriented programs create documents of virtually unlimited size, they can also automatically create footnotes, tables of contents, and indexes. Most code-oriented programs for the Mac also provide preview windows that show how the final product will appear. These programs are best for producing large publications that require a consistent appearance throughout, such as books and training manuals. And because their formatting codes are embedded in the original text, code-oriented programs are ideal for publications that need frequent revision. If you're producing complex technical publications that include mathematical equations, a program based on the TeX (pronounced *tek)* typesetting language may be your best bet. Another TeX package, OzTeX, is available free through user group libraries and on-line services.

With the boundaries increasingly blurred between text processing and publishing, the best desktop publishing program for your application may actually be a word processor. Microsoft Word, Ashton-Tate's FullWrite, Paragon Concepts' Nisus, and WordPerfect Corporation's WordPerfect can create footnotes, tables of contents, and indexes. Word also lets you create mathematical equations. FullWrite, WordPerfect 2.0, and Nisus include drawing features and the ability to wrap text around an irregularly shaped graphic. A word processor might be the best tool for jobs that don't require sophisticated layout features, but that undergo frequent revision.

Shopping for Software

The best way to find a desktop publishing program is to assess your needs, then find the program that best meets them — and whose operating style you can live with. Here are some features and factors to consider:

❖ *Document length* Early publishing programs were limited to short documents of about 16 pages. Today's programs support much longer documents — 999 pages in PageMaker's case, and as many pages as will fit on disk with Xpress and DesignStudio. Still, programs such as FrameMaker and Interleaf are better suited to the production of lengthy, structured documents such as books, catalogs, and manuals.

❖ *Positioning features* PageMaker relies exclusively on the mouse for positioning items on a page, while QuarkXpress and DesignStudio also let you type values that describe an element's position. Some people prefer typing these values to dragging with the mouse. Indeed, you'll often hear Xpress zealots praise their program for offering greater accuracy than PageMaker. The truth is, all publishing programs offer more positioning precision than a mechanical laser printer or imagesetter can provide. Claims of superior precision look good in advertising copy, but they won't show up in your printed pages.

❖ *Text-editing features* Unless you're using a workstation publishing program, you'll want to use a word processor to write your publication's text, saving your publishing program's text-editing features for simple tasks such as last-minute corrections and revisions. PageMaker, QuarkXpress, and DesignStudio each provide search-and-replace features and other rudimentary text-editing functions, but PageMaker tops them all. Its *story editor* is a mini word processor that makes it easy to revise text and even write small passages. PageMaker also provides *linking* options that let you easily update your original word processor files to reflect last-minute editing changes. Updating your original files to match the publication's text is important if you plan to use the originals again in other publications. (It's worth noting that System 7.0 provides a variety of additional features for moving data between programs. Today's publishing programs will be updated to take advantage of these features.)

❖ *Text spacing controls* The spacing between characters and between words plays an important part in determining a publication's overall legibility. Most publishing programs offer a variety of features that improve intercharacter and interword spacing. *Kerning* features let you move characters closer together to improve the spacing of certain letter combinations, such as To and AT. An *automatic kerning* feature enables the publishing program to kern characters based on *kerning tables* that are built into most fonts by their developers (see the figure "Kerning Characters"). A *manual kerning* function lets you fine-tune

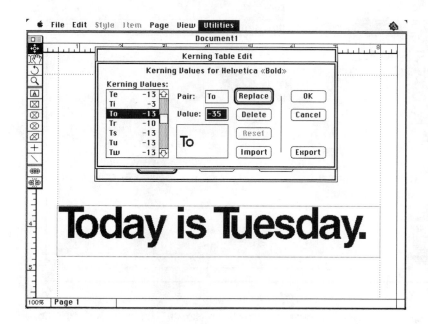

▲ **Kerning Characters**

The legibility of text, especially of large headlines such as the one visible here, is improved when key letter pairs are kerned. Automatic kerning features rely on kerning tables built into a font by its designer. QuarkXpress and Letraset's DesignStudio let you edit kerning tables to suit your typographic tastes. (QuarkXpress' kerning table editor is shown here.) You can also use third-party kerning table utilities such as The Software Shop's Kern-Rite and Pairs Software's KernEdit.

spacing by hand to improve the spacing of large text such as headlines. *Word spacing* features let you increase or decrease interword spacing. Finally, a *track kerning* feature lets the program uniformly decrease intercharacter spacing as the type size increases. Most publishing programs provide automatic and manual kerning, but only Aldus PageMaker, QuarkXpress, and DesignStudio provide track kerning. Ventura Publisher claims to provide tracking, but its tracking feature simply tightens intercharacter spacing, and isn't dependent on type size.

❖ *File-importing features* All publishing programs can import word processing and graphics files created by popular Mac programs, and some also support popular IBM PC file formats, such as that of WordPerfect. Ventura Publisher supports the largest number of PC file formats, however, making it a good choice for offices that use both Macs and PCs.

❖ *Third-party support* Aldus PageMaker and QuarkXpress users can choose from a large variety of software add-ons that enhance their programs. These add-ons range from color separation programs such as Aldus PrePrint to *database publishing* software such as ElseWare's DataShaper (for PageMaker) and Em Software's xdata (for QuarkXpress). These programs let you use the data stored by a database management program to create a variety of publications. For example, a video rental store might use its videotape database to produce catalogs for customers, inventory reports showing which tapes are checked out, and labels for the videotapes themselves. Database publishing simplifies the production of publications whose text is sorted and organized into categories. Typical database publishing applications include catalogs, classified advertisements, telephone directories, and television listings.

If you'll be creating advertisements, large headlines, or package designs, you might want a *display type* program such as Letraset's LetraStudio or

Adobe's TypeAlign. These programs let you stretch, condense, squeeze, and otherwise alter the appearance of text (see the figure "Special Text Effects"). Finally, if you plan to include graphics in your publications, see Chapter 8 for an introduction to graphics and drawing programs.

Putting the Issue to Bed

Before you take the desktop publishing plunge, prepare yourself: it's hard work. The Mac makes producing an attractive, readable page easier than it used to be, but that doesn't mean it'll be a breeze. To get results that do justice to your message, you will need to develop an awareness of design and typography.

One way to get off to a good start is to hire a graphic designer to create a conceptual framework — a foundation on which you can build each issue. Many desktop publishing software companies also sell canned *template* documents for common publishing jobs like newsletters and reports. Most programs also come with a library of templates that you can use as-is or modify to suit your tastes. Even with one of these approaches, however, the quality of your publication's typography is still up to you. We'll examine typographic considerations in detail in the next chapter.

You'll also need a standard dictionary (such as *Webster's Ninth New Collegiate Dictionary,* Merriam-Webster, 1986) and a style manual *(The Chicago Manual of Style,* University of Chicago Press, 1982, or *Words into Type,* Prentice-Hall, 1974) to get spelling, word breaks, grammar, and punctuation right.

When you start up that page-layout program you assume a responsibility for conveying ideas in an aesthetically pleasing way, both visually and verbally. Ignore that responsibility and you ignore centuries of printing tradition. And it isn't just the designers and typographers of the world who'll notice. They may not be aware of it, but your readers are excellent judges of good design and typography. Don't let them find you guilty of crimes against legibility. The sentences they'll impose will be to ignore yours.

Summary:

✔ Investing some time and effort in learning a sophisticated desktop publishing program can allow you to do what used to require several specialists and expensive equipment.

✔ The two most popular publishing programs are Aldus PageMaker and QuarkXPress, but for lengthy documents and technical manuals workstation programs like FrameMaker and Interleaf can be more appropriate.

✔ When shopping for desktop publishing software, features and factors to consider include document length, positioning features, text-editing features, text spacing controls, and third-party support.

✔ Although desktop publishing on the Mac makes producing attractive, readable pages easier, to get the best results you'll need to develop an awareness of design and typography.

Chapter 6
Typography

When you use the Mac, you're setting type. When you choose different fonts, sizes, or styles — be it in a publishing program, word processor, spreadsheet, or database — you're making the same decisions typographers have made for centuries. You're specifying the type characteristics that will convey your message clearly and attractively.

Or are you? Do you choose fonts that are appropriate to your message, or do you flit from font to font because the Mac makes it easy to do so? Do you choose type size, line spacing, and line length with readability in mind, or do you use whatever combination strikes your fancy?

The fact is, fine typography requires training and experience. Because type and fonts play such a large role in the Macintosh world, it's important to understand the basics of typography. In this chapter, I'll present some techniques for making your documents more readable. The sidebar "Type Terms" defines much of the typographic jargon used here.

Choosing a Font

The most basic typographic choice is usually that of a *typeface*. Each typeface has a personality; some are sophisticated, some are casual, and others are forceful and bold. Your goal is to choose typefaces whose personality complements your message.

Although some studies show little difference in legibility between *serif* and *sans serif* fonts, it's generally believed that serif typefaces are more legible and therefore better suited to lengthy text passages. I recommend that typographic newcomers follow this rule of thumb: Better serif than sorry (see the figure "Font Personalities").

Another issue concerns whether to use the same font for all the elements of a document, or to use a different font for headings and subheadings. One way to get good results is to use different fonts within the same *family.* For example, you might use Garamond for *body type* (or *body text*), Garamond Bold for headlines,

Type Terms

Ascender The part of characters such as *f* or *d* that rises above the body of the letter.

Base line The imaginary line on which the body of a character sits. Leading is measured from base line to base line.

Body type, or body text The typeface used for the main text of a job.

Descender The portion of characters such as *j* or *g* that drops below the base line.

Dingbat A decorative graphic element.

Downloadable font A font stored on a floppy or hard disk and downloaded into a laser printer's memory before use.

Em space A fixed amount of space equal to the point size of the typeface you're using. In 12-point type, an em space is 12 points wide.

En space Also called a *nut* space, a fixed amount of space equal to half an em space.

Family A group of related typefaces. For example, Times Roman, Times Italic, Times Bold, and Times Bold Italic are all members of the Times family.

Font All the characters for one typeface, and historically, in one size. Today, *font* and *typeface* are often used interchangeably.

Leading The amount of space between two base lines *(pronounced led-ing).*

Ligature Two or more connected characters, such as fi or fl.

Pica A unit of measurement that is equal to 12 points.

Point A unit of measurement equal to .01384, or approximately $1/72$, inch. The point size of a given typeface is the distance between the top of the highest ascender and the bottom of the lowest descender.

Pull quote A phrase extracted from the body text and set in large type to attract the reader's attention.

Sans serif A typeface without serifs. Sans-serif typefaces include Helvetica, Futura, and the Mac's Geneva screen font.

Serif A line crossing the main strokes of a character. Serifs lead the eye across a line of type. Serif typefaces include Times, Palatino, Century Schoolbook, and the Mac's New York screen font.

Small caps Capital letters with the same height as the lowercase characters.

Subhead A heading within the text that's used to split up lengthy passages and draw the reader's attention.

Thin space A fixed amount of space equal to half an en space.

x-Height The height of a typeface's lowercase letters, excluding ascenders and descenders.

ITC Franklin Gothic is legible and honest.

ITC Franklin Gothic Heavy carries weight.

Futura is geometric and "moderne," no?

ITC New Baskerville is delicate and graceful.

Helvetica Condensed is space-efficient, yet legible.

ITC New Century Schoolbook is easy to read.

Helvetica Condensed Bold Oblique is progressive.

ITC Lubalin Graph is sturdy and distinctive.

and Garamond Italic for captions. Or you could mix typefaces by using, for example, New Baskerville for body text and Helvetica Black for headlines. Just be consistent throughout a document, and don't mix with abandon.

The amount of copy you have may also influence your choice of typeface. To squeeze a lot of text into a small space, consider a space-efficient *condensed* typeface. The *downloadable font* libraries from Adobe Systems, Bitstream, Compugraphic, and other font vendors include attractive condensed versions of typefaces such as Helvetica, Univers, and Futura. A large selection of free or inexpensive, high-quality downloadable fonts is also available through user group libraries and on-line services and from software clearinghouses such as Educorp.

Line Length and Type Size

After choosing a font, you need to settle on the width of text columns and the type size. Both decisions are related and have one goal: putting a manageable number of words on each line.

Two rules of thumb exist for determining line length. One states that each line should have roughly from 8 to 11 words. Another says that a column should be just wide enough to accommodate 2½ lowercase alphabets in the typeface and size you plan to use (see the figure "How Long a Line?" on the next page). Experimentation with both rules reveals that they often provide the same results. The bottom line: strive for lines containing between 50 and 70 characters.

Most people read groups of three or four words at a time rather than individual words. If there are too many words on each line, the eyes tire as they journey from left to right. Too few words on each line, and the flow of the text becomes disrupted by line breaks and excessive hyphenation.

abcdefghijklmnopqrstuvwxyzabcdefghijklmnopqrstuvwxyzabcdefghijklm

One rule of thumb for determining line length states that a line should be wide enough to accommodate 2.5 lowercase alphabets in the typeface and size you plan to use. This works out to roughly 8 to 11 words per line—not so many that the eye gets lost, but enough to retain the smooth flow of the text.

▲ How Long a Line?

One way to determine the ideal line length for a given font and size is to type 2½ lowercase alphabets, as demonstrated here in 10-point Optima.

Your choice of type size will be influenced by the amount of text you have and the space into which it must fit. For documents duplicated on a laser printer or photocopier, you probably won't have a preconceived number of pages, or a *page count,* in mind. If that's the case, simply choose a type size that works with your column width to provide from 8 to 11 words per line.

For a document that will be commercially printed, however, you must determine the page count in advance — and make sure your text fits within it. Before WYSIWYG (what-you-see-is-what-you-get) screen displays, designers and typographers endured a complex *copyfitting* routine that involved crunching through formulas to calculate character widths. Today's WYSIWYG programs and displays let you adjust the type size as you work.

Of course, on-the-fly tweaking is effective only to a point. In a newsletter, for instance, you wouldn't adjust each article's type size to accommodate its text. That would destroy the publication's uniformity, and uniformity is a cornerstone of good typography and design. When an article is a tad long, try hyphenating more lines (this works best with text that's set ragged right). If it's still too long, consider cutting some text.

When an article is too short, try removing hyphenations, breaking long paragraphs into shorter ones, or narrowing the width of the columns. If these techniques fail, consider filling the leftover space with a graphic element such as a straight line (or *rule*) or an ornamental *dingbat.* Other possibilities include lengthening the article by using *subheads* or *pull quotes.* Or you can leave the space blank. Just as silence is an integral part of music, white space is an integral part of graphic design.

Leading Guidelines

Another way to do your readers a favor is through appropriate use of line spacing, or *leading.* For body text, the general rule is to lead at 20 percent of the type size. For 10-point type, for example, use 2 points of lead for a total of 12 points from one *base line* to the next. The Mac's fonts contain built-in autoleading specifications that use this 20 percent rule. When you specify "auto" in your word processor or desktop publishing program, the program uses the font's autoleading value.

The 20 percent rule is a good starting place, but many other factors should influence your choice of leading. Line length is one. With long lines, too little leading causes readers to occasionally read the same line twice, a phenomenon known as doubling. Longer lines benefit from more leading.

Type size should also influence how much leading you use. Headline type (14-point or larger) generally needs more leading than body type (8- to 12-point). Type that's smaller than 8-point sometimes needs more than 20 percent leading to make the tiny type appear less dense.

The rule, "Large type requires more leading," doesn't always apply to headlines. Headlines often look better when set *solid* — with no extra space. (For example, a 24-point headline set solid has 24 points of space between base lines.) With some fonts, you might even consider minus line spacing, such as 22-point leading with 24-point type. Just watch that one line's *descenders* don't touch the next line's *ascenders.*

When specifying type size and leading, designers write a kind of fraction in which the type size is the numerator and the leading is the denominator. For example, 10-point type and 12 points of leading from base line to base line is specified as 10/12, and pronounced *ten on twelve* or *ten over twelve.*

Alignment Issues

Another major aspect of type formatting concerns the alignment of the left and right margins. You're probably familiar with the three most common forms of alignment: *flush left, ragged right; justified;* and *flush right, ragged left.* But which to use, and when?

Traditionally, large passages of text have been set justified. Many designers believe that neatly aligned left and right margins are best suited to sustained reading because they give pages a quiet look that lets readers concentrate on content.

To justify text, word processors add space between each word. Some desktop publishing programs, including Aldus PageMaker and QuarkXpress, can also add space between each character, a process called *letterspacing.* Letterspacing helps eliminate the large word spaces and the *rivers* of white space that can occur (see the figure "Justifying Your Actions" on the next page). Hyphenation also helps, although you should never hyphenate more than two or three consecutive lines.

> Justified text, long preferred for its smooth appearance, is less readable when there's too much space between words. Distracting "rivers" of white space can appear. This problem is especially common with narrow column measures. Letterspacing and hyphenation can help eliminate the problem.
>
> Justified text, long preferred for its smooth appearance, is less readable when there's too much space between words. Distracting "rivers" of white space can appear. This problem is especially common with narrow column measures. Letterspacing and hyphenation can help eliminate the problem.

These days, ragged-right margins have become more popular, even in such bastions of justification as textbooks and magazines. Ragged-right text requires fewer hyphenations, and its consistent word and letter-spacing give it a clean, even texture (see the figure "Running Ragged"). And because

▲ Justifying Your Actions

Appropriate use of letterspacing and hyphenation can dramatically improve the appearance of justified type. Also note that because more text can fit on each line, the same amount of copy takes up less space. Adobe's Melior typeface is used here.

the eyes stop at a different point in each line, it can actually be less fatiguing to read than justified text.

As for the other alignment options — centered and flush-right, ragged left — both can be effective in small doses. Centering, for example, is ideal for short passages such as headlines. But because centered and ragged-left text force you to hunt for the start of each line, they can be hard to read in large doses.

Type on Display

Headlines and other large, attention-getting blocks of type are called display type. Showing attention to detail in display type is an important step in making documents look professionally typeset.

With display type intended to grab the reader's interest, you might be tempted to use all capital letters for added oomph. Resist the urge. A mix of upper- and lowercase characters gives words an overall shape that aids in recognition; text set in *all caps* lacks these patterns. It's generally better to capitalize only the first letter of important words, leaving conjunctions and articles such as and, in, and the lowercase. That way you won't put undue emphasis on less important words.

Once you've settled on case, concentrate on the space between characters and words. As I mentioned in the last chapter, most fonts produce too much space between certain character pairs, especially in large type sizes. You can improve the look by tightening those spaced-out pairs, a process called *kerning.*

In smaller type sizes, kerning usually involves tightening only certain letter pairs, such as *To* or *Av.* But in large sizes, almost every combination of characters is a

Whether a ragged-right margin is more readable depends in part on the contour, or *rag*, of the right margin. A good rag has a rhythm, with text alternating between longer lines and shorter ones. The best typographers ensure that each line ending contributes to the margin's profile, even if they have to break certain lines by hand.

Whether a ragged-right margin is more readable depends in part on the contour, or *rag*, of the right margin. A good rag has a rhythm, with text alternating between longer lines and shorter ones. The best typographers ensure that each line ending contributes to the margin's profile, even if they have to break certain lines by hand.

▲ Running Ragged

In the paragraph on the left, notice how most lines hover around the same width, making the right margin look poorly justified, not ragged. When the word with is brought down to the next line (right), the right margin assumes a more ragged contour. This example uses ITC New Baskerville.

candidate (see the figure "Kerned versus Unkerned"). Use the manual-kerning features in your desktop publishing program or word processor to remove space between characters until they are tight, but not touching. Also decrease the spaces between words. Just be sure to apply the same degree of kerning and word spacing throughout a document. Inconsistent spacing is worse than none at all.

A variation on the letter spacing theme in headlines involves adding space between each character to obtain an airy, elegant effect. This letterspacing technique can be effective when used sparingly. Be sure to also add more space between words so they don't run together, and avoid letterspacing heavy, condensed typefaces such as Adobe's ITC Machine. Type set in Machine actually looks better when certain characters touch slightly, or *kiss* (see the figure "Headline Spacing").

With body text, you usually let your word processor or publishing program end each line for you. With display type, however, you should take a more active role in determining line breaks. Good typographers end lines at logical stopping points, such as after a comma or a key phrase (see the figure "Breaking for Sense" on the next page). The best advertising typographers will also apply this technique to body text.

In headlines containing trademark or copyright symbols, the symbols are usually much too large and obtrusive. Use a smaller type size for the symbol itself, and then move the symbol so that its top aligns with the top of the text (again see "Breaking for Sense").

Kerned versus Unkerned

In display type, nearly every character is a candidate for kerning. Here, space was removed between the Y and the o, around the apostrophe, between the y and the comma, between each w, and between the period and the closing quotes. A little less space was removed between the a and the y. Notice how the kerned headline uses less space. This headline was created with Letraset's LetraStudio display-type program, which simplifies manual kerning tasks by allowing you to position individual characters by dragging them.

You'll say, "wow."

You'll say, "wow."

Headline Spacing

Top: Letterspaced headlines can create an airy, dignified effect, especially if you use a typeface with such elegant capitals as Italia's. Extra space between words keeps them from running together. Bottom: Heavy, condensed faces such as ITC Machine don't letterspace well and are best set tight. Note the kissing T and O, A and S, and S and T. In the bottom headline, the word spaces were tightened slightly, too. A period gives the slogan added authority.

ELEGANT AND SPACIOUS

TOUGH AS STEEL

TOUGH AS STEEL.

The Form Factor

One document that imposes unique typographic requirements is the form. Forms range in size and style from reply cards, with their blank lines for name and address, to tax forms, with their dozens of cubbyholes and instructions. If you use a database manager, you probably use on-screen forms to enter and view data.

A form's primary purpose is to obtain and present information in a structured format. The first step in creating that sense of order is to select clean, readable typefaces. Sans serif fonts such as Helvetica and News Gothic are particularly well suited to forms (just ask the IRS). Univers is another sans serif font that works well in forms.

When designing forms, group related information together. If the form will be filled out by hand, leave enough space for people to write comfortably. Put 18 to 24 points of space between each line, and make lines long enough to accommodate long names and addresses.

Creating on-screen forms for data entry requires similar considerations, with an added twist: most laser printer fonts don't have particularly readable screen fonts. The Mac's screen resolution is roughly one-fourth that of a

Breaking for Sense

Readability of display type (here 18-point Futura Extra Bold) is improved by breaking each line at a logical stopping point. Extra leading before the final sentence adds emphasis. This example also shows how to deal with a large, distracting register mark: select it, and then choose a smaller type size (in this case, 8-point). Then move it until its top aligns with the top of the text.

Today and tomorrow, the Southcom 300® will be there. We guarantee it.

**Today and tomorrow, the Southcom 300®
will be there.**

We guarantee it.

laser printer's, and that's insufficient to render the subtleties of most fonts accurately.

One solution is to use fonts designed for the Mac's screen, such as New York and Geneva. On laser printers, however, these fonts print poorly. The best method is to use separate forms for data entry and report printing. Use readable screen fonts such as New York and Geneva for on-screen data-entry forms, and laser-printer fonts for report-printing forms.

Character Cautions

One of the easiest ways to make documents look typeset is to replace the Mac's typewriter-like punctuation characters with ones typesetters use (see the sidebar "Type Tips" on the next page).

A few more cautions: Avoid gimmicky font styles such as shadow and outline. Also think twice about using the *small-caps* option that many programs provide. To create small caps, typesetting systems provide special fonts in which the small capitals are drawn to match the texture and line thickness of the large capitals. On the Mac, programs with small-caps options simply use a smaller type size for the small capitals. The resulting small caps have lighter *stem weights* than the large ones, giving the text an uneven appearance. If you want to use small caps, consider using a font that provides true small caps, such as those in Adobe's Adobe Originals series. These fonts also provide a variety of fractions, ligatures, and other characters that are mainstays of professional, high-quality typography.

Finally, avoid superimposing type over a gray-shaded background. Type is most legible when it's easily distinguished from the background; black-on-grey isn't exactly a high-contrast combination.

Recommended Reading

To learn more about typography, read the following books: *Designing with Type,* by James Craig (Watson-Guptill Publications, 1971); *Graphic Design for the Electronic Age,* by Jan White (Watson-Guptill Publications, 1988); *Basic Typography,* by John R. Biggs (Watson-Guptill Publications, 1968); *Design Principles for Desktop Publishers,* by Tom Lichty (Scott, Foresman and Company, 1989); and *The Mac is Not a Typewriter,* by Robin Williams (Peachpit Press, 1990).

Two more excellent sources of type tips are Adobe's *Font & Function* catalog ($6 from Adobe Systems, 1585 Charleston Road, P.O. Box 7900, Mountain View, CA 94039), and the International Typeface Corporation's free quarterly, *U&lc*

(write to *U&lc* Subscription Department, International Typeface Corporation, 2 Hammarskjold Plaza, New York, NY 10017).

As you create and format documents, remember that the best typography is always appropriate to the message it conveys. Every formatting command you issue should be aimed at improving your document's readability. Aaron Burns, chairman of the International Typeface Corporation, sums it up best: "In typography, function is of major importance; form is secondary; and fashion, almost meaningless."

Type Tips

I acquired an appreciation for fine typography while working for Davis & Warde, a 100-year old printing company in Pittsburgh, where I learned the trade from old-school masters who wore visors and referred to text as "matter." Headline matter, body matter, it didn't matter — no job was too complex. There an apprentice typographer started out melting down old type into lead bars, and loading and unloading 75-pound font "magazines" into Linotype machines. After six years, he (rarely she, in those days) became a journeyman.

"You learned your trade through association with experienced people," said Bill Darney, who started as an apprentice in 1959, then graduated to shop foreman and later, vice president. "There were shop standards for aesthetics and consistency you had to learn and live by — or die. Those standards are exactly what's lacking today. When you have so many people creating type in so many ways, [standards and consistency] fall by the wayside."

The death of hot-metal type forced Davis & Warde to make the painful transition to "cold" type — big phototypesetting machines, later to be supplemented by Macs. They succeeded, partly because they knew the basics of quality typography that transcend technology. Here are some ways to follow that tradition on the Mac:

❖ *Use em and en dashes.* Use these instead of double hyphens. To get an *em dash (—)* on the Mac, press Option-Shift-hyphen; for an *en dash(–)*, press Option-hyphen. An en dash is used to express a range, standing for *to* between numbers or words.

❖ *Use true quotes.* Press Option-] and Shift-Option-] for open and close single quotes; for double quotes, press Option-[and Shift-Option-[. (Also, put commas and periods inside quotation marks; colons and semicolons go outside quotes.) Most word processors offer a *smart quotes* option that inserts the proper quotes as you type. Desktop publishing programs also offer a "convert quotes" option that causes the program to automatically convert quotes when you import word processing files.

❖ *Don't put two spaces after punctuation.* Put only one space after periods, colons, and semicolons.

❖ *Don't use a lowercase l for the numeral 1.* Though similar on a typewriter, they look different in typographic fonts. And because the l is narrower than the 1 in most fonts, using the l will misalign number columns in tables.

❖ *Hyphenate judiciously.* Make sure words break correctly — between syllables. Try not to end more than two or three consecutive lines with hyphens, and avoid two-letter divisions (on-ly, un-til). **M**

Summary:

✔ Fonts and type play large roles in the Macintosh world, making an awareness of typographic basics especially important.

✔ The first step in choosing the appropriate typeface involves choosing between san-serif and serif designs.

✔ To arrive at the ideal line length, strive for an average of about 8–11 words per line.

✔ Body text generally looks best when you choose a program's autoleading option. Consider setting headlines with no extra leading.

✔ Justified body text can be prone to distracting rivers of white space, which you can eliminate with judicious hyphenation and letterspacing.

✔ In display type, almost every character combination can benefit from some kerning.

Chapter 7

Database Management

In This Chapter:

✔ The basics of database management.

✔ A look at the types of fields data managers provide.

✔ Details on how to locate data in a database.

✔ An introduction to creating "personalized" form letters.

✔ Single-file versus relational databases: which will meet your needs?

✔ A look at some specialized database programs.

L ife is filled with facts to file. In any office, near the "You don't have to be crazy to work here, but it helps" sign, file cabinets entomb paper that has run the course from in-box to out-box. Rolodex files swell with cards and Post-it notes spread like moss on the surface of an overcrowded folder holder. And "while you were out" messages stack up in a corner, each one a clear reminder of *why* you were out.

If this describes your workplace, the notion that a computer can get you organized and keep your head above paper can be enticing enough to inspire a purchase. But this inspiration is often built on the vague idea that computers have miraculous powers of organization, that putting one on your desk will somehow give you one-key access to those tedious tidbits you have to root for now.

Speed, disk storage, and eraserless revisions do give a computer powerful filing capabilities — when they're tapped by a *database manager*. These electronic file clerks let you store, sort, retrieve, revise, and print information. You can store an entire file drawer of facts and figures on a floppy disk, and locate any one of them in the time it would take you to open the drawer.

But a database manager isn't a panacea for organizational ills. For one thing, a computer database can't create itself. You have to decide how to organize your information and then set up the database manager accordingly. And information

A Matter of Record

In a database, a field is a single piece of information for an entry; together, the fields for an entry make up a record. Here, the top window shows a single record from a Microsoft Works database. The bottom window shows five records displayed in a spreadsheet-like, row-and-column format.

doesn't file itself in a database; you (or someone else, if you're lucky) have to set aside time for the tedious task called data entry. A database may allow effortless retrieval, but it requires endless maintenance.

Data Basics

Unlike a file folder, database managers don't let you stuff information anywhere just to get it out of sight. They hold data within a rigid structure, and planning that structure is the most important step in setting up your database. You can reorganize an electronic database after you've entered data, but it's not much easier than reorganizing a paper filing system.

A database structure is formed by two building blocks: *fields* and *records*. A field is a single piece of information for an entry; together the fields for an entry make up the record (see the figure "A Matter of Record"). In a database version of a Rolodex, for example, all of the information on a single card is a record and each element — first name, last name, company, zip code — is a field. When you define a database's structure, you create fields and give each one a name that reflects its contents, such as First Name or Street Address.

In addition to defining the structure, creating a database involves specifying how information will be presented on screen. The screen layout of fields and their names is called a *form*. Most programs provide a preset, quick-and-dirty form layout to use when you just can't wait to start entering data, and also let you design your own forms that mimic the paper forms you're trying to avoid (see the figure "In Fine Form"). Macintosh database managers tend to offer more design options than a decorator supply house, allowing you to choose fonts and

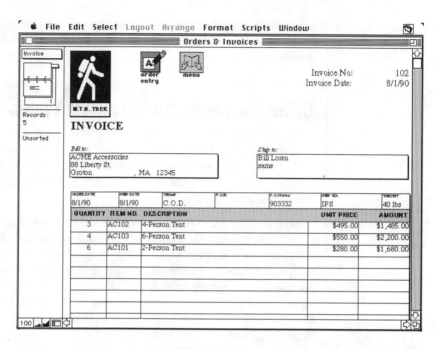

In Fine Form

Many Mac database managers provide layout features that let you create sophisticated forms for data entry and reporting. This invoice form was created using the powerful form-design features in FileMaker Pro. The bottom window shows the form in FileMaker Pro's layout mode. Note the tools (at left) for drawing shapes and creating text items, and the rulers for aiding in precise positioning.

styles, draw lines and boxes, and add graphics, such as company logos. Many database managers also let you view and enter data in a spreadsheet-like, row-and-column format.

Different Fields for Different Yields

Database managers provide different types of fields for different kinds of information. All data managers offer two basic types. *Text fields* hold letters, numbers, and any other keyboard character. *Number,* or *numeric, fields* hold numeric values — an employee's hourly wage in a personnel database, or a balance-due value in an accounting database.

Most data managers provide additional field types. *Date fields* hold only date values. *Picture fields* hold graphics that you paste in from the Clipboard. *Logical fields* hold only one of two values: yes or no. For instance, you might create a logical field called Past Due, which would indicate whether a client's account was paid up. *Formula fields* obtain their values not from the keyboard, but by processing values in other fields according to a formula you specify. One typical formula field is a Gross Pay field that multiplies the value in an Hours Worked field by that of an Hourly Wage field.

One way to improve your accuracy in data entry is to use a program that lets you assign *range checking* values to fields. You might specify, for example, that an error message be displayed if someone enters only five digits in a Social Security Number field. If your company opened in 1990, you could tell the data manager to reject employee hire dates earlier than January 1, 1990.

If text fields can hold any character, why are there special fields for numbers, dates, and yes or no values? One reason is to guard against inaccuracy. Most database managers won't let you store a text value in a number field, and would, therefore, thwart someone typing a lowercase *l* for the number 1, or an uppercase *O* for a zero. Similarly, a program that provides date fields rejects entries that aren't valid dates. And having numeric fields simplifies generating totals and subtotals in reports.

Better database managers offer data-entry shortcuts that cut down the amount of typing you need to do for some fields, thereby reducing the chance for error. Some programs can automatically copy a given field's value from the last record you entered. Others let you specify a preset value for a field when you're creating it.

A Sorted Tale

Using appropriate fields is also important when it comes to sorting data. Say you want to sort an employee database according to each employee's date of birth. If you stored the birthdate values in a text field, your database manager would place

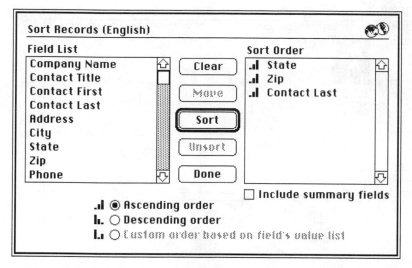

values beginning with December ahead of those beginning with September, because *D* precedes *S*. When you use a date field, however, the program recognizes that September precedes December, and sorts your records accurately.

A database manager's ability to sort information in alphabetic or numeric order makes your data more useful by letting you look at it from different perspectives. In a personnel database, you can view a list of employees sorted according to salaries, date of hire, or number of sick days taken. You can view a database of videotapes according to title, star, running time, or genre.

▲ **New Levels of Sorting**
This FileMaker Pro database is being sorted on three levels: first by state, then by zip, then by last name. The rising bars next to each field name denote an ascending (A–Z) sort.

But what if you want to view an employee list organized by salary within each department, or an alphabetized list of horror movies presented in the order they were made? That's where sorting levels come in. Most database managers let you sort data according to multiple levels: last name, then first name; last name, then first name, according to hire dates, according to department; last name, then first name, according to age group and income, sorted by city. Multiple sorting levels multiply the angles from which you can view your data (see the figure "New Levels of Sorting").

Golden Retrievers

Unlike the file cabinets I have known, a database manager doesn't teleport information it receives into the Twilight Zone. When you want to find something, you can do so in a few ways. The simplest is browsing: moving from one record to the next, either to view the records you just sorted, or to admire how much better they look on a screen than in a box of index cards. When you locate the record you want, you can alter it or just move on to the next.

When you're looking for something specific instead of just browsing, you use what are called *search specifications* or *search criteria,* phrases that tell

Search for Data

Many Mac data managers, including FileMaker Pro (top), let you search for data by typing the values you're looking for in the appropriate fields.

Here, a search is being specified for all contacts in California that did not receive a Christmas card. Also note the variety of search operators at the left edge of the window. At bottom, a quick-and-dirty search method from Microsoft Works.

```
     File  Edit  Select  Layout  Arrange  Format  Scripts  Window

                              Contacts

Data Entry           CONTACTS                    new  name    menu

                                              ENTER DATE:
                          CONTACT CODE:        FAX:
  M.T.H. TREK
                              COMPANY:
Requests:                     ADDRESS:
  1          CHRISTMAS CARD?  CITY, STATE, ZIP:           CA
             O Yes  ● No
   Find                    OTHER ADDRESS:
                          CITY, STATE, ZIP:
 □ Omit
  <    ≤     FIRST NAME  LAST NAME     TITLE          PHONE
  >    ≥
  =  Exact  NOTES:
 ...  Range
  !  Dupl's
 //  Today  REFERRAL       INDUSTRY      CREDIT       CONTACT TYPE

100
```

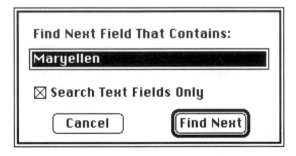

Find Next Field That Contains:

Maryellen

☒ **Search Text Fields Only**

Cancel   **Find Next**

your database manager what to look for. A search can be simple ("find Dave Byrd's record"), complex ("find all male employees in accounting earning more than $35,000"), or downright impossible ("find all Reds fans in Oakland").

When you perform a complex search, you use *search operators,* characters like the greater-than and less-than signs (> and <), to find entries above or below a certain value. You also use the *logical operators* AND, OR, and NOT to combine search criteria. In the complex search example above, the logical AND appears twice: "find all employees whose Sex field is male AND whose Department field is accounting AND whose Salary field is greater than 35,000." With the logical AND, all the criteria must be true for a given record to be considered "found." With a logical OR, only one need be true: "find all clients in Minneapolis OR St. Paul."

Fortunately, complex searches aren't complex to conduct. Most Mac database managers provide dialog boxes that make performing complex searches a matter of clicking the desired options, typing the data you're looking for, and then clicking OK (see the figure "Search for Data").

The results of all this searching is usually a *report,* a printed copy of the records meeting your search criteria, sorted in a specific order. While a report can be a form that shows just one record, it's more typically a *columnar report* showing many records, with each field in its own column and each record in its own row, like baseball team standings or stock exchange tables.

A Merger of the Mails

Between hosting *Star Search* and haunting the *Tonight Show,* how does Ed McMahon find time to personally address those publisher's giveaway mailings? He's discovered *mail merge,* a variation on the reporting theme that involves merging a stock form letter with a database to produce "personal" form letters. Mail merge is often performed with powerful word processors like Microsoft Word, but a database manager that lets you create lengthy text items on a form can also do the job.

With mail merge, you first type the stock portion of a letter, inserting field names where the custom text will appear. Using *conditional statements* such as IF...THEN, you can create different letters based on information in the database, congratulating clients with paid-up accounts, or telling clients whose accounts are overdue to reach for their checkbooks.

Let's Get Relational

When searching for a database manager, you'll run head-on into the brick wall known as *relational* database management. Though the term causes great confusion, the difference between the two types of databases is actually simple. The type I've discussed so far is the *single-file,* or *flat file,* database, where one file contains all the fields and records in the database. A relational database, however, comprises two or more files linked by the database manager to allow one file to access data in the others. Relational databases also provide the most headaches for newcomers to computer databases.

Unlike a single-file database, a relational database isn't easily compared to a real object like an index-card file. If you squint and pretend, however, you can compare it to a cross-referenced filing system. In such a system, an employee's personnel entry might say "see the payroll file for this employee's salary history." In the payroll file, each employee salary history could be accompanied by a note saying "see the personnel files for this employee's address and Social Security number." By cross-referencing the two files, you eliminate the need to store each employee's address and Social Security number in the payroll file and the

File Edit Form Organize

need to store payroll information along with the personnel history (see the figure "Filing Pictures"). Elimination of redundancy is a relational database's strong suit.

Another relational-database plus is that cross-referencing is automatic. An employee's address and Social Security number can appear on screen next to his or

▲ **Filing Pictures**
This Microsoft File database stores personnel information, with picture fields holding the employee picture and signature. File is one of many database managers that lets you store pictures and create forms that resemble paper forms.

her payroll information. When employees leave, you can expunge all references to them by deleting their records in just one file.

But these strengths don't mean that every data-management task demands a relational program. Unfortunately, there is no sharp boundary separating single-file applications from multifile applications, so deciding when to make that leap can be difficult. As a rule, consider a relational data manager such as Acius' 4th Dimension or Fox Software's FoxBASE+/Mac when the data you're storing could be used in more than one way, or when you find that you're entering the same information in separate files. If those programs are too daunting (and they can be), consider Claris' FileMaker Pro. Technically speaking, it's a flat-file database manager; however, it provides a lookup feature that allows one file to access data in another. And it's far easier to learn and use than a full-blown relational program.

At the head of the relational data management class are *applications generators,* programs that enable you to create data-management applications tailored for specific tasks such as inventory management or client billing. Such applications, often custom designed for a single company, allow people who don't need to understand the technicalities of data management or file structures to use the information on the database.

With an application generator, someone sets up the needed file structures, relationships, range-checking routines, and search-and-sort specifications, and then ties them all together with (ideally) self-explanatory pull-down menus and dialog boxes. The advantage: anyone can use the application immediately, without having to master the data manager. The drawback: a change in reporting needs or business practices requires that the application be modified, and that could bring work to a halt while the changes are made.

Variations on the Theme

Every database manager handles the details of field formatting and range checking in its own way, but most work within the standard framework of fields and records. There are some interesting exceptions. Foremost among them is HyperCard, Claris' "software construction set" that Apple includes with the Mac. As we'll see in Chapter 9, HyperCard much more than just a database manager, but it certainly can sort, search, and store, and many Mac users have embraced its ability to be customized.

Another filer with a twist is Symmetry Corporation's PictureBase, an "art manager" that can keep track of a library of graphics. You assign keywords to pictures — Outdoor Scenes, Company Symbols, and so on — to use for searching. PictureBase includes a desk accessory named Retriever that lets you search for and retrieve graphics from the library while using another program.

If you're determined to replace your Rolodex with something a bit more electronic, check out Power Up Software's Address Book Plus or Portfolio Systems' DynoDex. Both are simple data managers that can also dial the phone for you (provided you have a modem). The Dynodex package even includes 100 sheets of Dynodex paper, alphabetized divider tabs, and a six-ring binder with a see-through slipcover for custom cover designs and labels. A binder is optional for Address Book Plus. Several free or shareware address book programs are also available.

And as we saw in Chapter 4, spreadsheet programs make serviceable database managers, thanks to their sorting and searching features and their libraries of functions for manipulating data. But where most true database managers allow you to store as much data as will fit on disk, most spreadsheets allow you to store only as much as will fit in memory. Try to maintain a huge database using a spreadsheet program, and you risk running out of memory or at the very least, slowing the spreadsheet program to a crawl. Most spreadsheets also lack the built-in error checking features that data managers provide. You can construct error-checking routines yourself by creating formulas, but if you must resort to doing that, chances are you'd be better off using a database manager to begin with.

Before shopping for a database manager, first assess the way you work with information now, then try to find the program that will make the transition to electronic filing as smooth as possible. If you need to create data entry forms that resemble their paper counterparts, you'll need a program with complete form-layout features, such as FileMaker Pro. For complex accounting or inventory applications, a relational program such as 4th Dimension is in order. For maintaining a mailing list, a simple filer such as Software Discoveries' RecordHolder Plus may be all you need. For simple mail merge tasks, consider an integrated program such as Microsoft Works.

A database manager can streamline your filing, provided you realize it isn't a surefire cure for disorganization. If you learned filing from Oscar Madison, that slob's slob of a sportswriter from the *Odd Couple*, your records will be as disorganized electronically as they were on paper.

And some tasks are better handled on paper. Flipping through Rolodex cards is still often faster than typing search criteria. And until the Mac has a sauce-proof keyboard, recipes belong in card files and cookbooks. Don't try to shoehorn the computer into areas of your filing life that work efficiently now.

Summary:

✔ A database may allow effortless storing, sorting, retrieving, revising, and printing of information, but it requires endless maintenance.

✔ The most common type of fields used in a database are text fields for holding letters and numbers, and number fields for holding numeric values. Other fields hold data values and graphics.

✔ You can locate data in a database by browsing, or moving from one record to the next; or by using search criteria, which tells your database manager what to look for.

✔ Mail merge is the process of merging a form letter with a database to produce "personal" form letters.

✔ In a flat-file database, one file contains all the fields and records in the database; relational databases use two or more files linked by the database manager to allow one file to access data in others.

Chapter 8

Graphics

In This Chapter:

✔ A look at the two basic types of graphics programs: bitmapped and object oriented.

✔ An introduction to image processing programs.

✔ A comparison of drawing and painting programs: pixels versus objects.

✔ Deciding between a paint or draw program.

✔ Creating three-dimensional images.

✔ The pros and cons of various graphics file formats.

Word processors might be the Macintosh world's most popular applications, but graphics programs are the most appealing. Start up a word processor for a few friends and they'll probably show lukewarm interest. But fire up a graphics program and watch them line up for their turn at the mouse. People who would never dream of standing in front of an easel and canvas suddenly become artists-in-training, spilling paint all over the screen.

Perhaps graphics programs are enticing because people view a computer as a tool for calculating, not an artistic medium. Or maybe it's the sense of experimentation that draws you in. Move the mouse, get a circle. Oops, erase that mistake. Hey, the little spray can works just like a real one.

Ever since MacPaint blazed the trail in 1984, graphics programs have been instrumental to the Mac's success. Indeed, there are more ways to create images with the Mac than there are to process words — proof of the machine's graphical bent. In this chapter, I'll explore some of the technicalities behind Macintosh graphics and spotlight the features you'll find in the current crop of graphics programs. And because not everyone has artistic aspirations, I've included some tips on other ways to put graphics software to work (see the sidebar "Ten Ways to Use a Graphics Program" on the next page).

(Continued on page 100)

Ten Ways to Use a Graphics Program

You don't have to be a modern-day Monet to benefit from a graphics program. Here are some project ideas for using paint or draw programs (or both) for something other than painting or drawing.

1. *Spruce up a business graphic.* The graphs and charts created by programs like Microsoft Excel, Informix's Wingz, and Ashton-Tate's Full Impact are actually object-oriented drawings. You can use the Clipboard to move them into a draw program for further polishing, such as replacing the bars in a bar chart with icons representing the data (for example, using automobile icons in a car-sales chart).

2. *Make quick-reference cards.* Can't remember which dialog box contains that certain option or which menu holds the command you need? Use the Mac's snapshot feature (press Command-Shift-3) to create a MacPaint image of the screen, then annotate the image with text. Print the result and you have a custom quick-reference card. The Mac names snapshot files Screen0, Screen1, Screen2, and so on, through Screen9. (After that, you must rename or delete snapshot files to take more.) To capture color screens or pulled-down menus, you'll need a special utility, such as Mainstay's Capture. (Snapshots work a bit differently in System 7.0: the snapshot files are in PICT, not MacPaint, format, and they're named Picture 1, Picture 2, and so on. Also, the snapshot feature can capture color screens, although it still can't capture pulled-down menus.)

3. *Make a start-up screen.* You can replace the "Welcome to Macintosh" message with any image you like. Many paint programs, including MacPaint 2.0 and SuperPaint 2.0, can create start-up screens. The image must reside in the System Folder and be named StartupScreen.

4. *Create a logo for a database form.* Most database managers let you create custom forms and paste images from the Clipboard into your form designs. Use this technique to add your logo to a form; create the logo in a program, then copy and paste it into the form.

5. *Retouch scanned images.* You can use any paint program to retouch a scanned image saved in MacPaint format. To retouch a grey-scale image saved in TIFF format, you'll need a program that can handle TIFF files. All color paint programs can, but for serious electronic retouching, you'll want an image processing program.

6. *Create special text effects.* It's easy to stretch or condense text by using a draw program in conjunction with a desktop publishing program or word processor. First, type the text using the draw program. Next, select the entire block of text (not its individual characters) using your draw program's arrow-shaped selection tool and then copy the selection to the Clipboard. Switch to a word processor or publishing program and choose Paste, and you have a picture of the text that can be resized (see the figure "Transforming Text"). If you don't have Adobe Type Manager, the resized text will probably look ragged on screen, but it will print with sharp edges on a PostScript printer, GCC Personal LaserPrinter, or Apple Personal LaserWriter LS or StyleWriter. Note that this technique may not work with every combination of word processor and drawing program. For example, when you paste MacDraw II text into Microsoft Word or MacWrite II, it appears as ☞

Transforming Text ▶

At top is the text (18-point New Baskerville) as it appears in the draw layer of SuperPaint 2.0; at bottom, the stretched text in a PageMaker document. Note that you can't edit a picture of text; to correct a typo or change the text, you'll need to return to the drawing program.

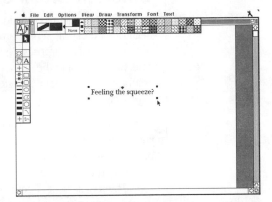

conventional text, not as a graphic. This problem doesn't occur if the original text is created in SuperPaint 2.0 or Drawing Table.

7. *Make a poster.* Most draw programs can print poster-size drawings by tiling — printing sections of the drawing on individual pages that you attach to each other. You can use this feature to create large posters — up to 81 square feet in Canvas. However, some programs limit maximum type size to 127 points. If you need larger text, use the previous tip to stretch a picture of text to the size you need.

8. *Create a publication.* With their rulers, line-drawing tools, and alignment features, draw programs make serviceable DTP programs, especially for small jobs such as brochures or one-page fact sheets. Canvas and MacDraw II 1.1 even have spelling checkers.

9. *Create a presentation.* MacDraw II 1.1 provides several features for creating overhead transparencies and slides. Electronic Arts' Studio/1 (for monochrome Macs) provides impressive yet easy-to-use mono-chrome animation features. Studio/1 and Studio/8 also include a slide-show application that lets you move from one image to the next by clicking the mouse. You can also specify special transition effects, such as dissolves and wipes, between images. With a dissolve effect, one image fades out while the next fades in;

with a wipe, one image appears to push the previous one off the screen.

10. *Modify clip art.* Many companies sell libraries of canned illustrations that you can use in desktop publications. Instead of just using a clip art drawing as is, copy it to a graphics program and personalize it — add some shading or flip it horizontally. Or autotrace a bitmapped clip art image to improve its appearance. **M**

Different Brush Strokes

Graphics programs come in two basic flavors: *bitmapped* and *object oriented*. Because of their different approaches to storing and printing images, each is suited to specific purposes. Some programs combine both approaches. In any case, understanding the differences between bitmapped and object-oriented graphics is an important first step in choosing graphics software and using it effectively.

Bitmapped graphics, or paint, programs store images as a series of bits — ones and zeros — in the Mac's memory. With monochrome (black-and-white) paint programs such as MacPaint, each screen dot, or *pixel*, in an image corresponds to one bit in the Mac's memory. If a dot is black, its bit is a one; if a dot is white, it's a zero. Think of a sheet of graph paper. Each square is a bit, and you create images by darkening some squares and leaving others white. To change part of the drawing, you change its black squares to white ones, and vice versa.

Color paint programs such as SuperMac's PixelPaint work similarly, except they assign more than one bit to each pixel. It's as if you laid several sheets of graph paper on top of each other, and selectively blackened squares on each layer. The on-off combinations of a pixel's bits tell the Mac what color that pixel is (see the figure "Bitmaps versus Objects").

Darkrooms on a Disk

Close cousins to paint programs are *image processing* programs such as Letraset's ImageStudio or ColorStudio, Adobe Photoshop, Silicon Beach's Digital Darkroom, or MicroFrontier's Enhance. Like color paint programs, they work with bitmapped images containing multiple bits per pixel. But image processing programs are designed for retouching and modifying scanned images (see Chapter 39 for an introduction to scanners). Digital Darkroom, Enhance, and ImageStudio work with grey-scale images, allowing you to adjust brightness and contrast, retouch flaws, create special effects, and choose from a variety of halftoning options to get the best possible output.

On Macs with color or grey-scale video hardware, these programs display true shades of grey. On monochrome Macs, they simulate grey by combining black pixels and white pixels into patterns, a process called *dithering* (see the figure "True Grey" in Chapter 1).

Photoshop and ColorStudio can also work with grey-scale images, but color is their forte. They provide all the image processing features I just mentioned, plus

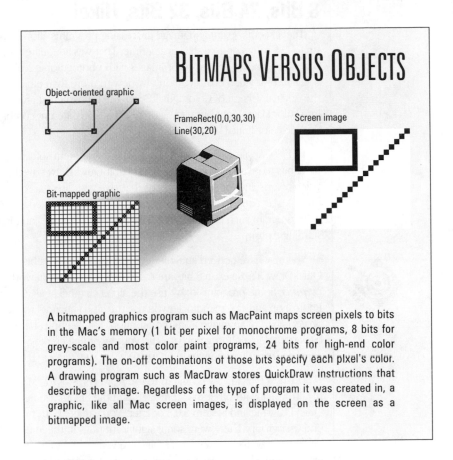

BITMAPS VERSUS OBJECTS

Object-oriented graphic

FrameRect(0,0,30,30)
Line(30,20)

Screen image

Bit-mapped graphic

A bitmapped graphics program such as MacPaint maps screen pixels to bits in the Mac's memory (1 bit per pixel for monochrome programs, 8 bits for grey-scale and most color paint programs, 24 bits for high-end color programs). The on-off combinations of those bits specify each pixel's color. A drawing program such as MacDraw stores QuickDraw instructions that describe the image. Regardless of the type of program it was created in, a graphic, like all Mac screen images, is displayed on the screen as a bitmapped image.

options for adjusting an image's color balance and printing a color separation — four pieces of film that break an image into cyan, magenta, yellow, and black layers. Professional printers use these separations to produce the plates used to print color images on printing presses. Until recently, features like these were available only on ultraexpensive graphic arts workstations. Now they're available on ultraexpensive Macs. To use these features effectively, you'll need a fast Mac, such as an SE/30, LC, or a member of the II family, with several megabytes of memory and a *24-bit video board* like SuperMac's Spectrum/24 or Apple's Video Card 8•24. And to be able to store the colossal files that such products create, you'll want a high-capacity hard disk and perhaps some *compression* hardware such as SuperMac's SuperSqueeze board, which SuperMac says can compress images by ratios of up to 65 to 1, resulting in storage space savings of up to 98 percent.

8 Bits, 24 Bits, 32 Bits, Hike!

The first color paint and image processing programs allowed you to work with up to 256 colors or grey shades at a time. That was adequate for grey-scale images, but not enough to display color images with photographic realism. The Mac II's original color video board couldn't work with more than 8 bits per pixel, nor could the original version of Color QuickDraw, the fundamental graphics routines built into color Macs. Eight bits can be on or off in 256 different combinations — hence the 256-color limit.

In 1989, Apple released its 32-bit QuickDraw system software, which allows up to 32 bits to be assigned to each pixel. 32-bit QuickDraw paved the way for 24-bit video boards and for paint programs that give you direct access to over 16 million hues. A Mac equipped with 32-bit QuickDraw, a 24-bit video board, and a 24-bit paint program such as SuperMac's PixelPaint Professional can display images with startling realism.

You may have noticed an 8-bit discrepancy between 24-bit color and 32-bit QuickDraw. Those extra 8 bits are reserved for an optional work area, the *alpha channel*. Some programs don't use the alpha channel at all. Others, including Photoshop and ColorStudio, let you use the alpha channel to create a *mask* that protects part of an image from modification. For example, before working on the background in a photograph of a car, you might first create a mask for the car to avoid accidentally altering it.

The new QuickDraw is built in to the ROM chips of the Mac LC, IIsi, IIci, and IIfx. To use it with other Mac II models and the SE/30, you need Apple's 32-bit QuickDraw file and System 6.0.3 or later. You can get both from an Apple dealer or a user group. There were some significant bugs in the initial release of the 32-bit QuickDraw file; for reliable results, use version 1.1 of 32-bit QuickDraw along with System 6.0.5 or a later version. System 7.0 contains 32-bit QuickDraw.

Drawing Distinctions

When you create an image — such as a circle — with a paint or image processing program, as soon as you release the mouse button the circle loses its identity as a circle and becomes simply a series of pixels. You can't change the circle's size, line thickness, or any other characteristics; instead, you must erase its pixels and create a new circle.

Not so with images created by an object-oriented, or draw, program. Programs such as Claris's MacDraw II and MacDraw Pro treat images not as a series of bits, but as a series of drawing instructions for QuickDraw. When you draw a circle, the program stores a set of QuickDraw instructions describing the circle's characteristics. To change the circle's size, you simply select and resize it. The program then updates the circle's QuickDraw instructions. In essence, you create images not by blackening squares on graph paper, but by creating instructions that tell your pen — the electron beam in a monitor, the print wires in an ImageWriter, or the laser in a LaserWriter or typesetter — how and where to move.

The same pixels-versus-objects issue also applies to text. With paint programs, editing or reformatting text means retyping it. Draw programs let you use the same editing and formatting techniques as a word processor.

Hard Copy Differences

Another big difference between paint and draw programs becomes evident when you print images, especially on a laser printer or typesetter. With paint programs, images are tied to a specific resolution, or number of dots per inch (dpi). A paint image's resolution generally matches that of the Mac's screen — 72 dpi. Print a 72-dpi image on a 300-dpi LaserWriter, and you'll notice jagged-edged text and shapes. (You can even out the jaggies somewhat by using the Page Setup dialog box's Smoothing option, but the results still aren't great.)

Some paint programs let you create bitmaps with up to 300 dpi, but that isn't a perfect solution either. For one thing, a 300-dpi image is still locked into a specific resolution. For another, 300-dpi bitmaps devour memory and disk space — an 8½-by-11-inch monochrome image uses about a megabyte. The storage toll increases for color and grey-scale images.

ImageWriters are prone to a subtler problem when printing bitmapped images. When you choose the ImageWriter's Faster or Best print-quality options, the ImageWriter prints roughly 80 horizontal dots per inch. When you print a 72-dpi bitmapped image on an ImageWriter, the slight difference in resolution can cause bitmapped images to appear distorted, compressed by about 13 percent — not a lot, but enough to turn a circle into an oval. The solution: select the Tall Adjusted option in the Page Setup dialog box. Tall Adjusted compensates for the difference in resolution, but at a price: text is widened along with the adjusted picture. A five-inch column of text expands to over 5½ inches.

Images created with draw programs, on the other hand, tend to use far less disk space and memory, and they're not tied to a specific resolution. You can print the same image on an ImageWriter, LaserWriter, or 2540-dpi Linotronic typesetter and get progressively better results. You're playing back the same drawing instructions each time you print, but with a progressively sharper electronic pen.

Object-oriented graphics can also be resized without the distortion and undesirable patterns bitmapped graphics are prone to. And because draw programs know that text is text, they can take advantage of the tack-sharp outline fonts used by PostScript printers, Adobe Type Manager, and Apple's System 7.0. (See Chapters 25 and 35 for details on printer font outlines.)

Paint or Pen?

So how do you decide whether you need a paint or a draw program? A paint program is the tool of choice when you need to create images with photographic details, fine shading, or brushlike effects. Paint and image processing programs are also required for working with scanned images, since these are always bitmapped.

All paint programs also provide tools for drawing simple shapes, for selecting a portion of an image to move or copy to the Mac's Clipboard, and for zooming in on an image to work with individual pixels. Simple monochrome paint programs offer a variety of brush shapes, a pencil tool, and a spray can for creating on-screen graffiti. Advanced color paint programs provide these tools as well as tools for obtaining charcoal and watercolor effects.

Draw programs are better suited to creating line drawings such as architectural floor plans, newspaper graphics, and technical drawings. Programs like Deneba Software's Canvas and Claris' MacDraw II and MacDraw Pro provide features that help you create drawings to scale. In most draw programs you'll also find dimensioning features that automatically display an object's dimensions in your choice of measuring systems. Layering features let you divide a drawing into layers you can selectively show or hide, and symbol libraries let you store and retrieve often-used shapes. MacDraw II, MacDraw Pro, and Canvas approach the power of computer-aided design, or CAD, programs — sophisticated drawing programs used by engineers and architects. CAD is covered in detail in Chapter 16.

Adobe Illustrator, Aldus FreeHand, and MacDraw Pro approach drawing from the standpoint of a graphic designer or technical illustrator, not a draftsperson. The technical illustrations you see in *Macworld* and in this book (such as the figure "Bitmap versus Objects") are produced using FreeHand or Illustrator. You won't find automatic dimensioning or symbol libraries in these programs, but you will find extensive text-manipulation features that let you take full advantage of PostScript's printing prowess. For example, all three programs can create *graduated fills* — patterns in which one shade smoothly blends in to another. (The shading that appears behind many of the illustrations in this book is a graduated fill.) These programs can also bind text to an arbitrarily shaped path — handy for printing text in a circle on the label of a phonograph album. The figure "Crazy Characters" shows other text effects both programs can create.

Crazy Characters
Aldus FreeHand and Adobe Illustrator
88 let you create interesting text
effects. At top is a zoom effect; below
that, text bound to a curved path; at
bottom, a stroke-and-fill effect, in
which characters are outlined with one
type of pen (here, a 1-point-wide black
pen) and then filled in with a color or
pattern. The reflection effect was
created by duplicating the words
Stroke&Fill and then using FreeHand's
reflect tool to create a mirror image
below the original text. Finally, the
skewing tool was used to angle the
text's reflection.

Illustrator 3.0 also lets you "dissect" Type 1 printer font outlines to reshape characters — perhaps to create a company logo or package design. Version 3.0 of FreeHand and of Deneba Software's Canvas, both due for release in the spring of 1991, can also dissect Type 1 fonts. (See chapters 35 and 36 for details on Type 1 fonts.)

All three programs also let you choose colors based on the Pantone Matching System, the printing industry's most popular color-specification system. Several paint programs support Pantone colors, too. But working with Pantone colors on the screen introduces a potential problem: your color monitor may not render the colors accurately. The answer? More hardware — specifically, *color calibration* hardware such as Radius' PrecisionColor Calibrator, RasterOps' True Color Calibrator, or SuperMac's SuperMatch Professional Color Matching System. A calibration device uses a small sensor cup that attaches to the screen surface of your monitor and provides feedback to the video board, which adjusts its signals to provide accurate on-screen colors.

Mixed Media

Fortunately, choosing between paint and draw graphics isn't an either/or proposition. A number of programs, including Deneba's Canvas and UltraPaint and Silicon Beach's SuperPaint 2.0, combine painting and drawing features. You can also move images between separate paint and draw programs using the Clipboard. You might paste a bitmapped image into a drawing program to annotate it with text or to trace it to create an object-oriented version. You can also paste an object-oriented drawing into a bitmapped program, but it will become just another bitmap floating in a sea of pixels.

Several drawing programs also provide autotrace features that enable you to create an object-oriented version of a bitmapped image. For example, you might scan your corporate logo, and then autotrace the resulting bitmapped image.

And remember, you can combine paint or draw programs with other types of software. You can use the Clipboard to paste images into word processors, page-layout programs, data managers, and any other program that supports graphics. You can also use disk files instead of the Clipboard to shuttle images. If you take this route, familiarize yourself with Macintosh graphics-file formats to choose the one that will represent your image accurately and take up the least amount of storage space (see the table "Storing Pictures").

Picto Graphs

Future archaeologists may be unable to decipher our written languages, but at least they'll have pie charts to learn where our tax dollars went. Charts and graphs from spreadsheet-and-graphics programs like Microsoft Excel, Informix's Wingz, and Ashton-Tate's FullImpact have become the hieroglyphics of our time. Printed as-is or spruced up with a drawing program, they provide at-a-glance insights into tables of yawn-worthy numbers.

Charting programs require data in tabular form, which is one reason why they're often paired with spreadsheets. The combo works well: you can select a row of data, perhaps final sales figures for the past four quarters, choose a command or two, and the program creates a chart. Each value is a *data point;* together, a set of values is a *data series.* The column headings act as *category names,* which, in a bar chart, appear below their corresponding bars.

You can create additional data series — perhaps to contrast this year's sales figures with last year's — by using more than one row of values. In such cases, you'll probably add a *legend* — a box adjacent to the chart that shows category names alongside the patterns in which their data points appear.

As the sidebar "Ten Ways to Use a Graphics Program" explains, the graphs that spreadsheet and charting programs create are actually object-oriented images. You can use the Clipboard or disk files to move these images into drawing programs to add dramatic shading effects or other embellishments.

The Third Dimension

Perhaps the most fascinating graphics programs to tinker with are ones that produce three-dimensional images — or, more accurately, simulate them on the screen through accurate perspective and shading.

Storing Pictures

Format	Best For	Comments
EPS	Text and Bitmapped or object-oriented graphics to be printed on Postscript printer.	Widely supported in both Mac and PC worlds. Generally used to export images from Postscript drawing programs or scanning applications to desktop publications.
GIF	Bitmapped images.	Developed by CompuServe for exchanging graphics between different systems. Allows up to 8 bits per pixel. GIF translators are available for most microcomputers.
MacPaint	72-dpi bitmapped images.	Widely supported, even by some IBM PC graphics and publishing programs.
PICT	Bitmapped or object-oriented graphics.	Usually used to transfer object-oriented graphics between programs.
RIFF	Bitmapped images, especially scanned.	Developed by Letraset and used by ImageStudio and ColorStudio. Supported by QuarkXpress and DesignStudio, but not by PageMaker or many other graphics programs. Files are usually smaller than TIFF counterparts.
TIFF	Bitmapped images, especially scanned.	Widely supported in both Mac and PC worlds. Able to represent color and grey scale images at virtually any resolution. Files can be large.

For someone used to the click-the-tool-and-go ease of most Mac drawing programs, a 3-D program is a foreign land with its own language. Creating a 3-D image usually involves combining *primitives* — basic shapes such as cubes, cones, and spheres — with shapes you draw (see the figure "Another Drawing Dimension"). Creating a complete 3-D scene usually means drawing separate shapes with these tools, then *merging* or *linking* them. The final step in the process might involve creating and adjusting the position of the light sources that illuminate the scene.

After building a scene, you can rotate it, look down on it or up at it, and alter the position and darkness of shadows. Your vantage point is sometimes called the *camera view;* many programs let you see the scene from several views at once. You can print drawings on an ImageWriter or a LaserWriter, with the latter producing dramatic shading effects.

Beyond that, the operating styles of 3-D programs vary enough to make generalizing impossible. Paracomp's ModelShop is designed to allow architects, landscape architects, and urban designers to draw three-dimensional sketches buildings, sites, or other structures. Silicon Beach Software's Super3D and Paracomp's Swivel 3D are designed for graphic artists, engineers, and designers who need to create complex models for use in presentations, desktop publications, and schematic designs.

To create 3-D images with that high-tech, computer graphics look, combine a 3-D modelling program with a *rendering* program such as Pixar's RenderMan, Strata's StrataVision 3d, MacroMind Three-D, Byte for Byte Corporation's Sculpt 3D, or Visual Information Development's Dimensions Presenter. Rendering programs let you create photorealistic 3-D scenes and add light sources of varying type, color, intensity and direction (see the figure "3-D for Real" on page 110). Most also let you apply *texture maps* to surfaces to add, say, marble and wood grain textures to walls and floors. Some also can do *ray tracing,* a complex technique for rendering shadows, reflections, and highlights.

MacroMind Three-D and Visual Information's Dimensions Presenter also have animation features that let you put your scenes into motion. And all rendering programs can *export* image files that you can use along with animation programs such as MacroMind Director (see Chapter 12).

As you might expect, rendering and animation are jobs that make microprocessors sweat. A Mac II-class machine is all but necessary, and a Mac IIfx with 8MB of memory wouldn't be overkill. Throw in a high-capacity hard disk for storing the large color files you'll be creating, too. The software isn't cheap, either. MacroMind Three-D, for example, retails for $1495. Still, a Mac-based rendering and animation setup goes for a fraction of the cost of the kinds of animation

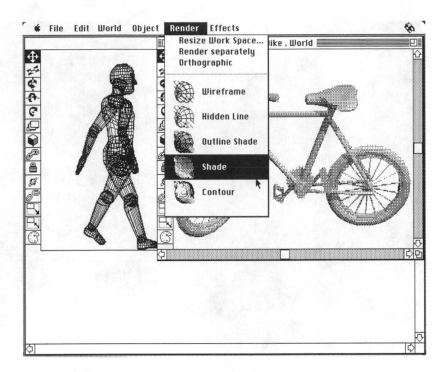

Another Drawing Dimension

Paracomp's Swivel 3D (top) and Silicon Beach's Super3D (bottom) are two graphics programs that let you create images with a three-dimensional appearance. Swivel 3D's Render menu shows the various ways the program lets you view a 3-D image. Each method requires more time to draw the image than the method preceding it; the wireframe view (used in the leftmost window) is the fastest. Both programs also provide animation features that let you put 3-D drawings into motion.

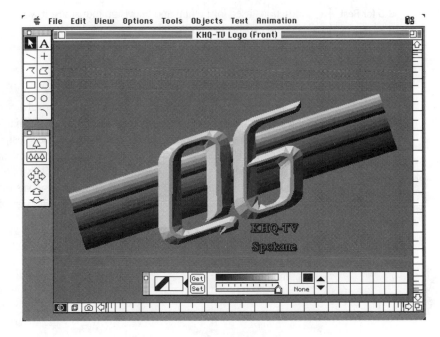

3-D for Real

Ray-tracing features, provided by many rendering programs, can create photo-realistic images. This ray-traced image illustrates numerous rendering concepts, including multiple light sources (the bright dots) with shading and shadows, texturing (the brick pattern), mirrored reflections (the bricks reflected in the clear spheres).

workstations used in the film and television industries. It won't have all their speed and capabilities, but it will come remarkably close.

Picasso Hated Mice

Finally, if you're serious about electronic art, you might consider supplementing your mouse with a *graphics tablet*, such as Personal Writer's PW10 SL or Wacom's SD-420L. Graphics tablets have a flat surface (usually 12 by 12 inches or thereabouts) upon which you draw using a pencil-like stylus (see Chapter 37). The Wacom tablet is especially appealing: its wireless stylus responds to pressure. When used with Adobe's Photoshop or Deneba's UltraPaint, you can press harder and get darker or wider lines. Many artists find graphics tablets more natural than the mouse for drawing and tracing.

But beware — if you think graphics programs are appealing when used with a mouse, wait until your friends start scribbling with a stylus. They may never go home.

Summary:

✔ Bitmapped graphics programs store images as a series of bits, one (or more) for each pixel on the screen. Bitmapped, or paint, programs are best for working with subtle shading and scanned images.

✔ Object-oriented, or draw, programs store images as a series of instructions for QuickDraw. An object-oriented image can take full advantage of your printer's resolution.

✔ Novel uses for graphics programs include sprucing up a business graph, making a quick-reference card or start-up screen, creating logos for database forms, retouching scanned images, creating special text effects, making posters, creating a simple publication, and creating a presentation.

✔ Image processing programs are bitmapped graphics programs that specialize in working with color or grey-scale scanned images.

✔ Some graphics programs let you create images that simulate three dimensions through use of perspective and shading.

Chapter 9
HyperCard

HyperCard defies simple definitions. Call it a database manager, and you short-shrift its MacPaint-like painting features. Call it a paint program, and you ignore its ability to store and retrieve information. HyperCard isn't educational software or a game, but it can educate and entertain. It isn't part of the Mac's System Folder, but like the Finder, it can start applications and open documents. It isn't a programming language, but it has introduced thousands of people to the fun and frustration of programming.

Appreciating HyperCard's versatility is easier if you consider the code name it bore during its gestation: WildCard. In poker, a wildcard represents any card and can make a winning hand. Similarly, HyperCard can be sculpted into nearly any kind of application, thus rounding out your computing toolbox.

In this chapter, I examine this software wildcard and spotlight some of the stellar ways in which HyperCard has been used. For those who haven't gone beyond browsing around in HyperCard, I've included a short exercise that introduces customizing basics. And if you've used version 1.x of HyperCard but haven't upgraded to version 2.0, which was released in late 1990, see the sidebar "HyperCard 2.0: What's the Difference?" for some incentive.

The Three Keys to HyperCard

Three factors combine to give HyperCard its wildcard versatility: its card-and-stack metaphor, its painting features, and its built-in programming language, *HyperTalk*.

HyperCard presents and stores information on *cards*. In an electronic address book, for example, each person's name and address is stored on its own card. Cards that accept information from you contain *fields*, each of which stores a piece of information, such as a name or a phone number. A card can also contain *buttons* — hot spots you click on to perform an action, such as moving to a different card for more information. A collection of related cards — such as all the cards in the address book — form a *stack* (see the figure "Fields, Cards, and Stacks").

HyperCard's painting tools do everything MacPaint's tools do, and more. You use them to create text and graphics on individual cards, and to draw *backgrounds*, which appear beneath cards in a stack (see the figure "In the Back-

HyperCard 2.0: What's the Difference?

HyperCard 2.0 addresses most of the requests made by HyperCard users since the program's first release. Here's a summary of the biggest improvements in version 2.0.

❖ Variable card sizes. In HyperCard 1.x, card sizes were fixed to match the size of a 9-inch Macintosh screen. Version 2.0 lets you create cards of any size up to 18 inches tall or wide.

❖ Mixed text styles. HyperCard 1.x let you format field text in just one font, size, and style. Version 2.0 lets you mix fonts, sizes, and styles within a single field.

❖ Multiple open stacks. HyperCard 1.x could open just one stack at a time; 2.0 can have numerous stacks open simultaneously, each in its own window.

❖ Hypertext links. In HyperCard 2.0, you can define a word or other text as "hot" so that something happens — a definition appears, a different card is displayed, and so on — when a user clicks on that text. In HyperCard 1.x, script authors had to fudge this feature, usually by using transparent buttons.

❖ Improved programming features. HyperCard 2.0 provides an improved script editor window, many of which can be open at once, unlike the script editor in 1.x. HyperTalk scripts in 2.0 are compiled rather than

interpreted, allowing them to run faster. There's also a *debugger* that makes it easier to track down problems in scripts. And the way in which XCMDs and XFCNs work with HyperCard has been improved in ways that will make more powerful XCMDs and XFCNs possible.

❖ Color support — sort of. HyperCard 2.0 doesn't provide the degree of color support some users would have liked, but it does allow you to display color PICT images in separate windows.

❖ Free technical support. Apple has turned HyperCard 2.0 over to Claris, its software subsidiary, and Claris offers free technical support for registered users. Users were on their own with HyperCard 1.x.

HyperCard 2.0 also includes expanded documentation and a larger variety of more powerful example stacks. Version 2.0 is also compatible with stacks created in earlier versions. In all, it's a worthwhile upgrade, and a must-have for anyone who uses HyperCard 1.x even occasionally. For upgrade pricing and availability information, contact Claris at 800/3CLARIS. **M**

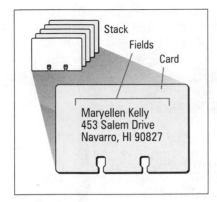

Stack

Fields

Card

Maryellen Kelly
453 Salem Drive
Navarro, HI 90827

Fields, Cards, and Stacks

HyperCard presents and stores information on cards. Cards that accept information from you contain fields. A collection of related cards forms a stack.

ground"). You can also paste graphics from the Clipboard to create a scrapbook of drawings — or to store a scanned photo of each person listed in your address book.

HyperTalk ties HyperCard's features together. By creating HyperTalk *scripts* — short command sequences that control HyperCard's actions — you determine how a stack responds to its users. A script for a button named Next might tell HyperCard to advance to the next card when the button is clicked. A script for a field named Date might tell HyperCard to display an error message if someone enters an invalid date, such as February 31. You can also design HyperCard scripts to control videodisc players and music synthesizers, or to play digitally recorded sound (see the figure "Hearing Hyper-Card" on the next page). I'll spotlight some of these advanced applications of HyperCard when I examine multimedia in Chapter 17.

A complete HyperCard stack — be it a business-management application, a children's story, or an introduction to bird anatomy — makes extensive use of the three elements I've just described. The stack's cards use text and graphics to convey information. The cards may also contain fields for accepting new information, and buttons for moving to other cards or otherwise controlling the stack. Behind the scenes, HyperTalk scripts define each button's action, calculate numbers, display messages, produce sound, and do whatever else the stack requires.

In the Background

A stack's background holds fields, graphics, and buttons that appear on every card (in this case, HyperCard's Address stack). To view a stack's background, choose Background from the Edit menu. HyperCard displays stripes in the menu bar to indicate that you're working with the background.

 File   Edit   Go   Tools   Objects   Font   Style   Utilities

Addresses

Name
Company

Street
City & State
Zip Code

Telephone

⇦ ⇨

Find...

Show Notes

New Card

Delete Card

Appointments   Home

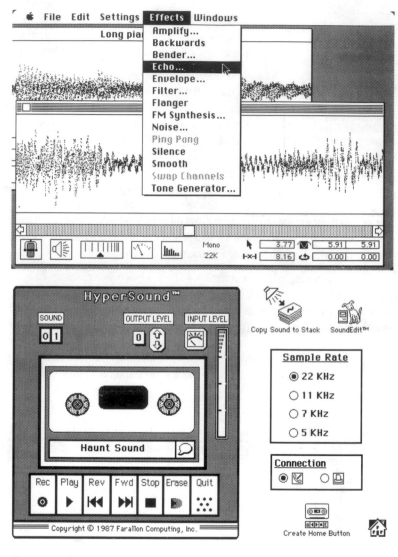

Hearing HyperCard

The easiest way to record sounds for playback in HyperCard is to use a Mac IIsi or LC, both of which provide sound-recording circuitry and a microphone. These Macs include a Sound Recorder desk accessory that lets you easily add sounds to HyperCard stacks. For other Macs, you can use Farallon Computing's MacRecorder. MacRecorder's SoundEdit application (top) lets you record sounds and modify them using numerous digital effects. It graphically displays a sound's waveform; you can cut, paste, and combine pieces of sounds using the mouse and the Edit menu. MacRecorder's HyperSound stack (bottom) lets you record sounds and add them to stacks without quitting HyperCard. SoundEdit versions 2.0.3 and later are also compatible with the Mac LC's and IIsi's recording circuitry and are available separately from the MacRecorder hardware. Finally, for more ambitious applications of digital audio, there's The Voyager Company's Voyager CD AudioStack, which allows HyperCard to play audio from a compact disc in a CD-ROM drive. With the tools in the AudioStack, you can create HyperCard stacks that incorporate the audio from a CD.

From the Obvious to the Subtle

If all HyperCard did was provide fields, store graphics, and contain a programming language, it would be no different than many Mac database managers. What makes HyperCard different is the myriad ways its components can work together. Everything in HyperCard seems to have obvious applications and subtle ones.

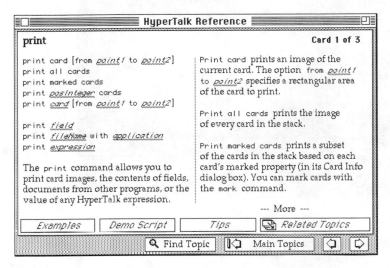

Take buttons, for example. Their obvious use is to provide icons for moving to the next or the previous card, or for returning to the *Home* stack. (The Home stack serves as your base of operations in HyperCard — just as the Finder does for the Mac.) Navigation buttons often appear as icons, and always have HyperTalk scripts that run when the buttons are clicked (see the figure "Navigation Buttons").

▲ Navigation Buttons

With the HyperTalk Reference stack that accompanies HyperCard 2.0, you use navigation buttons to access information about the HyperTalk language. The buttons at the bottom of the window let you display examples and related topics, search for topics, and move to the next and previous cards. The script for the "Examples" button is shown at bottom.

You can specify that a button not have an icon or text, but be *transparent*. By placing transparent buttons over key portions of a graphic, you can define a relationship between each area of the graphic and other cards, fields, or stacks. Thereafter, when you click on a portion of the graphic, HyperCard will take you to a different card or stack.

Many educational stacks use this technique. One superb example is a stack called Bird Anatomy, created by Yale University's Patrick Lynch and published by The Voyager Company (an earlier version of Bird Anatomy is available through BMUG, Yale MUG, and Boston Computer Society). This stack combines beautifully drawn images with transparent buttons that, when clicked, display additional details on avian anatomy (see the figure "See-Through Buttons" on the next page). On the lighter side, Amanda Stories, a delightful series of children's stacks by Amanda Goodenough, uses buttons to allow kids to travel through the worlds of Inigo the Cat and Your Faithful Camel. Amanda Stories are also published by The Voyager Company. The freeware version of Inigo Gets Out is available through user groups.

```
on mouseUp
  set cursor to 4
  visual zoom open
  go to card "Eye and Bill-Sparrow"
end mouseUp
```

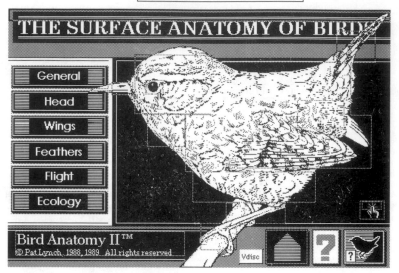

See-Through Buttons

In Patrick Lynch's Bird Anatomy II stack, transparent buttons are placed over key anatomical areas and become temporarily visible when you press Command-Option. Here, the Browse tool is pointing at the button whose HyperTalk script appears above the screen. Clicking this button tells HyperCard to go to the card shown at bottom, which also contains transparent buttons that, when clicked, reveal additional details.

Fields have their obvious and subtle uses. As in any database manager, they accept and store information. But they can also serve a read-only role — displaying text you can't edit — and they can be displayed or hidden using HyperTalk scripts. Combine both traits with buttons, and you have another way to convey information: *pop-up fields* that appear when you click a button (see the figure "Pop-Up Fields" on the next page).

Buttons and fields can appear on individual cards or on the background. Stack-navigation buttons are usually on the background, so they appear on each card and provide a consistent way for you to navigate. Transparent buttons that lead to other cards or display pop-up fields generally appear on individual cards and correspond to a graphic.

Designing Stacks

Knowing your way around HyperCard and HyperTalk doesn't guarantee you stunning stacks. The best guide to stack design I've seen is Apple's *Stack Design Guidelines* (Addison-Wesley, 1990). Its nine basic guidelines provide sound advice for budding stackware authors.

❖ Determine your audience. Do they have experience with computers and HyperCard? Imagine designing stacks about dinosaurs for kids and for paleontologists. How would the stacks differ?

❖ Focus the subject matter. Decide how detailed the stack will be. From this, you'll get ideas about how to present it. Your decisions may be influenced by disk space and scheduling considerations.

❖ Decide how to present the subject. Doodle on paper and on screen. Solicit opinions. Consider a metaphor. A book metaphor might use a table of contents as a gateway to various cards. A videotape metaphor might use on-screen rewind, stop, play, and fast-forward buttons.

❖ Teach people how your stack works. Provide help screens that explain the stack's workings, but make them unobtrusive so experts won't be slowed down.

❖ Make the stack easy to navigate. Consider how users will access other cards. Put key navigation buttons on backgrounds so they appear in the same place on each card. Use visual effects such as dissolves and wipes to convey a sense of movement within a stack.

❖ Integrate text, graphics, and audio design. Avoid amateurish graphics and sound effects. Use text sparingly. Put navigation buttons near the screen edge.

```
on mouseDown
    play "screech"
    show card field "screech owl"
end mouseDown
```

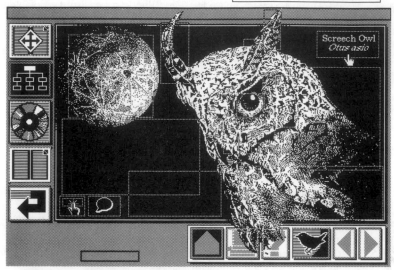

Pop-up Fields

Pop-up fields are an ideal way to convey small tidbits of information. Shown here is another card from Bird Anatomy II. Clicking the Screech Owl button executes the HyperTalk script shown above the card (top), which plays back a digitized recording of a Screech Owl and then displays the card field shown at bottom. That card field contains another HyperTalk script (not shown) that causes HyperCard to hide the field when you click within it.

❖ Change the stack as you think of new presentation styles and navigation methods. As Apple says, "Your goal should be to produce the best possible stack, not to defend your first beloved idea."

❖ Test early and often. Don't wait until the stack is done before soliciting feedback from users to find out where they — and you — are stumbling.

❖ When you've finished, check the stack again. Make sure there are no typographical or grammatical errors, and that all your buttons, dialog boxes, and scripts work.

▼ **HyperCard User Levels**

HyperCard offers five user levels, each providing more access to HyperCard's programming and customizing features than the level beneath it. The Blind Typing option lets you type messages without having to open the message box. Checking the Power Keys option enables HyperCard's power keys, a number of keys on the keyboard you can press to choose a command when a paint tool is active.

So You Want to Be an Author

Because the best way to learn about HyperCard is to play with it, I've put together an exercise that will expose you to HyperCard customizing. For a hands-on introduction to *authoring* — Apple's term for HyperCard customizing — see the sidebar "A HyperCard Tutorial" at the end of this chapter.

You might think this exercise is too simple, that HyperTalk scripts are usually longer. Not so. HyperTalk is an efficient language; scripts rarely exceed 10 or 20 lines, and often have just a few. To see for yourself, explore the scripts in HyperCard's stacks (see the figure "HyperCard User Levels"). To quickly open any button's script, press Command and Option while clicking on the button. (Note that your user level must be set to 5, the Scripting level, for this to work.)

HyperTalk contains a large vocabulary, but no programming language meets every need. Knowing that, HyperTalk's designers devised a way for HyperTalk to access routines written in conventional programming languages. These *external commands (XCMDs)* and *external functions (XFCNs)* can perform specialized jobs that exceed HyperTalk's capabilities, such as controlling a

Home

Preferences   Home

Your Name: Trixie

Click the user level you want: Other settings:

▶ **5** Scripting — Edit scripts of buttons, fields, cards, backgrounds, and stacks.   ☐ Blind Typing

4 Authoring — Create buttons and fields. Link buttons to cards and stacks.

3 Painting — Use the Paint tools to change the appearance of cards and backgrounds.   ☐ Power Keys

2 Typing — Enter and edit text in fields.

1 Browsing — Explore stacks but make no changes.   ☒ Arrow Keys in Text

videodisc player or adding custom menus to HyperCard's menu bar. Hundreds of free or inexpensive XCMDs and XFCNs are available from user groups and online information services such as America Online and CompuServe. Libraries of XCMDs and XFCNs are also available from a variety of sources, including Heizer Software (415/943-7667), Trendware (203/926-1116), Clear Lake Research (713/523-7842), TechAlliance (206/251-5222), and APDA (800/282-2732; 408/562-3959 international). And to augment HyperCard's report-printing features — which, especially in HyperCard 1.x, are too Spartan for serious data-management stacks — consider Nine to Five Software's Reports, a set of XCMDs and XFCNs for creating everything from mailing labels to inventory reports.

A variety of excellent books is available to help teach you HyperTalk. The best place to start is with the extensive documentation that accompanies Claris' HyperCard Development Kit.

As you become proficient with HyperCard and HyperTalk, you might want to sample one of the HyperCard-like programs available for the Mac: Spinnaker Software's Plus and Silicon Beach Software's SuperCard. Both products can open and use HyperCard 1.x stacks, and provide some features that even HyperCard 2.0 lacks. SuperCard boasts impressive animation features and the ability to create standalone applications (ones that users can run directly from the Finder, without having to open them using SuperCard). SuperCard and Plus provide more support for color and object-oriented graphics than does HyperCard 2.0. And Plus is also available for the IBM PC, allowing you to develop stacks that can be used by Mac and PC users alike. Finally, there's Symmetry's HyperDA 2.0, a desk accessory that lets you work with stacks from within any program. HyperDA lacks all of HyperCard's power and customizing features, but it's a handy way to access stacks without using HyperCard — and all the memory HyperCard requires.

Go Home

Is HyperCard a revolution? Or has it succeeded simply because it's included with the Mac? I'm less impressed by HyperCard's data-management applications than I am by its education and entertainment possibilities. HyperCard is a useful data manager if you have enough memory to keep it open all the time. Otherwise, shuttling between HyperCard and other programs takes too much time.

But for presenting information — as a medium for electronic publishing — HyperCard excels. And it's a boon to people who want to tinker with buttons and other aspects of the Mac interface without grappling with conventional programming.

Another way to assess HyperCard's significance might be to ask someone who has learned to read thanks to a stack called Alphabet for Adults by Michael Giamo. Developed for Drexel University's adult literacy program, this stack combines graphics and digitized sound to familiarize users with letters and words.

A software wildcard that teaches adults to read: who can say that isn't revolutionary?

A HyperCard Tutorial

In this exercise, we'll exploit HyperCard's ability to start other programs by adding a button to HyperCard's Home card that, when clicked, uses a HyperTalk script to open MacWrite or the word processor of your choice. To ensure you have enough memory for this task, don't use MultiFinder if your Mac has only 1MB of memory. Also, you must know the exact name of your word processor as it's stored on your hard disk. If you aren't sure, return to the Finder and find out. And finally, for insurance, use the Save a Copy command in HyperCard's File menu to make a backup copy of your Home stack.

One more thing: The following instructions assume you're using HyperCard 2.0 or a later version. Some instructions differ for versions prior to 2.0 and are preceded by the text "version 1.x:".

Changing Your Level

You can use HyperCard on any of five levels, each of which provides more access to HyperCard's customizing features than the one before it. To work with HyperTalk, go straight to the most powerful level: to the *scripting* level (see the figure "HyperCard User Levels"). Here's how:

1. With the Home stack open, choose Preferences from the Home menu to display the User Preferences card (Version 1.x: choose Last from the Go menu). If you're using the version of HyperCard 2.0 that

accompanies the Mac, you'll need to perform some extra steps to get to the scripting level. Specifically, open HyperCard's message box (type Command-M or choose Show Message from the Go menu), and then type **set userlevel to 5** and press Return. To be able to see the Scripting button, activate the button tool and delete the opaque button that covers it.

2. Click the Scripting button in the User Preferences card, two new menus, Tools and Objects, appear.

3. Return to the first card of the Home stack by choosing Home Cards from the Home menu (version 1.x: Choose First from the Go menu).

HyperCard remembers which user level you chose, so you need only perform these steps once.

HyperCard's Tools menu contains its painting, button, and field tools (see the figure "HyperCard's Tools"). The Objects menu lets you create, examine, and change information and scripts for buttons, fields, cards, backgrounds, and stacks.

Create a New Button

Now that you have the authority to author, you can create the new button on the first card of the Home stack.

1. Choose New Button from the Objects menu. A button named New Button appears in the center of the screen.

2. Drag the button to a free area of the Home card.

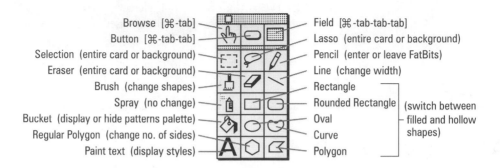

Browse [⌘-tab]
Button [⌘-tab-tab]
Selection (entire card or background)
Eraser (entire card or background)
Brush (change shapes)
Spray (no change)
Bucket (display or hide patterns palette)
Regular Polygon (change no. of sides)
Paint text (display styles)

Field [⌘-tab-tab-tab]
Lasso (entire card or background)
Pencil (enter or leave FatBits)
Line (change width)
Rectangle
Rounded Rectangle
Oval
Curve
Polygon

(switch between filled and hollow shapes)

Don't worry about its exact position; you'll fine-tune it shortly.

Refine the Button

Your next step is to make the button look like the other buttons in HyperCard's Home stack: icons with text below them.

1. Choose Button Info from the Objects menu, or simply double-click the new button and HyperCard's Button Info dialog box appears.

2. In the Button Name text box, type MacWrite (or your word processor's name). Because the dialog box's Show Name option is checked, the button name will appear on the card.

3. Click the Auto hilite check box. This tells HyperCard to invert the button (turn white areas black and vice versa) when you click on it. This way, the button provides visual feedback and operates like a standard Macintosh button.

4. In the Style area of the dialog box, choose the Transparent option. Don't click OK yet. When using this option to create an invisible button over a graphic, uncheck the Show Name option.

Add an Icon

Next, you'll add an icon to the button from one of the dozens built into HyperCard.

1. In the Button Info dialog box, click the Icon button. A dialog box showing HyperCard's built-in icons appears. For your word processor, use the icon located in the upper-right corner of the dialog box.

2. Select the word processor icon by clicking on it and then click the OK button.

The button changes to reflect its new icon. But because the button is rectangular, it obscures part of the icon.

In the next steps, you'll resize the button to see the entire icon, and you'll fine-tune the button's position.

1. To resize the button, point to any of its four corners, then click and drag until the entire icon and the text below it appears.

2. Drag the button as needed to align it with any adjacent buttons.

Create the Script

If you click on the new button now, HyperCard highlights it, but nothing else happens. In this final phase, you'll create the HyperTalk script that tells HyperCard what to do when the button is clicked.

1. Choose the button tool from the Tools menu.

2. Double-click on your new button to reopen the Button Info dialog box.

3. Click the Script button to access HyperCard's *script editor.* ☞

A script consists of one or more *handlers*. A handler is a collection of HyperTalk statements that are executed when HyperCard receives a *message* that an event has occurred — in this case, when the new button has been pressed.

A message handler for a button always begins with on mouseUp and ends with end mouseUp. The commands between these two lines tell HyperCard what to do when the mouse button is pressed and released while the browsing pointer is within the button's boundaries.

Note that a blinking insertion point exists between the two lines. You type the script there.

1. Type (include the quotes) **open "MacWrite"** (or the name of the word processor of your choice).

Be sure to type the name exactly as it appears in the Finder.

2. Check your work, then click the script window's close box and click Yes when asked to save changes (version 1.x: to close the script editor, click OK or press Enter).

3. Choose the browse tool — the pointing finger — from the Tools menu, or from the keyboard by pressing Command-Tab.

Test the button now. Depending on how you've organized your disk folders, one of two things will happen: HyperCard will dutifully start the word processor, or a dialog box will appear asking where the application is stored. If the latter happens, use the dialog box to aim HyperCard in the right direction. From now on, HyperCard will look for applications in that folder. (By editing the Search Paths cards in the Home stack, you can also add folder names to the list of folders that HyperCard automatically searches.)

When you quit the word processor, you return to HyperCard instead of the Finder. (This doesn't apply to MultiFinder, nor does the following tip.) To return to the Finder, press and hold the Option key immediately after quitting. **M**

Summary:

✔ Three key factors combine to give HyperCard its versatility: its card-and-stack metaphor, its painting features, and its built-in programming language.

✔ A collection of related cards in HyperCard is called a stack. Stacks should be designed with a particular audience in mind and should be easy to navigate. Integrating text, graphics, and audio design into your stacks and testing them early and often during their creation will produce the best results.

✔ HyperTalk is HyperCard's built-in programming language used to customize HyperCard. Specialized jobs that exceed HyperTalk's capabilities are performed by external commands and functions accessed from conventional programming languages.

✔ The improvements made in HyperCard 2.0 include variable card sizes, mixed text styles, multiple open stacks, Hypertext links, improved programming features, color support, and free technical support.

Chapter 10
Presentations

In This Chapter:

✔ Presentation graphics versus desktop publishing: what's the difference?

✔ A description of the three basic elements of a visual.

✔ Sorting, arranging, and presenting visuals.

✔ A look at the hardware used to present visuals.

✔ Specialized presentation programs.

Now and then, everyone dons a Willie Loman outfit and becomes a salesperson. Some sell products, others sell ideas and concepts. Whatever the wares, the steps are the same: you gather your facts, shine your shoes, and present your argument.

The Mac won't shine your shoes, but it can help with the rest of the process. *Desktop presentation* software can help you refine your ideas and create presentation aids such as slides, overhead transparencies, and audience handouts. The whole process smacks of desktop publishing, and indeed, there are many parallels between publishing and presenting, but there are also significant differences. In this chapter, we'll tour the world of presentation graphics software and hardware.

Present or Perish

Desktop publishing implies a permanence to your work: you're preparing documents that will be printed and kept — at least for a while. With presentation graphics, however, your efforts are often more transitory: each visual is seen just briefly, then it's gone. Because of their fleeting nature, it's important to create visuals with impact and to plan your presentation so that your message sinks in.

Another key difference between desktop publishing and presentation graphics lies in the output media. With desktop publishing, your efforts rest on paper. With

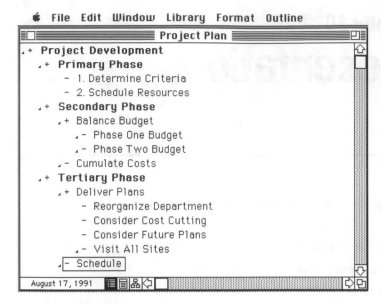

presentation graphics, your results are usually projected onto a screen, the most common types of output media being 35mm slides and overhead transparencies. The Mac itself is another medium: using hardware I'll discuss later, you can project Mac screen images onto a large screen.

Combining text and graphics is something most Mac programs do with ease. So do you really need a presentation program? The truth is, if you make only one or two presentations a year, you can probably get by with a drawing program such as MacDraw II, a spreadsheet program such as Ashton-Tate's FullImpact or Informix's Wingz, or a word processor or desktop publishing program. But if presentations are a regular part of your job, you'll come to rely on the specialized features of a presentation program.

▲ **Outlining Ideas**
More (shown here) and Aldus Persuasion offer built-in outlining features that let you organize your thoughts before creating visuals. Both can turn outlines into bullet charts with one command or mouse click.

Software to Present By

Word processors and publishing programs are generalists; presentation programs are specialists: their text-editing and graphics-manipulation features are geared specifically toward producing presentation materials. Toward that end, most presentation programs play three primary roles: they help you develop and refine your ideas, create visuals, and structure and deliver your pitch.

When you're first developing a presentation, you need to organize and reorganize your ideas on the fly. Built-in outlining features, found in Aldus Persuasion and Symantec's More, help you do just that (see the figure "Outlining Ideas") If you use a presentation program that lacks built-in outlining, team it with Symmetry's Acta Advantage outliner desk accessory, or do your brainstorming with a word processor that has outlining features.

Presentation programs encroach on word processing territory in other ways. Many provide search-and-replace commands for making wholesale changes to

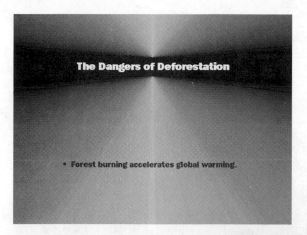

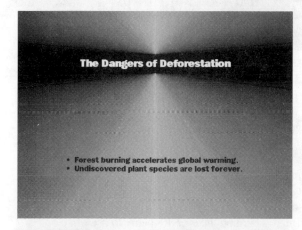

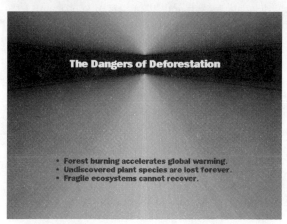

Bullet Charts

Bullet charts present their information in short phrases, organized in bulleted list form. Many presentation programs let you specify that the bulleted items in a list appear one at a time on consecutive visuals, as shown here. This technique is called a build.

your text. And because typos can turn a presentation into an embarrassment, you'll find spelling checkers in Microsoft PowerPoint, Aldus Persuasion, More, and Claris' MacDraw II version 1.1. But remember, spelling checkers aren't usage checkers. They don't know "capital" from "capitol" or "its" from "it's," so keep your dictionary handy.

Visual Components

After you've refined your ideas, you're ready to produce visuals, which can contain three basic elements:

❖ *Text* Usually short passages, often organized as *bullet charts* for fast reading (see the figure "Bullet Charts"). More and Persuasion let you turn outlines into bullet charts with one command or mouse click. Many programs also let you specify that the bulleted items in a list should appear one at a time on consecutive visuals, a technique called a *build.* By using builds, you can make your case and discuss it point by point.

❖ *Graphics* A picture is often worth a thousand bullets. Graphs can visually depict trends or market shares, organization charts can spell out the corporate pecking order, and diagrams and drawings can illustrate complex

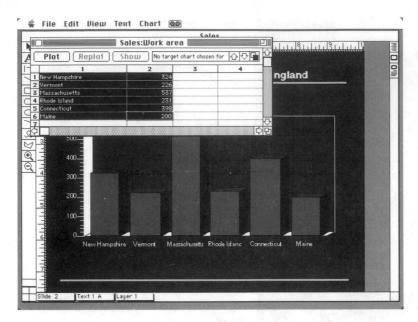

concepts. Persuasion and More provide built-in graphing features that let you create graphs from numerical data that you type in or import from a spreadsheet (see the figure "Built-In Graphing"). Other programs let you import graphs created in other programs such as Excel, but that isn't as convenient. As for other types of graphics, More and Persuasion can automatically generate organizational charts based on the indent levels in an outline. All presentation programs have drawing tools for making diagrams, and most can also import images created with a scanner or a drawing program.

▲ **Built-in Graphing**

Persuasion provides built-in graphing features that let you create graphs from numeric data that you type or import from a spreadsheet. A three-dimensional bar chart is shown here.

❖ *Backgrounds* On printed documents, text and graphics generally appear against the white background of paper. But presentation visuals are usually projected on a white screen in a darkened room, and in that setting dark text against a white background is hard on the eyes. It's better to use white or brightly colored text against a dark background. All presentation programs let you specify such schemes. Many also provide special background effects that give visuals an elegant, professional look (see the figure "The Right Background").

For assembling these components, presentation programs provide drawing and layout features that let you position text, create boxes and borders, paste graphics created in other programs, and draw various shapes. Most also provide on-screen rulers and alignment guides for precise positioning.

True, these features are all found in publishing and drawing programs. But presentation programs put a different spin on many of them. For example, publishing programs don't know overheads from slides, but presentation programs provide page-setup options for both. Thus, instead of having to

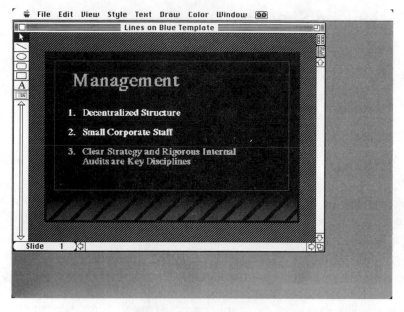

calculate the proper dimensions for a slide or overhead and then type them into a Page Setup dialog box, you simply choose your output medium from a dialog box.

A presentation is more effective if its visuals are designed with care. Well-designed visuals use a consistent background and color scheme, and have a uniform layout to give the viewer's eye familiar points of reference. One way to

▲ The Right Background

Most presentation programs provide canned templates that you can use to create your visuals. These templates often include a selection of attractive backgrounds, such as this one from Microsoft PowerPoint.

achieve this continuity is to repeat a company logo or graphic on each visual. Most presentation programs let you store such repetitive elements on a *master page* (see the figure "Master Slides").

For typographic consistency, many programs also provide word processor-like *style* features that let you store and recall text formats. Persuasion, More, PowerPoint, MacDraw Pro, and MacDraw II version 1.1 let you create *templates* to store your formatting preferences for future use. These programs also include an assortment of attractive predesigned templates.

Most presentation programs let you assign descriptive titles to each visual in a presentation, so you can tell at a glance what the slide or transparency contains. You can also use these names to sort and organize the visuals using your program's sorting features.

Master Slides

Presentation programs use master slides to hold elements that repeat on each slide, such as a company logo, a set of lines, or a background. The contents of a master slide are combined with each individual slide to create a composite containing the text and graphics on both.

Sorting and Showing

What ultimately separates presentation programs from most of their publishing and drawing kinfolk are features that let you sort and arrange visuals and present them using the Mac's screen.

People who work with slides often use an illuminated stand called a slide sorter to view and organize their images. On-screen slide sorters — provided by PowerPoint and Persuasion — perform the same role by displaying numerous slides reduced to fit within a window (see the figure "Sorting Slides").

Within the slide sorter window, you can change the sequence of slides in your presentation simply by dragging them to different positions. The slide sorter window in PowerPoint also lets you cut or copy slides to the Clipboard for pasting elsewhere in the same presentation or into a different one altogether. Most programs also provide title sorters that display only the slides' titles.

Finally, presentation programs provide *slide show* features to help you exhibit your visuals. Choose your program's Slide Show command, and the Mac becomes a projector, displaying each visual on the screen without the menu bar and tool palettes. In slide-show mode, the mouse becomes a remote control: click it to advance to the next visual. More and Persuasion also let you use visual effects such as a *wipe*, which causes one visual to "push" the previous one off the screen.

Sorting Slides
PowerPoint and Persuasion (shown here) provide on-screen slide sorters, which display numerous slides reduced to fit within a window. You can reorganize the sequence of the presentation by dragging the visuals within the sorter window.

Output Alternatives

Now we come to the output: once you've created your visuals, how do you screen them for your audience? I've just mentioned the Mac-as-slide-projector technique. With this route, however, you'll probably need some additional hardware — unless you can convince a roomful of people to crowd around your Macintosh.

One option for Mac II, LC, and SE/30 owners is a 19-inch color monitor like those offered by Apple, SuperMac, RasterOps, Radius, and many others. If you can spare about $8000, you might consider Mitsubishi's gargantuan XC-3715C, whose 37-inch color video screen is guaranteed to get noticed.

But giant monitors weigh — and cost — a great deal. And in a large room even a 37-inch screen can seem small. A more practical solution may be an *LCD projection panel* such as those offered by nView Corp. (Newport News, VA), Sayett Technology (Rochester, NY), and In Focus Systems (Tualatin, OR), and others.

LCD projection panels work with an overhead projector. You attach the panel to your Mac and then lay the panel on the projector as though it were a transparency. The Mac creates a video image on the panel's liquid crystal display (LCD) screen, and the projector shows the image on the room screen. Some LCD panels create monochrome (black and white) images only; others support color. Some panels even contain memory into which you can load your visuals, eliminating the need to carry your Mac along.

A better way to project color images is to use a *video projector* such as PDS Video Technology's Project-A-Mac. Video projects can create wall-sized images with the same vivid color and fast screen updating you see on the screen. As you'd expect, they're costly — the Project-A-Mac series, for example, starts at over $14,000. Many LCD projection pads, by contrast, start at just over $1000.

The biggest drawback to most video-oriented presentation hardware is that you need to lug your Mac along. When portability, color, and economy are important, overhead transparencies and slides are better alternatives.

Overheads and Slides

If you're like me, you probably slept through a few overheads in high school. Ah, but old Mr. Crusty didn't have the output options we enjoy today. By printing your visuals on *transparency film*, you can produce overheads that would impress even Mr. Crusty. For laser printers, use 3M Type 154 Transparency Film; for ink jet printers such as Apple's StyleWriter or Hewlett-Packard's

DeskWriter, use 3M CG3480 Transparency Film. Need color? Use one of the new breed of affordable color printers, such as Hewlett-Packard's PaintJet or Tektronix's ColorQuick. Bigger budgets might spring for a printer such as QMS' PostScript-based ColorScript 100 or Tektronix' QuickDraw-based Phaser II SX or PostScript-based Phaser II PX. (Chapters 35 and 36 detail the differences between PostScript and QuickDraw printers.)

Overhead transparencies are eminently portable — dozens of them will fit in a binder — and overhead projectors are almost as ubiquitous as photocopiers. But overheads have drawbacks, too. You must manually flip from one transparency to the next, and that can make an otherwise sophisticated presentation seem amateurish — especially if the projector's fan blows half your visuals off the table. (Don't laugh, it happens.) What's more, overheads can scratch and smudge, and the colors produced by inexpensive color printers can't approach the vividness of the ultimate presentation output medium — the color slide.

Slides are portable, too, and you can carry them in a tray, where they're always properly sequenced and ready to show. Slides are also inexpensive to duplicate, so it's easy to prepare extra sets as backups or for colleagues. And slides give you the vivid colors that only film can provide. Slides also have the greatest dazzle potential. By combining two or more slide projectors under the control of a *dissolve unit*, you can create impressive presentations containing fancy visual effects (see the sidebar "Professional Presentations").

To create slides with a presentation program, you need a *film recorder* such as GCC Technologies' ColorFast. A film recorder is a special kind of printer that creates images not on paper, but on film. Most film recorders contain a camera

Professional Presentations

Two slide projectors and a dissolve unit (available from photographic and audio-visual suppliers) give you the ability to create professional-looking presentations with special visual effects. When used with a dissolve unit, one projector's tray holds all even-numbered slides; the other holds odd-numbered ones. By alternating between projectors and fading the lamps in and out, a dissolve unit creates smooth transitions between slides, eliminating the jarring on-and-off flash between slide changes. By varying the speed of the lamps' fade-ins and fade-outs, the dissolve unit can create slow, graceful dissolves, or instant cuts.

The most sophisticated multimedia audio-visual applications combine a dissolve unit, multiple slide projects, one or more motion picture projectors, and a multitrack audio tape recorder. One track of the audio recording holds inaudible pulses that control the dissolve unit and projectors, while the remaining tracks hold narration, sound effects, and music. **M**

Genigraphics Driver Job Instructions

Copies:	1	sets, 35mm Slides (plastic mounts)
	0	sets, 35mm Slides (glass mounts)
	0	sets, 8"x 10" Overheads
	0	sets, 8"x 10" Prints

Send via: ◉ Modem ○ Diskette
Return via: ◉ Courier ○ Mail ○ Hold for Pickup
Save As: Geni-Genigraphics Disk

[OK]
[Cancel]
[Custom]

Genigraphics Billing Information

		Ship to:	Bill to: (if different)
Company	*		
Contact	*		
Mail Stop/Dept			
Street Address	*		
City	*		
State/Zip	*		
(Area) Phone	*		

* Always Required

◉ AMEX ○ VISA ○ MC   ○ Genigraphics Account   ○ COD

Acct #   Acct #
Expiration mo [ ] yr [ ]   PO#

Tax Exempt ID #   [Cancel] [OK]

aimed at a video tube. Sandwiched between those components is a wheel containing red, green, and blue filters. The film recorder paints an image on the video tube, making separate passes for red, green, and blue light — three primary colors for video with which it can create a palette of over 16 million hues. A complete exposure usually takes a few minutes.

Not only do film recorders provide spectacular color, they offer tack-sharp resolution — usually in the ballpark of 4000 horizontal lines per slide. By comparison, a Mac II's screen display contains 480 horizontal lines; commercial television has 525-line resolution.

▲ **Dialing for Dazzle**

Most presentation programs include a driver that lets you transmit visuals to a nationwide slide service bureau such as Genigraphics. Note the options for delivery time. With the Genigraphics driver shown here, after you OK the Print dialog box (top), a second dialog box (bottom) appears for you to enter payment and delivery information.

Hardware this sharp isn't cheap — film recorder prices generally start at about $6000. A less expensive alternative is to use a slide-service bureau. Most cities have service bureaus and large copy shops that can create slides for you from documents you supply on a floppy disk. As an alternative, you can send a disk to the bureau or transmit your visuals via modem. Your slides arrive from one to several days later, depending on the turnaround time you are willing to pay for. Service bureaus also provide other types of output, such as high-resolution overhead transparencies and color prints.

Most publishers of presentation software have cooperative arrangements with nationwide slide-service bureaus. Included with the software is a driver for the type of film recorder the bureau uses. You copy the driver into your System Folder, and use the Chooser desk accessory to select it prior to creating your visuals. Most publishers also include a special communications program that uses straightforward dialog boxes to automate communications with the service bureau (see the figure "Dialing for Dazzle").

For some tips on choosing between and designing slides and overheads, see the table "Presentation Pointers" on the next page.

Presentation Pointers

	Overhead Transparencies	Slides
Best Applications	Informal presentations to small groups.	Formal presentations to large groups; repeating presentations at trade shows or public places.
Advantages	Inexpensive; can be shown in lit room, allowing interaction; can be written on.	Vivid colors; impressive looking; special effects possible with multiple projectors; easy to duplicate; remain sorted in trays.
Disadvantages	Can scratch and smudge; bland colors; can become disordered.	Relatively expensive; turnaround time required for service bureaus; less personal — requires darkened room, which discourages interaction.
Design guidelines	One concept per transparency; use about 7 words per line, and no more than 7 lines per overhead.	One idea per slide; use bulleted lists and "builds" for complex topics; avoid more than four lines of type per slide. Use the same orientation for all slides — don't switch between horizontal and vertical slides.
Typographic guidelines	Avoid type sizes smaller than 18-point. Text should be readable from 10 feet away before projection.	Set type tight but not touching; use reversed type (light type on dark background); avoid centering; avoid varying type size from one slide to the next.
Presentation guidelines	Be sure visuals are in order before beginning.	Be sure slides are properly sequenced and oriented in their trays; use a large number of slides — don't force the audience to stare at one image.
Graphic guidelines	Use bar graphs to show relationships between data; use line graphs to show trends; use pie charts to show percentage relationships.	
Typeface guidelines	Use bold, san-serif fonts such as Helvetica Bold and Franklin Gothic Heavy. Also consider the square serifed Lubalin Graph. Don't use more than two typefaces per visual, and use the same typefaces throughout the presentation. For slides, use reverse type (light type on a dark background).	

Presentation Variations

Most presentation programs are geared toward brainstorming and producing visuals, but some specialized ones also deserve mention. Programs such as Visual Information's Dimensions Presenter allow you to create three-dimensional animated presentations. For example, architects can use these programs to take clients on simulated walk-throughs of their designs, and industrial designers or interior decorators can allow clients to view their proposals from literally any angle. MacroMind Director can produce animated presentations that incorporate sound effects and music (see chapters 12 and 17).

Then there's HyperCard. As a presentation program, Claris' software toolkit has serious limitations, most notably, limited color support. But it does provide a selection of visual effects and it can play back recorded sounds. And by combining its built-in programming language with on-screen buttons, you can create dynamic presentations that people can use and navigate through on their own. Silicon Beach Software's SuperCard and MacroMind Director 2.0 provide superior animation and color features, making them potentially better choices for interactive presentations.

Before I began researching the world of presentation software, I was skeptical. The entire category struck me as being one created by software companies looking for another way to sell programs that provide drawing and layout features. But once I had worked with the programs a little and had seen what they're capable of, I thought of all the meetings I've snoozed through — where monotonal voices droned on and on in conference rooms, curing insomnia. Some interesting visuals and better planning certainly would have enlivened those proceedings.

It's true that a presentation program can spawn uninteresting visuals when used by a graphics philistine. And it's true that a presentation program's brainstorming features won't help someone in a mental drought. But it's also true that every day thousands of people stand up and try to sell their ideas and products to others. That's hard work, and when I'm in that spot, I'm glad to have all the help I can get.

Summary:

✔ There are many parallels between desktop publishing and desktop presenting. The major differences between the two are that desktop publishing implies a permanence to your work while desktop presenting is more transitory. Also, the output in publishing is on paper — in presenting, it's usually projected on a screen.

✔ Visuals contain three elements: text, often organized into bullet charts; graphics, including graphs, organizational charts, diagrams, and drawings; and backgrounds, used to make text more readable on a screen.

✔ The ability of the presentation program to sort, arrange, and present visuals sets it apart from a desktop publisher. Slide sorters let you arrange the order of slides which can then be output using the slide show feature built into a presentation program.

✔ There are several hardware output devices you can use to present your visuals depending on your budget. For the occasional presenter, using the Mac as a slide projector might suffice. Other alternatives include using a large color monitor for larger crowds, or an LCD projection panel, which attaches to a Mac and is used with an overhead projector. One of the best ways to project color images is with a video projector, which can create wall-sized images with the same vivid color and fast screen updating you see on the screen.

Chapter 11
Music and MIDI

In This Chapter:

✔ A summary of the many musical roles a Mac performs.

✔ Music programs for any level of Mac musician.

✔ Details on the MIDI specification that makes advanced Mac music possible.

✔ An introduction to the most popular kinds of MIDI software.

✔ Miscellaneous MIDI programs and programming tools.

✔ How to connect your Mac to MIDI equipment.

For Mac owners with a musical bent, this is a wonderful time to be alive. The Mac may be best known for changing the way people publish, but it's becoming a prominent force in the way people make music, too. Whether you're a beginner who has trouble pecking out *Chopsticks*, a film score composer, or lead guitarist for the Bleeding Eardrums, there's a place for the Mac in your musical life.

And you don't have to break the bank to find it. You can sample the world of computer music applications for nothing more than the price of a program and a cable to hook your Macintosh into a stereo system. When you're ready to move up to a synthesizer you'll be pleasantly surprised. The same electronics advances that have spawned $9.95 digital watches have made possible synthesizers that cost less than a color television. In this chapter, we'll look at the ways in which you and a Mac can make beautiful music together.

Music to the Macs

The Macintosh is a multitalented performer. In fact, a Mac can play so many musical roles that it might help to briefly audition each role before taking a closer look.

❖ *Sequencing* Several programs turn the Mac into an electronic multitrack recorder that records, edits, and plays back performances using one or more synthesizers attached to the Mac. The alchemy that makes this possible goes by the name Musical Instrument Digital Interface (MIDI), a synthesizer-communications standard built into virtually every synthesizer and electronic instrument made today.

❖ *Scoring* The process of putting notes on paper is traditionally a grueling task for composers, who must wrestle with staff paper and white-out, and for music publishing houses, which often use a mutated typewriter called a Musicwriter. Scoring programs do for composers what word processors have done for writers.

❖ *Composition* A fascinating new genre of programs lets the Mac collaborate with you, storing groups of phrases you have entered, analyzing their structure, and rearranging the notes into new rhythms and patterns based on the originals.

❖ *Sound editing* With many electronic instruments, adjusting the many knobs and buttons required to produce a desired sound is so difficult that many players stick with the instruments' built-in sounds, often called *patches* (named in honor of the pioneering synthesizers of the sixties, whose many sound-generating modules were linked by patch cables like those for a telephone switchboard). *Patch editor* programs let you draw and manipulate the waveforms that describe a sound's qualities, then transfer them to a synthesizer's memory.

❖ *Patch management* Most synthesizers can store dozens of patches, but that isn't enough for real sound hounds. *Patch librarians* are database managers for patches; these programs transfer the settings making up each patch to or from a Macintosh disk. Patch librarians also let you cut and paste patches from one file to another, so you can organize sounds according to your performance needs. Most patch editors also provide librarian features.

❖ *Sound track production* For years, film and recording studios have used a timing standard called the *SMPTE edit time code.* (SMPTE, pronounced *simpty,* stands for Society of Motion Picture and Television Engineers.) The SMPTE code allows engineers to synchronize a sound track with an action. Many sequencers, as well as a variety of *cue* programs, work with the SMPTE code to simplify the chore of calculating how long a musical passage must be in order to fit a given scene.

Songs for Beginners

You say you're neither a synthesizer owner nor a sound track composer? You can still choose from a combination of programs designed to let you sound off with a minimal musical background and no additional equipment.

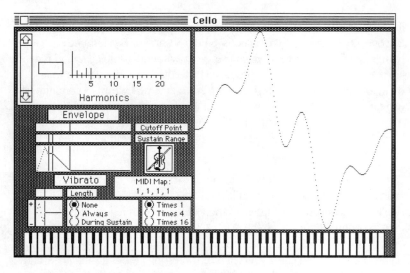

Foremost among such packages is Great Wave Software's ConcertWare+. With ConcertWare+, you enter music on conventional staves by using the mouse and on-screen palettes, which provide one-click access to note and rest values. ConcertWare+ also lets you cut, copy, and paste passages and print your compositions. The program isn't intended to be a full-fledged scoring tool, however, so don't expect to find more esoteric elements of music notation like tremolo slashes or glissando symbols. Such elements are the province of music scoring programs, which I'll examine later.

▲ **Designing Instruments**
ConcertWare+MIDI's instrument maker program lets you design instruments by specifying the characteristics of their waveform, harmonics, and envelope. You can hear your efforts by clicking on the on-screen piano keyboard, and you can save instruments for use with ConcertWare+MIDI's Music Player program.

ConcertWare+ is also an ideal tool for learning about sound. Using the package's Instrument Maker program, you draw and edit waveforms and define a sound *envelope*, which governs a sound's percussiveness (see the figure "Designing Instruments"). For example, a piano has a sharp *attack* (as the hammers hit the strings) and a gradual *decay* (as the strings stop vibrating and the sound fades out). Wind instruments have a gradual attack and little decay — until the musician runs out of breath.

Aural Gratification

Considering the Mac's limited sound-synthesizing capabilities, the end product of Instrument Maker is surprisingly good. But if it's not good enough for you, ConcertWare+MIDI can send songs to a synthesizer — or let you enter songs from a synthesizer. If the notion of playing a song and then printing out its score sounds too good to be true, it is. Any performer's rendition of a piece varies from the precise timing specified by music notation. ConcertWare+ MIDI — and professional sequencer and scoring packages as well — must attempt to round off variances in timing through a process called *quantization.* Generally the process works well, but you still must fine-tune the final score.

If you don't have a synthesizer and you aren't happy with the Mac's attempt to imitate one, consider Bogas Productions' Studio Session or Brødurbund Software's Jam Session, both of which use *sampled* sound. Sampled sound is a digitized version of the real thing, produced by feeding an audio signal into a hardware device called an *analog-to-digital converter,* which turns a continuously varying (analog) sound wave — the kind our ears recognize — into a series of numbers stored by sampling software. If you've ever marveled at a compact disc's startling clarity, you've experienced the most common application of sampled sound.

The instrument sounds included with Studio Session and Jam Session can't approach a compact disc's realism. Still, both are remarkable programs. Jam Session includes numerous songs in a variety of styles, from reggae to rock to classical to country. Each key on the Mac's keyboard is assigned to a "canned" riff (a series of notes) or a sound effect such as a cheering or applauding crowd; you can improvise solos (and cheer yourself on) by pressing keys as a song plays, and Jam Session works to ensure that everything you play is in the right key and tempo. And on the screen, an animated band boogies to your beat.

Studio Session includes additional features, including a music editor that lets you create new songs. CompuServe, America Online, and user group libraries are brimming with songs and additional instrument sounds. You can also create your own sounds using a Mac with sound-recording features such as an LC or IIsi, or any other Mac equipped with a sound digitizer such as Farallon's MacRecorder.

More on MIDI

In 1982 the largest companies in the electronic music industry overcame their normally secretive and competitive urges and agreed to cooperate. The result of their collaboration was not a hot new musical instrument, but a 13-page document that has literally changed the way the world makes music.

That document described the MIDI specification. MIDI was developed to enable musicians to connect electronic instruments to each other and to computers. The MIDI specification spells out the types of wires and connectors that unite musical instruments, as well as the commands and codes that MIDI-equipped instruments transmit and respond to. Generally, any piece of equipment with MIDI — whether a musical instrument or a computer — can talk with any other piece of MIDI gear.

On a basic level, MIDI lets you create a network of two or more instruments that you can play from just one instrument. Musicians often use this technique, called *layering,* to play multiple instruments simultaneously to obtain a richer sound. On a somewhat more advanced level, MIDI lets you connect one or more instruments to a computer to record and play back music and add accompaniments. This aspect of MIDI has helped create a new phenomenon — the home recording studio. And at its most advanced level, MIDI lets you combine a computer-controlled network of instruments with audio equipment and even stage lighting to automate an entire performance environment.

MIDI Basics

MIDI data can travel in two directions at the same time — from an instrument to a computer and from a computer to an instrument, for example. To accommodate this two-way traffic, every MIDI device has two connectors: *MIDI In* and *MIDI Out.* Some devices have another connector as well, *MIDI Thru,* which can be used for chaining MIDI devices together.

Peer behind the Mac and you'll notice there are no such connectors. Unlike some personal computers (specifically a few Atari models), Macs don't come equipped for MIDI but need a separate piece of hardware — a *MIDI interface,* which connects to the Mac's modem or printer port and provides MIDI In and MIDI Out connectors. Several are available for the Mac, ranging from Apple's $99 Apple MIDI Interface to Mark of the Unicorn's $495 MIDI Time Piece and J.L. Cooper Electronics' $349 SyncMaster. The high-end MIDI interfaces provide more MIDI In and MIDI Out connectors and allow the Mac to be synchronized with an external device such as an audio tape recorder (see the table "Mac MIDI Interfaces").

Mac MIDI Interfaces

Model	Company	MIDI In Connectors	MIDI Out Connectors	Sync Support	Retail Price
Altech 1 x 3	Altech Systems	1	3	no	$ 99.95
Altech 2 x 6	Altech Systems	2	6	no	149.95
Apple MIDI Interface	Apple Computer	1	1	no	99.00
MacNEXUS	J. L. Cooper Elec.	2	6	yes	69.95
SyncMaster	J. L. Cooper Elec.	2	6	yes	349.00
MIDI Time Piece	Mark of the Unicorn	8	8	yes	495.00
Professional Plus	Opcode Systems	1	3	no	125.00
Studio 3	Opcode Systems	2	6	yes	495.00
Studio Plus Two	Opcode Systems	2	6	no	225.00
MH-01M	Passport Designs	1	1	no	130.00
MIDI Transport	Passport Designs	2	4	yes	495.00

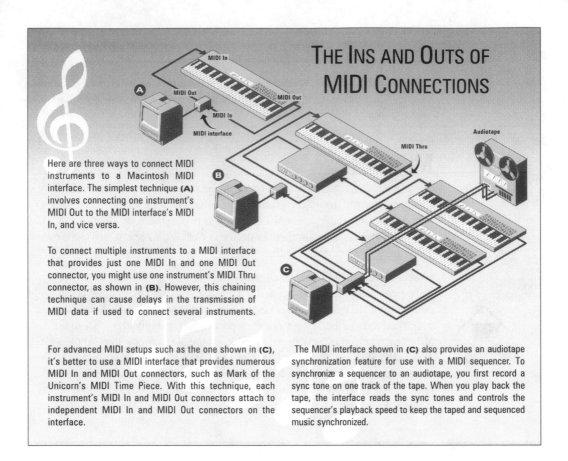

THE INS AND OUTS OF MIDI CONNECTIONS

Here are three ways to connect MIDI instruments to a Macintosh MIDI interface. The simplest technique **(A)** involves connecting one instrument's MIDI Out to the MIDI interface's MIDI In, and vice versa.

To connect multiple instruments to a MIDI interface that provides just one MIDI In and one MIDI Out connector, you might use one instrument's MIDI Thru connector, as shown in **(B)**. However, this chaining technique can cause delays in the transmission of MIDI data if used to connect several instruments.

For advanced MIDI setups such as the one shown in **(C)**, it's better to use a MIDI interface that provides numerous MIDI In and MIDI Out connectors, such as Mark of the Unicorn's MIDI Time Piece. With this technique, each instrument's MIDI In and MIDI Out connectors attach to independent MIDI In and MIDI Out connectors on the interface.

The MIDI interface shown in **(C)** also provides an audiotape synchronization feature for use with a MIDI sequencer. To synchronize a sequencer to an audiotape, you first record a sync tone on one track of the tape. When you play back the tape, the interface reads the sync tones and controls the sequencer's playback speed to keep the taped and sequenced music synchronized.

The figure "The Ins and Outs of MIDI Connections" shows three different ways to connect MIDI instruments with an interface to relay MIDI data (also called *messages* or *events*) between instruments and a Mac.

But what kind of data? First and foremost, *note data*. When you play a MIDI instrument's keyboard, it tells the Mac which keys were pressed and for how long. *Velocity-sensitive* keyboards also note how hard each key was pressed, letting the Mac capture the varied dynamics of your performance.

Incidentally, MIDI instruments don't necessarily have to have piano-like keyboards. They can take other forms, ranging from the self-explanatory *MIDI guitar* and *drum pad* to the not-so-self-explanatory, saxophone-like *wind controller*. MIDI-equipped accordions are available, as are retrofits that add MIDI to organs and acoustic pianos. Instruments that generate MIDI data are often called *controllers*. Many musicians combine one controller with several *sound modules* — boxes containing sound-generating circuitry and MIDI connectors, but no keyboards.

E-mu Systems' remarkable Proteus is one popular sound module; Roland Corporation's MT-32 is another. A visit to a local music store will turn up many more.

MIDI instruments can receive or transmit data on any of 16 independent *channels* — electronic mailing addresses that accompany MIDI data and specify its destination. Not only can you specify the channel MIDI instruments use to transmit data, you can also configure them to respond to data sent on all MIDI channels (*omni* mode) or only to certain ones (*poly* mode).

This ability to channel MIDI data is important because many MIDI setups comprise more than one instrument, some of which may be *multitimbral* — capable of simultaneously producing different types of sounds, such as those of a drum set and a horn section. If you couldn't assign certain MIDI data to certain channels, there'd be nothing to stop one instrument from playing another's part.

Note data is by no means the only kind of information that can travel on MIDI cables. Here are some MIDI messages that instead of playing notes play other roles in the performance.

❖ *Program changes* instruct an instrument to switch sounds — from piano to strings, for example.

❖ *Continuous data* generally modifies the way a sound is played. For example, many instruments have *pitch bend* wheels or levers that let you slide between pitches the way guitar players do when they bend a string. Another kind of continuous data is *aftertouch*, which describes how hard a note key is being held down. By pressing harder on a key after you've pressed it, you might add vibrato or cause a string sound to get progressively louder. Not all keyboards send aftertouch, but those that do allow for a greater range of expression.

❖ *Clock* or *sync data* carries information about the timing of a MIDI performance. It's often used to synchronize a network of MIDI instruments to an audio tape recording.

❖ *System-exclusive data* is information pertinent to a specific model of MIDI instrument, such as the contents of its internal memory, or the MIDI-channel assignments of its sounds. By transferring system-exclusive data to the Mac, you can store and alter an instrument's sounds, and then transfer the data back to the MIDI instrument.

Software to Make Music By

Without a computer, MIDI data plays a valuable but limited role — it lets you play numerous instruments using just one controller. MIDI data becomes much more useful when it's combined with a computer and software that can store and

File Edit Change Windows Songs Layout Goodies

Track Editor

Tk	P	R	S	L	Name	Chnl	Prg	Vol
1	▶				Bass & Synth	A1	-	127
2	▶				Chords	A2	-	-
3	▶				Opening Snare	A3	-	-
4	▶				Bass Drum	A3	-	-
5	▶				Crash Cymbal.	A3	-	-
6	▶				Congas	A5	-	-
7	▶				Melody Horns	A4	-	-
8	▶				Horn Accents	A4	-	-
9	▶				Latin Perc	A5	-	-
10	▶	•			Vibes	A6	-	-
11						A -	-	-

Conductor

Offset Tempo = 160

♩ = 160

Reggie MIDI file

Measure Beat Clock
14: 1:000

Current Time
0:00:20:00

◀◀ ▶ Play ▶▶ Punch Auto Thru A6

‖ Pause ■ Stop ● Record Count In Click INT Sync

▲ **Laying Down Tracks**

Sequencers (such as Passport Designs' Pro 4, shown here) let you record and play back MIDI data. The dark bars on the right indicate the presence of MIDI data in those measures. At the top of the window is a marker (here named Verse 2), which you can create to quickly access a specific point. Most sequencers provide these basic features.

manipulate it. The most popular kind of MIDI software is the *sequencer,* a kind of tapeless tape deck that lets you build your own arrangements by recording parts one *track* at a time. You might start with a drum or bass track to establish a rhythm, and perhaps specify that it *loop,* or repeat continuously. Next, you might add a guitar melody, then some strings to sweeten things up. During playback, you route the tracks to the appropriate instruments — or to the appropriate sounds within a multitimbral instrument — by specifying a different playback channel for each one (see the figure "Laying Down Tracks").

On the surface, a sequencer seems similar to a multitrack tape recorder or to a digital audio-recording system such as Digidesign's Audiomedia or Sound Tools. But a sequencer doesn't store sound; instead, it stores the sequence of MIDI data that describes what you played.

That storage technique has a few significant pluses. First, MIDI data requires far less disk space than digital audio data does. A ten-minute stereo recording made with Sound Tools requires 100MB of disk space; a ten-minute MIDI sequence might use 30K or so. Also, because the MIDI data in a sequence isn't tied to a particular sound, you can change an instrument's settings before or during playback to hear how that electric guitar part sounds when played by an acoustic guitar — or maybe an oboe. Or, you can work up an arrangement using an economical home system and then take your disk into a recording studio and play the sequence using state-of-the-art gear.

And because you're working with MIDI data, you can continue adding tracks without compromising the sound quality. With an audio recording, each time you *bounce* two or more tracks to a single track to free up a track for recording, the sound quality of the older tracks suffers. With a sequencer, the tracks exist in the Mac's memory, not on audio tape. So you can add as many tracks as you have memory for, and every playback is an original performance.

Perhaps best of all (at least for those of us who can't practice eight hours a day), you can use a sequencer's extensive editing features to correct misplayed notes or to add more dynamic expression. You can cut and paste sections of a recording — for example, to remove extra verses or repeat a part. And with a sequencer's *step recording* mode, you can manually enter difficult parts one note at a time, or slow down the tempo and record them at a more leisurely pace. Is it cheating? Some might say so, but it lets you make better music, and the results go a long way toward soothing your guilt.

Sequencer Features

Here's a closer look at the kinds of features you'll find in Macintosh sequencers.

For correcting or inserting notes in existing tracks, two basic schemes exist. *Graphic* editing displays a track's contents on a music staff-like grid, except that notes are shown as horizontal bars, with longer bars representing longer notes. Graphic editing lets you select and drag notes from one position to another using the mouse. Because a graphic editing display resembles a player piano roll, it's often called a *piano roll* display. (Mark of the Unicorn's Performer supports a third scheme that displays a sequence in standard music notation.)

Event list editing displays a track's contents as a table of MIDI data. It doesn't give you the click-and-drag convenience of graphic editing, but it allows for greater precision, since you can type and edit the exact values that describe individual notes or other MIDI data. Better sequencers provide both types of editing windows (see the figure "Editing Tracks" on the next page).

For tweaking the timing of notes, sequencers provide *quantizing* features, which cause the program to move notes to the nearest note value you specify. If used excessively, however, quantizing can give sequenced music an overly mechanized feel; after all, no one plays every note *exactly* on time. To eliminate this undesirable side effect, most sequencers let you specify a margin within which notes aren't quantized, and thus you can neaten up your playing without making it sound robotic. Some sequencers also provide a *humanize* option, which does the opposite of quantizing: it nudges notes off their exact beat values to improve the feel of a passage that was overly quantized or entered using a step-recording mode.

Many pieces of music don't have the same tempo throughout. To accommodate such pieces, sequencers provide a special track, often called a *conductor track*, that stores tempo information. Using the conductor track, you can create a *tempo map* that describes the tempo changes in the piece. With some sequencers — including Mark of the Unicorn's Performer, Opcode Systems' Vision, Steinberg-Jones's Cubase, and Electronic Arts' Deluxe Recorder — you can specify the tempo by tapping a key on a MIDI keyboard.

Editing Tracks

At top, the graphic (upper right) and event list (lower left) editing windows in Mark of the Unicorn's Performer. The entries reading #64 indicate the press and release of a MIDI keyboard's sustain pedal. In the middle, the quantizing dialog box in Opcode's Vision. At bottom, Performer's Split Notes dialog box, which lets you extract certain notes from a track. One use for Split Notes would be to separate the left- and right-hand parts of a track.

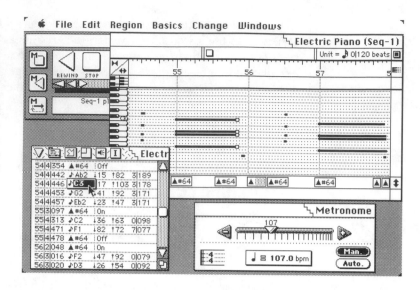

If you combine a sequencer with external equipment, such as a multitrack audio tape recorder, you'll need a sequencer that can be locked to synchronization codes sent by that external source. By recording a *sync track* on a tape recorder and feeding that track into a sync-supporting MIDI interface such as MIDI Time Piece, you keep the sequencer and recorder in exact synchronization. You can use sync to add sequenced electronic music to an acoustic recording, or to create a multitrack audio recording using a single MIDI instrument to record one track at a time, synchronizing the sequencer's playback with the tracks you've already recorded on tape. Sync features are commonly used in TV and movie soundtrack production, in which MIDI sequences of music or even sound effects are synchronized to visual action. In these cases, a sequencer is synchronized to a film editor or videotape recorder using the industry standard SMPTE time code.

At the leading edge of the sequencer world, you'll find Opcode's Studio Vision and Mark of the Unicorn's Digital Performer, which can combine MIDI data and digitally recorded audio in the same file, enabling you to add vocals or acoustic instrument recordings to a sequence. To record audio, you need appropriate digital audio hardware such as Digidesign's Sound Tools and Audiomedia (both discussed in Chapter 32).

If you're a pro, you might end up using more than one sequencer. Fortunately, virtually all support the standard *MIDI file* format, which enables sequencers — even ones running on different computers — to exchange recordings (see the sidebar "Choosing a Sequencer"). Often MIDI files are also used along with *scoring* programs — the next stop on our MIDI tour.

Music Processors

Scoring programs let you print music using conventional notation. They do for composers what word processors do for writers — they let you easily correct and revise a piece without a lot of erasing (see the figure "Scoring Software" on the next page).

Even more exciting, scoring programs can transcribe music as you play it on a MIDI keyboard. Real-time music transcription has been a fantasy of musicians for years, and the dream still hasn't been completely fulfilled. The primary problem is one I mentioned before — nobody plays every note exactly on time. A real-time transcription is likely to have a large number of awkward rests and

Choosing a Sequencer

Sequencer software firms keep a close eye on the competition, releasing updates so often that you'll rarely find any one program well ahead of the others. Given that, here are some issues that are likely to influence your buying decision.

❖ *Program design* As with any kind of program, some sequencers are easier to use than others. I'm partial to Performer and Pro 4. Vision provides a few more features, but it's harder to learn. Try a few programs and pick the one you feel comfortable with.

❖ *Memory requirements* Memory efficiency is critical with sequencers, since the length and complexity of your songs is limited by the amount of free memory available. Performer, with its flashy user interface, requires 2MB of RAM for serious work; most other programs can run comfortably with 1MB.

❖ *Copy protection* Most software makers stopped this practice years ago, but this inconvenience persists in the sequencer world. Before a protected sequencer will run, you have to insert a master floppy disk or perform a convoluted installation process on your hard disk. It's annoying, and potentially devastating if you use a sequencer at live jobs ("Sorry, folks — no music tonight. The band's master disk went bad."). Of the sequencers shipping at this writing, only Pro 4, Deluxe Recorder, and Dr. T's Music Software's Beyond are not copy protected.

❖ *Cost* For most musicians, money is an object. The best buy in sequencers is Passport Design's $99.95 Trax. **M**

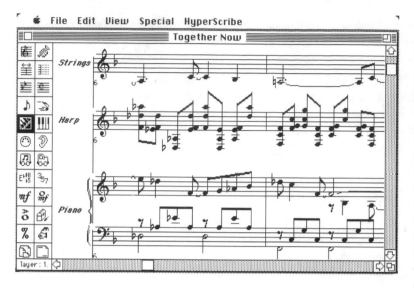

unusual note values you'll need to clean up using the scoring program's editing features. Scoring programs help you get better results by quantizing data as you play it (or load it from a MIDI file), but don't expect perfect notation the first time around. These real-time entry features are most effective when used as a starting point.

▲ Scoring Software

Notation programs such as Finale, shown here, let you commit music to paper by entering notes individually from a tool palette, playing a MIDI instrument, or importing a MIDI file created by a sequencer. The latter two approaches sound especially appealing, but music entered directly from a performance often requires extensive quantizing to compensate for minor timing inaccuracies.

Numerous scoring programs are available for the Mac, including Mark of the Unicorn's Professional Composer, Passport Designs' NoteWriter and Encore, Coda's Finale and MusicProse, Electronic Arts' Deluxe Music Construction Set, and Great Wave Software's ConcertWare+MIDI. Deluxe Music Construction Set and ConcertWare+MIDI provide beginner- to intermediate-level scoring features. The rest are geared toward professionals and offer more control over the elements of a score.

All of these programs take advantage of Adobe Systems' Sonata music font to produce sharp copy on LaserWriters and other PostScript printers. (Coda's programs include additional PostScript fonts for producing specialized notation symbols such as guitar chord patterns.) Beyond that, each program provides its own notation strengths; if you're a serious composer, you'll want to evaluate them all to find the one that best handles the notation requirements of the style of music and the instruments you're writing for. While you're at it, you may want to investigate free or shareware scoring programs such as Lime, from the CERL Music Group at the University of Illinois and the Department of Computer and Information Science at Queen's University. Lime and a large selection of music notation fonts are available through most user groups and on-line services.

Sounds Good

As mentioned at the beginning of this chapter, editor/librarians let you manage, alter, and save a MIDI instrument's sounds by manipulating system-exclusive MIDI data. You might use an editor/librarian to tweak an existing

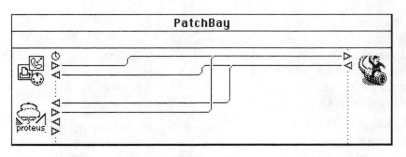

MIDI Patching

Apple's PatchBay application graphically depicts the connections between the MIDI Manager (upper left icon) and your MIDI hardware and software. Here, connections have been established between the MIDI Manager and Digidesign's MacProteus (far right), and the MacProteus' Front Panel application, which lets you adjust instrument settings and MIDI parameters. MacProteus is a version of E-mu's Proteus that plugs into a Mac II's NuBus slot.

sound to your liking or to create a new sound from scratch. You can alter a MIDI instrument's sounds using its front-panel knobs and switches, but an editor/librarian makes it easier by taking advantage of the Mac's graphical operating style. For example, giving a sound a sharper, more percussive quality might require 15 minutes of twiddling with an instrument's knobs while squinting at its small, calculator-like display. With an editor/librarian, you can edit an on-screen version of the sound, clicking and dragging its components until you get the sound you want.

Editor/librarians are available for all popular MIDI instruments. Some, such as Opcode's Galaxy, can work with numerous instruments, and are often called *universal* editor/librarians.

Similar to editor/librarians are *sample-editing* programs such as Digidesign's Sound Designer II or Passport Designs' Alchemy or entry-level Sound Apprentice. Sample editors let you manipulate the digital sound samples that sampling instruments such as Ensoniq's EPS and E-mu Systems' Emulator III play. (For details on digital sound and samplers, see Chapter 32.)

If you have a sampler, you might also want to investigate Digidesign's Turbo-synth software, which lets you design synthesized sounds on the Mac and then transfer them to a sampler for playback. Turbosynth gives a sampler — whose normal purpose is to play back digital recordings of real instruments — the sound-generating versatility of a synthesizer.

Every Combo Needs a Manager

If you try to run several MIDI programs simultaneously under MultiFinder (or System 7.0), you may experience compatibility problems. That's because some MIDI programs monopolize the Mac's communications chips, preventing other programs from using them.

But chances are all your MIDI programs will peacefully coexist if you use Apple's MIDI Manager, an enhancement to the Mac's system software that lets multiple MIDI programs run under MultiFinder and even share the same MIDI data. Instead of accessing the hardware directly, programs access the MIDI Manager, which in turn deals with the hardware. You can establish "connections" between the various MIDI programs and hardware you use by using Apple's PatchBay application (see the figure "MIDI Patching").

For users of the Mac Portable, MIDI Manager isn't an option, it's a necessity. The Portable's battery-conservation features make it incompatible with MIDI software that directly accesses the machine's communications chips. If you have a Portable, use MIDI Manager version 1.2 or later. Apple also recommends using System 6.0.5 or a later version to eliminate other possible compatibility problems with the Portable's modem and printer ports.

Most MIDI software vendors have updated their products to be compatible with MIDI Manager. Nonetheless, if your setup requires that you use MIDI Manager, it's a good idea to verify that a given piece of MIDI software is compatible with it before you buy.

Smart Songsters

One of the most fascinating categories of MIDI software almost defies categorization. I'm referring to *performance software*, programs that you interact with to improvise compositions, and in some cases, that store and analyze phrases and then improvise music with some characteristics of the originals.

Musical Luddites who aim their noses skyward at the notion of computer-composed music haven't played with Jam Factory, one of three intelligent instrument programs from Dr. T's Music Software. In Jam Factory, four "players" store notes you play at a MIDI keyboard, and then the program analyzes the music. From there, the program generates new passages that contain the notes you played, but in a more random order. The order isn't completely random, however, because the probability of a given note occurring depends on how often it occurred in the original phrase. That's what allows Jam Factory's improvisations to resemble the original phrases.

66 ...even Mozart once experimented with random composition, using dice to choose notes, then building a melody and supporting harmony based on those selections. 99

The basic concepts behind Jam Factory aren't new. In 1961, computer music scientists developed what they called an analog composing machine. In one experiment, they used it to analyze Stephen Foster songs and compose new songs that had that Dixie flavor. And even Mozart once experimented with random composition, using dice to choose notes, then building a melody and supporting harmony based on those selections.

Jam Factory would make the flamboyant Amadeus squeal with glee. The screen is jam-packed with *performance controls*, buttons, and graphs for altering the phrases Jam *Factory* plays — their tempo, rhythm, randomness, key signature, and more. Jam Factory turns the Mac into a musical instrument, letting you change the program's renditions of your phrases by "playing" the on-screen controls. You can store the results of a performance to commit that flash of brilliance to disk, and replay it later.

If it sounds to you like there's more to Jam Factory than I've described, you're right. Dr. T's Music Software wisely offers a $5 demonstration disk that lets you experience the program for yourself. While you're at it, get the demo disks ($5 each) for Jam Factory's cousins — M, a composition and performance program, and UpBeat, an intelligent rhythm program designed for use with drum machines. UpBeat takes basic rhythms that you enter and devises accents and fills that take the mechanized "boom-chaka-boom" feel out of drum synthesizers.

My favorite program in this category of performance software is Scorpion Systems Group's Sybil. Sybil works like a musical instrument, allowing you to produce complex, multi-part compositions on the fly, in real time. In short, you don't use Sybil, you play it.

On one level, Sybil lets you play back series of notes and chords that you assign to the pads on a MIDI drum controller, the keys on a MIDI music keyboard, the frets on a MIDI guitar, or even the keys on the Mac's keyboard. For example, once you've assigned a chord to a particular pad, you can play that chord by striking the pad. You can also set up Sybil to respond to how hard you strike a pad — strike it gently, and one set of notes plays; strike it hard, and another set plays.

On another level, you can tell Sybil to play your stored notes differently when you strike a particular pad twice in succession. The first hit might play a chord, while the second hit might transpose the chord to a different key. By combining stored notes with these toggles, as they're called, you can create remarkably rich compositions with surprisingly little effort.

Sybil is being used by all types of musicians, but drummers in particular have embraced it because it gives them the ability to make tonal music. Indeed, one of the things that makes Sybil special is that, in the words of Steve Lipson, one of Sybil's creators, "it breaks down the distinctions between instrumentalists."

Music Miscellany

Sequencers, editor/librarians, and scoring programs are the primary players in the MIDI software world. On the fringes, you find programs such as Ars Nova Software's Practica Musica, Coda's Perceive, and Hip Software's Harmony Grid, which are all designed to help you train your musical ear and learn music theory. And for creating slick drum and rhythm pattern, check out Coda's MacDrums, Primera Software's Different Drummer, and Dr. T's Music Software's UpBeat.

There are also MIDI programming tools such as Altech System's MIDI Basic and MIDI Pascal, and Hip Software's fascinating HookUp, a graphical programming language that lets you create MIDI-accompanied animations not by typing arcane programming commands, but by attaching icons to each other.

You can even find prerecorded MIDI sequences, such as Passport Design's Music Data series, which includes elaborately produced sequences of hundreds of Top-40, rhythm-and-blues, country, and classical music pieces. You might use a canned sequence to fine-tune your arranging or improvisation skills, or as an accompaniment to a live performance. And you can also find MIDI support in multimedia programs such as MacroMind's Director. Director's MIDI support lets you trigger a sequenced piece of music or a sound effect at a particular time during an animation. HyperCard users can also choose from a variety of XCMDs and XFCNs to add MIDI-control features to stacks.

Fade Out

If you want to learn more about computer music applications and synthesizers, consider a subscription to *Keyboard* magazine (Cupertino, CA) or *Electronic Musician* (Emeryville, CA). Both magazines review the latest in synthesizers and computer software, but not at the expense of the creative aspects of music making. For a complete guide to making music on the Mac, read *Macworld's Music and Sound Bible* (IDG Books Worldwide, due to be published in 1991).

The Mac has quickly become the computer of choice for music applications, and the future sounds even better. The Mac II, with its faster processing and expandability, plays a large role in sampling and professional audio applications. Synthesizer makers will continue to cram more and better sounds into less-expensive packages, and increasingly intelligent music packages will enable music lovers with less-than-virtuoso keyboard skills to experience the joy of listening to their own music.

And in the end, joy is what making music is all about.

Summary:

✔ The Mac is fast becoming a prominent force in the way people make music. A Mac can perform many musical roles, including sequencing (recording, editing, and playing back performances), scoring (putting notes on paper), composition (storing and analyzing groups of phrases), sound editing (manipulating sound quality), patch management (patch librarians), and sound track production.

✔ You don't have to be a professional musician to benefit from various programs designed to let you make your own kind of music with a minimal music background and no additional equipment.

✔ The Musical Instrument Digital Interface (MIDI) was developed to let musicians connect electronic instruments to each other and to computers. MIDI allows you to create a network of two or more instruments that you can play from just one instrument (layering). Or a more advanced level, MIDI lets you combine a computer-controlled network of instruments with audio equipment and even stage lighting to automate an entire performance environment.

✔ The most popular MIDI software is the sequencer, a kind of tapeless tape deck that lets you build your own arrangements by recording parts one track at a time. Scoring programs let you print music using conventional notation; some can transcribe music as you play it on a MIDI keyboard. Editor/librarians let you manage, alter, and save a MIDI instrument's sounds by manipulating system-exclusive MIDI data.

Chapter 12
Animation

In This Chapter:

✔ A look at the different uses of animation.

✔ How Mac animation programs simplify the animation process.

✔ Details on how to add sound to your animations.

✔ Additional hardware requirements for creating sophisticated animation.

✔ A hands-on look at animating with HyperCard.

You will see some animation today. It might be a Bugs Bunny cartoon or a NASA simulation of a space station. It might be a three-second TV station identification or a fifteen-minute battle scene from a science-fiction flick. Or it might be an elaborate Disney classic, a satellite's view of an approaching storm system, or a simple list of credits crawling up a movie screen.

Animation is everywhere — and it has been since newspaper cartoonist Winsor McCay thrilled turn-of-the-century theatergoers with his Gertie the Dinosaur cartoon. So novel were McCay's efforts that audiences "suspected some trick with wires," he later wrote.

Today's public is less naive but remains enchanted by watching inanimate objects take on lives of their own. Animation is hot, and computer animation is helping to fuel the fire. Enter the Mac, stage left. The Mac's sharp graphics and fast processor make it a natural platform for creating moving pictures. In this chapter, I'll explore the concepts and challenges behind animating on the Mac and spotlight some animation products.

Why Animate?

You might think the only people who could benefit from Mac animation are in the entertainment business. There's no denying that Mac animation is making show biz inroads. Advertising agencies and production houses use Mac animation programs to mock up animations that will be created on broadcast animation equipment such as the Quantel Paintbox, a broadcast titling and animation workstation commonly used in the video industry. Film and video artists use the Mac to make animated art. Television stations use Mac animations for on-screen graphics.

But the truth is, you don't have to have delusions of Disney to use an animation program. Consider the following scenarios.

❖ To explain the benefits of solar water heaters for a trade show, a marketing manager for a solar heating firm uses an animation program to create a moving diagram in which blue (cold) water enters a solar collector, is heated (it turns red), then flows into a storage tank. This is followed by animated graphs that show how much money and energy customers will save. The complete presentation runs continuously at the show booth.

❖ A developer of educational software wants to show how events combined to create the Cuban missile crisis. The firm creates an animation that uses maps of Cuba and the United States to depict the key events: the missiles arriving on Cuban soil, the spy photos, the naval blockade. The final animation is recorded on a videodisc that students can control using HyperCard. The result is far more engaging than a lecture and reinforces the geography and timing behind the crisis.

❖ An architect bidding on a project creates an animated walk-through that lets clients look at the building from various angles and that simulates entering the lobby from the central courtyard. The clients can better visualize the final product than they could by examining blueprints.

Visualization is the key to each of these scenarios. It's said that more than half the brain's neurons are involved in processing visual input; animation speaks directly to the brain's vision center, allowing — in theory, at least — faster, more complete comprehension of complex concepts and events.

Frame by Frame

Animation relies on a mental phenomenon called *persistence of vision*, which causes an image to remain visible for a fleeting moment after it's disappeared. By presenting the eyes with a rapid sequence of changing images, you create the illusion of motion.

Smooth animation requires that the viewer see at least 16 images, or *frames*, per second. That's easy for any Mac, but creating the frames themselves is, for the most part, your job. Some programs can automatically create certain types of animation, but creating a realistic moving picture still takes time and effort.

Animation programs such as Electronic Arts' Studio/1 and MacroMind Director electronically recreate the techniques behind *cel animation*, the conventional film animation technique patented in 1914 (by another newspaper cartoonist, Earl Hurd) and still used today. With cel animation, a background is drawn or painted on paper, over which are laid transparent sheets of celluloid containing only those components of the frame that have moved since the previous frame. The resulting composite is photographed, a new cel is laid in place, and the process is repeated. Cel animation saves animators time and effort by eliminating the need for them to redraw the background for every frame (as Winsor McCay did for all 10,000 frames of Gertie the Dinosaur).

▲ **Make it Move**
Studio/1's animove feature lets you quickly animate an object. First, specify the number of frames desired (32, in this example). Next, move the selection to its starting position and click Start Key, then move the selection to its ending position and click End Key. Finally, click OK, and Studio/1 generates the intermediate frames.

Studio/1 is an inexpensive monochrome (black and white) paint program with several easy-to-use but powerful animation features. Studio/1's *animpainting* feature works in two ways. You can define any selection — for example, a car — as a brush and then draw the path that you want the selection to follow. Studio/1 then creates the frames needed to move the selection (see the figure "Make it Move"). You can also define a short animated sequence as a brush. For example, if you had a bird that took 20 frames to fully flap its wings, you can define those 20 frames as a brush and then drag it across the sky, thereby eliminating the need to laboriously animate the entire sequence.

Studio/1 provides another animation technique, called *animoving*, that lets you create simple three-dimensional (3-D) animations, such as a company logo that appears in the distance and spins toward you. Creating an animation with the animoving technique involves selecting an image or some text, choosing the Anim 3D command, and then typing values that describe the object's path (see the figure "From Here to There" on the next page).

From Here to There
Studio/1's Anim 3D command lets you create 3-D animations by specifying the direction of a selected object. The Distance boxes let you specify the total distance that a selected object is to move along the X, Y, and Z axes. The Rotation boxes let you specify the total angle (in degrees) that a selection is to be rotated about the three axes.

```
═══════════════════ Anim 3D ═══════════════════
                X        Y        Z      Axes
Distance   [0]      [0]      [0]     [ Object ]    [ Clear ]
Rotation   [0]      [0]      [0]     [ Screen ]    [ Handle ]
─────────────────────────────────────────────────
[ Begin At #1 ]   [ Key #1 ]   Ease In  [0]   [ Preview ]
☐ Chained         [ Key #2 ]   Ease Out [0]   [ Done ]
Mode: [ Normal ]  [ Save ]     Count  [32]   [ Draw ]
```

MacroMind Director

The most popular — and one of the most powerful — Mac animation programs is MacroMind Director. In Director (as well as in its predecessor, Video Works II), the components in an animation — backgrounds, animated objects, sound effects, and so on — are stored in the Cast window. The Cast window is a cinematic data base, an electronic casting office that holds the audio and visual cast of characters in an animation. You add a cast member to an animation by dragging it from the Cast window to the *stage*, or by using the Score window, which graphically depicts the events in the animation (see the figure "In the Director's Chair").

If all this sounds complex, it can be. Fortunately, Director provides a host of labor-saving features for creating animated titles, bar charts, bullet charts, and other special

In the Director's Chair
MacroMind Director stores the components of an animated sequence — objects, sounds, backgrounds, and so on — in the Cast window (bottom right). Behind the Cast window is the Score window, which graphically depicts the events in the sequence. Behind the Score window is the Stage, where the animation takes place.

Automatic Animation

MacroMind Director provides labor-saving features that create animated titles, bar charts, and various text effects. After selecting the desired effect in the Auto Animate dialog box (top), you specify the text style, animation speed, and other options (bottom). Here, the From Right option, which causes each bulleted item to slide into place from the right edge of the screen, is selected.

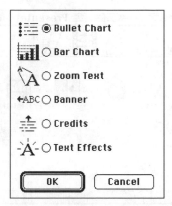

- ● Bullet Chart
- ○ Bar Chart
- ○ Zoom Text
- ○ Banner
- ○ Credits
- ○ Text Effects

[OK]   [Cancel]

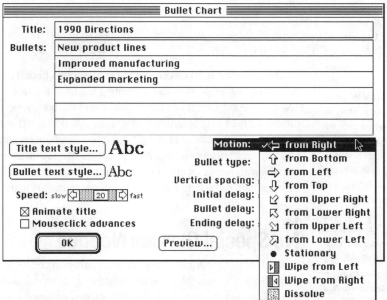

Bullet Chart

Title: 1990 Directions

Bullets:
New product lines
Improved manufacturing
Expanded marketing

[Title text style...] Abc
[Bullet text style...] Abc

Speed: slow ◁ [20] ▷ fast
☒ Animate title
☐ Mouseclick advances

[OK]   [Preview...]

Motion: from Right

Bullet type:
Vertical spacing:
Initial delay:
Bullet delay:
Ending delay:

- from Right
- from Bottom
- from Left
- from Top
- from Upper Right
- from Lower Right
- from Upper Left
- from Lower Left
- Stationary
- Wipe from Left
- Wipe from Right
- Dissolve

effects (see the figure "Automatic Animation"). Director's Overview application lets you streamline the process of creating animated presentations by allowing you to easily combine still graphics, animations, and sounds (see the figure "An Overview of Animation" on the next page).

Director also offers the computer animator's best friend, an *in betweening*, or *tweening*, feature. Tweening lets you animate without crafting every frame by hand. You create the first and last frames (the *key frames*) of a sequence, specifying the beginning and ending appearance of an object, as well as the total number of frames desired for the sequence. Director does the rest, creating the specified number of frames and moving the object from one frame to the next.

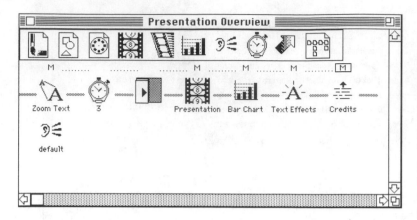

Director (and Studio/1) can also print the frames in an animation. You could film an animation by printing one frame on each page, and then punching the pages with a three-hole paper punch. Next, mount a movie camera on a tripod and point it at a copy stand containing pins that will hold the pages *in register*. Insert each page into the stand, snap a frame, and repeat the process.

There's far more to Director than I've described here. For creating your silicon cast, the program provides color painting features that rival those of a high-end, 32-bit paint program. It has impressive sound features, which I'll describe later. It provides a built-in programming language, called Lingo, that lets you create interactive animations containing HyperCard-like buttons and other on-screen hot spots on which users can click. And it can exchange images and even entire animation sequences with other programs. That latter talent lets you combine Director with three-dimensional drawing programs to create 3-D animations.

No Special Glasses Needed

Much of today's computer-generated animation creates the illusion of three dimensions. A network logo spins toward you, its letters thick and glittering as though cast in platinum. A telephone company commercial takes you on a fantastic voyage through the circuits of a fiber optic network. Seen on a big screen, 3-D animation can almost give you motion sickness.

3-D animation is also complex enough to give a computer headaches. Simulating depth, lighting, and shading requires time-consuming calculations that tax even the fastest Macs. A Mac II-class machine can easily take ten seconds or more to display a complex 3-D image. Multiply that figure by the number of frames needed for smooth animation (at least 16 per second), and the time factor behind 3-D animation becomes all too real. Consequently, no Mac 3-D graphics program provides real-time animation features. You can't draw a car, for example, and watch it move as you move the mouse.

▲ An Overview of Animation

Director's Overview window lets you quickly create and reorganize productions by dragging icons and choosing files. This example production begins with a title that zooms to fill the screen. After a three-second pause, a visual transition leads to a Director animation, which is followed by a bar chart created in Director. Finally, a sparkling title appears followed by a list of credits.

But if you're patient, you can still create stunning 3-D animations. Many 3-D programs let you create animation sequences that you can save and play back or, better still, import into VideoWorks or Director for further embellishment. You'll find animation-oriented features in numerous 3-D programs, including Abvent's Zoom; DynaWare's DynaPerspective; Strata's StrataVision 3d; Visual Information's Dimensions Presenter; Paracomp's ModelShop, Swivel 3D, and Swivel 3D Professional; Silicon Beach Software's Super 3D; and MacroMind Three-D and RenderWorks. And as I mentioned earlier, Electronic Arts' Studio/1 provides reasonably powerful monochrome 3-D animation features.

The most basic way to create frames for 3-D animation is to alternate between moving the objects (or the *camera*, the 3-D world's term for your vantage point) and issuing a command that saves the screen in a graphics format such as MacPaint or PICT. You can then move the resulting frames into Director, VideoWorks, or HyperCard.

An easier alternative to this move-and-save process is to use a program's tweening feature to create frames. Some programs provide a variation on the tweening theme by allowing you to specify not just the beginning and ending key frames, but also *intermediate frames*. Intermediate frames let you use a program's tweening talents to create more complex animation sequences, such as entering a building, turning left, then climbing stairs.

You can save the frames generated by a tweening session in a number of ways. Some programs, including Super 3D and Dimensions Presenter, let you save frames in a document that you can play back using an accompanying projection program. Swivel 3D lets you save frames in the Scrapbook file. Super 3D also supports a special file format for exchanging animation sequences called *PICS*. MacroMind Director can import (and export) animations in numerous formats, including Scrapbook and PICS. Studio/1 can also save animations in PICS format. Some screen saver utilities, including Berkeley Systems' After Dark, can play PICS files. Using this feature, you could create an animated version of your company logo that the screen saver would play. (Screen savers and other utilities are discussed in Chapter 19.)

Animating with HyperCard

You can get a feel for Mac animation techniques using HyperCard. By following the tutorial in the sidebar "Creating a HyperCard Animation" on the next page, you'll be using a method that closely mimics the process of traditional cel animation; it's also similar to the frame-by-frame animation techniques you can use in MacroMind's VideoWorks and Director.

Another way to animate using HyperCard is to create HyperTalk scripts that select objects and move them on the screen. One such script is shown in the figure "Remote-Control Painting." This second technique usually provides faster animation than the frame-by-frame approach. Yet another animation technique involves assigning an icon to a button and then moving the button and changing its icon. You can see this technique in action by playing with the Train Set stack that accompanies the version of HyperCard 2.0 that Claris ships. The puffs of

Creating a HyperCard Animation

To try this tutorial, your HyperCard user level must be set to the Painting level. If it isn't, use the Home stack's arrows to get to the User Preferences card, click the Painting button, then return to the Home stack's first card.

Phase 1: Casting Call

First, you need a character. For this exercise, use the pickup truck in HyperCard 2.0's Art Bits stack.

1. In HyperCard's Home stack, click the Art Bits icon. When the Art Bits index appears, click the entry that reads *Transportation.*

2. Open the Tools menu and activate the selection tool.

3. Find the pickup truck (it's near the upper left corner of the card), and select it by enclosing it within the marquee. Don't select any extra space below the truck's tires.

4. Choose Copy Picture from the Edit menu.

Phase 2: Create a New Stack

Now you're ready to create the stack that will contain the animation.

1. Choose New Stack from the File menu.

2. Uncheck the Copy Current Background box by clicking within it, then type a name such as **Animation Test**, and press Return.

Before pasting the truck into place, you must create a background.

3. Choose Background from the Edit menu. (Stripes appear in the menu bar to indicate you're working on the background.)

4. Open the Tools menu and select the line tool.

5. Hold down the Shift key and draw a horizontal line from one end of the card to the other. This line will be the street upon which your silicon truck will roll.

6. You're finished with the background, so choose Background from the Edit menu again.

Remote-Control Painting

Another way to animate in HyperCard is to use HyperTalk scripts to control HyperCard's painting tools. The script shown here selects an object located near the left edge of the card and roughly 1⅛ inches from the bottom, drags it to the right, reverses its direction, and drags it to the left.

```
on mouseUp
  choose lasso tool
  click at 25,270 with commandKey -- lasso
  set dragSpeed to 200 -- adjust for desired speed
  drag from 25,270 to 490,270 -- move
  doMenu "Flip Horizontal" -- turn around
  drag from 490,270 to 25,270 -- move it back
  doMenu "Flip Horizontal" -- turn it around again
  click at 0,0 -- deselect
  choose browse tool -- restore the browse tool
end mouseUp
```

smoke that spew from the engine are different icons, while the engine itself is a button that moves around the screen.

The best way to add animation to stacks is to create it using an animation program, and then use the HyperCard driver that accompanies MacroMind Director to play the animation from within a stack. The driver uses an XCMD named playMovie that adds to HyperTalk a command of the same name.

7. Add the truck to the scene by choosing Paste Picture.

8. Drag the truck (don't scratch the paint) until it's at the left edge of the card. *Do not deselect the truck; keep it within the marquee.*

9. As it stands, the truck is headed in the wrong direction, so flip it by choosing Flip Horizontal from the Paint menu.

Phase 3: Create the Frames

Now you're ready to create each frame. To do so, you will repeatedly move the truck, copy it to the Clipboard, create a new card, and paste the truck into the new card.

1. Choose Copy Picture from the Edit menu to put the truck and its new position on the Clipboard.

2. Choose New Card from the Edit menu or press Command-N.

3. Paste the truck into the new frame using Command-V.

4. Hold down the Shift key and drag the truck slightly to the right.

5. Copy the truck's position by pressing Command-C.

6. Repeat Steps 2 through 5 at least 20 times. The more frames you create, and the smaller the movements in each frame, the slower the truck will appear to move.

Phase 4: Action!

1. Return to the first card in the movie by choosing First from the Go menu.

2. Display HyperCard's message box by choosing Message from the Go menu.

3. In the message box, type **show all cards** and press Return.

Disney it isn't, but it's a start. From here, you might spruce up the background and add more characters. You might also create a background button whose script shows the movie for you (see the figure "Roll 'Em"). **M**

Roll 'Em

The top script, when attached to a background button, will show all the cards in a HyperCard stack when clicked. For faster animation, add the bottom script to your animation stack. It causes HyperCard to load the images into memory without showing them.

```
on mouseUp
    show all cards
end mouseUp


on openStack
    lock screen      --turn screen updating off
    show all cards --load images into memory
    unlock screen  --restore screen updating
end openStack
```

Read My Lips

With Bright Star Technology's interFace, you can create animated talking heads, called actors, whose mouth movements are synchronized with digitized or Macintalk-generated speech. One aspect of creating an actor involves assigning a different facial expression to a variety of sounds (top). Expressions can be scanned images or ones drawn using interFace's painting tools. After creating an actor, you can use interFace's Speech Sync mode (bottom) to convert text into phonetic codes and create the HyperTalk commands needed to play back digitized sound. The numbers in the HyperTalk command represent timing values that control how many sixtieths of a second each mouth and facial expression appears. As shown here, you can use Farallon Computing's MacRecorder to sample sounds without quitting interFace.

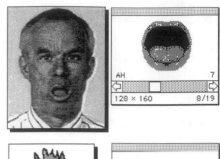

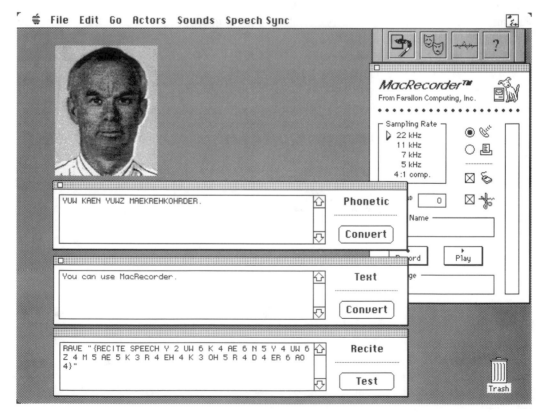

If you're serious about incorporating animation into stacks, you may want to use Silicon Beach's SuperCard instead of HyperCard. Besides offering superior color support and object-oriented drawing features, SuperCard has numerous animation-oriented features, including the ability to *compile* an animation so it runs faster and more smoothly, and the ability to import and export PICS files.

What About Talkies?

The extent to which you can add sound to an animation depends on your animation program, on the nature of the sound, and on your Mac's memory and storage capacities. MacroMind Director has the most impressive audio capabilities of any Mac animation program. Director can use Apple's Macintalk speech driver to produce synthesized speech, and it includes a library of synthesized sound effects. Some are convincing, but most have a decidedly electronic sound to them.

A better way to sound off is to exploit Director's ability to play back sounds that you digitally record, or *sample*, using Farallon Computing's MacRecorder, the microphone provided with the Mac LC and IIsi, or Digidesign's professionally oriented Audiomedia or Sound Tools systems (described in Chapter 32). Director can also control music synthesizers by transmitting commands using the Musical Instrument Digital Interface (MIDI). If you have a MIDI-equipped sampling keyboard, you can use the keyboard to record high-fidelity sound effects and brief snippets of narration, and then trigger the audio by having Director transmit MIDI commands to the keyboard. As for Studio/1, it can't control external MIDI devices, but it does let you add sampled sound to animations.

Animators using HyperCard or Silicon Beach's SuperCard can include synthesized and sampled sound in animations, too. And with Bright Star Technology's interFace, you can create animated "talking heads" whose mouth movements are synchronized with sampled or Macintalk-generated speech (see the figure "Read My Lips"). Animations created with interFace are generally used with HyperCard, but they can be used with most any program that supports HyperCard XCMDs. interFace also provides "hooks" that Pascal and C programmers can use to include interFace-created animations in their programs. Disney Studios recently used interFace (and its predecessor, HyperAnimator) to create the character of Albert in Disney's remake of *The Absent-Minded Professor.* Bright Star Technology says interFace is a preview of an era when computers will use talking heads, sometimes called *agents,* to assist and inform users. We shall see. In the meantime, interFace is a unique product that may appeal to anyone developing educational software.

Farallon Computing's MediaTracks is a specialized animation package designed for creating Macintosh training materials. MediaTracks includes a desk accessory called ScreenRecorder that captures Mac screen activity. You can then use the MediaTracks application to sequence the screens you've captured and add sound recorded with Farallon's MacRecorder or with the microphone that accompanies the Mac IIsi and LC. The MediaTracks Multimedia Pack includes the MacRecorder hardware and its accompanying software.

No Bargain Matinees Here

With its digital audio, color, and 3-D capabilities, the Mac makes a mighty impressive screening room. Unfortunately, the price of admission is high. Sophisticated animation and 3-D drawing programs are costly, and they have nearly insatiable hardware appetites. MacroMind Director, for example, retails for $695 and needs a minimum of 2MB of memory for color work; 4 or 5 MB is a more reasonable amount, especially if you use sampled sound.

To transfer your work to videotape, add a specialized video board that outputs video signals in the *NTSC* format used by consumer and professional video gear (see Chapter 18). If you want to videotape an animation on a frame-by-frame basis — the technique that yields the best quality — you'll need a controller board such as Diaquest's DQ-Animaq. Throw in a high-capacity hard disk for storing your movies, and you may not be able to afford popcorn.

Of course, cost is relative. A maxed-out Mac IIfx costs less than the down payment on a Quantel Paintbox. For animation professionals, a Mac animation system is a bargain.

And I don't want to discourage would-be animators on a budget. If you're content to create black-and-white animations and view them on-screen (or even film them frame-by-frame from the screen), you can get by with a smaller system. Some of the programs I've discussed run — or at least trot — on a 1MB Mac Plus. And if you have HyperCard, you already have a serviceable animation program.

Some traditionalists in the animation world decry computer animation, just as some musicians deride synthesizers and MIDI. I'd hate to see traditional cel animation disappear (and it shows no signs of doing so), but I also enjoy the distinctive, ethereal look that 3-D computer animation provides. Computer animation combines the magic of moving pictures with the art and science of mathematics and technology. Winsor McCay would have loved it.

Summary:

✔ While it's true that the entertainment and advertising industries use animation extensively, you don't have to be a film or video artist to use an animation program. Animation can be used to visualize something in 3-D, or simply to illustrate a concept.

✔ An image created in an animation program is called a frame. Smooth animation requires that the viewer see at least 16 frames per second. Many animation programs electronically recreate the techniques of cel animation, the conventional film animation technique patented in 1914.

✔ The extent to which you can add sound to an animation depends on your animation program, the nature of the sound, and your Mac's memory and storage capacities. One way to add sound is to use Apple's Macintalk speech driver to produce synthesized speech. Another way is to use a program like MacroMind Director to play back sounds that you digitally record.

✔ Sophisticated animation and 3-D drawing programs are costly and have nearly insatiable hardware appetites. Additional hardware to consider includes a video board that lets you transfer your work to videotape, a controller board to videotape an animation frame-by-frame, and a high-capacity hard disk for storing your movies.

Chapter 13
Telecommunications

In This Chapter:

✔ Two different approaches of telecommunicating.

✔ Details on what you'll find on most information services.

✔ How to choose an information service that meets your needs.

✔ The modem: a computer's link to the online world.

✔ A look at the two basic categories of communications software.

With some inexpensive hardware and software, your Mac can use a phone line to reach out and touch other computers. You can exchange files with a colleague at the office or a friend in another city. You can dial up *bulletin boards*, electronic meeting places for hobbyists and user group members. You can send *electronic mail* to friends and coworkers, even if they don't have computers. You can transmit documents to desktop publishing service bureaus for output on their typesetting equipment. And you can subscribe to any number of *information services* from which you can access current news and vast libraries of free and nearly free software.

Computer bulletin boards and information services have been around for years, but until recently they didn't take advantage of the Mac's appealing graphics and easy operating style. Information services were designed to communicate with any brand of computer, and that meant forgoing the mouse and returning to the dark ages of typed commands such as **cat/des/age:90/key:Mac.**

That's changing. The Mac has inspired a new generation of communications services that you control using icons and all the other trappings of the Mac's graphical interface. Some clever programmers have also managed to graft friendly interfaces to older, text-oriented services. In this chapter, I'll explore the new look of Mac communications and what you need to go online.

Private Lines and Party Lines

You can telecommunicate on two basic levels: directly with another computer (which may be anything from another personal computer to a Cray supercomputer), or through an intermediary such as an information service or bulletin board (see the figure "Two Ways to Connect"). With the direct route, you arrange the communications session ahead of time by determining who will call whom, and then setting up your communications gear accordingly. A business traveler might use this technique to transfer a file to a colleague at the home office.

Communicating directly costs only the phone call, but it forces you to contend with several communications technicalities, such as the choice of a *file-transfer protocol*, which causes data to be "proofread" to eliminate garbled files as it's received. Plan on making a troubleshooting call to iron out the wrinkles. Also plan for some scheduling predicaments: you and your fellow communicator should be at your machines to ensure that things go smoothly, and that's inconvenient if you're in different time zones.

An information service is a more convenient and more flexible way to communicate. When connected to one, your Mac is talking to a room full of refrigerator-size *mainframe* computers. Those mainframes may, in turn, be talking to thousands of your fellow subscribers simultaneously, divvying up their time between each one. It's called *timesharing,* and it's one of the

Two Ways to Connect

Access number

Switching network

Information service

One way to communicate is to call another modem-equipped computer directly (top). Most people, however, use information services as intermediaries. To connect to a service, you dial the *access number* closest to you to connect to a *switching network,* which, in turn, communicates with the service's computers. Some services operate their own switching networks, while others use commercial networks such as Telenet, Tymnet, and in Canada, Datapac.

oldest ways of getting computer power to individuals and small companies. (Indeed, some information services, including the largest, CompuServe, began life years ago by selling mainframe computer time to businesses for payroll management and similar tasks.)

Information services, especially ones with graphical *front ends* — Mac software programs that help you access and navigate through the service — provide some insulation from the cold world of communications technicalities. And information? It's there, too — in quantities that may overwhelm you at first and cost you a fair sum in *connect charges* after that.

Information, Please

An information service is a post office, library, stock broker, travel agent, meeting hall, computer club, and software flea market all rolled into one phone call. Here's what you'll find on most services.

❖ *Electronic mail* You can exchange messages and disk files with other subscribers in a flash, and cut your express courier bills in the process. Simply *upload* files and messages to the service; recipients can *download* them at their convenience. With many services, you can exchange *E-mail* with other subscribers only. Some services, however, provide *gateways* to other services. CompuServe and Connect users, for example, can exchange mail with MCI Mail subscribers. Other services, including MCI Mail and GEnie, can combine E-mail with paper mail: transmit your message to the service, and it's laser printed and then mailed or delivered by courier. MCI Mail can also send your E-mail to any fax machine.

❖ *News* Most services offer up-to-the-minute news from wire services such as Associated Press, United Press International, and Reuters; and from newspapers such as the *Wall Street Journal* and the *Washington Post*. The NewsNet information service specializes in government and industry news, offering the full text of hundreds of specialized newsletters. Most services let you locate items of interest by typing sets of *keywords.* For example, the keyword phrase "offshore and regulation" would snag stories on offshore drilling laws. Some services also let you set up electronic clipping folders: specify your keywords, and the service constantly scans the wires for you and saves stories containing them. When you go back online, you'll find the relevant stories waiting.

❖ *Research* CompuServe has the largest electronic research room of all the major consumer information services. You can summon detailed information on nearly 10,000 publicly traded companies and demographic reports on thousands of towns and cities. Also available are data from the Bureau of the Census, transcripts of television news programs, thousands of articles from *Consumer Reports* and numerous computer publications (including *Macworld*), and online versions of *Books in Print* and *Who's Who*. And on several services, you'll find all ten million words of *Grolier's Academic American Encyclopedia*. There are also specialized research-oriented services such as Knight-Ridder Company's Dialog.

❖ *Travel information* Most services have online travel agents that can help you plan trips. On CompuServe, you can search for fellow subscribers willing to swap houses for vacations. Frequent flyers can access the Official Airline Guide (OAG) database, the same flight-information service travel agents use.

❖ *Shopping* Yes, you can say "charge it" online. CompuServe and GEnie both have online malls containing music and video stores, florists, pharmacies, and cookie shops. On CompuServe you'll find the Boston Computer Exchange, a network that matches used computer equipment with potential buyers. GEnie and America Online offer gateway access to Comp-U-Store, which offers member discounts on 250,000 products.

❖ *Special-interest forums* Here you can communicate with other subscribers on a wide range of issues, including technical questions on using Mac hardware and software. You can also download megabytes of software, including fonts, scanned images, digitized sounds, utilities, desk accessories, and the latest version of the Mac's system software. Most programs are free, but some are *shareware*. You're expected to pay a modest fee (usually under $25) if you decide to keep a shareware program. Most major software and hardware firms also operate forums, offering technical tips and program updates. All the major services have lively Mac forums, but CompuServe's is the largest.

Choosing a Service

Choosing an information service involves assessing your budget as well as your information needs and then deciding how important a Mac-like interface is to you. Initial membership costs and connect charges vary depending on the service and when you use it. With most services, evening and weekend rates are lower than daytime weekday rates. One exception is the Prodigy service, a joint effort between IBM and Sears (you've heard of them), which charges a fixed rate of $9.95 per month instead of an hourly rate. But Prodigy lacks a Mac-like front end, so you pay for its potentially lower cost by forgoing much of the Mac's friendliness. (See the table "At Your Service" for information on each service's sign-up and connect charges.)

Your online intentions should be a major factor in your choice. Businesspeople might lean toward MCI Mail, Dow Jones/News Retrieval, and NewsNet, while Mac hobbyists who want access to shareware may find CompuServe or GEnie more appealing. People who work in the Mac field as consultants, dealers, writers, and developers might use AppleLink, Apple's worldwide communications network. Businesses and organizations might consider Connect; although it's sold to individuals, it's primarily geared toward

At Your Service

	America Online	CompuServe	Connect	GEnie
Sign-up fee*	none	$39.95 (includes $25 connect time)	$99.95 (includes one free hour)	$29.95
Includes communications software	yes	no	yes	no
Prime hours	6 am - 6 pm	—	7 am - 7 pm weekdays	8 am - 6 pm
Prime connect charge	$10 per hr. (all speeds)	$12.50 per hour (all speeds and times)	9600 bps, $14 per hour; other speeds $10 per hour plus 3¢ per 1000 characters sent	$18 per hour (all speeds)
Discount hours	6 pm - 6 am plus weekends and major holidays	—	7 pm - 7 am plus weekdays and major holidays	6 pm - 8 am plus weekends and major holidays
Discount connect charge‡	$5 per hour	—	9600 bps, $7 per hour; other speeds, $5 per hour plus 2¢ per 1000 characters sent	300 bps, $5 per hour 1200 bps, $6 per hour 2400 bps, $10 per hour
Monthly fee	$5.95 (includes one free discount-time hour)	$1.50 $10 for Executive Service (provides additional options)	none	none

* Many modems and communications-software packages include coupons offering reduced or no sign-up fee. Also, Connect offers volume discounts.

‡Charges listed do not include switching network fees or local phone charges, if any. Prices are current as of early 1991.

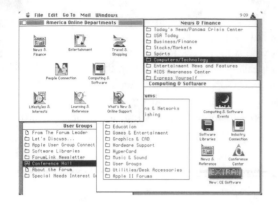

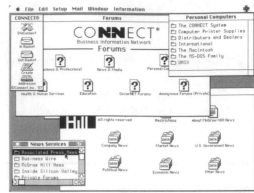

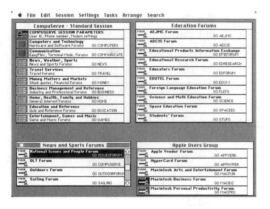

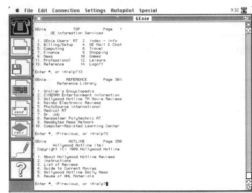

The Face of Communications

Four information services: (top left) the Mac-like America Online; (top right) Connect Business Information Network; (bottom left) CompuServe, as seen through CompuServe's Navigator front-end program; and (bottom right) GEnie, a text-only service, seen here through Hayes's Smartcom II.

organizations wanting to set up forums for their members. Connect can even create customized windows and icons for your group. A sales staff, for example, might use a forum whose icons let them file sales reports and read news and product information from the home office.

Then there's the interface issue. Some services take better advantage of the Mac's operating style than others (see the figures "The Face of Communications"). America Online takes the prize, with an attractive and easy interface that makes excellent use of the Mac's personality traits. The Connect service sports an attractive interface, too, with another bonus: it's also available for IBM PCs and compatibles. The service looks and works the same on both systems, making it a good choice for businesses that mix Macs and PCs. (A PC version of America Online is also in the works.)

As for CompuServe, MCI Mail, Dow Jones, and GEnie, their interfaces are, well, not so pretty. All are text-oriented services that require typed commands in response to text menus. However, Mac front-end software is available for each

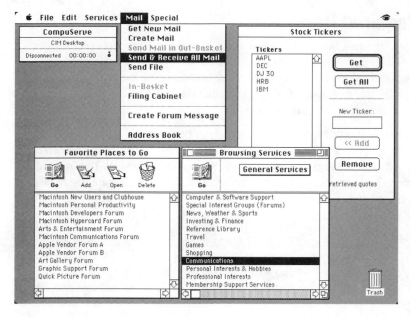

one. CompuServe's Navigator provides point-and-click access to some (but not all) of the service's nooks and crannies. Navigator can't compare to America Online or Connect, but it is an alternative to typing commands. A Mac front-end program called CompuServe Information Manager is more powerful (see the figure "CompuServe Makeover"). For MCI Mail and Dow Jones, consider Dow Jones Software's Desktop Express and E-Z Online packages. GEnie users can download a free (although somewhat crude) program called MacGEnie from the service's Mac forum.

▲ **CompuServe Makeover**

The CompuServe Information Manager is a friendly facade for CompuServe. You choose menu commands and double-click on forum names, and CompuServe Information Manager sends the commands that CompuServe expects to see. The program also offers a terminal mode that lets experienced users control CompuServe conventionally.

My personal picks? If you want to subscribe to just one service, make it CompuServe. Its interface isn't the prettiest, but its range of services is unmatched. It also boasts the largest number of subscribers, with over a half-million compared to less than 100,000 for most of the other services. If an easy, Mac-like interface is important to you, choose America Online. America Online is a good choice for *Macworld* readers, too: *Macworld* has a forum on America Online called Macworld Online, where you can search through and read reviews and news stories from past issues of *Macworld* and exchange ideas with *Macworld* editors, contributors, and fellow readers.

But limiting yourself to just one service is like reading only one newspaper or watching only one television station. Because you use the same hardware (and in some cases the same software) to communicate with each service, and you're generally only billed for the time you spend online, subscribing to additional services probably won't greatly increase your communications expenses.

Required Hardware

A computer's link to the online world is a *modem* (pronounced *mow*-dem). A modem converts, or *modulates*, the data coming from the Mac into audio tones that phone lines can carry, and *demodulates* the incoming tones into data the Mac can comprehend. Indeed, the word *modem* is a short form of the words *modulate* and *demodulate*.

Direct connect modems attach between a phone jack and the Mac's modem or printer port, and have a jack into which you can plug a telephone. *Acoustic* modems contain cups into which you snug a telephone handset. They're nearly extinct due to their susceptibility to background noise, but they are handy in such places as hotels, where phones are often wired directly instead of plugged into jacks.

Most direct-connect modems are small external boxes that you attach to the Mac's rear-panel modem connector and a telephone jack. The Mac Portable and the SE and II families can also accommodate *internal modems,* which live inside the case, providing more portability and a less-cluttered desk, but no *status lights,* which help you monitor the flow of data between machines. If you're shopping for an external modem, look for one that provides status lights. They aren't essential, but they can help you troubleshoot a sticky file-transfer session by showing when a connection exists and when data is being sent and received. Like a car without gauges, a modem without status lights doesn't tell you much when problems arise.

Place of residence aside, the primary difference between modems is the speed at which they transfer data. Most modems transmit data at 1200 bits per second (bps) or 2400 bps. 9600-bps modems are available, but most information services don't support this transmission rate. And because their standards are still evolving, not all 9600-bps modems can talk with each other. For general-purpose communications, a 2400-bps modem is your best bet. (For some background on how modems transfer data and how their speed is measured, see the sidebar "Bits and Bauds").

Although the industry standards are the ruggedly built (and pricey) Hayes Smartmodems by Hayes Microcomputer Products, you'll probably do just as well with a less expensive modem. But make sure that it's fully *Hayes-compatible* — that it understands the *Hayes command set* of dialing and connection commands.

A modem's price depends on its speed and brand. The 1200-bps, Hayes-compatible Apple Personal Modem retails for $279; the faster Apple Modem 2400 lists for $499. Hayes-compatible 2400-bps modems from firms such as

Prometheus, Anchor Automation, and Practical Peripherals often sell through mail-order firms for under $200. Some modems also include *communications software*, which tells the modem when to dial and hang up and helps you manage everything in between.

Several modems are available that do more than just modulate and demodulate. If you have several Macs interconnected on a network, consider Shiva's NetModem, which can be shared by all the machines on your network (see Chapter 40). And if you'd like to exchange faxes as well as files, you'll want a *fax modem* such as Dove's DoveFax, Orchid Technology's OrchidFAX, or Abaton's InterFax 12/48 or 24/96. A fax modem lets you send documents you create to a standard fax machine without having to print the documents and run them through a scanning device. If you do have a scanner, you can scan hard copy and transmit the results using the fax modem, too.

Software for Communicating

Communications software falls into two basic categories: customized front-end programs such as those used by Connect and America Online (as well as Navigator and Desktop Express); and *terminal emulation* programs such as Hayes's Smartcom II, Software Venture's MicroPhone II, and The FreeSoft Company's White Knight.

Bits and Bauds

The speed at which modems exchange data is measured in terms of *baud rate*, also called *bit rate*. Any character on the Mac's keyboard can be represented by a combination of eight bits, or a *byte*. Internally, the Mac shuttles these bits between memory and microprocessor and disk drives in *parallel*: The eight bits travel alongside each other, each in its own wire, like marchers in a parade striding eight abreast. When conversing with a modem or printer, however, the Mac sends bits in *serial* form — one bit after another, in single file, like commuters threading through a subway turnstyle.

To show the computer at the other end of the line where one byte ends and the next begins, a communications program adds extra bits, a *start bit* and a *stop bit*, to the eight bits in the byte itself. This means that it takes roughly ten bits to send one character. One "baud" equals one bit per second, so you can calculate how many characters a modem sends per second by dividing the bit rate by ten. Many people prefer the acronym *bps* because *baud* is old-fashioned and less precise. **M**

Front-end programs are tailored to a specific service; you can't use America Online's software to access Connect any more than you can use your front door to enter your neighbor's house. Terminal-emulation programs, however, are general-purpose communicators: they can talk to just about any computer that answers. You can use terminal-emulation programs to access CompuServe, MCI Mail, Dow Jones, and GEnie in their native text modes and to tap into hobbyist bulletin boards. You can't use a terminal-emulation program to access a strictly graphical service such as America Online, Connect, or AppleLink.

Both types of communications software are intermediaries between the Mac and the modem. When you start a communications session, the program transmits dialing commands to the modem, then waits for the modem to report when a connection is made and at what speed.

After the connection is made, however, each type of program works differently. A front-end program performs much of its work behind the scenes, receiving instructions from the service telling it what icons and windows to display and sending commands to the service as you click icons and choose menu commands. A terminal-emulation program, in contrast, simply displays incoming text on the screen and transmits your typing to the other computer.

Most terminal-emulation programs also provide features that streamline your online sessions. *Script languages* let you automate communications sessions by transmitting commands for you (see the sidebar "Automating Communications"). A script might dial a service in the middle of the night (when rates are low), sign on, retrieve waiting mail, and then sign off. Less ambitious scripts might simply take you to a specific forum when you choose a menu command or type a Command-key shortcut. With careful scripting, you can create your own front end for text-oriented services. (Indeed, Dow Jones's E-Z Online software was created using the powerful scripting language in Prometheus Products' MacKnowledge.)

Hayes's Smartcom II is my favorite terminal-emulation program. It's elegantly designed and easy to use, although it lacks some of the features found in MicroPhone II and White Knight. (The latter was formerly called Red Ryder and is the Mac world's shareware success story. Its fervent followers have inspired programmer Scott Watson to release updates at frequent intervals. Some joke that you don't buy White Knight, you subscribe to it.) If you plan to explore text-only services and bulletin boards extensively, you might be better served by MicroPhone II or White Knight.

Toward the Online Age

When the first information service appeared, industry gurus began forecasting a day when people would do all their banking, learning, and shopping online. That day hasn't arrived — partly because the refinement and widespread acceptance of a technology always takes longer than its initial birth, but mostly because you can't endorse a check, go on a field trip, or try on clothes over the phone.

Automating Communications

Script languages let you automate communications sessions by transmitting commands to the service that you would otherwise have to type. Here are portions of two scripts that sign on to CompuServe — the script as it appears in MicroPhone II (top), and in Smartcom II (bottom). Both scripts wait for certain incoming text (such as "Password:") and then transmit text you specify as if you typed it.

Smartcom II's script language is easier to use but less powerful than those of MicroPhone II, White Knight, and Prometheus Products' Acknowledge. The latter three programs also offer *learn modes:* they can watch over your shoulder and record scripts based on your actions. You can use the resulting script as is or modify it by adding a delay or additional features. MicroPhone II and MacKnowledge also provide features that let you execute scripts one step at a time — useful when a script isn't behaving as you expected.

The script languages in MicroPhone II, White Knight, and MacKnowledge also let you create custom pull-down menu commands and icons that, when chosen, execute scripts. You could use these features to create your own customized front end for a text-oriented service such as CompuServe. Prometheus's MacKnowledge software does just that for not only CompuServe, but also for Dow Jones/News Retrieval, MCI Mail, GEnie, and other services.

Creating graphical front-end software isn't a trivial task. For one thing, you need familiarity with basic Mac

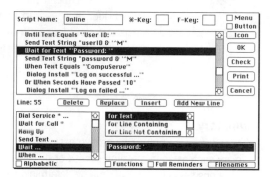

programming concepts such as creating and responding to choices in pull-down menus and dialog boxes (see Chapter 33). What's more, you need to anticipate every event that might occur during a session — from data-garbling static to busy signals. If you don't, your scripts will operate unreliably. **M**

Still, communications is slowly becoming a consumer commodity. Many banks offer bank-by-modem services, and the Internal Revenue Service is expanding a test program wherein taxpayers can file their returns by modem and get their refunds faster. But to some people, the real consumer communications age won't arrive until telecommunications meets television. Imagine looking up the latest online news and seeing a television news report instead of a window full of text, or browsing an online encyclopedia and not only reading about Martin Luther King Jr. but also seeing and hearing him give his most famous speeches. This kind of interactive news and video exists today, thanks to videodiscs and HyperCard, but it's unlikely to meet the online world for some time.

This doesn't mean today's world of communications doesn't have a great deal to offer. It does, and I encourage you to sample it. If you do, drop me an E-mail note and let me know how you use it. On CompuServe, I'm 76174,556; on America Online, I'm JimHeid; and on MCI Mail, JHEID.

Summary:

✔ You can telecommunicate on two basic levels: directly with another computer, or through an intermediary such as an information service or bulletin board. Using the direct route, you manage the communications session ahead of time by determining who will call whom and then setting up the communications gear accordingly. A less direct but more convenient way to telecommmunicate is to use an information service.

✔ Most information services provide electronic mail (exchanging messages and disk files with other subscribers); news (from popular newspapers and wire services); research (consumer articles and demographic reports, for example); travel (online travel agents); shopping (online malls); and special-interest forums (communicating with other subscribers on a wide range of issues).

✔ Choosing an information service involves assessing your budget as well as your information needs and then deciding how important a Mac-like interface is to you.

✔ A modem is the computer's link to the online world. It converts, or modulates, the data coming from the Mac into audio tones that phone lines can carry, and demodulates the incoming tones into data the Mac can comprehend.

Chapter 14

Optical Character Recognition

In This Chapter:

✔ An explanation of how OCR bridges the gap between the Mac and the printed page.

✔ A sampling of the various OCR applications.

✔ Trainable, nontrainable, and automatic OCR software: which will meet your needs?

✔ Scanners: the hardware half of the OCR equation.

✔ What to look for when shopping for OCR software.

Every so often, you're reminded that the Mac is incompatible with the most widely used data-storage medium in the world: paper. This revelation might dawn when you have to laboriously retype a financial table from last year's annual report, or when you spend hours pawing through magazines to locate something you read a few months ago. Wouldn't it be wonderful if you could apply the Mac's sorting, searching, and storing skills to the printed material that touches your life every day?

I have some good news and some bad news. The good news is that you can bridge the gap between the Mac and the printed page, thanks to *optical character recognition,* or *OCR,* software. When teamed with a hardware add-on called a *scanner,* OCR software lets a Mac read, or *recognize,* printed pages and create files containing their text. You can edit the resulting text, reformat it, run it through spelling checkers, save it, or paste it into databases or HyperCard stacks for quick searching. Pop a page into your scanner, click a button, and voilà — instant text, ready to be sliced and diced as you see fit.

The bad news is that it isn't as rosy as all that. Some OCR programs read certain kinds of text better than others, and to get the fastest, most accurate results, you need to match the program to the OCR task at hand. What's more, OCR software craves memory and processing power. Many OCR programs will run (albeit slowly) on Mac Pluses and SEs, but extensive OCR work almost demands one of the fastest Macs, the IIci or the IIfx.

Finally, OCR isn't a magic potion that automatically saves time and keystrokes. The best results come from practice and experience, and still require careful proofreading. If you're compiling a digital library of text scanned from publications, you must develop an electronic filing system that lets you find what you've scanned. You also need a hard disk that can hold it all, and a backup regimen to keep it safe. In this chapter, I'll describe how OCR programs work, and spotlight some of the features you'll find in them.

Who Needs to Read?

OCR isn't a panacea, but that doesn't mean it isn't useful. Here's a sampling of OCR applications.

❖ A printing service bureau or typesetting company uses OCR for clients who submit copy on paper rather than on disk. Of course, proofreading is still essential — no matter how you use OCR — but not having to retype all that text can save a lot of time, thereby cutting typesetting costs.

❖ A law firm scans legal briefings and contracts that were produced before the office became computerized. Having those old documents on disk allows the firm to reuse sections of them as needed, and it allows for fast searching of client histories.

❖ A stock brokerage scans company prospectuses and pastes the numeric data into Microsoft Excel to generate graphs that show companies' financial status. The text from the prospectuses and from annual reports is pasted into a HyperCard stack that brokers can use to advise their clients.

❖ An office that used to distribute weekly photocopies of newspaper and trade-magazine clippings now scans them and stores the resulting text files on a network file server, where they are available to everyone. Employees can quickly search the electronic clippings and copy key sections for inclusion in reports or distribution to others. The information is more accessible, and the office saves filing space as well as paper and photocopying costs. And cutting paper use benefits the environment as much as it does the bottom line.

❖ A corporation's human resources department receives hundreds of résumés each day. They're scanned, and the resulting text is imported into a database manager, which sorts them into job categories and then creates a text file for each category. The resulting files are forwarded via electronic mail to appropriate personnel managers in offices across the country. No photocopying, no express courier charges, just increased efficiency.

These scenarios share a common thread: OCR used department-wide or company-wide, not at individual desks. That isn't to say individuals can't benefit from OCR; they can, if they have enough text to scan or their typing is bad enough. But given its cost and the time required to use it, OCR makes the most sense when a group of people can share its benefits — as they do with the office photocopier.

How OCR Programs Work

The aforementioned scenarios involve a variety of hard-copy originals, from manuscripts and contracts to résumés and magazine pages. Manuscripts and contracts aren't too tricky; they are often produced in a simple typewriter font such as Courier. Magazine and newspaper pages are another matter. They can use just about any font and any format, from justified left and right margins to irregularly shaped columns that wrap around a photograph or illustration. And résumés might be the ultimate formatting wild card. You never know what fonts you'll find, and you might receive a photocopy rather than an original.

It's this variety of hard copy that makes it important to match the OCR program to the scanning task at hand. The figure "OCR Approaches Compared" on the next page illustrates the differences between the three basic categories of OCR software: *nontrainable, trainable,* and *automatic,* also known as *omnifont.* (The sidebar, "Choosing OCR Software" on page 187 describes some additional issues to consider when shopping for OCR software.)

Mix 'n' Match

Nontrainable programs generally use the simplest recognition technique, *matrix matching,* in which the program compares each character to a library of *templates, type tables,* or *matrices* for specific fonts and type sizes. Think of those tests where children insert different-shaped pegs into matching holes in a pegboard. Now imagine the OCR program trying to insert each character it has scanned into a hole shaped like a letter, number, or other symbol. When a character seems to fit a particular hole, the OCR program calls it a match.

Matrix matching is relatively fast and doesn't require a great deal of memory or processing power — matrix-matching programs run comfortably on a 1MB Mac Classic, Plus, or SE. (Comparing each character to hundreds of shapes seems arduous, but it's a breeze compared to the recognition techniques used by automatic programs.) Matrix matching is also quite accurate — provided you try to read only those fonts and type sizes your program knows about. If you try to scan a different font or size, performance slows and errors soar as the program attempts to hammer characters into holes they don't quite fit in.

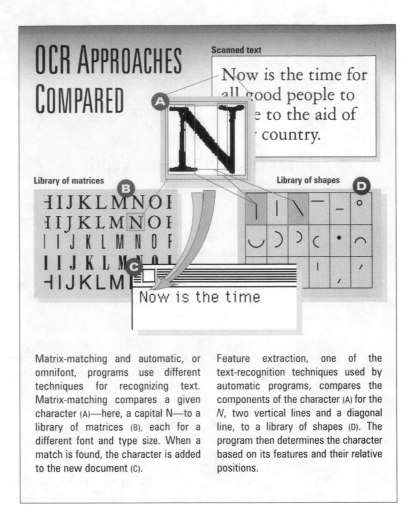

OCR APPROACHES COMPARED

Scanned text

Now is the time for all good people to e to the aid of country.

Library of matrices

HIJKLMNOF
HIJKLMNOF
IIJKLMNOF
IIJKLMNOF
HIJKLME

Library of shapes

Now is the time

Matrix-matching and automatic, or omnifont, programs use different techniques for recognizing text. Matrix-matching compares a given character (A)—here, a capital N—to a library of matrices (B), each for a different font and type size. When a match is found, the character is added to the new document (C).

Feature extraction, one of the text-recognition techniques used by automatic programs, compares the components of the character (A) for the N, two vertical lines and a diagonal line, to a library of shapes (D). The program then determines the character based on its features and their relative positions.

One of the better nontrainable packages for the Mac is DEST Corporation's Publish Pac. It recognizes common typewriter fonts — Courier, Elite, Letter Gothic, Pica, and so on — as well as 10-point Times Roman and the output of several popular dot matrix printers, including Apple's ImageWriters. DEST also offers an automatic program called Recognize, which is unique among OCR programs in that it works with Claris Corporation's XTND file-translation technology. This allows you to save scanned text in a vast variety of formats that can be read by Mac and IBM PC programs. Other OCR programs support only a few popular Mac word processing and spreadsheet formats. (For more information on XTND, see Chapter 29.)

Reading Lessons

Trainable programs are matrix matching programs that can learn. With programs such as Olduvai Corporation's Read-It and Inovatic's ReadStar II Plus, you can create your own digital pegboards for new fonts as you encounter them. Trainable programs combine the less-demanding hardware requirements of matrix-matching programs with at least some of the flexibility of automatic programs.

But *trainable* means you train it, and that means work. It might take only a few minutes to train a program to read a document with one or two fonts, but it could take an hour or two to teach it to read a typical magazine page. The program will be able to apply its newfound knowledge to future documents, but that's no consolation if you never need to scan those fonts and sizes again.

Choosing OCR Software

Here's a checklist of useful features to look for when you go chopping for OCR software:

❖ *Direct support for your scanner* lets you scan pages and recognize text using just one program. If an OCR program can not directly control your scanner, you need to scan pages using the software that accompanies the scanner, and then save them in a format the OCR program can read — a time-consuming approach.

❖ *A built-in editor* lets you review and alter the resulting text without switching to a word processor. Search-and-replace commands are useful for correcting problems that occur throughout, such as when a *w* is read as *vv*.

❖ *Format recognition* retains formatting attributes such as boldface, underlining, italics, centering, and justification. Some programs can also distinguish between multiple columns, allowing you to read them as a single table or as snaking (magazine-style) columns.

❖ *Support for multiple file formats* increases the odds that you'll be able to move recognized text into another application while retaining its formatting. Some programs can save documents in text-only format; others support popular word processing and spreadsheet formats.

❖ *A spelling checker* helps with (but doesn't eliminate) proofreading. Some OCR programs provide spelling checkers that are tuned to look for substitution and other typical OCR-oriented errors.

❖ *Graphics recognition* lets you save the graphics that appear in an original document. This can be useful if, for example, you're producing a new version of a printed manual containing illustrations.

❖ *Background operation under MultiFinder or System 7.0* lets the OCR program decipher a page while you work in another application. Some programs also offer a *batch* mode that lets you scan a stack of pages, but defer the actual recognition process until a later time.

❖ *Landscape support* lets you scan documents printed in landscape orientation (for example, 11 by 8½ instead of 8½ by 11). **M**

Still, there are applications for which a trainable program is best. Consider a manuscript produced on a typewriter that types a defective character — for example, an *e* whose crossbar always prints too lightly. An automatic program will probably always misidentify the character as a *c,* but a trainable program can be taught to recognize it. Trainable programs are also well suited to large projects that involve a lot of scanning, such as books or catalogs. The program will be finely tuned to the fonts at hand, and that can boost performance and accuracy. Finally, if you don't have a multimegabyte Mac II, a trainable program might be your best bet; most will run on 1MB Mac Pluses, Classics, and SEs.

Pick a Font, Any Font

The most versatile OCR programs are automatic packages, such as Caere Corporation's OmniPage, Xerox Imaging Systems' AccuText, and CTA's Scan-Reader. Instead of simply searching through those electronic pegboards to find a hole that seems to be a match, automatic programs use a whole bag of recognition tricks to read just about any font and type size.

With one such technique, *feature extraction,* the program studies the shape of a character's components — its stems, loops, bowls, and so forth — and compares them to the program's internal knowledge of letterforms. For example, if an automatic program sees a character with a vertical stem that descends below the baseline and has a loop attached to its upper-right side, the program knows it's found a *p.* There are significant variations between fonts — some have ornamental serifs, some have heavier stems than others — but generalized descriptions like this one apply to all characters.

But there are typefaces that bend these rules, and poor-quality documents that make them difficult to enforce. In such cases, an automatic program may resort to additional techniques such as: *topographical analysis,* which examines the character's shape for recognizable characteristics, and *context recognition* (also called *context intelligence*), which uses built-in rules and *dictionaries* that know, for example, that if the program recognizes a *q,* the next character is likely to be a *u.* Many nontrainable and trainable OCR programs also use this latter technique.

Automatic programs employ other tricks in their quest for text, but just the techniques I've described require a considerable amount of memory and processing punch. Caere's OmniPage and Xerox's AccuText, for example, demand a 68020- or 68030-based Mac and 4MB of memory.

And even setups like these don't deliver top OCR performance. For that, there are products like Calera Recognition Systems' TopScan for the Macintosh software and Compound Document Processor (CDP) hardware, which contains four 68020 microprocessors and a battery of other specialized chips designed for OCR. According to Calera, a CDP with TopScan can recognize about 2700 words per minute.

Another high-end package, Caere's Parallel Reader, uses not a Macintosh, but an IBM-compatible computer containing four processor boards, each of which packs the computing power of a Mac IIcx. The four processors work together to provide, according to Caere, a scanning speed of 2500 words per minute.

CDPs cost between $17,000 and $30,000, while the Parallel Reader goes for $10,995. They're steep, to be sure, but if shared in a large office where someone would otherwise do a great deal of retyping or photocopying, they can, over time, pay for themselves in labor savings.

Scanning the Field

I've said little about the hardware half of the OCR equation — the scanner, which uses a mechanism not too different from a photocopier or fax machine to examine a page and create a digital image of its contents. I'll examine scanner technology in detail in Chapter 39, but from an image-scanning, not OCR, perspective. Until then, here's a quick look at the field.

Sheetfed or *edge-feed* scanners such as DEST Corporation's PC Scan 2000 and the 2020 accept a page through a front-panel slot and move it through the scanner using a set of rubber rollers. *Flatbed* scanners such as Hewlett-Packard's ScanJet Plus and the Apple Scanner look like small copiers, with a lid covering a piece of glass upon which you lay the original document. Flatbed scanners can accommodate books and other originals too thick to fit through a sheetfed scanner's rollers. For accuracy, it's important to keep the glass spotless. Many sheetfed and flatbed scanners accept *automatic document feeders,* which hold a stack of pages and feed them to the scanner as needed — useful for high-volume OCR work.

Hand-held, or *hand,* scanners such as Logitech's ScanMan Model 32 and Thunderware's LightningScan 400 are small boxes that you roll across an original page. Costing only a few hundred dollars, hand scanners are inexpensive compared to the other types (whose prices start at $1000), but hand scanners have limitations. You need to move the scanner at a slow and steady pace — about an inch per second — to get good results, and you can scan only a few inches of a document at a time.

When you're buying a scanner for image-scanning tasks, it's important to assess how many levels of grey it recognizes — Apple's, for example, recognizes only 16 compared to 256 for Hewlett-Packard's ScanJet Plus. For OCR work, grey levels aren't important, since you always use the scanner's high-contrast, or *line-art*, mode. Still, you'll probably want to do some image scanning, too, so keep that grey-level figure in mind.

Meeting and Adjusting Your Expectations

When shopping for an OCR system, take along several test documents, preferably ones similar to the documents you plan to scan. Don't just take war-torn, barely legible documents in an attempt to stump the OCR software — you'll succeed. If you have trouble reading a page, an OCR program will, too. That's especially true if the document contains any fine print — OCR programs have more trouble with it than I do.

After you scan a test page, proofread it carefully. Some errors are easy to spot — a capital *D*, for example, can be misread as a vertical bar followed by a parenthesis — |). And the OCR program itself flags characters it doesn't recognize, usually by substituting a bullet (•) or tilde (~).

Substitution errors are the hardest to find. A *w* can become *vv*, an *m* can become *rn*, *S* can become *5*, and an italic *h* can become a *b* — to name only several ways OCR programs can suffer from mistaken identity. In a document I once scanned, OmniPage turned PS/2 (a model of IBM personal computer) into P512. Catching that kind of blunder requires not only a watchful eye, but an experienced one. A secretary unfamiliar with IBM computers might not know that P512 isn't a valid model number. And every field — from law to medicine to plumbing — has these kinds of specialized terms and ciphers.

The moral? No OCR program is 100 percent accurate, regardless of its developer's claims. But no typist is 100 percent accurate, either. If you approach OCR with the knowledge that the results will not be perfect and will require careful proofreading, you won't be disappointed.

As for me, I'm sold on the keystroke-saving benefits of OCR, but I haven't made it a part of my day-to-day business life. I once fantasized about scanning all the press releases that litter my office, but I soon realized that it would take far too long to be practical. A hand-held scanner might streamline the process by allowing me to scan just the portions of a press release that interest me, but as I mentioned before, hand scanners are second-best OCR devices.

With one exception. Caere Corporation's Typist is the first hand scanner designed for OCR. Typist isn't as finicky about speed as other hand scanners.

Better still, Typist inserts the text it reads directly into whatever application you're using — no grappling with a separate OCR program, no cutting and pasting or fussing with file formats to move text into the program where it will ultimately be used.

It sounds appealing, but don't believe it until you see it in action with the types of documents you plan to scan. Indeed, that's a good way to approach OCR in general — believe it when you see it. And when you proofread it.

Summary:

✔ Optical character recognition software teamed with a scanner lets a Mac read, or recognize, printed pages and create files containing their text.

✔ The simplest recognition technique an OCR program can use is called matrix matching, in which the program compares each character to a library of templates, one for each font and type size. Nontrainable OCR programs contain a fixed number of templates, while trainable OCR programs can be taught to recognize additional fonts and sizes. The third type of OCR software, automatic, recognizes text using feature extraction, topographical analysis, and other sophisticated techniques that demand a fast processor and plenty of memory.

✔ The scanner is the hardware half of the OCR equation; it uses a mechanism not too different from a photocopier or fax machine to examine a page and create a digital image of its contents. Types of scanners include sheet fed (accepts a page through a front panel slot and advances the paper using rubber rollers); flatbed (looks like a small copier and can scan pages from books, magazines, and other bulky originals); and hand-held (rolls across the page, scanning in narrow swaths).

Chapter 15
Project Management

Business life is full of goals, and each one breaks down into milestones that must be performed in sequence. Want to build a building? First you need to buy land, get permits, and draw plans. Introducing a new product? You need to build a manufacturing line, design packaging, and develop a marketing plan.

Each milestone in a project often breaks down into steps of its own. You can't buy land until you've met with real estate agents. You can't design packaging until you've hired a designer. Fleshing out all the steps involved in meeting a goal is like opening one box and finding another — and another, and another.

Project-management programs — or *project managers* — are designed to help you keep track of all those boxes, called *tasks.* Project managers can also help you allocate a project's *resources,* such as the people who will perform the tasks. And most important, project managers let you superimpose this cast of characters on a calendar to help you make sure things happen when they're supposed to.

The promise of project-management software is appealing: type in lists of tasks, resources, and dates, and out come fancy charts that graphically depict a project's steps and schedule. Consequently, you can't help but meet a goal on time and within budget.

And if you believe that, there's a big bridge in Brooklyn I'm taking offers on. Project management is one area where the old computer maxim, "garbage in, garbage out" applies in spades. Charts and graphs won't help you meet a goal if the dates and data you supply are incomplete or unrealistic. What's more, project-management programs impose a kind of rigid order on projects that you might find too restrictive or just too much trouble. All in all, they're specialized programs: not for everyone, but priceless for some — and required by most government agencies and subcontractors.

How They Work

A project-management program is part database manager, part spreadsheet, and part graphics program. Like a data manager, a project-management program lets you store and retrieve data — the tasks that make up a project, the time they'll take, the names of the people or companies who will perform them, the costs of materials and labor.

Like a spreadsheet program, even the most basic project-management software lets you perform *"what-if" analysis* by plugging in different numbers to see their impact on the bottom line. After specifying relationships between the data you enter, you can then ask "what-if" questions by entering new values and examining their effect on the project's schedule. What if it takes two weeks instead of one to get permits? What if we hire only five carpenters instead of eight? What if costs increase by 10 percent? These are questions many planners ask themselves frantically in the middle of the night; unlike a ceiling, a project manager can provide some answers. And if none of the scenarios you've set up seem to work, you can always revert to your saved project document to restore the original numbers.

Like a graphics program, a project manager can take all the numbers you supply and generate charts that depict a project's schedule, cash flow, and resource allocation. You can see at a glance whether you're on budget or whether you've assigned too much work or too little to a particular person or group.

Using a project manager involves specifying three kinds of information: a project's tasks, the amount of time each task will take, and the resources required to perform them. You can then create, distribute, and study the resulting charts and graphs to make sure your assumptions are realistic and to make adjustments where needed. After the project is under way, you revise the data to accommodate unexpected delays or changes in the project or your resources.

A Juggler's Assistant

A project-management program's real strength isn't generating pretty graphs and schedules; it's showing the options for meeting your goals and helping you juggle the trade-offs that must often be made between a project's tasks, your resources, and the time allotted to the project. To meet a goal, do you add resources (more employees, more money, longer work hours)? Do you delay the completion date or start earlier? Or do you simplify the project by scaling down your plans?

As the following scenarios show, the project itself often dictates which trade-off is the most viable.

❖ A business planning an exhibit at a trade show is dealing with a time-constrained project, since the show's starting date can't be changed. The manager in charge of the exhibit plugs in the starting date of the show, and then specifies the tasks behind the goal — designing, building, and shipping the booth; making travel and lodging arrangements; printing brochures; and setting up the booth. Resources in such a project include the company building the booth, the printing company, the brochure's designers and copywriters, and the budget. After meeting with representatives of each group to determine how long its job will take, the manager uses the project-management program to work backward and determine the best date for starting the project, adjusting resources and/or the scope of the project (perhaps choosing a simpler booth design) as needed to ensure that everything is ready for opening day. In project-management parlance, this type of project presents a *backward-scheduling* challenge.

❖ A contractor is building a house and facing strict budget constraints — the buyers can afford only so much, and they're approaching that figure fast. The contractor meets with them to determine which amenities they're willing to forgo; he then removes the associated tasks from the project's model until its cash-flow figures agree with the buyers' budget. This is a *cost-constrained* project.

❖ An electronics manufacturer is planning to unveil a new gizmo at the next major trade show, but the date is looming and the product isn't ready. The development team managers can't scale down the project or delay the launch date, so they meet with the product's engineers to find out which tasks are causing the delay. Then they use a project-management program to determine how many additional engineers will be required to complete the *critical* tasks on time.

There's a common denominator in each of these scenarios: before turning to the project-management program, the project leader must first prioritize the project's budget, timeline, and scope — by heading into the trenches to meet with the people who will be performing or paying for the work. A good project leader performs this vital step before the project is under way and then uses the project-management software to spot problems before they arise.

Managing the Jargon

The project-management world has its own jargon, most of which sounds like the rantings of a business school graduate who's had a bit too much caffeine. Project management has indeed been embraced by many MBA types, but much of

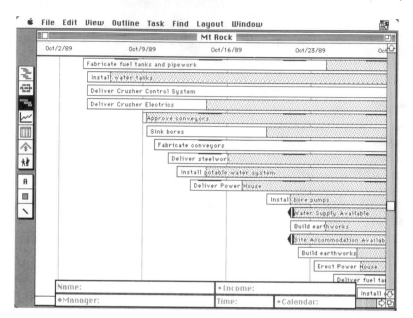

its terminology was created decades ago by that greatest of jargon generators, the government. Indeed, government, construction, and highly technical manufacturing industries are today's largest users of project-management software.

Many project-management techniques were developed to manage shipbuilding efforts during World War I, when Henry Laurence Gantt devised a kind

▲ Tasks and Timelines

Gantt charts, such as this one created by Symmetry's KeyPlan, display a project's schedule as a bar chart. The shaded portion of each bar represents that task's *slack time*, within which the task's start date could slip without delaying the project's completion date.

of bar chart that illustrates a project's tasks and timelines. All popular project-management programs can create these *Gantt charts* (see the figure "Tasks and Timelines").

In the 1950s, Du Pont and Remington Rand developed the *critical path method*, or *CPM*, project-management technique, which isolates the tasks that directly affect other tasks and ultimately the finish date of the entire project. In a construction job, for example, a delay in obtaining permits will delay the start of construction. The critical path is project management's game of dominoes — delay one task on the path, and those that follow are delayed, too.

The U.S. Navy incorporated CPM into its *program evaluation and review technique*, or *PERT*, created to manage the development of the *Polaris* nuclear submarine. *PERT charts* graphically display a project's steps by placing each task within a box and using lines to interconnect related tasks. The critical path is usually highlighted using bold lines (see the figure "Treading the Critical Path").

Another common planning technique involves creating a *work breakdown structure*. A work breakdown structure, often abbreviated WBS, looks much like

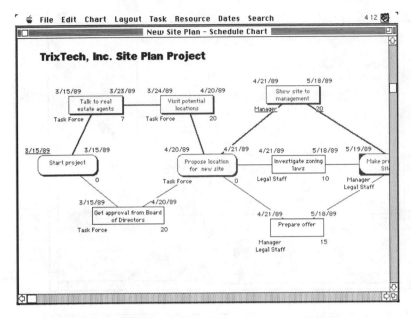

an organizational chart and shows the phases, milestones, and tasks needed to complete a project.

Some related tasks are known as *dependent tasks,* which means their completion is dependent on that of other tasks. For example, the task "eat dinner" is a dependent task of "cook dinner." In most project-management programs, you indicate these *dependency relationships* by drawing lines between the task boxes. The entire arrangement of tasks and their interconnecting lines forms a *dependency network.* Since only a PERT chart can visibly display dependency relationships, that's the format preferred by project managers.

▲ **Treading the Critical Path**

In a PERT chart, the critical path is denoted by bold lines. Rectangles represent tasks; each round-cornered rectangle represents a *milestone,* a goal or significant point in the project. Claris's MacProject II is shown here.

Clock Watching

When specifying a task in project-management software, you supply several time-oriented pieces of information that the program uses to calculate schedules and workloads. One such tidbit is a *duration* value, which tells the program how long that task will take. It's important to supply accurate duration values, since the program uses them to calculate many aspects of the project's schedule. You might also specify *lag times,* which are delays between tasks. A contractor might specify a two-day lag time between the tasks "pour foundation" and "erect walls" in order to allow the concrete to set.

And you might specify an *earliest start date,* the earliest date on which work on that task can begin. Generally, you specify an earliest start date for the first task in a project and let the program calculate the earliest start dates for remaining tasks based on the duration and lag-time values you supply. You can, however, specify explicit earliest start dates for tasks that are midway through the project — if, for example, a given resource won't be available until a specific date.

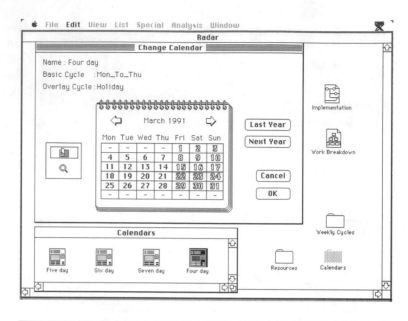

Making Dates

More sophisticated project management programs such as Micro Planner Xpert (top) let you define multiple resource calendars to accurately describe when a given resource is available. This calendar indicates the resource works four-day work weeks. To make the project model more manageable, Micro Planner Xpert uses a Finder-like window whose folders contain calendars, lists of resources, charts, and reports. At bottom, a three-day, 9-to-5 work week is being defined in Claris' MacProject II.

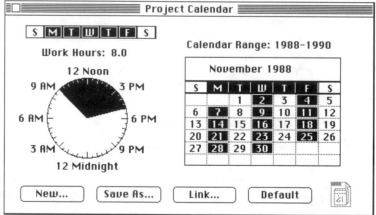

For these time calculations, you can specify durations, lag times, and the like in any time interval that's appropriate for your project, from hours to days to weeks to months. To let you be even more specific, project-management programs also allow you to define *resource calendars* that describe when a particular resource is available (see the figure "Making Dates"). For example, certain engineers may be available only on Mondays, Wednesdays, and Fridays. Or your overseas team may work six days a week while the local team works only five. Creating separate calendars for such resources makes the dates calculated by the project-management program more accurate.

To help you keep track of the demands made of a particular resource at a particular time, most project-management programs let you create *resource histograms.* These charts are useful when you've assigned a group of people many different tasks because they make it possible to see at a glance whether or not you've given them too much work to complete in a given amount of time. For example, if you've assigned a variety of tasks to a group of engineers, you could create a resource histogram that would show whether x number of engineers could perform those tasks within the timeframe allotted to them (see the figure "Are We Overworked Yet?" on the next page).

When the histogram indicates that you've overloaded a particular resource, you might invoke the *resource leveling* options that you'll find in Claris's MacProject II, Scitor's Project Scheduler 4, Welcom Software Technology's Open Plan/Mac, and Micro Planning International's Micro Planner series. A resource leveler first scans a project chronologically and locates over-allocated resources. An *automatic* resource leveler then reschedules tasks and juggles resources to resolve the over-allocation. An *interactive* resource leveler queries you along the way, allowing you to pick and choose which tasks and resources to juggle. Many project planners prefer interactive leveling because it leaves the decision making up to them, rather than the program. The aforementioned programs provide both leveling options.

A Project-Manager Sampler

Before personal computers became powerful enough to handle all the data and calculations involved in project management, project planners often calculated dates and costs by hand or with mainframe computers, and then hand-drew — and endlessly revised — blueprint-size charts. (Some masochists still work this way.) The Mac family has not only enough processing punch to handle the complex calculations required by project management, but the text and graphics skills needed to create all those charts and graphs as well as the detailed reports that more sophisticated programs can produce.

At the low end of the project-management spectrum, you find Gantt chart–generating programs such as Mainstay's MacSchedule and MacSchedule Plus, AEC Software's (formerly AEC Management Systems) FastTrack Schedule, and Varcon Systems' Great Gantt. These aren't project-management programs as such; they lack the ability to track dependencies and analyze relationships between tasks and resources. (MacSchedule Plus does provide several cash-flow analysis features.) They're most effective for someone who wants help in developing schedules and wants to create Gantt charts for presentations and reports, without getting mired in project-management jargon and concepts.

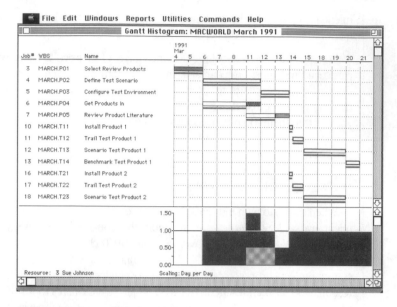

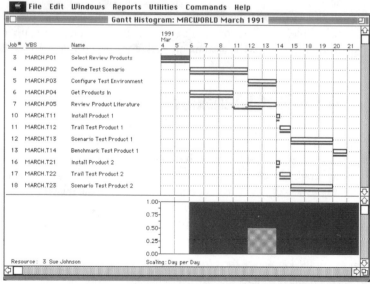

Are We Overworked Yet?

Project Scheduler 4's resource-leveling features in action. In the first screen, the resource histogram shows that Sue Johnson is over-allocated on March 11 and underallocated on March 13 — by 50 percent. In the Gantt chart, the shading represents one day of *free-float* time — a period within which the task could be delayed without affecting other tasks. The light shading represents *total-float* time, which would delay subsequent tasks but not the project's completion. In the second screen, the triangle shows a one-day delay for starting Review Product Literature, using up the free-float time. The baseline represents the original schedule. The revised histogram shows that Sue Johnson is no longer over- or underallocated. The light rectangle indicates that 50 percent of Sue Johnson's time is allocated to Review Product Literature.

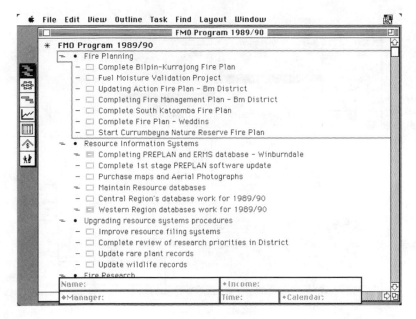

At the next level — a big step up from these programs — you'll find (in order of sophistication) Symmetry Software Corporation's KeyPlan, Claris's MacProject II, and Micro Planning's MicroPlanner. KeyPlan provides such project-management essentials as PERT charts and multiple resource-calendars, and wraps them around an easy-to-use interface that features a text-oriented outliner similar to Symmetry's Acta Advantage (see the figure "Outlining Projects"). It can also read outlines created with Acta and Symantec's More.

MacProject II, the most popular Mac project manager, has all these features plus resource leveling, a larger variety of reporting options, and support for *subprojects*. A subproject is a project within a project, stored as a separate document and opened when you double-click on the subproject's box. A complex project — the design of a new airplane, for example — is more easily managed when broken into a number of smaller subprojects.

MacProject II also has an excellent manual that teaches project-management basics as well as the program itself. Claris offers a $25 trial package, which includes a demonstration version of the software, a videotape tutorial, and a workbook. It's a great way for a beginner to sample the murky waters of project management. Claris also offers corporate training courses for MacProject II.

Micro Planner offers more features than MacProject II, including a larger variety of reporting and searching options that let you focus on specific resources and tasks. But Micro Planner's interface is a bit tricky to learn, and the program uses a somewhat confusing project-diagramming format, the *activity on arrow* method, in which task descriptions appear alongside the arrows that interconnect tasks. (Most other programs use the *precedence diagramming* method, in which task

▲ **Outlining Projects**

Symmetry's KeyPlan lets you view a project's tasks as a text outline. To sketch out the steps in a project without resorting to a project management program, you might consider using an outlining program such as Symmetry's Acta Advantage or Symantec's More, or the outlining features provided by many word processors.

Xpert Reports

Informed decisions require information, and that's where high-end project managers excel. Programs such as Open Plan and Micro Planner Xpert (shown here) can create a large variety of detailed, customized reports. Micro Planner Xpert's Job Card report is designed to ensure that cost information is accurately reported by the project team. The report lists the resources required for a given task and their cost, and provides boxes in which the actual time spent on the task is written. The project leader then uses the completed report to update the project model.

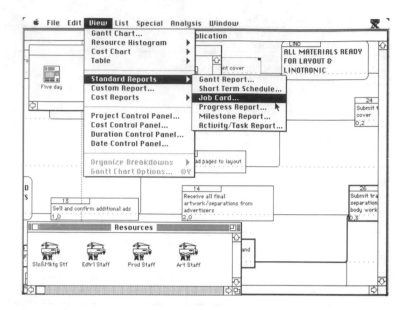

descriptions appear within boxes.) Micro Planning International is working on a new version of the program that is expected to smooth out some of these rough edges.

At the high end are programs such as Scitor's Project Scheduler 4, Micro Planning International's Micro Planner X-Pert, and Welcom Software Technology's Open Plan/Mac. These programs range in price from about $700 for Project Scheduler 4 to over $4000 for Open Plan/Mac. Their primary strengths? The ability to manage projects comprising thousands of tasks and to have multiple projects in memory simultaneously, more analytical features for fleshing out schedules and allocating resources, and the ability to apply those features across multiple projects. They can also produce more types of reports, allowing you to examine a project from more angles (see the figure "Xpert Reports"). The developers of these programs also offer training services.

But buying one project-management package doesn't preclude using another. Many programs can read files created by competing products, and all high-end project-management vendors offer customizing services that may include developing translation utilities. For example, Boeing recently commissioned Micro Planning International to create a utility for swapping data between Micro Planner X-Pert (which Boeing uses to manage development of its 777 jetliner) and Open Plan/Mac (which some of Boeing's subcontractors use). With these built-in or extra-cost data-transfer features, a company can use a variety of project-management programs, choosing midrange products such as MacProject II for managers who aren't project-management veterans, and kitchen-sink products such as Micro Planner X-Pert or Open Plan/Mac for the gurus in the corporation's project-management department.

In the end, you'll need to weigh a program's sophistication against your level of experience. If you're new to project management, you'll probably get better results from MacProject II or KeyPlan than from Micro Planner X-Pert or Project Scheduler 4. After all, a high-end project manager's extra features won't help you if you find the program too daunting to use in your day-to-day work.

Worth the Trouble?

I've spotlighted the key concepts behind project management, but the discipline is too complex to be covered in detail in one chapter. If you are interested in learning more, I suggest a book called *Getting Organized with MacProject II* (Van Nostrand Reinhold, 1990). Written by Peggy J. Day, a project-management consultant and educator in Portland, Oregon, it describes project-management concepts in detail and provides good advice for what to do before you start up your project-management program. I've included some of her insights in the sidebar "Project-Management Tips" on the next page.

Can project-management software help you? That depends. Some projects don't break down into tidy tasks as neatly as others. In many organizations, goals are redefined and resources are reassigned on the fly in order to meet urgent needs or respond to the competition. Project-management software doesn't handle this on-the-fly managing style well; it thrives on order and structure. On the flip side, a project model that's kept current can project the results — in time and costs — of an on-the-fly decision, which is often a sobering experience for its proponents. As Peggy J. Day says, "Nothing grounds a knee-jerk decision faster than a project-management program." Alas, many managers are so bogged down by their daily duties that they don't have time to keep the project model up-to-date as the project progresses.

In the project-management world, as in business, the object of the game is to meet your goals. Whether a computer program can help you do that is something only you can decide. One project management expert who read this chapter told me, "The statement 'garbage in, garbage out' doesn't even begin to cover the situation, since you can put in completely valid but incomplete data. [I've seen] managers fudge, manipulate, and obfuscate using [project management software.] The thing that most users do not understand about proper utilitization of a project management system is that it is every bit as much a programming or engineering exercise as designing the interface...for HyperCard or for putting together the design specifications and bill of materials for a major construction project. Your information must be organized and complete, otherwise you will be lying to yourself." Amen.

Project-Management Tips

Effective project-management doesn't come from Gantt and PERT charts, but from careful planning and experience. Here are some insights gleaned from Peggy J. Day's book, *Getting Organized with MacProject II,* and from the excellent manual that accompanies MacProject II.

❖ *Specify a goal* Write a charter describing the project's exact purpose. Don't be ambiguous. For example, the goal "build a better mousetrap" might mean "build a trap that kills mice more effectively" or "build a trap that costs less to manufacture." Distribute the resulting charter to team members so that everyone knows your objective. Revise the charter as needed when plans or goals change.

❖ *Determine phases and tasks* Break the project into phases — planning, design, implementation, testing, and so on — and then break each phase into its tasks. Make each task as small and specific as possible; this enables you to provide more precise resource and duration information. Jot down the phases and tasks in outline form; to do this you could use KeyPlan's outline view, Symmetry's Acta desk accessory, or the outlining feature within a word processor.

❖ *Use history when planning* You know the old saw: Those who ignore history are doomed to repeat it. Consult company records from previous similar projects; problems that surfaced then may well surface again. Remember to adjust for inflation and any changes in company procedures.

❖ *Allow time for the unexpected* Build extra time into the schedule, and add slack time following tasks you don't have direct control over, such as the delivery of a key part by an outside vendor. It's easier to figure in slack time before a project begins than to make up for lost time later. Have contingency plans that you can invoke if the worst happens. Start with the critical path, since that's where you're most vulnerable.

❖ *Update project records often* When schedules, resources, or costs change, update the project model so it's up-to-date. Too often, a project begins with a sharply defined schedule that dissolves into chaos as the project progresses and the real world intrudes. Keep the project model current, and you'll increase your chances of staying on track and within budget. Be sure to distribute current versions to everyone involved.

❖ *Meet early and often* Before plugging in duration dates for tasks, meet with the people who will be performing the tasks and solicit their input. When the project is under way, schedule regular meetings to make sure that things are on track — and be sure to include the time required for those meetings in the schedule. Document unanswered or unresolved issues to create a list of action items that describes who's responsible for resolving each item. If a task slips, inform the appropriate higher-ups before someone else beats you to it. Peggy J. Day says it best: communicate, communicate, communicate. **M**

Summary:

✔ A project-management program is part database manager, part spreadsheet, and part graphics program. It lets you store and retrieve data, perform "what if" analysis, and take all the numbers you supply and generate charts depicting schedules and workloads.

✔ Using a project manager involves specifying three kinds of information: a project's tasks, the amount of time each task takes, and the resources required to perform the tasks.

✔ The real strength of a project manager is its ability to show you options for meeting your goals.

✔ When specifying a task in project-management software, you supply several time-oriented pieces of information that the program uses to calculate schedules and workloads. These include duration value, which tells the program how long that task will take, and earliest start date, which tells the program the earliest date on which work on that task can begin.

✔ Some projects (such as house remodeling job) are cost-constrained — the timeline and ending goals may be flexible, but the budget isn't. Other projects, such as designing a booth for a trade show, are time-constrained — the project's ending date can't be changed.

✔ A project-management program's charts, graphs, and reports are worthless if the original data you supply is inaccurate or unrealistic. Effective use of project-management software requires constant updating of the project model and regular meetings with the people performing the work.

Chapter 16
Computer-Aided Design

In This Chapter:

✔ The three categories of CAD — mechanical, architectural, and electrical engineering — and what they do.

✔ A survey of the special labor-saving features that CAD programs provide.

✔ Some popular file formats used to exchange files between CAD systems.

✔ Printing to plotters, the LaserWriter, and the ImageWriter.

✔ The cost of CAD: what it takes to get started and go professional.

✔ Where the Mac fits in to the world of CAD.

✔ CAD variations: three-dimensional modeling, finite-element analysis, vertical-market systems.

This is not a good time to be in the T-square manufacturing business. Computers are replacing traditional drafting tools in the same way that word processors are supplanting typewriters. *Computer-aided design* (CAD) programs can turn computers into electronic drafting tables that make it easier than ever to create and revise complex drawings.

CAD was born in the sixties, when some automobile and aircraft manufacturers began augmenting their pencil-and-paper drafting methods with floor-sagging mainframe computers tied to large graphics terminals. These systems — which had a fraction of the Mac's speed, memory, and graphics resolution — cost millions of dollars to buy, and hundreds of dollars an hour to run. Because of their cost, CAD systems' benefits were reserved for the designers of such complex beasts as cars, planes, and missiles. Everyone else used T-squares, triangles, mechanical pencils, compasses, and protractors.

As the cost of computers shrank and their capabilities grew, CAD became feasible for smaller firms. Shortly after microcomputers debuted, CAD appeared on desktops, thanks largely to two IBM PC programs — Autodesk's AutoCAD and VersaCAD Corporation's VersaCAD. The Mac, despite its superior graphics, wasn't part of the picture. Using the original Mac's 9-inch screen to view blueprint-sized CAD drawings would be like viewing the ceiling of the Sistine Chapel through a keyhole.

Today, thanks to the arrival of large-screen monitors and faster machines, the Macintosh is becoming a major force in microcomputer CAD. In this chapter, I'll explore the basic concepts and terminology behind CAD. I'll also spotlight a few programs, but because CAD programs are usually quite complex, I won't provide an in-depth look at specific programs. Use this chapter as a guide to the jargon and a starting point for your own investigation.

Categories of CAD

At its foundation, CAD is *object-oriented* drawing — a term you may recall from Chapter 8. To recap briefly, object-oriented drawings are stored as a series of individual objects — circles, boxes, arcs, lines, and so on — that can be easily resized and otherwise altered. Object-oriented graphics contrast with *bitmapped* graphics, in which images are stored as a series of on and off bits corresponding to the black and white pixels on the screen.

CAD programs provide tools for drawing shapes, and they provide commands for altering those shapes and calculating and displaying their dimensions. When it's time to revise, leave your eraser in its drawer and make your changes on screen using the mouse. You can also create boilerplate designs and adapt them as needed. Fast-food chains, for example, use CAD programs to adapt their basic building designs to specific sites, allowing their buildings to maintain that "Anytown, USA" look while still adapting to the characteristics of a specific site.

Three basics categories of CAD exist: mechanical, architectural, and electrical engineering (see the figure "Three Faces of CAD"). Mechanical CAD is the broadest category. It involves the design of objects: cars, planes, trains, machine parts, lamp shades, thumbtacks — you name it. Most mechanical CAD programs create two-dimensional drawings that, like soap opera characters, have height and width, but no depth. Only a few programs can create three-dimensional drawings (see the sidebar "CAD Variations" on page 210).

Architectural CAD, as you'd guess, involves the design of buildings. Architects create many kinds of drawings: *elevations* depicting a building's profile; floorplans showing room dimensions, door locations, and furnishings; and maps of the building's plumbing, heating, and electrical systems. Many CAD programs provide drawing tools for creating parallel lines, making it easy to draw walls. Some architectural CAD programs let you create a 3-D view that you can rotate and examine from different angles.

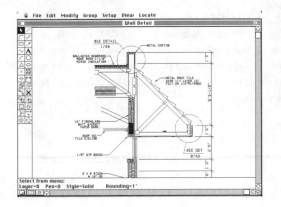

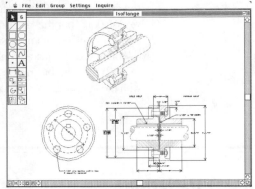

Three Faces of CAD

Three primary categories of CAD exist: architectural, mechanical, and schematic capture. At top left, an example of an architectural CAD drawing created with PEGASYS. At top right, a mechanical CAD created in VersaCAD. At right, a schematic diagram created in PEGASYS.

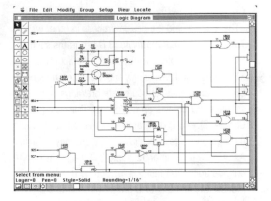

Electrical engineers use CAD programs to design circuits and *schematics* — those symbols and lines that show how electronic components are interconnected. CAD programs designed specifically for circuit design are often called *schematic capture* programs. In addition to letting you easily draw a schematic diagram, these programs work behind the scenes to keep track of what's connected to what. When you're finished, you have not only a schematic drawing, but a parts list and a list of connections. That list of connections can go to a circuit board layout program such as Douglas CAD/CAM Professional System, which can map out the copper highways and byways that traverse a multilayer printed-circuit board.

At this advanced level, CAD programs play a direct role in executing a design. Many programs can shuttle their data directly into *computer-aided manufacturing* (CAM) equipment, which uses the measurements and specifications in the CAD drawing to control industrial robots or machining tools to create the parts in the drawing. Such Buck Rodgers CAD/CAM is primarily the province of six-figure workstations, but the Mac is making inroads. At a recent CAD/CAM trade show, Apple conducted an impressive demonstration in which a Roland machining mill — connected to a Mac II running MGMStation CAD/CAM — ground, drilled, and carved an automobile piston rod out of a block of wax, based on a drawing created with the Macintosh version of VersaCAD.

CAD Variations

CAD doesn't always mean blueprints and schematics. The Mac can aid the design process in other ways.

❖ *Three-dimensional modeling* 3-D programs such as Silicon Beach Software's Super 3D, Paracomp's ModelShop and Swivel 3D, and Visual Information's Dimensions series let you create drawings that simulate 3-D objects on the Mac's 2-D screen (see Chapter 8). A 3-D program lets architects stroll through their latest creations — before they're built. As we saw in Chapter 12, some 3-D programs also provide animation features for putting designs in motion. Several 2-D CAD programs include 3-D features. 3-D CAD programs are often used by package designers. The Scitex Cornerstone Design System is a high-end 3-D package-design system comprising a maxed-out Mac IIfx and software for drawing package designs and managing other aspects of their production.

❖ *Finite-element analysis* You've designed a bridge and want to know how it will endure rush-hour stress. If you know the steel's basic properties, you can use this CAD technique to divide the bridge's surface into a finite number of tiny sections called *elements*, then electronically apply stress to the elements and see how they fare. It's a CAD technique developed for NASA in the sixties by engineers who later formed MacNeal-Schwender Corporation, which has developed finite-element analysis software for micros, minis, and mainframes. Cosmos/M, from Structural Research and Analysis Corporation, is a finite-analysis package that shows stress levels in color. Cosmos/M works with any CAD program that can export IGES or DXF files.

❖ *Specialized CAD* In the IBM PC world, over 400 independent developers have created AutoCAD templates for designing everything from kitchens to piping systems to oil wells. Those kind of *vertical-market* applications — ones tailored to specific professions — are becoming more and more popular on the Mac. Some are template collections for general-purpose programs like AutoCAD. One example is LandCADD's Irrigation Design, an AutoCAD-based system for designing irrigation systems. Other specialized CAD programs are designed from the disk up for specific trades. Graphic Magic's MacSurf, the leading CAD package for boat design, was used to design two America's Cup winning yachts. Another specialized CAD program, Compuneering's Landesign, is designed for creating survey maps and road construction blueprints. **M**

Life With a CAD Program

If you suspect software with this kind of power is complex, you're right. Forget diving into a CAD program without opening the manual. You'll need days or weeks of practice to master the hundreds of drawing, measuring, and annotating features that a powerhouse CAD program provides.

If you've used any version of Claris' MacDraw, you have a head start. From the features standpoint, MacDraw is to a CAD program what a tricycle is to a Harley Davidson. But there are similarities in their basic approaches to electronic drafting. You begin with a blank, untitled document window, and create a drawing by choosing tools from on-screen palettes, using the mouse to draw shapes. (Many CAD devotees shun the mouse in favor of a *graphics tablet* — a flat surface on which you scrawl with a *stylus*. A stylus and tablet feel more like a pen on paper, and they provide greater precision than a mouse. Graphics tablets and other alternative input devices are discussed in Chapter 37.)

To help you draw straight lines and position objects accurately, MacDraw and CAD programs provide a *snap-to* feature that causes the mouse pointer to be drawn to an invisible grid as it moves. But CAD programs offer more ways to snap. For example, most programs let you specify that an object snap to a particular point on another object, or to the point where two objects intersect.

MacDraw provides tools for drawing several different shapes, but a CAD program's palettes bristle with specialized tools that make creating complex drawings easier. A CAD program's *geometric facilities* replace compasses and protractors and allow you to quickly draw objects requiring calculations or measurements. Need to measure an angle or calculate the midpoint of a line? Want to draw a line perpendicular to a slanted line? Or parallel to it? Or tangent to an arc (such as a belt connecting two pulleys)? Such chores are a common part of an engineer's or architect's life. A CAD program reduces them to a mouse click.

CAD programs also simplify altering the objects you draw. As with MacDraw, you can move or resize an object by selecting it and dragging the mouse. Many CAD programs also let you enter measurement or position values from the keyboard for greater precision. You can rotate objects in single-degree increments and you can create mirror images of objects. An architect could use a mirror-image feature to turn a left-hinged door into a right-hinged one. Most programs also provide on-screen rulers and *coordinate windows* that display the mouse pointer's position as it moves within the drawing window.

A more advanced level of object altering involves creating *chamfers* and *fillets*. A chamfer is a beveled corner formed by a diagonal line that connects two lines. If you chamfer all four corners of a box, you get an octagonal shape similar to that of a stop sign. A fillet (pronounced *fill-it*) is similar, except the object connecting the two lines is an arc, not a diagonal line. If you fillet all four corners of a box, you get a box with round corners or, if the arcs are large enough, a circle. Geometrically speaking, a fillet is an arc tangent to two objects.

Other Labor-Saving Features

CAD programs also give you more ways to tame complex drawing jobs. One such life simplifier that nearly all CAD programs provide is a *layering feature*. Engineers and architects often build drawings using layers of transparent acetate, each showing a particular component or system. An architect might show a plumbing system on one layer, walls on another, electrical systems on a third, and room dimensions on a fourth. CAD layering features work similarly. You can move objects between layers and selectively show and hide layers, depending on how much detail you want to see. On a color Mac, you can usually assign a color to each layer to color code the systems in a drawing. Many CAD programs also let you open bitmapped graphics and place them on one layer, then trace over them using the CAD program's tools. You could use this technique to transfer old blueprints or schematics into a CAD program: first digitize the images using a scanner, then import them and trace over their bitmaps.

Mechanical drawings and architectural blueprints always show the dimensions of their components. CAD programs provide *dimensioning* features that create those dimension values for you. Simply choose a command or click a palette icon, select the item you're measuring, and the CAD program adds the dimension to the drawing, complete with arrows and *extension lines* (see the figure "CAD Dimensions"). All programs that provide dimensioning features let you choose the measuring system in which dimensions appear, and many also let you choose from several styles of arrows and extension lines. Most programs that provide dimensioning also provide *auto-dimensioning*. When an auto-dimensioning feature is active, the program changes dimension values for you when you change an object's size.

The kinds of objects you can measure vary between programs. Some programs provide only *linear* dimensioning — measuring the distance between two points. Others also support *angular* dimensioning — measuring the size of angles. Still others go a step further, offering *radial* dimensioning — the ability to measure the radii of circles.

Drawings and schematics often contain multiple copies of the same object, be it a bolt, a sink, or a transistor. Most CAD programs offer *symbol libraries* that make it easy to create, store, and reuse often-used symbols of your trade. Some programs come with libraries of common architectural or electronic symbols; with

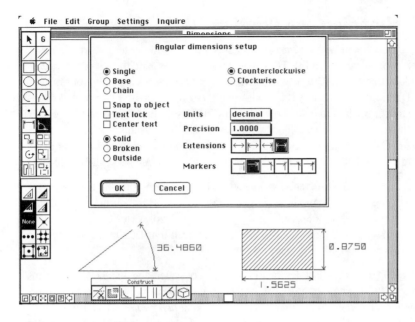

 File Edit Group Settings Inquire

Angular dimensions setup

- ● Single
- ○ Base
- ○ Chain

- ● Counterclockwise
- ○ Clockwise

- □ Snap to object
- □ Text lock
- □ Center text

- ● Solid
- ○ Broken
- ○ Outside

Units: decimal
Precision: 1.0000
Extensions
Markers

[OK]   [Cancel]

36.4860

0.8750

1.5625

Construct

▲ CAD Dimensions
Most CAD programs provide auto-dimensioning features that add dimensions to drawings. VersaCAD, shown here, provides linear (point-to-point) dimensioning and angular dimensioning, measuring the size of angles. The dialog box shows the variations of extension lines and arrows VersaCAD provides.

others, libraries are extra-cost options available from the program's developer or from third parties. With many programs, you can assign a name to each symbol, such as "3-inch carriage bolt" or "conference chair." Some programs can use those names to print parts lists showing how many times a given component appears in a drawing, allowing you to easily generate a parts list and bill of materials. This feature is often called *attribute tracking* or *associativity*. Some high end CAD programs can export these lists to database managers.

And because even a large-screen monitor can't show an entire blueprint-sized drawing at actual size, all CAD programs offer *zoom* commands that let you move in for a close-up look or zoom out to get the big picture. But redrawing an image containing thousands of objects takes time, even on a Mac II-class machine. To eliminate the wait, most programs offer a *redraw halting* feature that lets you stop the redrawing process. You might use redraw halting to stop further redrawing after the object you've zoomed in to see appears.

One potential solution to the problem of slow screen updates is a *vector accelerator* board such as Radius' QuickCAD, which greatly speeds up the process of drawing the objects that comprise a CAD image. Vector accelerators differ from graphics accelerators such as Apple's Macintosh Display Card 8•24GC. As we'll see in Chapter 38, graphics accelerators boost the Mac's overall performance at drawing bitmapped screen images. They take a lot of the wait out of working with 24-bit color bitmapped graphics, but they do little to speed up object-oriented drawing. Vector accelerators, on the other hand, don't improve bitmapped drawing performance, but are fine-tuned to speed up object-oriented drawing. But there's a catch: You need to verify that the CAD program you choose is compatible with the QuickCAD board, which, at this writing, is the only vector accelerator available for the Mac.

Exchanging and Printing

If you work in an organization that already uses a CAD system — whether a large workstation or an IBM PC — you'll want to investigate the data-exchange options that Mac CAD programs provide. There is no single standard for moving CAD drawings between systems, but there are some established formats. Perhaps the most popular is *IGES*, short for Initial Graphics Exchange Standard, developed by the American National Standards Institute (ANSI). You'll find support for IGES files in CAD systems running on micros, minis, and mainframes. Another popular format is the DXF file, popularized by Autodesk's AutoCAD package for IBM PCs.

Some Mac CAD programs can import and export IGES and DXF files. With others, file-translation modules are extra-cost options. Most advanced CAD users have come to rely on translation programs such as Claris' Claris Graphics Translator and Kandu Software's CADMover, both of which translates between IGES, MacDraw, PICT, DXF, and many other formats.

A CAD drawing's final destination is a piece of paper, and some CAD programs can get it there in more ways than others. In the CAD world, the dominant output device isn't a LaserWriter or an ImageWriter, but a *pen plotter*, which prints by zipping special felt-tipped pens across a sheet of paper or mylar film. Most plotters can hold between 4 and 12 different colored pens in a turret mechanism, switching between them as instructed by the CAD program. Plotters are often described according to their maximum paper size, with each size labeled by a letter: an *A-size* plotter can create 8½ by 11-inch drawings. *B-size* drawings measure 11 by 17; *C-size*, 17 by 22; *D-size*, 22 by 34; and *E-size*, 34 by 44. Nearly all Mac CAD programs can print to a plotter and support plotters from such industry leaders as CalComp, Hewlett-Packard, Houston Instruments, and Roland.

Plotters take too long to accurately render the subtle serifs and fine details of Mac fonts, so most CAD programs with plotter support include *stroke fonts* for their output. Stroke fonts allow the plotter to quickly draw text using — you guessed it — single strokes of its pens. Stroke fonts, sometimes called *vector fonts,* resemble the letters created with a Leroy lettering set, a stencil lettering kit popular in the drafting world.

Mac CAD programs also support ImageWriters and LaserWriters, but to varying degrees. Some can print in only low-resolution draft modes, but most offer both low- and high-resolution ImageWriter and LaserWriter output. Low-resolution output is useful for producing quick proofs of a drawing. High resolution takes longer, but takes advantage of your printer's maximum resolution.

The Cost of CAD

If you're drooling at the prospects of working CAD into your life, dry up — at least until you check your bank balance. Software with the capabilities I've described doesn't come cheap, and it does come with a voracious appetite for hardware.

Some CAD programs run on a Mac Plus, SE, or Classic, but slowly. For serious, day-in, day-out CAD, you need a Mac II-class machine with several megabytes of memory. If you'd prefer to spend your time drawing rather than scrolling, you'll want a large-screen monitor. Throw in a vector accelerator if you'll be working with extremely complex images.

Then there's the cost of the programs themselves. Their complexity and a relatively small market combine to place CAD programs among the Mac's most expensive software. High-end CAD programs such as Gimeor's Architrion II, Autodesk's AutoCAD, and InterGraph Corporation's MicroStation Mac each cost over $3000. Between $1000 and $3000, you'll find programs such as Schlumberger's MacBravo, Versacad's VersaCAD/Macintosh Edition, and IGC Technology's PEGASYS II, to name only a few.

You can also get capable programs for less than $1000. Examples include Claris' Claris CAD (one of the most popular Mac CAD packages), Engineered Software's PowerDraw, VersaCAD's VersaCAD Drafter, Forthought's Snap, and Graphsoft's MiniCad+. But be aware that some programs in this under-$1000 ballpark don't include the plotter support and file-exchange features included with their higher-priced brethren. If you need those features, be sure to tally up the total cost before buying.

The most reasonable CAD programs are Generic Software's CADD Level 1, Graphsoft's Blueprint, and Abracadata's Design Your Own Home Architecture, all of which retail for less than $300. These programs can't match the capabilities of an AutoCAD or Architrion II, but they're ideal tools for exploring the CAD world. And if you outgrow them, chances are you'll be able to import their drawings into a more powerful program.

Besides the features I've described here, other factors may influence your choice in a CAD program. For example, if you need to exchange drawings with IBM PCs, you'll get more consistent results with a program that has a PC counterpart, such as AutoCAD. If you've used Schlumberger's Bravo on a Digital Equipment Corporation VAX minicomputer, you'll feel comfortable with MacBravo. If you're an architect, you'll want to lean toward Architrion II, Blueprint, or Design Your Own Home Architecture. If you're buying CAD software that will be used by people with varying levels of CAD experience, a mid-range product such as Snap, Claris CAD, or PowerDraw may be in order. And don't forget to match the program's appetite for hardware to the systems you have. Try to run a high-end CAD program on a mid-range Mac, and you'll be disappointed with the results.

Where Mac CAD Fits In

Despite the amazing talents of today's CAD programs, the Mac isn't about to send expensive CAD workstations to the scrapheap. CAD systems exist that can show animated, three-dimensional views of a jetliner in one window, while you zoom in on single rivets in another. Today's Macs — even the IIfx — lack the processing speed required for such tasks.

Most Mac CAD programs are better suited to designing things that are easily visualized in top-view, side-view fashion, rather than in three-dimensional views. Clearly, that covers quite a few jobs. And in large engineering departments, Mac CAD programs can lighten the load on those expensive workstations by handing the simpler jobs that can monopolize a workstation's time — freeing it up to do what it does best. As one CAD expert once told me, "I see a lot of Ferraris on the road, but many of them are only doing 55 miles per hour." The Mac may not be a CAD Ferrari, but even a Chevy beats a horse and buggy.

Summary:

✔ The three primary categories of computer-aided design (CAD) are mechanical (designing objects for manufacturing); architectural (designing buildings); and schematic capture (designing circuits and schematics).

✔ CAD drawings are object-oriented — their components are stored as individual objects, such as circles and boxes, rather than as bitmaps.

✔ CAD programs make creating complex drawings easier by providing powerful geometric drawing tools, precise measuring and positioning features, and libraries that store often-used symbols for quick recall.

✔ To speed up the process of redrawing complex images, some CAD programs can use a vector accelerator board such as the Radius QuickCAD board.

✔ CAD output is most commonly pen plotters. Most Mac CAD packages support stroke fonts for quicker labeling on plotters. Laser and dot-matrix output is used mainly for quick proofs.

✔ The Mac won't replace dedicated CAD workstations for all tasks, but they can lighten the load by taking over the simpler jobs.

Chapter 17
Multimedia

In This Chapter:

✔ The different levels of sophistication of multimedia.

✔ A look at interactive versus passive multimedia.

✔ Details on multimedia's potential as an educational tool.

✔ The hardware and software components involved in multimedia.

✔ An analysis of the possible roles multimedia will play in the future.

Multimedia is many things — literally and figuratively. Literally, multimedia is the integration of more than one communications medium. It's the use of words, sounds, and still and moving pictures to convey ideas, sell products, educate, and entertain. It's built around the premise that anything words can do, words, sounds, and pictures can do better. The more, the media.

Figuratively, what multimedia is depends on who you talk to. Some say it's the future of computing, a harbinger of an era when computers will convey information using sound and motion as well as text and static images, and when television will become more interactive and less passive. Some say multimedia is the future of communication itself, the ideal way of conveying the complex ideas and concepts of the twenty-first century.

But others say multimedia represents the victory of television over literature, the triumph of sound bites and flashy visuals over the slow-moving but more thought-provoking printed word. Multimedia, they say, is just one more technological diversion for a society addicted to entertainment and distracted by trivia.

Multimedia is many things — it can be all these things. Multimedia brims with potential and the potential for misuse. Multimedia can also be technically complex and, in its most advanced forms, quite expensive. In this chapter, I'll explore the world of multimedia, spotlighting some ways in which it's used as well as the components that form a complete system.

The Multi Levels of Multimedia

At its most basic level, multimedia might involve jazzing up a slide presentation with background music or narration. This kind of multimedia doesn't require a great deal of equipment or technical expertise. You can create title slides and other visuals using a presentation program such as Aldus Persuasion or Microsoft PowerPoint, and then use a stereo cassette deck to record and play the soundtrack. Not long ago, the combination of soundtrack and visuals was about all there was to multimedia.

Today, multimedia generally means using an *authoring* program such as HyperCard or MacroMind Director to create a production and play it back. Using such a program allows a production to have animation, such as bullet chart items that slide onto the screen, and flashy *transitions*, such as dissolves and fade-outs between visuals. Creating a presentation that uses these basic visual tricks isn't difficult, but the results can be livelier and more engaging than a simple slide show.

A more advanced level of multimedia might involve using animation sequences that illustrate complex concepts, such as how a steam engine works or how heart valves operate. At this level, your role as producer becomes more demanding. Designing and executing a complex animated sequence requires artistic skills and some knowledge of animation techniques. It also requires software with more advanced animation features than HyperCard's — more about that later.

A sophisticated multimedia production might also incorporate *digitized* still images captured from a video camera or videocassette recorder. A corporate presentation might include shots of the new factory; a medical tutorial might show images captured from a videotape of a surgical operation. For this, you'll need additional hardware as well as some knowledge of video and lighting techniques.

Then there's sound, which authoring programs support in a few ways. They can play back short sound passages you record directly into the Mac using an add-on such as Farallon Computing's MacRecorder or using the recording circuitry built into the Mac LC and IIsi. So, your animated heart can beat to the sound of a recorded heart, and the animated steam engine can chug as a locomotive sound plays. Authoring programs can also control electronic synthesizers and *CD-ROM* players, which can store hundreds of megabytes of data as well as CD-quality audio. Thus, a corporate presentation can play to the sound of CD-quality background music, or a music tutorial can display text on the screen while a piece plays.

Passive versus Active

Multimedia productions can be linear affairs — watched from start to finish, like a slide show or a TV program. But the most significant aspect of Mac multimedia — and the thing that gets its evangelists and doomsayers so excited — is *interactivity*. The most advanced multimedia productions are non-linear and interactive. Instead of passively sitting through them from beginning to end, you use the Mac to interact with them, setting your own pace and branching to different topics and areas as they interest you. With interactive multimedia, the Mac and programs like HyperCard become more than devices that present various media — they become tools for navigating through the media themselves.

The primary tools of multimedia navigation are on-screen buttons and other *hot* areas that, when clicked, take you to other screens, display windows containing additional information, or play sounds — or even video sequences. Yes, interactive multimedia often makes use of yet another piece of hardware, a *videodisc player*, whose discs look like a cross between a phonograph album and a compact disc.

Videodiscs and interactive multimedia complement each other beautifully, primarily because, unlike a videocassette, a videodisc is a *random-access* medium. One side of a videodisc contains 54,000 numbered *frames*, and a player under the Mac's control can skip to any one of them almost instantly. The player can play frames continuously to show up to 30 minutes of moving footage, or freeze on any one frame to show a still. Thus, a multimedia production can include moving and still pictures stored on the same videodisc — along with up to 30 minutes of two-channel audio per side. Those two audio channels can be used for stereo, or they can be used separately to hold, for example, narration in two languages.

Multimedia in Education

Clearly, interactive multimedia has tremendous potential as an educational tool. Nowhere is this better illustrated than in a series of videodisc packages produced by ABC News Interactive and Optical Data Corporation. In the Martin Luther King Jr. package, you use HyperCard to explore a videodisc brimming with footage of civil rights protests, vintage news reports, and King's speeches, as well as still photographs, maps, and charts (see the figure "Interactive History"). You can watch the entire "I Have a Dream" speech while reading King's prepared text on the Mac's screen — and you can see where, half-way through, he diverged from the prepared text to capture the attention of millions. Other ABC News Interactive presentations include The '88 Vote, In the Holy Land, The Great

Interactive History

Three cards from the HyperCard stack that controls ABC News Interactive's Martin Luther King Jr. program. Clicking a topic (top) displays a card containing a timeline (middle). Clicking a subject on the timeline displays a card (bottom) with descriptive text and buttons that display accompanying visuals from the videodisc. Another click displays definitions of any terms or biographies of any names that appear in boldface.

Mar 28 1968

Memphis:
King supports sanitation workers strike

In early March 1968, **James Lawson** , chairman of the **Community on the Move for Equality** , invited King to come to Memphis, Tennessee, to support the black sanitation workers' strike. King arrived March 28, to lead a protest march to city hall. Shortly after the march began, turmoil erupted at the back of the column and the situation deteriorated into a riot. Stores were looted and more than 200 people were arrested. One black youth was killed by police. King was strongly criticized in the newspapers. The Memphis Commercial Appeal accused King of fleeing the melee instead of trying to stop it, that "King's pose as leader of a non-violent movement has been shattered."

Still: Newspaper — "Guardsmen Back Riot Curfew"

File video: King marching with strikers

Quake of '89, and AIDS. The state of Florida recently decided to distribute the latter package along with videodisc players to all its schools.

Each package in the ABC News Interactive series also includes a "documentary maker" with which students can assemble their own documentaries based on the videodisc's images and news footage. It's this feature that also raises red flags among interactive multimedia critics, who wonder, Are students learning about Martin Luther King Jr. or are they learning how to produce TV documentaries and splice sound bites? Are they learning about AIDS? Or are they learning that "learning can take the form of an entertainment, and ought to," in the words of professor and media critic Neil Postman, author of *Amusing Ourselves to Death: Public Discourse in the Age of Show Business* (Penguin, 1985).

Another example of interactive instructional media is Warner New Media's Audio Notes series, which use CD-ROM discs and HyperCard to allow you to listen to and learn about music. One three-disc package presents Mozart's opera *The Magic Flute*; a one-disc package called *The String Quartet* presents a Beethoven string quartet. As the latter plays, you can use an accompanying HyperCard stack to view any of several measure-by-measure commentaries on the music, each assuming different levels of musical knowledge (see the figure "Listen and Learn" on the next page). Other parts of the stack contain biographical information on Beethoven and additional tutorials on music theory. In The Voyager Company's *Igor Stravinsky: The Rite of Spring* a UCLA music professor provides real-time analysis and commentary as the ballet plays. Whether you're a music student or a casual listener, a few minutes with any of these products will give you a new appreciation for the music — and for the potential of interactive multimedia.

Optical Data Corporation produces packages that teachers can use out-of-the-box or as toolkits for creating their own instructional materials. The *Planetscapes* package, for example, contains a videodisc laden with images of planets taken by the Voyager spacecraft, of North America taken by Landsat satellites, and of space shuttle missions and components. Accompanying stacks let you browse the Voyager images, view Landsat images by clicking on a map, and learn about the space shuttle. You can also create your own stacks that use the videodisc images.

To give educators a hands-on overview of interactive multimedia's potential — and to allow them to create their own multimedia materials — researchers at Apple's Multimedia Lab spent two years developing a package called The Visual Almanac. It comprises a CD-ROM containing 25MB of HyperCard stacks and digital audio; a workbook; and a videodisc laden with 7500 sounds and moving and still images — what the workbook not-so-humbly calls "the basic audiovisual vernacular of our culture." The HyperCard stacks include 14

Listen and Learn

Warner New Media's *The String Quartet* lets you listen to a digitally recorded Beethoven string quartet playing on a CD-ROM drive while reading on-screen text in any of several levels, each assuming more musical knowledge than the last. Level 1 (top) is for listeners with little musical knowledge; level 4 (bottom) analysis the structure of the currently playing segment. In the upper-right corner, a counter displays elapsed time as the music plays.

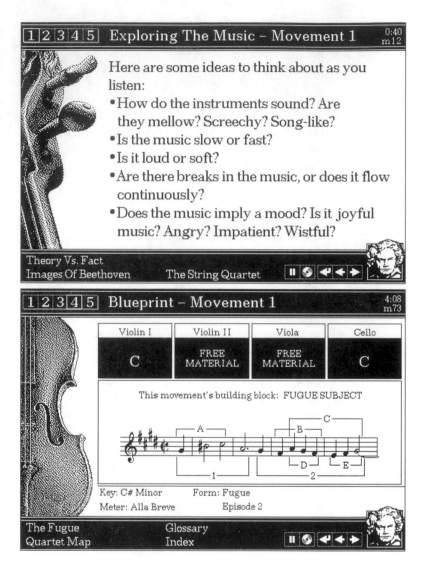

student activities in science, the arts, social studies, and mathematics. There's also a "composition workspace" that lets you search for images and sounds based on keywords you type, and then assemble them into stacks. The Visual Almanac was previously available to educators on an award basis only, but now it's available to anyone for only $100 from the Optical Data Corporation (800/524-2481 or 908/668-0022). It's the best introduction you'll find to the educational applications — and implications — of interactive multimedia.

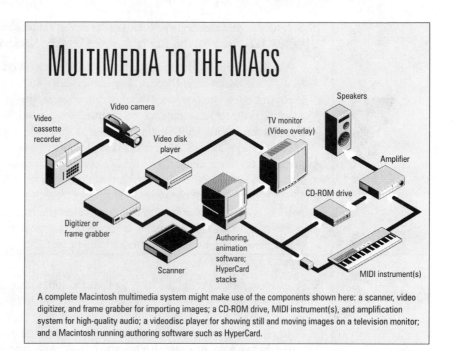

MULTIMEDIA TO THE MACS

Speakers

Video camera

Video cassette recorder

Video disk player

TV monitor (Video overlay)

Amplifier

CD-ROM drive

Digitizer or frame grabber

Authoring, animation software; HyperCard stacks

Scanner

MIDI instrument(s)

A complete Macintosh multimedia system might make use of the components shown here: a scanner, video digitizer, and frame grabber for importing images; a CD-ROM drive, MIDI instrument(s), and amplification system for high-quality audio; a videodisc player for showing still and moving images on a television monitor; and a Macintosh running authoring software such as HyperCard.

Of course, interactive multimedia has applications beyond the classroom. Interactive information kiosks in airports, shopping malls, or trade show floors can provide directories and profiles of cities, stores, or exhibitors. Interactive presentations can spotlight a concept, company, or product in a more engaging way. Interactive museum exhibits can enliven potentially dry subjects. In San Francisco's Exploratorium, you can fly over the Bay Area, viewing aerial footage and setting your own course using a trackball.

A Closer Look at the Pieces

I've mentioned in passing many of the software and hardware components involved in multimedia. The figure "Multimedia to the Macs" illustrates how they interrelate. Here's a closer look at the pieces and a partial list of products from each category.

❖ *Authoring* The key player in multimedia, authoring software is the stage that lets you direct your production's cast of audio and visual characters. HyperCard is the most popular authoring program; its relatively easy-to-learn programming language, HyperTalk, lets you create simple animations and establish links between on-screen hot spots and other cards. Silicon Beach's SuperCard is more sophisticated, with better color support and the ability to create stand-alone applications, which you can distribute to people who don't have

SuperCard. Spinnaker Software's Plus offers similar features and is also available for IBM PCs. You can move Plus productions between Macs and PCs.

More specialized authoring programs include Farallon Computing's MediaTracks, MacroMind Director, and Authorware's Authorware Professional. MediaTracks lets you produce Macintosh training materials by recording screen activity and then adding graphics and digitized sounds and on-screen navigation buttons. MacroMind Director began life as an animation program, but version 2.0 adds a HyperTalk-like language, Lingo, that lets you create interactive animations containing navigation buttons. Director includes a "player" application that lets others use your productions without having to own Director. Authorware Professional is a high-end ($8050) authoring package that provides sophisticated animation features and lets you create interactive productions without programming by drawing links between the production's components. Authorware also provides training, customizing, and production services for its clients.

❖ *Animation programs* In addition to Director and Authorware, there's Bright Star Technology's interFace, which, as we saw in Chapter 12, lets you create "talking heads" whose mouths move and facial expressions change as digitized speech comes from the Mac's speaker. Electronic Arts' Studio/1 is a monochrome paint program that lets you create simple black-and-white animations that you can play back within HyperCard and other authoring programs. 3-D drawing packages such as Silicon Beach's Super3D and Paracomp's Swivel 3D can create 3-D animations that you can play back within authoring programs. A high-end animation program, Linker Systems' Animation Stand, includes 3-D drawing features, a programming language, and compatibility with high-end animation hardware such as Diaquest's DQ-Animaq, a Mac II board that can control professional video recorders on a frame-by-frame basis.

❖ *Video hardware* Multimedia can make use of every category of video hardware. For recording a presentation on video tape, you might use a board that outputs *NTSC* video, such as those from RasterOps, Mass Microsystems, and Radius, to name just a few of the firms that offer such hardware. For capturing video images from camcorders, videodiscs or VCRs, you might use *digitizer* such as Koala's MacVision. For faster digitizing (MacVision takes several seconds to capture an image), use a board with *frame grabber* features such as RasterOps' FrameGrabber 324NC, Orange Micro's Personal Vision, Workstation Technologies' Moonraker, or Mass Microsystems' ColorSpace IIi (see the figure "Digitizing Video").

With boards such as Aapps' DigiVideo and Radius' RadiusTV, you can display video from VCRs, videodiscs, or TV stations in a Mac window. To combine

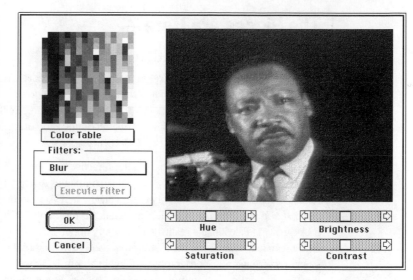

Macintosh-generated graphics and text with a video source, you'll need *video overlay* hardware such as Mass Microsystems' ColorSpace IIi, Truevision's NuVista+, or Computer Friends' TV Producer Pro.

Then there are VCRs and videodisc players. NEC Technologies' PC-VCR is an S-VHS videocassette recorder that you can attach to the Mac and control much like a videodisc player. VHS videocassettes cost far less to produce in small quantities than videodiscs, so a PC-VCR could be an economical alternative for an organization that produces its own video materials. The drawback: The videocassette isn't a random-access medium; it can take as long as 2½ minutes to locate a given point on the tape. As for videodisc players, Pioneer and Sony make the largest assortment of players that provide RS-232C serial interfaces that you can connect to the Mac.

❖ *Audio* I've discussed CD-ROM players and entry-level recording hardware such as Farallon's MacRecorder. To record and play back CD-quality audio, you'll need Digidesign's Audiomedia board. Throw in a big, fast hard disk, too, because CD-quality stereo requires 20MB of disk space per minute. As an alternative, use a MIDI interface to connect your Mac to one or more MIDI synthesizers and play back MIDI sequence files, which use a small fraction of the space. You might also consider Digidesign's MacProteus board, a version of E-mu Systems' remarkable Proteus MIDI instrument that you can plug into a Mac II. And if you don't want to write original music, Passport Design's Music Data Company sells hundreds of prerecorded MIDI sequences. See Chapter 11 for more details on MIDI and MIDI gear.

The Pieces are Here —
Can You Afford Them?

It's obvious that going for broke in interactive multimedia can mean going broke. Indeed, until the prices of its various pieces come down — or until a new generation of televisions is introduced that incorporate some of the pieces — full-blown interactive multimedia will remain confined to corporations and educational institutions for some time to come.

But the larger issue is the impact that interactive multimedia will have on schools and students. The workbook that accompanies Apple's The Visual Almanac waxes about how "history comes alive when you can hear the voices of the past and see the world's leaders at significant moments." Will seeing a clip of rock-throwing Palestinians really help students understand the roots of the Arab-Israeli conflict? What about the history that took place before the inventions of sound recording and photography? And what about disciplines that don't benefit from computer graphics and old news clips, such as literature? How can students concentrate in an expository writing class when they know they'll be flying around the solar system or watching Ted Koppel in their next period? After a few years of non-linear, TV-based education, will they be able to concentrate at all?

Smart educators and curriculum planners should definitely be in on the ground floor of interactive multimedia — not only to prepare for what appear to be tomorrow's teaching techniques, but to shape those techniques into being more than technological diversions. To paraphrase Neil Postman, instead of asking, How can we use television and the computer to control education? they should ask, How can we use education to control television and the computer?

Summary:

✔ Multimedia is the use of words, sounds, and still and moving pictures to convey ideas, sell products, educate and entertain.

✔ At its most basic level, multimedia might involve adding background narration or music to a slide presentation. More advanced levels of multimedia might involve using animation sequences to illustrate complex concepts.

✔ The most advanced multimedia productions are interactive — you use the Mac to interact with them, setting your own pace and branching to different topics and areas as they interest you.

✔ Listening to your favorite classical composer's music on the Mac while viewing measure-by-measure commentaries on it is but one way in which multimedia's tremendous educational potential can be exploited.

✔ The key player in multimedia is authoring software, the stage that lets you direct your production's cast of audio and visual characters.

✔ Multimedia can make use of every category of video hardware. For recording a presentation on video tape, you might use a board that outputs NTSC video; for capturing video images from camcorders, videodiscs, or VCRs, you might use a digitizer; and to combine Macintosh-generated graphics and text with a video source, you'll need video overlay hardware.

Chapter 18
Desktop Video

In This Chapter:

✔ A look at why you might want to record Mac screens.

✔ The difference between Mac video and TV signals.

✔ An introduction to the Macintosh II Video Card utility.

✔ How the Macintosh II Video Card can be used for economical desktop video.

✔ Getting rid of the horizontal line: Apple's VideoSync utility.

What looks like a television, but isn't? A computer screen. On the surface, the Mac's screen seems similar to a television set's — it uses a video tube that you definitely do not want to break, and it creates images by drawing hundreds of narrow horizontal lines. But beyond that, the Mac and a TV set take very different approaches to creating images. Normally, you don't need to worry about these differences. Your Mac and your TV lead separate lives, with little in common between them.

But then the day comes when, for reasons I'll describe shortly, you would like to videotape what you see on the Mac's screen. It's then that the differences between Macintosh video and *broadcast video* become critical.

In the last chapter, we looked at some of the desktop video hardware that's often used in multimedia applications: frame grabbers and video cards that can output NTSC video, superimpose Mac graphics over live or taped video, and show television images in a Macintosh window. In this chapter, I'll explain some of the technical differences between Mac video and broadcast video, and I'll let you in on two of the best-kept secrets in the Macintosh world: two Apple utilities — one free, one that costs only $35 — that let you videotape the Mac's screen.

The free utility lets you attach a standard Macintosh II Video Card directly to a video recorder using a simple cable, which you can make yourself or have a TV technician make for you. The results aren't 100 percent *broadcast quality,* as they say in TV, but they're quite close. The second utility modifies the output of a Mac's video circuitry to enable you to videotape the screen by pointing a video camera at it. Both are wonderful ways to try your hand at videotaping Mac images and to learn a bit about how television works.

Why Mac TV?

Before we look at the hows and whats of recording Mac screens, it might be useful to spotlight the whys. Here are some project ideas to stimulate the TV producer within you.

❖ Record a presentation. Perhaps you'd like your employees in the field to see that presentation you gave to the home office. Create your visuals using a presentation program such as Microsoft PowerPoint or Aldus Persuasion, and then use the program's slide-show feature to advance through the visuals while videotaping them. Because you're recording directly from the Mac, you'll get better quality than if you just aimed a video camera at the screen and podium. You can also record your speech by attaching a microphone or public address system to the video recorder. This technique can also help you fine-tune your presentation — and your presentation skills.

❖ Record animation. As we saw in Chapter 12, products like MacroMind Director and Apple's HyperCard allow artists to create impressive computer animations. If you're one of these digital Disneys, you can videotape your efforts and not have to fire up a Mac to show them off. Other pluses: you can see your work on a larger screen and add a sound track. And you can create a longer animation than would otherwise fit in memory or on disk by creating it in several sections and then videotaping each section in turn, pausing the video recorder while loading each one.

❖ Create a training video. Perhaps your company uses custom-developed Macintosh software, or maybe you'd like to educate new employees on the fine points of your electronic-mail system or network file server. By videotaping your own software or system in action, you can create a custom training video that reflects exactly how your company or department uses the Macintosh.

❖ Record Macintosh demonstrations. A school in Los Angeles videotapes the HyperCard stacks that students create so they can show their efforts to parents. Indeed, videotaping the Mac is an ideal way to show someone else what it can do. Just ask Apple, Microsoft, Adobe Systems, and Letraset. They're among the firms that have produced video demonstrations of their products in action.

❖ Create a promotional video. By mixing videotaped footage of live action with static or animated visuals created on the Mac, you can create a promotional video that can run in stores or be sent to prospective customers. Some advice: if you don't have any TV production experience, you might want to consult with someone who does. An amateurish promotional video may do more harm than good.

❖ Create titles for home videos. Let's be honest — this is really want we want to do with our Macs and video recorders, isn't it? And why not? Titles can lend a finishing touch to a home video, and they can be fun. Some video cameras have built-in titling features, but they're often hard to use and their typefaces aren't nearly as attractive as the Mac's. One catch: you can't superimpose a Mac-generated title over a videotaped image without specialized hardware, which I'll describe shortly.

❖ Set up an emergency monitor. If you attach a Mac to a video recorder that's attached to a TV set, you can use the TV as a Mac monitor. The results aren't great — you wouldn't want to use a TV as a monitor for very long — but they might be good enough to get you through an emergency if your main monitor breaks.

TV Technicalities

So there are several good reasons to put the Mac on TV. But why can't you just aim a video camera at the Mac's screen?

Actually, you can, but you may be disappointed by the results. For one thing, you're likely to pick up glare or reflections from the screen. For another, your videotape will have a fuzzy, out-of-focus appearance, even if you're extremely careful about positioning the camera. Worst of all, because of technical differences between Mac video and TV, your videotape will have a horizontal line running through it every few seconds. The bottom line: you'll get the cleanest recording of the Mac's screen when you attach the Mac directly to a video recorder.

To unite a Mac and video recorder, you need to attach the Mac video board's video-output connector to the video recorder's video-input connector. You also need to be sure that the Mac is sending a signal that the video recorder can receive. And that's when you encounter the differences between Mac video and TV.

The first of these differences concerns those horizontal *scan lines* that form video images. On all video tubes, these lines are formed by an *electron gun* (or, with most color monitors, three electron guns) within the video tube. The gun fires a stream of electrons at the tube's inner surface, causing its phosphor coating to glow briefly.

On a Mac II with Apple's standard Macintosh II Video Card, there are 480 horizontal scan lines, and they're painted one at a time, from left to right, from the top of the screen to the bottom. One complete set of scan lines is a *frame*. The Macintosh II Video Card repaints the entire frame 66.67 times per second (which translates into a *frame rate* of 66.67Hz).

By contrast, American television uses 512 horizontal scan lines, painted in a very different manner. Instead of painting one frame's worth of scan lines from top to bottom, a TV set paints them in two separate passes, or *fields*. First, all the odd-numbered lines are scanned, and then all the even-numbered lines are scanned. Each field is painted 30 times per second, giving broadcast video a frame rate of 30Hz. Thanks to *persistence of vision* — the same phenomenon that makes movies appear to move — we see the two fields as one image. This two-fields-per-frame approach is called *interlaced video*. The Mac's approach of painting all the scan lines in one pass is called *noninterlaced* video.

Mac video and TV also handle color differently. In the Mac, the signals for red, green, and blue — the primary additive colors from which all colors are created — each travel on a separate wire. Other wires carry synchronization, or *sync*, signals. This approach is called *RGB* video.

In the TV world, the red, green, and blue signals are merged with the sync signals into a *composite* signal that's technically simpler but lacks the sharpness and clarity of RGB video. The rules that describe the format of a composite broadcast video signal were developed about 30 years ago by the National Television System Committee, or NTSC. Broadcast video is often referred to as *NTSC video*, or by the name of the standard itself, *RS170*.

Lowering Your Video Standards

So in many ways, an NTSC signal is technically inferior to a color Mac's video signal. That's to be expected, given the less-demanding nature of television — a TV image doesn't have to be sharp enough to display small text that's legible at arm's length. To record a video signal directly from the Mac, we need, in essence, to tell the Mac to lower its standards.

Hardware add-ons such as Mass Microsystems' ColorSpace IIi (for the Mac II family) and ColorSpace Plus/SE (for the Plus and SE) do this by outputting a true NTSC video signal. Often such products also include a *genlocking* feature that lets you superimpose a Mac video image over an existing video image. When you see an announcer's name appear at the bottom of the screen as he or she speaks, you're seeing genlocking in action.

But specialized video hardware starts at about a thousand dollars and goes way up from there. It's hard to justify such an expenditure if you do desktop video only occasionally.

That's where the Macintosh II Video Card Utility comes in. If you have the original Macintosh II Video Card — the first color video card Apple released for the Mac — you can get reasonably good results with no additional hardware, except the cable. Alas, the utility doesn't work with the built-in video circuitry of the IIci, LC, or IIsi, nor does it work with the three new video boards Apple unveiled in 1990: the Macintosh Display Card 4•8, 8•24, and 8•24GC.

How the Video Card Utility Works

The Apple video utility relies on the Macintosh II Video Card's ability to be reprogrammed to put out a different kind of video signal. The utility is a system extension (an INIT) that reprograms the video board to output a signal that's very close to the NTSC standard. The signal isn't completely NTSC-compatible, says Jack Palevich, the utility's creator, because "the video card isn't infinitely program-mable." Because he couldn't completely reprogram the board, Palevich was forced to "round off" certain aspects of the modified video signal and, as a result, some video equipment may not be able to receive the signal perfectly. I had no prob-lems tuning in the Mac's signal on a Sony VCR. If you have problems, you may be able to resolve them by adjusting the video recorder's fine-tuning controls.

The utility supports each of the Mac II Video Card's modes (2, 4, 16, or 256 grey shades or colors), but in black and white only. So, you can record grey-scale images or use the fade-in and -out effects of programs like MacroMind Director, but you can't record in color.

Whether you use Apple's video utilities or a sophisticated desktop video board, one of the most serious problems with recording Mac screens is that any horizontal lines that are 1 pixel wide — like the lines in the title bar of a Mac window — flicker like a 1930s cartoon. This distracting flicker occurs because of the NTSC standard's interlaced approach — a horizontal line that's one scan line wide will appear in only one of the two fields that make up each frame. Thus, the line flashes on and off 30 times per second.

The Apple video utility fixes this by providing a *flicker filter,* a software routine in which each scan line is evaluated and averaged with lines adjacent to it. This is similar to the Apple Convolution feature built into Apple's latest video boards (described in Chapter 38). The Apple Convolution routine was based on the flicker filter in this free and humble utility.

But filtering flicker isn't free — it uses 48K of memory and slows the Mac by 20 to 40 percent. Pull-down menus become ooze-down menus. Animations run in slow motion, although you can often adjust for that by playing the animation back faster. (This performance penalty doesn't apply to Apple's new video boards.)

Using the Video Card Utility

The Apple video utility includes several pages of clearly written documentation, so I won't describe how to get it up and running here. I will, however, describe what you need to use it and provide some tips gleaned from my own experiments. The utility itself is available for downloading from CompuServe and America Online. It should also be available through user groups. Keep in mind that the utility is unsupported, though. Apple, your local dealer, *Macworld*, and IDG Books are not responsible for, or obligated to help you with, any problems you have.

Besides the Mac II Video Card, you need System 6.0.3 or a later version, along with the 32-Bit QuickDraw and Monitors files that accompany those versions. You'll also need to make a simple cable (see the figure "Making the Connection").

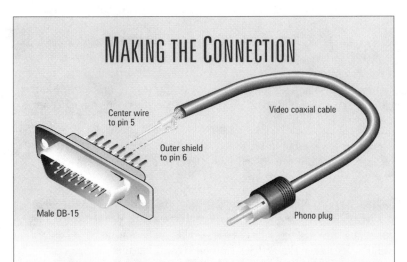

MAKING THE CONNECTION

Center wire to pin 5

Video coaxial cable

Outer shield to pin 6

Male DB-15

Phono plug

To attach the Macintosh II Video Card to a video recorder, construct a cable as shown here. The Macintosh end of the cable requires a male DB-15 connector. Many video recorders use a female RCA phono plug for their video inputs; in such cases, the recorder end of the cable should use a male RCA phono plug. You can use a shielded audio cable as a starting point for your cable, cutting the plug from one end and attaching the wires to the DB-15. The center wire of the cable attaches to pin 5, while the outer shield wire attaches to pin 6. Caution: You can damage your Macintosh and your video equipment by constructing the cable improperly. Consider having a video technician construct the cable for you.

You may need to flick a switch on your video recorder to tell it that video is coming from the video-input connector, not the video recorder's built-in TV tuner. On my Sony VCR, for example, I move a switch labeled Input Select from the Tuner to the Line position. Check your recorder's manual for details.

Video Boundaries

Because of overscan, not all of the Mac's screen will fit on a television screen. Of the Mac's standard 480 horizontal lines, only about 360 appear on a TV screen. For this reason, avoid using the outer 15 percent or so of the screen, positioning your titles and graphics within the rough boundaries shown here.

Note that when you activate the Apple video utility's flicker filter, the utility shrinks the Mac II's screen so it has the same dimensions as a compact Mac's — 512 by 342 pixels. This allows you to videotape a full Mac screen — handy if you're taping a Mac training video or HyperCard stack.

To record sound coming from the Mac, attach its audio-output jack to the video recorder's audio input jack. (For details on connecting the Mac's sound jack to other audio devices, see Chapter 32.) You can also record sound from a different source — such as a public-address system or stereo — by connecting the sound source's line-output jack to your video recorder's line-input jack.

To create titles for a video, consider using a paint program (I used PixelPaint 2.0) that lets you hide the menu bar and its tool palettes. Another good choice would be Adobe Photoshop or another program that creates *anti-aliased* screen fonts — ones whose jaggies are smoothed through the use of subtle shading. Create the title using the program's text-editing tools, and then hide its menu bar and tool palettes before recording the title.

Because of a television industry practice called *overscan,* in which the image projected onto a television's video tube is larger than will fit, the outer edges of the Mac's screen won't appear on the television or videotape (see the figure "Video Boundaries"). So it's best to design the title to occupy the center of the Mac's display — although you still may need to adjust the position of the text after you've connected the Mac to the VCR and TV.

Most commercial desktop video products compensate for overscan. Also, when you activate the flicker filter in the free Apple video utility, the utility shrinks the Mac II's screen so it has the same dimensions as a compact Mac's — 512 horizontal pixels by 342 vertical pixels. This allows you to videotape a full Mac screen, which is especially useful if you're taping a training video or HyperCard stack.

Overscan was born in television's early days, when the image on a picture tube would gradually shrink as the tube aged. Today's picture tubes don't suffer from this flaw, but overscan remains, partly to accommodate the elderly televisions still among us and partly because television manufacturers would rather fill an entire screen than have a black border around its image. On the other hand, computer monitors *underscan* — they project an image smaller than the tube's surface in order to show every precious pixel.

Designing for Television

To learn about the unique requirements of television graphic design, I talked with Anne Healy, graphic artist for NBC's "Late Night with David Letterman." Her advice: Keep it simple. "On television, everything looks soft," she says. "There's no real accuracy because of the [limited] resolution."

Some specific tips:

❖ *Avoid thin lines.* Lines that are one scan line wide will flicker badly, and even lines that are two scan lines wide tend to break up. Use horizontal lines that are an even number of pixels (2, 4, 6, 8) high.

❖ *Avoid tightly spaced parallel lines, small boxes, and tight concentric circles.* All three are prone to flicker because they conflict with the TV's scan lines. Make them heavier and space them farther apart than you might for a printed graphic. Think of stock market graphs you see on the news: they're often superimposed over a grid, but the grid boxes are large. Healy recommends a minimum box size of 1 square inch, as seen on a 19-inch television.

❖ *Avoid lightweight fonts such as Helvetica Light or Univers 45.* Serif typefaces are also risky in small sizes because the serifs tend to become blurred and hard to see. Bodoni, for example, doesn't work well in small sizes because the serifs and thin portions of characters are too thin. Times and Caslon don't always work well, either. Century Schoolbook is better, because its thins aren't very thin.

❖ *Don't space characters too tightly.* Avoid excessively close kerning. The edges of characters "bloom" when televised, so the characters appear closer together than they really are. To compensate, space characters so that they look a bit too loose on the Mac's monitor.

❖ *Choose colors carefully.* As a general rule, combine colors that are very different, like a light blue and a dark red, not a medium red and a medium blue. "Once I used a full range of pastel colors," Healy says, "and they all ended up looking the same." Also, avoid colors that are too hot, like hot pink or lemon yellow. If you want yellow, use a more golden yellow. If a color is too hot, it can bleed past its borders or appear to vibrate.

❖ *For titles that will not be superimposed over an image, use a black background and white or colored text.* Black or colored text on a white background is rarely used in television — for the same reason that it's rarely used in presentation graphics: an all-white background tends to be too glaring and harsh.

❖ *For titles that will be superimposed over an image, keep the text simple.* Use a font such as Univers 65 or Helvetica Medium — and choose a color that will allow the text to be visible over the background. Don't use white text, for example, if the background is a snow-covered ski slope. **M**

And that brings up the issue of designing titles for television, whose technical limitations impose some restrictions on graphic designers. You'll find some tips from a professional in the sidebar "Designing for Television."

Apple's VideoSync Utility

Apple's VideoSync utility is designed to let you videotape directly from the Mac's screen without having a distracting horizontal line appear every second or two. The utility adds an icon to the Mac's Control Panel that lets you adjust the timing of an Apple video card. The resulting Macintosh monitor image appears stable when photographed by an NTSC video camera.

VideoSync requires System 6.0.4 or later (or A/UX 2.0) or later; an AppleColor High-Resolution RGB Monitor; and a Macintosh Display Card 4•8, 8•24, 8•24 GC, Apple High Resolution Video Card, or Macintosh II Video Card. The utility is also compatible with some third-party displays that support Apple video cards. At this writing, the utility doesn't work with the built-in video circuitry in the Mac IIsi, LC, or IIci.

The VideoSync utility is available for $35 from the Apple Programmers and Developers Association (APDA). If you're interested in obtaining a copy of VideoSync and its documentation, contact APDA in the United States at 800/282-2732.

Signing Off

If you try either of Apple's utilities, drop me a line and let me know how they worked for you. Write to me in care of IDG Books Worldwide, or send electronic mail to 76174,556 on CompuServe, or to JimHeid on America Online.

Thanks to specialized video hardware, the Mac is playing a role in professional video production. Thanks to Apple's two video utilities, the Mac can play a role in the amateur video world, too.

Summary:

✔ You might want to videotape your Mac's screen to record a presentation; to record animation; to create a training video; to create a promotional video; to create titles for home videos; or to set up an emergency monitor.

✔ The rules that describe the format of a composite broadcast video signal were developed about 30 years ago by the National Television System Committee (NTSC). In many ways, the Mac's video signal is superior to an NTSC signal.

✔ To get reasonably good desktop video results without buying additional hardware, you can use the Macintosh II Video Card Utility, which can reprogram Apple's original Macintosh II Video Card to output a signal that imitates the NTSC standard.

✔ To use the Macintosh II Video Card utility, you need System 6.0.3 or a later version, along with the 32-bit QuickDraw and Monitors files that accompany those versions.

✔ To record sound coming from the Mac, attach its output jack to the video recorder's audio-input jack. To record sound from a different source, connect the sound source's line-output jack to your video recorder's line-input jack.

✔ Apple's VideoSync utility adds an icon to the Mac's Control Panel that lets you adjust the timing of an Apple video card. This allows you to videotape directly from the Mac's screen without having a distracting horizontal line appear every second or two.

✔ To design titles and other graphics to look their best within the limited resolution and 30Hz frame rate of NTSC video, avoid thin parallel lines and choose fonts and colors carefully.

Chapter 19
Utilities

Utilities are the spice of computing life. I refer not to the local telephone or gas company, but to *utility software* — programs that make using the Mac easier and more convenient. Utilities form the supporting cast of a computer setup; they work together with the Mac's system software and with your application programs to improve the Mac's performance and enhance its operation.

Want to customize your favorite programs' keyboard shortcuts? Need help managing the files on your hard disk? Longing for a way to resurrect that file you accidentally threw away? Want to customize the colors your Mac displays? Need an easy way to move files between programs or between a Mac and an IBM PC?

Utilities can perform these feats and many more. In this chapter, I examine the most popular categories of utility software and spotlight several products from each group. Because there's such an abundance of utilities for the Mac, I don't have room to mention each one; so if I've left out a particular program, don't assume it's under par. Computer dealers, user groups, and mail-order software advertisements are good places to learn about the gamut of utilities available in each class. For a look at some first-rate free and shareware utilities, see the sidebar "Utilities for Less."

Many of the utilities I'll describe in this chapter are designed to work with System 6.x. Because utilities work closely with the Mac's system software, there's a good chance that some won't run under System 7.0, or that they'll be supplanted by new features included in 7.0. If you use System 7.0 and you encounter a utility that sounds appealing, be sure to verify that it's compatible with System 7.0 — and, of course, that its features aren't already present in the system software.

Utilitarian Approaches

Utilities can provide Mac-enhancing benefits in several ways. Utilities that work together with your application programs may operate as *INITs* or as *desk accessories* (sometimes called DAs, these small programs are accessed from the Apple menu). Utilities may also take the form of *F-keys*, those small

Utilities for Less

Although a large selection of commercial utilities is available, the best place to shop for utilities, INITs, and desk accessories might be a user group or online information service. While most large software publishers have concentrated on full-blown applications, Mac programming hobbyists and small software firms have churned out more utilities than Dick Clark has TV shows. Here's a small sampling of the most popular free or shareware utilities that I haven't mentioned elsewhere in this chapter.

❖ Boomerang by Hiroaki Yamamoto — enhances the Mac's Open and Save dialog boxes with options that let you navigate files and folders quickly. An improved version of Boomerang, SuperBoomerang, is included with Now Software's Now Utilities 2.0 — along with such goodies as an INIT manager, a pop-up menu utility, an Open and Save dialog box enhancer, a menu bar clock, and much more.

❖ Compactor by Bill Goodman — a compression utility similar to the StuffIt series.

❖ Floppy Fixer by Frank Beatrous — recovers files from damaged disks.

❖ GooPanel by Steve Bollinger — a System 7.0-like substitute for the System 6.0.x Control Panel that

enables you to open cdevs one at a time in their own window, either by directly double-clicking on the cdev icon in the Finder or by launching the GooPanel application and opening as many cdevs as you like.

❖ MaxAppleZoom by Naoti Horii — enlarges the Mac II display area from the standard 640 by 480 pixels to 704 by 512 pixels.

❖ miniWriter by David Dunham — a simple text editor desk accessory. Another popular DA word processor is the shareware McSink by John Carpenter. Preferred Publisher's Vantage is a commercial version of McSink with more features.

❖ SuperClock by Steve Christensen — adds a digital clock, calendar, and stopwatch to the Mac's menu bar.

❖ Switch-A-Roo by Bill Steinberg — lets you switch between any two video modes (such as color and black and white) without having to use the Monitors Control Panel option.

❖ Tidy It Up by Guy Fiems — an application that organizes all the icons packed inside your System Folder into categories, making it easier to keep track of a fully stocked System Folder. **M**

Some utilities are
Control Panel devices,
or cdevs. In System
6.0.x, Control Panel
devices line the left
edge of the Control
Panel desk accessory
(top). When you click a
cdev, the right side of
the Control Panel
window changes to
reflect the cdev's
options. In System
7.0, Control Panel
devices live in the
Control Panel's folder,
which is located in the
System Folder. With
System 7.0, you open
a cdev by double-
clicking it. When you
do, the Mac displays
the cdev in its own
window (bottom).

software routines you run by pressing
Command-Shift along with a number
key. Or, they may work as *RDEVs*,
which are accessed using the Mac's
Chooser desk accessory, or as *Control
Panel devices (cdevs)*, which show
up in the Control Panel (see the
figure "Accessing a Utility").

INITs, also called *startup documents* or *system extensions*, reside in
the System Folder of a hard or floppy
disk and load into memory each time
the Mac starts up. A desk accessory or
INIT might also add its own menu to
the Mac's menu bar. In Chapter 30,
I'll provide some background on how
INITs load and operate and I'll pass
along some advice on troubleshooting INIT-related problems.

Utilities in this class have one
common characteristic: their benefits
can surface in any application, from a
word processor to a CAD program.
One example of an application-
spanning INIT is Apple's
MacroMaker, which lets you create
your own keyboard shortcuts
(although it's incompatible with
many applications). Another example
is Apple's Find File desk accessory,
which lets you locate a misplaced file
by searching for text that appears in
its name. And an example from the F-key camp is the snapshot F-key, which
creates a file containing the Mac's screen image when you press Command-
Shift-3.

The way in which you install these application cohorts depends on the type
of utility. In System 6.x, desk accessories are usually installed using Apple's
Font/DA Mover utility, which is included with the Mac. (I've included brief
instructions for using the Font/DA Mover in the sidebar "A Moving Experience"
on the next page.) You install an INIT by copying it to the System Folder of
your startup disk, and then restarting your Mac. (If you're using System 7.0,

copy the INIT to the Extensions folder, which is located within the System Folder. To save time, just copy the file to the System Folder: System 7.0's improved Finder will stash it in the Extensions folder after asking you for confirmation.)

Instead of working together with your applications, some utilities perform their work alone. Separate applications you start from the Finder, these self-contained job specialists perform specific tasks, such as backing up hard disks, resurrecting lost files, or transferring files between Macs and other computers.

A Moving Experience

The Font/DA Mover's workings are clearly explained in the manual that accompanies your Mac. But because many used or borrowed Macs lose their manuals along the trail, I've summarized its use here.

To start the Font/DA Mover, double click its icon. A list of fonts installed on the current startup disk will appear in the left-hand list box. To see a list of desk accessories instead, press and hold an Option key as the Font/DA Mover loads.

❖ To remove a desk accessory:
1. Select its name (the Font/DA Mover tells you how much space it uses).
2. Click Remove.
3. Click OK when asked if you're sure you want to remove the selected item.

❖ To copy a desk accessory to a new desk accessory file:
1. Click the Open button under the right list box.
2. Click the New button that appears in the file list box.
3. Type a name for the new desk accessory file and click Create.
4. Select the desk accessory to be copied, then click the Copy button.

❖ To copy a desk accessory to an existing desk accessory file:
1. Open the desk accessory file by clicking the Open button, then double-clicking the file's name. The names of the desk acces-sories in that file appear in the list box.
2. Select the desk accessory to be copied and click OK. That desk accessory is added to the others.

❖ To install a desk accessory in a System file:
1. Open the desk accessory file by clicking the Open button, then double-clicking the file's name.
2. Make sure the System file is open. If it isn't, use the other Open button to open it.
3. Select the desk accessory to be installed, then click Copy.

❖ To install a desk accessory in an application:
1. Press and hold an Option key while clicking the Open button.
2. Locate the application that will hold the desk accessory and double-click its name.
3. Select the desk accessory to be copied and click Copy.

You can remove, copy, or install more than one desk accessory at once by Shift-clicking on each. **M**

A well-stocked utility toolkit will combine programs from both camps. (For a summary of utilities described in this chapter, see the table "Utility Toolbox.") Not listed are those that perform obvious tasks, such as hard disk backup and file recovery. We'll look at these disk-related utilities in Chapter 27.

Navigation Copilots

As you become experienced with the Mac, you'll start wishing for easier ways to control your programs. You might long for more keyboard shortcuts to eliminate reaching for the mouse. Or you might want to automate frequently performed tasks, such as quitting one program, starting another, choosing a command, and then typing some text.

Navigation utilities let you streamline the Mac's operation to suit your work habits and preferences. For creating keyboard shortcuts and automating repetitive tasks, use a *macro* or *keyboard enhancement* utility such as Affinity Microsystems' Tempo II or CE Software's QuicKeys 2. Both let you record and play back keystrokes and mouse movements, and QuicKeys 2 also lets you choose from a roster of built-in shortcuts, such as scrolling to the beginning or the end of a document.

To test the macro waters, try Apple's MacroMaker, which comes with version 6.x of the Mac's system software. MacroMaker pales next to Tempo II and QuicKeys 2, but it can create simple macros that choose menu commands, enter often-used text passages, or click on icons in a tool palette. And its price is right. (Keep in mind that MacroMaker doesn't work with all programs, however.) For those who prefer mouse clicking to key stroking, there's Tactic Software's Icon-It, which adds to any program a bar of customizable icons to which you can assign key sequences.

If you use MultiFinder or frequently quit one program and start another, consider ICOM Simulations' On Cue. On Cue adds a menu to the right edge of the menu bar, where MultiFinder's small program icons normally appear. Add the names of frequently used applications and documents to On Cue's menu, and you can open them by simply choosing their names. You can even configure On Cue to display its menu at the mouse pointer's location when you click the mouse while pressing Command and Option — a boon for large-screen users who get tired of making the long trip to the menu bar. CE Software's Tiles offers similar features, but wraps them around an attractive, icon-oriented interface.

Speaking of saving trips to the menu bar, large-screen users might also want Magic Software's Powermenus, which turns the Mac's menu bar into a pop-up

Utility Toolbox

Utility	Company	Best Uses
Text-Retrieval		
Gofer	Microlytics	File locating, text retrieval, occasional research
On Location	On Technology	Text retrieval
Sonar	Virginia Systems	Research
Sonar Professional	Virginia Systems	Advanced research, index compiling, text retrieval
Navigation		
Tempo II	Affinity Microsystems	Keyboard customizing, task automation, program switching
QuicKeys 2	CE Software	Keyboard customizing, program switching
MacroMaker	Apple Computer	Simple keyboard customizing, task automation
Powermenus	Magic Software	Convenient menu access for large-screen users
TOM INIT	Advanced Interface	Convenient menu access for large-screen users
Icon-It	Tactic Software	Navigation for users who prefer mouse
On Cue	ICOM Simulations	Fast program and document opening
Disk and File Management		
Shortcut	Aladdin Systems	File locating, StuffIt archive manipulation, disk navigation
Findswell	Working Software	File locating
DiskTop	CE Software	Convenient file-and-disk management, program switching
DiskTools	Fifth Generation Software	Convenient file-and-disk management, program switching

Utility	Company	Best Uses
System Resource Management		
Suitcase II	Fifth Generation Systems	System resource management
MasterJuggler	ALSoft	System resource management
SuperLaserSpool	Fifth Generation Systems	Print spooling
Inix	Natural Intelligence	INIT management
Aask	CE Software	INIT management
INITPicker	Microseeds Publishing	INIT management
Data Exchange		
SuperGlue II	Solutions International	Text and graphics exchange between Mac applications
LapLink Mac	Traveling Software	File transfer between Macs and IBM PCs
MacLink Plus/PC	DataViz	File transfer between Macs and IBM PCs
DOS Mounter	Dayna Communications	Direct Finder access of 3½-inch IBM disks and Bernoulli Box cartridges
DOS Access	Insignia Solutions	Direct Finder access of 3½-inch IBM disks
Network/Workgroup		
MarkUp	Mainstay	Document annotation for approval and comment
Timbuktu	Farallon Computing	Training, remote control of Macs on network
In/Out	CE Software	Employee tracking and messaging
DiskPaper	Farallon Computing	Document annotation and exchange

menu (see the figure "Moving Menus"). Another navigation aid is Advanced Interface Programming's TOM INIT, which lets you turn any menu into a *tear-off menu*, which you can detach from the menu bar and drag anywhere on the screen — like the Tools and Patterns menus in HyperCard.

Managing Resources in System 6.x

Fond of fonts? Daft about desk accessories? If so, you've probably been frustrated by the Mac's inability to accommodate more than 500 font sizes and 15 desk accessories. The answer? A *resource manager* such as Fifth Generation Systems' Suitcase II or ALSoft's MasterJuggler. Also called *font/DA extenders*, these godsends let you laden your Font and Apple menus with a nearly unlimited number of fonts and desk accessories. They work with other types of system resources, too, such as F-keys and digitized sounds.

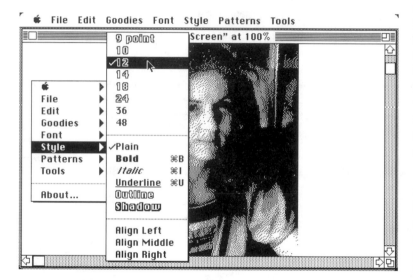

Resource-management utilities also make it easier to add and remove system resources. Instead of using Apple's Font/DA Mover (included with the System) or ResEdit

▲ **Moving Menus**

Magic Software's Powermenus turns the Mac's menu bar into a pop-up menu that appears when you Command-click, eliminating the need to move the mouse pointer up to the menu bar.

(available from user groups and online services) to install or delete resources in the System file, you simply access them via the resource utility's Open and Close commands. The utility tricks the Mac into thinking the resources are in the System file. The results: you can access more resources than the Mac normally permits, and the System file remains lean and therefore easier to back up and copy to other disks.

Both MasterJuggler and Suitcase II offer other goodies. Suitcase II can display the actual typefaces in a program's Font menu, instead of simply showing font names in the Mac's Chicago font. (Dubl-Click Software's MenuFonts 2 does this, too, as does Now Software's Now Utilities.) MasterJuggler lets you assign a sound to any of nine events, such as inserting or ejecting a disk. (A shareware INIT called SoundMaster, by Bruce Tomlin, also does this. It's described along with some other sound-related utilities in Chapter 32.) And both Suitcase II and MasterJuggler can *compress* fonts and sounds so they take up less disk space. When a compressed font or sound is needed, the utility automatically *decompresses* it while loading it into memory, leaving the compressed version intact on your disk.

If you use System 7.0, you don't need a font/DA extender. As we'll see in Chapter 25, System 7.0 makes installing and removing system resources easier and adds new versatility to the Apple menu.

Lost in Disk Space

Hard disks can be hard work. It's great having megabytes of fast storage on tap, but as a hard disk fills up, managing its contents becomes increasingly difficult.

Fortunately, an entire class of utilities is devoted to simplifying life for hard-disk owners. The Mac's Find File desk accessory is one example. Find File is handy, but its file-locating features are minimal compared to those of disk managers such as CE Software's DiskTop, Fifth Generation Systems' DiskTools (part of the File Director package), Aladdin Systems' Shortcut, and Working Software's Findswell.

DiskTop and DiskTools are desk accessories that mimic many functions of the Finder (see the figure "Surrogate Finders" on next page). Both let you copy, rename, and delete files, as well as start programs and open documents. But unlike the Finder, both also let you search for files according to a variety of criteria. With DiskTop, for example, you can search for all text-only files larger than 10K created by a program other than Microsoft Word between January 1 and January 15. Both programs provide some navigation benefits, too, allowing you to quit one program and start another without returning to the Finder. Tactic Software's MasterFinder provides similar features and includes both application and desk accessory versions.

Shortcut and Findswell offer an even more convenient way to locate files. Both utilities are INITs that modify the standard Open dialog box all Mac programs use — a logical place to put file-searching features (unless you need to locate a file when using the Finder, whose Open command doesn't display the standard dialog box). Findswell adds a small button; click it, and a dialog box for searching appears. Shortcut turns the disk name that appears above the Eject and Drive buttons into a menu whose commands let you search for files, create new folders, and more (see the figure "One-Stop Searching" on page 249).

Surrogate Finders

Fifth Generation
Systems' DiskTools
(top) and CE Software's
DiskTop (bottom) allow
you to manage disks,
start programs, search
for files, and open
documents without
having to return to the
Finder.

Phrase Finders

The aforementioned file ferrets are useful only when you know part or all of the file name you're looking for. When you don't, consider a *text-retrieval* utility such as Microlytics' Gofer, On Technology's On Location, or Virginia Systems' Sonar or Sonar Professional. These utilities can search for text contained *within* files. Besides offering another way to locate lost files, a text-retrieval utility can turn the Mac into a powerful research tool. An attorney, for example, might use one to search case-history files for references to a specific case or litigant.

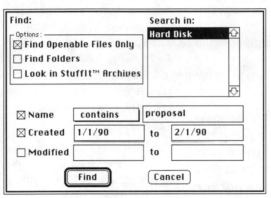

One-Stop Searching
Working Software's Findswell and Aladdin Systems' Shortcut modify the standard Open dialog box that Mac programs display. Click Findswell's button (top left) and a dialog box appears (top right) that lets you search for text appearing in a file's name or Get Info text. Shortcut turns the disk name above the Drive and Eject buttons into a menu (bottom left). Shortcut can't search Get Info comments, but it does let you search for files created or modified between two specified dates (bottom right).

The Sonar programs operate as separate applications; Gofer is a desk accessory. All three utilities let you perform simple searches for a single word or phrase, or complex *Boolean* searches, in which you separate multiple words or phrases with OR, AND, or NOT, as in: "locate all files containing 'baseball' AND 'pitcher' OR 'football' *AND* 'quarterback' but NOT 'hockey' AND 'goalie.' "

Because Gofer and On Location work as desk accessories, they're more convenient than the Sonar series for day-to-day use. The Sonar programs, however, offer more sophisticated searching features. Sonar Professional, in particular, is the program of choice for serious researchers. It can assemble an index of words and phrases; search for synonyms; and even search for words that are within a certain distance of other words, such as each occurrence of *trade* that appears within five words of *deficit*.

More Hard-Disk Tamers

Another way to tame a hard disk's frontiers is to use a *partitioning* utility such as ALSoft's MultiDisk or Symantec's SUM Partition, included with SUM II. Partitioning utilities let you divide a hard disk's capacity into two or more *logical volumes*, each of which is treated as a separate disk that you can electronically insert and eject. Some people prefer to divide a a large-capacity hard disk into several volumes, believing that doing so makes it easier to manage and back up files.

As you use a hard disk, its contents become *fragmented* — scattered across separate areas of the disk. *Defragmentation* utilities, also called *disk optimizers*, keep a hard disk running at top efficiency by rearranging its contents so that all files are stored contiguously. Symantec's SUM II, Norton Utilities for the Macintosh, and Central Point's MacTools Deluxe offer this feature; ALsoft's DiskExpress II is another popular disk optimizer.

Organizing a hard disk is one thing; keeping its files safely backed up is another. Backing up a hard disk involves copying its contents to another storage medium — usually to a dozen or so floppy disks. It's drudgery, to be sure, but you can make the process tolerable by using a *backup utility* such as Dantz Development's Retrospect, SuperMac's DiskFit, Microseeds Publishing's Redux, or Fifth Generation Systems' Fastback II. With a backup utility, you start by backing up the entire hard disk, inserting fresh floppies when necessary. After that, run the utility at regular intervals (every day or so) to back up new or modified files.

❝ Even if you back up religiously, you'll probably lose a file now and then. You might trash one by mistake or encounter a damaged disk between backups. ❞

Chances are your backup routine will be as simple as the one I just described. You might, however, want to take advantage of the remarkable array of backup options that some programs — particularly Retrospect and Fastback II — provide. With Retrospect, for example, you can click on an on-screen calendar to specify backup intervals — once a week, every day, every other day, and so on. Subsequently, Retrospect automatically backs up your work at the specified intervals.

Even if you back up religiously, you'll probably lose a file now and then. You might trash one by mistake or encounter a damaged disk between backups. At such times, you'll want a *file-recovery* utility such as Symantec's SUM II, Norton Utilities for the Macintosh, or Central Point Software's MacTools Deluxe. By working intimately with the technical information that the Mac relies on to keep track of files, these wonder workers can often (though not always) recover deleted files or files stored on damaged disks.

Disk backup and recovery programs are complex enough to warrant a separate chapter. I'll take a closer look at these utilities and the concepts behind disk backup and disk maintenance in Chapter 27.

Utility Potpourri

We've toured the most popular utility categories, but I can't wrap up without giving a few more programs their due.

❖ *Cosmetic* utilities let you customize the appearance of the Mac's interface. Palomar Software's Colorizer adds color to scroll bars, menus, and every other element of the Mac's user interface. Microseeds' Screen Gems lets you replace the Mac's grey desktop pattern with a color image. Dubl-Click's ClickChange and Preferred Publisher's Personality let you create 3-D windows and buttons as well as animated mouse pointers.

❖ *Screen savers* blank the Mac's screen after a specified period of inactivity, preventing an image of the menu bar from being burned into the monitor's phosphorous coating. Popular screen savers include Berkeley Systems' After Dark, Fifth Generation Systems' Pyro, and Microseeds' Dimmer (part of the Screen Gems package).

❖ *Clipboard enhancement* utilities add features or conveniences to the Mac's Clipboard data-exchange mechanism. Solutions' SmartScrap (illustrated in Chapter 2) provides more features than Apple's Scrapbook desk accessory, as does Mainstay's ClickPaste.

❖ *Font utilities* streamline the way the Mac works with type fonts. Foremost among them is Adobe's Adobe Type Manager (ATM), which uses PostScript outline font files to provide tack-sharp screen fonts at any size — no more jagged-edged type if you choose a size that doesn't exist in your System file. ATM also lets you use PostScript printer fonts with non-PostScript printers such as GCC's Personal LaserPrinter and Apple's Personal LaserWriter LS, ImageWriter II, and StyleWriter. Adobe's Adobe Type Reunion sorts and organizes fonts by family names, eliminating Font menus that sag to the bottom of the screen. Tactic Software's FontShare lets the Macs on a network share downloadable printer fonts stored on a file server. Jim Lewis' free theTypeBook program is one of several utilities that let you quickly create font-specimen books that graphic designers and desktop publishers rely on to help them choose typefaces.

❖ *Screen capture* utilities replace the Mac's feeble Command-Shift-3 F-key by providing a slew of options for saving a screen image on disk. Mainstay's Capture lets you copy part or all of the screen — including pulled-down menus — or save it as a disk file, and Capture supports color displays and large screens. Preferred Publishers' Exposure provides similar options.

❖ *Workgroup* utilities let you turn LocalTalk network cabling into a medium for coworker communication and brainstorming. If you're using LocalTalk cables only to connect Macs to laser printers, you're wasting your wires.

Farallon Computing's remarkable Timbuktu lets you control one Mac from another Mac on the network, or simply observe how others are using their Macs. It's also ideal for transferring files between machines. (Claris' Public Folder is another excellent network file-transfer utility; it's free to registered users of Claris software.) CE Software's In/Out lets you keep track of who's in the office — it's an electronic version of the message boards many offices use. Mainstay's MarkUp allows group editing of documents as they journey through the approval loop — it's an electronic red pencil that works on networks. Solutions' SuperGlue II provides document-annotation features, too. Farallon's DiskPaper lets you "print" an electronic copy of any document to your hard disk. After creating the document, you can include a recorded sound cover note containing instructions, comments, or additional information.

❖ *Spoolers* make the long wait for a slow printer less annoying by intercepting and storing documents on disk and then sending them to the printer as it becomes available. Although you won't get your output any faster, at least your Macintosh won't be tied up, leaving you waiting while files print. MultiFinder and System 7.0 provide *background printing*, too, but only to PostScript laser printers and Apple's Personal LaserWriter LS, not to ImageWriters, StyleWriters, or Hewlett-Packard DeskWriters. Fifth Generation Systems' SuperLaserSpool supports these printers, and it doesn't require MultiFinder — good news if your Mac has only 1MB of memory.

❖ *File-transfer* utilities — such as DataViz's MacLink Plus/PC and Traveling Software's LapLink Mac — bridge the gap between the Mac and the IBM PC and many popular laptops. Both include a cable and software for your Mac and PC. (I'll look at these file-translation utilities again in Chapter 29.) If your Mac has Apple's 1.4MB SuperDrive floppy drive, consider Dayna Communications' DOS Mounter or Insignia Solutions' DOS Access. Both are INITs that let you insert 3½-inch PC disks in a SuperDrive and work with them using the Finder.

❖ *File-compression* utilities such as Aladdin Systems' StuffIt Deluxe and the shareware StuffIt Classic let you compress files so they'll use less disk space. They're priceless for archiving lesser-used files and for sending and receiving files via modem. Salient Software's Disk Doubler is another popular file-compression utility. A variety of *disk labelling* utilities is also available to help you keep track of what's on your disks. Several labelling programs are available that read disks you insert and then generate labels that you can print on Avery peel-and-stick label stock.

❖ *Security* utilities let you keep sensitive files away from curious eyes. File-encryption programs scramble documents according to a password you supply. Some popular security utilities include SuperMac's Sentinel; Kent-Marsh's MacSafe II, FolderBolt, and NightWatch; FWB's Hard Disk DeadBolt; and Fifth Generation's DiskLock. StuffIt Deluxe and Disk Doubler also allow you to assign passwords to archives. To keep wandering hands off your Mac, consider a utility such as Kent-Marsh's QuickLock or Casady and Greene's Access Managed Environment (AME), both of which let you electronically lock the keyboard, screen, and mouse.

❖ *Virus detection* utilities such as Symantec's SAM, Microcom's Virex, and John Norstad's Disinfectant help guard against a virus attack. Viruses and virus detection utilities are covered in Chapter 28.

❖ *INIT managers* let you selectively disable INITs without having to drag them out of the System Folder. Popular INIT managers include CE Software's Aask (part of the MockUtilities package), Microseeds' INITPicker, and Natural Intelligence's Inix. I use a free INIT manager called Init, by John Rotenstein. You can get a copy through online services such as CompuServe or from a local user group or shareware clearinghouse.

Utilities that let you manage utilities — now that's the sign of a thriving marketplace. There's no shortage of utilities for the Macintosh, and that's proof of a few things: the gaps still present in the Mac's system software, the vitality of the Mac itself, and most of all, the desire of Mac users to personalize and customize their machines.

Summary:

✔ Utilities form the supporting cast of a computer setup; they work together with the Mac's system software and with your application programs to improve the Mac's performance and enhance its operation.

✔ Utilities that work together with your application programs may operate as INITs (system extensions), desk accessories, F-keys (function keys), RDEVS (accessed from the Mac's Chooser desk accessory), or cdevs, which show up in the Control Panel.

✔ Navigation utilities, like Apple's MacroMaker and CE Software's QuicKeys 2, let you streamline the Mac's operation to suit your work habits and preferences by creating keyboard shortcuts and automating repetitive tasks.

✔ Resource management utilities allow you to store a nearly unlimited number of fonts and desk accessories and make it easier to add and remove system resources.

✔ File-searching utilities like the Mac's Find File desk accessory let you find a particular file among the many you may have on your hard disk.

✔ Defragmentation utilities, or disk optimizers, help speed up a hard disk by rearranging its contents so that all files are stored contiguously.

✔ The fact that there are so many utilities available for the Mac indicates that there are still gaps in the Mac's system software and that Mac users enjoy personalizing and customizing their machines.

Section Two
MASTERING THE MAC

Chapter 20
Basic Maintenance

In This Chapter:

✔ Tips on how to keep your keyboard and mouse free of dust and liquids.

✔ Floppy drives: to clean or not to clean?

✔ How to avoid damaging your screen when cleaning it.

✔ Maintaining the electronic parts of your Mac.

✔ Mac ergonomics: setting up your system for maximum comfort.

✔ Power-related maintenance tips.

In computing's primeval period (30 years ago), computers used vacuum tubes — those glowing glass bulbs. One IBM SAGE computer, several dozen of which formed the backbone of the United States' air defense system from 1958 to 1983, used 25,000 tubes. Maintenance was hellish. A staff of technicians worked full-time keeping the four-story behemoth running, and even with a battery of built-in diagnostics, finding a faulty tube often meant turning the room lights off and looking for its weakened glow.

Today you can service a computer with the lights on. But despite the reliability of solid-state electronics, computers like the Mac still have some mechanical parts that require routine attention. Still, you'd be surprised at how many people ignore the basics of setup and maintenance vital for a healthy Mac. Or maybe you wouldn't. If you're part of the group that believes preventative maintenance should be prevented, this chapter is for you.

You'll be glad to know that keeping your Mac and its peripherals in tune doesn't require any fancy equipment or technical background. There isn't a single acronym in this chapter. In fact, Mac maintenance can be summarized in one phrase: keep it clean and cool.

Clean Up Your Mac

Although a layer of dust can do damage by acting as a blanket that keeps heat in, electronic chips don't have to sparkle to work. The only items on a Mac that need regular cleaning are the screen and the mechanical parts — the keyboard, mouse, and possibly, the disk drives.

Keeping the keyboard clean involves keeping it free of dust and liquids. Each key is a switch with two contacts that close; the key generates a signal when you press it. Dust or spilled maple syrup will either prevent that signal from being generated, or will cause a kind of keyboard stuttering: you'll press *c* and get six of them as the contacts intermittently make and break their connection through the grime.

To dust a keyboard, first turn off the Mac, and then unplug the keyboard. Take the keyboard into a different room (one without computers), turn it upside down, and blow into the keys with short, powerful breaths. Keep those breaths dry by swallowing a couple of times beforehand, and don't think about Grandma's cookies as you work. Better still, rest your lungs and buy a can of compressed air such as Falcon's Dust-Off at a camera store. Read the directions on the can first: with some products, holding the can upside-down or at other odd angles causes icy wet liquid to escape. Don't substitute a bicycle pump, air compressor, or other unfiltered air source. It could make matters worse by blowing dust into the keyboard.

Compared to liquids, though, dust is a minor enemy to keyboards. Crying over spilt milk may serve no purpose, but orange juice or soda spattered on a keyboard is definitely weep-worthy. When a sugary liquid dries, it leaves behind a sticky residue that will seal or even corrode the key's contacts. If you commit this cardinal sin, take your keyboard to a dealer for a complete cleaning.

If you're in the middle of a big project and can't do without the keyboard, however, there is one small hope. It's a desperate measure that won't replace professional service, but it may get you through a crunch. Buy a bottle of spray contact cleaner (not tuner cleaner) at an electronics store, then unplug the keyboard (with the Mac's power off), hold it over a sink, and spray a generous amount of cleaner into the keyboard while repeatedly pressing its keys. Quickly turn the keyboard upside down to let it drain. Wait half an hour or so, then reconnect the keyboard and try typing. If the keyboard works, say a prayer of thanks and vow to take it in for service as soon as possible. If it doesn't, or if one or two keys still act up, try again. If you can't locate contact cleaner, try a bottle of tape-recorder head cleaner. But remember that this technique is a last-ditch effort. If you can live without your keyboard for a while, having it properly cleaned is the best solution.

The mouse is another spill-prone component. Liquid spilled on it will seep in around the button and gum up its switch. Again, professional cleaning is the best remedy, but you can probably make due by disassembling the mouse and spraying contact cleaner into its switch. A mouse can also take in liquid from the bottom. If you roll it through a puddle, its rubber ball will pick up liquid and transfer it to the contact points, causing sluggish pointer movement or none at all. If that happens, turn the mouse upside down, remove the retaining plate that surrounds the ball, then invert the mouse and catch the ball as it falls out. Clean the ball with a lint-free cloth and clean the rollers inside the mouse with a cotton swab moistened with tape head cleaner or alcohol. In any case, cleaning the mouse regularly is a good habit to get into, since the mouse picks up dust and lint as it's used.

Dusty Drives and the Screen

The debate over whether or not to clean floppy disk drives frequently has been known to spark brawls at user-group meetings. Some say regular cleaning helps prevent disk errors by removing dust and particles that occasionally flake off a disk's surface. Clean-drive advocates swear by disk drive cleaning kits, which contain a disklike item that houses a circular pad of fiber-based cleaning material. You moisten the pad with cleaning fluid, then insert it in the holder, and put the holder in the drive, where it spins like a disk and cleans the heads.

Others say, leave the drives alone unless they're acting up. They claim that cleaning can do more harm than good because of too much or too little fluid, or because dirt and grime in the cleaning pad can act like sand paper on the drives' heads. I'm from that school. Some of my Macs are approaching their seventh birthdays, and their drives have never been cleaned and have never misbehaved — after near-constant use in houses plagued with woodstove dust in the winter and pollen in the summer. I'm not saying that cleaning is bad for drives, mind you: I'm just presenting both sides of the story. I believe cleaning is unnecessary if you use high-quality disks and prevent an accumulation of dust in your work area.

The screen is another area where improper cleaning can do damage. Most screens have a non-glare coating that common glass cleaners will promptly dissolve, turning the screen's finish from matte to glossy. You can keep the screen clean with lint-free tissues (such as Kimwipes) or photographic lens-cleaning tissue. If you must use a liquid to remove sticky fingerprints, use a cleaning fluid made for computer screens. It won't harm the finish, and some of those products repel dust — at least according to the companies that sell them. Although you can use window cleaner to clean the Mac's case, be sure to spray it on a cloth (not a linty paper towel) rather than directly on the case.

Beat the Heat

Cleaning is important for the Mac's mechanical parts; cooling is vital for its electronic ones. Electronic components have self-destructive lifestyles. Heat is their worst enemy, yet they generate heat as they work. To keep its parts cool, a computer's case must be ventilated so that cool air can replace hot. The designers of the first Macs (ones preceding the SE and II) placed cooling vents at strategic locations in the machine's case to provide what's called *convection cooling:* the heat created inside the machine rises and exits through the vents in the top of the case, drawing in cooler air through the vents at the bottom.

This clever arrangement allows air to circulate through the case without requiring a noisy fan. But you can easily thwart the process by blocking a set of vents. If you cram a Mac between books or magazines (or use it on a bearskin rug), you'll block the lower vents, preventing the intake of cool air. If you put it under a shelf or set books or papers on top of it, you'll block the top vents, trapping the hot air inside. Either way, the result is the same: you'll choke off the flow of air, allowing heat to build to potentially damaging levels. And damaging doesn't have to mean chip meltdown. Even if it doesn't damage the hardware, too high a temperature can cause a system crash.

To beat the heat, then, give any Mac — but especially the fanless Mac Plus — room to breathe: an inch or two on the sides and several more on the top. Keep it away from a radiator or other heat source. Also, keep it out of sunlight. Direct sunlight will bake a Mac and cause screen glare to boot. If you have a Plus or earlier model, be especially careful to keep the left side of the machine cool — that's the side where the heat-generating power supply lives.

Fans for the Mac Plus

An especially effective way to chill the chips in a Mac Plus is to add an external fan such as Kensington Microware's System Saver. External fans usually fit in the gap that forms the Mac's carrying handle, which may be a drawback if your Mac moves around with you.

A fan increases the flow of air through the machine, although keeping the vents clear is no less important. Some people think fans are for ballparks and hate the idea of losing the Mac Plus's aural unobtrusiveness, but if you work in a large office or use a hard disk or other fan-equipped gear, you won't notice a fan's extra decibels.

But don't feel like you must have one. The Mac Plus's fan-free cooling scheme will keep it temperate provided you follow the ventilation rules. You should consider a fan, however, if your Mac Plus contains several megabytes of memory or an accelerator board, or if you live in a tropical climate.

The Complete Mac Wardrobe

Cleaning and cooling will keep your Mac healthy, but what about you? Your equipment should be set up to allow you to use it without having to hire a live-in ophthalmologist and chiropractor. Fortunately, several companies have come to the rescue with gadgets and gizmos that all the well-dressed Macs are wearing. The figure "A Workstation that Works" illustrates ergonomic issues.

❖ *Tilt and swivel stand* For me and many others, the screen in a Mac Plus, SE, or Classic is too low to look at for hours on end without developing a pain in the neck. Swivel stands made by firms such as Curtis Manufacturing and Kensington raise the Mac and let you tilt it to a more comfortable viewing angle. You can also try propping up the front of the machine by placing something under it, such as the lid of a disk box or two 1½-inch-high plastic furniture leg-tips (my personal choice). Incidentally, you'll be glad to know that tilting a Mac does not affect the operation of pinball or billiard games.

❖ *Mac II stands* The original Mac II, the IIx, and the IIfx are big Macs that take up a lot of desk space. You can set up these Macs on their sides alongside your desk by using metal stands such as Kensington's Macintosh II Stand, which is also available with extension cables for the keyboard and monitor. Set up the Mac so that the power light is closest to the floor. This puts the floppy drive and programmer's switch within reach. (It also gets the floppy drive away from the dusty floor.) Don't set a big Mac on its side without a stand; you'll block the cooling vents. This doesn't apply to the Mac IIcx and IIci, by the way. They're designed to work in either vertical or horizontal orientations.

❖ *Mouse pads* These are squares of rubber that protect furniture and, according to their proponents, smooth mouse movement. They're just the thing if you're forced to set up shop on an antique desk. You can also make a mouse pad yourself from wet-suit neoprene or even a piece of clean cardboard, such as the backing on a pad of paper.

❖ *Anti-glare screen* If you work near a bright window or under a bank of flourescent lights, screen glare may take its toll on your eyes. Several firms make filters that attach to a monitor's screen. Some filters distort or blur the screen image, however, so be sure to evaluate several before buying one. It might be smarter to rearrange your work area or change its lighting to eliminate the glare. As you shop for screen filters, you'll encounter some that are advertised as reducing the low-frequency radiation that video tubes give off. There's little evidence that screen filters are effective at blocking monitor radiation. A safer practice is to be sure you sit at arms' length from the front of the Mac's screen, and at least four feet away from the sides or back of any other monitor. Keep that latter recommendation in mind if you work in an office: partitions and even walls won't stop low-frequency monitor radiation.

A WORKSTATION THAT WORKS

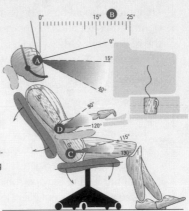

Today's ergonomists recognize that there is no perfect position that workers can maintain all day. For most people, a comfortable workstation is one that can accommodate two or more positions, enabling you to adjust your chair, monitor, and keyboard to fit your current task or inclination. Most people find the upright and slightly reclined positions portrayed here best for computer use. If you do a fair amount of traditional desk work, you'll probably want a chair that supports a forward-leaning position as well.

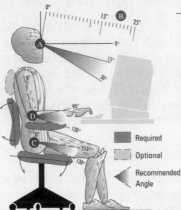

- ■ Required
- ▨ Optional
- ◀ Recommended Angle

Screen Posture always follows the eyes; screens placed too low or angled improperly are a major source of slouching **(A)**. The distance from the screen to your eyes should be only slightly greater than the distance you normally maintain between reading material and your eyes **(B)**. (Bifocal wearers may require a steeper screen angle than the ones portrayed.)

Chair Seat contours should follow the contours of your back. Adjust chair height so that you don't feel pressure on your tailbone (seat too low) or lower thighs (seat too high). Ergonomists used to recommend 90 degrees as a good angle between thighs and spine, but recent research shows that more people favor a more open posture **(C)**.

Keyboard Your arms should be relaxed at your side, with elbows a few inches from your body **(D)**. Position your chair and keyboard to minimize reaches. When you change position, from upright to reclined for example, be sure to reposition your keyboard (and screen). An adjustable keyboard stand, which enables you to use the mouse without a stretch, is useful for this purpose, but you can also place the keyboard in your lap.

Desk A comfortable desk height is particularly important if you keep the keyboard on your desk. If you don't have a keyboard stand and you work at a nonadjustable surface that's too high, try raising your chair and putting a platform or box beneath your feet. If your desk is too low, try fastening blocks to the ends of the legs.

Copy Stand If you often look at paper documents when you work, use a copy stand, mounted so that it puts your work in the same plane and at the same height as the screen. If you look at the hard copy more than the screen, orient your chair or screen such that the copy stand, rather than the Macintosh, is directly in front of you.

You Keep moving—motion makes the blood flow. And remember to take a break from computer work every hour.

Prepared with the assistance of Eileen Vollowitz, PT, of Back Designs, in Oakland, California.
—Joe Matazzoni

❖ *Typing desk* Many desks are too high for comfortable typing. To avoid back and neck strain, a typing desk should be roughly 27 inches high. Get a desk intended for typing, and avoid those so-called computer tables with shelves that place the screen at forehead level. To protect your neck and your ego, you should look down slightly on a computer.

❖ *Surge suppressor* To guard against lightning bolts and power surges (very brief but potentially very damaging increases in the power company's voltage), you might want to consider a surge suppressor. Some surge supressors also contain power filters, which smooth out the incoming voltage and help remove "noise" that power equipment or nearby thunderstorms can cause.

Some engineers I've talked to say a more common power problem is a voltage sag, also called a brown-out, which can occur when a power-hungry device like a clothes dryer or air conditioner comes on. Surviving voltage sags requires more complex and more expensive circuitry. The best power security is a device called an uninterruptible power supply or standby power supply, which contains batteries that provide a minimum of five minutes of juice after a power failure — not a lot, but enough to save your work and shut down safely. Chapter 31 discusses power problems and power-protection devices in detail.

Odds and Ends

While we're talking electrons, there are some other electricity-related mainte-nance tips to pass on. One concerns the battery that goes in the slot above the power switch on pre-SE Macs and powers the built-in clock and saves your Control Panel settings when the machine is off. It looks like a 1.5-volt AA flashlight battery, but it isn't. It's a 4.5-volt battery, an Eveready 523 or equivalent. If your Mac Plus's clock starts losing track of time, the battery is probably exhausted. You can buy a replacement, which should last about two years, at a camera store. Post-Plus Macs have lithium batteries that last for many years.

Then there's static electricity, which can be more disastrous to an integrated circuit than heat. If you've just shuffled across a wool carpet on a dry winter day, touch a metal lightswitch plate, a radiator, or a cat's nose before touching the Mac. That's especially vital if you're about to install or remove a memory upgrade or an expansion board. The closer you get to integrated circuit chips, the more important it is to be static-free. If you live in a static prone area (one where the humidity is very low), consider using an anti-static wrist strap, available through most computer dealers and mail-order houses, when working with your Mac's innards.

Static electricity can also zap disks, scrambling just enough information to make the disk unreadable. Speaking of floppy disks, they warrant their own special care, which, as we'll see in Chapter 27, boils down to no heat, no dust, no bending, and no magnetic fields. And if you have an external floppy disk drive, don't set it to the left of a Mac Plus or SE (near its power supply) or underneath a high-intensity desk lamp (the kind with a transformer in its base). Both items generate magnetic fields that can cause disk errors.

All in all, Mac maintenance isn't a full-time job. It certainly beats the hoops I had to jump through to keep my first computer, a 1977 Radio Shack Model I, afloat. Its copper connectors corroded faster than an old Chevy in an acid bath, causing frequent system crashes. The solution: a weekly "Pink Pearl treatment," which involved polishing three sets of connectors with a pencil eraser. Happily, the only erasers I see these days are in painting programs.

Summary:

✔ Despite the reliability of solid-state electronics, computers like the Mac still have some mechanical parts that require routine maintenance.

✔ Exposing a keyboard or mouse to dust or liquids can result in unreliable operation — or worse.

✔ Some people believe regular cleaning of floppy disk drives helps prevent disk errors while others believe you should leave them alone unless they act up — the decision is yours.

✔ Improper cleaning of your screen can damage the non-glare coating, turning the screen's finish from matte to glossy. Lint-free tissues and cleaning fluid made for computer screens can be used to avoid this problem.

✔ Proper ventilation must be provided for the electronic components of your Mac. Earlier Macs achieve this using convection cooling (heat escapes from the top while cool air is drawn through vents at the bottom). If you have a Mac Plus, another way to achieve this is to add a fan to your system.

✔ Anti-glare screens and tilt and swivel stands are examples of accessories you can buy to maximize your comfort in your working environment.

✔ To avoid ruining your Mac's integrated circuitry, touch a grounded metal object before working inside the Mac, or consider using an anti-static wrist strap.

Chapter 21
Memory

In This Chapter:

✔ An explanation of the difference between read-only memory (ROM) and random access memory (RAM).

✔ A look at the vital roles RAM plays.

✔ How to use RAM to boost your Mac's performance.

✔ When to use a RAM disk and when to use a RAM cache.

✔ Virtual memory: a RAM disk in reverse.

I n 1946 at a lecture at the Los Alamos National Laboratory, a mathematician named John von Neumann presented his vision of future computers: they would contain internal storage space for holding the results of calculations until the data could be permanently stored on punched cards. This temporary work space, which he called *internal memory,* would also allow a computer to hold sequences of instructions, eliminating the need to rewire the machine to perform a different type of calculation. Yes, in that computer Stone Age, to run a different program, you got out your wire cutters.

Since those early days memory has evolved from room-size circuits that could store a sentence to fingernail-size chips that can store a book. And someone reading this 20 years from now will probably chuckle at my quaint descriptions of today's memory. But it's likely that memory will still serve the same basic role: storing the programs we use and the data we create. In this chapter, I'll look at this role as it applies to the Mac, and I'll describe ways to use memory to improve the Mac's performance. The sidebar "Coming to Terms with Memory" defines the most common memory-related terms. For details on choosing specific upgrades, see Chapter 34.

Memory Minutiae

There are many types of memory, but most fall into either of two broad categories: *ROM* and *RAM.* You can't venture into the Mac world without encountering these two acronyms, so it helps to understand the concepts behind them.

ROM stands for *read-only memory:* the Mac can read the contents of a ROM chip, but it can't change them. A ROM chip's software is in there for good, prerecorded at the factory like the music on a phonograph album or compact disc. The only real threat to ROM is an electrical mishap such as a power surge or a spark of static electricity.

In most computers, ROM holds only a small amount of *system software,* that program code that enables the machine to run. The Mac's ROM plays a much more significant role. It contains software that programmers call on to create pull-down menus, windows, dialog boxes — all the trappings of the Mac's user interface. (These routines are often collectively described as the *Toolbox.*) This

Coming to Terms with Memory

Access Time   The time required, in nanoseconds (billionths of a second; abbreviated *ns*) to successfully read to or write from a RAM chip. Some Macs require faster RAM chips than others; the IIci needs 80ns RAM chips, while the Plus and SE can use slower chips. (Some static RAM chips provide access times as fast as 25ns.) You can use chips with a faster access time than your Mac needs, but they won't speed up processing; the computer's circuitry is designed for chips with a specific access time.

Bit   Short for *binary digit,* the smallest unit of computer storage. Another of John von Nuemann's contributions to computing, a bit can represent one of two states: 1 (on) or 0 (off).

Byte   The workhorse of information storage, equal to 8 bits. One byte can represent any of 256 values, since its 8 bits can be on or off in 256 different combinations. A byte can represent a single

character; for example, storing the alphabet requires 26 bytes.

Density   The capacity, in bits (not bytes), of an individual RAM or ROM chip. The most common densities are 256 kilobits and 1 megabit. By tying RAM chips together in groups of eight, a SIMM board can store 256 kilobytes or 1 megabyte. A 1MB Mac contains four 256K SIMMs; a 4MB Mac has four 1MB SIMMs. SIMMs that hold 4MB are becoming increasingly popular, especially among Mac IIsi owners.

Gigabyte   1024 megabytes; abbreviated as *GB.*

Kilobit   1024 bits; abbreviated as *Kbit.* The capacities of individual RAM chips are measured in Kbits.

Kilobyte   1024 bytes; abbreviated as *K.*

Megabit   1,048,576 bits; abbreviated as *Mbit.*

Megabyte   1024 kilobytes; abbreviated as *MB.*

built-in personality is what makes almost all Macintosh programs look and operate in the same basic way. ROM also stores diagnostic routines that swing into action when you switch the Mac on, testing its hardware for problems and then displaying the familiar where's-the-disk? icon.

RAM: Memory that Forgets

If a ROM chip is like a phonograph album, a RAM chip is like a cassette tape or floppy disk — it's initially blank, and its contents can be changed over and over again. RAM stands for *random-access memory.* Because it can be written to as well as read from, it's sometimes called *read-write memory.*

RAM performs the vital job of storing the documents you create and the software you use to create them. RAM is the Mac's temporary workspace — when you start a program, one of the Mac's first jobs is to copy the program from disk into RAM. Similarly, the Finder — the disk-management software that gives you the Mac's desktop, folder filing system, and trash can — loads into RAM when you start up the Mac.

When you're creating a document using a word processor or other program, RAM also holds some or all of your document. Most graphics and spreadsheet programs store an entire document in RAM. Most word processing, desktop publishing, and data-management programs swap information between RAM and a disk. The program keeps in memory only the portion of the document you're working on at the moment. This approach lets the program create documents larger than the available memory. On floppy disk systems, the disk-and-RAM shuffle slows performance, since the program must frequently access the disk to save or read part of a document. Because disks are mechanical beasts, they can't transfer information as quickly as RAM chips.

RAM is versatile but vulnerable. Cassettes and floppy disks store information using magnetic particles oriented in patterns that remain intact until another magnetic field comes along to change them. A RAM chip, on the other hand, uses millions of microscopic electronic switches that stay in place only as long as the chips have a steady, reliable supply of power. That's why programs have Save commands — and why it's a good idea to use them often.

Incidentally, RAM chips are often referred to as *DRAM* (pronounced *dee-RAM*) chips. *D* is for *dynamic* and reflects the chip's need for a periodic electronic nudging, or *refresh signal,* that allows it to retain its contents. The other major type of RAM chip, *static RAM,* doesn't require a refresh signal and therefore uses less power. That's one reason Apple used static RAM in the Mac Portable. But static RAM chips are more expensive than their dynamic counterparts; as a result, most deskbound computers use DRAM chips.

Actually, a special part of the Mac's memory does retain its information when the power goes. The Mac's battery-powered *parameter RAM* remembers Control Panel settings such as how quickly key characters repeat when you hold a key down, or how much time can elapse between two mouse clicks before they're considered separate clicks rather than a double click. The battery also powers the Mac's built-in clock.

The RAM chips used in deskbound Macs are connected in groups of eight on small plug-in circuit boards called *Single Inline Memory Modules,* or *SIMMs.* (The Mac Portable uses its own specialized memory boards, and in the discontinued 128K and 512K Macs, RAM chips are connected directly to the computer's main circuit board.) As mentioned earlier, in their least-expensive configuration, some Macs include 1 megabyte (MB) of RAM. One megabyte was a limitless expanse in John von Neumann's computing world, but as we'll see shortly, today it's barely enough.

Cramped RAM

The Mac's RAM and ROM chips work together — ROM supplies the carved-in-stone software that helps the Mac run, and RAM provides the storage space to hold, well, everything else. You might think the Mac's RAM holds only applications and their documents. Not so. RAM is like a shared closet — it's crammed with odds and ends that reduce the amount of space left over for your stuff. These odds and ends include the following.

❖ *RAM-based system software* Some of the Mac's system software isn't frozen in ROM but is instead loaded from disk during start-up. Apple omitted some of this RAM-based software from ROM in the interest of flexibility. (For example, if the Finder was in ROM, Apple couldn't release updated versions of it without requiring everyone to buy new ROM chips.)

Other RAM-based system routines bypass older ROM-based ones. Many ROM routines are designed to be replaced by newer ones, called *patches,* that load into RAM during start-up. A patch might fix a bug discovered in a ROM routine, or it might add new ROM-based features to an older Mac — for example, Apple's 32-bit QuickDraw software, which lets older Mac IIs use the latest color video hardware. The LC, IIci, IIsi, and IIfx have 32-bit QuickDraw software in ROM. Other Mac IIs that don't have 32-bit QuickDraw in ROM need the patch in order to use certain programs and video boards. The price for this interface lift? About 80K of RAM.

❖ *System extensions* These ubiquitous programs load during startup and let you customize keyboard shortcuts, exchange electronic mail, and more (see

Chapter 19). They're an effective way to customize and enhance the Mac, but they take their toll on free RAM.

❖ *MultiFinder* System software that lets you run multiple programs simultaneously. In System 6.x, it requires 160K of RAM — enough to accommodate an array of INITs or to help feed a memory-hungry program.

❖ *The RAM cache* This Control Panel option can boost performance, but it uses RAM to do so.

The upshot of all this is that a 1MB Mac doesn't have 1MB of *free* memory; instead, it has only 600K to 700K — less if you use MultiFinder or memory-consuming INITs such as network or electronic-mail software. If yours is a 1MB Mac, you'll need to do some careful tweaking to get acceptable performance, and you should choose programs that use memory sparingly.

Boosting Performance with RAM

By adding to the Mac's memory, you can run several programs at the same time and switch among them with a mouse click. You can also use extra memory to speed up the Mac's operation.

Extra memory can boost performance by reducing the need for the Mac to access both hard and floppy disks. When a program's code or data is stashed in memory instead of on disk, data transfers occur much faster than the leisurely pace of a spinning disk and its mechanical read-write heads.

There are three techniques you can use to improve performance by reducing disk accesses:

❖ *Give an application more memory* The Finder's Get Info window lets you fine-tune how large a chunk of memory MultiFinder gives a program. If you increase this amount, more of the application's program code will be able to reside in memory at once. Otherwise, the Mac will have to swap portions of the program into and out of memory as you work. Large, complex programs such as Microsoft Word, Excel, QuarkXpress, and Aldus Page-Maker are especially appreciative of more memory. Use this rule of thumb: if the Mac frequently accesses the disk when you choose commands or click on icons, chances are the program you're running can benefit from extra memory. (Incidentally, a very handy shareware INIT called AppSizer lets you change memory size values when you start a program without having to use the Get Info command.)

❖ *Activate the RAM cache* The RAM cache stores the most recently accessed portion of the disk in memory in case its program code or data is needed

FAST CACHE

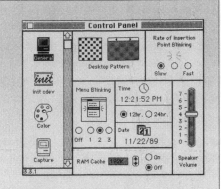

By activating the Control Panel's RAM cache option (top), you set aside memory (up to 25 percent of the total RAM) that the Mac uses to hold recently loaded program code and data. If that code or data is needed again, the cache supplies it, eliminating a disk access. The chart (bottom) shows how a 256K cache improves performance on a 1MB Mac SE without a hard disk. It takes less time to start Word 4.0 and quit to the Finder a second time because part of each is stored in the cache. In System 7.0, use the Memory Control Panel to set the cache. With any system version, restart the Mac after activating the cache or changing its size.

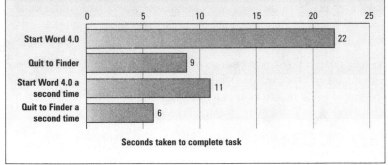

Seconds taken to complete task

again. If it is, the Mac retrieves it from the cache instead of accessing the disk. In System 6.x, the Control Panel's General option lets you activate the RAM cache and specify its size. In System 7.0, use the Memory Control Panel. Generally, the larger the cache, the better the performance boost, until the cache equals about 25 percent of the Mac's RAM (see the figure "Fast Cache").

❖ *Use a RAM disk* A RAM disk is a pseudo disk that you create in the Mac's memory using a RAM-diskutility (see the figure "Electronic Disks"). Such a utility is often included with a memory upgrade. You can copy an application to a RAM disk and run it at lightning speed. If the RAM disk is large enough, you can stash the System Folder there too, and improve performance even more. Unless you have more than 2MB of RAM, however, chances are you won't be able to create a RAM disk large enough to hold the System Folder and a couple of applications. Incidentally, you should never store documents on a RAM disk; if the power goes off (or even fluctuates briefly) or if the Mac crashes, you'll learn the hard way just how pseudo a RAM disk is.

RAM Disk or RAM Cache?

RAM caches and RAM disks sound similar; after all, both improve performance by replacing disk accesses with memory accesses. But beyond that the similarities

Electronic Disks

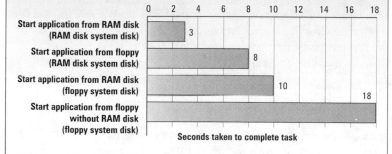

A RAM-disk utility such as Roger Bates's RamDisk+ (top) lets you set aside an area of memory as an electronic disk drive that works at lightning speed. (Another popular shareware RAM-disk utility is George Nelson's RAMStart.) RamDisk+ lists the minimum and maximum practical RAM disk size for the Mac it's running on (in this case, an 8MB Mac II) and also tells you how much memory is being used by the RAM cache and any programmer's debugging aids such as MacsBug. The chart (bottom) compares a RAM disk's effect on performance when it holds just an application (in this case, WriteNow), just the System Folder, and both the System Folder and an application against performance without a RAM disk.

	0	2	4	6	8	10	12	14	16	18
Start application from RAM disk (RAM disk system disk)			3							
Start application from floppy (RAM disk system disk)					8					
Start application from RAM disk (floppy system disk)						10				
Start application from floppy without RAM disk (floppy system disk)										18

Seconds taken to complete task

end. A RAM cache is dynamic; its contents change as you use the Mac. A RAM disk contains only what you put in it.

What's more, the effectiveness of each depends on how you use the Mac. If you generally run only one or two programs and you want maximum performance from them, try a RAM disk. If you routinely switch between two or more applications using MultiFinder or System 7.0, or if you regularly repeat certain tasks, a RAM cache may be the better choice. But if your computing habits are haphazard rather than repetitive — if you never know which command or program you'll be using next — a RAM cache won't help much, since much of the program code it holds may not be needed again.

Some Macs can get the performance-boosting benefits of a RAM cache without donating some of the RAM that holds the programs. The IIci has a slot designed to accept an optional *cache memory* board, which holds a small amount of static RAM that can supply data several times faster than the machine's conventional dynamic RAM chips. Apple's cache memory board provides 32K of cache memory and makes the IIci about 20 percent faster. The Mac IIfx contains built-in cache memory that's fine-tuned to work together with the machine's 68030 processor.

Those of us who don't drive a IIci or IIfx can still benefit from cache memory. Orchid Technology's MacSprint II is a 32K cache memory board for the original Mac II that boosts performance by about 30 percent — not bad for a $299 add-on. You'll also find cache memory on some *accelerator boards* — those brain transplants that replace the Mac's central processor chip with a faster one (see

Chapter 34). For example, the Radius Accelerator 16 and Accelerator 25 boards for the SE both contain 32K of static cache memory.

The Virtues of Virtual Memory

One of the most exciting recent developments in Macintosh memory has almost nothing to do with RAM. I'm referring to *virtual memory,* a software sleight of hand that can make a Mac act as though it had far more memory than it actually does.

Virtual memory is essentially a RAM disk in reverse: instead of treating part of RAM as a disk, it treats part of a hard disk as RAM. Virtual-memory system software and the Mac's *memory management* hardware work behind the scenes to swap program code and data between the Mac's RAM and the hard disk. Because hard disk space costs less per megabyte than RAM, virtual memory is an economical way to banish those out-of-memory messages.

System 7.0 adds virtual-memory features to the SE/30, IIx, IIfx, IIcx, IIsi, and IIci. The 68030 processor in these Macs contains built-in memory-management hardware. To use virtual memory on a Macintosh II or LC, you need to add an additional chip, the Motorola 68851 *Paged Memory Management Unit,* or *PMMU.*

If you have a Mac Plus or SE containing a 68030 accelerator board, consider Connectix Corporation's Virtual software, a system extension (INIT) that adds virtual-memory features to any Mac with memory-management hardware. (The Mac II version of Virtual includes the 68851 PMMU chip, which anyone with steady, static-free hands can install.) Virtual performs some fancy technical tricks that can give you the equivalent of 14MB of memory — even though version 6.x of the Macintosh's system software supports only 8MB. And Virtual runs on 1MB Macs; System 7.0 requires 2MB. Connectix also offers other noteworthy memory-related utilities, such as Maxima, which lets Macs use up to 14MB of memory as application memory and includes a RAM disk utility that supports RAM disks of up to 120MB.

But virtual memory isn't complete nourishment for a memory-starved Mac. For one thing, it's not as fast as real memory — remember, hard disks are mechanical beasts. A Mac with 8MB of real RAM will be faster than the same machine with 2MB of RAM and 6MB of virtual memory. (The exact difference in performance depends on the programs you run and on the speed of your hard disk.)

What's more, virtual memory works best when your Macintosh contains enough RAM to accommodate your largest programs. For example, if one of your programs needs 4MB, your Mac should have 4MB of RAM, even if all your other programs use less than 1MB. If you try to use virtual memory to shoe-horn a huge program into a 1MB Macintosh, you'll be forced to endure frequent slowdowns due to *thrashing*, the nearly constant swapping of data between the Mac's memory and its hard disk.

And finally, virtual memory uses hard disk space that could otherwise hold documents or application files. If you have a 20MB hard disk, you may not be willing to donate a third of its capacity to virtual memory.

But then again, you may. If you use only one or two programs — but they're memory-hungry ones — trading disk space for fewer memory problems may be worthwhile. And the low cost of virtual memory can make its slower performance tolerable.

That's the thing about memory — deciding how much you need and how to use it effectively is a game of trade-offs. You must set aside enough memory to accommodate system software and system extensions such as INITs, yet retain enough to run your applications — while your budget stares over your shoulder. The game isn't easy, especially if you're just getting started with the Mac.

But look at it this way; at least you don't have to use wire cutters to change programs.

Summary:

✔ The two basic categories of memory are ROM (read-only memory) and RAM (random-access memory).

✔ In a Mac, ROM contains the software that programmers use to create pull-down menus, windows, dialog boxes — all the trappings of the Mac's user interface. ROM also stores the diagnostic routines that are performed when you switch the Mac on.

✔ RAM performs the vital job of storing the documents you create and the software you use to create them. It is the Mac's temporary workspace — when you start a program, one of the Mac's first jobs is to copy the program from disk into RAM.

✔ RAM is like a shared closet — it's crammed with odds and ends that reduce the amount of space left over for your stuff. These odds and ends include RAM-based system software, system extensions, multitasking system software, and the RAM cache.

✔ Adding to the Mac's memory enables you to run several programs at the same time and switch among them with a mouse click. You can also use memory to speed up the Mac's operation.

✔ A RAM cache stores the most recently accessed portion of the disk in memory in case its program code or data is needed again. The cache should be used if you are using MultiFinder or System 7.0, or if you regularly repeat certain tasks.

✔ A RAM disk is a pseudo disk that you create in the Mac's memory using a RAM-disk utility. If you store a program on a RAM disk, it will run at top speed.

✔ Virtual memory is a new memory development that can make a Mac act as though it has far more memory than it actually does. Virtual memory is essentially a RAM disk in reverse: instead of treating part of RAM as a disk, it treats part of a hard disk as RAM.

Chapter 22

Acronyms and Other Jargon

In This Chapter:

✔ ADB: The Apple Desktop Bus.

✔ SCSI: Small Computer Systems Interface.

✔ CPU: Central Processing Unit.

✔ Math, graphics, and other specialized coprocessors.

✔ A list of some of the most common acronyms used in the Macintosh world.

The computer field abounds with arcane terms, the worst of which are acronyms. Acronyms are those leftovers in language's bowl of alphabet soup — cryptic letter combinations often thrown together without the courtesy of a vowel to make them pronounceable. And pronouncing them is only part of the problem; understanding them is the other. The phrase "the new ROMs contain HFS and the SCSI drivers, which used to be loaded into RAM" is enough to baffle anyone attempting to grasp a computer's modus operandi.

But behind every acronym are real, sometimes comprehensible words. Understanding those words and their meanings is an important first step in mastering the Macintosh. In the last chapter, we looked at two common acronyms: RAM and ROM, which refer to the two basic kinds of memory the Mac uses. In this chapter, I'll descramble some more acronyms and look at some of the other jargon you're likely to encounter in the Macintosh world.

ADB: The Apple Desktop Bus

As we dig into our bowl of alphabet soup, the first acronyms we encounter refer to some of the Mac's rear-panel *ports,* also called *connectors,* to which you attach your keyboard and mouse, as well as other add-ons.

The Mac's *input devices* — its keyboard and mouse — attach to its *ADB* connector. ADB stands for *Apple Desktop Bus*, an expansion system designed for input devices. (In the computer world, a *bus* is a set of wires that form a common pathway for data.) The Mac Classic, LC, and IIsi each provide one ADB connector; all other Macs made after the Plus provide two. (The Plus and earlier Macs used a different, less versatile method to communicate with their mice and keyboards.)

Mac keyboards provide two ADB connectors. That's how Macs with only one ADB connector can accommodate both a keyboard and a mouse — you plug your mouse into one of the keyboard's ADB connectors, and then use a cable to connect the keyboard's second ADB connector to your Mac. This technique is called *daisy chaining*.

You can use the daisy chaining technique to attach up to three ADB input devices to a single ADB connector. In Chapter 37, I'll take a closer look at alternative input devices and ADB.

SCSI: Small Computer Systems Interface

The ADB is a relatively slow bus; it transfers only about 4,500 bits — or 90 words — per second. That's certainly faster than anyone can type, but it's pretty slow as buses go. It's far too slow for performance-oriented add-ons like hard disks. At about 90 words per second, loading a 10-page document into memory would take over 27 seconds. You'd grow old waiting for large programs to start up.

One way the Mac accommodates high-performance add-ons is with the *SCSI* bus. Short for *Small Computer Systems Interface* and inelegantly pronounced *scuzzy*, the SCSI bus can transfer millions of bits per second. SCSI is most commonly used for hard disks, but it's also used by image scanners, CD-ROM drives, some printers, and tape-backup drives — all add-ons that benefit from fast data transfer.

Like ADB, the SCSI bus lets you daisy-chain peripherals to connect numerous add-ons to a single, rear-panel connector. While the ADB is limited to three devices, SCSI supports up to seven. Nearly all external SCSI devices have two 50-pin connectors, although some use 25-pin connectors like the one on the back of the Mac's case. In either case, you connect the first peripheral to the Mac's SCSI port. Then, if the peripheral has a 50-pin connector, use Apple's *Peripheral Interface Cable* to attach a second peripheral to it. If the device has a 25-pin connector, use another SCSI system cable.

When connecting multiple SCSI devices to the Mac, you'll need to contend with the black art of SCSI *termination*, which involves using small connectors called *terminators* to tell the Mac where the SCSI bus begins and ends. The sidebar "A SCSI Primer" provides more details on SCSI addressing and termination.

The CPU and its Sidekicks

RAM, ROM, and the rest would be nothing without the *central processing unit,* or CPU. The CPU is the microprocessor chip that executes the individual instructions

A SCSI Primer

Every Mac from the Plus on has a SCSI connector, a 25-pin female receptacle called a DB-25. Every Mac from the SE on also has a 50-pin SCSI connector inside its case for use with an internal hard disk.

In the SCSI world, every device has an *ID number* that ranges from 0 to 6. A device's ID number acts as its address — when the Mac sends data to a device, it transmits the device's ID along with the data. All the devices on the SCSI bus constantly "listen" for data, but only the device to which the data is addressed responds.

Besides being an electronic house number, an ID number also specifies a SCSI device's priority. The higher the ID number, the higher the device's priority. When two devices vie for the Mac's attention at the same time — as might occur when a scanning program saves an incoming image on disk during a scan — the Mac turns its attention to the device with the higher ID number. The Mac, which is the first device in the SCSI chain, has a priority of 7. Address number 0 is reserved for an internal hard disk.

Usually, you specify a device's ID number by setting a switch on the device, although with some devices you change the ID by running a program. (Some users recommend avoiding the latter type of device; if address conflicts prevent the Mac from starting up, you may not be able to run the program to change the address.)

Terminating the Chain

For the SCSI bus to work properly, the Mac must know where the SCSI chain begins and ends. These vital boundaries are formed by *terminators,* special connectors that absorb the SCSI signals when they reach the end of the line.

The number of terminators you need in a SCSI chain depends on the number of devices you're using — one terminator for one device; two terminators for two or more devices. Some devices (such as internal hard disks) include built-in terminators; others don't.

The only specific termination guidelines I can offer are these: never use more than two terminators, whether internal or external; and never change a connection while any device (including the Mac) is on. Doing either may damage the Mac.

Chapter 30 contains an illustration showing how to connect terminators; you can find numerous examples of how to use them in the Macintosh's manual. Check your peripherals' manuals to find out if they contain internal terminators so you'll know whether you need to add an external one. Chapter 30 contains more tips for setting up SCSI devices. **M**

that form a program, and that shepherds data between disk and memory and between memory and other components. In short, the CPU has a hand in almost every task performed by the computer.

A microprocessor's activity follows the beat of an extremely stable electronic metronome. Many factors govern a computer's speed, but the number of times per second the machine's metronome ticks is foremost among them. The clock governing the Mac Classic's microprocessor ticks roughly 8 million times per second, giving the Mac a *clock rate* of 8 million hertz (cycles per second), or 8*MHz* (pronounced *megahertz*). By contrast, the clock for the Mac IIfx's processor ticks at a sprightly 40 million times per second, or 40MHz.

Macs have grown faster and more sophisticated over the years; one key to their evolution has been Apple's use of increasingly powerful CPU chips. The Mac family uses Motorola's 68000 series of microprocessors. The Mac Classic and the Mac Portable use the Motorola MC68000, usually just called *68000* for short. This chip also drives the Mac SE and Plus and the primordial Macs that preceded them.

The Macintosh LC uses the 68020, often pronounced *sixty-eight-oh-twenty,* or simply *oh-twenty,* for short. The original Macintosh II, introduced in 1987 and discontinued in 1988, also used the 68020. This chip is superior to the 68000 for a few reasons. It's a true *32-bit* microprocessor, which means it works with information in 32-bit chunks. The less-sophisticated 68000 is a hybrid 16- and 32-bit processor: it handles information in 32-bit chunks internally, but transfers it to external components such as RAM chips in 16-bit chunks. The 68020, by working with 32 bits of information internally and externally, can shuttle twice the data in the same amount of time. (In the Mac LC, however, this feature isn't fully taken advantage of. The LC uses 16-bit external data paths.)

Another 68020 advantage is its built-in, 256-byte *instruction cache,* high-speed memory that holds the instructions that the CPU used most recently. If those instructions are needed again, they're supplied by the cache, eliminating the need for the CPU to access RAM, which takes more time. Motorola says the instruction cache boosts the chip's performance by about 40 percent.

The 68030 is used by the remaining members of the Mac family: the SE/30 and the IIsi, IIci, and IIfx. The 68030 also drives the now-discontinued IIcx and IIx. The 68030 has the same advantages of the 68020, and adds some pluses of its own. One is a built-in *paged memory management unit,* or *PMMU.* The PMMU is used by System 7.0's virtual memory feature, which we encountered in previous chapters. Apple's AU/X, a version of the *Unix* operating system popular in many universities and engineering and research settings, also uses the PMMU. As mentioned earlier, Macs that use the 68020 do not support virtual memory unless you buy an optional PMMU chip, the Motorola 68851.

Chapters 25 and 34 contain more details on which Macs do and do not support System 7.0's virtual memory feature.

The 68030 also provides a built-in 256-byte data cache, which holds the most recently used data just in case it's needed again. The instruction cache present in the 68020 is here, too. (Note the difference between instructions and data: instructions tell the CPU what to do next, while data is what the instructions affect.)

The 68030 also contains twice the number of internal data pathways than the 68020, and they work in parallel, allowing the CPU to do several things at once — such as access its instruction cache, data cache, and your RAM chips. Adding more data pathways to a chip is like adding lanes to a freeway — it lets more traffic move in the same amount of time.

Finally, the 68030 is capable of faster clock rates than the 68020. The 68020 can run at up to 33MHz, while the 68030 can run at up to 50MHz — the clock rate used by some Mac II accelerator boards. (Apple's top-of-the-line Mac IIfx uses a 40MHz 68030). Future high-performance Macs are likely to use the Motorola 68040, which is faster and more sophisticated still.

Coprocessors: CPU Sidekicks

Any good business manager knows that being able to delegate work to specialists makes a manager more productive and efficient. Ditto for a computer's CPU. The 68020 and 68030 are able to delegate certain tasks to specialized microprocessors called *coprocessors*. Coprocessors lighten the load on the CPU, freeing it to do what it does best: supervise the overall operation of the computer's components.

The most common coprocessor is a *math coprocessor*, a chip with a head for figures. A math coprocessor can perform complex calculations far more quickly than a general-purpose processor like the 68020 or 68030. Specifically, math coprocessors excel at *floating point* calculations — calculations involving numbers with decimal portions, such as 3.1415926. The Mac SE/30, IIci, IIcx, and IIfx contain the Motorola *68882* math coprocessor. This chip is also available as an option for the Mac IIsi and LC. The original Mac II used the 68882's predecessor, the 68881.

The Mac IIfx uses several specialized coprocessors that assist in transferring data to and from the computer's modem, printer, and SCSI ports. In other Macs, the CPU has to be intimately involved in the transfer of data to or from these ports. In the IIfx, specialized *input/output processors (IOPs)* handle data transfers to and from the modem and printer ports, while a chip called the *SCSI/DMA Controller* shuttles information between RAM and the SCSI port. By lightening the load on the IIfx's CPU, these specialized chips help contribute to the IIfx's blazing speed.

If you plan to do high-end color graphics work on your Mac, you'll probably encounter *graphics coprocessors* like American Micro Devices' *AMD29000* chip. Graphics coprocessors specialize in performing the types of calculations and data transfers involved in drawing complex color graphics on the screen. Apple's Macintosh Display Card 8•24GC uses the AMD29000. We'll look at graphics acceleration in Chapter 38.

Alphabits

ANSI American National Standards Institute. This is the standards organization that, through subgroups, defines such standards as SCSI.

ASCII American Standard Code for Information Interchange. A standard that defines the way letters, numbers, special characters, and certain control characters (such as tabs and carriage returns) are stored in the computer. ASCII often represents the only common ground between different models of computers. It enables various personal computers to communicate via modems and exchange ASCII files, which do not contain any codes or characters specific to a particular brand of computer. In the Mac world, ASCII files are usually called *text-only* files.

cdev Control Panel device, a file that appears in System 6.x's Control Panel or in System 7.0's Control Panels folder (located within the System Folder).

DB-9 A nine-pin connector used for the modem and printer ports on Macs preceding the Plus. Some third-party hardware and network cables still use DB-9 connectors; to use them with the Mac, you

need a DIN-8-to-DB-9 adaptor. Apple calls this cable a *Macintosh Peripheral Adapter*; its part number is M0199.

DIN-8 Also called *mini-8* or *circular-8,* the type of connector used for the Mac's modem and printer ports.

HFS Hierarchical File System, the disk-management software used by the Macintosh. HFS is what allows you to create folders and organize files within them.

INIT Short for *initialization resource,* software that loads into memory when the Mac starts up. An INIT can be a standalone file or it can be a resource within a cdev or RDEV file. In System 6.x, INITs (and files containing INIT resources) are stored in the System Folder. In System 7.0, they're stored in the Extensions folder within the System Folder.

MFS Macintosh File System, the disk-management software used by the original Mac and by the Macintosh 512K. MFS could keep track of only approximately 128 files on a disk. (I say "approximately" because the number varied according to the length of the file names.) That was sufficient for the limited capacity of a 400K floppy disk, but woefully 🖝

Yet another type of coprocessor is a *digital signal processor (DSP)* chip, such as Motorola's *56001* chip. In the Mac world, DSP chips are most commonly used by digital audio expansion boards such as Digidesign's Audiomedia card, which lets Mac IIs record and play back sound with the fidelity of a compact disc. We'll look at digital audio again in Chapter 32.

Letter Rip

I've covered the most common Mac acronyms and terms in this chapter, but there are many others, as well as a world of abbreviations, that you may encounter. I've included some of them in the sidebar "Alphabits." When you

---

inadequate for hard disks, which can hold thousands of files. When the Mac Plus and 512K Enhanced appeared, MFS was replaced by HFS, which remains in use today.

PICT A format in which many Macintosh programs can save graphic documents (see Chapter 8 for details on PICT and other graphics file formats, including TIFF and RIFF).

PRAM Short for *parameter RAM,* the battery-powered memory that stores key Control Panel settings.

RDEV Also called *Chooser device* or *Chooser resource,* an RDEV is a file whose icon appears in the Chooser window. The Mac's ImageWriter, LaserWriter, and StyleWriter printer drivers are RDEVs. RDEVs may also contain INIT resources that load into memory during startup; an example of such an RDEV is the AppleShare file that lets you connect to AppleShare file servers (described in Chapter 40).

RIP Rest in peace. Also *raster image processor,* the portion of a laser printer or typesetter that interprets

printing instructions (in PostScript or another language) and controls the printing mechanism to produce a page.

RS-422A The type of serial communications interface used for the Mac's modem and printer ports. RS-422A is a faster version of the RS-232C standard, the type of communications port found on IBM PCs and many other computers.

SIMM Single In-line Memory Module, the small circuit board that holds individual RAM chips (usually eight). You expand a Mac's memory by adding SIMMs.

VRAM Video RAM — the memory that stores the bits that form a Macintosh screen image. NuBus video boards contain their own VRAM. In a Mac containing built-in video circuitry, part of the machine's main RAM is used as VRAM.

XMODEM A *file transfer protocol* — a method of transferring files over a modem that ensures that no data is lost or garbled. **M**

run into one that isn't covered in this chapter, consult the index to find where it's discussed.

In the end, most acronyms are just someone's nasty way of turning a few understandable words into a mysterious jumble of letters. You simply have to find out what the letters stand for.

Of course, pronunciation can also be a problem. SCSI may be pronounced as a word, but you'll get strange looks if you ask someone what kind of cippu his or her Mac contains.

Summary:

✔ Behind every acronym are real words; understanding those words and their meanings is an important first step in mastering the Macintosh.

✔ ADB stands for Apple Desktop Bus. You attach your keyboard and mouse, as well as other add-ons, to the Mac's rear-panel ADB connector.

✔ SCSI is an acronym for Small Computer Systems Interface. The SCSI bus is used for high-performance add-ons, such as hard disks, image scanners, CD-ROM drives, some printers, and tape-backup drives.

✔ The CPU, or central processing unit, is the microprocessor chip that executes the individual instructions that form a program, and that shepherds data between disk and memory and between memory and other components.

✔ Increasingly powerful CPU chips have helped the Mac family to grow faster and more sophisticated.

✔ Coprocessors are specialized microprocessors that lighten the load on the CPU, freeing it to do what it does best: supervise the overall operation of the computer's operation.

Chapter 23
The System Folder

In This Chapter:

✔ An introduction to the basics of the System Folder — and why you should know them.

✔ The Mac's approach to controlling specific printers.

✔ A look at the System file and other files in the System Folder.

✔ Extending your Mac's capabilities with system extensions.

✔ Tips for using MacroMaker, Map, CloseView, and Easy Access.

I n the last chapter, I mentioned that the Mac's operation is a joint effort between the system software that's frozen into its ROM chips and the system software that loads from disk into the Mac's memory during startup. That disk-based system software lives in a variety of files located within the folder named System Folder.

One of the Mac's strengths is that you don't have to understand the contents of the System Folder in order to use the machine. Still, knowing what's inside the System Folder can be a big help when you want to troubleshoot a problem, customize the Mac, or just understand how it works. In this chapter, we'll open the System Folder and explore what's inside. The table "Inside System 6.x" shows the name, and purpose of all the files that comprise the System 6.x release of the Mac's system software. We'll also look at the four System Folder files that often confound inexperienced users — MacroMaker, Map, CloseView, and Easy Access.

Unless noted otherwise, the information in this chapter applies to system versions 6.x and 7.0. We'll explore the unique features of System 7.0 in Chapter 25.

Inside System 6.x

File Name	Purpose
Finder	Disk and program management
MultiFinder	Runs multiple programs simultaneously
System	Holds fonts, desk accessories, system software and resources
Scrapbook File	Holds contents of Scrapbook desk accessory
Note Pad File	Holds contents of Note Pad desk accessory
Clipboard File	Provides auxiliary storage for Clipboard
Backgrounder	Looks for spool files created by MultiFinder
DA Handler	Runs desk accessories under MultiFinder

Printer Resources

ImageWriter	Allows printing to ImageWriter
AppleTalk ImageWriter	Allows printing to AppleTalk-equipped ImageWriter IIs
ImageWriter LQ	Allows printing to ImageWriter LQs
AppleTalk ImageWriter LQ	Allows printing to AppleTalk-equipped ImageWriter LQs
StyleWriter	Allows printing to StyleWriters
Personal LaserWriter LS	Allows printing to Personal LaserWriter LSs
LaserWriter IISC	Allows printing to LaserWriter IISCs
Personal LaserWriter SCs	Allows printing to Personal LaserWriter SCs
LaserPrep	Prepares Postscript printers for printing by LaserWriter driver
LaserWriter	Allows printing to PostScript printers
Print Monitor	Print spooler for Postscript printers, Personal LaserWriter SCs, Personal LaserWriter LSs, and LaserWriter IISCs

Control Panel Devices (cdevs)

Startup Device	Selects startup hard disk (not for Plus)
Monitors	Selects number of colors/greys, change configuration of multiple monitors
Mouse	Adjusts mouse tracking and double-click speed
Keyboard	Adjusts key repeat rate and delay until repeat
General	Provides basic Control Panel settings

File Name	Purpose
Sound	Allows selection of system alert sounds. In System 6.0.7, allows recording and cutting and pasting of alert sounds.
Color	Allows selected text to appear in color
Map	Displays world map and allows resetting of built-in clock/calendar
Closeview	Enlarges screen image

Other Files

File Name	Purpose
Key Layout	Provides keyboard layout for Key Caps desk accessory
Easy Access	Allows issuing of multi-key sequences without holding down modifier keys
MacroMaker	Allows recording and play back of mouse and key sequences
Macros	Stores macros created by MacroMaker
MacroMaker Help	Contains MacroMaker help screens
Finder Startup	Stores your Set Startup command choices
Startup Screen	When present, its image replaces "Welcome to Macintosh" startup screen

Utilities

File Name	Purpose
Font/DA Mover	Installs and removes fonts and desk accessories
TeachText	Lets you create text-only files and read files containing last-minute update information
Installer	Updates System Folder to latest version or adds new system software
Apple HD 20 Setup	Tests and initializes Apple SCSI hard disks
Disk First Aid	Tests disks and performs minor repairs
HD Backup	Backs up and restores hard disks
Apple File Exchange	Allows access to non-Macintosh disks and translates between various file formats

TrueType Files*

File Name	Purpose
TrueType	Enables use of TrueType fonts
(various font files)	Contain mathematic descriptions of typefaces

*TrueType files can be used with System 6.0.7 only.

System Folder Basics

System software, whether that of a Macintosh, an IBM PC, or a room-sized mainframe computer, transforms a collection of chips and circuits into a working computer. System software controls the computer's parts and responds to external input from a keyboard and, in the Mac's case, the mouse.

The System Folder is the folder with a small Mac icon on it. Disks that contain System Folders are called *system disks;* a disk whose System files are currently in use is called the *startup disk*. The startup disk's icon always appears in the upper-right corner of the Finder's desktop. You can move it elsewhere, but it will revert to its original location the next time you start up your Mac.

The most visible member of the Mac's system software is the Finder, the software for which is stored in a file by the same name. As mentioned in previous chapters, you use the Finder to start, or *launch*, applications; to copy, rename, and delete files; and to copy, eject, and erase disks. The Finder also provides disk-management conveniences — the Get Info command for attaching descriptive text to files, for example. The Finder also lets you organize a disk's contents by creating folders and dragging documents or programs into them. And the Finder's Print Directory command (in the File menu) lets you print *directory* print-outs that show what's on a disk or in a certain folder.

In System 6.x, a close cousin to the Finder file is the file named MultiFinder, which contains the program code that enables the Mac to run numerous programs simultaneously. MultiFinder works together with two other System Folder files, Backgrounder and PrintMonitor, to provide the background printing capability that lets you continue to work while the Mac converses with a laser printer. We'll look more closely at how MultiFinder performs these juggling acts in the next chapter.

Printer Resources

Speaking of printing, obtaining hard copy would be considerably harder without *printer resources* like the files called ImageWriter and LaserWriter. Also called *printer drivers,* printer resources contain the commands that control a specific brand or model of printer. When your System Folder contains drivers for more than one printer, you use the Chooser desk accessory to select which printer you want to use. After choosing a printer, you'll see options pertaining to that printer in the Page Setup and Print dialog boxes that all programs use (see "Choosing a Printer").

The Mac comes with a disk called Printer Tools, which contains printer drivers for Apple's printers: the PostScript-based LaserWriter IINT, IINTX, and Personal

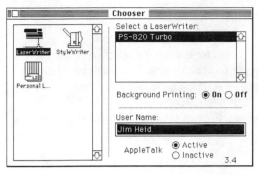

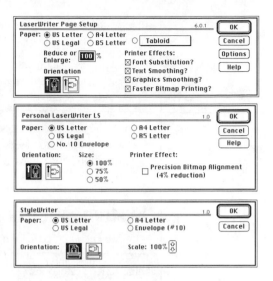

Choosing a Printer

The Chooser desk accessory (left) displays a list of all the RDEV files in your System Folder. When you choose a particular printer, the Mac changes the Page Setup and Print dialog boxes to reflect that printer's capabilities. At right, the Page Setup dialog boxes for Apple's LaserWriter, Personal LaserWriter LS, and StyleWriter.

LaserWriter NT; the non-PostScript Personal LaserWriter LS and SC; the dot-matrix ImageWriter II and ImageWriter LQ; and the ink-jet StyleWriter. Printer drivers for non-Apple laser printers such as Hewlett-Packard's LaserJet series and for numerous dot-matrix printers are available from companies such as GDT Softworks (see Chapter 36). And third-party, non-PostScript printers such as GCC Technologies' Personal LaserPrinter II series include their own drivers. Generally, you use a third-party printer driver in the same way that you use an Apple printer driver: Copy the driver into the System Folder of your startup disk, and then use the Chooser to select the driver you want. (In System 7.0, printer drivers are kept in the Extensions folder, located within the System Folder.)

As we'll see in Chapter 36, printing to a PostScript-based printer requires two printer files, named LaserPrep and LaserWriter. LaserPrep prepares the printer for accepting the PostScript printer commands sent by LaserWriter, the driver itself.

The System File

The lead player in the System Folder is the System file, which contains much of the Mac's system software. The System file also holds *resource* information that lets Mac programs display currency, time, and date values in the format required for various countries. And the System file holds your fonts and desk accessories. In System 6.x and earlier versions, you install or remove fonts and desk accessories using Apple's Font/DA Mover utility (instructions for using the Font/DA Mover appear in Chapter 19). In System 7.0, you install or remove fonts by simply dragging them to and from the System file, and you install desk accessories by moving them into the Apple Menu Items folder.

Awaiting installation into your System file is a massive selection of fonts, from Hebrew typefaces to special-purpose fonts containing math symbols to headline fonts for desktop publishing. Many fonts are available free through user groups; others are sold by companies such as Adobe Systems and Bitstream. The same applies to desk accessories: As we saw in Chapter 19, turbocharged calculators, scaled-down word processors, and disk- and file-management tools are just a few of the desktop adornments available.

System Extensions

We've encountered system extensions in previous chapters: they're files that extend the Mac's capabilities or enhance its operation. System extensions fall into three general categories:

❖ *Control Panel devices*, or cdevs (pronounced *see*-dev). These work along with the Control Panel in System 6.x. When you open the Control Panel, it looks for cdevs, then displays the icon for each one it finds. Click on an icon, and the cdev swings into action, adding whatever buttons and options to the Control Panel's window that are necessary for the device you chose. When you buy a new piece of hardware — such as a high-end video board or a CD-ROM player — it might come with a cdev that you copy to your System Folder. In System 7.0, cdevs reside in the Control Panels folder.

❖ *Chooser extensions*, or *RDEVs* (pronounced *are*-dev). These are files that appear in the Chooser window. The most common RDEVs are printer drivers. RDEVs are also often used to provide access to the devices on a network, such as laser printers and file servers (hard disks that are available to all the machines on a network).

❖ *Initialization resources,* or *INITs*. INITs contain software that loads into memory when the Mac starts up. INITs may be separate files (such as Apple's MacroMaker and Easy Access), or they may be part of a cdev or RDEV file. One example of an RDEV that also contains an INIT resource is the AppleShare RDEV, which lets you access AppleShare file servers on a network (see Chapter 40). In System 7.0, INITs live in the Extensions folder (within the System Folder).

What's with the four-letter abbreviations — RDEV, cdev, and INIT? These are the technical terms for system extensions and the way they're identified by the Mac's operating system. Apple would probably prefer that everyone call these files Chooser extensions, Control Panels, and initalization resources, but most advanced Mac users prefer the techie abbreviations. Maybe it's because they take less time to say.

The Supporting Cast

The remaining players in the System Folder have bit parts or do an occasional cameo, but they can enhance the performance. You may see a file called StartupScreen, which contains a picture that appears instead of the "Welcome to Macintosh" startup message. You can make your own startup screen by creating an image using any of several painting programs (see Chapter 8).

Another member of the system team, the Clipboard file, occasionally stores the contents of the Clipboard, the Mac's mechanism for exchanging information between applications. I say "occasionally" because the contents of the Clipboard are often held in the Mac's memory and not stored on disk. An application can instruct the Mac to save the Clipboard on disk if it contains more information than will fit in memory. If you use Microsoft Word, for example, you may occasionally see the message "Save large Clipboard?" when you quit the program. If you choose Yes, Word saves the Clipboard's contents in the Clipboard file.

Lastly, you might encounter specialized system files such as Macintalk, a *speech driver* that lets specially written applications produce somewhat convincing speech. You can access Macintalk from within HyperCard and with Bright Star Technology's interFace, which we looked at in Chapter 12.

The System Folder also holds a variety of other files that your programs may use as they run. For example, some programs with spelling checkers require that their dictionary files be stored in the System Folder. Many programs also create *preferences files,* which store your current application settings and which often have the text "prefs" or "settings" in their names. In System 7.0, preferences files are stored in the Preferences folder.

You may also see specialized font files used by a particular printer. Downloadable PostScript printer font files have odd-sounding names such as FrankGotBoo for Adobe's Franklin Gothic Book. You might be tempted to rename these files to make their names a bit more comprehensible. Don't do it — the Mac's LaserWriter printer driver won't be able to find the files during a print job.

And you're likely to see *temporary* files that application programs create as they operate. Microsoft Word's temporary files, for example, have names like Word Temp 1, Word Temp 2. Never delete a temporary file if the program that created it is still running — you'll be pulling the rug out from under the program and you'll probably lose work or cause a system crash. If you suspect that a program has left a few temporary files in your System Folder, be sure to quit the program before deleting them.

Making Macros

Now let's look at some of those confounding system files, starting with MacroMaker, which I introduced in Chapter 19. MacroMaker lets you record keystrokes and mouse actions, then play them back later by choosing a single command or using a key sequence. Using macros, you can add your own Command-key shortcuts to commands or store frequently typed text for quick retrieval. Although MacroMaker has been criticized as having compatibility problems with some programs, many people find it a handy way to automate simple repetitive tasks. For that reason, I've included an introduction to it here.

▲ Macro Making
MacroMaker's cassette recorder window lets you name, store, and retrieve macros. Here, a global macro (one available in any application) named Chooser has been loaded. The Info area contains a brief description of the macro, and the Keystroke area shows the macro's key assignment. Tip: to display MacroMaker's help screens, click on the version number in the bottom-right corner.

MacroMaker lets you create *global macros*, available in all programs; *Finder macros*, on tap when the Finder is active; and *application-specific macros*, which work only when the application you used to create them is active. MacroMaker loads into memory during startup and adds a menu (a cassette tape icon) to the menu bar. To record a macro, choose Start Recording from MacroMaker's menu, then perform the tasks you want to record. The cassette icon flashes while you're recording. When you've finished, choose Stop Recording from MacroMaker's menu, and MacroMaker's window appears (see the figure "Macro Making").

The MacroMaker window lets you save and name macros. Macro names appear in MacroMaker's menu. You'll probably also want to assign the macro to a key sequence to be able to play it without reaching for the mouse. You can use Command-key sequences to summon macros, but in doing so, you risk disabling a program's built-in Command-key shortcut. For example, if you use your word processor to record the text *Sincerely*, and you assign the macro to the Command-S key sequence, you'll disable the keyboard shortcut for your word processor's Save command.

For a good surrogate Command key, try the Control key present on all Mac keyboards (except those of the Plus and earlier machines). If you use the Apple Extended II keyboard — the big, 105-key beast — you can also assign macros to its fifteen function keys. For the Mac Plus, whose keyboard lacks a Control key and function keys, use Command along with the Shift or Option keys. Or just examine your program's menus before assigning the key sequence to be sure your sequence won't override an existing one.

MacroMaker does have limitations. You can't stop recording when a modal dialog box (one you can't click outside of) is open. Thus, you can't record a macro whose last act is to issue an Open command — you can't tell MacroMaker to stop recording without pulling down its menu, and you can't get to its menu without cancelling the dialog box. Also, MacroMaker can't record a pause, so you can't use it to automate a telecommunications session or other activity that involves waiting between two tasks. Two commercial macro packages — CE Software's QuicKeys 2 and Affinity's Tempo II — don't have these shortcomings. If you become addicted to macros, you'll probably graduate to one of these. But MacroMaker is ideal for automating simple tasks and putting the extended keyboard's function keys to work. And it's free.

Map: Are They Awake in Ankara?

I recently read of a Gallup poll in which three out of four Americans couldn't locate the Persian Gulf on a map. Perhaps the Map cdev will help to change that. Map adds to the Control Panel a world map and options for finding cities and determining the distance and time difference between them and your location (see the figure "The Mac's Map" on the next page).

Besides being useful and educational, the Map cdev illustrates Apple's commitment to making the Mac a truly international computer. When you use the Set button to specify your location, Map stores the location in the Mac's parameter RAM — that battery-powered area of memory that holds the time, date, and other Control Panel settings. Take your Mac to a different time zone, and you can use the Set button to adjust the Mac's built-in clock accordingly.

Apple's goals for dealing with time go far beyond making it easier to reset the Alarm Clock. More businesses are using modems and long-distance links to connect their offices to remote Macs, and as they say on Star Trek, that disrupts the space-time continuum. For example, if you create a file at 9:00 am in Boston, then transmit it to San Fransisco, it arrives three hours before it was created — at least according to the Mac's current file-dating mechanism. Future versions of the Mac system will be better able to deal with multiple time zones.

The Mac's Map

The Map cdev displays a world map and lets you determine the distance and time difference between cities. To determine the shortest distance between two points, Map performs a *great circle* calculation, which involves placing an imaginary plane through the center of a sphere so that it touches both points, then drawing and measuring an arc between the points.

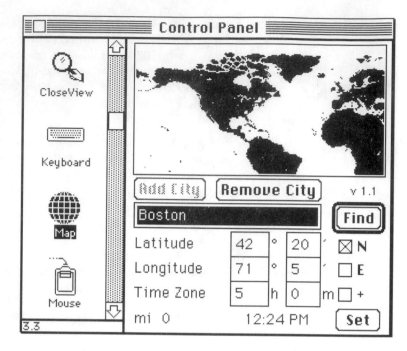

By the way, you can open an enlarged version of the map by pressing the Option key while clicking on the Map icon.

Up Close with CloseView

Another cdev that sometimes mystifies new users is CloseView, which lets you enlarge the screen image up to 16 times its normal size. CloseView is one of those cdevs that contains an INIT resource; when you start your Mac, CloseView loads into memory, ready to be summoned from the Control Panel. CloseView is intended to make the Mac's screen easier for visually impaired users to read, but it's also handy for precise drawing or positioning.

CloseView's mysterious side surfaces if you aren't aware of what it does. If you've ever started up your Mac and found a large black rectangle on the screen chances are you or someone else inadvertently activated CloseView. Similarly, if you're working away and a black rectangle suddenly appears, you probably typed CloseView's keyboard-activation sequence, which is Command-Option-X.

In either case, you can deactivate CloseView by opening the Control Panel, locating and selecting the CloseView cdev, and then clicking its Off button. But

Key Icons

Six icons that represent th e Mac's numeric keypad and its keyboard modifier keys.

⊞ Keypad

⬒ Caps Lock

⌘ Command

⇧ Shift

⌃ Control

⌥ Option

Example: ⌘ ⌥ ⇧ A

means Command + Option + Shift + A

because CloseView activates automatically each time you start up, you'll want to drag it out of your System Folder or disable it using an INIT manager.

By the way, if your Mac has color or greyscale video hardware, avoid using CloseView in the 16- or 256-color or grey modes. CloseView doesn't perform well with more than 8 colors or greys.

Incidentally, in CloseView and in MacroMaker, you'll notice icons representing the Option and Control keys (see "Key Icons"). It's a good idea to become familiar with these icons, because some programs (including Microsoft Word) use them to indicate keyboard shortcuts.

Not-So-Easy Access

If there's one INIT that causes more head scratching than any other, it's probably Easy Access. Easy Access provides two keyboard-modification features. The *sticky keys* feature makes the keyboard more accessible for physically challenged users. To invoke the sticky keys option, press the Shift key five times. When sticky keys is active, you can type combination keystrokes (such as Command-S, or Shift-A) without having to press two keys simultaneously. Instead, first press the appropriate modifier key (Command, Option, Shift, or Control), then the appropriate letter key.

The Keys to the Pointer ▶

The Easy Access file's "mouse keys" feature lets you move the mouse pointer using the keyboard's numeric keypad. To activate mouse keys, press Command-Shift-Clear. Subsequently, the keypad's keys move the pointer as shown here. The longer you hold a key, the faster the pointer moves; tapping a key moves the pointer one pixel at a time. Pressing the 5 key is equivalent to clicking the mouse button; pressing 0 is like holding down the button, while pressing the period key is like releasing it. To deactivate mouse keys, press the keypad's Clear key.

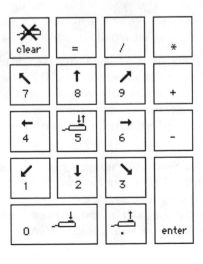

Easy Access' other feature, obtained by pressing Command-Shift-Clear, is called *mouse keys*. Mouse keys lets you move the mouse pointer using the keyboard's numeric keypad (see the figure "The Keys to the Pointer"). The mouse keys feature not only makes it easier to precisely position items in a

Easy Access in Use ▶

When Easy Access's sticky keys feature is active, a small icon appears at the right edge of the menu bar (left). When you press a modifier key (such as Shift or Command), an arrow appears in the icon (right). You can then type a character and Easy Access will combine it with the modifier key you pressed.

publishing or painting program, it could be a godsend if your mouse dies when you're on a deadline.

It's fairly easy to accidentally type the key sequences that invoke Easy Access's mouse keys or sticky keys features. If you aren't aware that Easy Access is in memory, you might think your keyboard has gone haywire. You'll always know if the sticky keys feature is active by examining the right edge of the Mac's menu bar: when sticky keys is active, Easy Access displays small icons there (see the figure "Easy Access in Use").

If you don't need or want Easy Access' features, yank Easy Access out of your System Folder or disable it using an INIT manager. Remember to restart the Mac after disabling Easy Access.

It's worth mentioning that the version of Easy Access that accompanies System 7.0 has new features. You can disable mouse keys or sticky keys using the Easy Access Control Panel, and audio feedback lets you know when Easy Access is active.

Matching the System to the Mac

Apple has released numerous versions of the Mac's system software, and it's important to use the version that's recommended for your Mac. The table "Recommended System Versions" lists the versions Apple suggests for each model of Macintosh. Not listed in the table is System 7.0, which works on any Macintosh from the Plus on, provided you have at least 2MB of memory and a hard disk.

If your Mac is running a system version prior to 6.0, updating to System 6.0 (or 7.0, if your Mac supports it) should be at the top of your to-do list. You can get the System 6.0 update from user's groups; by downloading its files from CompuServe, America Online, or other information services; or from an Apple dealer. The System Update 6.0 package sells for $49 and includes excellent manuals. Most dealers will also let you copy their System 6.0 disks if you supply your own disks.

The System 6.0 package includes a program called Installer that updates the System Folder on your hard disk or on startup floppies. The Installer uses special documents called *scripts*, each tailored to a particular model of Mac. You choose the script for your Mac, and the Installer reads it to determine which modifications to make to your System Folder. To ensure your system is updated properly, start

Recommended System Versions*

Macintosh Model	Recommended Versions	Acceptable Versions
128K	System 2.0/Finder 4.1	
512K	System 3.2/Finder 5.3	
512K	System 3.2/Finder 5.3	System 4.0/Finder 5.4
512K Enhanced	System 3.2/Finder 5.3	System 4.0/Finder 5.4
	System 3.3/Finder 5.4	System 4.1/Finder 5.5
	System 3.4/Finder 6.1	
	(for use with AppleShare)	
Plus	System 6.0.2/Finder 6.1	System 3.2/Finder 5.3
	System 6.0.3/Finder 6.1	System 3.3/Finder 5.4
	System 6.0.4/Finder 6.1	System 4.1/Finder 5.5
		System 4.2/Finder 6.0
Classic	System 6.0.7/Finder 6.1	
SE	System 6.0.2/Finder 6.1	System 4.0/Finder 5.4
	System 6.0.3/Finder 6.1	System 4.1/Finder 5.5
	System 6.0.4/Finder 6.1	System 4.2/Finder 6.0
	System 6.0.5/Finder 6.1	
SE/30	System 6.0.3/Finder 6.1	
	System 6.0.4/Finder 6.1	
	System 6.0.5/Finder 6.1	
LC	System 6.0.7/Finder 6.1	
II	System 6.0.2/Finder 6.1	System 4.1/Finder 5.5
	System 6.0.3/Finder 6.1	System 4.2/Finder 6.0
	System 6.0.4/Finder 6.1	
	System 6.0.5/Finder 6.1	
IIx	System 6.0.3/Finder 6.1	
	System 6.0.4/Finder 6.1	
	System 6.0.5/Finder 6.1	
IIsi	System 6.0.7/Finder 6.1	
IIcx	System 6.0.3/Finder 6.1	
	System 6.0.4/Finder 6.1	
	System 6.0.5/Finder 6.1	
IIci	System 6.0.4/Finder 6.1	
	System 6.0.5/Finder 6.1	
IIfx	System 6.0.7/Finder 6.1	
Portable	System 6.0.4/Finder 6.1	
	System 6.0.5/Finder 6.1	

*You must use System 6.0.7 or a later version in order to use the enhanced sound features in HyperCard 2.0 or Apple's Personal LaserWriter LS or StyleWriter printers.

up with the System 6.0 disk. In Chapter 30, I'll provide more tips for installing system software for reliable results.

The System 6.0 package also includes several *minimum scripts* that create scaled-down System Folders. The minimum Mac SE script, for example, creates a system containing only the Control Panel and Chooser desk accessories, just a few fonts, and no printer drivers. You'll want to use the minimum scripts if you have a Mac with no hard disk or to create an emergency startup floppy disk that you can use if something happens to your hard disk. I'll elaborate on the virtues of an emergency startup floppy in Chapter 27.

Summary:

✔ You don't have to understand the contents of the System Folder in order to use the Mac, but knowing what's inside can be a big help when you want to troubleshoot a problem, customize the Mac, or just understand how it works.

✔ System software controls the computer's parts and responds to external input from a keyboard and, in the Mac's case, the mouse.

✔ Printer resources contain the software that control a specific brand or model of printer.

✔ The System file, which contains fonts and much of the Mac's system software, also holds resource information that lets Mac programs display currency, time, and date values in the format required for various countries.

✔ System extensions (files that extend the Mac's capabilities or enhance its operation) fall into three general categories: control panel devices, or cdevs, found in the Control Panel; Chooser extensions, or RDEVS, found in the Chooser window; and initialization resources, or INITS, which contain software that loads into memory when the Mac starts up.

✔ Apple's MacroMaker lets you record keystrokes and mouse actions, then play them back later by choosing a single command or using a key sequence.

✔ Map is a cdev that adds to the Control Panel a world map and options for finding cities and determining the distance and time difference between them and your location.

✔ CloseView is a cdev that enlarges the screen image up to 16 times its normal size. Originally created for visually impaired users, it can be handy for precise drawing or positioning.

✔ Easy Access is an INIT whose sticky keys feature allows you to type combination keystrokes without having to press two keys simultaneously.

✔ Apple has released numerous versions of the Mac's system software, and it's important to use the version that's recommended for your Mac.

Chapter 24
Multitasking

In This Chapter:

✔ Multitasking using MultiFinder.

✔ A background discussion on the multitasking operating systems.

✔ How time and money figure into multitasking equation.

✔ Memory conservation: choosing your programs wisely.

✔ How to adjust memory requirements to fit more programs into memory.

✔ Survival tips to get the most out of the Mac's multitasking features.

Future computer historians will note the late 1980s as the period when *multitasking* began to make its way from mainframes and minicomputers to microcomputers like the Mac. Multitasking — a computer's ability to run numerous programs simultaneously — has been around on big computers for years, but microcomputers lacked the processing speed and the memory capacity needed to load and switch between numerous programs.

But that has changed. Multitasking has burst onto the microcomputer scene, throwing it into an era of transition. In the IBM PC world, new system software called Operating System/2 (OS/2) adds multitasking capabilities to certain IBM machines, but can't efficiently run many of the programs available for PCs. As a result, PC users and developers are grimacing from growing pains that began in 1987 and haven't let up yet.

Apple has made the transition to multitasking less painful by introducing multitasking features to the Mac in gentle steps. The first step was taken in 1987, when Apple released MultiFinder, which provided the most important features of a multitasking operating system — the ability to run several programs at once and to print documents and perform other time-consuming jobs while you continue to work. MultiFinder hasn't changed much from its initial release to the version that runs under System 6.x. As proof of Apple's desire to gently introduce the Mac world to multitasking, the Finder's Set Startup command gives you the option of not even running MultiFinder.

The next major step was the development of System 7.0. As we'll see in the next chapter, System 7.0 adds enhancements that many people expect of a powerful multitasking operating system, including features that allow programs to communicate with each other to exchange data and commands. As proof of Apple's commitment to Mac multitasking, System 7.0 doesn't give you the option of running under the "single Finder." In System 7.0, MultiFinder is always active; indeed, MultiFinder and the Finder are one and the same.

Even with System 7.0, the Mac's system software doesn't yet have all the capabilities of OS/2. But it doesn't have all its compatibility and performance headaches, either. In this chapter, I'll examine some of the technicalities behind the Mac's ability to run several programs at once. I'll also present some memory-conservation tips that will help you squeeze more out of — and into — MultiFinder. Unless noted otherwise, this memory information also applies to System 7.0.

The MultiFinder Difference

Even before MultiFinder, the Mac provided a scaled-down form of multitasking: desk accessories, those small programs you can summon from the Apple menu. But the Mac's system software places a limit on how large a desk accessory can be, and while some skilled programmers have managed to cram a lot into some desk accessories, no desk accessory can match the capabilities of a standalone program. Desk accessories are just that: accessories, complements to a full-scale application.

MultiFinder lets you have more than one program on the screen simultaneously and switch between them with a mouse click. When you start an application on a Mac running MultiFinder, the Finder doesn't disappear as it does without MultiFinder. Instead, it remains in memory and is visible behind the application's window. If you want to switch back to the Finder — perhaps to start another program or organize some disk files — you need not quit the program you're running. Instead, simply click on a disk icon or on the small icon at the right end of the menu bar, or choose Finder from the Apple menu. Once you've returned to the Finder, you can start another program. You can continue this process until you run out of memory — which, on a Mac with 1MB of memory, often happens after starting only one application.

In the computer world, the process of putting one application on hold and activating a different one is called *context switching*. It's important to understand that context switching isn't multitasking. Programs that are put on hold don't perform any work; they simply hang around on the sidelines, waiting to be called back into action.

MultiFinder's multitasking features surface when you use programs designed for them. When a program is written to recognize and use MultiFinder's capabilities, it can work *in the background* — that is, when it isn't the active application. A communications program can transfer a file over the phone lines while you type away in a word processor. A database manager can sort a database. A spreadsheet program can crunch through a complex calculation. And almost any program can print to a Personal LaserWriter LS or to any PostScript laser printer, thanks to PrintMonitor, a background printing program included with the Mac (see the sidebar "Background on Printing").

Any program that performs time-consuming tasks that don't require your attention is a candidate for background operation. You aren't likely to see

Background on Printing

Printing to a laser printer is like standing in line to buy vodka in Russia: the result is great, but you hate the wait. The PrintMonitor application that accompanies MultiFinder lets the Mac print to a Personal LaserWriter LS or any PostScript printer in the background. PrintMonitor won't make your pages appear more quickly — indeed, they'll probably take longer, since PrintMonitor must share processor time with other applications. But PrintMonitor, like any *spooler* (computerese for software that handles background printing), lets you resume work sooner by intercepting data en route to the printer, saving it on disk, then returning control of the Mac to you while it talks to the printer in the background.

To activate background printing, use the Chooser desk accessory to select the LaserWriter or Personal LaserWriter LS print driver, and then select the Background Printing On button. (If the Background Printing buttons are disabled, you aren't running under

MultiFinder.) Subsequently, when you issue a Print command, the Mac creates a *spool file* containing the document's contents. A small and always-active application called Backgrounder (located in the System Folder) constantly scans for the creation of a spool file. When it detects one, it starts PrintMonitor, which sends the spool file's contents to the printer in the background. As we'll see in Chapter 40, PrintMonitor's window lists the documents waiting to be printed and lets you postpone printing, schedule printing for a specific time, and rearrange the order of the waiting documents.

For now, background printing from Apple isn't in the cards for Apple's ImageWriter dot-matrix or StyleWriter ink-jet printers. However, Fifth Generation Systems' SuperLaserSpool does print to ImageWriters and StyleWriters in the background, and is fully compatible with MultiFinder. **M** support for background operation in highly interactive applications such as painting programs. The only time-consuming, hands-off task such programs perform is printing, and PrintMonitor takes care of that.

What Multitasking Is — And Isn't

How can the Mac run foreground and background programs simultaneously? It can't. The Mac's system software is a master of deception — it switches its attention from one program to another so quickly that all the programs *appear* to be running at once.

To understand how multitasking operating systems create this illusion, let's step back and look at how computers run programs. Nearly all computers, from Macs to mainframes, execute one instruction at a time, in sequence. The exceptions are today's ultra-powerful supercomputers, which use a new computing technique called *parallel processing*, wherein multiple processors execute instructions simultaneously.

In a multitasking operating system, each program you run is called a *task*, or a *process*. When a multitasking operating system is running several programs, the computer is still executing one instruction at a time, in sequence. However, the operating system switches its attention from one program to the next, executing a certain number of one program's instructions before putting that program on hold and turning to the next one (see the figure "Multitasking on the Line"). This *task switching* occurs so quickly that all the programs appear to run simultaneously.

Time to Run

You don't have to understand how the Mac divides its time between programs in order to use it, but a bit of background will help you appreciate the complex juggling that goes on inside a multitasking operating system.

The portion of an operating system responsible for dividing the computer's resources among tasks is called a *task scheduler*. Two basic approaches to scheduling tasks exist: *preemptive* scheduling and *cooperative*, also called *non-preemptive*, scheduling.

With preemptive scheduling, the task scheduler is tied to the internal "heartbeat" that all microcomputers use to govern their operation. The task scheduler gives each task control of the computer's resources for a specific number of heartbeats. When they've elapsed, the computer's operating system puts the current application on hold, turning its attention to the next one.

MULTITASKING ON THE LINE

Single-Tasking

Cooperative Scheduling

Parallel Processing

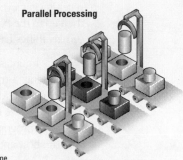

One way to understand computer operating systems is to compare them to factory assembly lines. A single-tasking operating system sequentially executes one application's instructions at a time; it's similar to a conventional assembly line, in which work passes from one operator to the next.

MultiFinder divides the microprocessor's time among applications, which is comparable to one worker switching between two assembly lines, each dedicated to a different operation.

True multitasking operates like a factory with separate assembly lines, each functioning independently.

With cooperative scheduling, the task scheduler plays a more passive role in allocating processor time. The responsibility for dividing the processor's time is shared among all the applications that are running. An application must be "well behaved" — it must return control of the processor to the operating system at frequent intervals so that other applications get their turn to run. If one program hogs too much of the processor's time, others slow to a crawl. Worse, if a program crashes, the whole system is likely to crash, since the haywire application may never return control to the operating system. An operating system that uses cooperative multitasking is a chain that's only as strong as its weakest link.

The differences between preemptive and cooperative multitasking are like the differences between traffic lights and yield signs. Traffic lights govern the flow of cars in a rigid way: traffic from each side of the street gets a chance to flow only as long as the traffic lights allow it. (Assuming some yo-yo doesn't run a red light.) Yield signs, however, turn driving into a cooperative effort. Traffic flows smoothly only when all the drivers cooperate and take turns using the intersection.

IBM's OS/2 and Apple's A/UX — a Macintosh version of UNIX, an operating system popular in academic, scientific, and engineering environments — use preemptive multitasking schedulers. But MultiFinder and System 7.0 use the cooperative scheduling approach because it jibes well with the way Macintosh programs operate. A Mac program spends much of its time waiting for an *event* such as a keystroke or a mouse movement to occur. MultiFinder and System 7.0 sense when a foreground application isn't receiving any events, and say, in essence, "Attention, background task #1! The foreground application isn't receiving any events at the moment, so now's your chance to do some work." It's then up to the background task to say, "OK, I accomplished something. I'm turning things back over to you, Mac."

Some multitasking gurus criticize cooperative multitasking as not being "true" multitasking. A true multitasking operating system, they contend, must maintain more control over the allocation of processor time among tasks. Let them whine. The bottom line is that the Mac's cooperative multitasker yields excellent results as long as program developers follow Apple's programming guidelines, which stipulate how applications that perform background tasks should operate.

The Price of Multitasking

The more projects you take on, the more time you need to finish each one. The same applies to the Mac, whose performance slows when applications run in the background. An application usually runs slower in the background than in the foreground, and a foreground application runs somewhat slower than it would if no background application were running. I say "usually" and "some-what" because the specific performance penalties depend on what the background and foreground applications are doing. As a general rule, the Mac's overall performance slows with each background task you add.

An example: If you're running PageMaker and also printing a document in the background using PrintMonitor, PageMaker will feel less responsive — you may notice a slight delay between the time you press a key and when its character appears, or the mouse pointer's movement may seem sluggish and erratic. You'll also wait longer to see your hard copy, because PrintMonitor slows down each time the Mac returns its attention to PageMaker in order to respond to those keyboard and mouse events. Of course, on faster Macs, the slowdown will be less noticeable. A Mac with a 68020 or '030 processor is better at multitasking than a Plus, Classic, or SE.

On the other hand, when an inactive application isn't performing a background task, it doesn't impose a performance penalty on the currently active application. For example, if Microsoft Word and PageMaker are both running, neither imposes a direct performance penalty on the other, since neither is written to perform work in the background.

While one drawback of multitasking affects your stopwatch, the other hits your bank account. Keeping multiple programs close at hand requires a hard disk, and keeping them in memory at the same time requires lots of memory. After loading

MultiFinder, a 1MB Mac becomes, for all practical purposes, a 512K. With 2MB of memory, you'll have enough room to combine two applications, provided they aren't too complex. With multitasking and memory, the phrase "the more, the merrier" applies in spades. And with System 7.0, 2MB is the bare minimum.

Shopping for Slender Software

One way you can cram more into your Mac's memory is to choose the applications you combine carefully. If you have only a megabyte or two of RAM, you'll need to choose programs that use memory sparingly if you want to run more than one program at once. Some recommendations:

❖ For word processing, T/Maker's WriteNow is the unchallenged champion of memory conservation. It's the only currently shipping word processor I know of that runs on every Mac ever made — even the primordial 128K (if you want to use WriteNow's spelling checker, you'll need at least a 512K Mac). By comparison, Microsoft Word 4.0 requires a minimum of 512K and Ashton-Tate's portly FullWrite Professional, with its designer interface and kitchen-sink mix of features, barely fits within 1MB and all but demands 2MB.

❖ For spreadsheet analysis, check out Bravo Technologies' MacCalc. It runs on all Macs from the 512K (enhanced or not) on up, and needs just 272K. It's also fast, well designed, and packed with features. And it's inexpensive.

❖ For database management, a good choice is Software Discovery's RecordHolder Plus, which requires just 300K. Microsoft File is a capable filer that runs in as little as 200K. It offers excellent color support and works well with Microsoft Word's print merge features.

❖ For personal finance management, consider Quicken's Intuit. It packs check writing, checkbook balancing, budgeting, and tax record keeping into a compact application that uses only 375K and runs on unenhanced 512K Macs.

❖ For graphics work, well, good luck. Graphics programs are inherently memory hungry. For example, Silicon Beach Software's SuperPaint 2.0 needs 700K, and Claris' MacDraw II and MacPaint 2.0 need 537K and 384K, respectively. And for MacDraw and MacPaint, those figures are bare minimums that limit your document size and the number of documents you can open simultaneously. One noteworthy alternative: Zedcor's Desk, a collection of desk accessories that pack impressive painting, writing, filing, and drawing features into your Apple menu.

```
┌─────────────────────────────────────┐
│ ▣▭▭▭▭▭▭▭▭ Info ▭▭▭▭▭▭▭▭ │
│                              Locked ☐ │
│      Aldus FreeHand                   │
│                                       │
│    Kind: application                  │
│    Size: 716,421 bytes used, 700K on disk │
│                                       │
│   Where: Hard Disk (SCSI #1)          │
│                                       │
│                                       │
│  Created: Mon, Nov 21, 1988, 6:13 PM  │
│ Modified: Mon, Nov 21, 1988, 6:15 PM  │
│  Version: 2.0, © Altsys Corporation, 1988 │
│                                       │
│  ┌─────────────────────────────────┐ │
│  │                                 │ │
│  │                                 │ │
│  │                                 │ │
│  └─────────────────────────────────┘ │
│                                       │
│  Suggested Memory Size (K):  750      │
│                                       │
│  Application Memory Size (K): [1200]   │
└─────────────────────────────────────┘
```

```
┌─────────────────────────────────────┐
│ ▣▭▭▭ QuarkXPress® Info ▭▭▭ │
│                                       │
│      QuarkXPress®                     │
│      QuarkXPress® 3.0                 │
│                                       │
│    Kind: application program          │
│    Size: 1.6 MB on disk (1,724,901 bytes │
│          used)                        │
│   Where: System 7.0 Startup: QuarkXPress │
│          Folder: QuarkXPress®         │
│                                       │
│  Created: Fri, Aug 3, 1990, 10:38 AM  │
│ Modified: Mon, Dec 24, 1990, 3:48 PM  │
│  Version: 3.0 © 1986-1990 Quark, Inc. │
│                                       │
│  Comments:                            │
│  ┌─────────────────────────────────┐ │
│  │                                 │ │
│  │                                 │ │
│  └─────────────────────────────────┘ │
│                    ┌─Memory──────────┐│
│                    │ Suggested size: 1,500 K││
│  ☐ Locked          │ Current size: [1,500] K││
│                    └─────────────────┘│
└─────────────────────────────────────┘
```

▲ Memory Suggestions

By using the Get Info window, you can adjust a program's current memory size value. If the current memory size is greater than the suggested size, you can safely reduce the current size to match the suggested size. If both memory size values are identical, you can try reducing the current size value, but the program may not run reliably. A Get Info window from System 6.x is shown at left; System 7.0's Get Info window appears at right.

Squeezing More into Memory

Another way to fit more programs into memory is to adjust their memory requirements using the Finder's Get Info command, which, among other things, lets you tell the Mac how much memory to give an application. Giving an application less memory than the recommended amount will probably slow its performance, but it will free memory for other programs. Giving an application more than the recommended amount can improve its performance.

How can you tell how much memory a program needs? It isn't easy. Software firms rarely list minimum memory requirements on their boxes. They tell you if a program runs on a 1MB machine, but they don't say how much of that 1MB the software actually uses. Determining that requires some detective work on your part.

The easiest technique involves selecting the application's icon and then choosing the Finder's Get Info command. Two values appear at the bottom of the Get Info window: the program's *suggested memory size*, the minimum amount its developer recommends, and its *application memory size*, the ideal amount its developer recommends (see the figure "Memory Suggestions"). In System 7.0, the suggested memory size is called the *suggested size*, and the application memory size is called the *current size*. I'll use these terms here because they're clearer.

There is not enough memory to open "Microsoft Excel" (1,024K needed, 1,023K available). Do you want to open it using the available memory?

OK   Cancel

With many programs, the suggested memory size is usually less than the current memory size. Sometimes, however, the two values are the same, as is the case with

▲ Take What You Can Get

When you start a program, the Mac consults its SIZE resource to determine how much memory the program would like to have. If less than the ideal amount is available, the Mac determines if at least the minimum amount is available. If it is, this dialog box appears asking if you want to run the program within that amount.

SuperPaint 2.0, QuarkXpress 3.0, and FileMaker II, to name a few. In any case, the suggested size is the value to watch, since it reflects the minimum amount of memory the developer recommends for the program.

When you start a program, the Mac consults these values to determine how much memory the program would like to have, and how much it will settle for if that ideal amount isn't available. If less than the ideal amount is available, the Mac determines if at least the minimum amount is available. If it is, a dialog box appears asking if you want to run the program within that amount (see the figure "Take What You Can Get"). If even the minimum amount isn't available, the Mac informs you that the program couldn't be opened and suggests quitting another application to free up memory.

By lowering a program's current memory size value, you force the program to accept less memory. Doing so increases your chances of being able to run your favorite programs simultaneously within the amount of memory available.

But how much of a change should you make? That depends:

❖ If the current memory size is greater than the suggested size, you can safely reduce the current size to match the suggested size.

❖ If both memory size values are identical, you can try reducing the current size value, but the program may not run reliably. Because the potential for problems exists, the Finder asks for verification when you supply an application memory size value that's below the suggested memory size.

What are the effects of reduced memory sizes? The program will probably run slower, and it will access the disk more frequently as it loads and discards portions of its program code in order to fit its cramped confines. If the program keeps open documents entirely in memory (Microsoft Works and drawing and painting programs do), you'll be restricted to smaller documents and you won't be able to have as many documents open simultaneously.

(Incidentally, you can also increase a program's application memory size. If you can spare the memory, you can boost a program's performance by giving it more memory. For programs that keep open documents in memory, this lets you create larger documents and have more documents open simultaneously.)

Of course, the best way to get more programs into memory at once is to buy a memory upgrade. Memory prices have fallen dramatically since their peak in the late eighties, and today you can buy a 4MB upgrade for less than what you'd pay for a major software package. And as we saw in Chapter 21, more memory opens the doors to a variety of performance-boosting techniques.

Multitasking Survival Tips

Here are some more tips to help you get more out of the Mac's multitasking features.

❖ *Save when switching* These days, all major Mac programs are written to coexist with MultiFinder and other programs. Nonetheless, it's always a good idea to use the active application's Save command before switching back to the Finder or to another open application. If switching programs causes a system crash, at least your latest work will be saved. For that matter, saving often is a good idea regardless of what you're doing.

❖ *Master MultiFinder navigation* MultiFinder makes it easy to create a messy electronic desktop; when several programs are open, switching to a specific window can be difficult. Remember that you have three ways to switch: clicking within an application's window, repeatedly clicking the icon at the right end of the menu bar, or choosing the application's name from the Apple menu. Under System 7.0, the icon at

Applications on the Menu
System 7.0's application menu (located at the right edge of the menu bar) lets you quickly switch between programs and avoid screen clutter by hiding windows of applications you aren't using.

the right end of the menu bar is actually a menu — the *application menu.* You can use it to switch between open applications and better still, to hide the windows of other applications and the Finder. Hiding other windows is a good way to avoid screen clutter (see the figure "Applications on the Menu"). Alas, it requires a bit more memory, since the Mac must save the state of each program's windows before hiding them.

❖ *Open desk accessories in an application layer when memory is tight* When you use a desk accessory under MultiFinder, the Mac runs a system program called DA Handler, which creates a "layer" in which all desk accessories run. But because DA Handler requires about 18K of its own memory to run, you may not be able to run it when little free memory remains. The solution: Open a desk accessory in an open application's layer by pressing Option while choosing the desk accessory's name from the Apple menu. With this approach, the desk accessory opens in the same layer as the active application, and therefore, uses the memory that MultiFinder has already allocated for that program.

❖ *Don't use MultiFinder if you don't need it* If you use System 6.x and your Mac has only 1MB or 2MB of memory, consider not using MultiFinder. You'll forgo one-click program switching, but your system will have more free memory, allowing large programs like 4th Dimension and PageMaker to run. To specify that your Mac start up under the single Finder, be sure your startup disk's icon is selected, then choose Set Startup from the Finder's Special menu. Click the Finder button, click OK, and then restart. Also remember that you can bypass MultiFinder during startup by holding down the Command key until the menu bar appears. If you need background printing but not fast application switching, use a print spooler such as Fifth Generation's SuperLaserSpool. And use a surrogate Finder desk accessory such as CE Software's DiskTop or Fifth Generation's DiskTools to move between programs without having to quit and return to the Finder. (Both DiskTop and DiskTools are illustrated in Chapter 19.)

Summary:

✔ Multitasking is a computer's ability to run numerous programs simultaneously.

✔ MultiFinder represented Apple's first step into the multitasking world with the ability to run several programs at once and perform time-consuming jobs while you continue to work.

✔ The two basic approaches to scheduling tasks are preemptive and cooperative scheduling. With preemptive scheduling, the computer gives each task control of the computer's resources for a specific amount of time. With cooperative scheduling, the responsibility for dividing the processor's time is shared among all the applications that are running.

✔ A Mac's performance slows when several applications are run in the background.

✔ Multitasking with a Mac requires at least 2MB of memory, preferably 4MB or more.

✔ Choosing software that uses memory sparingly and adjusting a program's memory requirements using the Finder's Get Info command are two ways to get the most from your Mac's available memory.

Chapter 25

System 7

The Mac's system software has seen numerous revisions since 1984, but System 7.0 tops them all. The latest version of the Mac's system is the ultimate Mac makeover and has something for everyone. Beginners will find it easy to learn and use. Experts will find a world of powerful new features to explore. For that matter, System 7.0 may excite Mac veterans even more than newcomers who didn't have to cut their teeth on earlier versions of the system.

System 7.0 is such an important milestone that it won't be long before it makes its way to the hard disk of every Mac user, sending System 6.x to that great Trash icon in the sky — just as System 6.x meant curtains for its predecessors. But until then, the Mac world will be in transition. Fortunately, the transition shouldn't be too painful. The Mac's basic operating style hasn't changed and Apple did a fine job of adding new features while retaining compatibility with most existing programs that ran under System 6.x.

In this chapter, I'll spotlight the new features in System 7.0 and I'll pass along some tips and ideas for using them. If you've used previous versions of the Mac's system, you'll have to break some old habits and learn some new ones. The sidebar "Transition Tips" summarizes the differences you'll need to adjust to. If you're new to the Mac, you may want to read Chapter 2 and Chapter 23 before reading this chapter for some background on basic Mac operations.

I won't go into detail on the process of installing the System 7.0 software; that information is described in detail in the excellent manuals that accompany System 7.0. For information on obtaining the System 7.0 upgrade, contact your local Apple dealer. For more details and insights on the features of System 7.0, check out my colleague Lon Poole's book, *Macworld Guide to System 7* (IDG Books Worldwide, June, 1991).

Transition Tips

Although the Mac's basic operating style is unchanged in System 7.0, there are several changes you'll need to adjust to if you've used earlier system versions:

❖ Open and Save dialog boxes. In System 6.x, Open and Save dialog boxes contain a button called Drive that lets you switch between the different disks on your desktop. In System 7.0, the Drive button is replaced by the Desktop button. When you click Desktop, the list box shows an icon for everything on your desktop — disks, folders, even the Trash (see the figure "The Desktop Level"). One benefit of this scheme is that it lets you quickly jump to a particular disk — no more clicking Drive time after time. Expect to see more and more programs adopting the new Open and Save dialog box design shown in the figure "The Desktop Level." Among other things, the dialog box contains a button for creating a new folder.

❖ The application menu. In System 7.0, you don't use the Apple menu to switch to a different open application; you use the application menu at the right edge of the menu bar instead. Also, because the application menu is no longer a simple icon, you can't rotate between each running program by clicking it. Don't forget you can hide the current application by pressing Option while choosing a different application's name (see the Quick Reference card at the back of this book).

❖ Renaming icons. In System 6.x, you could click on an icon once and then begin typing to rename it. That was handy, but it also made it easy to accidentally rename an icon. System 7.0's Finder makes it more difficult to accidentally rename an icon. To enter the renaming mode, you must click on the icon's name (not the icon itself). As an alternative, you can click on the icon and then press the Return key. To do everything from the keyboard, select the icon by typing the first few characters of its name, and then press Return to enter renaming mode. Finally, type the ☞

The Desktop Level

In System 7.0, Open and Save dialog boxes no longer have a Drive button. In its place is the Desktop button, which lets you view the items that are on the Mac's desktop, including disks, folders, documents, and the Trash. To access a different disk, click Desktop and then double-click the disk's name. In this Save dialog box, also note the new button for creating a folder and for creating a stationery pad. Expect to see this style of dialog box in more and more Mac programs.

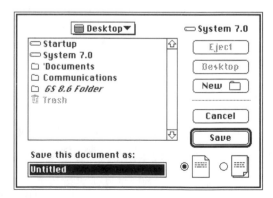

What's New?

System 7.0's new features fall into two broad categories: enhancements you'll enjoy as soon as you've installed the software, and ones that are dependent on the development of new versions of application programs.

Let's start out with an overview of the out-of-the-box enhancements:

❖ *TrueType outline fonts* System 7.0 boasts a signficant new font technology that allows the Mac to display sharp text regardless of the point size you choose, and to print that text on virtually any printer. This new font technology, called TrueType, works with all existing Mac programs.

new name. Regardless of how you select an icon, you'll always know you can rename it when a box appears around its name.

❖ Accessing Control Panels and extensions. In System 6.x, the Control Panel desk accessory was your gateway to all Control Panel options, including ones with INIT components. In System 7.0, these items can be scattered throughout a few different folders within the System Folder. You can access them all from one place by creating aliases, however, as described in this chapter.

❖ System extension loading order. In System 6.x, all INITs live in the System Folder and load alphabetically. In System 7.0, they still load alphabetically, but from a few different places. First, System 7.0 alphabetically loads the extensions in the Extensions folder, followed by those in the Control Panels folder, and then those in the top level of the System Folder. You'll need to keep this loading order in mind when troubleshooting INIT conflicts. Also, if you use an INIT management utility such as INIT Picker, you must put it in the Extensions folder so that it loads before other INITs.

❖ Working with system resources. As described in this chapter, you install and remove fonts and sounds by dragging them into and out of the System file. No more fussing with Font/DA Mover, ResEdit, or Suitcase utilities.

❖ Solving the Puzzle. Finally! You can cheat to solve the Puzzle desk accessory. Open the Puzzle, choose Copy from the Edit menu, and then choose Show Clipboard to see the Puzzle's picture intact. You can also customize the Puzzle by pasting a picture into it.

Existing Disks and System 7

Floppy and hard disks that you've used with earlier system versions work with System 7.0, but when you insert a disk, you'll see a message saying "Updating disk for new system software." When you see this message, the Finder is creating a desktop database file that will enable it to locate the disk's contents. For high-capacity disks, the desktop database file replaces the DeskTop file, which we've looked at in other chapters. The DeskTop file is still used for disks whose capacity is less than 2MB — in other words, for floppies.

If you use a hard disk or removable high-capacity cartridge with System 7.0 and then move it to a Mac running System 6.x, you'll notice two new folders: Desktop and Trash. These are folders that Finder 7.0 creates to store any icons you had moved to the desktop and to store the contents of the Trash. (Yes, under System 7.0, the Trash is actually a folder — which is why it isn't emptied until you explicitly choose Empty Trash.) You can delete these folders, but Finder 7.0 will create them again the next time you use that hard disk or cartridge on a Mac running System 7.0. **M**

❖ *An all-new Finder* System 7.0's Finder provides the same basic electronic desktop as earlier versions, but is faster, easier to use, more customizable, and far more powerful. And for the first time, the Finder can find — a new Find command lets you locate files using a variety of criteria.

❖ *Better System Folder organization* The System Folder in System 7.0 organizes related files into folders of their own, eliminating much of the confusing clutter that previous System Folders suffered from (see the table "Inside System 7.0").

❖ *File sharing* If you have more than one Mac, you can use inexpensive cabling kits to unite them in a *network.* That isn't new — Macs have always had networking hardware built into them. What *is* new, however, is built-in file sharing software — System 7.0 lets you make the folders on your hard disk available to other members of your network, and they can make their folders available to you.

❖ *Improved multitasking* System 7.0 still doesn't provide the preemptive multitasking I described in the last chapter, but it does go beyond MultiFinder. System 7.0 makes it easier to manage and switch between multiple programs, and it can copy files and perform other time-consuming file-management tasks in the background.

❖ *Access to more memory* With System 6.x, the Mac family is limited to accessing a maximum of 8MB of memory. With System 7.x, 32-bit Macs — the Mac IIsi, IIci, and IIfx — can access hundreds of megabytes of memory. Virtual memory — the System 7.0 feature that enables the Mac to treat part of a hard disk (not an ejectable, removable media drive)as an extension of RAM — is limited to a maximum of 15MB on the IIx, SE/30, and IIcx. (See Chapter 34 for more details on virtual memory and specific Macs.)

Let's take a closer look at some of these innovations.

Truth in Type

One of the biggest shortcomings of System 6.x and earlier versions is their reliance on bitmapped screen fonts. Bitmapped fonts require a separate, disk-

Inside System 7

Folder Name	Purpose
Apple Menu Items	Holds items that appear in Apple menu
Control Panels	Holds Control Panels (cdevs)
Extensions	Holds system extensions (INITs, RDEVs)
Preferences	Holds system and application preferences files
Startup Items	Holds items you want the Mac to open automatically during startup

Not So Smooth

With bitmapped fonts, you need a separate, disk-consuming font description for each size. Available sizes appear in outlined type. When you use a size for which no bitmap description exists (in this example, any size but 12-point), the Mac scales an existing size, which results in jagged-edged text.

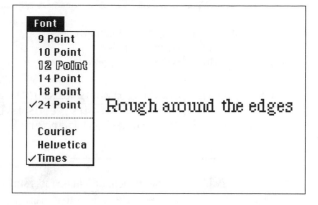

consuming description for each size — if you want to see smooth 24-point Times on the screen, you need a 24-point Times font in your System file. If you don't have one, the Mac approximates the required size by enlarging or shrinking an existing size (see the figure "Not So Smooth").

TrueType outline fonts change all that. Instead of describing a font in terms of how many pixels make up a given character in a given size, TrueType describes fonts mathematically. For example, in a bitmapped font, an uppercase *T* might be described as an object ten dots high with a crossbar eight dots wide. In a TrueType outline font, however, the *T* might be described as an object whose crossbar is 20 percent shorter than its vertical stem. This is a bit of an oversimplification, but it illustrates that an outline font is like a recipe that lists ingredients in proportions instead of measurements: the cook can use math to *scale* the final product to any size.

▼ Outlines on Tap

With TrueType outline fonts, the Mac can use one mathematical description to create text in any size — for the screen and for PostScript and non-PostScript printers. Note that all sizes appear outlined.

When fonts are described as outlines, the same font description can be used to create character bitmaps in any size. Indeed, when you choose a TrueType font and then examine a program's Size menu, you'll notice that all sizes — not just some — appear outlined, as shown in the figure "Outlines on Tap." (By the way, don't confuse the outline text style with an outline font — they're different beasts. It just so happens that the Mac has always used the outline style to indicate which sizes you've installed.)

Just as a cook can change the flavor of a dish by changing the proportions of its ingredients, a device that uses outline

Expanding or condensing text can give a typeface a new personality. This is ITC Garamond, condensed 20 percent.

Expanding or condensing text can give a typeface a new personality. This is ITC Garamond, expanded 20 percent.

fonts can change the look of a font by altering its proportions. As the figure "Changing Proportions" shows, fonts can assume different personalities when *expanded* (widened) or *condensed* (narrowed).

▲ Changing Proportions

Since TrueType outline fonts are described mathematically, the Mac can apply calculations to a font's description to expand or condense it, giving the font a new personality. Many desktop publishing programs, including PageMaker, QuarkXpress, and Design Studio, can exploit this capability.

Another benefit of outline fonts surfaces when you use the zoom-in and zoom-out viewing scale options that many programs provide. For example, in System 6.x, if you zoom in on a PageMaker document for a closer look, the Mac must scale its bitmapped fonts to create the large sizes required. The results are usually unattractive and contradict the Mac's what-you-see-is-what-you-get operating style. With TrueType, the Mac is able to create characters in exactly the size required by the magnification scale you chose. You can zoom in and out to your heart's content, and you'll always see sharp text on the screen.

How TrueType Works

How does TrueType perform these feats? When you choose a given size, TrueType reads the outline font recipe and then stirs up characters in the size required, a process called *rasterizing*. Part of rasterizing involves tweaking the appearance of each character to look as good as possible given the size you chose and the resolution of the screen. That's a tall order: the Mac's screen isn't sharp enough to accurately render every little detail of a typeface, so TrueType must compromise by adjusting the position of the pixels that form each character so that the end result is legible and as faithful as possible to the original type design. This process is often called *grid fitting*, since TrueType must create text whose pixels fit within the grid of horizontal and vertical pixels that will ultimately form the character.

To enable this text tweaking, every TrueType font contains internal instructions, sometimes called *hints*, that tell TrueType how to make that font look as good as possible at each size. It all sounds complex, and indeed, it is. But fortunately, you don't need to concern yourself with it — just choose the type size you want, and TrueType does the rest.

If you've collected a foundry full of bitmapped fonts over the years, take heart: they still work under System 7.0. The only difference is that they're much easier to install and remove — more about that shortly.

TrueType and PostScript Fonts

It's important to note that the concepts behind outline fonts aren't new. Printers that use the PostScript page-description language have PostScript outline fonts built into their ROM chips, and they automatically substitute those fonts instead of using the bitmapped fonts in the Mac's System file. What's more, using Adobe's Adobe Type Manager (ATM) utility, System 6.x users can can get the benefits of outline fonts on the Mac's screen. TrueType is also available with System 6.0.7 and the Apple StyleWriter and Personal LaserWriter LS printers. This version of TrueType exists as a system extension (INIT) — like ATM, it loads into memory when the Mac starts up and modifies the way the Mac creates fonts.

ATM uses downloadable PostScript printer font files to create sharp character bitmaps for the Mac's screen. When you choose a font for which a downloadable font file exists, ATM performs many of the same tasks as TrueType — it reads the font file and creates the bitmapped characters in the sizes required, using the font's internal hints for best results. ATM works beautifully, but there's a catch: it works only for those fonts that have corresponding PostScript printer font files in your System Folder. Choose a font for which you don't have the printer font file, and it's back to the bitmap world, with all its ugly artifacts.

If you use downloadable PostScript fonts and ATM, you'll be glad to know that TrueType coexists peacefully with them. Indeed, as we'll see in Chapter 35, TrueType and its fonts work well with PostScript printers. You may, however, want to avoid putting the same TrueType and downloadable PostScript typeface — for example, each format's version of Times — in the same System Folder.

TrueType and Printers

TrueType fonts bring even bigger benefits to printers that don't use PostScript, such as the ImageWriter and Personal LaserWriter SC. When used with System 6.x, these printers use the Mac's bitmapped screen fonts to produce text. To print in best-quality mode in System 6.x, an ImageWriter II requires your System file to contain a font that's twice the size you actually used — to print sharp 12-point Times, you need 24-point Times, too. At printing time, the ImageWriter driver reduces the larger size by 50 percent to obtain sharper text. The LaserWriter IISC and Personal LaserWriter SC work similarly, but require fonts that are four times the size you actually used: to print sharp 18-point text, you need a 72-point font. You could almost fill a hard disk by outfitting a System file with a wide range of font sizes.

TrueType fonts eliminate those burgeoning bitmaps. Like ATM, TrueType is as skillful at creating sharp characters for printers as it is for the screen. And yes, those internal hints play a role in the process by allowing TrueType to optimize the appearance of the text to best match the printer's resolution. The bottom line: non-PostScript printers can produce text whose quality matches that of a PostScript printer. The "SC" in Personal LaserWriter SC no longer stands for "second class." And the new fonts are used by Apple's newest affordable printers, the Personal LaserWriter LS and the little StyleWriter inkjet printer.

No More Font/DA Mover

TrueType font outlines reside in the System file, along with any bitmapped fonts you might also have. But the good news is that System 7.0 makes adding fonts to or removing them from your System file a breeze. There's no need to grapple with the old Font/DA Mover utility.

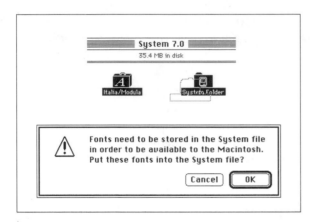

To install a font, first quit any programs and close any desk accessories that are running. (You can't modify the System file when programs or desk accessories are running.) Next, drag the font to the System Folder icon, and the Finder asks whether you want it put into your System file. Click OK or press Return, and the font is installed (see the figure "Font Moving Made Easy").

You can also see what fonts and sounds are in your System file by double clicking on the System file icon. In System 6.x, an error message appears when you double-click on the System file. In System 7.0, a window appears listing the contents of the System file, with different icons representing TrueType and bitmapped fonts (and sounds).

▲ Font Moving Made Easy

No more Font/DA Mover — to install a font in System 7.0, drag its icon to the System Folder (top). When the Mac asks if you want to put the fonts in the System file (bottom), click OK. One catch: You must quit any open programs and close any desk accessories in order to install or remove a font.

The System file window looks and works much like a disk or folder window — icons represent each font, and you can use the Finder's View menu to look at the window's contents sorted according to icon, name, date, size, and so on. To remove a font, simply drag it out of the System file window. You can even double click on a sound to hear it and on a font to see a sample (see the figure "Free Type Samples"). You can also install a font by dragging it to the System file's window or to the icon of the System file.

As you can see, installing and removing fonts is similar to copying a file to a different folder or disk, although it takes a bit longer. That's because, behind the

Helvetica 14

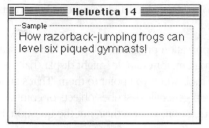

Helvetica 14

—Sample—
How razorback-jumping frogs can
level six piqued gymnasts!

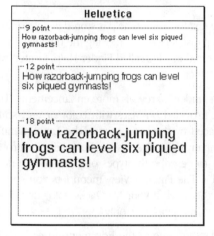

Helvetica

—9 point—
How razorback-jumping frogs can level six piqued
gymnasts!

—12 point—
How razorback-jumping frogs can level
six piqued gymnasts!

—18 point—
How razorback-jumping
frogs can level six piqued
gymnasts!

▲ **Free Type Samples**

When you double-click on a font in the System file's window, a window appears containing a sample. Only one size appears with a bitmapped font (top); a few sizes appear for a TrueType outline font (bottom). Also note the different font icons.

scenes, the Finder is working to modify the System file — it's another example of how System 7.0 puts a friendly veneer on a complex process.

Incidentally, the new Finder may not need the Font/DA Mover, but it does know about it. You can double-click a Font/DA Mover document (often called a *suitcase file* because of its icon), and a window appears showing the desk accessories or fonts within.

This Finder's a Keeper

Making fonts easy to install and remove is just one of the many ways System 7.0's new Finder streamlines the Mac's operation. The System 7.0 Finder also makes it easier to find and select files, to view the contents of disks and folders, and to customize the Mac's operation to suit your tastes and work habits.

One of the most visible differences in the new Finder is that there's no more Set Startup command for choosing between MultiFinder and the one-program-at-a-time Finder. The Mac always runs in the multitasking mode I described in the previous chapter. The small icon that MultiFinder displayed at the right edge of the menu bar has evolved into a menu — the *application menu,* which lists the name of each program you're running and lets you switch between them (see the figure "Programs on the Menu" on the next page).

As I mentioned in the previous chapter, you can also use the application menu to avoid screen clutter by hiding the windows of other applications and the Finder. It's important to know that hiding a program doesn't suspend its operation. You can, for example, start a lengthy file-transfer session with a communications program, and then hide the program without interrupting the file transfer.

To the left of the application menu is the *Help menu,* the gateway to another of System 7.0's innovations: *balloon help.* When balloon help is turned on, the Mac displays small, cartoon-like balloons containing descriptive text as you point to different items or menu commands (see the figure "Help is Just a Balloon Away"). The Finder contains some 1300 different help balloons for everything

from the Trash can to the One Sided and Two Sided buttons in the Erase Disk dialog box.

More and more application programs will provide their own balloon help — a painting program, for example, might display balloons explaining its palette tools when you point to them. That's an important point: balloon help generally describes objects or commands, not tasks. It answers the question, What is this?, not the question, How do I do that?

In most cases, the text for balloon help is stored in a separate disk file, so you can free up disk space by removing the help file if you like. The Finder's help balloons are stored in a file called Finder Help, located within the System Folder's Extensions folder.

Browsing the other menus in Finder 7.0 reveals more enhancements. The Color menu (which System 6.x provided on Macs with color or grey-scale video hardware) has been replaced by the Label menu. The Label menu lets you assign text labels to accompanying colors. Using the Labels Control Panel, you can create your own labels to describe the types of items you work with (see the figure "Read the Label"). The Finder's View menu lets you sort a disk or folder window according to the label. If your Mac lacks color or grey-scale hardware, the Label menu shows the label text only.

The Finder's Edit menu looks the same as the Edit menu in earlier Finders, but in System 7.0, it's available even when a dialog box is open. (In System 6.x, the Mac beeps if you try to pull down a menu when a dialog box is open.) Thus, you can cut, copy, and paste text within a dialog box.

Strolling over to the left edge of the menu bar, we find the new and improved Apple menu. In System 6.x, the Apple menu allows you to open desk accessories. In System 7.0, the Apple menu lets you open anything — programs, desk accessories, documents, folders, and more. You can add virtually any item to the Apple menu by putting the item in the Apple Menu Items folder, which is located within the System Folder. Choosing an item's name from the Apple menu tells the Mac to open that item. Thus, the Apple menu provides one-click access to whatever you use most.

▲ Programs on the Menu
System 7.0's application menu (located at the right edge of the menu bar) lets you quickly switch between programs and avoid screen clutter by hiding windows of applications you aren't using. Tip: to hide the current application when you switch, press the Option key while choosing the Finder or an application name.

Help is Just a Balloon Away
System 7.0's balloon help feature, activated by choosing Show Balloons from the Help menu, allows the Mac to identify the components of its programs. Shown here: a help balloon for the LaserWriter Print dialog box.

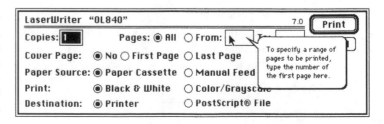

```
≣□≣≣≣ Labels ≣≣≣≣
┌─────┐ ┌─────────────────┐
│     │ │ Work in Progress │
└─────┘ └─────────────────┘
┌─────┐ ┌─────────────────┐
│ ███ │ │ Biz Letters      │
└─────┘ └─────────────────┘
┌─────┐ ┌─────────────────┐
│ ███ │ │ Personal Letters │
└─────┘ └─────────────────┘
┌─────┐ ┌─────────────────┐
│ ███ │ │ Macworld         │
└─────┘ └─────────────────┘
┌─────┐ ┌─────────────────┐
│ ███ │ │ To Do            │
└─────┘ └─────────────────┘
┌─────┐ ┌─────────────────┐
│ ███ │ │ Archive          │
└─────┘ └─────────────────┘
┌─────┐ ┌─────────────────┐
│ ███ │ │ Application      │
└─────┘ └─────────────────┘
```

▲ **Read the Label**
The Labels Control Panel lets you associate text with colors and assign those labels to icons to organize and identify programs, documents, and folders. Using the Views Control Panel, you can specify that labels be shown in list views (by name, by size, and so on).

The Amazing Alias

The Apple menu becomes especially useful when you combine it with one of the most powerful — and potentially confusing — features of System 7.0: *aliases*. An alias is a small file that points to a document, an application, a disk, or a folder. When you open an alias, the Mac opens whatever the alias points to, regardless of where that item is located — in a different folder, on another disk, or on a network a thousand miles away.

Think of an alias as an electronic remote control for the items you work with. For example, say you always work with a certain program that you've stashed within several folders. Normally, to access that program, you have to make your way through all the folders that contain it. In System 7.0, you can create an alias of the program and then move the alias to the Apple Menu Items folder. From then on, when you want to run the program, instead of "getting up from your chair" to locate the file, simply choose its alias from the Apple menu. Doing so tells the Mac to open the program, since that's what the alias points to.

To create an alias, select the original item and then choose Make Alias from the Finder's File menu. After a moment or two, a new icon appears adjacent to the original, with its name in *italics* to indicate that the icon is an alias (see the figure "Making an Alias" on the next page). An alias file has the icon of whatever it points to. Initially, an alias file's name is the same as the original item with the word *alias* added, but you can change the name to anything you like. An alias file itself is very small (about 1K), so feel free to create aliases by the bushel and not worry about wasting too much hard disk space.

In the example I just used, you might wonder why you couldn't simply move the program file itself to the Apple Menu Items folder. You could, but that would defeat the purpose of your filing system. That's one benefit of aliases: they give you one-click access to frequently used items while allowing you to store those items wherever you want to.

It's worth noting that an alias is a smart little critter — you can move and even rename the item an alias points to, and the Mac is still able to find it. You can even create an alias of an item that's on a floppy disk and then copy the alias to your hard disk. If you double-click the alias, the Mac asks you to insert the floppy disk containing the original. For more tips on how to tap the power and flexibility of aliases, see the sidebar "Alias Ideas" on page 321.

Making an Alias

To make an alias, select an icon (at top, the Sound Control Panel) and choose Make Alias from the File menu. A new alias icon (bottom) appears adjacent to the original, with its name in *italics*. You can rename the alias and move it elsewhere — perhaps to the Apple Menu Items folder.

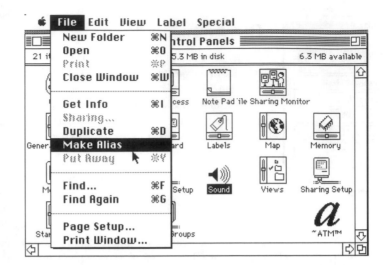

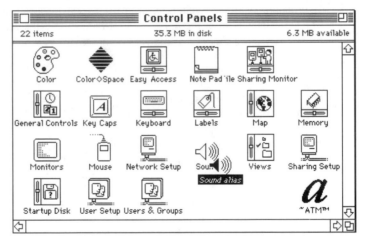

The Finder Can Find — Finally

The Finder in System 7.0 provides a powerful Find command that lets you locate files. When you choose Find or use the Command-F keyboard shortcut, a dialog box appears. Type part of the file or folder name you're looking for, and then click Find or press Return. The Mac locates the first item whose name contains the text you typed, and then selects the item for you while opening the folder or disk window that contains the item, if necessary. At that point, you can open the item by choosing Open or pressing Command-O, or you can continue searching by choosing Find Again or pressing Command-G.

Alias Ideas

There are almost as many ways to use aliases as there are ways to use the Mac. Here's a collection of ideas to get you started.

❖ *Put items in your Apple menu* Don't move an original program, document, or folder to the Apple Menu Items folder. Create an alias of it, and put the alias in the Apple Menu Items folder. Remember you can rename the alias if you like.

❖ *Access a frequently used folder* Perhaps you always use a certain folder that you keep buried within other folders. For fast access to that folder, make an alias of it and move the alias to your desktop. You can then open or modify the contents of the folder by opening its alias — not by opening folder after folder to get to the one you want. You can even copy items to the folder by dragging them to its alias.

❖ *Access a file server volume* An alias provides an easy way to mount an AppleShare file server volume or a disk or folder made available through System 7.0's file-sharing features. (See Chapter 40 for an introduction to AppleShare and file servers; System 7.0's file-sharing features are discussed elsewhere in this chapter.) First, mount the volume as you normally would, then select it and choose Make Alias. Rename or move the alias as desired. Thereafter, to connect to the server, simply open its alias, and you'll receive the standard AppleShare log-on dialog box. (You won't even see the log-on dialog box if you access the server as a guest when making the alias.) You can even use this technique to copy a file to a server volume that you haven't yet mounted: Just drag the file to the alias icon and respond to the log-on dialog box as necessary. The Finder connects to the server and then copies the file.

❖ *Access your hard disk from any Mac on your network* First, use the Finder's Sharing command to make your hard disk available. Next, make an alias of your hard disk, and then copy that alias to a floppy disk. To connect to your hard disk from a different Mac in your network, simply insert the floppy and double-click the alias.

❖ *Access an extension or a Control Panel from somewhere else* Normally, system extensions (INITs) reside in the Extensions folder, which is in the System Folder. If you want to access an extension from the Control Panels window, make an alias of the extension and move the alias to the Control Panels folder (also within the System Folder). Similarly, if you want to access a certain Control Panel directly from the Apple menu, make an alias of it and move the alias to the Apple Menu Items folder.

❖ *Start programs and open documents* If you make an alias of a program, you can start the program and open a document by dragging the document icon to the alias icon. When you do, you'll see the alias icon become highlighted — just as a folder or disk icon is highlighted when you copy an item to it. Release the mouse button, and the Mac starts the program and opens the document.

❖ *Quickly access all the programs on your hard disk* First, use the Finder's Find command to search for all applications at once. (See the section on the Find command in this chapter.) After the Mac has found and selected all the applications, choose Make Alias. The Mac makes an alias of for every application it found. You can then move those aliases into a single folder to have quick access to every program on your hard disk.

❖ *Automate access to archived files* Many people use file compression utilities such as StuffIt to compress ☞

Detailed Searching

When you click More Choices in the Finder's Find dialog box, a new dialog box appears whose pop-up menus give you more ways to search. Here, a search is being conducted for all items with the label Biz Letters. Clicking the All at Once button tells the Finder to find and select all the files rather than stopping after the first one it finds.

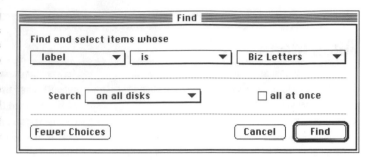

The Find dialog box contains a button called More Choices. When you click More Choices, the Find dialog box is replaced by a larger dialog box containing pop-up menus that allow you to search using a variety of different criteria (see the figure "Detailed Searching"). The table "Find Options" describes each search option and its criteria. To specify that the Finder locate and select all the items that meet the criteria, click the All at Once check box. When this option is unchecked, the Finder stops each time it locates and selects an item.

You can combine search criteria by conducting a second search as soon as the Finder locates the items that meet the first search. For example, say you want to find all documents modified after April 21, 1991. First, search for all documents (the Find pop-ups read "kind contains documents") with the All at Once option checked. After the Finder selects all the documents, change the pop-ups to read "date modified is after 4/21/91."

Alias Ideas (cont'd)

and archive older files that they copy to floppy disks and then delete from their hard disks to free up space. If you're in this group, you can use aliases to easily locate your archives — no more rooting through floppies trying to locate the disk that contains a certain archive. First, make your archive file as you normally would and then copy

it to a floppy disk. Next, make an alias of the archive on the floppy and then copy the alias from the floppy to your hard disk — perhaps to a folder called Archive Aliases. Finally, delete the archive from your hard disk. When you need to access the archive, just double click on its alias. The Mac will ask you to insert the appropriate floppy. **M**

More Info in Get Info

The Get Info command in Finder 7.0 provides more information and lets you customize certain aspects of the Mac's operation. Some examples:

❖ When you select an alias and choose the Finder's Get Info command, the Get Info window displays the location of the item that the alias points to. You can tell the Finder to locate and select the original item by clicking the Find Original button. You might do this if you wanted to rename the original, throw it away, or move it.

❖ The Get Info window for the Trash icon contains a new check box called Warn Before Emptying. Normally, this box is checked, causing the Finder to ask if you really want to delete the contents of the trash when you choose Empty Trash. If you uncheck the box, you won't receive this query.

Find Options

When searching by...	your options are...	and you specify...
Name	contains, starts with, ends with, is, is not, doesn't contain	part or all of a name
Size	is less than, is greater than	a size value (in K)
Kind	contains, doesn't contain	alias, application, document, folder, or stationery
Label	is, is not	a label name or None
Date Created	is, is before, is after, is not	the current date or use arrows to change to the desired date
Date Modified	is, is before, is after, is not	the current date or use arrows to change to the desired date
Version	is, is before, is after, is not	a version number
Comments	contain, do not contain	some text that appears in the Get Info comment
Lock	is	locked or unlocked

```
☰☐☰  Memo Boilerplate Info  ☰☰
```

Memo Boilerplate

Kind : Microsoft Word stationery pad
Size : 1K on disk (15 bytes used)

Where : System 7.0 :

Created : Thu, Feb 14, 1991, 9:11 AM
Modified : Thu, Feb 14, 1991, 9:11 AM
Version : not available

Comments :

☐ **Locked**   ☒ **Stationery pad**

You have opened a stationery pad, so a new document will be created.

Type a name for the new document:

Memo Boilerplate copy

(**Save In...**)   (**Cancel**)   ((**OK**))

▲ **Personal Stationery**

To turn a document into a stationery pad, click the Stationery Pad check box in the document's Get Info window (top). When you open a stationery pad, the Finder asks you to provide a name for the new document (bottom), which will be a copy of the original. To save the document in a different folder or on a different disk, click the Save In button.

❖ The Get Info window for a document contains a new check box called Stationery Pad. If you check this box, you turn the document into a *stationery pad*. The stationery feature lets you create masters for the types of documents you create — letterheads, business letters, fax cover sheets, newsletter designs, and so on. By creating a document and then turning it into a stationery pad, you can reuse its contents without worrying about accidentally saving over them. When you open a stationery pad, the Finder makes a copy of the document and asks you to name the new copy (see the figure "Personal Stationery").

❖ You can customize the icons of most files and folders by using the Get Info window. To replace an icon with a different design, first create the design in a painting or drawing program, and then copy it to the Clipboard. Next, open the item's Get Info window and click on the icon. If the icon can be modified, a box appears around it. Choose Paste, and the Mac replaces the icon with the graphic on the Clipboard, scaling it down to fit if needed. You can even use a scanned or digitized image as an icon, as shown in the figure "Picture an Icon."

Finder Tweaks and Enhancements

Many of the Finder's improvements fall into the "little things that mean a lot" category — they're tweaks and enhancements that make the Mac operate more smoothly. If you're a new or occasional Mac user, many of these improvements won't sound that significant. If you've used the Mac for a while, however, some of them will give you goosebumps. Some of the top tweaks include:

❖ "Dropping" a document into an application. You can open a document by dragging the document icon to an application icon. When you do, the application icon becomes highlighted — just as a folder icon is highlighted when you move an icon into it. When you release the mouse button, the Finder opens the document (and starts the application, if it isn't already running). This is a great way to start a word processor and import a text-only file. For example, to start Microsoft Word and open a text-only document,

```
▤☐▤  Things-to-do Folder Info  ▤▤▤
```
📁	Things-to-do Folder

Kind: folder
Size: 755K on disk (750,183 bytes used), for 21 items
Where: System 7.0:

Created: Sun, Oct 7, 1990, 4:58 PM
Modified: Tue, Feb 19, 1991, 8:22 AM
Comments:

```
▤☐▤  Things-to-do Folder Info  ▤▤▤
```
☑	Things-to-do Folder

Kind: folder
Size: 755K on disk (750,183 bytes used), for 21 items
Where: System 7.0:

Created: Sun, Oct 7, 1990, 4:58 PM
Modified: Tue, Feb 19, 1991, 8:22 AM
Comments:

▲ Picture an Icon

System 7.0 lets you customize the icons of most items by using the Get Info window. First, select the image in a graphics program and choose Copy. Next, select the icon in the Get Info window; if the icon can be modified, it appears within a rectangle (left). Finally, choose Paste, and the Mac scales the graphic to fit and turns it into an icon (right). The icon for this folder is from HyperCard 2.0's Icon Ideas stack.

drag the text-only document to the Word icon. This drop-to-open technique even works with Apple's ResEdit resource editing utility. To start ResEdit and open an application, drop the application icon into the ResEdit icon.

❖ Double-clicking desk accessories and cdevs. You can run a desk accessory or open a Control Panel device (cdev) by double-clicking it.

❖ Autoscrolling in directory windows. When you're dragging an item in a directory window, you can cause the window to scroll automatically by pointing at its edges with the mouse button still pressed. Autoscrolling is just the ticket when you're moving a file into a folder that isn't currently visible within the window's boundaries. It also works when you're selecting multiple files by drawing a selection marquee.

❖ A better marquee. In Finder 6.x, the selection marquee worked only in the icon and small icon views. In System 7.0, the marquee works in all list views, too. (List views are the text-oriented views of a disk or folder: by name, by size, by kind, and so on.) And items highlight as soon as the marquee touches them, even if the mouse button is still down. In earlier systems, the Mac didn't highlight selected items until you released the button. But this enhancement also means a bit of adapting for System 6.x users: You can no longer select an item in a list view by clicking anywhere on that item's line; you must click directly on the icon or its name.

❖ Improved list views. In Finder 7.0's list views, clicking a small triangle icon lets you look at disks and folders in outline form, with nested folders and files appearing indented (see the figure "Better List Views" on the next page). In list

Better List Views ▶
Finder 7.0's list views let you look at a folder's contents in outline form by clicking the triangle to the left of the folder's name. Here, the outline view shows the contents of the HyperCard 2.0 folder. Note that the HyperCard Help folder's outline is collapsed, while the HyperCard Stacks folder outline is expanded. Besides making it easy to see the contents of folders, the outline view also lets you select items that span folders — something System 6.x doesn't allow.

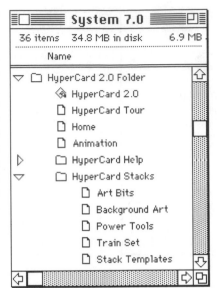

views, you can select a group of items that span different folders — you couldn't in Finder 6.x. You can also switch between different list views by clicking the desired view in the window's heading. You can also use the Views Control Panel to tell the Finder how much information to display in its list views, what font to use, and whether or not to automatically clean up icons when you drag them (see the figure "Improving Your View").

❖ Smarter zoom boxes. In Finder 6.x, clicking a directory window's zoom box caused the window to fill the screen — which led to some mighty big windows on large-screen monitors. In Finder 7.0, clicking a zoom box causes the window to become only as large as necessary to show its contents without scrolling.

Views

Font for views: **Geneva** ▼ **9** ▼

- - - Icon Views - - -
◉ Straight grid   ☒ Always snap to grid
○ Staggered grid

- - - List Views - - -
◉ ○ ○
☒ Show size
☐ Show kind
☐ Show label
☐ Show date
☐ Show version
☐ Show comments
☐ Calculate folder sizes
☒ Show disk info in header

Improving Your View ▶
The Views control panel lets you customize the way the Finder shows the contents of disks and folders. Select Always Snap to Grid for automatic icon clean-up. The List Views portion of the dialog box gives you three different list view sizes and lets you choose the information to show. Tip: to create small list view windows when you click a window's zoom box, uncheck most or all of the "show" options.

Dialog Boxes Compared
Finder 7.0 can copy files, conduct searches, and perform other tasks in the background while you work in other programs. When background option is possible, the Finder displays a movable modal dialog box (top), which lets you switch to another program, but not perform any other Finder tasks. In previous system versions, the file-copying dialog box lacked the movable modal's title bar (bottom).

Dialog Boxes Compared
Finder 7.0 can copy files, conduct searches, and perform other tasks in the background while you work in other programs. When background option is possible, the Finder displays a movable modal dialog box (top), which lets you switch to another program, but not perform any other Finder tasks. In previous system versions, the file-copying dialog box lacked the movable modal's title bar (bottom).

```
================= Copy =================

Items remaining to be copied:      1
Reading:   System

[███                              ]  [ Stop ]
```

```
Files/Folders remaining to be copied:  [    1 ]
Writing:   System

[▓▓▓                              ]  [ Cancel ]
```

❖ An improved Trash can. In System 6.x, the Trash emptied now and then, even if you didn't explicitly choose Empty Trash. In System 7.0, the Mac doesn't empty the Trash until you tell it to. This gives you a better chance of being able to recover something you threw away by mistake. (If you have a huge number of files in the Trash, the Finder will suggest that you empty it.) You can also move the Trash icon elsewhere on the desktop, and it will appear there the next time you start up the Mac.

❖ Background file copying. Finder 7.0 can copy files in the background while you work in other programs — great if you're copying a large number of files to a backup disk. To indicate that you can switch another program while something takes place in the background, System 7.0 introduces a new type of dialog box — the *movable modal* dialog box. As the first part of its name suggests, a movable modal dialog box can be moved around on the screen. *Modal* refers to the fact that you can't click outside of the dialog box. In the past, virtually all Mac dialog boxes were modal — you couldn't do anything until you confirmed or cancelled the dialog box. A movable modal dialog box works a bit differently: it won't let you do anything else in the current program, but you can switch to a different program and continue working. The new Find command also uses movable modal dialog boxes, as do a few other Finder operations. You can recognize a movable modal dialog box by the stripes that appear in its title bar (see the figure "Dialog Boxes Compared").

❖ Easier copying between windows. In System 6.x, copying an item from an inactive window to another window was often cumbersome. As soon as you clicked on the item, the inactive window would become active, often obscuring the destination window or icon. In System 7.0, the Finder doesn't activate the inactive window unless you release the mouse button while the pointer is still

More Choices
System 7.0's larger Chooser window has room to show more devices. Also note the subtle 3-D appearance that System 7.0 gives to windows and icons when running on Macs with color or grey-scale video hardware.

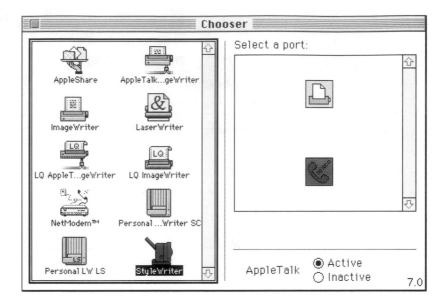

in the inactive window. If that sounds confusing, try it. Or just remember this: Finder 7.0 makes it easier to move and copy items between windows.

❖ Cleaner clean-ups. The Clean Up command in the Finder's Special menu works better and has new options that make it easier to organize the icons in a folder or disk window. By combining the Clean Up command with commands in the View menu, you can organize your icons according to two criteria. For example, say you want to organize the icons so that they're sorted according to their names. First, choose the By Name command from the View menu, and then switch to the desired icon view. Next, press the Option key while choosing Clean Up by Name from the Special menu. When you press the Option key while choosing Clean Up, the command organizes icons according to the last list view you chose.

❖ A better Chooser. The Chooser desk accessory in System 7.0 provides a bigger window that's better able to show the many devices and components that may be part of a large network (see the figure "More Choices"). The Chooser also lets you tab between its various list boxes and select devices using the keyboard arrow keys or by typing the first few characters of a device's name.

❖ More keyboard navigation options. The keyboard navigation enhancements found in the Chooser extend to other areas. You can select an item in a Finder directory window by using the arrow keys, the Tab key, or by typing one or more characters of the item's name. You can expand and contract outline views and open and close folders by using the arrow keys along with

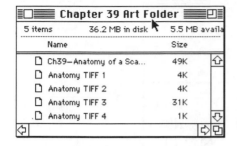

the Option and Command keys. For details on these and other Finder 7.0 shortcuts, see the Quick Reference card at the back of this book.

❖ Easier folder navigation. In the Finder, if you press the Command key while clicking on the title of a directory window, a pop-up menu appears listing the folders and disk that contain the current directory (see the figure "Pop-up Path"). This pop-up lets you quickly navigate the folders you use.

Personal File Sharing

As we'll see in Chapter 40, file server software lets you share a hard disk with other Macs on a network to provide a central repository for shared documents and application programs. Before System 7.0 appeared, the only official, Apple-developed server software available was AppleShare, which requires you to set aside, or *dedicate,* a Macintosh to file server duties. For less expensive, *peer-to-peer* file serving — which doesn't require a dedicated server — you had to buy third-party software that didn't always adhere to Apple's networking guidelines.

▲ Pop-up Path

When you press Command while clicking on a Finder window's title bar (top), a pop-up menu appears showing the path to the window (bottom). In this example, the folder Chapter 39 Art Folder is within the Chapter 39 folder, which is within Section III, on the disk System 7.0. Choose a folder or disk name to quickly display its contents.

System 7.0 changes that by integrating peer-to-peer file sharing into the Mac's system software. To turn file sharing on, use the Network Setup Control Panel. To share a hard disk or a folder, select its icon and choose Sharing from the Finder's File menu, and then click the check box labeled "Share this item and its contents." You can then use the Chooser desk accessory on a different Mac to connect to that shared folder or disk. Because System 7.0's file sharing software uses the same basic networking protocols as the AppleShare software, you can use a Mac running System 6.x to access a shared folder. Simply install the AppleShare workstation software on the 6.x Mac. You can even access a shared folder or disk using an IBM PC that's running AppleShare-compatible networking software.

The Finder uses different icons to indicate when a folder is available for sharing and when someone has connected to it (see the figure "Share and Share Alike"). For all but the smallest networks, you'll probably want to have some control over who can access which folders. Two additional Control Panels, User Setup and Users and Groups, allow you to specify the names of people who will be sharing your files and the access privileges they'll have. Another Control Panel, File Sharing Monitor, lets you see which disks and folders you've made available and who's connected to them.

```
┌────────────────────────────────────────────┐
│ ▤□▤══════════  'Documents ▤══════════════   │
│ ┌───┐                                        │
│ │   │  Where:      Startup:                  │
│ └───┘                                        │
│                                              │
│  ⊠ Share this item and its contents          │
│ ─────────────────────────────────────────── │
│                        See    See    Make    │
│                      Folders  Files Changes  │
│  Owner:  [ Jim Heid    ▼]  ⊠     ⊠     ⊠     │
│  User/Group: [<None>   ▼]  ⊠     ⊠     ⊠     │
│              Everyone      ⊠     ⊠     ⊠     │
│ ─────────────────────────────────────────── │
│  ☐ Make all enclosed folders like this one   │
│  ☐ Can't be moved, renamed or deleted        │
└────────────────────────────────────────────┘
```

Miscellaneous   Sharing isn't enabled for this folder.

Miscellaneous   Sharing isn enabled for this folder, but no users are connected to it.

Miscellaneous   Sharing is enabled for this folder, and the folder is being accessed by someone on the network.

System 7.0's file-sharing features are generally easy to use. But with any network software, it's a good idea to plan your file sharing scheme in advance and educate everyone who will be using it. Chapter 40 contains details on networking and provides tips for creating a reliable network.

One Program to Another: Can We Talk?

At the beginning of this chapter I mentioned that some of System 7.0's new features will require new versions of application programs. The most significant feature in this group is *interapplication communications,* or *IAC.* Like the Mac's Clipboard, IAC enables a program to exchange data with another program. But unlike the Clipboard, IAC enables the exchange to take place automatically, without you having to copy and paste information from one program to another.

IAC makes possible new ways of working with information and creating documents. Some examples:

❖ A financial report created in a word processor might include a chart generated by a spreadsheet program. Using IAC, you can automatically update the chart in the report when its underlying spreadsheet data changes.

❖ A desktop published catalog might include price information obtained from a database program. You could use IAC to automatically update the price lists in the catalog when the database is changed.

❖ A weekly executive status report might include summaries from several different managers. Using IAC, a secretary could assemble the report automatically by linking the report document to each manager's status report files.

The last example illustrates an important point: IAC can work together with System 7.0's file sharing features to enable different programs *running on different Macs* to exchange data. Thus, a work group can collaborate on a document that can be easily updated whenever one of its contributors makes a change in his or her section. Indeed, with IAC, you can create a document in which every single component — text as well as graphics — comes from programs running on other users' computers.

IAC is built around two key concepts: *publishing,* which involves making part or all of a document available to other programs; and *subscribing,* which involves including in a document information that has been published. If a program supports IAC, its Edit menu contains commands that allow you to publish and subscribe to information (see the figure "Publish and Subscribe Commands"). If a program's Edit menu doesn't contain these commands, the program doesn't support this aspect of IAC (although as we'll see later, it may support other aspects of it).

As a general rule, anything you can select — text, graphics, spreadsheet cells — you can make available to other programs. You publish something by selecting it, choosing Create Publisher from the Edit menu (see the figure "Becoming a Publisher" on the next page). When you publish some information, you create an *edition,* a separate file containing the information itself as well as data that allows the

Publish and Subscribe Commands

If a program supports System 7.0's publish and subscribe data-exchange features, its Edit menu has commands similar to these.

Edit	
Undo Typing	⌘Z
Cut	⌘H
Copy	⌘C
Paste	⌘P
Clear	
Select All	⌘A
Create Publisher...	
Subscribe to...	
Subscriber Options...	
Show Borders	
Show Clipboard	

Becoming a Publisher

To publish information, select it (top) and then choose Create Publisher from the Edit menu. In the dialog box that appears (middle), type a name for the edition. Note the preview of the information in the left portion of the dialog box. Programs indicate published information by drawing a border around it (bottom).

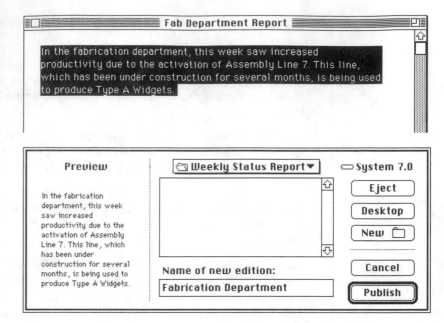

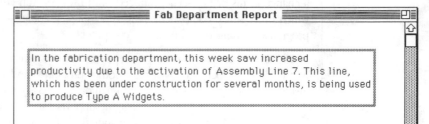

Mac to know where the information came from. The edition file acts as a conduit between the publisher and subscriber: Data always flows from publisher to edition to subscriber. Documents that contain publishers and subscribers don't have to be open at the same time to share data. When you save a document containing a publisher, the edition changes to reflect the current data from the publisher. Any number of subscribers can subscribe to a single edition.

To subscribe to an edition that you or others have created, choose Subscribe To from the Edit menu. Locate and choose the desired edition from the dialog box that appears and click OK, and the previously published information appears in your document, with a grey border around it to indicate that it comes from an edition (see the figure "Subscribing to Data"). Information that you've subscribed to is called a *subscriber*.

Using the Edit menu's Subscribe Options and Publisher Options commands, you can specify how the Mac handles the process of updating information that

Subscribing to Data

To subscribe to published information, choose Subscribe To from the Edit menu and locate the desired edition (top). The Mac reads the edition and inserts its contents into the currently open document (middle), with a dark border indicating that the information is from an edition. After you've subscribed to information, you can use the Subscriber Options dialog box (bottom) to specify when the information should be updated.

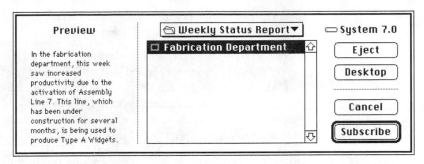

has been published and subscribed to. You might choose to automatically receive new editions as soon as they become available. This update mode is useful if you've subscribed to information in a spreadsheet consisting of daily sales figures, where you would want each version of the sales information as soon as it becomes available.

On the other hand, you might choose to receive a new edition only upon request — perhaps if you've subscribed to an edition consisting of an illustration that an artist in your office is working on. You probably don't need to have the illustration updated constantly, so you'd specify manual updating in the Subscriber Options dialog box. With manual updating, the Mac updates the subscriber with a new edition only when you specifically request it.

You can select, cut, and paste a subscriber. You can't edit a subscriber, although you can modify it as a whole. For example, you can underline or italicize subscriber text, but not delete or edit a word. This restriction protects you from losing changes to a subscriber when a new edition arrives.

The concepts behind publishers and subscribers sound complex, and indeed, they are quite a bit more complicated than cutting and pasting. For many tasks, you'll probably continue to rely on the Clipboard to move information between programs. Moving data using the Clipboard requires less memory, disk space, and processing time. But for those times when you need automatic updating, the publish-and-subscribe aspects of IAC are the answer.

AppleEvents

Another equally powerful aspect of IAC is *AppleEvents*, the ability of programs to send messages and data to each other. AppleEvents is built on the premise that multiple programs working together can be more powerful than multiple programs working in isolation. A word processor might use AppleEvents to "communicate with" a spelling checker. Instead of the word processor's developer having to write (and debug) spelling checker code, it could rely on a third-party spelling checker that supports AppleEvents. And if all your programs supported AppleEvents, they could access the spelling checker, too. Thus, one spelling checker would work with every program you have. Similarly, a spreadsheet could work together with a project management program to exchange data and create graphs, or a MIDI sequencer could collaborate with a scoring program.

AppleEvents are messages sent from one program to another. AppleEvents might request a service from another program ("Please check the spelling of the selected text"), respond to a request ("I've finished checking"), or send news and data ("The word 'occassionally' is misspelled — change it to 'occasionally'"). That last point is significant: Because AppleEvents can contain data, it can also be used to move information between programs.

AppleEvents' ability to shuttle data as well as instructions will make possible a kind of *distributed processing*, in which a task is divided among more than one Macintosh. For example, a complex statistical analysis program running on a Mac Classic could delegate number-crunching tasks to a Mac IIfx elsewhere on the network. Once the IIfx finished the calculations, it could pass the results back to the Classic. And AppleEvents will make possible a new generation of macro recorders that will enable you to create HyperTalk-like scripts to automate repetitive tasks.

AppleEvents and the publish-and-subscribe aspects of IAC will allow programs and networked Macs (and eventually, other computers) to work together in ways that are likely to amaze. With IAC, Apple has created the foundation for a powerful new generation of programs. It's up to the architects and carpenters of the software development world to build on that foundation.

A Bright-Sounding Future

Another of System 7.0's remarkable talents is the ability to play back multiple channels of sound from disk files in real time. Put another way, as I write this, a jazz ditty is playing through my Mac's speaker from a 17MB file located on a CD-ROM disc. System 7.0's enhanced sound features will make possible more powerful multimedia and sound-editing software and allow sounds to be compressed to use less memory and disk space. (We'll look at the latter in Chapter 32.)

But as I've shown in this chapter, IAC and improved sound features are only two of the many significant improvements in the Mac's latest interface lift. A better Finder, file sharing, more customizing options, aliases, TrueType fonts, keyboard navigation, and a tidier System Folder are pleasures you can enjoy as soon as you install System 7.0 — after verifying that your favorite programs are compatible with it.

Summary:

✔ System 7 enhancements you will enjoy immediately include: a better Finder, file sharing, more customizing options, aliases, TrueType fonts, enhanced keyboard navigation, and a tidier System Folder.

✔ TrueType is a new font technology that describes fonts mathematically, allowing the Mac to create sharp text at any size.

✔ Adding fonts to or removing them from your System file is much easier under System 7. The Font/DA Mover utility is no longer needed — you can simply drag the font to the System file.

✔ The System 7 Finder makes it easier to find and select files, to view the contents of disks and folders, and to customize the Mac's operation to suit your tastes and work habits.

✔ An alias is a small file that points to a document, an application, a disk, or a folder. When you open an alias, the Mac opens whatever the alias points to.

✔ System 7 allows for peer-to-peer file serving, — you can make your disks and folders available to other users on your network, and they can make theirs available to you.

✔ Interapplication communications (IAC) is a System 7 feature that enables a program to automatically exchange data with another program without having to copy and paste information from one program to another.

✔ Although the Mac's basic operating style is unchanged in System 7, there are several changes you'll need to adjust to if you've used earlier system versions.

Chapter 26
Mass Storage

In This Chapter:

✔ An introduction to how floppy disks and hard drives store data.

✔ A look at the different disk capacities of floppy disk drives — and their compatibility problems.

✔ The disk capacity and performance of a hard disk.

✔ Removable-media drives: combining security and portability.

✔ Technical specifications you'll encounter when shopping for a hard drive.

✔ Organizing files to maximize hard disk performance.

The Mac is a remarkable machine, but how quickly it forgets. The moment the juice is turned off, the Mac becomes a dark and silent box, and your efforts leave its memory chips like air from a bursting balloon.

Because memory forgets, computers have always been paired with *mass-storage* devices — originally punched cards, then paper or magnetic tape, and now the current standard, magnetic disks. Storage devices hold the documents you create and the applications you use. In this chapter, we'll tour the mass-storage world, with a focus on hard disks and other high-capacity media. I'll also provide some tips for organizing a hard disk to maximize its speed and efficiency.

A Magnetic Voyage

In the late seventies, personal computer users wept for joy as floppy disks replaced slow, unreliable cassette tapes as the standard storage device. Floppy disks transformed the microcomputer storage world by allowing *random access* to data. To appreciate that, locate a song in the middle of an album, then try locating a song in the middle of a cassette tape. You have to access a cassette *sequentially* by fast-forwarding and rewinding, but you can plop a turntable's tone arm in place at any point. Similarly, a computer can access any spot on a disk almost immediately by moving the drive's heads to that point.

Inside a floppy's plastic case is a disk of flexible — that is, floppy — plastic coated with iron oxide particles (see the figure "Inside a Disk"). This disk spins at 390 to 600 revolutions per minute as it is being accessed. When the Mac saves a document or copies a file, a read/write head in the disk drive generates a magnetic field that positions the disk's iron particles in patterns corresponding to the zeros and ones that comprise the information being written. When the Mac reads from the disk, the particles recreate the magnetic field in the head.

A disk is divided into 80 concentric circles called *tracks*, and each track is divided into wedges called *sectors*. The number of sectors in a track depends on the track's location; tracks located near the disk's outer edge have room for more sectors than the smaller tracks closer to the disk's center. The disk's rotation speed varies depending on which tracks the read/write head is accessing.

You can look at a phonograph album and see grooves, but you can't look at a disk and see tracks and sectors. A disk's divisions aren't physical ones; they're magnetic boundaries recorded on the disk when it's *initialized*, or *formatted*. This software approach to disk formatting allows many other computers to use the same 3-1/2-inch disks that the Mac uses. Fresh out of the box, the disks are identical lumps of storage clay. Each computer's system software sculpts the disk to its own needs by initializing it.

Part of the sculpting process involves creating the tracks and sectors; the other part involves reserving parts of the disk to hold special information. Some tracks hold start-up software— the instructions that either transfer control to the Finder when you start the Mac or eject the disk and display the blinking X icon to indicate that the disk can't start up the Mac. Other tracks hold information about the disk's contents, so the Mac can locate documents and applications and determine where a disk's available space is.

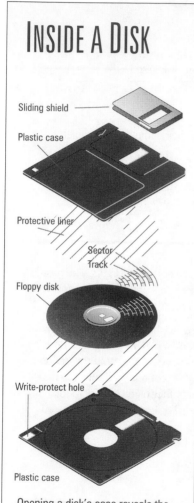

Inside a Disk

Sliding shield

Plastic case

Protective liner

Sector

Track

Floppy disk

Write-protect hole

Plastic case

Opening a disk's case reveals the floppy disk it protects. What you can't see is how the disk is divided into concentric rings, or tracks, containing sectors that store your data and programs.

Disk Capacities

The original Mac floppy drive stored 400K. The Mac Plus premiered with 800K disk drives, which doubled storage capacity by using both sides of a floppy disk. 800K drives have two read/write heads, one for each side of the disk. If you have a 128K or 512K Mac or if you choose the Single Sided button in the disk-initialization dialog box, only one side of the disk is used. One reason you might choose the Single Sided option is to create a disk that a Mac with a 400K floppy drive can access.

(Incidentally, it's worth mentioning that some of Apple's original 800K drives had an annoying habit of occasionally refusing to eject a disk completely. They sucked it back in, forcing you to pull out the Universal Disk Disgorger — an unbent paper clip — to rescue the disk, a job that always gets a chuckle out of onlooking IBM PC users. To use the Universal Disk Disgorger, insert it into the small hole next to the floppy drive and push. Don't pull on the disk — you'll risk damaging the drive mechanism.)

In 1989, Apple introduced the *SuperDrive*, also called the *FDHD* (short for floppy disk high-density) drive. SuperDrives, now standard equipment in all Macs and available as upgrades for older SEs and IIs, store 1.4MB on *high-density* disks, which have a thinner magnetic coating and smaller magnetic particles. A high-density disk has a small hole in its upper-left corner, opposite the write-protect hole. A SuperDrive looks for this hole when you insert a disk. If the hole is present, you can initialize the disk to store its full 1.4MB. If the hole isn't present, the SuperDrive will only allow you to create a 400K or 800K disk. And if you're curious, high-density disks spin at 300 rpm regardless of which track the Mac is accessing.

A high-density disk's differences can cause problems if you move disks between SuperDrives and 800K drives. If you use an 800K drive to initialize a high-density disk, the drive will create an 800K disk. That disk will work properly in 800K drives, but when you insert it in a SuperDrive, you'll get a message asking if you want to initialize the disk. The message appears because the SuperDrive notices that extra hole in the case, and tries to read the disk as a 1.4MB disk. What's more, once the disk has been initialized as an 800K disk, the chances of being able to successfully reformat it as a high-density disk are slim. The moral? If you'll be swapping files between 800K drives and SuperDrives, don't use high-density floppies as your transfer medium. Instead, format an 800K disk and use it to transfer the files.

Driving in the Fast Lane

These days, the *hard disk* has transformed floppies into a medium for backups and software distribution. A 20MB hard disk puts the contents of dozens of floppies on tap. 20MB units used to be the power user's choice. Today, as 80MB and 105MB drives become more popular and affordable, 20MB drives are at the bottom of the totem pole.

INSIDE A HARD DISK

High-capacity hard disk drives owe their speed to technology. These drives position the read-write heads with voice coil actuators, which are faster and more precise than the stepper motors used in smaller drives. Heads travel less on high-end disks, yielding faster access times, because data is packed more densely than on low-end disks.

The biggest speed boost, however, comes from the method used to position the

heads over the data tracks. This method, called dedicated servo surface, uses one disk platter solely for aligning the heads over data tracks on other platters. In contrast, lower-capacity disks may use part of the data platters for positioning information (embedded servo method) or they may use no positioning information (open-loop method).

With a dedicated servo surface, the drive positions its heads over the right track with fewer retries.

How the Servo System Works

A read-write head reads alignment information from a dedicated servo disk (A). The information is sent to a dedicated microprocessor (B) where it is analyzed to determine the current position of the read-write heads on the drive's other platters. The processor instructs an amplifier to vary the voltage in the servo coil (C). The strength of the magnetic field produced by the servo coil changes and

causes the coil to adjust its position relative to a permanent magnet (D). The read-write heads change their position in relation to the coil. With every change of position, the read-write heads send new signals to the servo disk, starting the loop over again.

A hard disk may have the capacity of a truck, but it offers the performance of a Porsche. Hard disks transfer data many times faster than floppy disks, and that means less waiting when starting programs and saving files.

A hard disk owes its stellar speed and capacity to several factors. First, its magnetic surface isn't a sheet of of flexible plastic, but a polished, precision-machined metal *platter* whose magnetic particles (and therefore, your data) are packed closer together. Most hard disks contain several platters, stacked like records in a jukebox and sealed in a dust-free enclosure (see the figure "Inside a

Hard Disk"). In most drives, the platters spin at 3600 rpm — six to nine times faster than a floppy disk. And finally, hard disk platters spin continuously; a floppy stops when it isn't being accessed and takes about a half-second to get up to speed when the next access begins.

Unlike the heads in a floppy drive, a hard disk's read-write heads don't touch the disk's surfaces, but ride a hair's width above them. If a hard disk's head *does* touch the surface, you've got trouble. That's a *head crash*, and it can occur when the drive is jostled during use, or even when a speck of dust gets between the platter's surface and the head. A head crash used to damage the platter as the head dug a ditch in the platter's coating. Improved platter surfaces make today's drives more durable (although you still should never move or bump a drive that's in use). *Thin film* coating, in which the platter is coated with a minutely thin film of metal, is one technology found in many of today's drives. Another safety feature is *automatic head-parking*, which retracts the drive's heads to a safe area when you shut down.

A hard disk can live inside or outside a Mac. Internal drives don't use any desk space, and they make moving your Mac more convenient. But an internal drive adds extra heat to the Mac's case, it usually requires dealer installation (assuming it wasn't installed at the factory), and if it breaks, your entire Mac must go to the shop. I'm partial to external drives. They don't change the climate inside the Mac, they move from one Mac to another in a flash, and with long cables, you can bury them out of earshot under your desk or in a nearby closet. And you don't have to part with your Mac if the worst happens.

Megabytes to Go

But the big drawback of hard disks isn't their vulnerability to head crashes, it's that they lack the portability and security of floppies. You can't pop an internal drive into your briefcase or lock it in a safe at night. External drives are a bit more portable and protectable, but moving one still means fussing with cables and transporting a delicate mechanism. And once you fill a hard disk, you face an electronic Spring cleaning, throwing away or copying musty old files and applications to floppies to make room for new ones.

Happily, there is a way to combine the security and portability of floppies with the capacity of a hard disk. Several manufacturers offer *removable-media* drives whose disks are encased in lightweight plastic cartridges.

The veteran of the removable-media world is Iomega Corporation, whose Bernoulli Box drives have been around since the mid-eighties. A Bernoulli Box uses principles of fluid dynamics discovered by an 18th-century mathematician and physicist named Daniel Bernoulli (pronounced *burn-ooly*). His Bernoulli

INSIDE A BERNOULLI BOX

Bernoulli cartridges closely resemble standard floppy disks. Bernoulli technology uses dual, single-sided platters. The drive heads--which move laterally, read from above and below. The Bernoulli does not filter dust particles, but circulates air to move dust away from the media. Unlike SyQuest and Ricoh removable-media drives, the read-write head do not actually contact the media, so head crashes cannot be caused by dust particles, and disk crashes also are rare. As seen in the detail, the platter flexes toward the head. An air cushion between the two floppy platters allow them to flex inward should a dust particle approach the head. The cartridge also locks in place while in use. This is necessary because unlike other removable-media, the Bernoulli cartridge protrudes from the drive during operation.

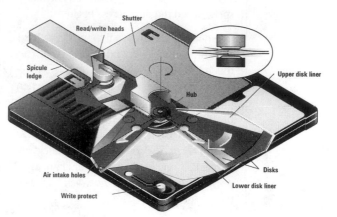

Theorem states that the pressure of fluid or air decreases when it's moving. In aircraft, the decreased air pressure around moving wings gives them their lift. In bathrooms, the decreased air pressure caused by the showerhead's stream pulls the shower curtain in.

In a Bernoulli cartridge, a rush of air causes a flexible disk to be drawn to within a few thousandths of an inch of a rigid metal plate located in the drive (see the figure "Inside a Bernoulli Box"). The disk floats firmly within this air flow, flexing no more than one-thousandths of an inch.

Until an intruder comes along. Because the disk is flexible, a foreign intruder isn't as threatening as it is to a hard disk. When something comes between a Bernoulli disk and its head, the disk flexes and the air flow blows the intruder away. The result is a temporary disk error that the Mac can detect and often correct.

Iomega produces several Bernoulli Box models, with the latest storing 44MB on a cartridge. Older Bernoulli Boxes used an 8-inch disk that held 10 or 20MB; newer models use 5¼ inch disks housed in more compact cartridges.

Other Removable Options

Iomega was the first company to produce removable-media drives, but Bernoulli cartridges aren't the only way to cache and carry. Indeed, the most popular removable-media drive is made by SyQuest and used in drives from Mass

Micro, Microtech, Peripheral Land, Ehman, and others. The Syquest drive borrows from the hard disk camp, using a single 5¼-inch rigid platter (spinning at 3280 rpm) that holds 45 megabytes. Bernoulli and SyQuest drives that store 80 MB are on the horizon. Putting a platter in a removable cartridge sounds as safe as playing with matches in a fireworks factory, but the Syquest mechanism has proven to be reliable. It has become especially popular in the desktop publishing world, where huge files are common and where users often need to carry them somewhere else (such as to a publishing service bureau).

Another removable-media device is the *tape drive*, which uses cartridges containing magnetic tape. Tape drives are designed to back up hard disks, but most are slow and expensive and can't be used as primary storage devices. Bernoulli and Syquest drives are far more versatile.

Speed Thrills

The speed at which its disk spins and the density of the data in its tracks aren't the only factors that contribute to performance. Here's a look at some other tech specs you'll encounter when shopping for a drive.

The *average access time* specifies how long it takes for the drive's heads to locate a given spot on the disk — the mass-storage equivalent to moving a phonograph's tone arm to a given spot on an album. The average access time is measured in milliseconds; the lower the value, the better.

The *data transfer rate* measures how quickly the drive can shuttle bytes to the Mac. The higher the value, the better, but only to a point. Mac Classics, SEs, and Pluses, for example, can't handle as high a transfer rate as a Mac II-class machine.

The *interleave ratio* describes the organization of sectors in each track (see the figure "Understanding Interleaving"). Generally, the lower the interleave ratio, the better. A 1:1 ratio is best — if your Mac can scarf up sectors at such a warp

---

UNDERSTANDING INTERLEAVING

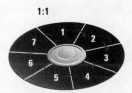

On a disk with a 1:1 interleave, the sectors are numbered and accessed in sequence. With a 2:1 ratio, the heads read from, or write to, every other sector. With a 3:1 ratio, every third sector is accessed.

speed. Drives that use Apple's standard SCSI driver can use a 1:1 ratio only with a Mac II-class machine. The SE needs a 2:1 ratio; a Mac Plus, a 3:1 ratio. But some drives include modified SCSI drivers that allow a 1:1 interleave with all Macs. Other units provide built-in *data caching* — the drive reads an entire track and stores it in a small reserve of memory. When the Mac requests subsequent sectors from that track, the drive sends the data from the cache.

Performance specs make for fun party talk, but they really aren't that important for most applications. In day-to-day use, the differences between most drives are minor. And if you started with floppies, you'll be pleased with the performance of any hard drive.

Managing Your Megabytes

What's more, you can make any drive operate faster by taking advantage of the Mac's ability to organize files and programs within folders. A file cabinet lets you create a storage hierarchy; so does the Mac. In this hierarchy, the file cabinet corresponds to the hard disk — it's at the top level of the hierarchy, with folders nested within it.

Beneath the Mac's friendly folder metaphor lie some technicalities that influence performance. When you open a disk's icon by double-clicking on it in the Finder, the Mac scans the disk in order to display its contents. The more files you store at the top level of the disk's hierarchy — that is, not within folders — the longer it takes for the Finder to display the disk's window. This also applies when you choose an application's Open command: to display a list of available files, the Mac must scan all the files in the current level of the disk's hierarchy. The more files present there, the longer the scanning process takes.

The Mac all but ignores files stored in a folder until you actually open the folder. So, by grouping documents and applications into folders, you'll boost the Mac's performance by reducing the number of files it has to scan at once. And there's the convenience factor: instead of having to electronically paw through dozens of word processor files, for example, you can go directly to the Proposals folder, the Memos folder, or the Seedy Novel folder, and quickly locate the file you need.

Another way to streamline storage involves using *partitioning* software, which electronically divides a drive into a number of smaller *logical volumes.* You can *mount* and *unmount* these volumes as though you were inserting and ejecting separate disks. Many hard disks include partitioning software, and most that do let you assign passwords to partitions, giving you a secure place to hide sensitive files.

ORGANIZING A HARD DISK

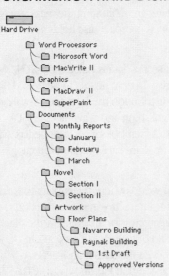

Hard Drive
- Word Processors
  - Microsoft Word
  - MacWrite II
- Graphics
  - MacDraw II
  - SuperPaint
- Documents
  - Monthly Reports
    - January
    - February
    - March
  - Novel
    - Section I
    - Section II
  - Artwork
    - Floor Plans
      - Navarro Building
      - Raynak Building
        - 1st Draft
        - Approved Versions

Extensive use of folders improves the Finder's performance and keeps better track of files. In this filing scheme, each application category (word processor, graphics, and so on) resides in its own folder. Another folder holds all documents, separated into related category folders. Not shown is the System Folder, which contains files the Macintosh needs to start up and run.

To create a folder, use the Finder's New Folder command (in the File menu). The Finder gives new folders the name Empty Folder (untitled folder, in System 7.0); you'll want to change that to something a bit more appropriate — Documents, Proposals, Graphics Programs, whatever best describes the folder's contents. At this point, you can open the new folder and follow the same process to create another folder inside it — just as you can nest one manila folder within another. This lets you develop a storage hierarchy that keeps your files orderly. You can nest folders more than a dozen levels deep, but navigating through more than five levels or so becomes cumbersome and time-consuming.

The number of folders you create and the names you give them is up to you. Some people create date-oriented folders — January Work, February Work, March Work, and so on — and then create folders within them for specific types of documents — Memos, Publications, Artwork. Some people create 26 folders, one for each letter of the alphabet, and file documents within them. You'll find a sample filing scheme in the figure "Organizing a Hard Disk." It's just a starting point, though — the best filing system is one you've personalized for your work style.

Even with an efficient filing system, you may occasionally misplace a file. When you do, use the Mac's Find File desk accessory to locate it. If you're using System 7.0, use the Find command in the Finder's file menu. You'll find powerful file- and text-searching features in a variety of utilities, too (see Chapter 19).

To keep a drive running at top performance, keep *fragmentation* in check. In its zeal to reuse space freed by deleted files, the Mac may scatter newly saved or copied files across physically discontiguous tracks. The longer you use a disk, the more likely it is that it contains fragmented files. When many files are fragmented, the drive's heads spend too much time in transit, and performance suffers. Two solutions exist: backup the entire disk, reformat it, and then recopy the files, starting with the System Folder and the applications you use most often. Or, run a defragmenting utility, which moves files around to make them contiguous (see Chapter 19). With the latter route, backup the drive first; the disk's contents can be damaged if something happens during defragmentation.

Speaking of backing up, *do it*. Electrocution aside, the loss of data is the most painful experience a computer peripheral can cause. It's an agony you can avoid by backing up faithfully. I'll present some guidelines in the next chapter.

Now Available on Compact Disc

Magnets' force in computer storage may be weakening. Compact discs, those silver platters that have made my stereo obsolete, are infiltrating the mass storage world. And we are talking *mass* storage: a 5¼-inch compact disc holds as much as 550 megabytes of data.

In the computer world, a compact disc that stores data is called a *CD-ROM*. A CD-ROM's data, like that of a ROM chip, is factory-frozen, unable to be erased. For this reason, CD-ROMs are used primarily as a distribution medium for software or data. Firms such as the Bureau of Electronic Publishing and Wayzata offer CD-ROM-based reference materials ranging from CIA factbooks to encyclopedias. CD-ROMs containing megabytes of fonts and free or shareware programs are also available.

CD-ROMs also play a part in the multimedia world, where their ability to hold digital audio as well as data makes them idea for interactive audio instruction (see Chapter 17). In addition to providing a SCSI connector for attaching to the Mac, CD-ROM drives provide standard RCA-type audio output jacks that you can connect to a stereo. Apple's AppleCD SC drive even includes a desk accessory that lets you play audio CDs and a system extension that lets audio-only CDs appear on the Mac's desktop (see the figure "Now Taking Requests"). And Apple's HyperCard CD Audio Toolkit provides HyperCard XCMDs and XFCNs that let you access an audio CD from within HyperCard stacks.

One problem with CD-ROMs is their slow access time. A typical hard disk has an access time of 20-40 milliseconds (ms), but most CD-ROM drives have 300–650-ms access times. (Apple's drive has a 650-ms seek time.) The sluggishness is due largely to the fact that a CD-ROM's laser head is heavier and takes more time to stop than a hard disk's magnetic read/write heads. CD-ROM drives are also costly, with most drives selling for between $700 and $1000.

These are just two reasons that optical-based storage isn't likely to replace magnetic storage any time soon. A more serious hurdle involves developing disks that can be erased and reused — data is written on a CD-ROM by a laser that burns pits into the disk's surface. One alternative is offered by *write once, read many times (WORM)* drives. With a WORM drive, once you save a file, it's there for good. Given that WORM drives hold 400–800MB, that may not be such a big drawback.

But the storage technology that best clears the read/write hurdle uses — you guessed it — magnets embedded in the disk's surface. I'm referring to *magneto-optical* drives such as those offered by Microtech, Mass Micro, Peripheral Land, and others. Also called *erasable optical (EO)* drives, these devices use mechanisms made by Sony, Ricoh, or Maxtor to store 500-600MB on 5¼-inch removable

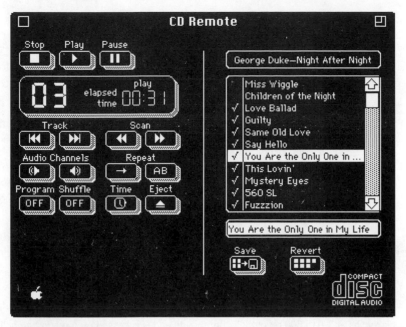

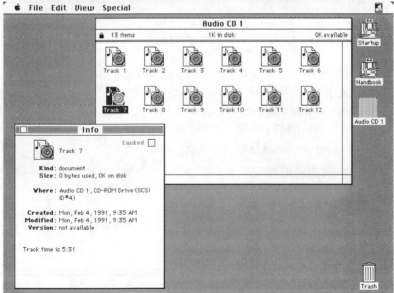

Now Taking Requests

Apple's CD Remote desk accessory (top) lets you play audio CDs inserted in a CD-ROM drive. You can also store and recall the names of the tracks on the CD and selectively enable or disable playback. With Apple's Foreign File Access INIT, you can view an audio CD's contents on the desktop (bottom). Note the Get Info window showing a track's playback time.

cartridges. To write to a cartridge, the drives use a high-powered laser and electromagnet to orient the media's magnetic particles. To read from the cartridge, the drive uses a low-powered laser. As with CD-ROM drives, however, access time is relatively slow, making EO drives better for long-term storage and retrieval than as substitutes for a conventional hard disk. And they're costly, with prices in the $3000–$5000 ballpark.

A new generation of 3½-inch EO drives is appearing that offers 60-ms access times on cartridges that hold roughly 125MB. Cartridges will cost about $60 and drives will retail for under $2000.

So the lowly magnet continues to serve us well and it looks like it will even have a place in tomorrow's disk drives. In the next chapter, we'll look at how to take care of your magnets.

Summary:

✔ Floppy and hard disks allow fast, random access to data.

✔ A floppy disk spins at 390 to 600 revolutions per minute and is accessed by a read/write head in the disk drive.

✔ A floppy disk is divided into 80 concentric circles called tracks, which are further divided into wedges called sectors.

✔ Disk capacities of Mac disks have steadily increased from the original drive, which stored 400K, to the 800K drive, and then to the SuperDrive, which allows you to store 1.4MB on a high-density disk.

✔ Unlike a floppy disk, a hard disk contains several metal platters, which are stacked like records in a jukebox and whose magnetic particles are packed closer together than those of a floppy disk.

✔ Hard disks transfer data many times faster than floppy disks.

✔ A hard disk can be internal or external to your computer. An internal disk saves desktop room, but adds extra heat to your Mac's case; an external one won't change the climate inside the Mac but will take up space.

✔ Removable-media drives such as Iomega's Bernoulli Box and SyQuest's drives combine the security and portability of floppies with the capacity of a hard disk.

Chapter 27
Disk Maintenance

In This Chapter:

✔ Backup basics: backing up floppy and hard disks.

✔ Performing full and incremental backups with backup utilities.

✔ A look at how different backup programs perform incremental backups.

✔ Shopping tips on what to look for in a backup utility.

✔ Restoring files from backup disks to a hard disk.

✔ A summary of file-recovery utilities.

A floppy or hard disk is like a friend you can't quite trust. Most of the time, disks are faithful computing caddies that hold our software and documents. Over time, it's easy to become smug about this give-and-take relationship. Then one of them develops a case of amnesia, and all of a sudden it's "Files? What files? I don't have any files." Just like that, you're forced to retype your documents from printouts (if you're lucky enough to have some) or worse, recreate them from scratch. Either way, it's *deja vu* in its ugliest form.

Disks can betray your trust in a variety of ways. Their microscopic magnetic particles can be led astray by magnetic fields produced by loudspeakers, telephones, electric motors, and the Mac's own power supply. They're susceptible to system errors and program bugs, both of which can cause inaccurate information to be written to the disk. They face physical threats from spilled soda to dust to extremes of heat and cold. And hard disks can fall victim to *head crashes,* in which the read-write heads strike and damage the media surface.

How do you maintain a relationship with such fair-weather friends? Use an umbrella — a *backup utility,* which stores copies of your files on floppy disks or other storage devices. Backups are to computers what vice presidents are to governments: they don't do much when the sailing is smooth, but when the worst happens, they're indispensable.

And since a good vice president isn't always around when you need one, every software library also needs a *file-recovery utility.* One of these rescue squads can save the day if disk problems occur or if you accidentally throw away a file in between backups.

In Chapter 19, we toured the world of utilities — programs that make the Mac easier and more convenient to use. In this chapter, I'll take a closer look at backup and file-recovery utilities, and show how to use both to make your disks more trustworthy companions.

Backup Basics

A file tucked away on a disk seems safe and sound; after all, the command reads "Save," not "Save until some unforeseen event." But the worst does happen. Disks are damaged or lost. Programs turn kamikaze, crashing and taking files with them. Power surges give hard disks amnesia. Fires start, and sprinkler systems sprinkle. Equipment is stolen. It's enough to make you want police protection, but only a faithfully followed backup strategy can help.

Backing up floppies is easy, especially if your Mac has two floppy drives. First, lock the original disk by sliding its plastic *write-protect* tab so you can see through the square hole. Then insert the original disk in one drive and the backup in the other and drag the original disk's icon to the backup's icon. When the Finder asks if you want to replace one disk's contents with those of the other, click OK. When the copy is complete, eject both disks; unlock the original if you plan to write to it again.

If your Mac has just one drive, the floppy copy routine is a bit trickier. To avoid excessive disk swapping, follow these steps. First, insert the backup disk and then choose Eject from the File menu or, in System 7.0, the Special menu. (The Finder dims the disk's icon to indicate it still "knows" about the disk.) Next, lock the original disk, insert it, and then drag its icon to the backup disk's dimmed icon. When the Finder asks if you want to replace the backup disk's contents, click OK. (You will need to swap disks a few times during the copying process.)

The techniques I've just described copy every file from your original floppy to the backup disk. As you work with the original (don't forget to unlock it first), you'll probably add to it or modify its files. You have two alternatives for keeping your backups up to date. You can drag only the new or modified files to the backup (clicking OK when asked if you want to replace the existing files), or you can simply recopy the entire disk. The latter takes the Mac longer, but is easier for you, since you don't have to keep track of which files you modified or added.

If you take the former route, use the Finder's By Date command (it's in the View menu) to look at the original disk's contents sorted according to their creation and modification dates, then copy only those files with dates past the backup date. You can also determine when a file was created and modified by selecting the file and choosing Get Info from the File menu or pressing Command-I.

How often should you back up a floppy disk that you use to store documents? As often as necessary for your work habits and your peace of mind. If you're using it constantly, you may want to back it up every day. The best rule may be to back up anything you aren't willing to recreate.

Hard Disks are Harder

Backing up a hard disk is, well, harder. A hard disk may streamline your day-to-day computing, but it turns into a ball and chain at backup time. A hard disk can hold hundreds of files, making the job of backing up modified files a logistical nightmare. Yet backing up a hard disk couldn't be more important. If you use a computer extensively, a hard disk tends to become a magnetic representation of your life. It's all there — your business plans, personal letters, drawings, programs, and more — and losing it in one fell swoop is about as traumatic an experience as you can have sitting in front of a computer.

To back up a full 40MB drive, you'll need about 50 800K disks — and about an hour. Most people can think of better ways to spend their time and disk money. Until their hard disks crash, that is. But thanks to the Mac's ability to keep track of the date and time files are created and modified, you need not back up an entire hard disk during each backup session. Backup utilities can read the Mac's digital datebook and back up only those files you've added or changed since the last *full backup*. This task, called an *incremental backup*, takes far less time than a full backup.

Backup Helpers

Every Mac comes with a barebones backup utility, HD Backup, that lets you perform full and incremental backups to floppy disks. Virtually all non-Apple hard disks include backup software, too. And several software firms offer backup programs that work with any SCSI hard disk. Each program handles the chore differently.

The most basic difference concerns how the backup program copies files to your backup media. Some programs, including SuperMac Technology's DiskFit and Magic Software's Backmatic, copy each file separately and then create on each backup disk a *catalog file* that the program can use to *restore* the files to the hard disk. On the backup disk you'll see each file just as it existed on your hard disk.

Need to restore a few files? Simply use the Finder to copy them from the backups to your hard disk. (If a given file won't fit on a single disk at backup time, the utility splits it across multiple disks; you must use the utility to restore such a file.)

Other programs, including Fifth Generation Systems' Fastback II, Dantz Development's Retrospect, and Microseeds Publishing's Redux, copy your files into one large file that spans all your backup disks. Instead of using the Finder, you run the backup utility and tell it to locate and restore the files you need.

With the separate-files approach used by DiskFit and Backmatic, you can restore any file that fits on a single backup disk without having to run the backup utility. You'll appreciate that if the utility's master disk becomes damaged, or if you take your backup disks to another machine but forget to take along a copy of the utility.

With the one-file-holds-all approach, if you don't have the backup utility, you don't have any backups — but it does make possible faster back-up sessions and some fancy backup gymnastics. Retrospect and Fastback II, for example, can *compress* files as they back them up, reducing the number of backup disks required. Fastback II can also record special error-correction codes that enable the program to recover data from damaged backups. Fifth Generation Systems claims Fastback II can recover all the data from a backup disk even if up to 10 percent of its contents are damaged.

Incremental Differences

Another factor to consider is whether the program saves or deletes older versions of files you back up. For example, say you begin writing a proposal on Monday morning and then do a full backup on Monday evening. You work on the proposal again on Tuesday and then do an incremental backup. What happens to the backup of Monday's version?

It depends on the program you use. DiskFit and Redux replace older versions of files with their newer versions. That keeps your mountain of backup disks from growing too high, but it also eliminates the option of going back a few days to an earlier version of a file. If you decide Tuesday's version of your proposal stinks — or worse, if your word processing program somehow scrambles the file, and you unknowingly back up the scrambled version — you don't have Monday's version to fall back on. (I'll present a workaround for this potential nightmare shortly.)

By contrast, Retrospect and Backmatic don't replace earlier versions of files. Fastback II lets you choose whether older versions should be deleted or saved. That gives you an extra-strong safety net, but it also means you need more disks to hold your backups. That could be significant if you're backing up large files such as scanned images.

Choosing Your Backup Weapon

Here are some other points to address before buying a backup utility.

❖ *Network support* If you use network software like TOPS or AppleShare, you'll want a backup utility that supports it. For example, to back up an AppleShare file server, look for a utility that backs up each folder's access privilege information. Retrospect and SuperMac's Network DiskFit do.

❖ *Backup selectivity* If you're willing to rely on your original application disks as backups, you can back up documents only and cut your backup time. But some programs give you more flexibility than others in choosing files to back up.

❖ *Specialized media support* If you plan to use a backup medium other than floppy disks, be sure to buy a program that supports your chosen medium. (To find out what other media are available, see the sidebar "Media Circus.") Retrospect can back up to virtually anything. Fastback II, DiskFit, and Redux support tape drives, as long as they display tapes as icons on the Finder's desktop.

Media Circus

If your hard disk holds more than 40MB — or if you lack the patience for shuffling floppies — consider an alternative backup medium. One possibility is a second hard disk. Today you can buy two 40MB drives for less than what one 20MB drive cost a few years ago. And you'll have a spare drive if the first one acts up.

Another alternative is a *tape drive* such as GCC Technologies' HyperTape or Archive Corporation's MaxStream. Their primary strength: capacity. Most tape drives store between 40MB and 300MB on cassette-like tape cartridges. Some drives, such as Personal Computer Peripherals Corporation's PCPC Tape Backup, use 8mm video cassettes that hold over 2000MB. Their primary weakness: performance. Locating a specific file on a tape cartridge can be slow since the drive can't randomly access any point on the tape.

The most versatile backup device is a *removable-media* drive such as Iomega's Bernoulli Box or Mass Microsystem's DataPak. (The DataPak uses a popular removable hard disk technology developed by SyQuest; many other drives use the same mechanism.) As we saw in the last chapter, removable-media drives combine a hard disk's speed and capacity with the insert-and-eject convenience of floppies. And unlike a tape drive, a removable-media drive can be used as a primary storage device. Bernoulli Boxes and SyQuest drives are also available in dual-drive units that allow convenient, cartridge-to-cartridge backup. **M**

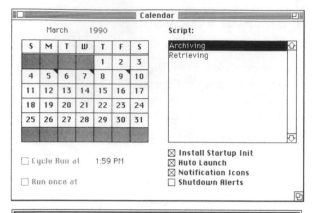

❖ *Unattended operation* If you use a file server in a busy office, you might want to back it up at night, when it's idle. If so, you'll need Fastback II, DiskFit 2.0, or Retrospect. All three let you specify intervals for unattended backups (see the figure "Scheduled Maintenance"). But since no one will be around to shuffle floppies, you'll need to use a high-capacity backup medium such as a second hard disk or a tape drive.

❖ *Programmability* If you have very specific backup needs — perhaps you want to back up all PageMaker and Excel documents at 8 p.m. every Tuesday — consider a program that lets you automate the types of backups you do. Retrospect and Fastback II offer the strongest automation features. Redux finishes second.

❖ *Ease of use* Backing up is boring; a program that's difficult to learn won't encourage the practice. Alas, ease of use and power are at opposite ends of the seesaw. The two most powerful backup programs — Fastback II and Retrospect — have steep learning curves. If your backup needs don't demand automation and sophisticated file-selection features, consider a simpler program. Redux, DiskFit, and Network DiskFit strike a balance between power and simplicity.

Backmatic is an elegant little utility. It's a system extension (an INIT) that intercepts the Mac's shut-down process. Choose Shut Down, and a dialog box asks if you want to back up the files you worked on that day. Click Yes, insert floppies as needed, and Backmatic does the rest. It also monitors battery power on the Macintosh Portable, suggesting you back up when power drops below a specified point.

Backup Plans

How will you use your backup program? You'll probably start by doing a full backup, following up with incremental backups at regular intervals. Here are some guidelines and tips.

❖ *Make two backups* Your backup disks are prone to the same ailments as your originals. For extra safety, make two backups, and alternate them (see the figure "Backup Strategies"). And don't store your backups along with your computer. Fire or water won't discriminate between the originals and the back ups, and chances are a thief won't either. Practice what the data processing industry calls "off-site storage." Keep your backups separate — in a different room, at home, at the office, in a fireproof box, or, if you want real security, in a safe deposit box.

❖ *Use the Mac's disk cache* Most backup programs run faster when the Mac's disk cache is on. If your program's manual doesn't provide cache-size guidelines, try 64K. In System 6.x, use the Control Panel's General option to set the cache. In System 7.0, use the Memory control panel. With all system versions, you must restart your Mac after adjusting cache settings to put them into effect.

❖ *Create an emergency-restore floppy disk* Put copies of the Finder, the System file, and your backup utility on a floppy disk. If your hard disk crashes, you can start up with this floppy and use it to restore your files. (Depending on how your hard disk crashed, you may first need to reinitialize it using the software that accompanied it.)

❖ *Don't forget customized files* To save time, you may want to tell your backup program to ignore files in the System Folder. That's generally a safe approach, provided you don't forget to back up the custom files that may also live in the System Folder. Such files include word processor spelling-checker dictionaries that contain your own entries, preferences files that store your application preferences, the Scrapbook file, and the System file itself, which contains your fonts and in system versions prior to 7.0, you desk accessories.

❖ *Verify your backups* Most backup utilities have a *verify* option, which, when

BACKUP STRATEGIES

S	M	T	W	T	F	S
28	29	30	31	1	2	3
	IB-1	IB-2	IB-1	FB	IB-1	
4	5	6	7	8	9	10
	IB-1	IB-2	IB-1	IB-2	IB-1	

▬ Full backup
▬ Incremental backup 1
▬ Incremental backup 2

One technique for backing up a hard disk is to rotate among three well-marked sets of back-up disks or other media. With this technique, if one set of backups goes bad, you have two other sets to fall back on.

active, causes the program to proofread its work as it backs up files. If a disk error causes a file to be written inaccurately, the verification process catches it, and the utility tries again. Verification lengthens the backup process, but that's a small price to pay for more reliable backups.

When to Restore

When will you need to restore the files from the backup disks to the hard disk? The obvious answers are after losing an important file or reformatting the hard disk, which might be necessary after a power failure or kamikaze program crash; after having a hard disk repaired, during which time it was probably replaced or reformatted; or if you're switching to a different hard disk or want a colleague to have a large number of your files.

Another incentive to restore is to improve the hard disk's performance. When you delete files from a disk (hard or floppy), the Mac frees their space for new files. When you save a large file or copy an application to the disk, the Mac, in its zeal to reuse the freed space, may save the file in pieces — scattered across physically separate tracks on the hard disk instead of in contiguous tracks. It takes longer for the drive's magnetic heads to leap between separate tracks than to stroll from one track to the next. As you continue deleting and adding files, performance begins to suffer as the drive's heads waste time *thrashing* around the disk saving or reading fragmented files.

To restore a hard disk so that its files are stored contiguously, first make a full backup (or two, for safety), then reformat the entire hard disk. Next, restore the system files, then the applications, then the folders and documents. Performing the restoration process in this order ensures that the frequently accessed system and application files will be stored contiguously.

Disk Doctors

What happens if you lose a file in between backups? If you're smart, you'll reach for a file-recovery utility such as Symantec's Symantec Utilities for Macintosh (SUM II) or Norton Utilities for the Macintosh, Central Point Software's PC Tools Deluxe for the Macintosh, or Microcom's 911. These products can often repair and resurrect damaged disks and files. They do so by working intimately with the *reserved areas* of a disk — areas that don't store documents or applications but instead hold information the Mac uses to keep track of files.

Reserved areas have technical names like *volume allocation bitmap* and *extents b-tree*. The Mac takes these magnetic tables of contents at face value; it assumes they're intact and contain valid data. When they don't — when a system crash, program bug, or stray magnetic field scrambles their contents — the Mac may be unable to retrieve part or all of the disk's contents. File-recovery utilities can analyze these areas and often correct inaccurate entries and thus retrieve files that the Mac thinks are gone (see the figure "Recovery Tools").

The aforementioned products can also save the day when you accidentally throw away a file. All three include INITs that spy on you as you use a disk. When you delete a file, the INIT makes notations on disk that indicate where that file is physically located on the disk. The file is still there; the Mac has simply removed its entry from the disk's electronic table of contents. Should you need to resurrect the file, you run the file-recovery utility, which reads those notations and recreates the file's table of contents entry. (Prosecutors for the Iran-Contra trial used similar techniques to resurrect memos Oliver North *thought* he'd deleted from his word processor.)

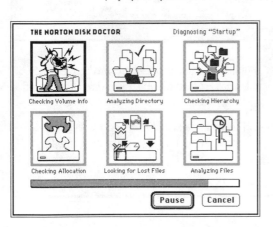

But there is a catch: if you worked extensively with the disk after deleting the file, some of its contents may have been replaced by newer files. So when you realize you've accidentally deleted a file, stop using that disk until you can run the

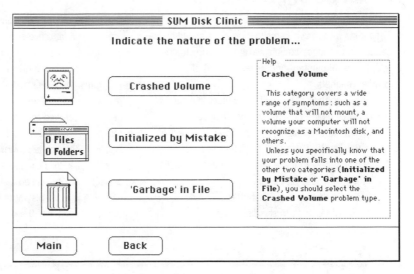

Recovery Tools ▲

Two software rescue squads in action: Norton Utilities (top) and SUM II (bottom). ▶

Disk Editing

When a file-recovery program's automatic recovery features fail you, turn to its disk editor (SUM II's is shown here). By searching for text present in the lost file, you may be able to locate some or all of its data and copy it to a new file — or at least retype it. The four-character columns in the left portion of the display show each character's hexadecimal value, while the rightmost column shows the characters themselves. The hexadecimal value selected here (6) is part of the two-digit value that represents the letter c.

```
┌─────────────────────────── Edit File : Chapter 5 ═══════════════════┐
│□▓▓▓▓▓▓▓▓▓▓▓▓▓▓▓▓▓▓▓▓▓▓▓▓                                             │
│ Data Fork              In Folder: Chapters                          │
│ NumSectors: 121        Current Sector: 30        ┌───────────┐      │
│ Size: 61952            Offset: 0                 │  Hex Edit  │      │
│                                                  └───────────┘      │
│ 00003C00  6364 6576 2077 6F72 6B73 206F 6E6C 7920   cdev works only ▲│
│ 00003C10  7769 7468 2074 6865 204D 6163 2053 4520   with the Mac SE  │
│ 00003C20  616E 6420 6C61 7465 7220 6D61 6368 696E   and later machin │
│ 00003C30  6573 2C20 616E 6420 6974 D573 2075 7365   es, and it's use │
│ 00003C40  6675 6C20 6F6E 6C79 2069 6620 796F 7520   ful only if you  │
│ 00003C50  6861 7665 206D 6F72 6520 7468 616E 206F   have more than o │
│ 00003C60  6E65 2053 4353 4920 7374 6F72 6167 6520   ne SCSI storage  │
│ 00003C70  6465 7669 6365 2E20 4966 2079 6F75 2064   device. If you d │
│ 00003C80  6F2C 2079 6F75 2063 616E 2075 7365 2074   o, you can use t │
│ 00003C90  6865 2053 7461 7274 7570 2044 6576 6963   he Startup Devic │
│ 00003CA0  6520 6364 6576 2074 6F20 7370 6563 6966   e cdev to specif │
│ 00003CB0  7920 7768 6963 6820 5343 5349 2064 6576   y which SCSI dev │
│ 00003CC0  6963 6520 7468 6520 4D61 6320 7368 6F75   ice the Mac shou │
│ 00003CD0  6C64 20D2 7374 6172 7420 7570 2066 726F   ld "start up fro │
│ 00003CE0  6DD3 2074 6065 206E 6578 7420 7469 6D65   m" the next time │
│ 00003CF0  2079 6F75 2072 6573 7461 7274 2E20 5768   you restart. Wh │
│ 00003D00  656E 2079 6F75 2072 6573 7461 7274 2061   en you restart a │
│ 00003D10  204D 6163 2C20 6974 2073 6361 6E73 2074   Mac, it scans t │
│ 00003D20  6865 2064 7269 7665 7320 636F 6E6E 6563   he drives connec │
│ 00003D30  7465 6420 746F 2069 7420 696E 2073 6561   ted to it in sea │
│ 00003D40  7263 6820 6F66 2061 2064 6973 6B20 636F   rch of a disk co │
│ 00003D50  6E74 6169 6E69 6E67 2061 2053 7973 7465   ntaining a Syste ▼│
└─────────────────────────────────────────────────────────────────────┘
```

recovery utility. Even if a recovery utility can't automatically resurrect a file, there's still hope. All three products include *disk editors*, which let you directly view and alter the disk's contents (see the figure "Disk Editing").

The previous paragraphs contain several *oftens* and *maybes*. The fact is, file-recovery utilities don't always succeed. A visit to a doctor isn't a substitute for good health habits, nor can a file-recovery utility replace a good backup routine.

An Ounce of Prevention

Here are some tips for taking care of floppy disks.

❖ *Keep disks away from items that produce magnetic fields* That includes audio speakers, electric motors, telephones, high-intensity desk lamps, and of course, magnets.

❖ *Keep disks comfortable* Don't leave them in a sun-baked car or near a radiator or other heat source.

❖ *Don't place an external floppy disk drive to the left of a Mac Plus or SE* Don't store floppies there, either. The power supply in these Macs generates magnetic fields that can cause disk errors.

❖ *Be gentle* Don't slide a disk's shutter open and touch the inside. Don't trust a disk's plastic case to

protect the disk in the mail; cardboard disk mailers are available at office-supply stores.

❖ *Buy quality disks* You've made an investment in your Mac and in the documents you create and the programs you buy; don't skimp on something as relatively inexpensive as a disk. With 800K drives, use disks certified for double-sided operation.

❖ *Use the write-protect tab to guard against accidental erasure* Slide the tab toward the disk's shutter to lock the disk. You can see straight through the write-protect hole of a locked disk. The Finder indicates a locked disk by displaying a padlock icon in the upper-left corner of the disk's window. **M**

And speaking of good health habits, keep disks — floppy or hard — away from excessive moisture, stray magnetic fields, extremes of heat or cold, and dusty environments (see the sidebar "An Ounce of Prevention"). Pack them securely for shipping. (Save your hard disk's original box or your Mac's box, if you have an internal drive.) If you move them from one temperature extreme to another, give them time to acclimate before using them. And never move or jostle a hard disk while it's on.

Following these common-sense precautions can lessen the chances that you'll need to restore data from backups or use a recovery program. In short, disks may be fair-weather friends, but you can control the weather.

Summary:

✔ Because of the large volume of files often found on hard disks, they are more difficult to back up than floppy disks.

✔ A full backup is a backup of all the files you have on floppy disks or a hard drive.

✔ An incremental backup is a backup of only those files you've added or changed since the last full backup.

✔ Every Mac comes with a backup utility, HD Backup, which lets you perform full and incremental backups.

✔ Some backup programs save older versions of files you back up while others delete them. A program that deletes older versions can help reduce the number of backup disks needed, but it eliminates the option of going back a few days to an earlier version of a file.

✔ Points to address before shopping for a backup utility include: network support (if you use network software); backup selectivity (backing up only documents and using application disks as backups, for example); and specialized media support (choosing a program that supports your backup medium).

Chapter 28
Virus Protection

In This Chapter:

✔ An introduction to viruses and how they spread.

✔ Names and symptoms of identified viruses.

✔ How to protect your Mac against viruses.

✔ Details on the virus-detection utilities available.

✔ Tips on what to do if you suspect your Mac is infected.

Have you had any viruses lately? I refer not to the cold-and-flu variety, but to *computer viruses,* programs that invade the Mac and slow its performance, cause system errors, or — at their most evil — destroy applications and documents.

The term *virus* implies a natural entity that you can't help but pick up now and then, like a cold. The truth is, computer viruses are tools of vandalism — they're bricks heaved through your Mac's windows by people with apparently nothing better to do with their time and programming skill. No cures exist for the viruses that cause colds, but computer viruses could be stopped dead if their creators turned their energies toward being productive, not destructive.

But then, so could war, crime, and pollution. And like them, viruses will be around for some time. What can you do? First, don't lose any sleep over viruses. They exist, but your chances of being victimized by one are small, especially if your Mac isn't on a network and you don't swap software with other users. Second, be prepared — just in case. Arm yourself with knowledge of how viruses spread, of their symptoms and remedies, and of the measures you can take to avoid them.

It Came from Ohio

Some of the technical concepts behind viruses have been around for decades, but the first microcomputer viruses appear to have been created in 1983 by Frank Cohen, a University of Cincinnati professor who was researching his doctoral thesis on computer security. Cohen's viruses were created under controlled conditions; none reached the outside world. Interviewed in 1988, when viruses enjoyed a burst of media attention, he admitted to being reluctant to publish his findings, but did so to warn the world of the virus threat. "I had planned to devote my thesis to ways to defend against viruses," he said. "Instead, I used it to prove that you can't defend against them."

Viruses are difficult to fight because they're designed to spread. A virus contains software instructions that enable it to copy itself into legitimate files, called *hosts.* Some viruses infect only application files, while others invade documents or the Mac's system files. Still others begin by infecting a system file and then copy themselves to uninfected applications.

Most viruses spread when you copy an infected file from one Mac to another, although some spread simply when you insert an infected floppy disk. Now imagine millions of Mac users exchanging files through user groups, office and university networks, and online bulletin boards and information services — the propagation possibilities are endless. In 1989, a new virus was discovered in Belgium in early December; by Christmas of that year, it had spread throughout the United States.

A virus doesn't just replicate itself, it also inflicts its own unique symptoms on the machines it infects. Viruses can be malicious or mischievous. A malicious virus might deliberately damage applications, cause system errors, or erase files on a hard disk. A mischievous virus might simply display a message or joke at a predetermined time; its creator is out to soap your windows, not smash them. To date, most Macintosh viruses have fallen into this second category.

But even a mischievous virus can be trouble. It might cause a system error by trying to use memory or resources that a legitimate program is already using. Its programmer may not have tested it thoroughly, or it might conflict with your Mac's combination of hardware and system extensions (especially INITs). The bottom line: There's no such thing as a benign virus.

Names and Strains

Most Mac viruses have odd-sounding names — nVIR, Hpat, INIT29 — that reflect the technical makeup of the virus's software. Others are named after their discoverers — Don Ernesto Zucchini was reportedly the first victim of the ZUC virus. Some viruses earn more pronounceable monikers, like the "Peace" virus, set loose by an attention-hungry editor of a Canadian Mac magazine. It was designed to display a "universal message of peace" on March 2, 1988, and then erase itself. Its victims — including Aldus Corporation, which inadvertently shipped a few thousand infected copies of FreeHand — didn't find the medium appropriate to the message.

Now and then a new strain of an existing virus appears. That's been the case with the nVIR virus, whose original program code was once posted on a computer bulletin board in an attempt to aid creators of antivirus software. It may have helped them, but it also gave budding virus creators a head start in creating new strains.

The table "Field Guide to Viruses" lists the names and symptoms of the viruses that have been identified as of early 1991.

Is Your Mac at Risk?

Generally, the more Macs your machine comes in contact with, the greater the risk of a virus infection. Consider yourself at risk if any of the following describe you.

❖ You swap programs, HyperCard stacks, or disks with other Mac users. Even an erased disk can carry the WDEF virus if you erase the disk by dragging its contents to the Trash. If a friend hands you a blank disk to fill with your latest shareware finds, be sure the disk was erased using the Finder's Erase Disk command before you insert it into your Mac.

❖ You download programs and HyperCard stacks from bulletin boards or information services. Most bulletin boards and information services check incoming files for viruses before making them available to subscribers, but a new virus can slip through undetected if the service's virus-detection software can't recognize it.

❖ You're connected to other Macs on a network. A network is an ideal transmission medium for viruses, especially if several users access applications stored on a file server.

❖ You use a desktop publishing service bureau or university laser-printer center. Some service bureaus have been criticized for taking a cavalier attitude toward virus checking and prevention. If you use a bureau or central printing station regularly, look into its virus-prevention measures.

Field Guide to Viruses

Virus Name	Nature of Infection	Symptoms	Comments
ANTI, ANTI-B, ANTI-ange	Infects applications only (including the Finder), not other system files or documents.	Nondestructive but may cause crashes due to its poor programming.	Disinfected applications aren't identical to original, but generally still run. Best approach is to replace infected application with an uninfected copy from its master disk.
CDEF	Infects DeskTop file only, not system files, programs, or documents.	Slows performance. AppleShare server performance slows significantly.	You can remove this virus from an infected disk by rebuilding its DeskTop file: Press Command and Option while inserting the disk. For hard disks, restart and hold down Command and Option until rebuild dialog box appears. To avoid infecting an AppleShare server, do not grant "make changes" privilege to the server's root directory (desktop level).
Frankie	Infects applications, not documents or system files. Infects only Atari computers containing certain Mac emulator hardware.	Draws bomb icon, displays, "Frankie says: No more piracy," then crashes.	Very rare. Doesn't infect genuine Macs. Doesn't spread under MultiFinder.
INIT 29	Infects any file (document or application) containing resources. Spreads only via applications and System files.	Its poor coding may cause printing problems, INIT conflicts, and MultiFinder crashes. If you insert a locked floppy disk, a dialog box appears saying the disk needs repairs. Normally, this dialog box doesn't appear with locked disks.	INIT 29 can spread very rapidly because it infects unlocked floppies as soon as they are inserted.
MDEF (strains A, B, and C; also called Garfield)	Infects applications, various system files, and documents.	System crashes. On Macs using CE Software's Vaccine, MDEF-A causes menus to work only in infected applications.	Often infects DeskTop, DA Handler, and Finder files. Strains B and C attempt to bypass watchdog INITs.

Virus Name	Nature of Infection	Symptoms	Comments
nVIR (strains A and B)	Infects System file first, adding code that subsequently infects each application you run. Finder and DA Handler files usually become infected.	System crashes. Files may disappear. Mac may beep when applications are started. "B" strain causes Mac to say "Don't panic" if System Folder contains the Macintalk file. Otherwise, you may hear random system beeps.	The original program code for nVIR was posted on some bulletin boards and information services. As a result, several "clones" have appeared: Hpad, nFLU, AIDS, MEV#, and F***, whose actual name can't be printed here. Their symptoms are generally the same.
Peace (also called MacMag, Drew, and Brandow)	Infects System file.	"Message of peace" appeared on March 2, 1988; virus then destroyed itself.	Rare these days, but still could be encountered on old disks.
Scores	Infects System file first, lies dormant for two days, then searches for and infects a new application at 3 ½ minute intervals. Adds invisible files called Scores and Desktop_ (_ character represents a space) to System Folder.	System crashes; printing problems. Miscellaneous problems with MacDraw and Microsoft Excel. May cause insufficient memory messages. Increases size of files it infects by 7K. Notepad and Scrapbook files may have generic document icons (dog-eared page).	System 6.0.4's System file is irrepairably damaged and must be replaced with an uninfected copy from its master disk.
WDEF (strains A and B)	Infects only the invisible DeskTop file contained on all floppy and hard disks. Spreads rapidly through the sharing of floppy disks.	Crashes Mac IIci and Portable. "B" strain causes Mac to beep each time a DeskTop file is infected.	See CDEF comments.
ZUC (strains A and B)	Infects applications only, not other system files or documents.	Strange pointer movement when mouse button is pushed down — pointer moves and bounces off the screen edges like a billiard ball. Can cause desktop pattern to change.	Applications don't have to be run to become infected. Spreads over networks.

How to Protect Yourself

If you don't fall into the preceding categories, you aren't immune from viruses, but the threat is minimal. Whether or not you're in the high-risk group, here's how to protect yourself.

❖ *Lock floppy disks whenever possible* A virus can't infect a locked disk. *Always* lock the original master disks of an application before inserting them; you'll need virus-free masters in case one of your programs gets infected. To lock a disk, slide its plastic write-protect tab so you can see through the square hole. If you don't have a hard disk, it won't be possible to work with locked floppies. Your best defense is to do the following.

❖ *Back up religiously* If the worst happens, you'll have something to fall back on — unless the backups are infected, too. To avoid that, keep at least two sets of alternate backups made at different times. Don't neglect to back up the files in your System Folder, too; most viruses attack them first, and by having a backup, you won't have to laboriously reinstall your favorite fonts and desk accessories. (See Chapter 27 for tips on backing up.)

❖ *Be wary of a new freeware or shareware program* Instead of trustingly copying it to your hard disk, run the program from a floppy first and watch for abnormal behavior, such as system crashes or significantly slowed performance. Use the Control Panel or Alarm Clock desk accessory to change the Mac's date setting, then run the program again; some viruses lie dormant until a certain amount of time passes. (The Scores virus, for example, waits four days before doing some of its dirty work.) Bypassing your hard disk protects you from *Trojan horse* programs, which appear to be legitimate applications, but which damage or erase files when you run them (see the sidebar "Attack of the Trojan Horses").

Attack of the Trojan Horses

A Trojan horse differs from a virus in that it isn't designed to spread by replicating itself; if a Trojan horse strikes, you can prevent future problems by deleting it. Trojan horses have been relatively rare in the Mac world, but there are several out there:

❖ Mosaic and FontFinder surfaced in early 1990 on a bulletin board system in Edmonton, Alberta. They appear to be utility programs, but when run, they erase the directory of the Mac's hard disk and display a message saying "Gotcha."

❖ Steriod appeared later in 1990. It's an INIT that promises faster screen displays on Macs with 9-inch, built-in screens. It wipes out disks.

❖ Sexy Ladies may have been the first well-known Mac Trojan horse. It's a HyperCard stack that displays cheesy images while erasing data from the disk it's stored on. **M**

❖ Protect your networks. Only applications known to be uninfected should be copied to a network file server. If you're in charge of running a server, establish guidelines to prevent anyone else from copying programs to the server. Also consider using the file server for document storage only, and running applications from local hard or floppy disks (not a bad approach in any case, given the less-than-blazing speed of LocalTalk cabling).

❖ Consider using one or more *virus-detection* utilities. These are programs you can use to scan suspect disks for viruses, remove viruses from infected programs, and guard against future infection. They're often described as the vaccines of the computer world, but the truth is, they're more like chicken soup — not guaranteed cures, but certainly worth trying if you're at risk.

If you suspect a virus infection, see the sidebar "When Infection Strikes" for some tips on what to do.

When Infection Strikes

Your Mac is acting up. Should you suspect a virus? Not at first, unless the problem is a dialog box containing a universal message of peace. Most system errors or other problems can be traced to non-viral causes: conflicting INITs, a damaged disk, loose or damaged printer cables, or application bugs (see Chapter 30 for more troubleshooting advice). I learned this the hard way a while back: I spent two days trying to eradicate an WDEF infection after my system slowed to glacial pace, but the problem turned out to be conflicting INITs. It goes to show that even the threat of a virus infection can impair your productivity.

After you've eliminated non-viral possibilities, compare your list of symptoms to those in the table "A Field Guide to Viruses." Run Apple's Virus RX utility, Disinfectant, and any other virus detectors you might have. If the detection utility identifies an infection:

❖ *Isolate the patient* If you're on a network, disconnect your LocalTalk connector where it attaches to the Mac's printer port. Inform other members of the network before disconnecting your Mac, and be sure

they know your machine is infected — theirs probably are, too.

❖ *Replace the infected files with healthy backups if you have them* You did back up yesterday, didn't you? If you don't have healthy backups, use a virus utility to try to repair the damaged files. First, because the disinfecting process itself could damage the files, backup the files the utility says are infected: Copy them to floppy disks and be sure to clearly label those disks as infected. If one utility fails to repair the files, try another. If you can't fix a file, delete it. Once you've successfully repaired or deleted all infected files, run the detection utility again.

❖ *After you repair the files, erase the infected backup disks* Don't use the Finder to erase the disks; you might reintroduce the virus when you insert an infected disk. Instead, use a magnetic bulk eraser such as Radio Shack's catalog number 44-232. A bulk eraser uses a strong magnetic field to scramble the disk's microscopic magnets, so don't use it near your good disks. **M**

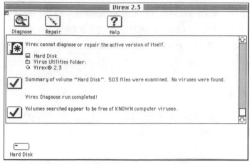

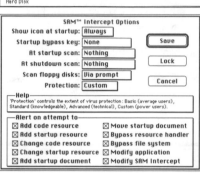

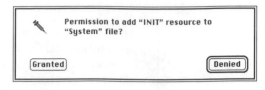

Virus Hunt

Commercial virus-detection utilities include a scan-and-repair application such as Microcom's Virex (top left) and a watchdog INIT such as Symantec's SAM Intercept (bottom left). When a program attempts to modify a file in the way that a virus would, a watchdog INIT displays a dialog box that lets you grant or deny access to the file. Above, a warning displayed by CE Software's free Vaccine watchdog.

Mac Medicine

After the Big Mac Viral Epidemic of 1988 (which snared more media attention than victims), programmers on the side of law and order began developing ways to detect, disable, and prevent viruses. Today, you can choose from several commercial virus-detection utilities and nearly a dozen shareware or free ones.

The commercial packages — Microcom's Virex, Symantec's SAM, Mainstay's AntiToxin, and Microseed's Rival — include an application for scanning suspect disks and repairing infected ones, and a *watchdog* INIT, which can help prevent infections (see the figure "Virus Hunt").

It's a good idea to use a virus-detection application's scan mode to check for viruses before backing up. Virex also has a Record/Scan command that saves information about the size and contents of one or more files. If you suspect infection, run the Record/Scan procedure again, comparing the results with the first scan. This is a useful way to spot a new virus that the utility might not otherwise detect.

Watchdog INITs provide several lines of defense against future infections. They automatically scan a newly inserted floppy disk for viruses; if one is found, you can eject the diseased disk and throw it away or you can try to repair it. The INITs also display a warning dialog box if you try to start an infected application. Virex's INIT also watches for the Mosaic and FontFinder Trojan horses.

SAM's watchdog INIT can also help prevent "unauthorized" modifications to applications and the System Folder. When a program (virus or otherwise) tries to modify an application or system file or attempts to add a new INIT to the System

Folder, a warning appears that lets you prohibit or permit the operation. (You can also tell SAM to automatically allow a specific type of modification, to eliminate unnecessary warnings.)

As for the free and shareware virus-detection utilities, the most popular are John Norstad's Disinfectant (a detection and repair application with watchdog INIT), Don Brown's Vaccine (a watchdog INIT), Jeffery S. Shulman's VirusDetective (a detection and repair DA), and Apple's Virus RX (a detection application). The table "Virus Fighters" (on the following page) summarizes the features of these and other virus-detection utilities.

At least one virus-detection utility belongs in every Macintosh user's software library. Start with Virus RX, Disinfectant, and Vaccine — they're free, and they may be all you'll need. For extra protection, consider one of the commercial packages.

If security is extremely important, you might also consider Casady & Greene's AME. Short for Access Managed Environment, AME provides more security than you'll find at a Secret Service company picnic. You can create a list of people permitted to use your Mac, and then define privileges — such as the ability to create or delete files, use printers, or insert floppy disks — for each user. For virus protection, you can register your healthy applications as "trusted," and then instruct AME to compare an application to its registration to verify that it hasn't been altered. If it has, AME won't allow it to run.

No Sure Cures

As I mentioned earlier, a virus-detection utility can't guarantee immunity. It's possible for a new virus to bypass a utility's detection and prevention features. When a new virus appears, a detection utility must be revised to recognize it. Many of the today's packages allow you to update the program yourself by typing cryptic character sequences that the utility will look for as it scans for viruses. But the virus has to be discovered before the utility's developer can tell its customers which characters to type.

Your other alternative is to buy individual program updates (often $15 to $25) or subscribe to a series of updates (around $75). If a few new viruses appear each year, you'll spend a small sum keeping your medicine cabinet up to date — and you'll be partially unprotected until the latest versions arrive.

It's also worth noting that watchdog INITs can cause problems if you're not careful. SAM's Intercept INIT, in particular, lets you intercept certain activities that some programs perform as part of their normal operation. SAM includes a list of over a dozen software and hardware products that Intercept may not work properly with — one of them is Microcom's Virex INIT. With virus utilities, two watchdogs do not necessarily offer twice the protection of one.

Virus Fighters

Product	Developer	Distribution	Description
AntiPan	Michael Hamel	free	Removes nVIR infections and prevents future nVIR infections. Detects nVIR clones.
Antitoxin	Mainstay	commercial	Includes watchdog INIT and scan/repair application.
Disinfectant	John Norstad	free	Scan/repair application with superb on-line help. Highly recommended.
Eradicat'Em	Dave Platt	free	INIT that repairs and protects against WDEF infections.
GateKeeper	Chris Johnson	free	INIT/cdev that protects system files and applications against infection. An alternative to Vaccine — more thorough checks, but requires some set-up time. Recommended for use with GateKeeper Aid.
GateKeeper Aid	Chris Johnson	free	INIT that repairs and protects against WDEF infections. Highly recommended.
Rival	Microseeds Publishing	commercial	INIT/cdev watchdog that repairs infected files you try to open. Bulk-erases disks.
Symantec AntiVirus for Macintosh (SAM)	Symantec	commercial	Includes watchdog INIT and scan/repair application. Configurable for new viruses.
Vaccine	Don Brown (CE Software)	free	INIT/cdev watchdog that warns you when a program attempts to modify system or application resources.
Virex	Microcom	commercial	Includes watchdog INIT and scan/repair application. Configurable for new viruses. Recommended.
Virus RX	Apple Computer	free	Detects Scores, nVIR, INIT29, ANTI, and WDEF. Doesn't repair infected applications.
VirusBlockade II	Jeff Shulman	$35 (shareware)	Control Panel device (cdev) for virus detection. Works with VirusDetective to scan inserted floppies for viruses.
VirusDetective	Jeff Shulman	$35 (shareware)	A powerful desk accessory you can configure to detect new viruses as they appear. Doesn't repair infected applications, but does cure WDEF infections.

Some people believe virus-detection utilities challenge virus writers to create new strains that can bypass their protection measures. They may be right; the WDEF virus contains a stealth mechanism that enabled it to evade most detection utilities when it first appeared.

What Are My Chances, Doc?

How likely are you to get a virus? In a *Macworld* reader survey that ran in the October 1988 issue, only about 8 percent of the readers who responded had been infected. I've never had a virus, and I hang out on a half-dozen information services and run untested shareware with abandon. OK, I'm a hypocrite — a doctor who tells you to watch your diet while his own cheeks bulge with M&M's.

Or maybe I simply give viruses the attention they deserve. The virus threat is minimal; you'll probably never see one. But they are out there, and new ones could appear at any time.

Summary:

✔ Viruses are tools of vandalism created by unlawful programmers and can cause damage to your computer's system software and applications, a mischievous message displayed on your screen, or both.

✔ Although viruses exist, your chances of being victimized by one are small, especially if your Mac isn't on a network and you don't swap software with other users.

✔ Generally, the more Macs your machine comes into contact with, the greater the risk of infection.

✔ A few tips to help protect your Mac from infection include: locking floppy disks whenever possible (a virus can't infect a locked disk), backing up religiously, running new freeware or shareware from a floppy disk first, protecting your networks, and using one or more virus-detection utilities.

✔ A virus-detection utility can help protect your Mac against infection by scanning suspect disks as well as repairing disks that have become infected. Choose a utility carefully, however, and don't combine virus utilities indiscriminately.

Chapter 29
Exchanging Data

I used to live in rural New England, where a too-often-told joke tells of a lost tourist who asks a taciturn Yankee for directions. Never looking up from his checker board, the Yankee retorts, "You can't get theyah from heeah."

If you've ever struggled to get data from one program or computer to another, you might wonder if that old Yankee's reply applies to computers, too. Perhaps you want to include a financial table created using a spreadsheet in a report created with a publishing program. Or you want to transfer some in-flight notes from a laptop computer to your Mac for editing. Or maybe you need to move data between similar Mac programs — perhaps to transfer a Microsoft Works database into FileMaker Pro.

Well, your data *can* get there from here. Moving files between programs and computers isn't as easy as using the Clipboard — the Mac's small-scale data-exchange medium — but it isn't as hard as finding a hidden New Hampshire hamlet, either. In this chapter, I'll examine data exchange basics and look at ways to transfer files between programs and computers.

Just Between Programs

In an ideal world, exchanging files between programs would be easy because all applications would create and save the same kind of documents. Alas, that world doesn't exist, and may never. Every application category — an word processor, spreadsheet, graphics program — has its own document-storage requirements. To understand why, let's look at how programs store documents.

When you choose a program's Save command, the program creates a file on disk and then copies data from the Mac's memory to the disk file. If you're saving a memo, the data includes the characters you typed, as well as codes that indicate *character attributes* such as font, style, and type size. If you're creating a spreadsheet, the program saves the values and the formulas you entered, as well as information that lets the spreadsheet recreate your column widths and cell formats. A MacPaint file's data includes a series of bits corresponding to the black and white areas of the image. A MacDraw file contains the QuickDraw graphics commands that represent the drawing.

Collectively, the organization of data in a disk file — the characters, their formatting codes, and the file signature — is called a *file format*. You might, for example, describe a document created with Microsoft Word as being "saved in Word format."

No standard exists that dictates how a program stores its data. Developers design file formats when creating their programs, and they usually keep the formats guarded secrets. (Indeed, programming journals have carried advertisements promising cash and confidentiality for information on a given program's file format.) If a competitor deciphers the format and creates a program that understands it, the original developer may lose business to a newcomer. This lack of *glasnost* in the software business results in the data-exchange headaches that occur when one program can't interpret another's file format.

Transfer Headache Remedies

Fortunately, there are some solutions. Some programs become so popular that their formats are deciphered and made public by independent programmers, or they're simply published by the program's developers. For example, most word processors can open and save MacWrite and Word files, most painting programs can open and save MacPaint files, and many spreadsheet programs can open and save Lotus 1-2-3 spreadsheets.

You can exchange files between two programs that can read a common format. Simply choose Program B's Open command, locate the document created by Program A, and then click Open. Why not simply double-click the document at the Finder? Because doing so would cause the Finder to attempt to open the *original* application. If the original application isn't on your disk and you do mistakenly double-click the document, you'll get an error message telling you that application can't be found for the document. Don't believe it: simply start the second application and use its Open command. (Incidentally, you can change this with file-launching utilities such as Software Innovations' HandOff, which allow you to assign documents to applications other than the ones that created them.)

Another way to move a file between programs is to save it in a data-exchange format — a file format designed for *exporting* and *importing* data. Such formats are usually designed by software developers, who publish the formats' specifications for other developers to use. Microsoft's Symbolic Link (SYLK) format is a popular exchange format for spreadsheet and database files. Microsoft's Rich-Text Format (RTF) for word processing documents allows you to swap text without losing its character formatting attributes. The table "Common Ground" lists several popular data-exchange formats.

These two approaches show that the secret to exchanging data between programs is to find a file format that both programs can understand. And the most desirable parcel of common ground is the one that retains the original file's formatting information — its font attributes, row and column widths, graphics, and so on.

Even if no such parcel exists, there's still hope. You can use a file-translation utility such as DataViz's MacLink Plus/PC or Apple's Apple File Exchange — provided the utility supports the file formats you use. If it doesn't, it's time to visit The Last Resort. Standards are rare in computing, but there is one that allows you to exchange data between any two computers. It's the American Standard Code for Information Interchange — ASCII, for short — and it's the least common denominator in the world of data exchange.

Nothing But the Text

ASCII (pronounced *ask-ee*) is a set of 256 codes, each representing a letter, number, special character, or a control code (a rudimentary formatting function such as a tab or carriage return). All computers use the ASCII character set, and thus, can exchange text and rudimentary formatting (tabs and carriage returns). Among the wonders that ASCII makes possible are text-oriented online services such as CompuServe, which can be accessed using any computer equipped with a modem.

Most programs that deal with text can save and open files containing only ASCII codes. In the Mac world, such ASCII files are called *text-only* files. By saving a document as a text-only file, you lose its formatting information, but at least you can transfer its text to another program.

To save a document as a text-only file, first be sure you've saved the document in its "native" file format. Next, choose the application's Save As command and select the text-only option (see the figure "How to Make Text Only"). Give the text-only file a different file name to avoid replacing the original. Avoid editing at this point, since any changes you make won't be saved in the original, formatted document. For this reason, it's best to create a

Common Ground

Format	Application	Pros	Cons
Document Content Architecture (DCA)	Word processing	Supported by many IBM PC programs and IBM word processors, and by MacLink Plus and Apple File Exchange	Font, style, and size information is lost
Data Interchange Format (DIF)	Spreadsheets and database management	Supported by many programs and by MacLink Plus	Cell formatting and widths are lost
Encapsulated PostScript (EPS)	PostScript graphics and special effects	Supported by IBM PC version of PageMaker	Applies to PostScript printers only
PICT	Object-oriented graphics	Supported by IBM PC version of PageMaker; translators available for converting to Microsoft Windows graphics	Minimal IBM PC support
Symbolic Link (SYLK)	Spreadsheets and database management	Retains some formatting information, including commas, column widths, and cell alignment	Font, style, and size information is lost
Tagged-Image File Format (TIFF)	Bitmapped graphics	Supported by many IBM PC and Macintosh scanners; not tied to specific computer or graphics resolution	Files can be large and time consuming to load
Rich-Text Format (RTF)	Word processing	Retains most formatting information, including font, styles, and sizes; supported by Mac and PC versions of PageMaker	Not supported by most Mac word processors

A
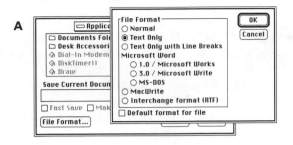

File Format
- ○ Normal
- ● Text Only
- ○ Text Only with Line Breaks

Microsoft Word
- ○ 1.0 / Microsoft Works
- ○ 3.0 / Microsoft Write
- ○ MS-DOS
- ○ MacWrite
- ○ Interchange format (RTF)
- ☐ Default format for file

[OK] [Cancel]

☐ Application
- ☐ Documents Fol...
- ☐ Desk Accessori...
- ◇ Dial-In Modem...
- ◇ DiskTimerII
- ◇ Draw

Save Current Docum...

☐ Fast Save ☐ Mak...
[File Format...]

B
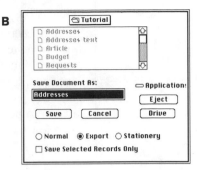

☐ Tutorial
- ☐ Addresses
- ☐ Addresses text
- ☐ Article
- ☐ Budget
- ☐ Requests

Save Document As:
[Addresses]

☐ Applications
[Eject]
[Save] [Cancel] [Drive]

○ Normal ● Export ○ Stationery
☐ Save Selected Records Only

C

☐ Startup
- ☐ Documents
- ☐ America Online
- ☐ Art 1 R...
- ☐ CIS 2-...
- ◇ Colori...
- ☐ Comm...
- ☐ Denni...

Save Wor...
[Workshe...]
Normal F...

File Format
- ○ Normal   ○ SYLK/Excel 1.5   ○ DIF
- ● Text   ○ WKS   ○ DBF 2
- ○ CSV   ○ WK1   ○ DBF 3

[OK] [Cancel]

Password: [   ]

☐ Create Backup File

D
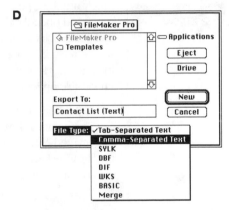

☐ FileMaker Pro
- ◇ FileMaker Pro
- ☐ Templates

☐ Applications
[Eject]
[Drive]

Export To:
[Contact List (Text)]

[New]
[Cancel]

File Type: | ✓Tab-Separated Text
Comma-Separated Text
SYLK
DBF
DIF
WKS
BASIC
Merge

E

Specify field order for export
- ✓ Company Name
- ✓ Contact Title
- ✓ Contact First
- ✓ Contact Last
- ✓ Address
- ✓ City
- ✓ State
- ✓ Zip
- ✓ Phone
- Other Address
- Other City
- Other State
- Other Zip
- Enter Date
- Referral Type

● Don't format output
○ Format output using current layout

[Cancel] [OK]

How to Make Text Only

Most Mac applications let you save documents in ASCII, or text-only, form. With Microsoft Word (A), choose Save As, then click the File Formats button and choose Text. With Microsoft Works (B), choose Save As and click the Export button. With Excel (C), choose Save As, then click the Options button and click Text. With FileMaker Pro (D), choose Export from the File menu, then choose the desired format from the pop-up menu. Next, select the fields to be exported (E) and then click OK.

text-only file only when you're ready to open the file with the importing application.

(Incidentally, some word processors make you perform an extra step when saving text-only files. After you confirm the Save As dialog box, they ask if a carriage return should be put at the end of each line or only between paragraphs. If you plan to open the document with a word processor or publishing program, choose Paragraphs. Choosing Line Breaks tells the program to place a carriage return at each line ending. All those extra returns will defeat the importing program's word wrap feature, making reformatting difficult.)

The steps required to open a text-only file in the importing application depend on the program. With most word processors and spreadsheets, you can simply use the Open command. If you haven't yet started the program, you can start it and open the document by selecting both at the Finder (click on one icon, then Shift-click on the other), and choosing Open from the File menu. This second technique doesn't work with all applications, however. Microsoft Works, for example, displays an error message and tells you to use its Open command's Import File option.

With publishing programs, you usually import text-only files using a Place or Get Text command. Most programs assign preset font, style, and size values to unformatted ASCII text, so you may want to adjust those presets before opening the file. Check the formatting and file-importing sections of your program's manual for details on such features.

Delimiters: Boundaries for Bytes

If you need to exchange a spreadsheet or a database file, use the exporting program's Save As or Export command to create a file in a format the importing program can interpret. If both programs support an exchange format such as SYLK, use it. Advanced data managers such as 4th Dimension, Double Helix, and FoxBASE+/Mac offer many ways to exchange data. You can, for example, often import data from and export it to ASCII files directly, or you can use a Print to Disk option to create an ASCII file containing those records that appear in a given report.

If you must resort to the lowly ASCII file, you'll encounter an additional data-exchange wrinkle. In order to separate the rows and columns of the spreadsheet or the fields and records of the database, the program must insert codes called *delimiters*. Delimiters are boundaries; they tell the importing program where one field or cell ends and the next begins.

The most common field or cell delimiter is a tab character (ASCII code 9); the most common row or record delimiter is a carriage return (ASCII code 13). A *tab-delimited text file* is an ASCII file whose data items (cells or fields) are delimited by tabs. Some programs and programming languages create text files that use commas as delimiters. Commas cause problems, however, since they can appear within values themselves ("10,000", "Raynak, Margaret"). Programs that delimit with commas will do what I did in the previous sentence: enclose each data item within quotes, and then separate each quoted item with a comma.

If you're working with two programs that don't support the same delimited format, don't give up. Massage the exported file using a word processor, changing the exported file's delimiters into ones the importing application understands. For example, if you bring a comma-delimited text file into Microsoft Works' database (which can import tab-delimited text files), open the text file in your word processor and use its search-and-replace feature to replace the quotes and comma delimiters with tab characters. You can use most any word processor to perform the alterations. Chapter 4 shows how to specify tab codes in the search-and-replace dialog boxes of several popular programs.

Between Macs and PCs

So far, I've covered exchanging files between Mac programs. Swapping files between Macs and IBM PCs involves traversing similar minefields, but to get to them you first have to move the files from one machine to the other. There are four basic ways to move documents between Macs and PCs.

❖ With a disk drive. Using special software, several floppy disk drives (including the 1.4MB SuperDrives built into today's Macs) can directly access 3½-inch MS-DOS floppy disks. There's also Dayna Communications' DaynaFile, which attaches to a Mac's SCSI port and can house one or two 5¼- or 3½-inch floppy drives, or one of each. You simply pop a PC floppy into the DaynaFile, and its contents appear on the Mac's desktop. The disk drive approach is easy and convenient, but it can be slow. Also, a floppy disk's limited capacity makes this option unsuitable for moving large numbers of files or large documents such as scanned images.

❖ With a file-transfer package. Products such as Traveling Software's LapLink Mac and DataViz' MacLink Plus/PC include a cable that connects to each machine as well as specialized communications software for each machine (see the figure "Transfer Tools" on the next page). With this technique, you can swap files that wouldn't fit on a floppy disk. Most packages can also use modems to transfer files over phone lines — handy when the machines aren't close enough for a direct cable connection. You'll often find niceties, too, such as a logging feature

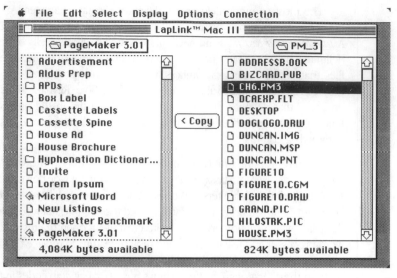

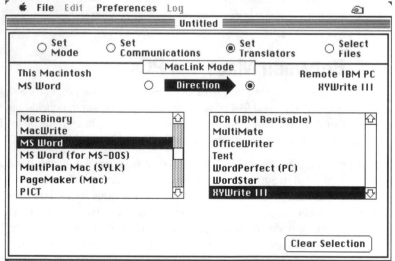

Transfer Tools

Top: The Mac and PC transfer software from Traveling Software's LapLink Mac uses a similar interface design and commands, making it easy to move between the two and allowing you to initiate transfers from either machine. The PC software also supports a mouse and can run under the Microsoft Windows environment. Bottom: With Dataviz's MacLink Plus/PC, you can't transfer files unless you first specify how (or whether) to translate them. When you click on a file format in one scroll box, the other scroll box changes to list only those formats MacLink Plus can translate to. Here, MacLink Plus/PC is set up to translate a Microsoft Word document into XyWrite III format. After choosing translators, you click the Select Files button to select the files to be moved.

that records who's accessed your machine, and password protection for guarding against unauthorized access. The cons: You need to learn the transfer software and juggle cables if you normally have different devices connected to your serial ports.

❖ With a network. Equip a PC with a LocalTalk expansion board, and you can connect it to your Mac using file-server software such as TOPS or AppleShare, or electronic mail software such as Microsoft Mail, Sitka's InBox, Lotus' cc:Mail, 3Com's 3+Mail, or CE Software's QuickMail. The pros: It's relatively fast and very convenient, especially if you transfer files frequently. You can access the other camp's hard disks as if they were connected to your machine, opening files directly or transferring them using the Finder. And a LocalTalk-equipped PC can share a PostScript laser printer with Macs. The cons: It's relatively expensive; PC LocalTalk boards cost a few hundred dollars, plus $50 to $75 for each network connector kit. Networks require setup and maintenance time, and their software reduces the memory available for programs.

❖ With communications software and a cable or modems. If you already have communications programs for your Mac and PC, you can swap files using modems or a null modem cable (the ImageWriter I cable works well). If you use modems, you can upload files to a communications service, and then download them to the other platform. Or you can call the other computer directly (see the sidebar "Computer to Computer" on the next page). The pros: It's generally inexpensive, since you may not need to buy any additional software. And communications services make convenient "drop boxes" that eliminate the need for two people to be at their machines at the same time to exchange files. The cons: It's slow and filled with technical hurdles. Communications services can be costly for large transfers, since you're charged for the time you spend online.

What's Your Signature?

Another aspect of Mac-PC file exchange involves associating transferred documents with the applications that can open them. On the Mac side, this lets you double-click on a transferred document's icon and automatically start the appropriate program. It also ensures that a transferred document will appear in a particular program's Open dialog box. Without this association process, transferred documents appear with the generic document icon (a blank page with one corner turned down). Double-click on a generic document and you'll get an error message saying the file couldn't be opened because its application is missing. The truth is, the Mac just doesn't know which program to start.

To associate documents with the programs that created them, the Mac uses invisible *file signatures*. A document has two four-character signatures; one specifies the document's creator, and the other specifies the document's type. For example, the creator code for an Aldus PageMaker 4.0 document is ALD4, while its type code is ALB4. When you double-click on a document, the Mac consults its creator signature to determine which application to start. When you choose an application's Open command, the application displays only the documents whose type code matches those the application can open.

The PC works similarly, albeit more crudely. With MS-DOS, file names are limited to eight characters plus a three-character *extension*, which appears after a period, as in FILENAME.TXT. The extension usually associates documents with their applications. For example, an Aldus PageMaker document has the extension PM4; its full name might be BROCHURE.PM4 or NEWSLETR.PM4. In the Mac-like Microsoft Windows operating environment, double-clicking on a file with the PM4 extension starts PageMaker and opens the file.

Most file transfer programs automate the document-association process with a technique called *extension mapping*, in which each PC file extension corresponds to a set of Macintosh signatures, and vice versa. When the Mac

Computer to Computer

Using a communications program to transfer files between computers can be a trying experience. Here are some tips that will help you try.

❖ *Get the right cable* For direct cable connections, be sure your cable is wired properly. Standard RS-232C cables don't work; your cable must be wired as a *null modem*, which tricks each machine into thinking it's talking to a modem. A competent computer dealer can supply the cable you need.

❖ *Check your settings* Both the receiving and transmitting programs must speak the same language at the same speed. Typical settings for cable connections are 9600 bps, 8 data bits, 1 stop bit, and no parity. For 1200-bps modems, use 1200 bps instead of 9600. And to see what you're typing, turn both programs' *local echo* options on.

❖ *Use transfer protocols* File-transfer protocols eliminate garbled data by "proofreading" data as it's sent. The most popular transfer protocol is called XMODEM. For Mac-to-Mac transfers, use MacBinary XMODEM; it transfers the special information in Mac files, such as their signatures and icons.

❖ *Plan ahead* For modem transfers, talk to the other person and settle on communications settings and transfer protocols, and on who should call whom. Next, the person at the receiving end puts his or her program in *answer* mode and the sender invokes his or her program's dial command. When a connection is made, type a few characters to verify settings, then invoke the transfer commands. **M**

**Swapping Files,
Apple Style**

Apple File Exchange,
included with the Mac's
system software, lets
you use the Mac's
SuperDrive to directly
access 3-1/2-inch MS-
DOS disks. The Mac to
MS-DOS and MS-DOS
to Mac menus list
available translators.
Here, a PC PageMaker
template file is being
transferred.

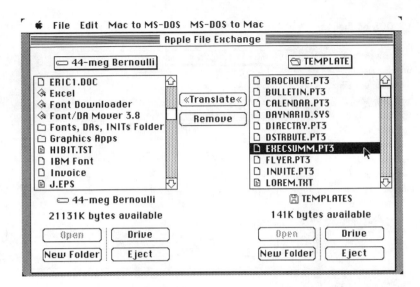

transfer program receives a PC file with a given extension, it automatically assigns
the corresponding type and creator codes to the Mac version of that file. Similarly,
when you move a file to the PC, it receives the appropriate extension. Most file
transfer products include extension maps for common dual-platform applications
such as Excel, Word, WordPerfect, and PageMaker, and also let you modify their
extension maps to better suit your software library. For example, if you use Full
Impact, you might want to modify the extension map so that transferred Lotus 1-
2-3 files acquire Full Impact's signature instead of Excel's.

Extension mapping is a great convenience, but it isn't essential. You can
change a file's type and creator codes yourself using Apple's ResEdit utility or a
disk-management desk accessory such as CE Software's DiskTop or Fifth Generation Systems' DiskTools. And you can usually force an application to open a
document with a different type code, provided the application supports that file
format using a technique I mentioned earlier: select the icons of both the
application and the document, and then choose the Finder's Open command. On
the PC, you can simply rename the file to change its extension.

Which Route to Take?

If you already have a SuperDrive-equipped Mac, use Apple File Exchange
for occasional transfers (see the figure "Swapping Files, Apple Style"). For
more convenient access to DOS disks, combine a SuperDrive with Dayna's

DOS on the
Desktop

With Dayna
Communications' DOS
Mounter, you can
work with MS-DOS
floppies using the
Finder. MS-DOS
subdirectories even
appear as folders.
Shown here: The
Templates disk from
the PC version
of PageMaker.

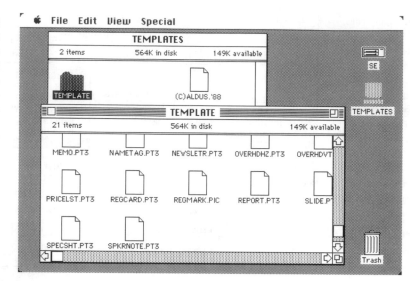

DOS Mounter (see the figure "DOS on the Desktop"). If you don't have a SuperDrive, Kennect Technology's Drive 2.4 external floppy drive and Rapport adaptor combination is a better buy.

To read 5¼-inch DOS disks, DaynaFile is the best choice. (Apple sells a 5¼-inch drive, but it's expensive, requires an expansion board to run, and doesn't show disks on the desktop.) If you use Bernoulli Box II drives on your Macs and PCs, use Dayna's DOS Mounter 2.0, which lets you work with PC Bernoulli cartridges inserted in a Mac Bernoulli drive.

It's also worth noting that you can equip a PC to read and write Macintosh disks using Central Point Software's Deluxe Option Board, which works with a PC's existing 3½-inch drive, or Micro Solutions' MatchMaker, which lets you attach an external Mac drive to a PC.

As for cable transfer products, you can't beat LapLink Mac for versatility and ease of use — provided you don't need extensive file-translation features. If you do, MacLink Plus/PC is a better choice. MacLink Plus/PC also includes MacLink Plus Translators, the most extensive set of translators available for Apple File Exchange. Claris' MacWrite II version 1.1 can use these translators to directly read and write a raft of PC word processor formats, including WordPerfect, MultiMate, WordStar, XyWrite, OfficeWriter, and Microsoft Word. Thanks to a new file-translation technology developed by Claris called *XTND*, installing the translators is as easy as copying them and a driver file called MacLink Plus/Bridge to your MacWrite II folder. If you use MacWrite II, this feature alone makes MacLink Plus/PC worth acquiring. XTND is supported by a growing number of programs, including WordPerfect Corporation's WordPerfect 2.0, Leonard Development Group's SmartWorks integrated package, and DEST's Recognize OCR program. MacLink Plus Translators is also available separately — consider it if you already have a way to access the other camp's files.

Versions of MacLink Plus are also available with translators for Wang and NBI word processors as well as Sun workstations and the NeXT computer. The DaynaFile drive and TOPS network software also include versions of MacLink Plus.

What's ahead for Mac-PC file swappers? Less work. The DOS-on-the-desktop approach offered by network software and the DOS Mounter/Apple SuperDrive combination is already making it easier to access PC files. The next step is transparent translation — the kind MacWrite II 1.1 provides when teamed with Dataviz's translators. As more developers adopt the Claris XTND file-translation technology, we can look forward to a day when translation occurs behind the scenes regardless of which program you use.

In the meantime, if you anticipate frequent Mac-PC swapping, you can minimize migraines by using programs that share formats, such as Microsoft Word, Excel, WordPerfect, and PageMaker.

When you transfer files, remember: the format's the thing. If the two swapping programs don't share a common format, use a file-translation program. If you strike out there, use an ASCII file. You'll have to do some reformatting, but you'll be spared retyping. And in the end, never typing the same text twice is what data-exchange is all about.

Summary:

✔ Every application category has its own document-storage requirements. The organization of data in a disk file — the characters, their formatting codes, and the file signature — is called a file format.

✔ Some programs become so popular that their formats are deciphered and made public by independent programmers, or they're simply published by the program's developers.

✔ The secret to exchanging data between programs is to find a file format that both programs can understand. This can be achieved by saving a file in a data-exchange format — a file format designed for exporting and importing data.

✔ ASCII (the American Standard Code for Information Interchange) is a set of 256 codes, each representing a letter, number, special character, or a control code. Most programs that deal with text can save and open files containing only ASCII codes.

✔ There are four basic ways to move documents between Macs and PCs: with a disk drive, a file-transfer package, a network, or communications software.

✔ If you already have a SuperDrive-equipped Mac, use Apple File Exchange for occasional transfers; for more convenient access to DOS disks, combine a SuperDrive with Dayna's DOS Mounter.

Chapter 30

Troubleshooting

In This Chapter:

✔ Symptoms and solutions for common Mac problems.

✔ Tips on setting up your system.

✔ Solving start-up and system problems.

✔ A look at disk and Finder problems and their symptoms.

✔ What to do if you experience printing and network problems.

The Mac is reliable, but not infallible. And when problems do occur, the Mac's friendly facade can even work against you by hiding technical difficulties behind error messages that provide few clues to the problem. At such times the Mac seems to say, "Sorry, something is wrong, but I won't bore you with the details."

This chapter is a guide to troubleshooting common hardware and software problems. I've organized symptoms into three general categories: start-up and system problems, disk and Finder problems, and printing and network problems; and I've provided at least one suggestion for each. (The sections that involve Font/DA Mover don't apply to System 7.0.) For some tips on how to set up a new Mac, see the sidebar "Setup Tips."

Start-Up Problems and System Crashes

You connected a hard disk, scanner, or some other SCSI device, but the Mac doesn't recognize it.

❖ Check all the SCSI devices to make sure they are connected properly, with the right number of terminators in the right positions. (See the sidebar "A SCSI Primer" in Chapter 22 for details.) Then with the power off, disconnect and firmly reconnect all SCSI cables. Use the metal cable snaps to lock them into place.

❖ Make sure each device has a unique SCSI ID number. If two or more SCSI devices have the same number, one or more of them may not work.

❖ Be sure you've installed any system extension software that accompanies the device. Some scanners, for example, won't work unless their system extensions are in the System Folder.

❖ Be sure the total length of the cabling in your SCSI chain is less than 30 feet (the shorter the better — some users say no longer than 20 feet) and that no single link between peripherals is more than 6 feet long (again, the shorter the better).

Setup Tips

Five years ago, setting up a Mac meant plugging it in, pouring some Perrier, and listening to the New Age music on the guided tour cassette. These days, you have to wrestle with SCSI cables, expansion boards, and a slew of system files. And when you're done, you may feel like sipping something a little stronger.

This section presents a roadmap to follow when setting up a system. These tips aren't intended to replace the setup instructions in your hardware and software manuals. Always consult your manuals first for information specific to your hardware and software.

Step 1: Install Expansion Boards

If you bought any expansion boards for your Mac, you'll want to install them first. The components on expansion boards and on the Mac's main logic board are extremely sensitive to static electricity, so be sure you're static-free before removing the Mac's case. (Don't shuffle across any carpets, and touch a metal light switch plate or other grounded object before starting. Consider using a wrist grounding strap if you're working in a very dry environment.)

Don't remove an expansion board from its static-free bag until you're ready to install it. You can install most NuBus boards in any slot, but check your boards' manuals to see if they have any special restrictions.

And be sure your Mac is unplugged before installing or removing any board.

Step 2: Tame the SCSI Bus

The next step in setting up a Mac is to properly connect it to its peripherals — the keyboard, mouse, printer, external hard disk, and any other add-ons. The most difficult aspect of Mac cabling involves interconnecting peripherals such as hard disks, scanners, and tape backup drives. These devices connect to the Mac's high-speed SCSI bus, which I introduced in "A SCSI Primer" in Chapter 22.

Keep two rules in mind when setting up SCSI peripherals:

❖ *Be sure each device has a unique ID number* Use the highest number (6) for an external hard disk. Use lower numbers for lower-priority hardware such as a scanner or tape-backup drive. You don't have to number devices sequentially; for example, you can use ID number 6 for a hard disk and ID number 3 for another device, skipping over numbers 4 and 5.

❖ *Be sure to terminate the SCSI chain properly* Determine whether your hardware contains internal terminators, and never place more than two terminators on the bus (see the figure "SCSI Wiring").

☞

The Mac won't start from a hard disk that was previously working.

❖ The disk's start-up information — its *boot blocks* — may be damaged. If the Mac's screen flashes the "where's the disk?" icon, or if the Mac crashes during start-up, displaying the frowning Mac icon instead of the "Welcome to Macintosh" message, bad boot blocks may be to blame (but also see the next section on misbehaving Inits). You can make repairs using a disk-repair utility such as Norton Utilities for the Macintosh, Microcom's 911, or Symantec's SUM II.

Step 3: Finish Wiring

Once you've tamed SCSI, your remaining wiring chores are child's play. They involve attaching the mouse and keyboard, and perhaps also connecting to an ImageWriter, StyleWriter, or LaserWriter printer.

On every Mac from the SE on, the mouse and keyboard use the *Apple Desktop Bus* (ADB). Like SCSI, the ADB lets you daisy chain numerous peripherals to a single connector. But unlike SCSI, ADB devices automatically configure themselves when you switch on the Mac; you don't have to fret with ID numbers and termination.

Your biggest decision when wiring the keyboard and mouse is whether to attach the mouse to the keyboard's ADB port or directly to the Mac's second ADB port. (If you have a Mac LC, Classic, or IIsi, you're spared even this decision — these Macs have just one ADB port.) I connected my Mac II's mouse to the keyboard. This allowed me to put my II on the floor (on a Kensington Macintosh II stand, which allows for adequate ventilation) without having to buy a set of extension cables. It also simplifies switching between left- and right-hand mouse operation, since it eliminates having to thread the cable over the top of the monitor and its cables.

As for printers, connecting to an ImageWriter, StyleWriter, or Personal LaserWriter LS is straightforward — each of these printers connects via a serial cable to the Mac's modem or printer port. But PostScript-based LaserWriters and other PostScript printers can be tricky. These printers use Apple's *LocalTalk* networking system to enable you to share their printing prowess with an office full of Macs and PCs.

The tricky part of LocalTalk wiring involves structuring the network properly. In a LocalTalk network, the network signals must run in a line, not a circle (see the figure "A Network Diagram"). And be sure to position cables and connectors so that people won't trip over them or inadvertently disconnect them by moving their Macs.

Step 4: Install System Software

After setting up your hardware, turn your attention to software. This step is especially vital if you have a hard disk or other large-capacity storage device. Time spent planning your software installation will be rewarded with faster, more efficient operation later on.

For the Mac to be able to access and start up from a hard disk, the disk must be *formatted* and it must contain a System Folder. The formatting process creates magnetic divisions on the disk that allow the Mac to keep track of files; the System Folder, as we saw in Chapter 23, contains files that allow the Mac to start up and run. ☞

❖ If a dialog box appears saying "Can't load the Finder!", a system crash may have damaged the Finder or the System file (or both). Start up with a floppy disk containing the latest System Folder, and copy its Finder or System file (or both) to the hard disk's System Folder. Note: After replacing the System file, you must reinstall any fonts and desk accessories you added (a chore you won't have to endure if you have a backup copy of your current System file).

❖ The hard disk's *driver software*, which allows the Mac to recognize and access the hard disk, may be damaged. If your hard disk came with a

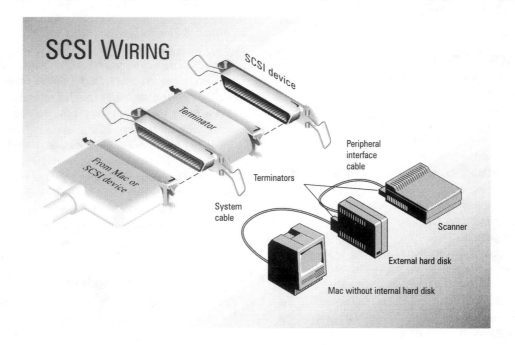

SCSI WIRING

SCSI device

Terminator

From Mac or SCSI device

Peripheral interface cable

Terminators

System cable

Scanner

External hard disk

Mac without internal hard disk

Some hard disk manufacturers format drives and install system software at the factory. You can use a preformatted drive immediately after connecting it. Switch on the drive first, then the Mac. If the smiling Mac icon appears and is followed by the Finder, you can proceed to the next step. If, instead, you see a disk icon and a flashing question mark, turn everything off and double check your SCSI cabling and ID numbering.

With unformatted drives and some removable-media drives, you use a special utility program included with the drive to format and test the drive or cartridge. Turn everything on (starting with the drive), then start your ☞

diagnostic program, run it. Many hard disks allow you to reinstall the driver software without reinitializing (which would erase the contents of the disk).

❖ The crash may have corrupted the contents of the Mac's *parameter RAM*, the battery-powered memory that holds Control Panel settings, such as the time, date, current start-up device. Try resetting the parameter RAM. To reset the parameter RAM under System 6.x, start the Mac with a different disk, then hold down the Command, Shift, and Option keys while opening the Control Panel. A dialog box asks if you want to "zap" the parameter RAM. Click Yes, then restart. To reset the parameter RAM under System 7.0, you'll need Apple's PRAM zapper utility, available through user's groups and on-line services.

Mac using the floppy disk that came with the drive. Locate and start the utility program, and follow the manufacturer's directions to test and format the drive or cartridge.

To install the System Folder and its contents on your hard disk, use Apple's Installer program, included on your System Tools disk. Although you can install system software by using the Finder to drag the files to your hard disk, it's better to use the Installer, which tailors your System Folder to match your model of Macintosh. If your hard disk was preformatted and already contains a System Folder that you want to replace, restart your Mac using the System Tools floppy disk. Then run the Installer.

If you connected a new printer in the previous step, you'll want to copy its driver file to your hard disk's System Folder. Printer drivers for Apple printers are generally located on a disk named Printer Tools. If you're using a non-Apple PostScript laser printer, use the driver named LaserWriter.

If you have any hardware that included INITs or other driver software, install the software now. Usually that means simply copying one or more system

extensions to the System Folder, although some hardware products include their own installer program.

Step 5: Install Applications

After installing your system software, you're ready to install your application programs. Installation routines vary between applications. You can install some programs by simply dragging their icons to your hard disk. Other programs come with their own installation programs. Be sure to follow the instructions in your program manuals. And watch that you don't copy a second System Folder to your hard disk. Having more than one System Folder (or more than one Finder or System file) on a hard disk is a common source of problems. Sometimes a superfluous System Folder can be buried within another folder, so to be sure you don't have more than one, use the Find File desk accessory (or System 7.0's Find command) to search for the files Finder and System.

See Chapter 26 for tips on creating a filing scheme that helps you find what you've stored. **M**

To zap the parameter RAM on a Mac Plus or earlier machine, you must remove the computer's battery — regardless of which system you're running. Leave the battery out for 20–30 minutes before reinstalling it.

You added a new system extension (INIT, cdev, or RDEV), desk accessory, or font, and now the Mac crashes during startup, when you try to use the system extension, or when you try to start a program that was previously working properly.

❖ System extensions that load during start-up can conflict with each other or with applications. First, remove the suspect extension from the System Folder (start the Mac with a different system disk if necessary), then restart. If the Mac doesn't crash, blame the extension. You can often cure system extension conflicts by renaming the offending extension so that it loads in a different order (the Mac loads system extensions in alphabetical order). If that fails, contact the extension's developer.

❖ If the Mac acts up after you add a desk accessory or a font, the System file (which holds both) may be damaged. Restart using a different system disk, and copy its System file to the damaged disk. Make sure you're using the latest version of Font/DA Mover (at this writing, version 3.8 for system versions prior to 6.0.7). If the problem persists, the desk accessory or font may be damaged. It's also possible that the desk accessory is incompatible with your version of the system software; check with the desk accessory's developer.

❖ When you run MultiFinder under System 6.x, newly installed fonts and desk accessories don't always appear in the Font or the Apple menu (if this happens, try restarting the Mac). It's best to install fonts and desk accessories from the Finder.

❖ If the Mac crashes only when you try to use the new desk accessory, the desk accessory itself may be damaged or improperly installed. Remove the desk accessory, then reinstall it. If the problem persists, it may be that the desk accessory's disk is defective, or the desk accessory may not be compatible with your system configuration; contact the desk accessory's developer.

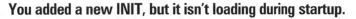

You added a new INIT, but it isn't loading during startup.

❖ Make sure that the new INIT is stored in the System Folder, then restart. If you're using System 7.0, be sure the INIT is in the Extensions folder, located within the System Folder.

❖ Don't press any keys during start-up, and be sure the Caps Lock key isn't depressed; often you can bypass loading a particular INIT by pressing certain keys.

The Mac crashes when you start a program or open a desk accessory, and the ID number in the bomb dialog box is 12, 15, 25, 26, or 28.

❖ An ID=15, ID=25, or ID=28 system crash often indicates insufficient memory (especially ID=15; ID=25 and ID=28 errors could be caused by other problems, too). Restart, then try one or more of the following: remove system extensions (especially INITs); use the Control Panel to disable or reduce the size of the RAM cache; or use the Finder's Set Startup command to specify that the Mac not use MultiFinder. Restart again to allow the changes to take effect.

❖ An ID=26 crash indicates that the Mac's attempt to start the program was unsuccessful, perhaps due to corrupted data in memory or a damaged application file. Restart and try again. If the Mac still crashes, reinstall the application from its master disk.

❖ An ID=12 crash indicates that the software you're attempting to run is making a toolbox call that isn't supported by your current hardware and/or system software combination. For example, you might be trying to run a color program on a Mac Classic, or you might be trying to run a program that requires System 7.0 under System 6.0.5. Check the program's system requirements and verify that your Mac meets them.

You tried to install a new version of the system software (or other software that uses the Apple Installer utility), and an error message appeared saying you "can't switch launch under MultiFinder."

❖ Versions 3.0 and earlier of Apple's Installer utility can't update system files that are currently in use. For this reason, the floppy disk containing these versions of the Installer must be the startup disk — the one whose System

Work File

Folder is currently active. You'll see the aforementioned error message if you start up MultiFinder from a hard disk and then try to run Installer 3.0 or earlier from a floppy disk that you've inserted. (*Switch launching* is the process of starting a program that's on a different disk and also switching to that disk's System Folder.) The solution: click Cancel to get rid of the error message, then start up your Mac using the floppy disk the Installer is on. This approach also results in a more reliable installation process, since any INITs or

The file "Work File" could not be opened/printed (the application is busy or missing).

OK

other extensions your hard disk might contain won't load into your Mac's memory, where they could interfere with the installation process.

Installer versions 3.1 and later support what's called a *live install* and don't attempt to switch-launch. These latest versions of the Installer are also to modify the active startup disk. It's still a good idea to start your Mac with the Installer disk, however, to avoid potential INIT-related problems.

Disk and Finder Problems

When you copy files using the Finder, an error message says that some files couldn't be written or read and were skipped.

❖ If the Mac couldn't write some files, the destination disk could be at fault. If you're copying multiple files, try copying one at a time. If that doesn't work, the destination disk may be magnetically or physically damaged. A temporary fix that usually works for me is to use the Finder's Duplicate command to duplicate a small file on the destination disk. This will cause subsequently copied files to be stored on a different area of the disk. But make sure you back up the disk as soon as possible and then erase it. If problems surface after erasing, the disk may be physically damaged. Throw out a damaged floppy; a damaged hard disk can be repaired.

❖ If the Mac couldn't read some files, the source disk may be the culprit. If it's a floppy or removable hard disk, try ejecting and reinserting the disk; it may not have been seated properly. If you have two floppy drives, insert the source disk in the other drive. If these techniques fail, the source disk may be damaged. Use a disk-repair utility to scan the disk for errors, a process called *verifying*. See Chapter 27 for more details on disk-repair and file-recovery utilities.

▲ **Generic Errors**
When you see this error message, it means the Finder was unable to locate the application that created the document. Oftentimes, this occurs when you try to open or print a document that isn't intended to opened from the Finder. Examples of such a document include an application's temporary work file or settings file, which stores your working preferences. Such documents often have generic document icons (top).

DeskTop

When you double-click on a document, the Finder says it can't be opened because "the application is busy or missing."

❖ If you don't have the application that created the document, you can't open the file from the Finder, but you may be able to open it from within another application. For

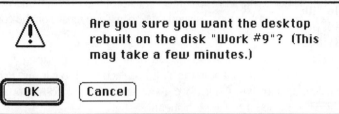

example, you can open MacWrite documents from within most word processors by using the word processor's Open command. You can also use utilities such as Software Innovations'

▲ DeskTop Details

Every disk that you use with System version 6.x or earlier contains an invisible file named DeskTop, which stores important information about the disk's contents and the way you view them. One solution to certain disk ailments involves rebuilding the DeskTop file by pressing the Command and Option keys while inserting the disk. Doing so causes the Finder to display the message shown here. Note, however, that rebuilding the DeskTop file causes the Finder to lose any Get Info comments you may have added to that disk.

HandOff to assign documents to a different program.

❖ The document may not be intended to be opened from the Finder (for example, a document that stores your working preferences or a spelling checker dictionary). If the document has a generic document icon, it probably can't be opened from the Finder (see the figure "Generic Errors"). But again, you may be able to open it from within an application.

❖ The document, its application, or the disk's DeskTop file, which contains information about the disk's contents, may be damaged (see the figure "DeskTop Details"). This is less likely than the previous situations, but it's possible. Every document file contains a 4-character *signature* that identifies the application that created it. If this signature is damaged, either in the document or in the DeskTop file, the Finder won't know which application to open. Try rebuilding the DeskTop file (as shown in the figure "DeskTop Details") or using a disk utility to examine the document's file signature. The DeskTop file is used in System 6.0.x and earlier versions only.

❖ A special file attribute called the *bundle bit* may be set (that is, turned on) for a file other than the application itself (such as a spelling checker dictionary). As a result, the DeskTop file has become confused. Most disk utilities can repair this problem.

When you insert a disk, the Mac tells you that it needs minor repairs and asks if it should perform them.

❖ This usually indicates a damaged DeskTop file. If you click OK, the Finder rebuilds the DeskTop file.

When you insert a disk, the Mac tells you that it's damaged or unreadable and asks if you want to initialize it.

❖ Just say no — unless you want to erase the disk. If the disk has important data on it, click Cancel to eject it. Then try inserting the disk again and/or restarting the Mac; if the same message appears, the disk is sick. Use a disk utility to diagnose its ailments and, if possible, recover its contents. (Use the utility to copy those contents to another disk and then try making repairs on the copy, in case the recovery process backfires.)

❖ If you elect to initialize the disk and the Mac displays a message saying "Initialization Failed!" you'll know the disk is defective. Throw it out. Even if the initialization succeeds, think twice about using the disk for important work. It could be about to fail permanently.

When you choose Empty Trash, the Finder says that "the Trash couldn't be emptied." Or, when you throw away a document or application, the Finder says that the "item is locked or in use and can't be removed."

❖ Verify that the file isn't really locked: using the Finder, select it and choose Get Info. If the Locked box is checked, click it to unlock the file. Then try throwing it away.

❖ These problems can occur when you throw away a file that the Mac is currently using — or thinks it is. When you open a file, the Mac alters the disk's directory to indicate that the file is in use. These notations may remain unchanged until you quit the application — even if you use the application's Close command. Try quitting the application, then throwing the document away. If that fails, hold down the Option key while dragging the document into the Trash. Then hold down Option again while choosing Empty Trash. If this fails, restart and then throw the file away. The restarting process should close the file properly. If you frequently encounter this problem with a specific disk, try rebuilding the disk's DeskTop file.

The Mac asks you to insert a disk that you ejected long ago.

❖ When you use the Eject command, the Mac remembers that the disk still exists, and may ask to see it again. Dragging an icon to the Trash causes the Mac to forget the disk, thereby guaranteeing that you won't be asked for it again. In System 7.0, you can also use the Put Away command.

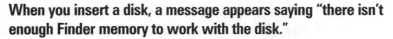

When you insert a disk, a message appears saying "there isn't enough Finder memory to work with the disk."

❖ If you have a large number of windows open on the desktop, the Finder must keep track of everything that's in them. When you insert the disk, the Finder doesn't have enough memory to read and keep track of its contents. One solution is to close some windows (and perhaps desk accessories and applications) and try again. If you can spare the memory, you may also want to allocate more memory to the Finder. Open the System Folder, select the Finder file, use the Get Info window to increase the amount of memory allocated to the Finder, and then restart your Mac. Increasing the amount of memory available to the Finder speeds up disk- and file-copying, too.

When you eject a disk, a Finder error message appears saying that "the disk is so full that the folder changes couldn't be recorded."

❖ If a disk is full or nearly full, there may not be enough free space for the Finder to record the changes you've made to the disk's icon arrangement, Get Info comments, or folders. Click OK to close the error dialog box, then reinsert thc disk, delete at least one file, and try again.

Printing and Network Problems

The Mac reports that it can't locate or access the printer.

❖ Verify that the start-up disk you're using is unlocked and that it contains at least 50K of free space. Many applications create temporary files during printing and can't print if the start-up disk is locked or nearly full.

❖ For ImageWriters and StyleWriters: Check to make sure that the printer is connected and online (press the Select button), and that its paper supply hasn't run out. Use the Chooser to make sure that the printer driver and the proper connection port are selected. Then choose the Page Setup command, verify your print settings, click OK, and try again.

❖ For laser printers: Be sure the printer is on and that its paper tray contains paper and is properly seated. Use the Chooser to select the printer's driver. If you're using a PostScript printer and the printer's name doesn't appear in the Chooser window, the printer may not be warmed up, or you may have a LocalTalk wiring problem (see the figure "A Network Diagram"). Once the printer's name appears in the Chooser, select it, then use Page Setup to verify print settings, and try again.

When you print to a laser printer, an error message appears saying that the printer was initialized with an earlier version and needs to be reinitialized.

❖ The Macs on your network have different versions of the LaserPrep and LaserWriter files. Each Mac on a network should have the same version. At this writing, version 6.0.1 is the latest for System 6.x. You'll find it on the Printer Tools disk in the 32-bit QuickDraw folder.

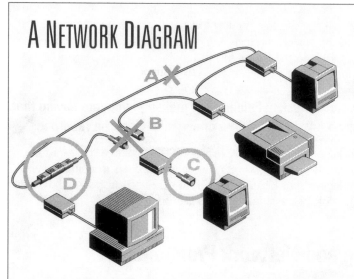

A NETWORK DIAGRAM

LocalTalk connectors attach cables to all the networked devices—Macs, printers, or IBM PC's equipped with LocalTalk expansion boards. Avoid a common wiring trap by never connecting the first and last device on a network and creating a closed loop **(A)**. Other problems include loose connections and dangling unconnected cables **(B)**. If you need to remove a device, either unplug its connector box **(C)** or insert a cable extender between the two dangling cables **(D)**.

You use TOPS, and some Macs occasionally lose contact with a server, causing TOPS to display the message, "Trying to connect to [server name]."

❖ Check your network wiring.

❖ Check to see if someone is using the server. Performing time-consuming tasks on a server — erasing a floppy, copying files, or installing a font or desk accessory — can cause *time-outs*. TOPS can usually reestablish the connection after the operation is completed. Avoid performing such tasks on a TOPS server that has *published volumes* (volumes that have been made available to other users on the network).

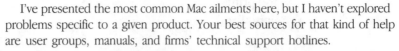

For More Help

I've presented the most common Mac ailments here, but I haven't explored problems specific to a given product. Your best sources for that kind of help are user groups, manuals, and firms' technical support hotlines.

But before you call the latter, be sure to compile the information the support technician will need to diagnose the problem. Take time before trouble strikes to write down your system configuration: the amount of memory, the System version (choose About the Finder or About this Macintosh from the Apple menu), the names of any INITs and desk accessories you've installed, and a list of your peripherals. When a problem occurs, note the steps that caused it.

And before you call, take a few deep breaths. A support technician can't help when all you can say are cartoonist's punctuation characters. When you're at that level of despair, you need a different kind of hotline.

Summary:

✔ If the Mac doesn't recognize a hard disk, scanner , or other SCSI device, check all the SCSI devices to make sure they are properly connected (the right number of terminators in the right position).

✔ If your Mac won't start from a hard disk that was previously working, the hard disk's start-up information may be damaged.

✔ When you copy files using the Finder and an error message says that some files couldn't be written and were skipped, the destination disk could be at fault.

✔ If you don't have the application that created a document you are trying to open, the Finder will say it can't be opened because "the application is busy or missing." You may, however, be able to open it from within another application.

✔ Should the Mac report that it can't locate or access the printer, check your cabling and verify that the start-up disk you're using is unlocked and contains at least 50K of free space.

✔ When setting up your system, perform the following steps in this order:
   1. Install expansion boards.
   2. Connect the Mac to any SCSI peripherals you may have.
   3. Complete remaining wiring for mouse and keyboard.
   4. Install the system software.
   5. Install the applications.

Chapter 31
Power Protection

In This Chapter:

✔ An introduction to power problems and their solutions.

✔ A look at the Mac's built-in power protection features.

✔ Reducing incoming surges with surge suppressors.

✔ Details on how standby and uninterruptible power supplies work.

✔ What to look for when shopping for surge suppressors and standby power supplies.

A nyone who has watched an hour's worth of unsaved work vanish into the black hole of a darkened screen knows how traumatic a power failure can be. One minute you're hard at work, and the next you're staring stupefied at a blank piece of glass. Mac Lesson Number One: The power to be your best only exists when there's power.

But of all the power problems that can occur, power failures constitute a relatively small percentage. A variety of gremlins lurk on the other side of a wall outlet, and some of them can turn a Mac's lights out for good. In this chapter, we'll look at the kinds of mishaps you might encounter, and we'll see just how susceptible your system is to them. Finally, I'll describe some add-ons that ensure the Mac a healthy flow of juice.

Current Events

The electricity that powers the Mac's chips, video tube, and other components is quite different from the current you get from a wall outlet. Most of the Mac's electronic components require small amounts of voltage — between 5 and 12 volts — but a wall outlet supplies roughly 120 volts (in the United States and Canada, that is; in Europe, 220 or 240 volts is standard, and elsewhere you may find either 120- or 220-volt systems).

What's more, the Mac's components require *direct current* (DC), while a wall outlet supplies *alternating current* (AC). DC travels continuously, while AC reverses its direction at regular intervals — generally, 60 times per second with 120-volt systems and 50 times per second with 220-volt systems.

All Macs contain a *power supply* that turns AC voltage from the wall outlet into direct current at the voltage levels needed by the Mac's components. The power supply also contains filtering circuits that smooth variations in the original current.

It's those variations that can cause problems. The electricity a power company supplies may seem like pretty consistent stuff, but it isn't. Its voltage fluctuates — sometimes dramatically — and it's prone to various types of *noise,* or interference. The figure "Power Problems" illustrates the most common types of power flaws:

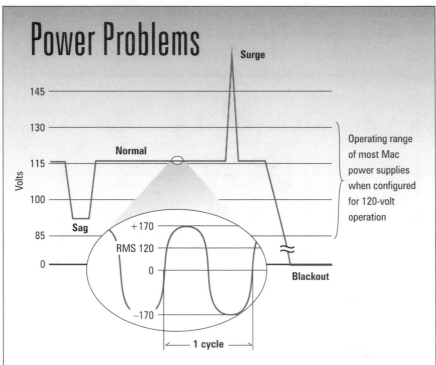

Power Problems

Incoming voltage averages 115 to 120 volts, but it drops during sags or brownouts, and momentarily soars during surges. The inset shows one cycle of alternating current (AC), 60 of which occur each second. Note that the sine wave's peak and trough reach values of +170 and −170 volts. The root-mean-square, or RMS, voltage value, which can be thought of as an average value, is 120 volts. Macintosh power supplies draw their power at the peak of each sine wave.

❖ *Outages,* or *blackouts,* occur when the power goes out completely. An overloaded circuit can cause a localized blackout in part of a house or building, while storms and downed power lines usually cause prolonged, area-wide outages. Momentary blackouts can also occur when a utility company switches between various power-distribution circuits while isolating a problem in the lines. Although such blackouts usually last only a fraction of a second, they can go on for several seconds (on the rural northern California coast where I live, longer ones are more common).

❖ *Sags* occur when the voltage available at the wall outlet drops below roughly 105 volts. Also called *brownouts,* sags can occur when a sudden load is placed on a circuit — such as when an air conditioner or some other power glutton is turned on. Sags can also occur when an electric utility company lowers the voltage in order to reduce demands on its generating equipment during periods of peak usage, such as sweltering summer days and frigid winter nights. Sags generally won't damage the Mac, although a very large one could cause a system error.

❖ *Surges* occur when incoming voltage increases by astronomical amounts for a very brief period (on the order of a few milliseconds, or thousandths of a second). Surges, also called *transients* or *spikes,* can occur when lightning strikes in your vicinity or when the power comes back on after a blackout. Small surges (under 1000 volts) can be caused by the electric motor in a refrigerator or other appliance turning off and are more common than large surges (1000 volts or more). A large surge can damage anything that's connected to the circuit; a small one generally won't cause permanent damage but could produce a system error and some lost work. Surges as a whole are less common than sags.

❖ *Noise* covers a range of flaws that affect the quality, not the quantity, of power present. A large electric motor can transmit noise into wiring that can interfere with radio or television equipment on the same circuit. This kind of noise, called *electromagnetic interference* (EMI), generally doesn't affect computer equipment.

The First Line of Defense

How vulnerable is the Mac to blackouts, sags, and surges? Judging from the number of *power conditioning* products available — and by the alarmist advertising some manufacturers use — you might think it's a sitting duck, ready to be humbled by the first surge or sag that comes down the wire.

Not so. The power supplies in the Mac family are designed with sags and surges in mind. Apple's power supplies are designed to work with as little as 85 volts, so the Mac shouldn't blink during brownouts.

Mac power supplies can even provide enough juice to keep the machine running during a very brief blackout, the kind caused when utilities switch distribution networks. Apple's power supplies are designed to provide 20 milliseconds of current to a Mac running at *full load* — all floppy and hard drive motors on, keyboard and mouse in use, all expansion slots filled, the processor hard at work, and all rear-panel connectors in use at the same time. Because a Mac rarely operates at full load, the power supply can carry you through an outage of a second or two — depending on what's connected to your Mac and how it's being used when the outage occurs.

All Macs are designed to withstand surges of up to 5000 volts. Indeed, the power supplies in most computer equipment have at least some surge protection built in.

So the Mac's power supply tolerates low-voltage conditions and stands up to surges. Why, then, does an entire industry revolve around power protection? For one thing, no power supply provides enough juice to span an outage lasting more than a couple of seconds. Also, surge resistance varies from one piece of equipment to the next; your Mac may withstand a surge, but will your modem, external hard drive, monitor, and scanner? And many power-protection devices offer convenient features, such as a single switch that turns everything on and off, or separate front-panel switches for each item plugged in to the device. Finally, there's the chicken-soup factor — a second stage of power filtering and surge protection can't hurt, and it may well help.

Suppressing the Urge to Surge

The most popular power-protection device is the *surge suppressor,* which you install between the wall outlet and your computer gear. It reduces incoming surges to innocuous voltage levels. Surge suppressors don't help when the power sags, but they are the least expensive power protectors.

When shopping for a surge suppressor, you'll face a barrage of jargon and a variety of features, some convenient, some essential. In the jargon department, the two most important specifications are *clamping voltage* and *response time.* The clamping voltage is the point at which the surge suppressor kicks in and starts suppressing; voltages below the clamping voltage are sent along to the equipment. Thus, the lower the clamping voltage, the better; a 340- to 400-volt clamping voltage is best.

Response time is the time required for the surge suppressor to close its electronic gate and prevent the surge from getting through. The faster the response time, the better, since it means less of the surge sneaks through to the computer. Look for a response time of about 10 nanoseconds or less.

You may also see an *energy dissipation* specification. This refers to how much juice the surge suppressor's circuitry can absorb before it fails and simply passes the surge on to ground, an event that won't harm your equipment but will blow out the surge suppressor. Energy dissipation is measured in joules; the higher the value, the more durable the surge suppressor. Inexpensive surge suppressors generally absorb about 50 joules, while heavy-duty suppressors can absorb 300 or more joules.

The easiest way to choose a good surge suppressor is to make sure it meets Underwriters Laboratory (UL) specification 1449. (UL 1449 refers to a battery of torture tests, themselves described in another cleverly named document, IEEE 587.) A suppressor that complies with IEEE 587 is desirable, but the UL 1449 designation is preferable, since it means an independent laboratory, not the suppressor manufacturer, tested the device. It isn't enough for a suppressor to simply be UL listed; look specifically for the UL 1449 designation.

Beyond tech specs, here are other factors you'll want to consider:

❖ *Connections between hot, neutral, and ground.* Inexpensive surge suppressors (in the $10 to $20 range) protect only between the hot (current-carrying) and the neutral wires of a wall outlet. For complete protection, you also need protection between the neutral wire and the ground wire (the round hole below the two rectangular ones on a wall outlet) and between hot and ground wires. This scheme is often described as providing "three-way" protection.

❖ *Modem protection.* A lightning-induced surge can enter the phone lines and fry a modem. Some suppressors provide jacks for a modem or fax machine, a desirable feature for lightning-prone areas. Another UL designation, UL 497A, indicates that a suppressor can successfully protect such communications equipment.

❖ *Number of outlets.* Most surge suppressors provide several outlets, and must also provide a master power switch. Some also provide individual switches for each outlet. Some suppressors, such as Curtis Manufacturing Company's Curtis Command Center, are designed to sit beneath a monitor, providing a swivel base for it, and they have a power switch for each outlet.

❖ *Failure alarm.* A surge suppressor can fail after absorbing too large a surge; better units provide an alarm that indicates when the suppressor circuit has failed. An alarm might consist of an indicator light (handy if the suppressor is close to your system), an audible buzzer (good if the suppressor is under your desk, out of eyeshot), or both (best).

Complete Power Protectors

For protection against sags and brief blackouts as well as surges, you'll want a *standby power supply,* which installs between your equipment and the wall outlet and contains batteries that provide from 5 to 30 minutes of power. That's more than enough power to span a brief outage or give you time to save and shut down during longer ones.

A standby power supply is often called an *uninterruptible power supply* (UPS), but in fact there's a difference between the two. With a UPS, computer equipment runs continuously from the power supply's batteries, which are constantly being recharged. By contrast, a standby power supply's batteries don't kick in until the power goes off (see the figure "How Standby and Uninterruptible Power Supplies Work"). A standby power supply generally costs less than a true UPS and is just as reliable. A standby supply kicks in within milliseconds of an outage or sag, and as I mentioned earlier, the power supplies in your hardware will continue to provide power during that period.

The amount of power a standby supply can provide depends on what's connected to it. The greater the load on the supply, the faster its batteries will

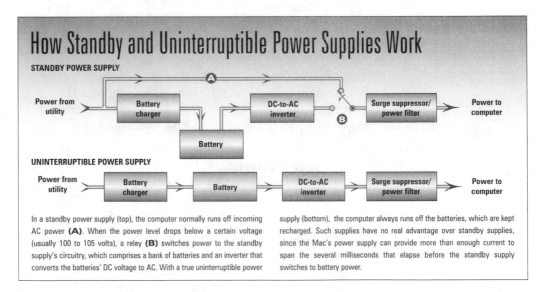

How Standby and Uninterruptible Power Supplies Work

STANDBY POWER SUPPLY

Power from utility → Battery charger → DC-to-AC inverter → Surge suppressor/ power filter → Power to computer

Battery

UNINTERRUPTIBLE POWER SUPPLY

Power from utility → Battery charger → Battery → DC-to-AC inverter → Surge suppressor/ power filter → Power to computer

In a standby power supply (top), the computer normally runs off incoming AC power **(A)**. When the power level drops below a certain voltage (usually 100 to 105 volts), a relay **(B)** switches power to the standby supply's circuitry, which comprises a bank of batteries and an inverter that converts the batteries' DC voltage to AC. With a true uninterruptible power supply (bottom), the computer always runs off the batteries, which are kept recharged. Such supplies have no real advantage over standby supplies, since the Mac's power supply can provide more than enough current to span the several milliseconds that elapse before the standby supply switches to battery power.

discharge. What's more, if you exceed a standby supply's current rating, you'll eventually blow a fuse in the supply. (Better-quality supplies have overload indicators that light when you're drawing too much current.) Thus, it's important to match the supply to your hardware.

Standby and uninterruptible power supplies are usually rated in *volt-amps*. A unit rated at approximately 100 volt-amps will power a typical Mac Plus or SE with a hard drive for at least 15 minutes (see the table "Current Requirements"). Such supplies generally cost between $200 and $400. For a Mac II– class machine with a 13-inch color monitor, you need a supply that provides 300 to 400 volt-amps, at a cost of $400 to $500. For a 19-inch monitor, make that at least 400 to 500 volt-amps and $500 to $700. Add another 100 volt-amps to include an external hard drive or tape backup device.

Don't bother providing standby power to your laser printer — you'd need a supply rated at 1000 volt-amps or more, and they cost between $1000 and $2000. And given the fact that you won't lose any work if the laser printer loses power anyway, it makes more sense to simply protect the printer from surges.

Shopping for Standby Power

Many of the shopping considerations behind surge suppressors apply to standby power supplies too. Some supplies provide only one rear-panel outlet; others provide several. Some (such as American Power Conversion's UPS 110SE and UPS 370ci) can sit beneath a Mac or a monitor, while others (such as Emerson Electric Company's Accupower Micro UPS series and Kensington Microware's Power Backer series) are designed to sit on the floor. The better ones have several indicator lights that warn you when you're overloading the supply, when your electrical wiring is faulty, and when you're running on battery power.

More-sophisticated supplies provide an interface connector that lets you attach the supply to the Mac's modem or printer port so that the supply can convey status information to the Mac. Such a feature is most useful when you want standby power for a network file server.

If you want standby power for an AppleShare network file server, consider pairing American Power Conversion's UPS 110SE or UPS 370ci with the company's PowerChute software. These well-designed supplies provide interface connectors that can attach to the server Mac's modem port. The PowerChute software monitors the status information; when the power fails and the power supply kicks in, PowerChute sends a warning to all Macs connected to the server telling them how long the server will

Current Requirements

Computer/peripheral	Power Consumption (volt-amps)
Macintosh Plus	75
Macintosh SE (no internal hard drive)	65
Macintosh SE (with internal hard drive)	80
Macintosh IIcx	120
Macintosh IIci	130
Macintosh IIx	150
Macintosh IIfx	180
13-inch color monitor	80
Full-page monochrome	80–90
Two-page monochrome monitor	130–170
Typical external hard drive	30–70
Typical laser printer	950

remain available. If the power doesn't return before the standby power is exhausted, all users are safely logged off the server, which is then shut down normally. Of course, only users who weren't victimized by the outage — or who have their own standby power supplies — will see the on-screen warning message, but the warning is only half the value of PowerChute anyway. What's equally important is that the server is safely shut down for you.

Before buying any standby power supply, make sure it provides either *sine wave* or *stepped-square wave* output. Inexpensive standby supplies often provide *square wave* output, which causes considerable electrical stress to monitors and hard drives that could make them wear out faster. Sine-wave output is the most desirable, since that's what wall outlets normally supply.

Power Protectors

Company	Phone	Comments
Surge Suppressors		
Computer Accessories Corporation	619/457-5500	Numerous models; ProLine is UL 1449 rated; Proxima Power Director series has multiple power switches; Proxima Power Director Plus protects modem. $49.95–$159.95.
Curtis Manufacturing	603/532-4123	Numerous models, all UL 1449 rated. $6.95–$149.95.
Intermatic	312/282-7300, 815/675-2321	Electra-Guard series UL 1449 rated. Numerous models, some with modem protection and front-panel switches. $89.95–$159.95.
Kensington Microware	212/475-5200, 800/535-4242	Numerous models; MasterPiece Mac II also protects modem and has monitor swivel and multiple front-panel power switches. $29.95–$159.95.
Practical Solutions	602/322-6100	Strip Switch enables SEs to be turned on using keyboard power-on key. $89.95.
Standby and Uninterruptible Power Supplies		
American Power Conversion	401/789-5735, 800/541-8896	UPS 110SE and UPS 370ci provide 110 and 370 volt-amps, UPS 110SE $299, UPS 370ci $499; several less sophisticated models available. PowerChute software for AppleShare servers, $99.

Finally, be aware that after several years, you'll need to replace your standby power supply's batteries, which can cost up to 30 percent of the supply's original price. You may want to investigate replacement costs before picking a unit.

Standby power supplies provide more complete protection than surge suppressors but are far less popular. One reason is their cost; another is that they provide only a brief reprieve from darkness. Still, if your power is as unreliable as mine, that reprieve can be priceless. The glow of a Mac screen in an otherwise darkened room is a heartening sight — especially if you haven't saved recently.

More Power Tips

The table "Power Protectors" lists some vendors of surge suppressors and standby power supplies. But neither device will help if your electrical wiring is faulty. Be sure your wall outlets' third-wire ground holes are connected to a good earth ground. (Check the point where the electrical service enters your house; you should find a copper rod driven into the ground with a heavy wire connect-

Company	Phone	Comments
CMS Enhancements	714/222-6000	UltraPower series provides 450–1500 volt-amps. UltraPower 800 and 1000 produce square wave output;others produce sine wave. $699–$2199.
Computer Accessories Corporation	619/457-5500, 800/582-2580	Proxima IPS 500+ fits under Mac II monitor and provides 400 volt-amps. $649.95.
Cuesta Systems Corporation	805/541-4160, 800/332-3440	DataSaver series provides 110–750 volt-amps. $495–$695.
Emerson Electric	714/380-1005	Accupower Micro UPS series provides 150–1400 volt-amps. $189–$998.
General Power Corporation	714/956-9321, 800/854-3469	Heavy-duty Unistar series provides 1000–10,000 volt-amps. $2795–$14,025.
Kensington Microware	212/475-5200, 800/535-4242	Power Backer series provides between 360 and 1200 volt-amps. $399–$1399.
Para Systems	214/446-7363, 800/238-7272	MM 1600SS provides 1600 volt-amps. $1999.

ing it to your wiring.) Also be sure that your hot and neutral lines are wired properly. You can check them yourself using an inexpensive *line checker* such as Radio Shack's catalog number 22-101. (American Power Conversion's standby supplies contain line-checking features.) To be extra sure, however, double-check with an electrician or your local utility company.

Also, avoid ground eliminators — those little adapters that let you plug a three-pronged power cord into the two-conductor outlets many older buildings have. Defeating the ground conductor makes the Mac more susceptible to power surges. Have an electrician install a properly grounded, three-conductor outlet.

The best way to protect equipment against lightning-induced power surges is to unplug the Mac and everything connected to it during a lightning storm. (Don't forget to unplug the modem from the telephone lines.) A lightning bolt is the ultimate surge; don't count on a surge suppressor to protect you from it.

In the end, one of the best ways to avoid losing work because of power problems is free. Simply follow the advice that Fred Parker, a power-supply veteran at Apple, passed along to me: Save often.

Summary:

✔ The most common types of power flaws are blackouts (power goes out completely), sags (wall outlet voltage drops below 105 volts), surges (incoming voltage increases dramatically for a brief period), and noise (degradation of the quality of power).

✔ Apple's power supplies are designed to provide a degree of protection against brownouts, sags, and surges for your Mac, but don't offer protection for other hardware you may have.

✔ The most popular and least expensive power-protection device is the surge suppressor, which reduces incoming surges to harmless voltage levels.

✔ When shopping for a surge suppressor, the two most important specifications to look for are the clamping voltage (the point at which the suppressor begins suppression) and the response time (the time it takes for the suppressor to close its electronic gate and prevent the surge from getting through).

✔ For protection against blackouts and sags, you can use a standby power supply, which contains batteries that provide from 5 to 30 minutes of power.

✔ An uninterruptible power supply (UPS) is one in which the computer equipment runs from the power supply's batteries, which are constantly being recharged.

Chapter 32
Digital Sound

In This Chapter:

✔ The roles digital audio plays in the Mac world.

✔ A look at how the Mac records and plays back sound.

✔ How to attach your Mac to a stereo system for better sound quality.

✔ Farallon Computing's MacRecorder: the most popular third-party recording hardware for the Mac.

✔ High-end audio applications: the Mac in recording studios.

✔ Information on a HyperCard stack that showcases the Mac's sound feaures.

Have you heard? Computers are transforming the way we record and listen to sound. More and more, music is stored not in fragile vinyl grooves but in bits and bytes on silvery compact discs (CDs). Scratches, clicks, pops, and skips are becoming relics of the past.

And if you've explored the Mac's Sound control panel, you've noticed that you can choose from several digitally recorded beep sounds: a simple beep, a clanking sound, a springy "boing" that reminds me of the suspension on my first car, or a monkey's squawk (which, Mac trivia buffs will be interested to learn, was actually created by a woman named Sandy Dobrowolsky, now a Claris employee). Compact discs and the Mac's monkey squawk may seem worlds apart, but the concepts behind them are similar.

 When you combine digital audio with a general-purpose computer like the Mac, suddenly the potential of digital sound goes beyond great-sounding Springsteen. The Mac's ability to record, manipulate, and play back sound opens doors to new applications in education, entertainment, music, business, and science.

In this chapter, I examine the roles digital audio plays in the Mac world and I spotlight some of the sound-oriented products available for the Mac. The sidebar "The Mac Sounds Off" explains how to modify your System file to add your own digitally recorded system beeps, and it reveals some sources for prerecorded sounds. And since the best way to appreciate the Mac's audio abilities is to hear them, I've created a HyperCard sound stack that aurally illustrates many of the concepts discussed here. Details on how to get the stack appear at the end of this chapter.

The Sound of Mac

Digital audio can play so many roles that it might help if I summarize each one before taking a closer look at just how digital sound is produced.

❖ Digital sound is used to teach concepts that are difficult to grasp through written words or pictures. What does a red-tailed hawk sound like? How are numbers pronounced in Spanish? What's the difference between *legato* and *staccato?* For explaining concepts like these, a sound is worth a thousand words.

❖ Digital sound enlivens games with realism that phony beeps and squawks can't match. In some arcade games, for example, you hear the screaming of fighter jets and the wash of helicopter blades. In Microsoft's Flight Simulator, you hear a digitized airplane engine and the skid of your landing gear.

The Mac Sounds Off

You can add to the Mac's repertoire of digital beep sounds by adding sound resources to your System file. Thousands of prerecorded sounds are available through online information services such as America Online and CompuServe, through user groups, and through public domain and shareware clearing-houses.

The MacRecorder's SoundEdit, Digidesign's Sound Designer II, and Passport Design's Alchemy and Sound Apprentice can save sound resources directly in the System file (or any other file, for that matter). You can also use SoundMover, a shareware utility by Riccardo Ettore, or Apple's ResEdit (versions 1.2 and later can even play sound resources).

Regardless of the program you use, be sure to make a backup copy of your System file in case something goes amiss during the modification process. After you've added a sound resource, use the Sound control panel to select it as the current system beep.

Using a variety of shareware system extensions (INITs), you can make your Mac sound off at other times, too. Two particularly noteworthy shareware sound INITs include SoundMaster (by Bruce Tomlin) and Chime (by Robert Flickinger; free). SoundMaster lets the Mac play sounds when you perform any of over a dozen tasks (such as inserting or ejecting a disk). Chime plays up to four separate sounds on the hour and at 15, 30, and 45 minutes past. **M**

❖ In music, digital sound plays three roles. On one level, it makes possible Brøderbund Software's remarkable Jam Session, whose digitally recorded instruments turn the Mac into a six-piece band that can make even novice musicians sound good (see Chapter 11). On another level, the Mac's sound features enable musicians to alter sounds played by digital sampling keyboards such as those made by Ensoniq, E-mu Systems, Roland, Kurzweil, and others. On still another level, some additional hardware can turn the Mac into a professional audio workstation that can record and play back sound with the fidelity of a compact disc.

❖ Digital sound can enliven business presentations and training software. It also plays a specialized role in a unique sales product, Magnum's TFLX, whose hardware and software turn the Macintosh into a sophisticated system for recording telephone messages and taking orders.

❖ Scientists and medical researchers use Mac sound products to analyze brain waves and study heart rhythms. And at Scotland Yard, some cutting-edge criminologists are using Macs to view and analyze voiceprints, which depict the characteristics of an individual's voice. Like fingerprints, no two are alike.

A Sampling of Technicalities

To understand how the Mac records and plays back sound, think of a movie. By taking 24 photographs per second, a movie camera captures a reasonably accurate *sample* of the action in front of it. When those samples are played back, the illusion of smooth motion is created.

Digital audio also samples motion — the moving air molecules that make up sounds. Vibrating objects — whether strings, saxophone reeds, or vocal chords — produce *sound waves*, variations in air pressure that travel outward from the sound source like the ripples from a stone dropped into a pond.

A digital audio recorder samples these sound waves thousands of times per second. Each sample is a digital image of the sound at a given instant (see the figure "Snapshots of Sound"). The samples, each recorded as a series of bits, are stored in memory and can be manipulated. Bits can be added or removed, their order can be altered, or their very values changed. Each modification alters the overall image of the sound wave, so when the samples are played back, you hear a different sound.

With movies, taking too few pictures per second results in jittery, unrealistic motion. With sound, taking too few samples per second results in a distorted recording that doesn't faithfully convey all the frequencies present in the original sound. The faster the *sampling rate*, the more accurate the recording, and the

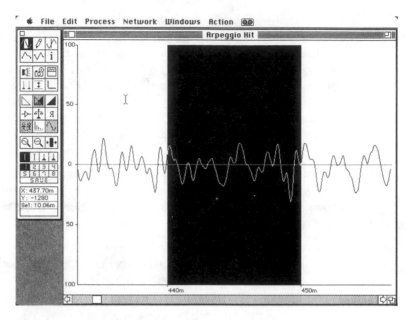

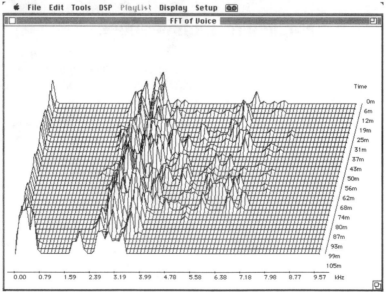

Snapshots of Sound

Sound-editing programs graphically display sampled sounds and let you edit them. At top, 10 milliseconds of a sampled piano arpeggio have been selected in Passport Design's Alchemy. At bottom, Digidesign's Sound Designer II depicts how a sound changes over time using a sound-analyzing technique called a fast Fourier transformation, or FFT.

better the recorder is able to capture the highest frequencies. Compact discs are recorded at a rate of 44,100 samples per second, or 44.1kHz. Without specialized sampling hardware, the Mac's maximum sampling rate is 22kHz — too slow for recording-studio quality, but fast enough to allow the Mac to sound at least as good as an ordinary table radio.

Another factor that influences digital sound quality is the *sampling resolution* — the number of bits assigned to each sample. These bits store information about the sample's *amplitude,* or loudness. The more bits assigned to each sample, the more accurately the recorder can store and recreate the original sound's variations in loudness. A compact disc player has a 16-bit sampling resolution, allowing it to reproduce thousands of distinct volume levels. The Mac has an 8-bit sampling resolution; it can store and re-create only 256 volume levels. When a given sample's amplitude lies between two levels, it's rounded to the nearest one. This rounding of amplitude information, called *quantization*, causes distortion.

Required Equipment

Before digitally recorded sound can be played back, the discrete bits of digital data generated during sampling must be translated back into continuously varying volume levels. This job is performed by a hardware component called a *digital-to-analog* converter. Because all Macs contain one, they can play digital sound without additional hardware. For better sound quality, however, you'll want to attach the Mac to a stereo system or external amplifier as shown in the figure "Wired for Sound" on the next page.

To record sound, the Mac needs an *analog-to-digital* converter, which measures the voltage levels coming from a microphone or other sound source and translates them into digital data. Such hardware is built into the Mac LC and IIsi, and will be standard equipment in future Macs.

Both the LC and the IIsi provide a three-conductor audio input jack that supplies power to the microphone, a sensitive electret condenser mic not much bigger than a large button. An adapter cable, available separately, lets you connect a stereo and other audio sources, and merges the left and right audio channels into a single channel.

In System 6.0.7 and later versions, the Mac's Sound Manager (the portion of the Toolbox that handles audio recording and playback) also offers a *compression* feature that decreases storage requirements (and fidelity) by assigning fewer bits to each sample. Called Macintosh Audio Compression and Expansion (MACE) scheme, it allows sound to be compressed by 3:1 or 6:1 ratios.

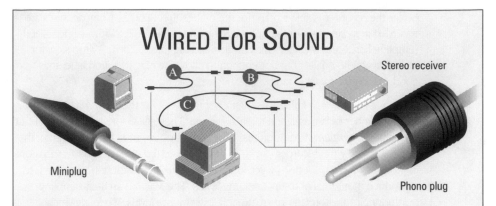

WIRED FOR SOUND

Stereo receiver

Miniplug

Phono plug

For better sound quality, connect a Mac to a stereo system. For monophonic Macs (the Classic, SE, LC, Plus, and earlier machines), one cable has a $\frac{1}{8}$-inch miniplug on the Mac end, and a phono plug (Radio Shack catalog number 42-2444) on the other end **(A)**. The other cable is a "Y" adapter with a phono plug on one end and two phono plugs (Radio Shack number 42-2435) on the other **(B)**. For stereo Macs (the Mac II, IIsi, IIx, IIcx, and SE/30), all you need is a cable with a $\frac{1}{8}$-inch stereo miniplug on the Mac end and two phono plugs (Radio Shack number 42-2475) on the other **(C)**. Important: Before turning your stereo on, turn its volume control all the way down and use the Mac's Sound Control Panel to turn the Mac's speaker volume all the way down. Then turn the stereo on and adjust its volume and the Mac's to a comfortable listening level.

System 6.0.7 also includes an improved Sound control panel that lets you record your own beep sounds, eliminating the tedium of using a separate utility to paste sound resources into the System file. When you click its Add button, a recording dialog box appears that lets you choose the desired recording settings and adjust the record volume (see the figure "Now Recording"). Apple also added support for sound resources to the Clipboard, so you can cut and paste sounds between applications that support them.

Although the input circuitry in the LC and IIsi support monophonic recording only, stereo recording is possible by combining the built-in mic with a Farallon Computing MacRecorder — the most popular third-party recording hardware for the Mac.

The MacRecorder

The MacRecorder hardware is a box slightly larger than a cigarette pack. Besides the analog-to-digital converter, it contains a filter that removes high frequencies that can't be accurately sampled at 22kHz. Completing the package are a small microphone, a volume control, and jacks for an external microphone, tape recorder, or other sound source.

Now Recording ►
System versions 6.0.7 and later include a standard record dialog box that appears when you click the Add button in the Sound control panel. Recording begins when you click the Record button, and its progress is indicated by the graph and seconds display below the speaker icon. When you've finished recording, you can click the Save button to name and save the sound.

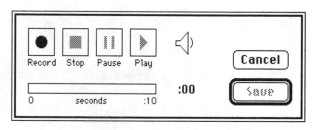

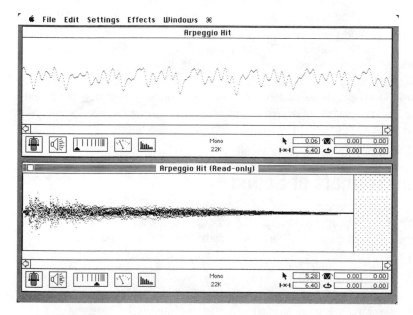

The MacRecorder software comprises several components: SoundEdit, a recording and editing application; Hyper-Sound, a HyperCard stack that lets you record and play back sounds from within HyperCard; and HyperSound Toolkit, a potpourri of Hyper-Card external commands (XCMDs) and external functions (XFCNs) that stack authors can use to give any stack digital

▲ Riding the Waveform

The graphic display of a sound is called its waveform. Here are two waveform displays of the same sound, displayed by SoundEdit (part of Farallon Computing's MacRecorder package). The bottom window shows the entire recording; the top shows a small portion of it.

recording features. You could use the HyperSound Toolkit to create an appointment stack that recorded spoken reminders and then played them back at a specified time.

The SoundEdit application is your primary link to the MacRecorder hardware. SoundEdit displays a recorded sound as a *waveform* (see the figure "Riding the Waveform"). You can zoom in on the waveform display to look at an individual *cycle* (one back-and-forth phase of the sound's vibration), or zoom out to see the entire recording. You can select part or all of the waveform and cut or copy it to the Clipboard to rearrange the notes in a musical passage or the words in a phrase. You can also modify the sound, adding reverb to simulate a concert hall, or filtering certain frequencies to improve the sound quality. You can even reverse the sound to make it play backwards.

The latest version of the MacRecorder also includes a system extension (an INIT) that lets you use the enhanced sound features in versions System 6.0.7

and later of the Mac's system software. With the MacRecorder hardware and driver software installed, your Mac acts as if it has the same sound hardware as a Mac LC or IIsi.

With two MacRecorders you can record in stereo. (In theory, you can record in stereo with one MacRecorder by recording each channel separately, but synchronizing the channels is difficult.) You can play back stereo sounds on any Mac with stereo playback features — the SE/30, II, IIsi, IIx, IIfx, or IIcx.

But be forewarned that digital sound devours memory and disk space. With a 22kHz sampling rate, one second of sound uses 22K of memory and the same amount of disk space (double that for stereo). A Mac with 2MB of memory has room for about 70 seconds of 22kHz audio. When you're willing to trade fidelity for longer recording times, SoundEdit lets you specify sampling rates of 11, 7, and 5kHz. On a 2MB Mac, these slower sampling rates provide recording times of 136, 204, and 273 seconds, respectively. SoundEdit also lets you use one of several compression ratios. Using the 8-to-1 compression ratio, a 2MB Mac can accommodate about 530 seconds of sound.

The Formats of Sound

Every program category has its standard file formats, and sound-editing software is no exception. Although the SoundEdit application has its own file format, it also supports two important standard formats: *SND resources* (also known as *sound* or *'snd'* resources) and *Audio Interchange File Format.*

If there's a sound you'd like to use as a system-error beep in a HyperCard stack, you must save it as an SND resource. Technically, two types of SND resources exist. *Format 1* resources are generally system beeps, while *Format 2* resources are used by HyperCard and other sound-playing applications. In the early days of digital Mac sound, the distinction was more important; you couldn't use Format 2 SND resources as system beeps. Beginning with System 6.0.2, however, Apple made the Mac's Sound Manager a bit less picky. With System 6.0.2 and later versions, you can use either format for system beeps.

The Audio Interchange File Format (commonly referred to as either AIFF or Audio IFF) lets one program open a digital recording created by another program. You'll find support for AIFF files in professionally oriented sound software such as Passport Designs's Alchemy and Digidesign's Sound Designer. AIFF is a preferred format for swapping files between such programs because it supports stereo recordings and 16-bit sampling resolution; SND resources can be stereophonic or monophonic, but they support only 8-bit resolution.

Sound at the High End

The MacRecorder and the microphone that accompanies the latest Macs aren't intended for professional audio applications. To reach the upper strata of Mac digital audio, you need more sophisticated hardware such as Digidesign's Audiomedia board, which is available for the SE/30 and Mac II family. Audiomedia contains a Motorola DSP56001 *digital signal processing* chip, a microprocessor designed for the data-shuffling demands of digital audio. (Steve Jobs's Next computer also contains a DSP56001).

The Audiomedia board allows the Mac to record and play back stereo CD-quality audio directly to and from a Mac's hard disk. Thus, sound length is limited only by available disk space. You still might feel rather limited, however: A one-minute monophonic recording uses 10MB of disk space; double that for stereo. Audiomedia also includes drivers that let you play back its recordings from within HyperCard as well as from MacroMind Director and other programs.

On the back of the Audiomedia board are a microphone jack and four RCA jacks, two of which are inputs that accept audio from a tape deck, compact disc player, or other sound source. Audiomedia can record from the RCA and microphone jacks simultaneously, allowing you to record a voice narration and background music in one step. The other two RCA jacks are outputs that connect to a stereo amplifier or mixer.

Audiomedia's software includes the Audiomedia application and a Hyper-Card stack called SoundAccess. The latter lets you record and play back Audiomedia recordings from within HyperCard and also install in your own stacks a external function (XFCN) called SoundPlay for recording and play-back. You can also use the Audiomedia board with MIDI sequencers that support digital audio recording and playback, such as Opcode's Studio Vision and Mark of the Unicorn's Digital Performer.

You use the Audiomedia application to record, alter, and play back recordings. Each recording, or *sound file*, appears in its own window (see the figure "In the Studio" on the next page). While recording, Audiomedia expertly shuttles incoming data from the Mac's memory to your hard disk — provided the hard disk has a 28ms or faster average access time. If the disk isn't fast enough, parts of the recording will be lost, and you'll need to try again with a slower sampling rate. (Audiomedia's manual includes a list of drives that meet its requirements.)

Audiomedia's editing features allow you to cut and paste portions of a recording and you can alter individual sound samples using a MacPaint-like pencil icon. To locate exact spots on the recording, there's a *scrub tool* that

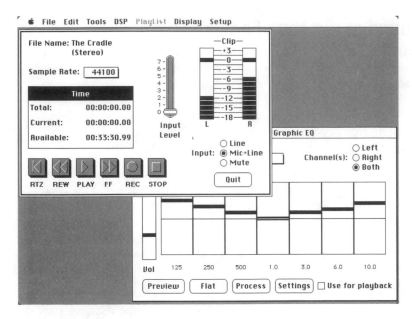

lets you slowly play the recording forwards and backwards — like rocking the reels of a reel-to-reel tape recorder back and forth.

The remarkable *playlist* editing feature lets you rearrange a recording — remove or rearrange words, cut or add verses to a song, or repeat a section — without changing the original sound file. You do so by selecting specific areas of the recording (such as a single verse), naming them, and then arranging those names in the playlist window. Just as a baseball manager can change the batting order by simply rearranging names on the lineup card, you can change how a recording plays back by rearranging names in its playlist window. You can create and save as many playlists as you like.

You can also mix two recordings or fade from one to the other. You can change a recording's tonal qualities using an on-screen graphic equalizer and hear each change as you make it. You can even change a recording's length without altering its pitch — handy if you have a 35-second music passage that has to fit a 30-second animation.

Tape Deck on a Disk

Another remarkable digital audio program from Digidesign is Deck, which works with an Audiomedia board to turn the Mac into a four-track digital stereo recorder. Deck's sole screen display is faithful to the multitrack recording metaphor, with volume meters that show sound levels, sliding faders that adjust recording and playback volumes, and transport controls that let you record, play back, fast forward and rewind (see the figure "Now On Deck"). If you've used conventional multitrack decks, you'll feel at home with most of what you see. And you'll be delighted with some of the differences, such as instantaneous rewinding.

▲ **In the Studio**
Audiomedia's record window (upper left) has a volume slider and dancing volume meters that let you adjust the input volume before recording. Familiar-looking "tape transport" controls let you record, rewind, fast-forward, and play back the recording. Audiomedia's on-screen graphic equalizer, which uses the DSP chip's processing power to change a recording's tonal qualities in real time, appears in the lower-right corner.

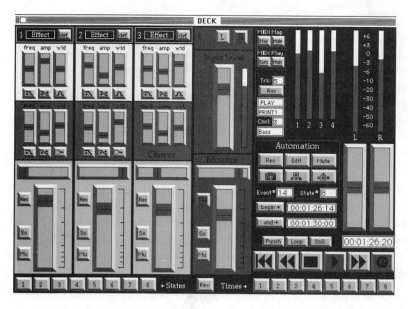

Recording a track with Deck involves selecting the desired track, adjusting the input volume to avoid clipping (which causes distorted sound), and then clicking the Record button. After you've recorded one track, you can record additional tracks. If you fill all four tracks and still need more, you can merge two or more tracks into one, freeing the others for reuse. This technique,

▲ Now On Deck

Digidesign's Deck turns the Mac into a multitrack digital audio recorder with automated mix-down features and the ability to import and play back MIDI sequences. Here, track 4 is being recorded while the remaining three tracks play back, and a chorus effect is being applied to track 3.

called *bouncing*, is often used with conventional multitrack decks, too. But bouncing tracks in the analog world degrades a recording's quality; not so with Deck.

Deck also exploits the digital signal processing features of the Audiomedia board to allow you to alter the sound of a track during playback. Several digital effects are supported, ranging from a digital equalizer, which lets you accentuate or attenuate certain frequencies, to a "stereoizer," which processes a monophonic recording to simulate stereo.

Another big difference between Deck and conventional recorders is that Deck can import and play back a MIDI composition created using sequencer software (described in Chapter 11). To include a MIDI sequence in a Deck recording, you save the sequence as a standard MIDI file, and then import it into Deck. Thereafter, when you play back your audio recording, Deck also plays the sequence, thereby controlling any MIDI instruments attached to your Mac. A musician might use this feature to combine sequenced instrumentals with vocals or acoustic instrumentals. A multimedia producer might use it to add voice narration to an instrumental sound track.

Deck reaches out to the MIDI world in another way: It lets you assign, or *map*, one or more of Deck's on-screen faders to the physical sliders on a MIDI *fader box* such as J.L. Cooper Electronics' FaderMaster. (A fader box contains slider knobs that transmit MIDI data when you move them.) With this feature, you can control the playback volume of one or more tracks by moving the sliders on the fader box instead of using Deck's on-screen sliders.

The final step in any recording session is the *mix-down*, which involves adjusting the playback volume of each track while recording in standard two-track stereo on a second deck. As the multitrack recording plays back, a recording engineer will often adjust the volume of certain tracks, change their apparent location in the left-right stereo spread, and make other fine adjustments to arrive at the best-sounding final product. Twiddling all those knobs while a piece plays back requires some dexterity, and twiddling them in the exact same way each time is all but impossible. For these reasons, professional recording equipment often provides automated mix-down features that "remember" the adjustments the engineer makes so the final mix can be recreated if needed.

Deck brings automated mix-down to the desktop. You can save and restore up to 200 different combinations of fader and effects settings. During playback, Deck's faders and other on-screen knobs move to the appropriate positions by themselves. Automation files are stored separately from the recording itself, allowing you to apply different automation files to a single recording to see which you prefer.

Deck provides some features that enable it to synchronize its playback to industry standard time-code signals such as SMPTE, but they're limited compared to the sync features in Digidesign's Sound Designer II software. Musicians working with film and video soundtracks will want to verify that Deck's limited sync features can meet their needs.

It's also worth noting that you can move recording files between Deck and Digidesign's Audiomedia and Sound Designer II software. Deck can also import AIFF files.

Sound at the Summit

At the summit of the Macintosh digital audio world, you'll find products such as Digidesign's Sound Tools system, which you can use to record and edit CD-quality digital audio, synchronize to motion picture and videotape sound tracks, and use digital audio tape (DAT) to create masters that you send to a compact disc manufacturer for pressing. It's a professional-quality digital audio recording and mastering system — and it runs on a computer that smiles when you switch it on.

Sound Tools comprises a NuBus board called Sound Accelerator, which holds the DSP chip and its support circuitry; and an external box called Pro I/O, which contains the analog-to-digital converter, circuitry for synchronizing audio to video, and Apogee anti-alias filters to improve sound quality. (Apogee filters are popular in the professional digital audio world.) Composer Philip Glass recently used the Sound Tools system to record a solo piano album for CBS Masterworks records.

The Sound Tools software — called Sound Designer II — graphically displays digital recordings and lets you alter them. Sound Designer II is similar to, but more sophisticated than, the Audiomedia software. With Sound Designer II, you can, for example, alter a recording's pitch without changing its tempo, or alter its tempo without changing its pitch.

Digidesign and Prosonus (a leading developer of sampled sounds for music samplers) have collaborated on a CD-ROM packed full of production music and sound effects designed for audio and multimedia productions. Called Clip Tunes, it contains 350MB of music in a variety of styles and 250MB of sound effects, all in Sound Designer II format.

Sampling Samplers

Just as digital sound has made its mark in the Mac world, it has also significantly influenced the music industry. Musicians are embracing a new generation of keyboards called *samplers*. Like a Mac equipped with a MacRecorder, a sampler digitally records and plays back sound. But with a sampler, you can play the sound at different pitches simply by pressing different keys. Record just one pitch of a given instrument, and you can instantly "play" that instrument from the sampler's keyboard.

Actually, most samples sound artificial when transposed too high or too low. Therefore, most sampling keyboards divide the range of notes into multiple samples, each of which plays a range of only an octave or so. This technique, called *multisampling*, avoids having to transpose a sample too high or low.

Programs like Sound Designer II let you simultaneously view and alter a sampler's sounds. This capability is especially useful for setting a *loop point*, a portion of a sample that repeats as long as a key is pressed. Because few samplers display waveforms graphically, it's difficult to find the perfect loop point using a sampler's editing commands. When you can see the waveform, however, setting loop points is far easier.

Another popular sample-editing program is Passport Design's Alchemy, which performs much of the same magic as Sound Designer II. One of Alchemy's primary strengths is its ability to change the sampling rate of a recorded sound. This *resampling* capability allows you to transfer sounds between samplers that use different rates. Musicians can store all their sound samples on the Mac and use Alchemy to shuttle them between samplers as needed for more versatility. (Digidesign's Sound Designer Universal also has this capability.)

Now Hear This

There's no better way to learn about digital audio concepts than to hear them. I've created a HyperCard stack that showcases the Mac's sound features, contains examples of various sampling rates and compression ratios, and spotlights some sound utilities. Jim Heid's Sound Stack costs $12.95 including shipping in the United States and Canada. For ordering information, see the coupon at the back of this book.

Incidentally, if you subscribe to America Online, you can download an earlier version of the stack that doesn't cover Apple's latest Macs. I've also encouraged its distribution through user groups, so you can probably copy it from someone else. But be advised: even in compressed form, the stack occupies an entire 800K floppy disk and will take a considerable amount of time to download.

And that illustrates a problem: At present, digital audio requires too much memory and disk space to be practical for many applications that could benefit from it. A talking tutorial that explains a program's features might be valuable, but would you be willing to donate half your hard disk to it?

Despite the storage crunch, sound is working its way into more types of applications. Several electronic mail packages let you send voice-mail messages to other users on a network. The latest versions of Ashton-Tate's FullWrite and FullImpact let you annotate documents with spoken comments. SecondGLANCE's SoundTack adds annotation features to QuarkXpress. And Information Presentation Technologies' VoiceFont lets you add sound to virtually any document. VoiceFont adds a "font" named Voice to a program's Font menu: Choose the Voice font's name, and a dialog box appears allowing you to record.

> **_66 Soon, you might protect sensitive documents with a password utility that recognizes only your voiceprint. 99_**

Sound is potentially useful for electronic mail, but I question its value for document annotation. For one thing, many people feel self-conscious about speaking into a microphone. For another, sounds require more time to transmit over a network than does text, and they devour disk space and memory. Then there are all the Macs out there without sound recording features. Companies that want to standardize on sound-based document annotation will need to buy a lot of MacRecorders. And finally, opening and playing back recorded annotations requires more effort than simply reading text.

In the future, we're likely to see even more sophisticated applications of digital sound. Soon, you might protect sensitive documents with a password utility that recognizes only your voiceprint. Or you might enjoy stereo sound effects in your quest to save the galaxy.

In other words, the Mac's audio features are impressive now, but we haven't heard anything yet.

Summary:

✔ The Mac's ability to record, manipulate, and play back sounds has opened doors to new applications in education, entertainment, music, business, and science.

✔ Digital audio can be used to teach concepts that are difficult to grasp with written words or pictures; to enliven games with realistic sounds; to turn the Mac into a six-piece band; and to enliven business presentations or training software.

✔ To record audio digitally, thousands of samples must be taken per second. Compact discs use a 44.1kHz sampling rate; the Mac's maximum sampling rate is 22kHz.

✔ Before digitally recorded sound can be played back, the digital data generated during sampling must be translated by a hardware device called a digital-to-analog converter.

✔ To record sound, the Mac needs an analog-to-digital converter, which measures the voltage levels coming from a sound source and translates them into digital data.

✔ Farallon Computing's MacRecorder contains an analog-to-digital converter and a filter that removes high frequencies that can't be accurately sampled at 22kHz.

Chapter 33
Programming

In This Chapter:

✔ What is programming?

✔ An introduction to low- and high-level programming languages.

✔ A look at the processes involved in programming.

✔ Using debugger programs to find errors in your program.

✔ Programming the Mac versus programming other computers.

✔ Where to learn more about programming.

✔ A hands-on HyperCard programming tutorial.

Good afternoon, Mr. Phelps. Your mission, should you decide to accept it, is to program a computer. You must assemble a series of instructions in perfect sequence — with no typographical errors — that perform their intended task exactly as planned. Fail on any one of these counts, and your mission will fail. Good luck. This chapter will self-destruct in about 2500 words.

Mission impossible? Not at all. It's done every day (although, as far as I know, not by Peter Graves). Programming is tricky, but without it, the Mac wouldn't exist.

Programming on the Mac can be a challenging, enjoyable, and yes, frustrating, experience. Macintosh programming is also far too complex to explain in one chapter, much less in one book. In this chapter, I'll introduce the concepts involved and show how Mac programming differs from that of other computers. I'll also spotlight some popular programming languages plus some products that simplify the process. Want to try writing a short program in HyperCard? You'll find instructions in the sidebar "A HyperCard Programming Project".

A HyperCard Programming Project

HyperCard includes a built-in programming language called HyperTalk. In this introduction to HyperTalk programming — or scripting, as it's called in the HyperCard world — you'll add a button to your Home stack that lets you calculate a car's gas mileage.

To try this example, you must set HyperCard's user level to Scripting. For details, see the sidebar "Creating a HyperCard Animation" in Chapter 12.

Phase 1: Create the Button

Here's how to create the button that, when clicked, will run your program. From the Objects menu, choose New Button. One (named New Button) then appears in the middle of the first card in the Home stack. Drag the new button to a blank area of the card.

Next, double-click on the new button to display the Button Info dialog box. Select the following options, but don't click OK yet: Show Name, Auto Hilite, and Rectangle. In the Button Name text box, type Gas Mileage.

Phase 2: Type the Script

You're ready to type the program, or script.

1. Click on the Script button.

HyperCard's script editor window appears, containing two lines: on MouseUp and end MouseUp. Notice that the insertion point is between the two lines; your script goes there.

2. Type the text shown in Script 1. (Note the ¬ [called a soft-return symbol] that appears at the end of several lines. If a statement is too long to fit on one line, put this symbol [type Option-Return] where you want the line to break so that HyperCard knows the statement continues on the next line.)

Proofread your work as you go; when you're finished, click OK or press the Enter key.

Phase 3: Try It

To try the program, choose the Browse tool (the pointing finger) from the Tools menu, then click on the Gas Mileage button. If all goes well, dialog boxes appear asking how many miles you drove and how many gallons of gas you used. Finally, a dialog box appears telling you your gas mileage.

If you got an error message beginning "Can't ☞

Script 1

```
on mouseUp
  ask "How many miles did you drive?"
  if It is empty then exit mouseUp else put It into ¬
      milesDriven
  ask "How many gallons did you use?"
  if It is empty then exit mouseUp else put It into ¬
      gallonsUsed
  divide milesDriven by gallonsUsed
  put milesDriven into gasMileage
  answer "Your car got" && gasMileage && "miles¬
      per gallon."
end mouseUp
```

understand," your script may contain some typographical errors. To display the script, press Command-Option while clicking on the Gas Mileage button.

Phase 4: Trap those Errors

A good program anticipates errors and traps them before they cause problems. This program already does some error trapping — the If...then statements check to see if you left a dialog box blank and stop the program if you did. But what if you type letters in the box instead of numbers? Try it, and you'll receive an error message when the script tries to divide the letters.

The solution is to scan each dialog box to make sure it contains only numbers. The code in Script 2 does just that. Insert those lines just before the line in Script 1 that asks how many gallons you used. Then copy all inserted lines (select them and press Command-C) and paste them (using Command-V) just before the line reading "divide milesDriven by gallonsUsed." Next, in the newly pasted section, change the two occurrences of milesDriven to gallonsUsed. Finally, try the program

again and type some letters to see the error trapping in action.

The error-trapping routine works by first determining how many characters you typed, and then examining each character in turn to verify that it's a number. If it encounters a character that isn't a number, it displays the error message.

Important Concepts

This script is simple, but it illustrates several important programming concepts:

❖ *Input/output statements* (ask and answer) to interact with a user.

❖ *Variables* (milesDriven and gallonsUsed), which are named storage places in memory.

❖ A *math operator* (divide) to perform math on values you enter.

❖ *Conditional statements* (if...then) to perform tests and act on the results.

❖ A *looping structure* (repeat...end repeat) to perform a task a given number of times. **M**

Script 2

```
Repeat with count = 1 to the length of milesDriven
    put the charToNum of char count of milesDriven¬
        into temp
    if temp <48 or temp >57 then
        answer "Sorry, you must enter numbers only."
        exit mouseUp
    end if
end repeat
```

BASIC Gas Mileage

This BASIC program, written in Microsoft's QuickBASIC, calculates a car's gas mileage. The top window shows the program's source code; the bottom one shows its output. As with many programming products, QuickBASIC displays keywords in bold. This isn't a Mac-like program, since it doesn't use dialog boxes for interacting with a user.

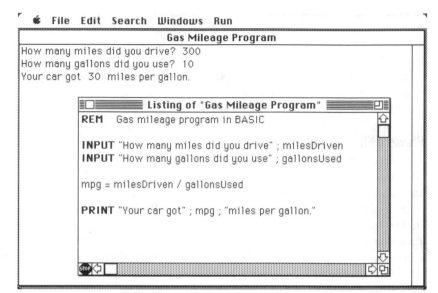

What is Programming?

Programming involves thinking about a problem, devising a list of steps for solving the problem, then supplying those steps to the computer in a form it understands. For example, let's consider the problem of calculating a car's gas mileage. First, let's list the steps needed to solve the problem:

❖ Find out how many miles were driven.

❖ Find out how many gallons of gas were used.

❖ Divide the number of miles driven by the amount of gas used.

❖ Record the answer.

Why can't you type those steps into the Mac and have a program? Because human languages are ambiguous. Consider the fourth step above: record the answer. Should the Mac send the answer to the screen? To a printer? Should it record the answer on disk? Or on a tape recorder? In human languages, a word can have many meanings. We pick the correct meaning (usually) when we hear or read the word in context.

Today's computers can't decipher a word's meaning from its context. That's one reason why the ultimate word processor — one that responds to dictation — doesn't yet exist.

Languages to Program By

You can't program the Mac in English, but you can use a reasonable facsimile — a *programming language*. These languages use vocabularies of English-like words, called *keywords*, combined with symbols for representing math instructions and other functions. To create a program, you assemble the keywords and symbols according to the rules, or syntax, of the language you're using. The figure "BASIC Gas Mileage" shows what our gas mileage problem looks like in *BASIC*, a popular beginner's language.

Just as human languages have standard parts of speech — nouns, verbs, adjectives, and so on — computer languages provide different categories of keywords for controlling the computer and processing information (see the table "Keyword Categories"). The keywords themselves, their exact spelling, and the ways they're combined are three factors that make each language different. The figure "Three Ways to Count" illustrates this point by showing, in three languages, a simple program that counts from one to ten.

A variety of computer languages have evolved over the decades. Many even have their own dialects, variations in syntax that programmers must keep in mind if they program for a variety of machines. Many beginners prefer BASIC because it's more like English; its syntax isn't as rigid as that of other languages. But this flexibility can lead to sloppy programs that are difficult to read and understand. Programming pros use more *structured* languages such as *Pascal* and *C*. Both

Keyword Categories

Category	Purpose	Example
assignment	assigns a value to a variable	NewYearsDay = "January 1"

conditional	tests for conditions and responds accordingly	IF cold THEN
		    wear overcoat
		ELSE
		    wear T-shirt

input/output	gets entries and displays results	INPUT "What's your sign?" PRINT "Buzz off, creep."
logical	tests relationship between two or more entities	IF lunchtime AND hungry THEN eat
looping	performs a task until a certain condition is met	WHILE plate contains food take a bite
relational	tests relationship between two entities	IF myPay < yourPay THEN me = "jealous"

Three Ways to Count

This is one program — it counts from one to ten in three languages: BASIC (top), C (middle), and Pascal (bottom). Note the differences in the keywords themselves, in their spelling, and in how they're arranged. The more rigidly structured C and Pascal require certain statements at the beginning of the program to set aside memory and control the compiler. This program also illustrates the concept of looping, executing a given set of statements repeatedly. The statements within the loop are indented to set them off from the rest of the program.

```basic
FOR count = 1 TO 10
    PRINT "This is number" ; count
NEXT count
```

```c
#include <stdio.h>

main()
{
int count;
for (count = 1; count < 11 ; count++ ) {
    printf("This is number %d\n", count);
    }
}
```

```pascal
program CountToTen;
  var
    count : integer ;

begin
  count := 0;
  for count := 1 to 10 do
    writeln('This is number', count);
end.
```

require more rigid syntax than BASIC, but they are better suited to creating legible, well-organized programs. That's important, because the person who modifies a program a year after it's written may not be the same person who wrote it.

Another difference between languages is the amount of programming required to perform certain tasks. *High-level* languages like Pascal and BASIC look most like human languages and let you perform complex tasks — such as reading something from a disk file — with relatively few lines of code. To the uninitiated, *low-level* languages such as *assembly* look like gibberish. More to the point, they require an intimate knowledge of the Mac's memory and microprocessor, and often require dozens of lines of code to perform even simple tasks. Some languages, such as C, straddle the fence between high-level and low-level. With C, you're not intimately involved with the Mac's memory and microprocessor, but you're very close friends.

Why use low-level languages if doing so means more work? Because the programs they create generally run faster than those created by high-level languages, and they often require less memory.

The Programming Process

The process begins with brainstorming, which might involve drawing a flowchart, a graphic blueprint that illustrates the components of the program and how it will work (see the figure "Follow the Flowchart").

After brainstorming, you're ready to write your program's instructions — its *source code* — using a *text editor*. These cousins to word processors provide specialized features designed for programming. For example, programmers indent certain program lines to indicate their relationship to the lines around them (see the figure "Three Ways to Count"). Lines nested within a loop, a portion of a program whose instructions repeat a certain number of times, are indented to allow someone reading the program to quickly identify them as instructions that repeat. Text editors provide formatting features that make these indents easier to create and adjust. The text editors built into products such as Symantec's Think Pascal and Microsoft QuickBASIC automatically indent lines and format keywords in boldface so they stand out.

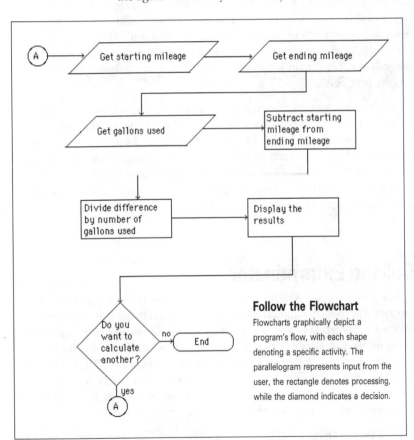

Follow the Flowchart

Flowcharts graphically depict a program's flow, with each shape denoting a specific activity. The parallelogram represents input from the user, the rectangle denotes processing, while the diamond indicates a decision.

After you've typed your source code, you'll be eager to test your program to see if it works. Here's where you'll encounter the most significant difference between programming packages: whether they use an *interpreter* or a *compiler* to translate your program into the instructions the Mac's microprocessor needs.

An interpreter translates source code on the fly — one line, or *statement*, at a time — as a program runs. To use your program, you must start the interpreter, open the program, and then tell the interpreter to run the program.

A compiler translates the source code into *machine code* — the internal language used by the Mac's microprocessor. From there, a component called a *linker* processes the machine code to create an *application file*.

A compiler's strength is its ability to create a complete application that you (or anyone) can start from the Finder — something an interpreter can't do. In addition to producing stand-alone applications, most compilers can also produce desk accessories (whose internal structures differ from application files') and other types of program code, such as HyperCard external commands (XCMDs) and external functions (XFCNs). And compiled programs generally run faster than interpreted ones, since that on-the-fly translation process isn't needed.

Another drawback of interpreters is that anyone who wants to run an interpreted program will also need a copy of the interpreter. But interpreters have their strengths as well. Because they translate and run a program one statement at a time, you can make changes in a program *listing* (the source code that comprises the program) and then immediately run the program to see the results. Compilers generally don't offer this start-and-stop programming convenience, although some, such as Think C and Think Pascal, come close.

Call the Exterminator

Few programs run perfectly the first time. It is more likely that your program will contain some errors, known as *bugs*. Perhaps you will omit a keyword or forget to type a symbol. With low-level languages, bugs can result if you handle the Macintosh's processor or memory carelessly (such as changing or moving information vital to the Mac's operation). These are only a few of the types of bugs that can surface; you might also create a program that performs calculations incorrectly (bad news if you are writing accounting software) or whose steps simply aren't in the proper sequence.

Most programming products provide *debugging* features to help you catch bugs. Some products offer *source-level* debuggers, which let you run your program one line at a time (see the figure "Stepping through Software").

A more advanced level of debugging involves watching how each machine-language instruction affects memory and the Mac's microprocessor. Think

Stepping through Software

A source-level debugger lets you run your program one step at a time and watch the results of each instruction. In Think Pascal, a pointing finger denotes the line that will execute next. If a syntax error is found, the pointing finger turns into a "thumbs down" icon and a dialog box appears describing the nature of the error. The Pascal code in this window is part of an application's main event loop.

```
 ⌘  File   Edit   Search   Project   Run   Debug   Windows

     🐞   Semicolon (;) or END expected after the previous statement.

      begin
        SetGrowZone(@MyGrowZone);
        OpenWindow('Clipboard', Null, 0, ClipBdWindow, ClipBdRect, wClipBd);
        OpenFile(FALSE)

        repeat
          UpdateClipBd(FALSE);
          SystemTask;
          HandleCursor;
          if GetNextEvent(EveryEvent, Event) then
            case Event.what of
              MouseDown:
                HandleMouse;
              KeyDown, AutoKey:
                HandleKey;
              ActivateEvt:
                HandleActivate;
              UpdateEvt:
                HandleUpdate;
              otherwise
            end
        until Done;
```

Pascal is one product that offers this *machine-level* debugging. Many advanced programmers also swear by separate debuggers such as ICOM Simulations' TMON, Jasik Designs' The Debugger, or Apple's MacsBug. Generally, only advanced programmers who are writing complex programs need to descend to this nitty-gritty debugging level.

Programming the Macintosh Way

Programming on the Macintosh differs from programming on most other computers. With most computers, a programmer must spend a lot of time designing the program's user interface — the way it interacts with the users. Programs for the Mac use standard user-interface elements — pull-down menus, dialog boxes, windows, and so on.

When programming the Mac, you don't have to design user interface elements, but you do have to know how to create and use the elements the Mac provides. That means becoming familiar with the Mac's *Toolbox*, a library of small, specialized snippets of software, often called *routines*.

The Mac's Toolbox routines are stored in the Mac's read-only memory (ROM) chips and in the System file, and are grouped into categories called *managers*. The Menu Manager, for example, contains routines that create, manipulate, and dispose of menus, while the Dialog Manager creates, manipulates, and disposes of dialog boxes and alert messages. Mac programmers use the Toolbox routines to create windows, menus, dialog boxes, and other user-interface elements.

Another concept that often trips up budding Mac programmers is the fact that Mac programs are *event driven*. A Mac program doesn't say to a user, "These are the things you're allowed to do now. Don't try to do anything else." Instead, it says, "I'm ready for whatever you might do. Go ahead, move my mouse. Click its button. Press a key. I can handle it." A Macintosh program is always ready to respond to anything.

But this flexible operating style means more work for programmers, and if you're used to programming other machines, it means rethinking some basic concepts of program design. A Mac program spends most of its time in an *event loop*, essentially running in circles, waiting for something to happen. When an event occurs, the program must determine what kind of event it is — a *mouse-down event*, a *keyboard event*, or another type of event — and then respond appropriately.

Yet another unique Mac programming concept is that of *resources*. In Mac programs, elements such as menus, dialog boxes, and text messages are stored separately from the program code, and they're called into use as needed by

A Beginning Programmer's Toolkit

So you want to learn to program. The first thing you'll have to do is choose a language. Start with Pascal, not because it's the best or easiest to learn, but because Apple's official technical manuals for the Toolbox — the *Inside Macintosh* series from Addison-Wesley Publishing Company (1985–1991) — use Pascal in their examples and instructions. If you end up programming in a different language, your familiarity with Pascal won't be wasted.

A great way to learn Pascal is to use Just Enough Pascal, a disk-and-book tutorial that you use with Think Pascal. In Just Enough Pascal, you build a Mac program step by step, pasting in new sections of code as you learn what they do. It's an excellent way to learn Pascal and to learn how to use Think Pascal.

You might also try a code-generating program such as Smethers/Barnes' Prototyper or Bowers Development's AppMaker. These programs let you click and drag to create menus, dialog boxes, and other user-interface elements. Choose a command, and the program generates the Pascal or C source code that

you'd otherwise have to type yourself. Both Prototyper and AppMaker can generate code for Think C and Pascal, and for the C and Pascal compilers that run under Apple's Macintosh Programming Workshop (MPW), a heavy-duty programming environment that Apple and many large software firms use.

If pecking out programming statements seems too daunting, consider starting out with a product such as Mainstay's V.I.P. or Maxem's Cause. With V.I.P. (short for visual interactive programming), you program by drawing a flowchart — interconnecting icons representing keywords and program functions. You can create a stand-alone V.I.P. application by using Translator to Think C, Mainstay's code-generation utility that turn V.I.P. programs into C code. With Cause, you create programs by drawing the windows and reports used for entering and viewing data and then specifying how they interact. Neither VIP nor Cause has what it takes to create and maintain a major-league program like Microsoft Word or MacDraw, but either is up to handling small programming tasks. And both are great ☞

the Mac's Resource Manager. This separation of code and resources allows programmers to create foreign-language versions of their software by editing the appropriate resources, without changing the code. For example, you might edit the menu resource to list choices in Spanish or French without having to change the code that tells the Mac when to display that menu. Indeed, resources are so easy to alter that even nonprogrammers can edit them using Apple's ResEdit resource-editing utility, available through user groups and communications services. You can also get ResEdit from the Apple Programmer's and Developer's Association (APDA).

As you learn to program the Mac, prepare to be frustrated. Grappling with Toolbox concepts, event loops, and resources can be taxing for those unfamiliar with the peculiarities of Macintosh programming. Fortunately, you don't have to start from square one. You can take advantage of the many sources of help available (see "A Beginning Programmer's Toolkit"). And don't try to do too much too soon. You wouldn't try to write a novel in a language you had just learned to speak; similarly, you shouldn't make your first programming project a complex one. Start small and master one concept at a time.

But first, turn the page before this chapter self-destructs. And good luck.

---

ways to hone your stepwise programming skills without doing a lot of typing.

And you'll need reading material. Volumes I through VI of *Inside Macintosh* are the standard reference bibles for the Mac's Toolbox. Apple's Tech Notes series are invaluable supplements to Inside Macintosh; they're available from the Apple Programmer's and Devel-oper's Association (800/ 282-2732). If you're new to Pascal, *Oh! Pascal!* by Doug Cooper and Michael Clancy (W.W. Norton, 1985) is an excellent introduction to the language.

If you're familiar with Pascal or another language but you're new to Mac programming, Stephen Chernicoff's four-volume set, *Macintosh Revealed* (Howard Sams, volumes 1–2, 1987; volume 3, 1989; volume 4, 1990), will get you up to speed. Scott Knaster's *How to Write Macintosh Software* (Howard Sams, 1988) and his *Macintosh Programming Secrets* (Addison-Wesley, 1988) will help, too. A first-rate guide to learning Think C is *Macintosh Programming Primer* by Dave Mark and

Cartwright Reed (Addison-Wesley, 1989; a second volume was published in 1990). An excellent Pascal version of the Mark and Reed book is available from Addison-Wesley. Addison-Wesley's Macintosh Inside Out series contains several excellent Mac programming books. And Apple's own *Programmer's Introduction to the Macintosh* is a superb primer for programmers who are new to the Mac.

Another excellent source of help and guidance is America Online or CompuServe. CompuServe's APPDEV and MACPRO forums contain source code for hundreds of programs that you can take apart and modify, as does America Online's MacDeveloper forum, which also has online "classes" in Pascal and C. Symantec also has a CompuServe forum for Think C and Pascal users (type GO THINK at any ! prompt). Also consider a subscription to MacTutor (P.O. Box 400, Placentia, CA 92670), a monthly Mac programming journal that covers all popular languages. **M**

Summary:

✔ Programming involves thinking about a problem, devising a list of steps for solving the problem, then supplying those steps to the computer in a form it understands.

✔ You can't program the Mac in English, but you can use a programming language, which uses English-like words called keywords to represent instructions and other functions.

✔ Many beginning programmers prefer learning with a beginner's language such as BASIC, while professionals use more structured languages such as Pascal and C.

✔ The three processes involved in creating a program include brainstorming, writing the instructions, and testing the program.

✔ Errors contained in a program are known as bugs, and can be caught using a programming product's debugging features.

✔ Programming on the Macintosh differs from programming on other computers in that the programmer need not design a user interface — the Mac already has one. Mac programs are also considered to be event driven (always ready to respond to any action) unlike programs on other computers, which pften restrict your available options.

Section Three
EXPANDING THE MAC

MACWORLD

Chapter 34
Upgrading

Buying into the Mac world is like boarding a moving train. You stand alongside the tracks, waiting until the right model comes along, then you time your leap and hold on as money flutters from your pockets. Whew — you made it.

But where are you heading? Toward a dead-end spur? Is a new model going to pass as you settle into your seat? And if this train can't take you to your destination, will you be able to transfer to one that can?

Every Mac owner has faced worries like these at one time or another — most likely in 1990, when Apple turned into Grand Central Station and released four new Macs while discontinuing another four. And Apple's System 7.0 software further complicates matters. Will your upgrade be compatible with all of System 7.0's features? Should you sell your old machine and buy a new one?

These aren't easy questions to answer, but one thing is certain: an old Mac may not be the newest or fastest train on the tracks, but it can still take many people where they want to go. (And it sure beats walking.) But more to the point, you can upgrade an old Mac to give it most, if not all, of the features in Apple's current offerings. And if you do have one of the newest Macs, hardware upgrades can make a good thing even better. In this chapter, I'll outline the most common upgrade options available for old and new Macs, with the goal of helping you map out an upgrade path that makes the most of your Mac and your money.

Assessing Your Hardware Options

Before you can devise an upgrade strategy, it helps to know what your options are. Hardware upgrades fall into two broad categories: ones that make your Mac faster, and ones that add new features such as color or additional storage. The most common upgrades within these categories (which often overlap) include:

❖ *Memory* More memory helps programs run faster and enables MultiFinder and System 7.0 to run more of them at once. More memory also lets you create larger documents with programs that keep entire documents in memory instead of swapping between memory and disk. (Examples include drawing programs such as MacDraw II, music sequencers such as Mark of the Unicorn's Performer, and most spreadsheet and integrated packages such as Microsoft's Excel and Works.) Memory prices have plummeted in recent years; at this writing, several mail-order retailers offer 4MB upgrades for a few hundred dollars, and some include an installation video and technical support. A 4MB upgrade consists of four 1MB single in-line memory modules, or SIMMs — small, plug-in boards, each containing eight memory chips (see the table "Memory Details").

❖ *Hard disks* With its vast storage capacity and swift speed, a hard disk is the most important upgrade you can buy. With one, your Mac will start programs and open documents far more quickly, and you'll be able to keep all your files in one place instead of swapping and waiting for slow floppy disks. Hard disks are cheap, too, with external units starting at less than $300. If you don't already have one, get one — then back it up often.

❖ *Accelerator boards and CPU upgrades* These silicon brain transplants replace your Mac's central processing unit (CPU) with a faster, flashier one. Accelerators for the Mac Plus, SE, and Classic usually replace those machines' 68000 CPU with a 68020 or 68030 — the CPUs that drive Apple's Mac LC and II series, respectively. (The original Mac II used a 68020 CPU.) Accelerators for the Mac II family replace the CPU with one that runs at a faster *clock rate*, and therefore allows your Mac to do more in less time. What's the difference between an accelerator and a CPU upgrade? Accelerator boards often include sockets for memory; memory installed there can run faster than memory installed on your Mac's logic board. CPU upgrades, on the other hand, simply replace the CPU, and thus, don't provide the same degree of performance enhancement. Costs range from several hundred dollars for an SE or Plus CPU upgrade to several thousand for a II-family accelerator.

❖ *Logic board upgrades* This upgrade involves an Apple dealer replacing your machine's logic board with a different one. Logic board upgrades are restricted to models that have cousins in the same basic case — you can upgrade a 128K and 512K Mac to a Plus; an SE to an SE/30; a IIcx to a IIci; and a II and IIx to a

IIfx (see the table "The Official Upgrade Path"). Logic board upgrades generally cost more than accelerators, but they have a significant advantage: All logic board upgrades either include or require the purchase of new read-only memory (ROM) chips, which contain some of the Mac's fundamental system software. When the ROM upgrade is sold separately from the logic board

Memory Details

Model	Total Memory	Configuration	Comments
Classic	1MB	logic board memory	150ns or faster chips required
	2MB	as above plus 1MB Memory Expansion Card with SIMM sockets empty	
	2.5MB	as above except 2 256K SIMMs	
	4MB	as above except 2 1MB SIMMs	
Plus, SE	1MB	4 256K SIMMs	150ns or faster chips required
	2MB	2 1MB SIMMs	
	2.5MB	2 256K, 2 1MB SIMMs	
	4MB	4 1MB SIMMs	
LC	2MB	logic board memory; SIMM Bank B empty	100ns or faster chips required
	4MB	as above except 4 1MB SIMMs in Bank B	
II, IIx, IIcx, IIci, SE/30	1MB	4 256K SIMMs in Bank A; Bank B empty	120ns or faster chips required (80ns for IIci); for best performance from IIci, put larger-capacity SIMMs in Bank B
	2MB	as above except 4 256K SIMMs in Bank B	
	4MB	4 1MB SIMMs in Bank A; Bank B empty	
	5MB	as above except 4 256K SIMMs in Bank B	
	8MB	4 1MB SIMMs in Bank A and in Bank B	
IIfx	4MB	4 1MB SIMMs in Bank A; Bank B empty	80ns or faster chips required; special SIMMs required; minimum SIMM size: 1MB
	8MB	as above except 4 1MB SIMMs in Bank B	
IIsi	1MB	logic board memory	100ns or faster chips required
	2MB	as above plus 4 256K SIMMs	
	5MB	as above except 4 1MB SIMMs	
Portable	1MB	logic board memory	100ns or faster, low-power chips required
	2MB	as above plus 1MB Memory Expansion Kit	

upgrade, the ROM upgrade sometimes also includes a SuperDrive floppy disk drive. A SuperDrive, also called the FDHD (short for floppy disk, high density) can use high-capacity, 1.4MB floppy disks in addition to the 800K disks used by most earlier Macs. Thus, your Mac not only gets faster, it gets new features. The SE-to-SE/30 upgrade, for example, gives you Color QuickDraw, which opens the doors to color video boards. The logic board upgrade will serve you with System 7.0, too (see the sidebar "System 7.0 and Upgrades"). Some people have whined about Apple's upgrade being pricey, but the fact is, no major manufacturer in the IBM PC world provides similar upgrade options.

❖ *Video boards* Their circuitry works along with display monitors to create the Mac's screen image. Most Macs include video circuitry on their logic boards, but can also accept plug-in video boards that control color or large-screen monitors or add other display talents, including the ability to attach the Mac to videocassette recorders (see Chapters 17 and 18).

The Official Upgrade Path

Upgrade	Cost	What You Get
For Pre-Plus Macs		
Macintosh Plus Disk Drive Kit	$299	800K internal floppy drive, 128K ROMs
Macintosh Plus Logic Board Kit	$599 for 512K Macs; $799 for 128K Macs (also requires disk drive kit above)	Mac Plus
For Macintosh SEs		
Macintosh SE FDHD Upgrade Kit	$449	1.4MB internal high-density floppy disk drive, new ROMs
Macintosh SE/30 Logic Board Upgrade	$1699	Mac SE/30
For Macintosh II		
Macintosh II FDHD Upgrade Kit	$449	1.4MB internal high-density floppy disk drive, new ROMs
For Macintosh II and IIx		
Macintosh IIfx Logic Board Upgrade	$2999 (requires new memory)	Mac IIfx
For Macintosh IIcx		
Macintosh IIci Logic Board Upgrade	$2399	Mac IIci

❖ *Coprocessors* These specialized microprocessors work along with the Mac's CPU, lightening its load. Math coprocessors speed up calculations in spreadsheets and other number-crunching programs. Math chips are often built into or offered for accelerator boards, and are available on plug-in expansion cards for the Mac LC and IIsi. (Other Mac IIs and the SE/30 include math chips; the LC can accept one via its expansion slot.) Graphics coprocessors, also called *graphics accelerators*, are generally used with or included on *true color*, or *24-bit*, video cards, which enable Macs to display images with photographic realism, but must move megabytes of data to do it. Without a graphics accelerator, true color can require true patience. Graphics accelerators, currently available for the Mac II series only, aren't cheap, with Apple's Display Card 8•24GC costing $1999.

❖ *Sound-recording hardware* The Mac LC and IIsi contain sound-recording circuitry that, with appropriate software, lets you "attach" recorded comments to documents and send voice mail messages to other Macs on a network. As we saw in Chapter 32, you can add sound-recording features to other Macs using external hardware such as Farallon's MacRecorders, which retail for $149 to $249, depending on the model. Other low-cost recording hardware includes Articulate Systems' Voice Link and Premier Technology's $59.95 MacMic.

❖ *Cache memory boards* These special-purpose memory boards boost a Mac's overall performance 15 to 30 percent by storing the most recently used instructions and data in a small amount (usually 32K) of high-speed memory

System 7.0 and Upgrades

Where hardware upgrades and System 7.0 are concerned, one area is of special concern: virtual memory, a feature that lets the Mac treat part of a hard disk as memory. In the past, it was believed that all you needed to use System 7.0's virtual memory feature was a Mac containing a 68030 processor or a 68020 combined with a paged memory-management unit (PMMU) chip. Not so. System 7.0's virtual memory software relies on certain ROM routines that aren't present in Pluses or SEs. Thus, the virtual memory feature works only with Macs designed around the 68030 processor, or with original Mac IIs equipped with the optional PMMU chip.

To work around this problem, many accelerator boards will (or already do) include Connectix Corporations' Virtual utility software, which implements virtual memory with today's system software, and which will be updated to be compatible with System 7.0. What does this mean for accelerator shoppers? If you want virtual memory in your 68030-accelerated Plus or SE, be sure a 68030 accelerator includes or is compatible with the Virtual utility before you buy. And if you want virtual memory without having to use a third-party utility, buy an Apple 68030 logic board upgrade or a new machine instead of an accelerator. **M**

that the processor can access faster than main memory. For a few hundred dollars, you can add a cache memory board to the original Mac II as well as to the IIci, which contains a slot designed specifically for one. Cache memory is built into the Mac IIfx and many accelerator boards for the SE.

Assessing Your Slot Options

Before you start musing over which upgrades to buy, it's important to know that some Macs are less receptive to upgrades than others (see the sidebar "Surveying the Slots"). The Classic, Plus, and earlier machines are especially resistant to improvement. They're sealed boxes, with no expansion slots for accepting plug-in boards such as video boards, accelerators, and high-speed networking boards. To work around this, upgrade developers generally use the *Killy Clip*, a clip that straddles the machine's processor and thus taps into the signals that would otherwise be provided by an expansion slot (for background on the benefits of expansion slots, see the sidebar "This Bus is Never Late").

Surveying the Slots

The SE, SE/30, IIsi, and LC each contain one expansion slot. The Mac II and IIx each contain six, while the IIfx contains seven. The IIcx has three slots and the IIci has four.

But all slots are not created equal. The SE's slot is much less sophisticated than those of its successors, although it's adequate for accelerator boards and large-screen video cards.

The SE/30, IIsi, and IIfx each provide one *030 Direct Slot*, which allows access to all of the control, address, and data signals of the 68030 processor that these machines use. In theory, you can use any board designed for an 030 Direct Slot in any of these three machines. In practice, physical and electrical compatibility problems can surface. For example, the IIsi's case is too short to vertically accommodate a card designed for the SE/30, where a card lies horizontally, parallel to the logic board.

Apple's 030 Direct Slot Adaptor Card contains its own slot into which you plug your 030 expansion card. Because the adaptor card is positioned at a right angle to the logic board, the 030 card you plug into it ends up being parallel to the logic board, and thus, fits within the IIsi's case. The 030 Direct Slot Adaptor Card also contains a 68882 math coprocessor chip.

The primary means of expansion in the Mac II family are *NuBus* slots, named for a standard that was developed at the Massachusetts Institute of Technology and refined in 1985 by a standards committee comprising representatives from MIT, AT&T, Texas Instruments, Apple, and others. The NuBus standard specifies everything from how expansion boards access the internal bus to such physical details as the distance between the slot's pins.

To use a NuBus board with the Mac IIsi, you need an ☞

This clip-on technique works, but it's not without potential problems. One risk is electrical: the Plus and earlier machines lack fans and their power supplies can be stressed by having to provide juice for extra hardware. The other risk is mechanical: accelerator clips can be jostled loose or develop unreliable connections, especially if you move your machine around. The Classic may be especially prone to this problem: according to several upgrade vendors I've talked to, the way in which its processor is soldered to the logic board makes it difficult to develop a clip that stays put.

The IIcx, IIci, IIsi, and LC also contain soldered rather than socketed CPU chips. This has hampered the accelerator board market for these machines, since most accelerator boards require you to remove the original CPU and plug the accelerator board into its socket. The physical design of these machines' CPUs complicates clip-on alternatives.

The accelerator-and-soldered-CPU issue aside, upgrading any other Mac is generally straightforward, since all other models provide at least one slot. With the single-slot SE, SE/30, LC, and IIsi, there isn't much room to grow, so you'll need to choose upgrade options carefully. Fortunately, several SE accelerators can accept large-screen video boards via piggyback connectors. And as the LC and IIsi

adaptor such as Apple's NuBus Slot Adaptor Card. This card contains a 68882 math coprocessor as well as Apple's custom-designed set of NuBus transceiver chips, which allow the IIsi to communicate with a NuBus card. And the card contains the standard, 96-pin NuBus connector into which you plug your NuBus board, which runs from front to back within the IIsi's case, parallel to the logic board. A bracket inside the IIsi's case helps support a NuBus board.

NuBus slots overcome two of the classic drawbacks of slots: forcing users to fuss with small switches inside the case that tell the computer what hardware you've installed, and making it harder for software developers to write software that runs on different system configurations.

Every NuBus board contains a *configuration ROM* — a read-only memory chip that identifies the board and describes its capabilities. When you switch on a Mac II, its Slot Manager consults each board's configuration ROM and then sets up your system accordingly. Thus, installation is usually a plug-and-play proposition.

Apple tackled the software compatibility problem by designing the Mac's system software to act as an intermediary between programs and your hardware. Properly written Mac programs avoid accessing hardware directly; instead, they use Macintosh Toolbox routines, which access the hardware. So as long as software developers follow Apple's guidelines, their programs will run on any Mac, regardless of the boards it contains. **M**

become increasingly popular, we'll probably see more *multifunction* cards that cram several upgrades onto one board.

Strategies for Discontinued Macs

Let's look at some specific upgrade strategies, starting with discontinued Macs. See the table "Where to Buy Upgrades" for a partial list of upgrade vendors and representative products.

128K, 512K, and 512K Enhanced You can upgrade a 512K Mac to a 512K Enhanced by buying Apple's 800K Disk Drive Kit, which also includes the 128K Mac Plus ROM chips. But the 512KE lacks the SCSI circuitry needed for fast hard disks and it lacks sufficient memory to run most of today's programs. For that reason, it's better to go all the way and buy both the disk drive kit and the Macintosh Plus Logic Board Upgrade to get a full-fledged Mac Plus. If you have a 128K or 512K Mac, you can also assemble the equivalent of a Plus by using Apple's Mac Plus ROM chips along with third-party SCSI and memory hardware from firms such as Computer Care, Dove Computer Corporation, and Newbridge

This Bus is Never Late

To understand the benefits of slots, you need to understand the *bus* — an internal freeway that carries data between the Mac's memory, its microprocessor, and a variety of support chips.

All Macs contain two primary buses: the *address bus*, which carries signals from the microprocessor that specify where in memory data is to be stored or retrieved, and the *data bus*, which carries the data itself. With only a few exceptions, all the data that moves within the Mac does so on its data bus. Thus, the speed of the bus is one of the many factors that determines a Mac's overall performance.

When you consider the significant role it plays, the advantages of tapping into the bus become clear. With direct access to the microprocessor, to memory, and to many of the timing and control signals inside the

Mac, a device connected to the bus becomes an integral part of the Mac. Accelerator boards are able to supplement or even supplant the Mac's microprocessor with their own.

Another advantage is speed. A device connected directly to the bus can transfer data and communicate with memory far faster than it could using one of the Mac's external connectors. In an SE, for example, the SCSI port transfers data at about 656,000 bytes per second; a card in the SE's expansion slot, however can access memory at over 3 *million* bytes per second. Yes, there's always a benefit to eliminating the middleman.

If the bus is a freeway, then a slot is a set of on and off ramps, ready to accommodate high-performance add-ons without clips, voided warranties, or fried power supplies. **M**

Microsystems. But act now or forever hold your peace, because rumor has it the 128K ROMs and Apple's upgrades may not be available for long. (Some upgrade firms are reporting ROM scarcities now.) Given this, the low price of the new Macs, and the fact that the Plus itself has been discontinued, it may make more sense just to buy a new Mac.

Where to Buy Upgrades

Company	Phone	Products
Aox	617/890-4402	DoubleTime-16 accelerator for SE
Apple Computer	408/996-1010	logic board, floppy disk drive upgrades
Aura Systems	619/438-7730	ScuzzyGraph series drives monitors via SCSI
Computer Care	800/950-2273	memory, video upgrades for 128K, 512K, 512K Enhanced, Plus, SE, Classic
Computer System Associates	619/566-3911	FasTrack accelerator for SE
DayStar Digital	404/967-2077, 800/962-2077	accelerators and cache boards for II series
Dove Computer	919/763-7918, 800/622-7627	accelerators and CPU upgrades for most Macs; SCSI and memory upgrades for pre-Plus Macs
Lapis Technologies	415/748-1600	video upgrades for most Macs, including Classic
Mac Doctor Electronics	415/964-2131	Brainstorm series of memory upgrades for 128K, 512K Macs
Mobius Technologies	415/654-0556	030 Display System adds 68030 CPU and large-screen video circuitry to SE
Newbridge Microsystems	613/592-5080	accelerators, memory, and CPU upgrades for most Macs, including 128K and 512K; graphics accelerator for II series
Novy Systems	904/427-2358	Mac20MX accelerator for 512K Enhanced, Plus, SE
Orchid Technology	415/683-0300	MacSprint II cache board for original Mac II
PSI Integration	408/559-8544	cache board, 030 slot adaptor for IIsi
Radius	408/434-1010	accelerators for Plus, SE; video upgrades for most models
Second Wave	512/343-9661	expansion chassis for most Macs
Siclone Sales & Engineering	408/263-8207, 800/727-8207	accelerators for Mac II, IIx, SE; memory upgrades for Portable
Sigma Designs	415/770-0100	Bullet 3040 accelerator for Mac IIci and IIsi
SuperMac Technology	408/245-2202	SpeedCard accelerator for SE
Total Systems	503/345-7395, 800/874-2288	accelerators for 128K, 512K, Plus, SE

Given the poor track record of Plus and pre-Plus power supplies, if you do opt for an upgrade, consider beefing up your machine's power supply using the $80 Power Up kit from Total Systems Integration (TSI), which replaces the supply's most failure-prone parts. You can either have your dealer install the kit or send your power supply board to TSI for installation ($148 including the kit).

Plus If you've outgrown the Plus, your best option is to sell it or supplement it with a new machine. Accelerators and large-screen adapters are available, but the Plus's weak power supply and lack of a fan make these upgrades somewhat risky. If you're determined, note the power supply comments above.

SE There's a brighter future for this recently canned Apple, whose expansion slot can reliably accept accelerator boards and large-screen monochrome monitor adapters (sorry, no color). Apple's SE/30 Logic Board Upgrade is even more appealing, providing Color QuickDraw, a more up-to-date expansion slot, and support for virtual memory under System 7.0. Keep in mind, though, that any SE expansion board you may already have (such as an accelerator or large-screen video board) won't work in an SE/30's slot.

IIcx This workhorse Mac II can last for years, thanks to three NuBus expansion slots and a large selection of boards to fill them. However, all but the very first IIcx machines contain soldered rather than socketed CPU chips, and as mentioned earlier, that means problems for accelerator boards. DayStar Digital is the only firm offering IIcx accelerators, and you need to send in your machine's logic board to have a CPU socket installed. (If you can't bear the down time, some DayStar dealers will swap logic boards for an extra charge.) A better upgrade alternative may be Apple's IIci logic board, which gives you faster performance, a slot for a cache memory card, and new ROMs that support more than 8MB of memory under System 7.0.

II, IIx With six NuBus slots, these big Macs may have the brightest future of all. Accelerators such as those from DayStar Digital and Siclone Sales and Engineering provide 68030s running at clock rates of 33MHz to 50MHz, yielding performance that rivals the top-of-the-line Mac IIfx. Speaking of which, Apple's IIfx logic board upgrade retails for just $2999 plus memory — a deal so good it's created a hot market for used IIs and IIxs and helped push down prices for II and IIx accelerator boards. A much less-expensive but still valuable upgrade for the original Mac II is a PMMU chip, while allows the II to take advantage of System 7.0's virtual memory feature.

Strategies for Current Macs

Just because a Mac is still being manufactured doesn't mean there isn't room for improvement.

Classic As mentioned earlier, the Classic uses a soldered rather than socketed CPU chip that promises to make life difficult for accelerator developers. Still, Dove Computer offers a 68030 upgrade, and others will probably follow suit. Large-screen video adaptors are also available. Given the challenges the Classic presents to CPU clip manufacturers, it might be prudent to wait a while before buying a product that clips on to the Classic's CPU to make sure the wrinkles have been ironed out.

SE/30 It's a good thing this Mac is reasonably fast, because no accelerator boards are available for the current model. (Dove's MaraThon 030 Accelerator is available for early SE/30s, whose CPUs were socketed.) Large-screen and color video boards are available, however.

LC At this writing, no accelerators had been announced for the fledgling LC, although Dynamac had announced its $99 LCDevice card, which contains sockets for a 68030 CPU and a 68882 math coprocessor chip. Dove has a similar card on the drawing board. DayStar Digital plans to develop an accelerator, but representatives told me the machine's small power supply presents a considerable design challenge — it supplies only 4 watts to expansion boards, versus 15 in the IIcx. The LC's soldered CPU complicates things, too. Video hardware is beginning to proliferate for the LC. One noteworthy product is Dynamac's LCDisplay, a liquid-crystal display (LCD) technology similar to that used by many portable computers. PSI Integration's Bus Adapter Card lets you use SE/30 expansion boards and provides a slot for a cache memory board. Finally, Second Wave is developing an adapter that will let you use one NuBus expansion board with the LC. The adaptor should be available by the time you read this.

IIsi Thanks to its unique expansion-slot design, this littlest Mac II can accept either a NuBus board or a board designed for the SE/30's 030 Direct Slot. NuBus compatibility means a huge selection of boards, but some, including Apple's own 8•24GC graphics accelerator, draw more current than the IIsi's power supply can deliver. (Apple says you can use the 8•24GC provided your home or office temperature doesn't exceed 90° F.) Determine the power requirements of any NuBus board you plan to buy for the IIsi. Also, some boards designed for the SE/30's 030 Direct Slot may not work in the IIsi. Whether you're shopping for a NuBus or 030 Direct Slot board, it's smart to verify compatibility before buying a board for the IIsi. DayStar Digital and Dove plan to support the IIsi with accelerator and CPU upgrade boards.

The IIsi's ability to use either an 030 Direct Slot card or a NuBus card introduces an important question for IIsi owners: Which expansion camp do I buy into? Organizations with other Mac IIs will probably want the NuBus adaptor in the interest of standardization. Also, there's currently a larger selection of NuBus cards to choose from. But the 030 Direct Slot has the potential to provide higher performance for data-intensive applications such as 24-bit color and digital sound processing. That's because the 030 Direct Slot runs at 20MHz versus NuBus' 10MHz. What's more, it's also likely that more multifunction expansion cards will be developed for the 030 Direct Slot, now that it's supported by three Mac models (the SE/30, IIsi, and IIfx), two of which provide just one slot. In the end, you'll want to do some research to determine which type of board to buy when both camps offer products with similar features.

IIci One of the most popular and inexpensive upgrades for this fast Mac is a cache card. Citing reliability problems, Apple yanked its IIci cache card from the market for a while, but released it again in February 1991. A large selection of third-party cards is available. Sigma Designs' Bullet 3040, a card that installs in the IIci's cache card slot, accelerates the IIci's performance by boosting its CPU's clock rate to 40MHz. Another way to speed up the IIci is to use a NuBus video board instead of the machine's built-in video, whose design can slow down the machine, especially in its 16- and 256-color modes (This speed-up tip applies to the LC and IIsi, too.).

IIfx Given its blazing speed and exotic design, it's not surprising that no accelerators are available for Apple's top-of-the-line Mac. (Another problem is that the Motorola's faster 68040 microprocessor generates a fair amount of heat. Developers creating 68040-based accelerators for the IIfx will have to find a way to dissipate that extra warmth.) IIfx memory, storage, and video upgrades abound.

Portable One of the most useful upgrades for the Portable is an external video monitor adapter. Aura System's Scuzzy Graph attaches to the Portable's SCSI port and can drive monochrome or color monitors. Generation Systems' Portable Publisher installs in the Portable's processor direct slot and can drive numerous Apple monitors. Computer Care's Video Mac Pac also installs in the processor direct slot and can drive numerous monitors designed for use with the IBM PC. Numerous memory upgrades are available for the Portable.

Finally, it's worth noting that Second Wave offers *expansion chassis* for most Mac models. The chassis are external boxes containing expansion slots and power supplies. The Plus and Portable chassis let you use SE expansion cards, while the SE/30 and II-family chassis support NuBus cards.

Upgrade or New Machine?

Buying the right upgrade requires pinpointing your present Mac's weaknesses: Do programs take too long to start, or documents too long to open? You might need a faster hard disk (or any hard disk, if you don't have one). Once a program starts, does it run sluggishly? What aspects of its operation are sluggish?

Do calculations take too long? A math coprocessor or an accelerator or logic board upgrade might be in order. Do true-color graphics ooze onto the screen? You might need a graphics accelerator. If you answer "all of the above," think about a new, faster machine.

Last but far from least, it's important to assess your financial options to determine which will cost less: upgrading an existing Mac or selling it and buying a new one. Before October 1990, upgrading an existing machine usually made better financial sense, since the only alternative was a considerably more expensive new machine. Now that Apple has lowered prices and introduced the more affordable Classic, LC, and IIsi, the decision isn't as easy. Given the cost of hardware upgrades — and the compatibility and reliability risks that sometimes accompany them — a new machine may be the smarter buy. That's especially the case if you want to take a big leap forward, from, say, a 1MB SE to a 4MB, 68030-based machine that supports sound recording. And even if a new machine costs slightly more, the extra features it provides may be worth the cost.

There's another plus to buying a new machine: you get a blank slate that's ready to accept all the upgrade options that will be developed for it. That knowledge will be comforting when the next convoy of new trains starts rolling out of Apple Station.

Summary:

✔ You can upgrade an old Mac to give it most, if not all, of the features in Apple's current offerings. You can also upgrade a new Mac to make a good thing even better.

✔ Hardware upgrades fall into two broad categories: ones that makes your Mac faster, and ones that add new features such as color or additional storage.

✔ The most common upgrades include: memory, hard disks, accelerator boards and CPU upgrades, logic board upgrades, video boards, coprocessors, sound-recording hardware, and cache memory boards.

✔ Some Macs are less receptive to upgrades than others. The Classic, Plus and earlier models do not contain expansion slots for accepting plug-in boards.

✔ If you've outgrown a Mac Plus or earlier model, your best option might be to buy a new machine due to the riskiness of upgrading these models.

✔ When considering whether to upgrade an older machine or buy a new one, you should first pinpoint your Mac's weaknesses and then assess your financial options to determine which will cost less.

Chapter 35
PostScript

Your boss is no smarter than you are, yet you're treated like a peripheral in the office. You sit in a corner, biding time, waiting for the boss to bark. When the orders finally arrive, you go into action, assimilating data, making decisions, crunching numbers, and turning out a finished product that makes the boss look stellar. What's in it for you? All the paper you can eat and a new toner cartridge now and then.

It's a good thing PostScript printers haven't unionized, or they might demand the attention they deserve. Sure, the Mac's graphics and friendly personality sparked the desktop publishing revolution. But it's PostScript-based laser printers that have fueled the fire. In this chapter, I'll examine PostScript and the part it plays in the printing world. This tour of PostScript will set the stage for our look at laser printers in the next chapter. I'll also look at how PostScript fonts can coexist peacefully with Apple's TrueType outline fonts, which I examined in Chapter 25.

PostScript's Place

What is PostScript? To most laser printer users, it's air: unseen and unheard, but indispensable. Technically, PostScript is a programming language — a vocabulary of English-like *keywords*, combined with symbols for performing math and other operations, that can be assembled into programs that perform a given task. With an all-purpose programming language like BASIC or Pascal, the task might be a game, an accounting program, or a word processor. With PostScript, the result is a page produced by an *output device* — a laser printer or imagesetter. PostScript is a *page-description language*, a specialized dialect whose vocabulary is tightly focused on the task of describing the appearance and position of text and graphics on a page.

Page description languages are recent developments, inspired by the burgeoning capabilities of computer printers and the increasing demands of their users. PostScript was born in 1982 at Adobe Systems, under the guidance of founders Charles Geschke and John Warnock. Before founding Adobe, they developed a similar page description language called InterPress at Xerox's Palo Alto Research Center, the research and development lab where many of the Mac's mouse, window, and menu concepts were first tested.

PostScript lives in the part of a laser printer called the *controller*. The controller accepts instructions and data from the Mac, interprets them, then controls the printer's *engine*, which produces the hard copy. This controlling process involves directing the pulsing of the printer's light source (usually a laser) as it scribes a series of fine parallel lines across a photosensitive drum or belt. The lines — 300 per inch on most laser printers — are similar to the scan lines visible upon close examination of a computer or television screen.

> 66 *PostScript is a* **page-description language,** *a specialized dialect whose vocabulary is tightly focused on the task of describing the appearance and position of text and graphics on a page.* 99

Indeed, the image on a video screen and a page of laser printer output are actually close cousins, both made of scan lines produced by a *raster* controller. Acronym buffs often call laser printer controllers *RIPs*, short for *raster image processor*.

All laser printers have controllers, but not all controllers use page description languages. Many laser printers, including the best-selling Hewlett-Packard LaserJet series, accept orders in the form of less-flexible *control codes*. A control code is a special command sequence sent by the computer that tells a printer, "Don't print what comes next; treat it as a command instead." Some control codes tell the printer to switch to bold or underlined type, or to a different font. Others may feed a sheet of paper, position text at a certain location, or draw lines on a page.

Control codes, also called *escape codes*, have been guiding print mechanisms for decades. They're fine for formatting the monospaced, "letter quality" characters of a daisy wheel printer or electronic typewriter, and they're adequate for instructing a printer to switch from one font to another. But as a printer's capabilities increase, so do the number of control codes required to access them. If you're a controller designer, one solution is to add new control codes to accommodate new features — at the risk of creating a dizzyingly high number of control codes that could be obsolete when tomorrow's print engines arrive. A better solution is to start from scratch and design a graphics- and printing-oriented language whose words can be combined in different ways to produce different results. That's the PostScript approach.

The Object is the Game

PostScript is built on a foundation that gives it complete dominion over a printer's capabilities. One cornerstone of that foundation is a powerful set of *graphics operators* — programming routines that allow PostScript to rotate, enlarge, reduce, shade, chop, slice, and dice graphic images. Another is the basic premise that everything on a page, including text, is a graphic. That means anything PostScript can do to a picture, it can do to text. And the mortar holding it all together is an *object-oriented* approach that lets PostScript create images on everything from video screens to laser printers to imagesetters.

Let's address that last point first. Back in Chapter 8, we looked at the differ- ences between bitmapped and object-oriented graphics. We saw then that a bitmapped graphic such as a MacPaint picture is a series (a map) of bits in the Mac's memory, each corresponding to a dot on the screen. An object-oriented graphic like a MacDraw drawing, however, is stored as a series of commands for QuickDraw, the Mac's built-in library of graphics routines. These commands describe each object's appearance, including its location, size, line thickness, and pattern. Because object-oriented drawings are stored as QuickDraw commands rather than as a fixed number of dots, they are *resolution independent* — they can take advantage of all the sharpness your printer has to offer. They aren't tied to the relatively coarse 72 dot-per-inch (dpi) resolution of the Mac's screen.

PostScript takes a similar route to resolution independence by acting as a middleman between the Mac and the printer's engine. A PostScript controller receives commands from the Mac that describe each object's location and appearance, interprets the commands, then creates a bitmapped image for the entire page in the printer's memory. Thus the Mac can remain blissfully ignorant of the printer's resolution; an image becomes tied to a fixed number of dots per inch only moments before it's printed, when its bit map is created in the printer's memory. (The one time this rule doesn't apply is when you're printing a MacPaint- type picture, whose resolution is already carved in the Mac's memory. That's why object-oriented programs like MacDraw give better results with laser printers.)

The biggest benefit of PostScript's resolution independence is that it frees the Mac from having to know how much resolution a given printer provides. That means you can use the same programs to print the same documents on a 300-dpi Personal LaserWriter NT, a 600-dpi Varityper VT-600, or a 2540-dpi Linotronic 300. The only difference between the output of each will be increas- ingly sharper images.

Well, almost. There can be some trials on the trail from LaserWriter to Linotronic. The most obvious is the appearance of grey shades, called *screens* in the printing trade. A screen comprises a group of dots; the more dots within the screen's area, the darker the shade of grey. On LaserWriters, each dot is about $\frac{1}{300}$-inch in diameter — the smallest dot the printer's engine can produce. But a Linotronic 300 can create a dot $\frac{1}{2540}$-inch in diameter. This size difference means that light screens print far lighter on a Linotronic than on a LaserWriter. Both devices are printing the same number of dots, but their size differs. Hairline rules, which are one dot wide, are finer on a Linotronic for the same reason. And as we'll see in Chapter 39, their smaller dots allow Linos and other high-resolution PostScript printers to deliver superior results when printing scanned images.

Also, some Linotronic users report problems with extremely complex pages taxing the controllers of older Linotronics, even though the same pages may print on a desktop laser printer without incident. That presents another potential compatibility wrinkle: Even though PostScript is designed for device independence, situations can occur where a document that prints on one printer chokes another. One printer may lack fonts another one has, or may have less free memory than another. Imagesetter veterans recommend printing test documents to verify font and memory compatibility. It's a lot harder to iron out compatibility wrinkles with a deadline staring you in the face.

Language of a Thousand Faces

A variation on the object-oriented theme gives PostScript enough font finesse to make a type hound howl. In PostScript printers, fonts are stored as mathematic equations called *outlines* that the controller can use to create characters of virtually any size — just as a Mac that uses TrueType or Adobe Type Manager can (see the section "Truth in Type" in Chapter 25).

And because PostScript can apply its graphics-manipulation skills to text, PostScript printers can shade text, rotate it, print text in circles or along a wavy line, and even print text within text, as shown in the figure "A C of PostScript."

Of course, all the type-transformation talent in the world is worthless if your fonts are ugly to begin with. Adobe's library includes hundreds of today's most beautiful faces, licensed from such titans of type as Mergenthaler and the International Typeface Corporation (ITC). Thousands of top-quality fonts are available from font developers such as Bitstream, Casady & Greene, and Compugraphic.

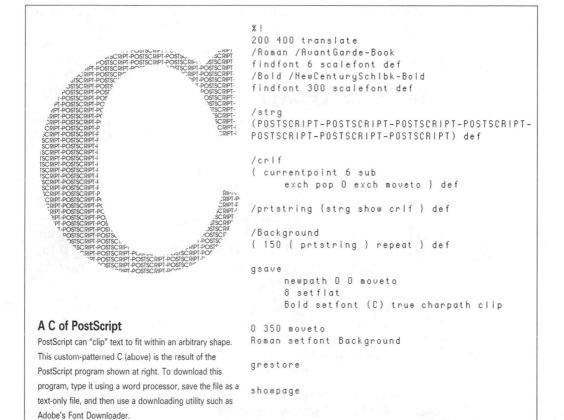

```
%!
200 400 translate
/Roman /AvantGarde-Book
findfont 6 scalefont def
/Bold /NewCenturySchlbk-Bold
findfont 300 scalefont def

/strg
(POSTSCRIPT-POSTSCRIPT-POSTSCRIPT-POSTSCRIPT-
POSTSCRIPT-POSTSCRIPT-POSTSCRIPT) def

/crlf
{ currentpoint 6 sub
     exch pop 0 exch moveto } def

/prtstring {strg show crlf } def

/Background
{ 150 { prtstring } repeat } def

gsave
     newpath 0 0 moveto
     8 setflat
     Bold setfont (C) true charpath clip

0 350 moveto
Roman setfont Background

grestore

showpage
```

A C of PostScript

PostScript can "clip" text to fit within an arbitrary shape. This custom-patterned C (above) is the result of the PostScript program shown at right. To download this program, type it using a word processor, save the file as a text-only file, and then use a downloading utility such as Adobe's Font Downloader.

The best fonts to use with 300-dpi PostScript printers are *Type 1* fonts containing *hints* that allow the printer's controller to tweak the appearance of text (especially small sizes) to look their best within the resolution available. Unhinted, or *Type 3,* fonts produce excellent results on high-resolution imagesetters, but can produce chunky-looking text on 300-dpi printers.

Most PostScript printers come with between 13 and 35 typefaces built into ROM chips, and organized into *families.* For example, the Times family comprises four typefaces: Times Roman, Times Italic, Times Bold, and Times Bold Italic. You can supplement a printer's ROM-based fonts with *downloadable fonts,* whose outlines are stored in individual files within your System Folder and downloaded into the printer's memory before use. A laser printer with 2MB of memory has enough room to hold a half-dozen or so fonts. Printers containing more memory have room for more. And as we'll see in the next chapter, some printers can accept their own hard disks that hold hundreds of downloadable fonts.

The Price of Power

The calculations involved in translating font outlines and interpreting graphics commands could keep a Mac busy for some time. Indeed, a Mac Classic, SE, or Plus is slower at running Adobe Type Manager or TrueType than is a Mac II-class machine. But a PostScript printer contains impressive computing hardware that liberates the Mac from much of that math. In a Personal LaserWriter NT, a 68000 microprocessor presides over 2MB of memory, roughly half of which is required to hold a full-page, 300-dpi bitmap. Another megabyte of ROM holds the PostScript interpreter and built-in fonts, while a cast of supporting chips manages communications between Mac and controller, and controller and engine. Before the Mac II was introduced, many joked that LaserWriters were Apple's most powerful computers. They weren't entirely wrong.

These smarts free the Mac from grappling with the myriad calculations necessary to describe a complex image. That's the primary reason why a PostScript printer's performance doesn't vary significantly depending on the kind of Mac you use it with. With a QuickDraw printer, by contrast, printing times vary significantly depending on what kind of Mac you have.

Sophisticated PostScript controllers are also one reason why PostScript printers cost more than non-PostScript printers. For example, the stripped-down version of Hewlett-Packard's LaserJet IIP uses the identical Canon-built print engine as the Personal LaserWriter NT, but is often sold for under $1000.

To make their purchase less painful, PostScript printers contain *print server* software that lets up to 32 Macs on a network share one printer. Server software lets a printer listen for print requests from any machine on the network, and service them on a first-come, first-served basis. Non-PostScript printers generally lack server software; multiple machines can share them only if you buy expensive splitter boxes and server software.

Despite having its own microprocessor and a good head for figures, a PostScript printer can seem slow at times. Documents containing large or complex graphics can bog down the controller. In the next chapter, we'll take a closer look at some of the factors that influence a PostScript printer's performance.

PostScript and Macs

To access a PostScript printer, a Mac running System versions prior to 7.0 needs two system files, LaserPrep and LaserWriter. The LaserWriter file is a *printer driver* that tells the Mac how to access a PostScript printer. The LaserPrep file is a *PostScript dictionary* that the Mac transmits to the printer at the beginning of the first job you print after starting the printer — it's what's being sent when the Mac displays the "Status: initializing printer" message. (You'll see this message only when you've disabled the Mac's background printing option or when the PrintMonitor window is open.)

LaserPrep actually adds new commands to the PostScript language that allow it to work with the LaserWriter driver, which doesn't send standard PostScript commands, but a special, pseudo-PostScript "shorthand" that takes less time to transmit over the network and is more compatible with QuickDraw. In essence, LaserPrep takes the printer aside and whispers, "Listen. We Macs use PostScript a bit differently. Here's what we do..." These *extensions* to the PostScript language remain in the printer's memory until it's shut off, which is why you only see the "initializing printer" message during your first print job.

Dictionaries get out of date and need to be revised from time to time. Apple has released several versions of the LaserWriter and LaserPrep files. The 6.x and 7.0 versions of the LaserWriter driver are faster than their predecessors, they have superior color- and greyscale-printing capabilities, they support more paper sizes, and they provide an option that lets you have an unlimited number of downloadable fonts in a document — at the price of performance.

It's important that you use the same version of the LaserWriter driver on every Macintosh in your network. Mix and match versions, and you'll frequently see error messages notifying you that the printer was initialized with an incompatible version of the driver, and needs to be restarted.

To use a PostScript printer with System 7.0, you need only the LaserWriter file. System 7.0 does away with the LaserPrep file, putting the PostScript dictionary in the LaserWriter driver itself. Version 6.1 of the LaserWriter driver (which works with System 6.0.7) also takes this approach. You can safely mix LaserWriter driver versions 6.1 and 7.0 on a network.

PostScript Programs

The LaserWriter driver may be all the Mac needs to access a PostScript printer, but it takes a special breed of application program to plumb the depths of PostScript's power. Illustrators and other graphic arts professionals swear by PostScript-oriented drawing programs such as Adobe Illustrator and Aldus

FreeHand, both of which let you trace pasted-in or scanned bitmapped images and then print the results or save them in a variety of formats, including PostScript code. Altsys Corporation's Fontographer lets you dissect and modify existing PostScript fonts (to add, for example, special characters or create symbols) or design entirely new ones. Chapter 6 discusses these and other font-altering programs.

Many desktop publishing and word processing programs let you incorporate PostScript effects created with these programs. Several methods exist for including PostScript effects in other documents, but the most useful are Encapsulated PostScript (EPS) files, and special PICT files containing embedded PostScript commands. The two files have technical differences, but both provide the same advantage: they store the PostScript programming statements the printer needs to create an effect, *as well as* QuickDraw commands that let the Mac approximate the effect on screen. In an EPS file, a portion of the file contains PostScript statements, while another part contains the QuickDraw commands. The PICT-with-PostScript format stores the PostScript statements needed to create an effect along with the QuickDraw commands all PICT-format files contain. With this approach, you can include PostScript illustrations and text effects in programs that don't support EPS files, such as Microsoft Word.

The common denominator between the aforementioned programs is that they're "PostScript aware." Their output contains instructions that go straight to the heart of a PostScript controller, instead of being simple bitmapped images or QuickDraw commands. Apple walks a fine line where the development of such PostScript-dependant products is concerned. On one hand, it recognizes the need to take full advantage of the PostScript printers it has helped popularize. But on the other hand, PostScript-oriented programs can be incompatible with (or at least deliver inferior results with) non-PostScript printers such as GCC's QuickDraw-based Personal LaserPrinter II and Apple's own Personal LaserWriter LS, LaserWriter IISC, and StyleWriter.

PostScript, TrueType, and TrueImage: Can They Coexist?

When Apple announced System 7.0 and TrueType fonts in May 1989, industry pundits began predicting chaos in the printer and publishing worlds. Would you be able to create a document using TrueType fonts and then print it on a PostScript-based printer? Would service bureaus face new technical hassles as customers began mixing TrueType and PostScript fonts? Was Apple weaning itself away from Adobe and PostScript?

Those flames of speculation were fanned in the Fall of 1989 when Microsoft announced that it was developing TrueImage, a clone of the PostScript language, and that TrueType fonts would be supported by future versions of the Microsoft Windows and Presentation Manager graphical environments.

Although the dust still hasn't completely settled, it looks like the pundits' predictions of doom and chaos will not come to pass. Apple continues to sell and develop new Adobe PostScript printers. More important, versions 6.1 and later of Apple's PostScript printer drivers allow TrueType and PostScript fonts to coexist peacefully. To understand how, let's look at what happens when you print a document using LaserWriter driver version 6.1 or later:

❖ First, the LaserWriter driver looks in the printer to see if the required fonts are located in its RAM or ROM or on a hard disk attached to the printer. If the fonts are found, the job proceeds.

❖ If the fonts aren't present in any of those places, the LaserWriter driver looks in the System Folder for downloadable PostScript fonts. If they're found, they're downloaded and the job continues.

❖ If the downloadable PostScript fonts aren't in the System Folder, the LaserWriter driver looks in the System file for TrueType outline fonts.

❖ If the TrueType fonts are present, the driver queries the printer to determine if it contains the TrueType rasterizing software, which enables the printer to translate TrueType outlines into the bitmapped sizes required. If the rasterizing software isn't present in the printer, the driver downloads it to the printer's memory, where it remains until the printer is restarted or switched off. The TrueType rasterizer uses about 50K of printer memory, reducing the amount available for downloadable fonts. You'll feel the crunch more if you have an older LaserWriter or the base models of Texas Instruments' microLaser PS17 or PS35, both of which contain just 1.5MB of memory.

❖ When the driver is satisfied that the printer contains the TrueType rasterizer, it downloads the fonts themselves. The printer's controller then uses the TrueType rasterizer software to create the sizes needed.

All of these steps sound complex, but they happen very quickly. More to the point, they occur automatically. You don't have to fret over which font formats to use with which type of printer. You can work with fonts as you normally would, and the LaserWriter driver will work behind the scenes to ensure that the right fonts get printed — in the right way.

And where does Microsoft's TrueImage fit into all of this? Because TrueImage is a PostScript clone, printers that use it will work with the LaserWriter driver in the way I've just described. But some printers, such as Microtek's TrueLaser, contain TrueType fonts and the TrueType rasterizer in ROM. When used with these printers, the LaserWriter driver won't have to download the TrueType rasterizer. That results in two small advantages: a slightly faster printing time for the first document you print after switching on the printer, and a savings of about 50K of printer memory. By themselves, these advantages aren't significant enough to give a TrueType/TrueImage printer a major edge over an Adobe PostScript printer or a different clone. Paper handling, overall performance, and print quality — points we'll address in the next chapter — are more important.

Considering QuickDraw

If you're laser printer shopping, you'll need to decide between a printer built around PostScript or one that uses QuickDraw, especially now that Adobe Type Manager and TrueType give QuickDraw printers the benefits of outline fonts. In the next chapter, I'll present some points of comparison that may help you make your decision.

In the meantime, it's important to note that the dawn of high-quality QuickDraw printing doesn't mean dusk for PostScript, which has gained unstoppable momentum in the past several years. Dozens of printer manufacturers are selling or developing PostScript devices. Hundreds of programs running on Macs, IBM PCs, minicomputers, and mainframes support it. And with PostScript printers proliferating and the price of memory chips continuing to drop, the cost chasm that separates non-PostScript and PostScript printers is shrinking.

What's more, PostScript itself is improving. In 1990, Adobe announced PostScript Level 2. Among other things, PostScript Level 2 boasts faster processing speed, vastly improved features for printing forms, improved support for producing four-color separations on imagesetters, better support for specialized paper-handling features such as dual paper trays, and more efficient use of printer memory. Also becoming available from firms such as Dataproducts, QMS, and Epson is a new generation of printer controllers that incorporate high-speed RISC processors instead of the general-purpose Motorola 68000 series processors. Most of these features will appeal primarily to the high end of the market, where sluggish imagesetters and color-separation hassles have frustrated publishing professionals already pushing today's technology to its limits, and where big businesses with large networks need faster text and forms printing.

In short, PostScript is evolving to meet the needs of the devices that speak it. That's exactly what a language is supposed to do.

Summary:

✔ PostScript is a programming language — a vocabulary of English-like keywords, combined with symbols for performing math and other operations, that can be assembled into programs that perform a given task. Postscript is a page-description language, a specialized dialect whose vocabulary is tightly focused on describing the appearance and position of text and graphics on a page.

✔ The part of a laser printer that contains PostScript is called the controller, which accepts instructions and data from the Mac, interprets them, and then controls the printer's engine, which produces the hard copy.

✔ Graphics operators are programming routines that allow PostScript to rotate, enlarge, reduce, shade, and otherwise alter graphic images.

✔ PostScript works on the basic premise that everything on a page, including text, is a graphic. This allows PostScript printers to apply their graphics operators to text in order to produce special effects.

✔ To access a PostScript printer, a Mac running System versions prior to 6.0.7 needs two system files, LaserPrep and LaserWriter. The LaserWriter file is a print driver that tells the Mac how to access a PostScript printer; the LaserPrep file is a PostScript dictionary that the Mac transmits to the printer at the beginning of the first job you print.

Chapter 36
Laser Printers

In This Chapter:

✔ The mechanical and electronic components of a laser printer.

✔ A look at the differences between laser printer controllers.

✔ Techniques laser printers use to produce text.

✔ PostScript versus QuickDraw printers.

✔ A summary of what to look for in a PostScript laser printer.

✔ How to determine which type of laser printer to buy.

The marriage of Mac and laser printer is a happy one — even if it does require a hefty dowry. But finding the perfect partner isn't easy. Today's laser printer shopper faces a raft of specifications and technical issues. In this chapter, I'll examine the technical processes behind laser printers and present the issues you'll want to consider when shopping for one.

Mechanics and Electronics

A laser printer's output results from a collaboration between an *engine* and a *controller*. The engine is the mechanical half of the duo; it works much like a photocopier. The engine helps determine print quality and speed, and it defines how well the printer can handle different kinds of paper, such as envelopes. The controller determines the printer's typographical features — the range and quality of the fonts, styles, and the sizes it can produce — as well as its compatibility with Mac applications and with other computers. The controller also guides the engine's imaging mechanism, telling it where to apply the *toner* powder that forms the image. And because describing the appearance of a page requires complex calculations, the controller also helps determine printer speed. In most printers, the controller is housed within the printer's case and contains its own microprocessor and memory chips. As I'll explain shortly, however, some less-expensive printers use the Mac's processor and memory as their controller.

Because the controller defines the printer's overall capabilities, your quest for the perfect printer should begin with a look at its brains.

Watch Your Language

The primary difference between laser printer controllers lies in the type of commands they respond to. *PostScript* controllers use commands written in PostScript, which, as we saw in the last chapter, is a programming language created by Adobe Systems for describing the appearance of pages. A PostScript controller is a powerful computer in itself. It typically has 2 megabytes of memory or more, a microprocessor, and ROM chips containing the PostScript language *interpreter* as well as a selection of *font outlines*, mathematical formulas the controller can use to create text in virtually any size and orientation. Apple's Personal LaserWriter NT and LaserWriter IINT and IINTX are both PostScript printers, as were the pioneering LaserWriter and LaserWriter Plus.

QuickDraw-based printers use the Mac as the controller, so they don't contain the complex controllers that PostScript printers require. And because QuickDraw printers make the Mac do more of the work, they generally cost less. But they often do less, too (see the table "PostScript versus Non-PostScript" for ten points of comparison). Only a few QuickDraw-based laser printers are available: Apple's LaserWriter IISC and Personal LaserWriter LS, and GCC Technologies' Personal LaserPrinter II (PLP II) and PLP IIs. (Incidentally, many of the technical details behind QuickDraw laser printers apply to other types of QuickDraw-based printers, such as ImageWriters, StyleWriters, and Hewlett-Packard DeskWriters.)

The Digital Type Foundry

Another important differentiating factor between printers is the *font mechanism* — the techniques they use to produce text. Outline fonts, combined with PostScript's wide array of graphics-manipulation commands (called *operators*), give PostScript printers tremendous typographic versatility. Need a 10-foot-high *W* filled with a checkerboard pattern? Want to produce a record label with the musician's name set in a circle? With a shadow behind it? Chores like these are a cinch for PostScript.

Apple's QuickDraw printers can use either TrueType or bitmapped fonts. GCC's QuickDraw printers use proprietary outline fonts (created by Bitstream) or bitmapped fonts. Although these printers use outline fonts, they still aren't as typographically talented as their PostScript cousins. The problem isn't the fonts, but the underlying language that positions them on the page:

QuickDraw lacks PostScript's wide array of graphics operators, and because of that, QuickDraw printers still can't produce all the special text effects of their PostScript competitors.

But this is changing, and ironically, Adobe itself deserves much of the credit. Its inexpensive Adobe Type Manager (ATM) utility gives QuickDraw printers access to thousands of PostScript outline fonts, and lets them print those fonts in virtually any size. And Adobe's Type Align program works with ATM to allow you to skew and distort text, attach it to a curving baseline, and create other exotic effects that users of QuickDraw printers could previously only dream of.

Although ATM and Type Align give QuickDraw printers a shot in the typographic arm, Quick Draw printers still deliver inferior results with Post-Script-oriented drawing programs such as Aldus FreeHand and Adobe Illustrator — unless you use PostScript emulation software such as QMS' UltraScript (see the sidebar "PostScript on a Disk" on the next page).

You can also supplement a PostScript printer's built-in, or *resident*, fonts with *downloadable* fonts, whose outlines are stored in separate files within your System Folder and down-loaded to the printer's memory before printing.

PostScript versus Non-PostScript

PostScript	Non-PostScript
Processing occurs in printer, requiring complex controller, but freeing Mac for other tasks	Processing occurs in Macintosh, allowing simpler, less expensive controllers, but requiring Mac memory and hard disk space
Many font outlines stored in printer's ROM	All fonts stored on Macintosh hard disk
Background printing built into the Mac's system software	Not all QuickDraw printers support spoolers or work with the Mac's background printing feature
Printer can be shared by up to 32 Macs	No built-in sharing capabilities
Large selection of fonts	Currently a smaller selection of fonts unless you use Adobe Type Manager
Controller can shadow text, and print along an irregular path	Some effects currently not available or are application-dependent
PostScript printers are ideal proofing devices for imagesetter output	Spacing of some fonts may not match PostScript counterparts, making proofs less accurate
Can use applications that generate PostScript effects	PostScript-specific applications may not work
Most PostScript printers can also emulate other printers, such as HP LaserJet	QuickDraw printers generally have no emulation features
Printer can be used with other PostScript-supporting computers	Printer must be used with Macintosh

They Don't Share Alike

The differences between printer-driving languages are also important if you plan to share a printer with other computers. Since QuickDraw is confined to Macs, you can't use a QuickDraw printer with an IBM PC or clone. And because QuickDraw printers attach to the Mac's SCSI or serial port, they can't be shared on a network.

PostScript printers are far easier to share. Every PostScript printer contains a LocalTalk connector and built-in print server software, which allow it to be used with up to 32 Macs (and PCs equipped with LocalTalk boards).

PostScript on a Disk

PostScript emulation software lets you overcome the language barrier between QuickDraw and PostScript. A PostScript emulator resides on your Mac's hard disk and acts as an intermediary between your application programs and a non-PostScript printer. After installing the emulator, you use the Chooser desk accessory to select its driver. Thereafter, when you issue a Print command, the emulator intercepts and saves on disk the PostScript instructions that would otherwise be sent to a PostScript printer. The emulator's PostScript interpreter then takes over, using the Mac's processor and memory to translate the PostScript into instructions your printer can understand.

Several PostScript emulation packages are available, including TeleTypesetting's T-Script, Custom Applications' Freedom of Press, and QMS' UltraScript Plus. All three support dozens of output devices, from dot matrix printers to ink jets to lasers. One of the most interesting features provided by all three packages is the ability to act as a print server for other Macs on a network. You can use another Mac's Chooser to select the emulator's driver, and then print as though you were printing to a LaserWriter. The emulator receives the PostScript instructions over the AppleTalk network, and then processes the job.

A PostScript emulator can be a remarkably inexpensive way to get PostScript output. An HP LaserJet IIP with GDT Softworks' ParaLink cable can be had for less than $1000. Throw in UltraScript Plus for another $300 or so, and you have a 4-ppm psuedo-PostScript laser printer. Substitute an HP DeskJet for the LaserJet IIP, and you've saved even more.

Of course, there are other prices to pay. A PostScript emulator's performance is dependent on your Mac's. A Mac II-class machine with a math coprocessor chip delivers acceptable performance, but lesser Macs will tax your patience. And because each of the three use non-Adobe PostScript interpreter software, there's always the chance that a complex PostScript document won't print.

Still, a PostScript emulator is less likely than a driver package such as MacPrint or JetLink Express to fall victim to application compatibility problems, since your programs think they're printing to a PostScript printer. And emulators are a great way to put an underused ImageWriter to work as a proofing device. There's no substitute for a real PostScript printer, but a PostScript emulator can come surprisingly close. **M**

Another PostScript plus is its industry-wide support. PostScript is available on output devices ranging from laser printers to typesetters, and it's supported by a wide range of computers. PostScript's popularity lets you move files between printers or computers while retaining file formatting. For example, you can print proofs of a document on a 300-dots-per-inch (dpi) PostScript laser printer, and then take your file to a service bureau for output on a 2540-dpi PostScript imagesetter. Similarly, you can transfer a document created using the Mac version of PageMaker to an IBM PC running PageMaker, and its line breaks and character spacing will remain intact.

It's worth noting that Microsoft's Windows and Presentation Manager graphical environments will someday support Apple's TrueType outline fonts. When TrueType becomes firmly entrenched in both the Mac and PC worlds, exchanging documents and retaining their formatting will be easier. In the meantime, PostScript is the best common denominator.

From Screen to Printer

Every page must ultimately be described as a *bitmap* — an array of bits, each corresponding to one dot on the page. A full-page bitmap for a 300-dots-per-inch printer is roughly 1MB in size. All that data has to be stored somewhere:

❖ PostScript printers and the LaserWriter IISC store it in the controller's *page buffer*, a 1MB area of printer memory.

❖ The driver for the GCC Personal LaserPrinter II series stores the bitmap in compressed form on the Mac's hard disk, then decompresses and transmits the bitmap to the printer via the SCSI bus, timed to match the rotation of the engine's drum. This approach eliminates the need for a page buffer in the PLP II, but it also eliminates the ability to print in the background.

❖ The driver for Apple's Personal LaserWriter LS first creates a file on disk containing the QuickDraw commands that describe the page. Next (and in the background, if you've enabled the background printing option), the driver divides the page into bands, and then creates a bitmap for a given band in the Mac's memory. The bitmap is then compressed so it takes less storage space and time to transmit. The compressed bitmap is sent to the printer, where a custom chip decompresses it. This process repeats for the remaining bands. (The more memory your Mac has, the larger the bands are, and the faster the printer's performance.) Some clever engineering allowed Apple to build only 512K of memory into the Personal LaserWriter LS — one key to the printer's low cost.

Printers that use outline fonts must translate those outlines into bitmaps in the type sizes needed for the page you're currently printing. Because some character bitmaps will probably be needed again later, PostScript printers, TrueType, and the PLP store them in an area of memory called the *font cache*. Retrieving a character bitmap from the font cache is much faster than creating a new one from the outline. On a PostScript printer, a fixed amount of printer memory is reserved for the font cache. The PLP creates a font cache in the Mac's memory; its size depends on how much memory the Mac has. TrueType also uses the Mac's memory for font caching.

Other PostScript Issues

All PostScript printers are compatible with the Mac, but there can be significant differences among printers. Some questions worth asking include:

❖ *Does it use an Adobe interpreter?* To avoid the cost of licensing PostScript interpreters from Adobe Systems, some manufacturers have developed their own. Some of these so-called *PostScript clones* provide faster performance, but some also deliver inferior results when used with *Type 1* downloadable fonts, the hinted font format used by Adobe and many other leading font developers. Moreover, PostScript is a complex language and incompatibilities can arise, especially if you print complex illustrations created with programs like FreeHand or Illustrator. If you print typographically simple documents such as memos, manuscripts, and legal contracts, you may never encounter problems. Of course, if you print simple documents, you may not need a PostScript printer to begin with.

❖ *How much memory is provided?* Most PostScript laser printers provide 2MB or 3MB of memory, divided into three areas: the page buffer, the *font cache*, and *virtual memory*, or *VM* — general work space that also holds downloadable fonts. (By the way, virtual memory as it applies to PostScript printers is unrelated to System 7.0's virtual memory feature.) The font cache holds the bitmaps for characters that have already been printed on a page. When the font cache fills — which can happen when you print a document with a large mix of type styles and sizes — the controller must purge some of the character bitmaps it has laboriously created, and then create the new ones it needs. If the purged characters are needed again, the controller must recreate their bit maps from the font's outlines. The more memory a printer provides, the larger its font cache and VM. A larger font cache means faster performance, and more VM means more room for downloadable fonts. Many printers also accept memory-expansion options.

❖ *Can it accept a hard disk?* Some printers can accept an optional SCSI hard disk. A hard disk attached to a printer stores downloadable fonts, making them available to all machines on the network and eliminating downloading time (20–30 seconds per font). A hard disk also acts as an extension to the font cache, which further improves printer performance. (Incidentally, if you're buying a hard disk to be used with a printer, verify that the model you're considering can be used as a font-storage hard disk. Some SCSI drives aren't compatible with the SCSI ports used on laser printers.)

❖ *Can it imitate other printers?* Older software for IBM PCs and other computers may not support PostScript, but it generally does support letter-quality printers or Hewlett-Packard LaserJets. Most PostScript printers provide *emulation modes* that allow them to respond to commands for such printers. If emulation modes are important to you, look for a printer that provides *automatic emulation sensing,* such as QMS' PS-410 or PS-2000. Emulation sensing enables the printer to switch into an emulation mode when it determines that incoming data isn't PostScript code. Without emulation sensing, you need to flick a switch or use a printer's front-panel buttons to switch between PostScript and emulation modes.

❖ *What ports does it provide?* All PostScript printers provide a LocalTalk port for connecting to Macs and LocalTalk-equipped IBM PCs (and compatibles). Most PostScript printers also provide RS-232C serial ports; some also have Centronics parallel ports — the dominant printer port in the IBM world. To use the printer with computers lacking LocalTalk, you'll need one of the latter two ports. Some high-end, heavy-duty PostScript printers also provide Ethernet connectors for tapping into high-speed networks.

Print Engine Considerations

A print engine forms images using a series of evenly spaced parallel lines that are painted on a photosensitive drum or belt by a laser beam or some other light source (see the figure "Inside an Engine" on the next page).

A print engine's design determines several important factors, including:

❖ *Resolution* Most of today's printers produce output containing 300 dpi. Compugraphic and Varityper offer Adobe PostScript printers that produce 400- and 600-dpi output, respectively, but they're costly. LaserMAX Systems' LaserMAX 400 is a 400-dpi printer built around the Canon LX engine. With a retail price of $1995, it sounds unbeatable, but there are catches. The printer's controller resides not within the printer, but on a NuBus expansion board that you plug into any member of the Mac II family. Thus, you can't use the 400 with a compact Mac or an LC unless your network has a Mac II containing the printer's controller board.

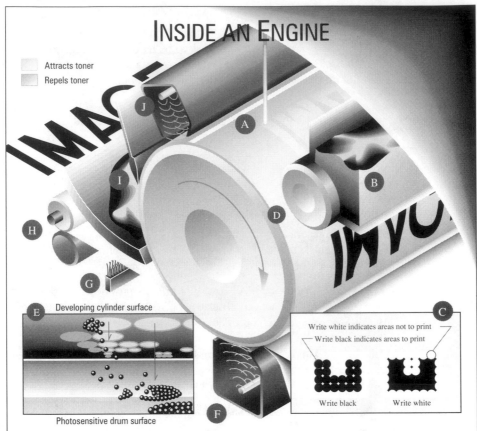

INSIDE AN ENGINE

Attracts toner
Repels toner

Developing cylinder surface

Photosensitive drum surface

Write white indicates areas not to print
Write black indicates areas to print

Write black   Write white

With the bitmapped image of the page as a guide, the engine uses a light source (usually a laser) to expose its photosensitive drum or belt **(A)**. In a write-black engine (shown here), the areas to be printed have an electrical charge that attracts toner as the drum rotates past the toner compartment **(B)**. In a write-white engine, the areas not to be printed have a charge that repels toner. Because written-to areas are not completely solid, write-white engines produce more solid blacks **(C)**. When the drum meets the developing cylinder **(D)**, charged toner particles are attracted to areas of the drum that have an opposite charge **(E)**. An electrically charged wire attracts toner from the drum onto the paper **(F)**. After a discharge brush removes all electrical charges from the paper **(G)**, heat rollers fuse toner to the paper **(H)**. A cleaning blade removes any remaining toner from the drum **(I)**, and a second wire neutralizes the drum's electrical charge **(J)** so that it may be written to again.

❖ *Engine speed* Most laser engines can push paper at a pace of between four and eight pages per minute (ppm). Generally, however, you'll see these speeds only when printing multiple copies of the same document or very simple documents such as manuscripts in the Courier font. With documents containing graphics or several fonts and sizes, performance is usually limited by the printer's controller, not its engine.

❖ *Engine life* If you churn out hundreds of copies of documents or share a printer in a busy office, you need an engine designed to take a beating and keep on feeding. Two specifications refer to an engine's durability: engine life, measured in pages; and *duty cycle,* the number of pages you can print per month. Heavy-duty printers such as QMS' PS-2000 have duty cycles in the 40,000 page per month range. Exceed the recommended duty cycle rating, and you're asking for mechanical trouble.

❖ *Ease of feeding* You'll need to replenish your printer's toner supply every few thousand pages or so. For no-fuss feeding, you can't beat the single-cartridge system used in Canon-built engines, which you'll find in Apple, Canon, QMS, and Hewlett-Packard printers. Other engines use multi-part consumables kits, which might comprise a toner cartridge, a photo-conductor belt or drum, and a small bottle that holds used toner. You install these components separately, a job that isn't difficult, but that can lead to messy spills if you aren't careful. Alas, the disposable cartridges used in Canon engines are an environmentalist's nightmare, each contributing several pounds of plastic to the local landfill. Happily, you can recycle cartridges — and save money in the process — by sending them to one of the growing number of cartridge remanufacturing services (see the sidebar "Saving Green" on the next page).

❖ *Paper handling* The features an engine provides for storing and feeding paper break down into several categories: maximum page size (usually 8½ by 14 inches); paper capacity (from 100 to 1000 sheets); number of paper trays (usually one, sometimes two); and manual-feed features. If you plan to feed envelopes or other nonstandard paper sizes frequently, look for a printer that offers a *self-centering* manual-feed slot. Such slots use two adjustable guides; move one, and the other moves accordingly.

Talking to PC Printers

Laser (and ink jet) printers designed for the IBM PC world often cost considerably less than their Mac-specific cousins. If you're willing to stray from the pack, you can use one of these PC printers with a Mac. All you need is the proper cable and driver software that the PC printer can understand.

The cheapest — and slowest — way to connect to a PC printer is through a serial cable. One is included with Insight Development's MacPrint and GDT Softworks' JetLink Express, two PC printer driver software packages. For better performance, you'll want to use the parallel interface that most PC printers provide. But because all Macs lack a parallel interface connector, you need a serial-to-parallel conversion cable such as GDT's ParaLink Express or Orange Micro's Grappler LX. (Mac II users might instead choose a parallel interface board such as Creative Solutions' Hurdler-CPI, which eliminates tying up your modem or printer port.)

For driver software, you can choose between a QuickDraw-based driver package such as JetLink Express or MacPrint, or a PostScript emulator such as QMS' UltraScript. Consider the latter if you have a Mac II-class machine with several megabytes of memory, or if you absolutely must have PostScript output and are willing to wait for it. For 68000-based Macs, a QuickDraw-based driver provides better performance. GDT's JetLink Express provides outline fonts that can be scaled to up to 127-point, versus MacPrint's 96-point maximum. JetLink Express also works with more printers than does MacPrint, which supports only Hewlett-Packard DeskJets, LaserJets, and compatibles. Both products work with Adobe Type Manager.

In the past, third-party PC printer drivers have had serious application compatibility problems. Most problems were caused by application developers that disregarded Apple's programming guidelines by assuming their programs would never print to anything but an ImageWriter or a PostScript-based LaserWriter. Now that QuickDraw-based laser and ink jet printers are becoming popular, most application developers have wised up and stopped making

Saving Green

A used toner cartridge isn't used up — many of its internal parts are good for tens of thousands of pages. By reusing or recycling toner cartridges, you can at least postpone all that plastic's journey into forever.

Toner cartridge remanufacturers disassemble cartridges, clean and replace parts as needed, and then replenish their toner supply — for about half of what new cartridges cost. Many remanufacturers are starting to handle non-Canon toner cartridges, too. Using a recycled cartridge won't void your printer's warranty, degrade print quality, or hurt your printer.

If you choose a reputable recycler, that is. Some fly-by-night operations simply drill a hole in the cartridge and fill it with toner — an approach that invites poor output quality at best, and printer damage at worst. Ask for recommendations at a user's group or desktop

publishing service bureau, or ask a remanufacturer for references. Or contact one of the trade organizations that promote cartridge remanufacturing: the American Cartridge Recycling Association (305/539-0701) and the International Computer Products Remanufacturing Association (503/222-3215). The latter organization can help you find sources for ink jet cartridge and dot matrix ribbon refills, too.

If you still prefer to buy brand-new cartridges, at least consider recycling your spent ones. You can send used Canon engine cartridges to Hewlett-Packard, which recycles many of their internal components and donates a dollar to the National Wildlife Federation and The Nature Conservancy for every cartridge received. For a free recycling kit, call HP at 800/752-0900 and ask for part 5952-2368. **M**

such assumptions. But you'll still find pages of warnings and workarounds in the JetLink Express and MacPrint manuals, so it's wise to verify compatibility with your favorite programs before you buy.

Picking Your Printer

Should you buy a PostScript printer? Will a clone suffice? Or should you buy a QuickDraw-based printer?

Apple's TrueType, Adobe Type Manager, and Adobe Type Align give QuickDraw printers greatly improved typographic features. If you don't need networking features, you don't use PostScript-oriented drawing programs, and you don't need to exchange formatted documents with other types of computers, a QuickDraw printer is probably a good choice.

If you need to share a printer — especially between Macs and PCs — go for PostScript. I would be wary of PostScript clones, however; to date, they haven't shown any significant advantage over Adobe PostScript interpreters, especially given their potential for compatibility problems.

System 7.0 gives QuickDraw printers improved typographic features, but it doesn't send PostScript printers to the breadlines. When it comes to providing plug-and-play print services to a network and maintaining consistent document formatting across different printers and computers, PostScript excels. That isn't going to change.

Summary:

✔ The output from a laser printer is the result of an engine, the mechanical device that helps determine print quality and speed, and the controller, the electronic component that determines the printer's typographical features.

✔ The primary difference between laser printer controllers lies in the type of commands they respond to. Some printers use the PostScript language, while less-expensive printers rely on the Mac's QuickDraw Language.

✔ A QuickDraw laser printer can't be used with an IBM PC or clone and also cannot be shared on a network as can a PostScript printer.

✔ If you don't need networking features, don't use PostScript-oriented drawing programs, and don't need to exchange formatted documents with other types of computers, a QuickDraw printer is probably a good choice — otherwise, you might want to consider a PostScript printer.

Chapter 37
Input Devices

In This Chapter:

✔ An overview of input device options.

✔ Non-Apple keyboards: more features and a different feel.

✔ The mouse and its alternatives.

✔ Drawing and drafting with a graphics tablet and stylus.

✔ Attaching input devices to the Apple Desktop Bus.

✔ Specialized input devices — the joystick and voice recognition hardware.

The Mac's *input devices* — its keyboard and mouse — are your links to the Mac, letting you move around the screen in the direction of your choice. And — like most Mac users — you've probably been content to use Apple's stock input devices. After all, one mouse or keyboard is the same as another, right?

Not quite. These days, Macintosh owners can choose from a large and varied selection of alternative input devices. Some are keyboards and mice that may appeal to people who find Apple's input devices uncomfortable or too expensive. Others fall into the different-strokes-for-different-folks category: *trackballs* don't require as much desktop space as mice, while *graphics tablets* offer penlike control for drawing and drafting applications. And then there's *voice recognition* hardware, which can make the Mac accessible to people with physical disabilities that prevent them from using a keyboard or mouse.

Although many alternative input devices are currently available for the Plus, most are designed for the Mac SE and Mac II families. These newer machines are equipped with the *Apple Desktop Bus (ADB)*, an expansion system designed for input devices (see the sidebar "The Inbound Bus" on the next page). In this chapter, I describe the most popular input devices available for the Mac family and spotlight some products from each class.

Keyboard Considerations

In the Mac world, most alternative input devices are alternatives to the mouse. True, a *pointing device* is the cornerstone of the Mac's graphical interface, but the keyboard is essential too, especially for typing-intensive applications such as word processors, data managers, and spreadsheets.

Apple offers several keyboards for the Mac: the Macintosh Plus keyboard (discontinued in October 1990), the Macintosh Portable keyboard, the Apple Keyboard, and the Apple Extended Keyboard II. The Mac Plus and Portable keyboards are included with their respective machines; the Apple Keyboard is included with the Classic and LC. Both the Apple Keyboard and Extended Keyboard II are also sold separately; when you buy a Mac other than a Classic, Portable, or LC, you'll need to choose a keyboard. The Apple Keyboard is similar to the Plus keyboard, with a standard typewriter layout supplemented by four *arrow keys* for moving the Mac's blinking insertion point, and a calculator-like *numeric keypad* for fast number entry. Many word processors also use the numeric keypad for scrolling.

The Apple Extended Keyboard II supplements the standard keyboard's typewriter, arrow, and numeric keypad keys with additional scrolling keys and a row of 15 *function keys.* Many programs, including Microsoft Word 4.0 and WordPerfect, use the function keys as keyboard shortcuts for often-used menu

The Inbound Bus

The Apple Desktop Bus (ADB), used on all Macs except the Plus, is a simple expansion system designed for input devices. The Mac provides two ADB connectors, as do many ADB input devices. You can attach multiple input devices to a single connector by *daisy-chaining* them — attaching one device to another. Although the ADB can accommodate up to 16 devices, Apple warns against attaching more than 3 to each connector because ADB signals deteriorate as the cable length increases.

The Mac's ADB connectors also provide a source of power, so you don't need a separate power supply or power outlet for each device. The battery-powered Mac Portable, however, requires low-power ADB devices designed to draw less juice.

Before connecting or disconnecting an ADB device, you must first shut off the Mac, or it may fail to recognize one or more of the devices. Another incentive to turn off the Mac is that ADB connectors may short-circuit momentarily when installed or removed, damaging the input device or the Mac itself. Some people who travel with a Mac have also reported problems with the connectors wearing out after repeated use, so it's wise not to attach and detach ADB devices too frequently.   **M** commands. You can also create your own function-key shortcuts using a macro utility such as CE Software's QuicKeys 2 or Affinity Microsystems' Tempo II (see Chapter 19).

I recommend an extended keyboard for anyone with enough desk space to accommodate it. Even if you never create any macros, you'll find its additional scrolling keys useful for navigating through documents. What's more, the Extended Keyboard II provides adjustable feet that let you tweak the keyboard's angle for comfortable typing and less hand fatigue. Its layout almost matches that of the latest IBM keyboards — useful if you switch between Macs and PCs or use Insignia Solutions' SoftPC software, which lets Macs run IBM PC programs.

(The Extended Keyboard II, as its name implies, represents Apple's second attempt at an enhanced keyboard. The original Extended Keyboard provided an identical layout, but lacked the angle-adjustment feet. If you're buying an extended keyboard, be sure to get the latest model. Its Apple part number is M0312; its predecessor's was M0115.)

Apple's ADB keyboards also offer a *power-on key* that turns on a Mac II-series machine. On the Classic, LC, SE, and SE/30, the power-on key has no effect. You can, however, put it to work by using Sophisticated Circuits' PowerKey — which provides three outlets that supply juice when you press the power-on key — or Practical Solutions' Strip Switch, which provides one outlet to which you can attach a power strip. Strip Switch also lets you turn off power by tapping the power-on key twice.

Competing Keyboards

If you haven't bought a keyboard yet, or if you're thinking of upgrading from a standard to an extended version, consider a non-Apple keyboard. Not only do these products cost less than Apple's Extended Keyboard II, many offer useful features — missing from Apple's models — providing even more value for the money.

One popular alternative keyboard is Datadesk International's Mac-101, available in an ADB and non-ADB version, which includes a macro utility and provides a layout nearly identical to that of the Extended Keyboard II. The primary difference is that the Mac-101 provides just one set of Control, Option, and Command keys, while Apple's keyboard provides two, one on either side of the spacebar.

key tronic Corporation's MacPro provides a layout similar to that of the Extended Keyboard II, but with a larger Return key that supposedly reduces data entry errors. The MacPro, available for ADB Macs only, also includes the

Tempo II macro utility. key tronic also offers a keyboard with a built-in pointing device.

If you're fond of function keys, you can't beat Northgate Computer Systems' 119-key OmniMac Ultra, which provides user-programmable function keys — 12 across the top and 12 along the keyboard's left edge. The OmniMac Ultra also provides a useful comma- and period-lock feature that prevents you from getting angle-bracket symbols (< or >) when you press the comma or period key while holding down the Shift key. OmniMac Ultra includes a scaled-down version of CE Software's QuicKeys, and the keyboard works with the Plus as well as with ADB-equipped Macs.

Possibly the most interesting alternative keyboard is Datadesk International's modular-design Switchboard. It lets you remove the keyboard's numeric keypad, for example, and replace it with a trackball, which I'll describe shortly. You can even get function-key modules that contain their own memory for storing macros and custom keyboard shortcuts.

But there's another, more subjective, reason to consider a non-Apple keyboard: how it feels. The pressure required to generate a keystroke, how well the keys respond to fast typing, the sound they make when pressed and released — these characteristics combine to give every keyboard its own personality. If you find Apple's keyboards uncomfortable or unresponsive, give

Three Apple Mice

Apple currently ships three mice, and only fate determines which one you'll get. One species is electro-mechanical, using the ball to drive two wheels whose edges are ringed with metallic encoders. A current is made and broken as the encoders spin past electrical contacts. The other mice use the opto-mechanical design described later in this chapter.

Here's how to tell the three rodents apart:

❖ The electro-mechanical mouse has a heavy grey ball with a sliding retainer ring and is made in the United States.

❖ The first opto-mechanical mouse has a lighter black ball with a rotating retainer and is made in Taiwan. Some people complain that this mouse's lightweight ball prevents smooth pointer movement.

❖ The second and latest opto-mechanical mouse (shipping since mid-1990) has a heavy grey ball with a rotating retainer and hails from Malaysia. Incidentally, the original Apple mouse — the non ADB mouse — was born in 1983 along with Apple's Lisa and the Apple IIe. The Macintosh 128K, 512K, 512K Enhanced, and Plus used this mouse. Apple still uses this mouse for the Apple IIe and IIc. **M**

the competition a try. But remember, you will be stroking those keys for years, so don't buy a keyboard until you've test-driven it.

Pointing Alternatives

Since its invention in 1964, the mouse has become the world's premier pointing device. Apple builds a first-rate rodent that meets most users' needs — and, unlike a keyboard, it's conveniently included with each machine (see the sidebar "Three Apple Mice"). But tastes in input devices do vary, and certain tasks benefit from a different approach to pointing.

Although Apple's mice are among the best, they're mechanical beasts prone to wear and breakdown. The mouse mechanism uses a rubber ball that requires a smooth surface on which to roll, lest the pointer jerk across the screen. The ball and the rollers it touches accumulate dirt and require periodic cleaning. An extremely dusty environment — a factory, a wood-heated house, or my office — can choke an Apple mouse to death.

A mouse that doesn't share these shortcomings is Mouse Systems Corporation's aptly named Little Mouse. Designed for ADB-equipped Macs, the Little Mouse is an *optical* mouse — rather than measuring the movement of a rubber ball, it measures the light reflected from a 7-by-8-inch pad covered with a grid of minute dots (see the figure "How Pointing Devices Work"). Aside from its button, the Little Mouse has no moving parts to wear out or get cheesy. It's also smaller and lighter than an Apple mouse. The required mouse pad does add to desktop clutter, but many people prefer to use a mouse pad even with a conventional mouse because the mouse glides nicely on a pad's smooth surface. I used a Little Mouse for a few weeks and found it a worthy alternative to an Apple mouse.

Another contender is Advanced Gravis's $129.95 SuperMouse, for ADB-equipped Macs. It has not one button but three, and lets you program them to issue Command-key sequences or execute macros (a scaled-down version of QuicKeys is included). People who use Apple's AU/X version of the UNIX operating system may like the SuperMouse especially well, since UNIX is often used with a three-button mouse.

For those who like the mouse but not its tail, there are Practical Solutions' Cordless Mouse and Basic Needs' The Cordless Mouse. Both use an infrared link instead of a wire. Each requires batteries and provides a sleep mode that conserves juice when the mouse isn't moving.

How Pointing Devices Work

Mechanical Mouse

In an Apple mouse, a rubber ball touches two capstans, which are connected to slotted wheels sandwiched between two light-source-and-photosensor pairs (**A** and **B**). When the ball rolls, the capstans turn the wheels, whose slots interrupt the light. Each interruption is interpreted by the Mac as one increment of movement. The sensors are offset slightly so that, as the wheels turn, they produce a pair of signals with a pause between. The direction a wheel turns is indicated by which sensor, **A** or **B**, produces the first signal in each pair. Trackballs work similarly, except only the ball (not the entire housing) moves.

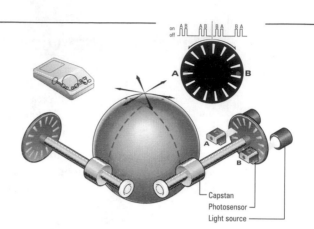

Capstan
Photosensor
Light source

Optical Mouse

In an optical mouse, light from two light sources (**A** and **B**) reflects off a pad covered with a fine grid of dots. The image of the grid is projected onto two separate photosensors. One senses vertical movement (**C**) and the other horizontal movement (**D**). As the reflection of the grid passes over the sensors, circuitry within the mouse counts the dots to determine the distance the mouse has moved in either direction.

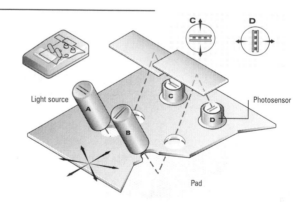

Light source
Photosensor
Pad

Tablet with Stylus

In a graphics tablet, a drawing stylus or cursor exchanges minute radio signals with the tablet through a grid of wires that crisscross the drawing area. The tablet determines the location of the stylus and transmits the location information to the Macintosh. The stylus doesn't need to touch the tablet surface itself; this means you can trace a drawing, even through several pages of a book.

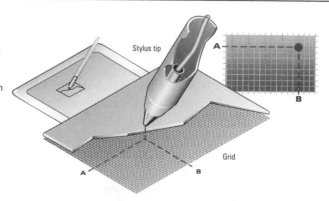

Stylus tip
Grid

Pointing without Rolling

But even a tailless mouse requires some desk space in which to roam. If you just can't spare that kind of real estate, consider a *trackball* — a plastic ball that sits on rollers housed within a small case that, like a keyboard, occupies a fixed location on your desk. To move the Mac's pointer, you roll your fingers across the trackball.

Most trackballs provide two buttons. One works just like a standard mouse button, while the other works like a mouse button that sticks. This second button lets you drag icons, windows, or other items without holding down a button: click the button once to start dragging, then click it again to stop. By giving your hand one less chore to perform, a locking-click button can help you make more precise pointer movements, and it eliminates the finger fatigue that hours of delicate dragging can cause.

Some trackballs — such as Kensington Microware's Turbo Mouse ADB — let you combine both buttons to perform special tasks. For example, you can configure it to issue an often-used keyboard command, such as Command-S for Save. This technique of pressing two or more buttons simultaneously is called *chording*.

Other ADB-compatible trackballs include Mouse Systems Corporation's three-button Trackball/ADB; Abaton's two-button ProPoint; MicroSpeed's three-button MacTrac; lynx Computer Products' two-button lynx Turbo Trackball and Kraft Systems' two-button Trackball ADB, which can accept an optional foot pedal for clicking. All but Kraft's trackball are also available for the Mac Plus.

Something to consider when trackball shopping is the size of the ball itself. Some people find that a smaller sphere, such as the lynx Turbo Trackball's, gives more control. See how comfortable you are with the size and position of the trackball's buttons. They're all different: Kensington's Turbo Mouse ADB's big buttons curve around the trackball itself, while Abaton's ProPoint has one large button and one small one to help you remember which is the locking one. And if you're left-handed, opt for a trackball that lets you reverse the functions of the single-click and locking-click buttons.

Absolute Pointing

As effective as mice and trackballs are, they still lack the familiar feel of a pen or pencil, making them second-best tools for drawing and drafting. For these tasks it's hard to beat a *graphics tablet,* also called a *digitizing tablet.* Tablets provide a flat drawing area upon which you scrawl using a penlike *stylus* whose tip contains a switch that mimics a mouse button. Most tablets have a drawing area that's covered with a clear plastic sheet, or *overlay,* under which you can tuck artwork to be traced. A newspaper artist might use a graphics tablet and a drawing program such as Aldus FreeHand or Adobe Illustrator to trace a map or diagram to accompany a story. Many tablet pens accept ink-filled cartridges, allowing you to place a sheet of paper on the tablet's surface to see on paper what you're drawing on screen.

Tablet work areas vary widely in size, and as the size increases, so does the price. One inexpensive tablet, CalComp's Wiz (for ADB-equipped Macs) provides a small work area — 7½ inches square. Midrange tablets have work areas of about 8½ by 11 or 12 by 18 inches. Large tablets can give as much work area as a drafting table. Wacom's SD-013L, for example, offers a 35-by-47-inch drawing surface.

But their pen-on-paper operating style isn't all that makes tablets superior drawing tools. Equally important, they're *absolute-motion* pointing devices, while mice and trackballs are *relative-motion* pointing devices. Your blind mouse can't report its physical location — it doesn't know whether it's at the edge of the desk or in the middle. When you pick up the mouse and set it down elsewhere, the pointer doesn't suddenly jump to a different spot on the screen. Mice and trackballs simply report that they're moving a certain distance in a certain direction.

❝ *The higher a pointing device's resolution, the better suited it is to precise drawing, since it's able to register even minute movements.* ❞

In contrast, each point on a graphics tablet corresponds to a point on the Mac's screen. Pick up a tablet's stylus and then touch it to a different part of the drawing area, and the Mac's pointer *does* suddenly jump to a different part of the screen. It's this operating style that makes tablets ideal for tracing and drawing. Most tablets also provide a relative-motion mode that you can use when you want mouselike operation.

Graphics tablets are also better able to discern small degrees of movement. Mice and trackballs can generally discern 200 to 300 units of movement per inch, but graphics tablets typically detect 1000 units or more per inch. The higher a pointing device's *resolution,* the better suited it is to precise drawing, since it's able to register even minute movements.

For artists, the most exciting graphics tablets are pressure sensitive. With tablets such as Wacom's SD series, pressing harder with the stylus gives you a darker or wider line. But there's a catch: you need a graphics program that responds to the pressure information the tablet sends. Wacom tablets include driver files that enable Deneba's UltraPaint and Silicon Beach Software's

SuperPaint 2.0 to respond to pressure. Adobe Photoshop supports Wacom tablets directly.

Another desirable, if costly, trait to look for in a tablet is the ability to work with a cordless pen. By eliminating the pen-to-tablet umbilical, tablets such as Wacom's SD series and Kurta's IS series take one more step toward providing a natural-feeling drawing surface. Most tablets, including Wacom's and Kurta's, also accept a mouselike *cursor* containing a lens with cross-hairs that aid in precise positioning.

Finally, to help earn their keep, many tablets accept *command templates* that give you one-click access to frequently used commands. A template package includes a disk and a printed sheet that slips beneath the tablet's plastic overlay and contains labeled boxes in which you click to issue commands. Of course, locating the right box and then clicking in it can take as long as choosing the command with the mouse. But it never hurts to have another option for choosing commands, and some people do find templates ideal alternatives.

I Said Cut, not Quit

Keyboards, mice, trackballs, and graphics tablets represent the mainstream of input devices. In the backwaters, you'll find some specialized devices, including *joysticks.* Anyone who's seen a video game has seen a joystick; it's a moving appendage similar to a car stick-shift with a button on top. Advanced Gravis's MouseStick and CH Products' Mach IV Plus also provide buttons alongside the stick. The MouseStick provides several goodies, including adjustable stick tension and programmable buttons that transmit commands when pressed. Both are available for ADB and non-ADB Macs. Joysticks remain best suited to game playing, but they can also be used as mouse replacements.

A distant cousin to the joystick is Altra's $169 Felix, for ADB-equipped Macs. Felix uses a short, stubby stick that moves within a one-inch area. Altra says the stick's tight area of travel makes it feel more precise and natural than a mouse or conventional joystick. Felix was previously marketed by Lightgate Systems, but Altra says it's improved the stick's precision and features considerably.

And then there's *voice-recognition* hardware like Articulate Systems' Voice Navigator II, available for the Plus on up, and MacSema's Voice Express, available for the Mac II family (an SE version is in the works at this writing). Both devices let you issue commands by speaking them. But first, you (and anyone else who will use it) must train the system by repeatedly speaking the words you want it to recognize. Thereafter, the system compares what you say to what it knows, looking for matches. Voice-recognition hardware can't yet take dictation and replace the keyboard for general data entry, but it can aid users who have disabilities.

Some people believe voice recognition represents the future. I doubt it. Today's systems are too primitive, unable to tell *two* from *too*, for example, and susceptible to background noise and variations in pronunciation.

Others claim handwriting recognition — already available in a limited form from Personal Writer's Personal Writer 15SL graphics tablet — is where we're heading. I don't think so. These days, more people can type than ever before, and most of them can type faster than they can write.

Until some as-yet-unforeseen breakthrough occurs, keyboards and mice will probably remain the preeminent input devices. Besides, who wants to work in an office full of people barking at their computers?

Summary:

✔ Although a pointing device is the cornerstone of the Mac's graphical interface, the keyboard is essential for typing-intensive applications such as word processors, data managers, and spreadsheets.

✔ The mouse can come in many forms, including the standard Apple mouse, an optical mouse (measures the light reflected from a pad covered with a grid of minute dots), a three-button mouse (extra button lets you issue Command-key sequences or macros), and a cordless mouse.

✔ A trackball is an alternative to the mouse that consists of a plastic ball that sits on rollers housed within a small case. The pointer is moved by rolling the trackball with your fingers.

✔ Many artists and draftspeople prefer a graphics tablet and its pen-like stylus to the mouse.

✔ Joysticks (moving appendages similar to a car's stick-shift, and most often used for video games) and voice recognition hardware (commands activated by voice) are two of the specialized input devices available.

Chapter 38
Color Video

In This Chapter:

✔ How color Macs display their images.

✔ Color look-up tables and how the Mac uses them.

✔ Details on the video circuitry of the various Mac models.

✔ How color fits into the Mac's user interface.

✔ A summary of the different kinds of color applications.

✔ Color printer and monitor options.

The retinas of your eyes are lined with small, light-sensitive nerve elements called rods and cones. Rods are especially sensitive to weak light, but can't distinguish colors. Cones can't detect low light levels, but they do respond to color. Some cones are especially sensitive to red light; others, to green; and still others, to blue. These three colors are *primary colors*, the basic building blocks of colored light.

When red light enters the eye, it stimulates the red-sensitive cones. Yellow light stimulates cones sensitive to red and green — the two primary colors that form yellow. White light stimulates all three types. When the cones are stimulated, they send impulses to the brain's vision center, which merges and interprets the red, green, and blue impulses to create the thought sensation we call color.

Until the Mac II came along, the Macintosh lived in a black-and-white, or *monochrome*, world — even though the color capabilities of the Apple II helped make that machine a classic. Did the Mac's original designers have an aversion to color? No. The Mac was born color blind more because of economics than aesthetics. Apple was determined to keep the Mac's size and cost down, but to give it a screen with enough resolution to display sharp graphics and a variety of fonts.

For reasons we'll explore shortly, color requires more memory than monochrome. Special high-capacity memory chips would have allowed Apple to shoehorn color capabilities into the Mac, but they were scarce and expensive in the early 80s. What's more, the additional processing demands imposed by color would have made the original Mac unbearably slow — a point it was approaching anyway.

But times change. Nowadays, high-capacity memory chips are plentiful and less expensive. And the 68000 microprocessor has speedier successors, the 68020 and 68030. Apple exploited these advancements when designing the Macintosh II, and refined the Mac's system software to provide a sturdy foundation upon which to build future color Macs. Today, the Macintosh family has several machines that can put your cones to work. In this chapter, I'll examine the technical concepts behind color and grey-scale video, and show how color fits into the Mac world.

What Eight Bits Will Buy

Let's start out by examining how color Macs display their images. You may recall from previous chapters that the Mac uses a *bitmapped* display. Each screen dot, or *pixel*, corresponds to one bit in the Mac's memory. When a given bit has a value of one, its corresponding pixel is on, or black. When a bit has a value of zero, its pixel is off, or white.

Because a bit can have only one of two values (1 or 0), a bitmapped display that uses one bit per pixel can display only two colors: black or white. Shades of grey can be simulated by *dithering*, in which groups of pixels are combined into patterns. The Mac's grey desktop is an example of a dithered pattern formed by evenly spaced, alternating black and white pixels.

The secret to displaying color or true shades of grey is to assign additional bits to each pixel — what many people refer to as increasing the *pixel depth*. Each additional bit lets a color Mac store more information about the pixel. Two bits per pixel can represent four colors. Four bits can represent 16 colors, and eight can represent 256 colors. You can tell a color Mac how many bits to assign each pixel by using the Monitors control panel (see the figure "Bits and Pixels").

But how can only two bits represent four colors, or eight, 256? In the video circuitry of a color Mac, the bits that represent each pixel can be on (assigned a value of 1) or off (assigned a value of 0) in different combinations. For example, when two bits are assigned to each pixel, four on-off combinations exist: both bits on; both bits off; one bit on, second bit off; and second bit on, first bit off.

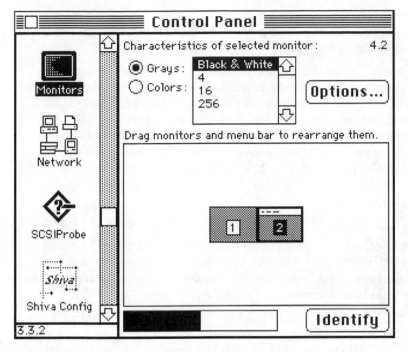

When four bits are assigned to each pixel, you get sixteen on-off combinations. With eight bits per pixel, you get 256 combinations. Internally, the Mac uses 24 bits to describe colors, giving it the ability to create more than 16 million different hues. But remember, the number of colors that can actually be *displayed* at once depends on the video board and monitor you use. Most Macs have color video circuitry that can assign a maximum of eight bits to each pixel, so they

▲ Bits and Pixels

The Monitors control panel lets you specify how many bits the Mac II should assign to each pixel, and whether it should display colors or shades of grey. If you have more than one video board installed (as is the case here), you can also specify where the menu bar should appear.

can display a maximum of 256 colors or grey shades simultaneously. (As we'll see shortly, there are exceptions.)

So a color Mac's first step in determining a pixel's color is to determine the value of each of the pixel's bits. If you're using four bits per pixel, the result of that operation is a number between 0 and 15. The Mac uses the resulting number to retrieve a color description from a *color look-up table* — the next stop on our tour of the Mac family's color capabilities.

I'd Like Three Pixels of Colonial Red...

If you've seen someone at a paint store mix a special color, you're well on your way to understanding color look-up tables (also called *CLUTs*). When you buy a custom color, the store's employee leafs through a paint-stained book until he finds the number of the color you want. Next to that number is a "recipe" listing the correct quantities of the appropriate pigments that must be blended to create the color.

Now imagine that the Mac's video circuitry is the paint store employee. Given a number that represents the state of the pixel's bits, the circuitry leafs through the color look-up table, which can hold the recipes for 256 different colors, to find the recipe corresponding to the number. The recipe consists of three numbers that tell the circuitry how much red, green, and blue light is required to create that color.

Next, the video circuitry generates electrical signals that control the red, green, and blue electron guns located in the back of the monitor's video tube. Each gun squirts a beam of electrons at the tube's display surface, which is coated with red, green, and blue phosphor dots. The phosphor glows briefly, but just long enough for your eyes to see the glow and detect varying degrees of red, green, and blue light. Because the dots are too small to be seen individually, they appear as a single colored pixel.

Satisfying Your Palette

Working with one color look-up table sounds hard enough, but a color Mac's capabilities don't end there. A system software component called the Palette Manager lets the Mac load different color look-up tables into and out of the video board's memory.

This capability is especially important for image scanning or color painting applications. The 256 color descriptions that a look-up table can hold might seem like a lot, but they aren't enough to accurately render gradual color shifts and variations in shading. The solution is to create custom palettes in which unused colors are replaced with ones customized for the task at hand. For example, a portrait artist might replace the brilliant blues and Day-Glo greens in the palette with an expanded choice of flesh tones, while a landscape artist would want numerous shades of green and blue to choose from. Most graphics programs that allow you to swap palettes also allow you to save them on disk for future recall.

True Color

But the best way to get more simultaneous colors is with a 24-bit, or *true color,* video board such as Apple's Display Card 8•24, Radius' DirectColor/GX, or RasterOps' 24S or 24L. These boards work with Apple's 32-bit QuickDraw to assign 24 bits to each pixel, giving you direct access to more than 16 million simultaneous colors. True color video cards take advantage of 32-bit QuickDraw's ability to directly drive the circuitry that controls the monitor's electron guns without having to use color look-up tables (see the figure "Looking Behind a Color Monitor").

But with prices in the $1000–$2000 ballpark, buying one of these boards can turn your bank balance bright red. What's more, because a true color video board must move megabytes of data in order to create its images, activities like

LOOKING BEHIND A COLOR MONITOR

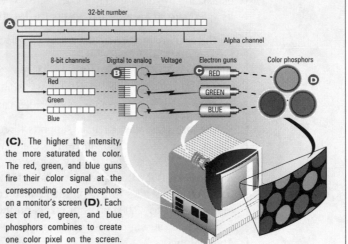

The digital information that represents an image goes through several transformations before appearing on the Mac's screen. Each screen pixel starts life out as a chunk of 32 bits **(A)**—8 bits define red, 8 define green, and 8 define blue. The remaining 8 bits (the alpha channel) are reserved for special effects that vendors may opt to support. Lines of 32- bit information are queued up in a buffer on the video display board; the lines are separated into 8-bit chunks, and each chunk is sent to a converter that transforms it from digital to analog information **(B)**. The board electrically intensifies each analog signal, so that it can drive its corresponding electron gun

(C). The higher the intensity, the more saturated the color. The red, green, and blue guns fire their color signal at the corresponding color phosphors on a monitor's screen **(D)**. Each set of red, green, and blue phosphors combines to create one color pixel on the screen.

scrolling and redrawing windows become sluggish when the board is in its 24-bit mode. For optimum true color performance, you'll want a board containing a *graphics accelerator,* such as Apple's Display Card 8•24GC. Thanks to the 8•24GC's dedicated graphics processor (an American Micro Devices 29000 running at 30MHz), true-color images snap into view instead of oozing onto the screen. Indeed, scrolling a 24-bit image with the 8•24GC is faster than scrolling an 8-bit image with Apple's original video card.

The 8•24GC board, like most true-color boards, provides general-purpose graphics acceleration. It doesn't cut the time required to render a complex, ray-traced image, although it does display the final product faster. Nor is the 8•24GC optimized for vector (object-oriented) drawing. If the only color application you use is a CAD program such as AutoCAD, you might be better served by a product such as Radius' QuickCAD board.

Although we've covered a lot of ground, we've only touched on the technicalities behind the Mac's color capabilities. Another of its talents is the ability to keep track of multiple palettes and screens, a skill that becomes vital when you have both a color and a monochrome monitor attached to a Mac. In such cases, the Mac must keep track of each monitor's color capabilities, and adjust its displays accordingly — even when you position a window so that it spans across a color screen and a monochrome one.

Built-in Video: Is it Really Free?

The Mac LC, IIsi, and IIci include 8-bit video circuitry on their logic boards, eliminating the need to buy a video card. When you start up any of these Macs, its video circuitry senses and adapts itself to the monitor you've attached.

The circuitry in the Mac IIci and IIsi displays up to 256 colors or grey shades on Apple's 12- and 13-inch color and monochrome monitors, and up to 16 shades of grey on the Apple Portrait Display. The video circuitry does not support Apple's Two-Page Monochrome Monitor, although you can use that monitor by buying a separate NuBus video card.

The Mac LC's video circuitry supports three Apple monitors. The LC can display 16 colors on the 13-inch AppleColor monitor; 256 colors on the 12-inch RGB Display; and 16 grey shades on the 12-inch Monochrome Display. A video RAM (VRAM) upgrade is available for the LC that boosts the number of colors or grey shades to 256 on the 13-inch color and 12-inch monochrome monitors, and to 32,000 greys or colors on the 12-inch color monitor. (These potentially confusing details are summarized in the table "Built-in Video and Apple Monitors.")

But for IIci and IIsi owners, there's a price to pay for free video. In its 16- and 256-color modes, the on-board video in the IIci and IIsi provides slower performance than does a plug-in video board, which provides its own video memory. That's because the Mac's CPU often has to wait to access memory because the video circuitry will be accessing the same bank of memory in the course of creating screen images. Two office workers can use the same filing

Built-In Video and Apple Monitors

	12" Monochrome Display	12" RGB Display	AppleColor 13" High-Resolution RGB Monitor	Macintosh 15" Portrait Display	Two-Page 21" Monochrome Monitor
Resolution (pixels)	640 by 480	512 by 384	640 by 480	640 by 870	1152 by 870
LC	16 greys (with VRAM upgrade, 256)	256 colors (with VRAM upgrade, 32,000)	16 colors (with VRAM upgrade, 256)	Not supported*	Not supported*
IIsi	256 greys	256 colors	256 colors	16 greys	Not supported*
IIci	256 greys	256 colors	256 colors	16 greys	Not supported*

* These monitors can be used with appropriate video cards, if available.

drawer to store different things, but not at the same time. What kind of performance penalty can you expect? In tests performed by Macworld Lab, a Mac IIsi using built-in video was almost twice as slow in 256-color mode as a IIsi using a NuBus video board (Apple's Macintosh Display Card 4•8). This performance penalty doesn't apply to the Mac LC, which uses dedicated video RAM.

And because the video circuitry uses part of the Mac's main memory to hold the screen image, less memory is available to run programs — up to 320K less in the 256-color mode (see the table "Built-in Video and Memory"). Given that 2MB of memory is the bare minimum required for System 7.0 (and for getting any real use out of MultiFinder in System 6.x), if you plan to buy a IIsi or IIci, you may want to buy a memory upgrade at the same time.

Pick a Color, Any Color

Another example of Apple's attention to color details is the way you choose and change colors. Rather than allowing application developers to design their own color-choosing schemes — which could result in dozens of different approaches — Apple incorporated into the Mac's system a standard way of changing colors called the *color wheel,* or *color picker,* dialog box. Just as the Open and Save dialog boxes give you a standard method for opening and saving documents, the color wheel dialog box provides a standard way to change colors.

The color wheel dialog box consists of a colorful circle with a scroll bar alongside it and six text-entry boxes filled with numbers (see the figure "Wheel of Color" on the next page). The easiest way to choose colors is to drag the mouse pointer within the wheel; as you do, the numbers in the left side of the dialog box change to reflect the internal recipe for the current color. To

Built-In Video and Memory

Type of Monitor	Screen size (pixels)	Memory Required for Video Mode			
		Black and White	4 colors/greys	16 colors/greys	256 colors/greys
12" Monochrome Display	640 by 480	38K	75K	150K	300K
12" RGB Display	512 by 384	24K	48K	96K	192K
AppleColor 13" RGB Monitor	640 by 480	38K	75K	150K	300K
Macintosh Portrait Display	640 by 870	68K	136K	272K	not supported

decrease a color's brightness, you use the scroll bar. You can also type values directly into the text-entry boxes; one reason for doing so would be to precisely duplicate someone else's color choices.

The text boxes reflect the current color setting in two different ways, each corresponding to a different *model* for describing colors. In the *RGB* model, a color is described by the amount of red, green, and blue light it contains. In the *hue, saturation, and brightness* model, a color is described by its hue (its color, formed by a single primary color or a combination of primaries), its saturation (its purity, or the degree of grey present in the color), and its brightness (the degree of lightness from white to black). Both models are

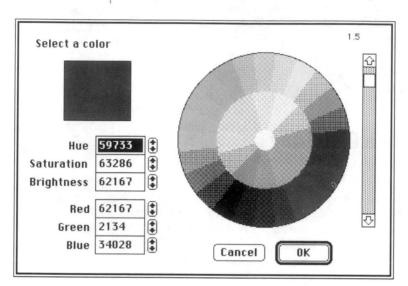

▲ Wheel of Color

Apple's standard color picker dialog box lets you choose colors by dragging the pointer within the color wheel or by typing values in the text-entry boxes. The color swatch above the text-entry boxes lets you compare the current color to the one you started with.

interrelated; change a number in one set of boxes, and one or more values in the other set change accordingly.

Understanding the hue, saturation, and brightness approach to color creation is easier if you pretend that the color wheel is cone-shaped. The outer rim of the cone contains vivid, fully saturated colors. As brightness decreases, the cone gets narrower, since there are fewer discernable dark colors than there are bright ones. (If that sounds fishy to you, consider the fact that most of the colors for which names exist are bright ones.) The cone's center axis always contains equal amounts of red, green, and blue, so it represents shades of grey ranging from white at the top of the cone to black at the bottom.

The color wheel, then, is simply a two-dimensional view of a three-dimensional hue, saturation, and brightness cone — it's as if you're looking at the cone from above. The wheel depicts the current color's hue and saturation, while the scroll bar to the right of the wheel takes the place of the third dimension — brightness.

Color and You

Enough of theory. What's it like to use a color Mac? In many ways, it's no different than using a monochrome one. Apple has done a superb job of providing remarkable color features while retaining the Mac's easy to use operating style. And it showed restraint in not using color for color's sake.

The first place you see color is in the familiar "Welcome to Macintosh" screen, in which the minimalist-style Mac drawing appears in color. When the Finder appears, don't expect to be dazzled. In System 6.x, the Apple menu appears in color and a Color menu appears in the menu bar, but those are the only giveaways that you're using a color Mac. In System 7.0, windows, scroll bars, and the Trash have an attractive 3-D appearance to them. But overall, Apple took a subtle approach to the use of color in the Mac's user interface. Color is a powerful and highly subjective conveyer of information, and Apple's user interface engineers feel strongly about not foisting a rainbow of colors upon users just because some Macs can display them.

But Apple did provide some options for colorizing the Mac environment. The General control panel lets you choose from several desktop colors or create your own. The Color control panel lets you choose a different highlight color — the color used to indicate a selected icon or text passage. Finally, the Color menu in Finder 6.x offers another way to organize your files, allowing you to assign any of eight colors to icons and folders. Finder 6.x's View menu includes an additional command, By Color, that lets you sort a disk's window according to its icon's colors.

In System 7.0, the Color menu is replaced by the more useful Label menu, which lets you assign color icons and attach text labels to color codes. And as we saw in Chapter 25, System 7.0 even lets you paste a color picture into an icon.

Colored desktops and icons are nice, but if you just spent several thousand dollars on a Mac and color monitor, you might wish there were more ways to work color into your electronic desktop. There are, thanks to Preferred Publisher's Personality, Dubl-Click Software's ClickChange, and Palomar Software's Colorizer. These utilities let you add color to every element of the Mac's user interface, from windows and menus to scroll bars and buttons. Colorizer includes many preset color combinations — like "Miami Vice," which turns your Mac into a palace of pastels, or "4th of July," which gives you a red, white, and blue workplace. Should you not share color preferences with Don Johnson or Ollie North, you can choose from over a dozen others or create your own. Colorizer also lets you install color start-up screens, and it includes an application that lets you add color to MacDraw or other PICT-format drawings, and a screen-capture FKEY that lets you commit full-color screen shots to disk. It's a package no owner of a color Mac should be without.

A Rainbow of Applications

Of course, you don't buy a color Mac just to have colored menus and scroll bars. Color fits into most popular application areas, and creates some new ones of its own. Color applications include:

❖ *Painting and drawing* Needless to say, color adds a whole new dimension to electronic canvases and drafting tables. The two classic categories of graphics software — bitmapped and object-oriented — still exist in the color world, and each has the same advantages and drawbacks as its monochrome counterpart: bitmapped programs are superior for rendering fine detail and shading, while object-oriented ones are better for electronic drafting and other applications in which images are represented by collections of shapes.

❖ *Business and presentation graphics* Bar graphs and pie charts speak louder when their bars and wedges are in color. As we saw in Chapter 10, some programs can generate brilliant color slides by printing to specialized (and expensive) output devices called *film recorders*.

❖ *Desktop publishing* Most desktop publishing programs let you assign *spot color* to elements such as headlines or rules. On color Macs, you can see the colors. Some publishing and illustration programs also let you specify colors using the *Pantone matching system*, a standard method of color specification in the printing industry. Of course, creating color separations for the final printing job still involves printing a separate, black-and-white page for each ink color.

❖ *Business applications* You'll also find color where you wouldn't expect it, such as in spreadsheet programs — when your budget's in the red, your spreadsheet figures can be, too. Many database managers can display fields and records in color.

❖ *Animation and broadcasting* Equipped with a *genlock* expansion board, a Mac can send video signals directly into video equipment. More and more, Macs are being set up alongside million dollar graphics workstations used for creating on-air graphics and animation. Check your local listings for details.

Color Me Compatible — Mostly

Considering the colorful capabilities of some Macs, you might expect to find a raft of incompatibilities between them and monochrome Macs. Actually, there are surprisingly few. Color QuickDraw, the fundamental software routines responsible for the Mac family's color capabilities, works together with the rest of the system software to keep the entire Macintosh family on speaking terms.

One potential incompatibility involves opening a color document on a monochrome Mac. The original QuickDraw has limited color capabilities — the only hues it can recognize are black, white, red, green, blue, yellow, magenta, and cyan. Many desktop publishing and graphics applications let you create documents containing these colors, and print them on color printers such as the ImageWriter II.

When you open a Color QuickDraw image on a monochrome Mac, the monochrome Mac discards any color information that the original QuickDraw can't recognize. Anything on one side of a given intensity will display and print as white; everything else will display and print as black. If the picture was created using the old, eight-color QuickDraw, everything that isn't white will display as black, although it should print correctly. Got all that? Don't worry — if you aren't moving documents between color and monochrome Macs, you won't encounter this incompatibility. If you're using a network and routinely shuttle documents between machines, however, beware.

The Money of Color

Other grey areas exist in the world of Macintosh color. One problem is a dearth of color printers, especially ones capable of doing justice to 8- and 24-bit color images. Hewlett-Packard's $1395, 180 dots-per-inch PaintJet is a good low-end color printer, ideal for producing color overhead transparencies. HP's PaintWriter XL is better still, able to handle 32-bit QuickDraw images and a larger variety of paper sizes. Mitsubishi, NEC, QMS, Seiko, and Tektronix all offer 300-dpi color printers that produce stunning results, but the printers' prices are in the four- and five-figure ballparks.

The high cost of color surfaces everywhere you look, from video boards to monitors to the high-capacity hard disk you'll need to store large color images. So if you're buying a Mac that's capable of displaying color, don't feel obligated to buy a color monitor and 24-bit video board. Color displays are beautiful, but they don't render text as sharply as monochrome ones. And the extra processing time required to work with all those colors slows the Mac's performance.

Of course, take my advice with a grain of salt. I bought a color monitor for my Mac, even though I spend most of my time gazing at text. Why didn't I go the less expensive monochrome route? Well, the excuse I gave my accountant — and she knows who she is — was that I need a color system to test and write about color software.

That's what you really need to buy a color Mac — a good excuse.

Summary:

✔ Displaying color requires more memory than monochrome (black and white), since more bits must be assigned to each pixel.

✔ The secret to displaying color or true shades of grey is to assign additional bits to each pixel — what many refer to as increasing the pixel depth.

✔ To find a particular color to display, the Mac uses look-up tables which list the "recipe" for blending the right pigments to create the desired color.

✔ Some Macs contain built-in color video hardware; with other Macs, you must buy a separate video board.

✔ For the IIci and IIsi, there's a price to pay for free video: slower performance as pixel depth increases. The primary reason for this is that the IIci and IIsi use part of their main memory as video memory, while other machines use plug-in video boards that provide their own video memory.

✔ Utilities such as Palomar Software's Colorizer let you add color to every element of the Mac's user interface.

Chapter 39
Scanners

In This Chapter:

✔ How scanners are used — and do you really need one?

✔ How scanners work.

✔ Advantages and disadvantages of sheet-fed and flatbed scanners.

✔ A look at scanner resolution and grey-scale scanners.

✔ Tips for getting the best results from your scanner.

O wning a scanner probably sounds enticing. Think of the possibilities — if your database manager supports graphics, you can put scanned images of products in your inventory database. A real-estate database could include an image of each property along with its description, allowing prospective buyers to search for — and see — houses meeting their needs.

Scanned images team up well with HyperCard, too. You might scan a map, then adorn it with buttons and scripts that describe a street or landmark when you click on it. Or you could scan a diagram of an engine, then create scripts describing each part's purpose.

But before you get out your checkbook, consider the drawbacks. Most scanners are expensive, and the images they create can devour memory and disk space. In this chapter, I'll explore the world of electronic imaging, with the goal of helping you decide if a scanner is for you. You'll find some tips for better scans in the sidebar "Toward Better Scans," at the end of this chapter.

A Scanner's Roles

Creating image files for desktop publications is the most common scanner application. Many graphic designers use scanners to create *for position only* scans that show clients or professional printers where final photos should appear. But most Mac programs can accept graphics from the Clipboard or can directly open MacPaint documents, allowing scanned images to show up elsewhere, such as HyperCard stacks, word processing documents, and databases. And scanners work well with *fax modems*, which allow the Mac to send and receive faxes (see Chapter 13). Indeed, without a scanner, you can't use a fax modem to send faxes of hard copy documents.

Scanners can also be used with *optical character recognition* (OCR) software, which I examined in Chapter 14. To recap briefly, OCR software turns a scanner into an electronic typist that can scan pages of text and turn out text files you can edit with a word processor. (Without OCR software, scanning text is like photocopying it — you can't edit or reformat the end product.) Law firms can scan reams of old contracts and save their text on disk. Publishing or typesetting companies can scan typewritten copy. Researchers can scan magazine or newspaper articles to create text databases.

When it comes to scanning images, originals come in two flavors: *continuoustone* images (such as photographs), which contain white and black areas along with many shades of grey: and *line art* (such as diagrams or pen-and-ink drawings), which is strictly black and white. As we'll see shortly, each type of original imposes its own demands on a scanner.

Scanner Species

Most scanners, like laser printers, are cousins of photocopiers. But a laser printer's resemblence is in the output department; a scanner's is in the input department. Like a photocopier, a scanner illuminates your original while a sensor called a *charge-coupled device*, or *CCD*, measures the light it reflects and generates a voltage (see the figure "Anatomy of a Scan"). Solid black areas reflect no light, resulting in a low voltage. White areas reflect the most light and generate the highest voltages. Grey areas create voltages whose levels depend on the shade of grey. The scanner's software translates the voltage values into data that represent the image.

Most scanners use one of two methods to perform the scanning process. With a *flatbed* scanner such as Apple's Apple Scanner or Microtek's MSF-300Z, the original remains stationary and the CCD mechanism moves across it during the scan. Some flatbed scanners, including Microtek's MSF-300Z, can scan in color by scanning an image in three passes, viewing the original through a different color filter (red, green, and blue) in each pass.

With a *sheet-fed* or *edge-feed* scanner, you feed the original into a slot, and a set of rubber rollers draws it past a stationary CCD mechanism. Sheet-fed scanners

ANATOMY OF A SCAN

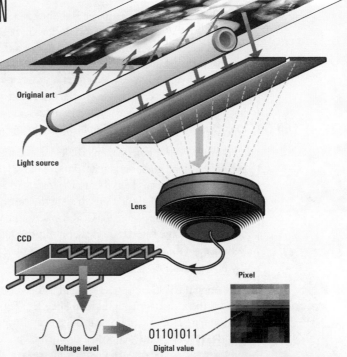

Original art

Light source

The scanner illuminates the original, and the CCD measures the amount of reflected light, generating higher voltage levels for lighter shades than for darker ones.

Lens

The scanner translates the incoming voltage levels into digital values, using a given number of bits to represent each dot. The more bits per dot a scanner uses, the better it can represent shades of grey.

CCD

Pixel

01101011

Voltage level   **Digital value**

When you specify a bitonal scan, the scanner doesn't save the grey-scale information. Instead, it determines whether a given voltage level represents an all-white pixel or an all-black one.

Selecting the scanner's halftoning option combines pixels into larger halftone cells, thus fixing the halftone resolution.

When you specify a grey-scale scan, the grey-scale information is saved in a TIFF file; halftone resolution is not specified until the image is printed.

include DEST's PC Scan 2000, Microtek's MS-II, and Datacopy's JetReader 220. Sheet-fed scanners are especially popular for OCR and fax applications.

Each approach has advantages and drawbacks. Flatbed scanners can scan pages from books and other originals too thick to fit between a sheet-fed scanner's rollers. Flatbed units also eliminate the risk of a delicate or irregularly shaped original jamming inside the unit. And they provide guides that make it easy to position the original. With a sheet-fed scanner, it's easy to insert something crookedly, causing crooked or *skewed* scans. Skewing is especially apparent with line art because it causes straight lines to assume a jagged-edged, stair-stepped look. With photos, skewing simply makes your photographer look sloppy.

But sheet-fed scanners often cost less, since they don't need a system of precisely aligned guides and rails to move the scanning mechanism. And their transport mechanisms lend themselves nicely to accepting *automatic document feeders*, paper-handling add-ons that shuttle originals into and out of the scanner for you — a real time-saver for OCR work. Automatic document feeders are available for some flatbed scanners, but they're much more common and often less costly in the sheet-fed world. Both types of scanners almost always attach to the Mac's SCSI port.

Sharing the field with sheet-fed and flatbed scanners are such unconventional units as the legendary ThunderScan Plus. The ThunderScan Plus's scanning hardware replaces the ribbon cartridge in an ImageWriter printer. You roll your original into the printer, choose a command, and the cartridge moves left and right, advancing the original slightly with each pass. ThunderScan was one of the first scanners available for the Mac; at $249 (plus a required $50 power pack if you have a member of the Mac II family), it's still the least expensive. But it's also the slowest. A full-page scan can easily take 20 minutes, versus the 30 seconds or so that other scanners require.

A step up from the ThunderScan Plus — but still a few flights down from a desktop scanner — is a *hand scanner* such as ThunderWare's LightningScan 400 or Logitech's ScanMan. A hand scanner looks like a small blow dryer on wheels. You slowly and carefully roll the scanner over your original, and the scanner transmits the image to the Mac via an external SCSI interface box. One drawback of hand scanners is that it's easy to lead the scanner astray as you roll it across the original, resulting in crooked scans. Another drawback is the scanner's narrow width, which restricts you to scanning in 4-inch wide swaths. Most hand scanners include software that allows you to piece together those swaths in order to scan wider originals. The process can be cumbersome, but still much faster than a ThunderScan — for not much more money.

Then there's the scanner's cousin, the *video digitizer*. As we saw in Chapter 17, digitizers such as Koala Technologies' MacVision accept video signals from a video recorder or camera and convert each horizontal video scan line into data. Their primary advantage over conventional scanners is that they don't require a photographic original. If you want highlights of the company picnic in the next newsletter, take a camcorder along and shoot, then digitize the high points later. But on the down side, scanning flat artwork with a video digitizer means buying a stand to hold the camera at the proper angle, and it means adjusting lights to illuminate the original evenly and focusing carefully to eliminate fuzzy edges.

At the upper end of the scanning spectrum are *slide scanners* such as Howtek's Scanmaster 35/II, Nikon's LS-3500, and Barneyscan's CIS•3515. These upper-class scanners create ultra-sharp color scans of 35-millimeter slides. With prices of between $5000 and $10,000, they're specialized tools that are only now coming into their own among professional publishers.

Looking Sharp: Resolution

Like video screens and laser printers, all scanners represent images by arranging a series of dots into a bitmap. The more dots per inch a scanner (or screen or printer) can work with, the higher its *resolution*, and generally, the sharper its images.

Scanners typically provide a resolution of 300 dots per inch (dpi), a value matching the resolution of most laser printers. A few scanners, such as Agfa's Focus II 800GSE, provide 400-dpi resolution, although for reasons I'll explain shortly, 300 dpi is usually more than adequate. The ThunderScan Plus's resolution with an actual-size scan (no enlargement or reduction) is only 72 dpi, but using some clever scanning tricks, you can boost an image's resolution to nearly 300 dpi.

Differences in resolution can be more apparent in scanned line art than in scanned photos. As resolution drops, sharply defined shapes in line art take on the jagged look (known as *aliasing*); to see for yourself, compare a circle on the Mac's screen to one printed by a laser printer.

Looking Shady: Grey Scales

Continuous-tone images impose their own demands. Because a bit can represent only white or black values, depicting shades of grey requires special techniques. The first scanners used a scheme called *dithering*, in which the scanning software combined black and white dots into patterns that simulated shades of grey. The Mac's desktop pattern is a good example of a dithered shade of grey.

The drawback of dithering is that the scanner software must assign each grey shade a specific number of dots. In the image-rendering world, when you assign a specific number of dots to anything, you lose the ability to take advantage of a screen or printer whose resolution is higher than resolution you've already chosen. That's why it's preferable to retain some *resolution independence* — to not lock the image into a specific number of dots per inch until it's actually printed.

The scanner world reached this vital milestone with the debut of *grey-scale* scanners. Grey-scale scanners represent grey in the same way a color Mac represents color: they assign more bits to each dot. By assigning four bits of data to each dot, a scanner can represent 16 different shades of grey (four bits can have 16 different on-off combinations). Six bits per dot can represent 64 grey levels; eight can represent 256. Among today's grey-scale scanners, most use four or eight bits per dot.

When you scan a photo with a grey-scale scanner, its software doesn't simulate shades of grey through dithering. Instead, it saves the incoming grey-scale information. The image is converted into dots when you print it, thanks to a process called *halftoning*.

Halftoning is what allows a printing press — which can't print shades of grey — to represent a continuous tone-image. In the printing world, halftoning involves photographing a continuous-tone image through a screen that converts the image into a series of tiny black dots that a press can print. The halftone represents different grey shades by varying the size of the halftone dots: larger dots for darker shades, smaller dots for lighter ones.

A laser printer handles halftoning differently: since it can't vary the size of its dots, it must combine several dots into a larger *cell* whose size it *can* vary (by turning some dots on and others off). You're able to print halftone images, but at a price: because the printer must combine dots to create the halftone cells, its effective resolution drops. For example, if 5 dots are assigned to each cell, a 300-dpi printer can print only 60 dots per inch — roughly the same resolution as a newspaper photograph. That's sobering: when you shelled out $1000 or more for your scanner, you may have had in mind an end product that would look better than a newspaper photo. It's because of the halftoning process that a 300-dpi scanner is more than adequate for most needs.

But because grey-scale images aren't locked into a specific halftone dot size, you can get sharper halftones by printing your image on a higher-resolution printer, such as a desktop publishing service bureau's imagesetter. Imagesetters such as Linotronics can print far more dots per inch, so they can create much smaller halftone cells. If a 1270-dpi Linotronic uses 5 dots per cell, its effective resolution is about 200 dots per inch — more than that of a high-quality magazine halftone. That's the beauty of not halftoning until printing time: your image can take full advantage of the printer's resolution (see the figure "There's More than One Way to Scan a Cat").

◄ **There's More than One Way to Scan a Cat**
The more dots per inch a printer provides, the better the
quality of its halftones. At top, output from a
300-dpi PostScript printer, using a 53-lines-per-inch
halftone screen. At bottom, the identical image printed on
a 1200-dpi Agfa Compugraphic CG 9400 Imagesetter, using
a 125-lpi halftone screen.

Of course, when you leave the
halftoning job to the printer, the
printer must be able to create
halftones. PostScript-based printers
contain halftoning routines, but
QuickDraw-based printers such as
GCC Technologies' Personal
LaserPrinter II series and Apple's
Personal LaserWriter LS do not. To
print grey-scale images as halftones
with these and other non-PostScript
printers, the program you use for
printing must do its own halftoning.
Many desktop publishing and grey-
scale graphics programs do; other
types of programs generally don't.

A Scanner's
Command Post

Let's take a closer look at your link
to the scanner's hardware. A scanner's
software lets you adjust settings
before scanning, edit the resulting
image, and save it in a variety of
formats. (See the table "Storing
Pictures" in Chapter 8 for a list of
common graphics file formats.)

To allow you to compensate for
imperfect originals, scanning programs provide buttons or sliders that

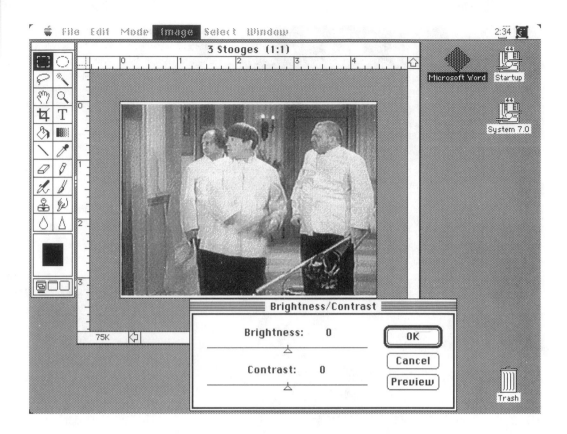

🍎 File Edit Mode **Image** Select Window 2:34 📖

3 Stooges (1:1)

Microsoft Word   Startup

System 7.0

75K

Brightness/Contrast

Brightness: 0

OK

Contrast: 0

Cancel

Preview

Trash

▲ **Scans on Screen**
Macs with color or grey-scale video hardware make ideal electronic retouching platforms. Here, Adobe Photoshop is used to adjust the brightness and contrast of an image captured using a video digitizer.

let you adjust brightness and contrast. These controls don't alter the lighting within the scanner; they cause the scanner software to assign different brightness and contrast values to the incoming grey-scale data.

Scanning software lets you specify the area to be scanned as well as an enlargement or reduction percentage to create scans larger or smaller than the original. You can also specify whether the original is line art or a continuous-tone image. If it's the latter, you can designate whether the software should halftone the incoming image (through dithering) or simply save the grey-scale data. Always choose the grey-scale option for best results with desktop publishing and image-processing programs; if your printer doesn't support halftoning or if you'll be exporting the image to a program that doesn't support grey-scale files, choose the dithering or halftoning option.

All scanning software also provides MacPaint-like editing features such as erasers, pencils, and line-drawing tools. But most programs' editing features are adequate for only simple retouching tasks. For serious editing, consider an image-processing program such as Letraset's ImageStudio, Silicon Beach's Digital Darkroom, Adobe's PhotoShop, or Letraset's ColorStudio. These programs' sophisticated drawing and retouching tools let you blend, soften, sharpen, and otherwise alter images. Because a Mac II or LC can display shades of grey, it's the best Mac for electronic retouching (see the figure "Scans On-Screen").

Another extremely useful image-processing feature is the ability to change a photo's brightness or contrast after you've scanned it. Because grey-scale images retain the grey-scale data sent by the scanner, image-processing programs can change the brightness and contrast by simply interpreting the data differently. This ability to *remap* the grey-scale data lets you compensate for brightness or contrast flaws in the original, and allows for special effects (see the figure "Fun with Grey Maps" on the following page). Most desktop publishing programs also let you remap grey-scale data, a process often called *gamma correction*.

It's also worth noting that many image-processing programs can drive a scanner directly. That's a handy feature that lets you scan and retouch without having to switch programs.

Is a Scanner the Answer?

With all the wonders scanners perform, why aren't I more enthusiastic about recommending them? Several reasons. First, you don't need one to include photos in a publication. You can use the standard graphic artist's technique: draw a black box — a *halftone window* — to indicate where the photo will appear. Then send the photo to a print shop for photographic halftoning. They'll make a *photomechanical transfer,* or *PMT,* from the photo that you can put into position on your pasted-up page.

Second, scanners are expensive: the money one costs will buy quite a few photographic halftones. (The one exception is the marvelous ThunderScan, which will do the job if you have the patience and the ImageWriter.) And if you don't already have a high-capacity hard disk and at least 2MB of memory, add their prices to the tally. For top-notch retouching, throw in a few hundred dollars for an image-processing program.

Finally, remember that the quality of laser-printed grey-scale images is far from *National Geographic* standards. An imagesetter gives better results, but some can take a long time to print halftones. Most typesetting service bureaus charge by the hour, so your digital halftones could cost a lot more than conventional ones.

Fun with Grey Maps

You can open grey-scale files with an image-processing program such as ImageStudio or Digital Darkroom, and remap the grey scale to adjust brightness and contrast (a process often called gamma correction) or to produce special effects. Here are two images along with their corresponding grey maps, as displayed by ImageStudio. At top, the grey map is unchanged. At bottom, a posterized version of the same image.

But if you work with images frequently and if you'd like to be able to retouch them electronically, then by all means consider one. And it's true that OCR software and fax modems allow scanners to earn their keep in other ways.

Scanners have always promised a lot, but only recently have they started to deliver. Whether one can deliver enough for you is a grey area that no scanner can detect. You're the one who has to assign a 0 or 1 to that question.

Toward Better Scans

Following two simple rules will help you get the most from your scanner and disk space.

❖ *Scan photos at lower resolutions* Most scanners let you scan at resolutions lower than 300 dpi. If you're creating a grey-scale image of a continuous-tone original, scan at a lower resolution — as low as 75 dpi if your final output will be laser printed, or 150 dpi if you'll be printing on a Linotronic. Because a printer's effective resolution drops when it halftones, you'll get virtually identical results. And you'll save a tremendous amount of disk space — a 75-dpi grey-scale scan is roughly $1/16$ the size of a 300-dpi one. For line art, which doesn't require halftoning, always scan at your scanner's maximum resolution.

❖ *Scan grey and save TIFF* If your scanner, its software, and your printer support grey scale and halftoning, always scan continuous-tone originals using your scanner software's grey-scale setting and save the result as a TIFF or RIFF file. Doing so will let you alter the image's grey map, change its halftone resolution and angle, and resize the image without distorting its halftone screen. If you use the scanning software's halftoning options instead, the settings of these key components will be carved in stone during the scan.

Finally, if you're still shopping, remember this: The more shades of grey a scanner and its software can detect, the better the image will look, especially if printed on an imagesetter or 600-dpi laser printer. Remember, too, that printer resolutions are likely to improve in the future. Scanned images containing 64 or 256 levels of grey will be able to take better advantage of future printers' ability to create smaller halftone cells. **M**

Summary:

✔ Creating image files for desktop publishing is the most common scanner application.

✔ Most scanners can work with either continuous-tone images (such as photographs), which contain white and black areas along with many shades of grey; or line art (diagrams or pen-and-ink drawings), which is strictly black and white.

✔ A scanner resembles a photocopier in that it illuminates your original while a sensor called a charge-coupled device (CCD) measures the light it reflects and generates a voltage.

✔ In a flatbed scanner, the original remains stationary and the CCD mechanism moves across it during the scan.

✔ In a sheet-fed scanner, the original is fed into a slot and a set of rubber rollers draws it past a CCD mechanism.

✔ A scanner's software lets you adjust settings before scanning, edit the resulting image, and save it in a variety of formats.

✔ If you work with images frequently and you'd like to be able to retouch them electronically, a scanner may be for you, but consider the drawbacks — the scanner's cost and the memory and disk space required by scanned images.

Chapter 40
Networking

In This Chapter:

✔ How networking lets you share expensive hardware such as printers and modems.

✔ The file server: the electronic version of an office file cabinet.

✔ Will your software work on a network?

✔ Tips for getting good performance and reliability from your network.

✔ Dialing for data: how to access your network when you're on the road.

✔ Networking at the high end — the Mac-to-VAX connection.

I f you use two or more Macs, chances are you can benefit from connecting them to each other to form a *network*. Wait! Don't turn the page. It's true that networking has its technicalities — bandwidths and bridges, twisted pairs and topologies — but even if you are new to the Macintosh you can set up a small network without immersing yourself in them. Small-scale Mac networking can be surprisingly easy and economical.

What's to gain? For one thing, your Macs can share an expensive add-on such as a laser printer or hard drive (see the sidebar "Hardware You Can Share"). It's easier to buy a big-ticket item when you know that all your Macs will be able to share it.

Beyond sharing hardware, you can share information and ideas. Using *file server* software, you can store in one place files everyone needs to access — client databases, product fact sheets, downloadable laser printer fonts, or boilerplate templates for frequently produced documents. Using *electronic mail* software, you can send messages and files to co-workers. And with *multiuser* database software, everyone can access the same database file at once, eliminating the need to store a separate copy on each user's machine — and fretting over whose version is the latest.

Many people are intimidated by networking not only because of the jargon that surrounds it, but also because it provides so many sharing options. The best way to conquer both fears is to start small and add new capabilities as you need them

— and as you master those you already have. In this chapter, I present a road map you might want to follow in your journey to a networked office. Along the way, I'll examine networking's benefits and look at some products.

Phase 1: Sharing a Printer

At its simplest level, Macintosh networking means sharing a PostScript-based printer such as Apple's LaserWriter IINT, IINTX, Personal LaserWriter NT, or any of the other dozen or so Mac-compatible PostScript printers. Like a co-op vacation home, a PostScript printer is a less painful purchase when a large group can enjoy it. Non-PostScript laser printers, such as Apple's Personal LaserWriter SC and LS and GCC Technologies' PLP II and PLP IIs, cannot be shared on a network because they attach to the Mac's SCSI or modem connector, neither of which is designed with sharing in mind, and because they lack the ability to respond to numerous machines.

Sharing a PostScript printer is a breeze because all you need are cables that interconnect the Macs and the printer. You don't need to purchase any special networking software; Apple's LaserWriter *printer driver*, included with the Mac's system software, contains all the smarts needed to communicate with any Mac-

Hardware You Can Share

Sharing hardware doesn't mean just hard drives and laser printers. Here's a sampling of the other types of hardware you can share on a LocalTalk network.

❖ *ImageWriters* Using Apple's ImageWriter II/LQ LocalTalk Option board, you can share an ImageWriter II or LQ.

❖ *Telephone modems* Modems such as Hayes's Smartmodem 2400M and Shiva's NetModem V2400 or high-speed NetModem V.32 can be shared on a network. A network modem can't serve an office full of communications junkies, but it is ideal for several people who just check their e-mail now and then.

❖ *Fax modems* You can share a fax modem such as Apple's now-discontinued AppleFax or Orchid Technology's OrchidFax by using Solutions' FaxGate

Plus software with the Microsoft Mail or CE's QuickMail. (Incidentally, you should always choose a fax modem that can both send and receive faxes; some can send them only.)

❖ *Serial devices* With Shiva's NetSerial or Solana Electronics' C-Server, you can put virtually any serial device — modem, pen plotter, daisy wheel printer — on a network.

❖ *Alternative storage devices* You can share tape backup drives, erasable optical drives, and removable-media drives such as Bernoulli boxes and SyQuest drives. You can even share CD ROMs via an AppleShare server, provided the server's hard disk has enough free space to keep track of the CD ROM's vast number of files. **M**

compatible PostScript printer. Similarly, all PostScript printers contain built-in *print server* software that allows them to listen for numerous machines and handle print jobs on a first-come-first-served basis. In short, the Macintosh and the printer already know how to talk with each other — your job is to add the lines of communication.

Those lines can take a few forms. If you want the Apple brand name, endow each Mac and printer with a $75 LocalTalk Connector Kit, which includes a 6-foot length LocalTalk cable and a small connector box that plugs into a Mac's rear-panel printer connector or into the printer itself. The connector box's nine parts electrically isolate the network's components, helping to prevent wholesale equipment carnage should one item short out. The cable itself isn't too different from what you'd find in a stereo system. It contains a pair of wires twisted around each other, surrounded by a braided wire shield that keeps electrical interference out and helps prevent the signals in the cable from interfering with nearby radios or TVs. Included with the connector kit is a small connector called a *cable extender,* used for attaching two cables to each other. If you need longer cable lengths — perhaps to reach a Mac in another room — Apple offers a 30-foot LocalTalk cable for $75, and a 75-foot cable for $125.

Apple's cabling is often discounted below the retail prices I've given, but you can save even more by using one of the LocalTalk cabling alternatives, such as Farallon Computing's popular PhoneNet cabling system. PhoneNet connector boxes, for example, retail for $59.95, but mail-order prices hover around $35. Another plus: PhoneNet uses ordinary telephone wiring rather than the special cabling LocalTalk requires. PhoneNet can even use the telephone wiring already present in a building. That can save you a fortune in cable costs, especially if your Macs are far apart. Other PhoneNet-like network connectors that use telephone wiring include Sitka's Teleconnector, Nuvotech's TurboNET, and Dayna Commu-nications' DaynaTALK. Adaptors are also available that let you mix LocalTalk and telephone cabling on the same network — helpful if you're already using one kind of cabling and decide to add more machines to your network.

Whether you use LocalTalk or a LocalTalk-compatible cabling scheme, you'll hook up your Macs and printers as shown in the figure "Network Wiring" in Chapter 30. Be sure each cable is snugly attached to its connector, and tuck the cables safely behind desks so people won't trip over them or jerk them loose with desk chairs. And avoid the common pitfall of leaving a cable dangling, without going into a connector. The end points of a LocalTalk network are connectors to which only one cable is attached. In this case, the network isn't properly termi-nated — its end point isn't defined, and it won't work properly.

After you unite the machines, you need to configure each Macintosh for network printing. First, be sure the laser printer is warmed up (wait until it prints its start-up page). Next, use each Mac's Chooser to turn on AppleTalk and select the LaserWriter printer driver icon. (If you don't see this icon, you need to copy it and the file named LaserPrep either from the Mac's system disks or from the disks that accompany the printer. Copy the files to the System Folder on the Mac's start-up disk. If you're using System 7.0, you don't need the LaserPrep file, as explained in Chapter 35.)

Before closing the Chooser, type a name in its User Name text box. (In System 7.0, use the Network Setup control panel.) Use the name of the person who uses that Mac, or a name that describes the Mac's purpose, such as Publishing Station. This name allows the LaserWriter driver to provide useful feedback when you're printing — more about that shortly.

Finally, activate the Background Printing option so you're not forced to wait while the Mac and printer communicate during each print job. Background printing intercepts data en route to the printer, saves it on disk in a *spool file,* and then quickly returns control of the Mac to you so you can get back to work. Then, a system program called PrintMonitor transmits the spool file to the printer in short bursts while you work (see the figure "Monitor Your Printing").

(If no icon appears at the right edge of the menu bar, you *aren't* using MultiFinder, and the background printing option isn't available. You can activate MultiFinder using the Set Startup command in the Finder's Special menu; see Chapter 2 for details.)

After you perform these steps, close the Chooser and try printing a short document. If you've activated background printing, you won't see any status messages (telling you who's printing what on which printer) unless you open the PrintMonitor window by choosing its name from the Apple menu (in System 6.x) or from the application menu (in System 7.0). If background printing is off or if PrintMonitor's window is open, you'll see status messages such as "processing job." If your test document doesn't print, retrace your steps and double-check the cables. If it does print, perform these steps on each Mac in the network.

If you always use the same printer, you need to perform the previous chores only once; the Chooser remembers that you've chosen the LaserWriter driver as well as the user name you typed and the name of the printer you selected. However, if you switch between two or more LaserWriters or other printers, you need to use the Chooser each time you change printers.

Phase 2: Electronic Mail

Once you've strung the lines between machines, you can add additional capabilities to a network by adding appropriate software. The next step might be to add software that lets you transfer files between Macs, enabling you to say

Monitor Your Printing

When you're using MultiFinder or System 7.0, selecting the Background Printing option in the Chooser (top) eliminates having to wait for the printer.

The PrintMonitor application (middle) displays the document names of jobs waiting to be printed. Status messages appear at the bottom of PrintMonitor's window (or at the top of the Mac's screen when background printing is disabled). By clicking on the Set Print Time button, you can delay printing until a specific time or postpone it indefinitely — using the pop-up dialog box (bottom).

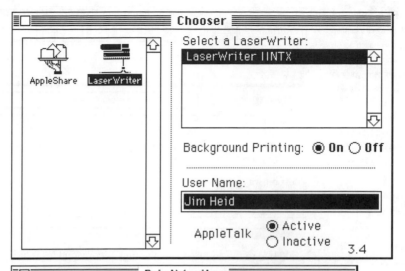

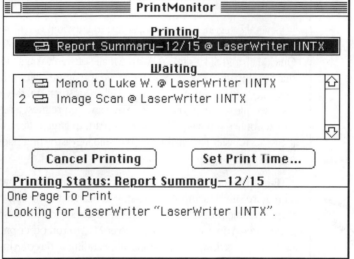

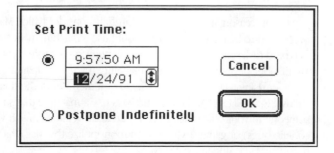

Files Enclosed

With electronic-mail software such as CE Software's QuickMail, shown here, you can enclose disk files with messages. The recipient clicks on the ENCL button to retrieve the file from the mail server.

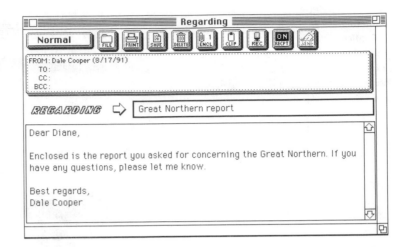

good-bye to the so-called sneaker net — copying files to floppy disks and carrying them to other machines in your office.

Several categories of network software let you move files between machines. One is *electronic mail,* or *e-mail* software such as Microsoft Mail, CE Software's QuickMail, and Sitka's InBox. With e-mail software, you send files as *enclosures* that accompany messages you type (see the figure "Files Enclosed"). When messages arrive at their electronic mailbox destination, the recipients can save the enclosed files on their own disks. You can even request a return receipt message, which notifies you when a message is read. In large offices, e-mail not only makes it easy to transfer files, it also helps eliminate distracting phone calls and annoying games of phone tag.

E-mail Details Each brand of e-mail software has its own operating style, but all require similar setup steps. First, you designate one Mac as the e-mail server, the electronic post office that stores messages and forwards them to their addressees. You can still use the server Mac to run other programs, but you'll notice it slows down when people are sending and retrieving mail as it divides its time between postal duties and running other programs.

For this reason, it's important to carefully consider which Mac in a network is best suited to being a server. You should use a machine with several megabytes of free hard disk space and at least 2MB of memory — more if you plan to use MultiFinder or System 7.0 on that machine. If you anticipate heavy mail volume, consider using a faster Mac — an SE/30 or a member of the II family — instead of a Plus, SE, or Classic. And make sure you use a machine that's reliable — if someone in your office likes to run prerelease versions of software (which may contain bugs) or games (which often monopolize the Mac's hardware), that person's Mac is not an ideal server.

Server Setup

Just as every post office needs a postmaster, every mail server needs an administrator — someone who sets up the mail system and keeps it in tune. The administrator's first job is to add users to the system (InBox is shown here). After the initial setup, the administrator's job becomes custodial. Using the administrator program, he or she adds and removes users as needed, helps users who have forgotten their passwords, and works to keep the mail moving. Each user can — and should — change his or her password when signing on to the system for the first time.

Configure Address List

InBox

Names	Passwords
BulletinBoard	
Maryellen Kelly	maryellen
Jim Heid	jim
Macintosh SE	se
IBM PC	ibm
Bo Jackson	bo
Harold Baker	harold
Luke Williams	luke

[Insert Mailbox]
[Cut Mailbox]
[Paste Mailbox]

[OK]
[Cancel]

After you choose a server, you set up the e-mail server software, which usually comprises a system extension (INIT) that loads the server software into the Mac's memory during start-up and an *administrator* program that you use to create a mailbox for each person in the network (see the figure "Server Setup"). Finally, install on each Mac the e-mail *client* software, which generally includes a desk accessory that lets the user read and send mail and a start-up document that lets the Mac notify the user when a message arrives.

Microsoft Mail, QuickMail, and InBox can each easily meet the needs of a small network. As your network and needs grow, however, you need to decide between Microsoft Mail and QuickMail, both of which currently provide more features than InBox. QuickMail wins the features derby, but it's harder to learn. An advantage to Microsoft Mail is that it lets you exchange mail and documents directly within Microsoft Word and Excel, Aldus PageMaker 4.0, and several other applications.

For a simpler variation on the file-transfer theme, investigate file-transfer utilities such as Traveling Software's LapLink Mac III Network Pac, Gizmo Technologies' Send Express, or Claris Corporation's Public Folder, which is free to registered users of Claris products. These utilities don't let you type in messages to be sent; they simply beam existing files from one machine to another.

And then there are more specialized products such as Farallon Computing's Timbuktu and Microcom's Carbon Copy Mac software (see the figure "I've Got You Now" on the next page). Both transfer files, but they aren't e-mail packages; instead, they let you control one Macintosh from another, for example, to help someone who's struggling to master a difficult program. You

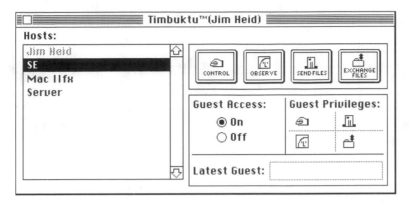

can take over all the screens in the office — great for group training sessions. And you can use one Mac's modem or Image-Writer printer from another Mac. With Farallon's Timbuktu/Remote, you can even control a Mac over the telephone lines, although you need a high-speed modem such as the Hayes Smartmodem 9600 for tolerable performance. Carbon Copy Mac includes remote-access features.

▲ **I've Got You Now**
Farallon Computing's Timbuktu software lets you transfer files between Macs and control one Mac from another. Timbuktu's desk accessory, shown here, also lets you specify passwords to protect against unauthorized access to your files or your Mac.

Phase 3: Creating a File Server

E-mail products can eliminate sneaker wear but not worries over whose version of a certain document is the most current. If anything, swapping files between different machines only fuels those fears. And having important files scattered across the hard drives and floppy disks in an office makes backing up difficult.

The solution? Use file-server software to make one or more hard drives available to the entire network. A file server is an electronic version of the office filing cabinet, providing shared storage for files that everyone needs (or that only certain people need — you can create private folders that can't be used without a password). Backing up is simplified, since all the important documents are stored in one place. And the entire office can take advantage of that high-capacity hard drive you just bought.

Or so go the claims. In reality, a network's hard drive isn't nearly as fast as a *local* one (attached directly to your Mac) because LocalTalk transfers data more slowly than the Mac's SCSI port does. For example, Microsoft Excel takes about 10 seconds to start from my local hard drive but over 30 seconds to start from my file server. What's more, putting all that extra data on a network's cabling slows down everything else that takes place on the network, such as printing and exchanging e-mail. Thus, it's best to use a file server to store only documents, not programs.

(It's worth noting that network cabling systems such as *Ethernet,* widely used with Digital Equipment Corporation's VAX minicomputers, are far faster

Server Approaches Compared

With distributed file serving (top), you can make any Mac in the network act as a server by publishing one or more folders or the entire contents of a hard drive. A server can still be used to run application programs, but its performance slows when other users access its hard drive. With dedicated file serving (bottom), a Mac is set aside to act as a server. A dedicated server can't be used to run programs, but it could run electronic-mail server software.

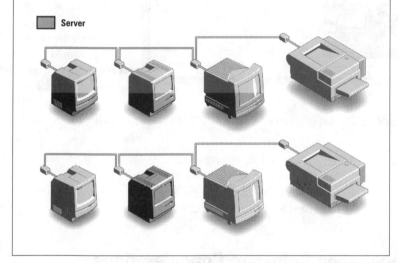

▮ Server

than LocalTalk cabling, but are too costly to be practical for small networks; Ethernet requires that you put $500-to-$1000 expansion boards in each Mac. What's more, to use most PostScript printers on an Ethernet network, you need a *protocol converter,* a kind of network interpreter that translates between the different communications rules used by Ethernet and LocalTalk. Only a few high-end printers, such as QMS' PS-2000, can accept Ethernet connectors.)

Two Ways to Serve File servers come in two flavors: *distributed* and *dedicated* (see the figure "Server Approaches Compared"). With distributed serving, anyone in the network can turn his or her machine into a file server by *publishing* one or more folders — or the entire contents of a hard drive. Once it's published, anyone on the network can *mount* it and use it as though it were a local drive. File-server software using this approach includes Sitka's MacTOPS and Apple's own System 7.0. Indeed, as we saw in Chapter 25, System 7.0's network features even allow you to link to remote programs to exchange data.

With the dedicated approach, you set aside, or *dedicate,* one Mac and its hard drive to act as a server for everyone. A dedicated server can't run applications because the server software all but monopolizes the Mac's hardware. A server can, however, run e-mail server software. Apple's $799 AppleShare software, which supports up to 50 users, is the only dedicated server software

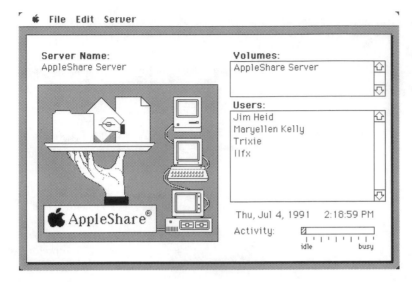

available that uses a Mac as the server (see the figure "Serving with Dedication"). I'll describe some products that let you turn an IBM PC into a server shortly.

Clearly, distributed file serving is the more economical approach. Neither Mac TOPS nor System 7.0 requires any extra hardware beyond cabling. With Mac TOPS, you simply buy a copy of the software for each user; it retails for $299 but is often discounted to around $190. Mac TOPS also includes the InBox e-mail software.

Serving with Dedication

A Macintosh running Apple's AppleShare file server software displays this screen, which lists the users who are signed on to the file server and shows the current activity. Some companies create a "headless server" by using a Mac II without a monitor, relying on Farallon's Timbuktu to control and configure the file server.

One downside to distributed file serving is that someone can *unpublish* a folder or hard drive at any time, with disastrous results for anyone using it. Mac TOPS and System 7.0 provide some safeguards for this, but it still can happen. And of course, a Mac acting as a file server slows down when others are accessing its hard drive.

Application Software Considerations

Because file server software turns a hard disk into a shared storage area, the possibility exists that more than one user could try to modify the same document at the same time. One part of a file server's job involves keeping track of who's opened what. It does so through *file-access protocols* — rules built into the file-serving software that specify how users can access files. A *file locking* protocol locks a file against alteration after one person has opened it.

But some tasks, especially database management and accounting, benefit from users being able to simultaneously modify a file. File servers can accommodate such applications when they work in concert with *multiuser software*. With a multiuser database manager, for example, a secretary can enter new client records, a sales representative can print a sales report, and a shipping clerk can update inventory figures — at the same time, from the same database.

A multiuser program handles these simultaneous requests without file clobbering through a *record-locking* protocol, which allows multiple users to access a file, but only one person to modify a given record. Apple's AppleTalk Filing Protocol (AFP) is a set of file-sharing rules that developers of network-compatible applications follow.

How do some of the leading software packages handle file and record locking? Here are some examples.

❖ Microsoft Works lets numerous users open the same file, but only the one who opened it first can modify it. Anyone else must use the Save As command to give it a new name. Microsoft Excel works similarly.

❖ Aldus PageMaker 4.0 lets numerous users open a template or a copy of a publication, but only one person at a time can open an original publication.

❖ Microsoft Word won't let more than one person open a document unless they all check the Read Only option in the Open dialog box. (As an alternative, you can use the Finder's Get Info command to lock the document.) To modify the file, you must save it under a new name.

❖ Claris Corporation's MacDraw II lets multiple users open a file, but only the person who opens it first can save changes normally (that is, by using the Save command). If others try to save changes they've made, a message asks if they want to save the changed document under a new name or not save the changes after all.

❖ Claris's FileMaker II and FileMaker Pro, Acius's 4th Dimension, and Fox Software's FoxBase+/Mac are multiuser database managers that let numerous users work simultaneously with a database file. However, only one person at a time can modify a given record (one entry in the database, such as someone's name and address). Multiuser data managers also provide security features that let you make certain information available to only certain people. In a personnel database, for example, you might want to give everyone access to employee names and phone extensions, but only certain managers access to salary information.

As you can see, not all programs behave in the same way on a network. After setting up a network for file serving, test your applications to see how they behave when more than one person tries to open a document.

Remote Control

If you have employees who travel frequently or work at home, you may want to give your network *remote access* features to allow those users to dial in and access the file server, e-mail system, and even laser printer. Shiva Corporation's NetModems include dial-in access software for Macs (see the figure "Calling Home"). Shiva's DOS Dial-In package allows PCs to call home. Farallon's Liaison software also allows dial-in access.

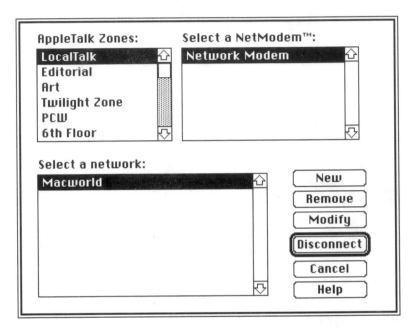

Because 1200-bits per second (bps) and even 2400-bps modems transmit data far slower than a network does, remote network access can seem as slow as the pony express. With a high-speed modem such as Hayes' Smartmodem 9600, however, performance is quite acceptable — not as fast as a local network node, but fast enough for electronic mail to still seem electronic. I used to use a 1200-bps modem for connecting to *Macworld*'s e-mail system (built around QuickMail), but I switched to a Smartmodem 9600 after a few too many cobwebs formed between me and my Mac.

CE Software's QuickMail takes an especially versatile approach to remote access by being able to talk to any computer with a modem. If you dial into a QuickMail server using a computer other than a Mac, QuickMail discards the Mac interface and presents special text menus for accessing the system. Combine that capability with a $300 Radio Shack laptop computer, and you have an inexpensive way to keep in touch.

Remote-node setups allow network e-mail systems to span the miles, but commercial e-mail and online services still have their place. For starters, their multiline phone networks can accommodate thousands of callers at once. With remote-node access, only one person at a time can call in to check his or her mail.

▲ **Calling Home**
With Shiva Corporation's NetModem, you can dial into a remote network to check e-mail, access a file server, and even print to a networked printer. The dial-in dialog box shown here also lets you select which of the remote network's *zones* you want to access. A zone is an individual network that's tied to other networks.

If you exchange e-mail via telecommunications services such as MCI Mail or CompuServe, you'll be glad to know that QuickMail, InBox, and Microsoft Mail provide *gateway* features that unite a network and a service by automatically dialing the service at specified intervals and sending or retrieving mail.

Other Networking Options

After you master printer sharing, electronic mail, and file serving, you might want to investigate more advanced networking options. If you use IBM PCs, PS/2s, or compatibles, you can tie them into the network using LocalTalk expansion boards such as Sitka's FlashCard, Farallon's PhoneNET Card PC•LocalTalk, or DayStar Digital's LT200 Connection PC and, for IBM PS/2s, LT200 Connection MC. Farallon's PhoneNET Talk lets LocalTalk-equipped PCs access an AppleShare server. You can also turn a PC into a server for Macs using software such as Novell's NetWare, DayStar Digital's FS100, and 3Com Corporation's 3+Share. Microsoft Mail, InBox, and QuickMail are available for PCs. And there are PC-oriented e-mail packages such as Lotus' cc:Mail, Dayna Communications' DaynaMail, and 3Com's 3+Mail for Macintosh.

Then there's *groupware,* a new genre of network-oriented software designed around the fact that people often collaborate on projects. Farallon's Timbuktu and Microcom's Carbon Copy Mac enable users to control each other's machines. Mainstay's MarkUp lets multiple users electronically annotate a document and keeps track of when comments were made. CE Software's In/Out lets you track the whereabouts of the employees in your office.

At the high end, you'll find products that allow the Mac to tap into minicomputer- and mainframe-based networks such as those from IBM and Digital Equipment Corporation (DEC). Macs are especially popular among users of DEC's VAX minicomputers — it's been estimated that over half of all VAX installations also use Macs (see the sidebar "Mac to VAX Connections" on the next page).

But before venturing into these waters, master the basics. Add one capability at a time to your network, and be sure everyone understands it before expanding further. And don't ignore your network-administration duties: Develop a filing system for your server. (For some additional tips on managing your network, see the sidebar "Network Etiquette" on page 528.) Be on the alert for viruses — as we saw in Chapter 28, networks allow them to spread easily. Use the same version of the LaserWriter driver on each Mac.

Follow these basic guidelines, and you'll have fewer technical problems and questions to answer. In short, you'll increase your net's worth.

Mac to VAX Connections

You might think that hooking a Mac to a minicomputer such as a VAX would be like giving Pee Wee Herman a spot on the Chicago Bears. Not so. Microcomputers, especially graphically talented ones like the Mac, can play several positions in the world of team computing.

The simplest form of connectivity is the sincerest form of flattery: *terminal emulation*. By tapping into a VAX— through either a telephone modem or a direct cable connection—and running terminal emulation software, you can make a Mac act like a DEC terminal, allowing you to access VAX applications from a Mac. The programs are still running on the VAX; you're just using the Mac to send them commands and view their responses. Usually, you forego the Mac's user interface and type commands as if you were using a DEC terminal. However, a clever product from Apple called MacWorkStation lets developers create Mac-like front ends for VAX applications. These front ends present you with pull-down menus and dialog boxes, then translate your selections into the typed responses that the VAX application expects.

You'll find terminal emulation features in most communications programs, including Apple's MacTerminal, Software Venture's MicroPhone II, Hayes' Smartcom II, and Synergy Software's VersaTERM series. But each package's emulation talents vary. Some emulate only DEC's older VT100 series, which are text terminals. More sophisticated emulators such as VersaTERM-Pro can emulate the newer VT200 series and VT-320, which can display graphics sent from the VAX using DEC's ReGIS commands (ReGIS stands for Remote Graphics Instruction Set, a set of graphics commands VAXs use to create images on graphics terminals).

Using a Mac as a terminal has several advantages. You can copy text and graphics from the VAX and paste them into Mac programs, and you can paste text from the Clipboard to the VAX. Terminal emulators also let you squirrel away incoming data on disk or commit it to paper. A Mac costs less than most DEC graphics terminals—and it can run Flight Simulator when you aren't online.

A more sophisticated way to combine Macs and VAXs is to link Macs into a VAX network. Even the smallest VAX provides hundreds of megabytes of hard disk storage. A VAX can be a formidable file server that can house (and back up) not only its own documents and applications, but those of a roomful of Macs, too.

Because Macs and VAXs store their files in different formats, Mac-to-VAX networking products work behind the scenes to unite the two disparate systems. Some products let you create *virtual disks*, which appear on the Mac's desktop like any other disk but that actually reside as single files on the VAX disk.

Coercing a VAX into storing Mac files is one thing; allowing VAX applications to *access* them is another. Products such as TechGnosis' SmartTalk bridge the gap between the two machines by providing file translation features that allow Mac users to work with files created by VAX applications, and vice-versa.

Many of the same firms that make Mac-to-VAX disk-sharing products also offer software that allows Mac users to access printers on the VAX, and VAX users to access PostScript printers attached to Macs. Some products also turn the VAX into a print spooler that intercepts Mac documents en route to the printer, stores them on the VAX disk, then sends them to the printer.

You Say 10011, I Say 11100

But all this happy sharing doesn't come without complications. The Mac and the VAX use different network protocols—those rules of the road that determine how chunks of data called *packets* travel ☞

on the network's wires. The solution? Teach one system to speak the other's language. Products such as Alisa Systems' TSSnet and Technology Concepts' CommUnity-Mac teach the Mac DECnet protocols, allowing Macs to join a VAX network. Macs that belong to a VAX network can run VAX applications and access the VAX's disk storage, printer, and electronic-mail systems.

Another approach is to add AppleTalk protocols to a VAX. A VAX that speaks AppleTalk can appear in the Chooser desk accessory as though it were a LaserWriter or an AppleShare server. Products that let you create virtual disks on a VAX generally use this second approach. Pacer Software's PacerShare and Alisa Systems' AlisaShare add the AppleTalk Filing Protocol to a VAX, allowing it to be used as an AppleShare file server.

The most ambitious way to join Macs and VAXs is to link an AppleTalk network to a VAX network using a hardware gateway such as those made by Dove Computer and Cayman Systems (see the figure "Power Sharing"). On the Mac end, the gateway plugs into a LocalTalk connector, a SCSI connector, or into a Mac II NuBus slot. On the VAX end, the gateway plugs into an Ethernet connector. The gateway translates the protocols of one network into those of the other.

The most promising dividend of a Mac-VAX merger is *distributed processing,* which lets you combine each system's strengths to create powerful applications that neither system could handle by itself. Odesta's Helix VMX is one example of Mac-VAX distributed processing. It combines the iconic approach of the Helix database manager with the file-serving prowess of a VAX. You design and access the database on the Mac using Helix's icons and form-design features, and the VAX handles the data-management dirty work—storing records and administering database access to numerous Mac users. Numerous other products allow the Mac to tap into VAX-based databases that use the Structured Query Language (SQL).

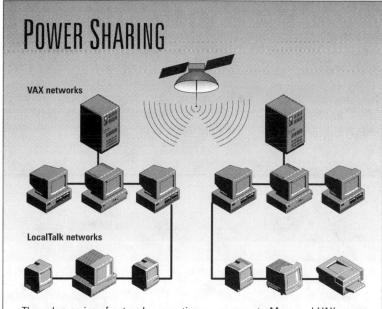

POWER SHARING

VAX networks

LocalTalk networks

Through a series of network connections, even remote Macs and VAXs can easily communicate with one another. Here, a LocalTalk network is bridged via an Ethernet gateway to a VAX network, which is then linked by satellite to a remote VAX network. The second VAX is also connected through Ethernet to a LocalTalk network.

Network Etiquette

Following some basic rules can help make communal computing work smoothly.

❖ *Run applications locally* Avoid running large applications from a server. They'll perform slowly and bog down the network. Small, fast-loading applications work well from a remote server, but a complex program like PageMaker can make a network snail slow. Run large applications locally, ideally from a hard disk; use the server primarily for sharing and storing documents.

❖ *Don't run unreliable software* Never run prerelease software or untested shareware on a network. A crash for one can mean a crash for all.

❖ *Don't delete indiscriminately* Don't throw away a file with a cryptic name; it might be a work file that another user's application has created. Check with others before deleting files you don't recognize.

❖ *Release volumes you don't need* When you're done with a server volume, release it by dragging the volume's icon to the Trash at the Finder.

❖ *Don't break connections* If you must unplug a LocalTalk connector, make sure all users have saved their work. Reliable network software can usually reestablish a connection, but don't count on that. If you must detach from the network, disconnect your machine by unplugging its network box from your Macintosh, not by unplugging the cables that go into the network box.

❖ *Use the RAM cache* You can reduce disk accesses by activating the Mac's RAM cache. In System 6.x, use the General control panel; in System 7.0, use the Memory control panel.

❖ *Use the same version of the LaserWriter drivers* If you don't, you'll see frequent messages telling you that the printer must be restarted and reinitialized.

❖ *Share applications carefully* Many programs weren't written with network use in mind, and can crash when used by more than one person at the same time. Be sure a program is designed for network use before storing it on a shared hard disk. And don't ignore the legal ramifications of networking. You may be required to buy a special license or purchase multiple copies of a program to use it on a network.

❖ *Back up religiously* The crash of one person's hard disk leads to depression; the crash of a shared hard disk can lead to a riot. **M**

Summary:

✔ Networking allows Macs and LocalTalk-equipped IBM PCs to share expensive hardware such as laser printers. You can also use electronic mail and file-server software to share ideas and information with coworkers.

✔ Sharing a PostScript printer is a relatively easy process: Apple's LaserWriter printer driver is included with the Mac's system software, and can communicate with any Mac-compatible PostScript printer. All you add are cables.

✔ Electronic mail software lets you transfer files between Macs as enclosures that can accompany messages you type.

✔ File server software lets you turn one or more hard disks into a central storage area that can hold documents or applications. Security features allow you to assign passwords to folders containing sensitive data.

✔ File server software provides file-locking protocols that prevent multiple users from trying to modify the same file. Record-locking protocols enable multiuser database managers to allow many users to access a file, but only one user at a time to modify a given record.

✔ Dial-in access features allow you to tap into your network using a telephone modem. For acceptable performance, however, you'll want a 9600-bps modem.

✔ A variety of networking products allow Macs and minicomputers such as VAXDECs to communicate and exchange data.

✔ Start small and add new capabilities to your network as you need them — and as you master those you already have.

Appendix A
Where to Buy

This appendix provides companies and phone numbers for the products mentioned in this book. Public domain, freeware, and shareware programs aren't listed here. They're available through online information services; user groups (call 800/538-9696 ext. 500 for information on a local user group); or mail order clearinghouses such as Budgetbytes (800/356-3551 for orders, 913/271-6022 in Kansas), Educorp (800/843-9497, 619/259-0255 in California), or the Public Domain Exchange (800/331-8125, 408/496-0624 in California).

3Com Corp.; 408/562-6400.
3M Visual Systems Division; 800/328-1371, 612/736-1285.

— A —

Aapps Corp.; 408/735-8550.
Abaton, a Subsidiary of Everex Systems; 415/683-2226.
Abracadata; 503/342-3030, 800/451-4871.
Acius; 408/252-4444.
Adobe Systems, Inc.; 415/961-4400, 800/833-6687.
Advanced Gravis Computer Technology Ltd.; 604/434-7274, 800/663-8668.
AEC Software; 703/450-1980.
Affinity Microsystems, Inc.; 303/442-4840, 800/367-6771.
Agfa-Compugraphic; 508/658-5600.
Aladdin Systems; 408/685-9175.
Aldus Corp.; 206/628-2320.
Alisa Systems, Inc.; 818/792-9474.
ALSoft; 713/353-4090.
Altech Systems; 318/226-1702.
Altra; 307/745-7538, 800/726-6153.
Altsys Corp.; 214/680-2060.
America Online (Quantum Computer Services, Inc.); 703/448-8700, 800/227-6364.
American Power Conversion; 401/789-5735, 800/443-4519.
APDA (see Apple Programmer's and Developer's Association).
Apple Computer, Inc.; 408/996-1010.
Apple Programmer's and Developer's Association (APDA); 800/282-2732, 408/562-3959.
Archive Corp., Data Storage Division; 800/237-4929.
Ars Nova Software; 805/564-2518, 800/445-4866.
Articulate Systems, Inc.; 800/443-7077, 617/661-5994.
Ashlar; 408/746-2980.
Ashton-Tate; 213/329-8000, 800/227-4866.
Authorware, Inc. 612/699-3095.
Autodesk, Inc.; 415/331-0356.

— B —

Barneyscan Corp.; 415/521-3388.
Basic Needs; 619/738-7020, 800/633-3703.

Berkeley Systems, Inc.; 415/540-5536.
Bitstream, Inc.; 617/497-6222, 800/522-3668.
Bogas Productions; 415/925-2561.
Bowers Development. 617/259-8428.
Bravo Technologies, Inc.; 415/841-8552.
Bright Star Technology. 206/451-3697.
Brøderbund Software, Inc.; 415/492-3200, 800/521-6263.
Bureau of Electronic Publishing; 201/808-2700.
Byte by Byte; 512/343-4357.

— C —

Caere Corp.; 800/535-7226, 408/395-7000.
CalComp; 714/821-2000.
Calera Recognition Systems, Inc.; 408/986-8006.
Casady and Greene, Inc.; 408/624-8716
Cayman Systems, Inc.; 617/494-1999.
cc:Mail; 415/961-8800, 800/448-2500.
CE Software, Inc.; 515/224-1995.
Central Point Software; 503/690-8090.
Claris Corp.; 408/987-7000.
Clear Lake Research; 713/523-7842.
CMS Enhancements; 714/222-6000.
Coda Music Software; 800/843-2066.
Compugraphic; 800/622-8973.
Compuneering Inc.; 416/738-4601.
CompuServe, Inc.; 614/457-8600.
Computer Accessories Corp.; 619/457-5500.
Computer Care; 800/950-2273.
Computer Friends, Inc.; 503/626-2291.
Connect, Inc.; 408/973-0110.
Connectix Corp.; 415/324-0727.
Cooke Publications; 607/257-8148.
Creative Solutions, Inc.; 800/367-8465.
CTA; 800/252-1442, 212/935-2280.
Cuesta Systems Corp.; 805/541-4160, 800/332-3440.
Curtis Manufacturing, Inc.; 603/532-4123.
Custom Applications, Inc.; 508/667-8585.

— D —

Dantz Development Corp.; 415/849-0293.
Datadesk International; 818/780-1673.
Dataproducts Corp.; 818/887-8000.
DataViz; 203/268-0030.
Dayna Communications; 801/531-0203.

DayStar Digital; 404/967-2077, 800/962-2077.
Deneba Software; 305/594-6965, 800/622-6827.
DEST Corp.; 408/946-7100.
Diaquest. 415/527-7700.
Digidesign, Inc. 415/327-8811, 800/333-2137.
Douglas Electronics; 415/483-8770.
Dove Computer; 919/763-7918, 800/622-7627.
Dow Jones Software; 609/520-4641, 609/520-4642.
Dow Jones/News Retrieval; 609/520-4641, 609/520-4642.
Dr. T's Music Software; 617/969-6657.
Dubl-Click Software; 818/700-9525.
Dynaware; 415/349-5700, 800/445-3962.

— E —

E-mu Systems, Inc.; 408/438-1921.
Ehman, Inc.; 800/257-1666, 307/789-3830.
Electronic Arts; 415/571-7171, 800/245-4525.
ElseWare Corp.; 206/547-9623.
Em Software; 800/253-8472.
Emerson Electric Co.; 714/380-1005.
Engineered Software; 919/299-4843.
Epson America, Inc.; 800/289-3776.

— F —

Farallon Computing, Inc.; 415/596-9100.
Fifth Generation Systems, Inc.; 504/291-7221, 800/225-2775.
Forthought, Inc.; 803/878-7484.
Fox Software, Inc.; 419/874-0162 ext. 650.
Frame Technology; 408/433-3311.
FWB, Inc.; 415/474-8055.

— G —

GCC Technologies; 617/890-0880, 800/422-7777.
GDT Softworks; 604/291-9121.
General Power Corp.; 714/956-9321, 800/854-3469.
Generic Software, Inc.; 206/487-2233, 800/228-3601.
GEnie (General Electric Information Services Co.); 301/340-4000, 800/638-9636 ext. 21.
Genigraphics Corp.; 800/638-7348.
Gimeor, Inc.; 202/546-8775.
Graphsoft; 301/461-9488.
Great Wave Software; 408/438-1990.

— H —

Hayes Microcomputer Products; 404/441-1617.
Heizer Software; 415/943-7667, 800/888-7667.
Heizer Software; 415/943-7667.
Hewlett-Packard Co.; 800/752-0900.
Hip Software Corp.; 617/661-2447.
Houston Instrument, A Division of Ametek, Inc.;
    800/444-3425.
Howtek; 603/882-5200.

— I —

Icom Simulations, Inc.; 708/520-4440.
Icom Simulations; 312/520-4440.
IGC Technology Corp.; 415/563-3612.
In Focus Systems, Inc.; 800/327-7231.
Information Presentation Technologies;
    818/347-7791, 800/233-9993.
Informix Software, Inc.; 913/599-7100,
    800/438-7627.
Inovatic; 703/522-3053.
Insight Development Corp.; 415/652-4115.
Insignia Solutions, Inc.; 408/522-7600.
InterGraph; 205/730-2000, 800/345-4856.
Interleaf Inc.; 617/290-0710.
Intermatic Inc.; 312/282-3700.
Intuit; 415/322-0573.
Iomega Corp.; 801/778-1000, 800/456-5522.

— J —

J. L. Cooper Electronics; 213/306-4131.

— K —

Kandu Software Corp.; 703/532-0213.
Kennect Technology; 408/370-2866, 800/552-1232.
Kensington Microware Ltd.; 212/475-5200,
    800/535-4242.
Kent-Marsh; 713/623-8618, 800/325-3587.
key tronic; 509/928-8000.
Koala Technologies; 408/287-6311.
Kraft Systems, Inc.; 619/724-7146.
Kurta Corp.; 602/276-5533, 800/445-8782.

— L —

LaserMAX Systems; 612/944-9696.
Leonard Development Group; 800/468-9143.
Letraset; Graphic Design Software; 201/845-6100.
Linker Systems; 714/552-1904.
Logitech, Inc.; 415/795-8500
lynx Computer Products; 213/590-9990,
    800/321-5969.

— M —

Macreations; 415/359-7640.
MacroMind, Inc.; 415/442-0200.
Magic Software; 402/291-0670, 800/342-6243.
Magnum Software Corp.; 818/701-5051.
Mainstay; 818/991-6540.
Mark of the Unicorn, Inc.; 617/576-2760.
Mass Microsystems, Inc. 408/522-1200,
    800/522-7979.
MCI Mail (MCI); 202/293-4255, 800/444-6245.
Micro Frontier, Inc.; 515/270-8109.
Micro Planning International; 415/389-1420.
Microcom Software Division; 919/490-1277,
    ext. 924.
Microlytics; 716/248-9620.
Microseeds Publishing; 813/882-8635.
Microsoft Corp.; 206/882-8080.
Microtech International; 203/468-6223,
    800/626-4276.

Microtek Lab, Inc.; 213/321-2121.
Mitsubishi Electronics America, Inc.; Information
    Systems Division; 213/217-5732.
Mouse Systems, Inc.; 415/656-1117.

— N —

Natural Intelligence; 617/266-7858.
NEC Technologies, Inc.; 708/86-9500,
    800/562-5200 ext. 632.
NewsNet; 800/345-1301.
Nikon, Inc.; 516/222-0200.
Nine to Five Software Co., Inc.; 303/443-4104.
Northgate Computer Systems, Inc.; 612/476-4400,
    800/548-1993.
Novell, Inc.; 408/747-4000.
Nuvotech, Inc.; 415/331-7815.
nView Corp.; 800/736-8439, 804/873-1354.

— O —

Odesta Corp.; 312/498-5615.
Official Airline Guides; 800/323-3537.
Olduvai Corp.; 305/665-4665, 800/822-0772.
On Technology; 617/876-0900.
Opcode Systems, Inc.; 415/321-8977.
Optical Data Corp. 800/524-2481, 908/668-0022.
Orange Micro, Inc.; 714/779-2772.
Orchid Technology; 415/683-0300.

— P —

Pacer Software, Inc.; 619/454-0565.
Palomar Software, Inc.; 619/721-7000.
Para Systems, Inc.; 214/446-7363, 800/238-7272.
Paracomp; 415/956-4091.
Paragon Concepts, Inc.; 800/922-2993 ext. 410.
Passport Designs, Inc.; 800/443-3210,
    415/726-0280.
PDS Video Technology, Inc.; 714/244-3521.
Peripheral Land; 415/657-2211, 800/288-8754.
Personal Computer Peripherals Corp.;
    813/884-3092.
Personal Writer, Inc.; 213/556-1001, 800/322-4744.
Portfolio Systems; 718/935-9501, 800/729-3966.
Power Up Software Corp.; 415/345-5900,
    800/851-2917.
Practical Solutions, Inc.; 602/322-6100.
Preferred Publishers; 901/683-3383.
Prescience Corp.; 415/282-5864.
Primera Software; 415/525-3000.
Prometheus Products; 503/624-0571,
    800/477-3473.

— Q —

QMS, Inc.; 205/633-4300, 800/631-2692, ext. 906.
Quark, Inc.; 303/932-2211.
QUME Corp.; 408/942-4000.

— R —

Radius, Inc.; 408/434-1010, 800/227-2795.
RagTime USA; 415/780-1800.
RasterOps; 800/468-7600.

— S —

Salient Software; 415/321-5375.
Sayett Technology, Inc.; 800/836-7730.
Schlumberger; 313/995-6000, 800/366-0060.
Scitor Corp.; 415/570-7700.
Scorpion Systems Group; 415/864-2956.
SecondGLANCE; 619/598-5225.
Shiva Corp.; 617/864-8500, 800/458-3550.
Silicon Beach Software, Inc.; 619/695-6956.

Silicon Beach Software, Inc.; 619/695-6956.
Sitka; 415/769-9669, 800/445-8677.
SmethersBarnes. 503/274-2800, 800/237-3611.
Software Discoveries, Inc.; 203/872-1024.
Software Ventures Corp.; 415/644-3232.
Solano Electronics; 619/573-0801.
Solutions International; 802/658-5506.
Sony Corporation of America; 201/930-6034.
Sophisticated Circuits, Inc.; 206/485-7979,
    800/827-4669.
Spinnaker Software; 612/944-3915.
Steinberg-Jones; 818/993-4091.
Strata; 801/628-5218, 800/678-7282.
Structural Research and Analysis Corp.;
    213/452-2158.
SuperMac Technology; 408/245-2202.
Symantec Corp.; 408/253-9600.
Symantec; 408/253-9600.
Symmetry Corp.; 602/998-9106.
Synergy Software; 215/779-0522.

— T —

T/Maker Co.; 415/962-0195.
Tactic Software; 305/378-4110.
TechAlliance; 206/251-5222.
TechGnosis Inc.; 407/997-6687.
Technology Concepts; 800/777-2323,
    508/443-7311.
Tektronix; 503/682-7377, 800/835-6100.
TeleTypesetting Co.; 617/734-9700.
Texas Instruments; 800/527-3500, 214/995-6611.
The FreeSoft Company; 412/846-2700.
The Voyager Company; 213/451-1383.
ThunderWare, Inc.; 415/254-6581.
Traveling Software; 206/483-8088, 800/662-2652.
Trendware; 203/926-1116.
Truevision; 800/858-8783.

— V —

Varcon Systems, Inc.; 619/563-6700.
Varityper; 800/631-8134, 201/887-8000.
VersaCAD Corp.; 714/960-7720.
Virginia Systems, Inc.; 804/739-3200
Visual Information Development; 818/918-8834.

— W —

Wacom, Inc.; 201/265-4226, 800/922-6635.
Warner New Media; 818/855-9999.
Wayzata Technology Inc.; 612/447-7321,
    800/735-7321.
Welcom Software Technology; 713/558-0514.
WordPerfect Corp.; 801/225-5000.
Working Software; 408/423-5696.
Workstation Technologies, Inc.; 714/250-8983.

— X —

Xerox Imaging Systems; 415/965-7900.

— Z —

Zedcor, Inc.; 602/881-8101, 800/482-4567.

Appendix B
Production Notes

This book is a superb example of what you can do with Macintosh technology. The Mac was used in virtually every aspect of this book's production.

To write the original columns, I used versions 1.05 through 4.0 of Microsoft Word. To revise and expand the columns, I used Microsoft Word 4.0. I wanted each chapter to be based on the column exactly as it appeared in print, but that introduced a problem: many older columns had been produced using an outside typesetting firm, and electronic versions of the text files weren't available.

The answer? Optical character recognition. Using Caere Corporation's OmniPage and a DEST sheet-fed scanner, I scanned tear sheets of the older columns. After much proofreading and correcting, I had the files I needed. OmniPage was even able to retain formatting such as italics and bold, which also saved some time.

My next step was to get electronic versions of the more recent columns, beginning with the May 1989 issue (the first to be desktop published). *Macworld*'s production department supplied me with the final column files in Aldus PageMaker format, and I used PageMaker 3.01 and 4.0 to export their text to Microsoft Word files.

While all this was going on, *Macworld* Senior Design Associate Arne Hurty was using his Mac IIfx and Aldus FreeHand to create the beautiful illustrations in this book. Thanks to telephone modems and dial-in network software, Arne was able to instantly transmit his masterpieces from San Francisco to my office located on California's rugged north coast. To be more specific, we corresponded and exchanged the files using CE Software's QuickMail. At first, I called in to the magazine's mail server using QuickMail's QM Remote program and a 2400-bps Hayes-compatible modem. Later, I switched to a 9600-bps modem that allowed me to dial directly into *Macworld's* network and even access the AppleShare file servers.

I used America Online to transmit completed chapters to technical editor Dennis Cohen in Sunnyvale, California. He edited them on-screen and returned the edited chapters to me via America Online. When I had technical questions on System 7.0 or Apple's new Personal LaserWriter LS and StyleWriter printers, I used Apple's AppleLink communications service to correspond with the appropriate Apple product managers and engineers. Using electronic mail

eliminated annoying games of telephone tag and enabled Apple's experts to put together more comprehensive answers to my queries.

To create the screen shots, I used Mainstay's Capture utility, which unlike Apple's snapshot FKEY, is able to capture pulled-down menus. I used Claris' MacPaint 2.0 to tweak the monochrome screen dumps and Letraset's ImageStudio and Adobe Photoshop to polish up the gray-scale illustrations. To reduce the amount of disk space required by the illustrations (and the chapters, for that matter), I used Aladdin Software's StuffIt Classic file-compression utility.

I then submitted final chapters and art to IDG Books using AppleLink and old-fashioned overnight couriers. IDG Books turned my electronic materials over to University Graphics, the production house. Their crack staff assembled the final pages with PageMaker 4.0 and output them to an Agfa-Compugraphic image-setter. The body text in this book is Bitstream's ITC Garamond. The illustrations, subheads, tables, and figure captions use typefaces from Bitstream's Zurich family, a Univers lookalike.

After wrapping up the chapters, I created the quick reference card using PageMaker 4.0. By doing the layout myself, I was able to see exactly what would and would not fit, and adjust accordingly. I used AppleLink to transmit preliminary versions to IDG Books Production Manager Lana Olson, who checked the margins and positioning of text to verify that everything would fit.

This book's cover illustration was created by sketching the figure on paper, then scanning it with a Microtek scanner which was used as a template to redraw the figure using Adobe Illustrator 3.0. This illustration was created by Ron Chan — Bay Area residents will recognize Chan's distinctive style from the covers of the San Francisco Examiner's weekly TV magazine. Mac aficionados encounter Chan's work frequently: his illustrations appear in *Macworld* and other Mac periodicals on a regular basis, as well as on Mac product packaging (his illustration on the MacroMind Director box is just one example).

There you have it — a remarkable collaboration involving over a dozen people scattered across hundreds of miles. And, as I'm fond of saying, it all happened on a computer that smiles when you switch it on.

Index

You've read about the Mac's sound features.
Now hear them!

Reading about the Mac's sound features is one thing. With Jim Heid's Sound Stack, you can hear them for yourself. This HyperCard-based audio tutorial will provide the background you need to understand the Mac's digital sound features and use them effectively. You'll learn—and hear:

- How various sampling rates affect sound quality
- The pros and cons of audio compression
- How you can use sound-editing software to create startling digital audio effects such as reverb and flanging
- How to "attach" voice comments to your documents
- Which sampling rates to use for voice and music recording
- How to connect your Mac to a stereo system for stunning sound quality.

Version 1.0 of Jim Heid's Sound Stack received a "four-Apple" rating from the Boston Computer Society. Version 2.0, available only through this offer, is bigger and better, with more audio examples and coverage of the latest developments in Mac digital sound. If you're curious about the Mac's sound-making capabilities, you'll want this amazing tutorial.

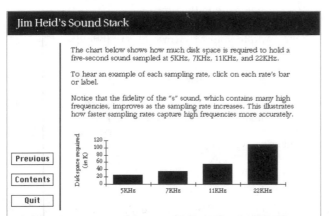

Now With Bonus Sounds and Audio Clips!

With your order, you'll also receive Jim Heid's Sound Disk, a disk jam-packed with top-quality sound resources that you can use and modify. You'll find hilarious replacements for your system beeps, sound effects that you can use along with utilities such as SoundMaster, and musical backgrounds for use in HyperCard or any program that plays sound resources. These are all-original sounds that are not available through user groups and online services.

Two Disks and a Library of Sound—For Just $12.95

Jim Heid's Sound Stack and Jim Heid's Sound Disk are available to *Macworld Complete Mac Handbook* readers for just $12.95, including shipping in the United States and Canada. Use the coupon below to order—and start hearing what your Mac can do!

System Requirements
- Macintosh Plus, Classic, or above with a hard disk and 1MB of memory (2MB recommended) running System 6.0.7 or a later version
- HyperCard 2.0 or a later version
- External amplifier and speakers not required, but recommended for better sound quality
- To modify the sounds on Jim Heid's Sound Disk, you'll want a sound-editing application such as Farallon Computing's SoundEdit

IDG Books Worldwide Registration Card

MACWORLD
COMPLETE MAC HANDBOOK

Fill this out—and hear about updates to this book & other IDG Books Worldwide products!

Name _____

Company/Title _____

Address _____

City/State/Zip _____

What is the single most important reason you bought this book? _____

_____

Where did you buy this book?
- ❑ Bookstore (Name _____)
- ❑ Electronics/Software Store (Name _____)
- ❑ Advertisement (If magazine, which?_____)
- ❑ Mail Order (Name of catalog/mail order house _____)
- ❑ Other: _____

How did you hear about this book?
- ❑ Book review in: _____
- ❑ Advertisement in: _____
- ❑ Catalog
- ❑ Found in store
- ❑ Other: _____

How many computer books do you purchase a year?
- ❑ 1
- ❑ 2-5
- ❑ 6-10
- ❑ More than 10

What is your favorite computer book? _____

How would you rate the overall content of this book?
- ❑ Very good   ❑ Satisfactory
- ❑ Good   ❑ Poor
- Why? _____

What chapters did you find most valuable? _____

What did you find least useful? _____

What kind of chapter or topic would you add to future editions of this book?_____

_____

Please give us any additional comments. _____

_____

❑ I liked this book! By checking this box, I give you permission to use my name and quote me in future IDG Books Worldwide promotional materials.

❑   FREE! Send me a copy of your computer book and book/disk catalog.

Thank you!

Thank you!

- -
Fold Here

IDG Books Worldwide, Inc.
155 Bovet Road
Suite 730
San Mateo, CA 94402

Attn: Reader Response

Tape or staple bottom here.

Readers cheer Jim Heid's "Getting Started" Column in *Macworld*...

"I can remember...one of your articles explaining that mysterious wonder, PostScript, and for the first time understanding what it was. I laugh now, because everyday I have to reach for that simple explanation as a software training specialist at Adobe Systems."   —Danielle Beaumont

"Your article on the new system was fantastic....You hit such a perfect tone.... Thanks again for great writing."   —Nancy Anderson

"Your article was clear, easy to read, and was particularly useful in understanding the design constraints of NTSC video."   —John Fox & Richard Fox

"Your article...helped me most in choosing my telecommunications software."
    —Albert Su

"Excellent...has given me facts and insight unavailable elsewhere."
    —Lloyd Haugh

"Very informative and helpful."   —Jack Karnes

"Superb...interesting and useful."   —Milton Spencer

"Thanks a heap for your help!"   —Scott Roberts

"Well done!....Thank you for all your help, support, concern and assistance"
    —Dick Owens

"An article like yours really stimulates the imagination to explore the topic further."   —Quinton Friesen

"Your articles are one of the...reasons I maintain my subscription to Macworld... Your articles...are excellent and useful."   —Geoff Kloster

"Your article was much appreciated."   —Marc Matthews

"Well done!"   —Steve McIntosh

Book Level:
Beginner
through
Advanced

MACWORLD
COMPLETE MAC HANDBOOK

"Very enjoyable reading. It's an excellent beginner's introduction, along with plenty of useful tips & shortcuts, that *any Mac user* will appreciate ."

–MARVIN CARLBERG, Designer of Norton Utilities for the Macintosh, Peter Norton Computing

This is your complete guide to getting started, mastering, and expanding your Mac with expert advice on:

Buying a Mac • Word Processing • Spreadsheets • Desktop Publishing • Typography • Database Management • Graphics • HyperCard • Desktop Presentations • Music & MIDI • Animation • Telecommunications • OCR • Project Management • CAD • Multimedia • Desktop Video • Utilities

Plus, get the ins and outs of:

Basic Maintenance • Memory • System Folder • Multitasking • System 7 • Disk & Maintenance • Viruses • Data Exchange • Troubleshooting • Digital Sound • Programming • Printers & Fonts • Alternative Input Devices • Expansion Slots • Video • Scanners • Networking

BONUS – Macworld Quick Reference Card for System 7!

About the Author: Jim Heid's *Getting Started* column in Macworld is read by over 400,000 Mac users each month. He is a respected Macintosh authority and the bestselling author of *Inside the Macintosh*.

Maximize your Mac skills with these other fine IDG Books:
Macworld Guide to System 7 by Lon Poole
Macworld Music & Sound Bible by Christopher Yavelow

$26.95 USA
$35.95 Canada
£24.95 UK

ISBN 1-878058-17-7

52695

IDG Books Worldw
An International Data
Group Company
San Mateo, CA 944

Computer Book
Shelving Category:

MACINTOSH/GENERAL

9 781878 058171

Printed on recycled paper.

Cover Design by Owens/Lu
Cover Illustration by Ron C
created in Illustrator on the
Macintosh